Handbook of Grammatical Evolution

Conor Ryan • Michael O'Neill • JJ Collins
Editors

Handbook of Grammatical Evolution

 Springer

Editors
Conor Ryan
Department of Computer Science
and Information Systems
University of Limerick
Castletroy, Limerick, Ireland

Michael O'Neill
School of Business
University College Dublin
Dublin, Ireland

JJ Collins
Department of Computer Science
and Information Systems
University of Limerick
Castletroy, Limerick, Ireland

ISBN 978-3-030-08772-2   ISBN 978-3-319-78717-6   (eBook)
https://doi.org/10.1007/978-3-319-78717-6

Printed on acid-free paper

This Springer imprint is published by the registered company Springer Nature Switzerland AG
The registered company address is: Gewerbestrasse 11, 6330 Cham, Switzerland

To my parents, who still inspire me every day; you gave me the schemata to take on the world in all its multi-modality.

– Conor Ryan

To Nancy, Joseph, and Daniel; your collective patience is a virtue that I deeply value.

– JJ Collins

Preface

In the Fall of 1997, under pressure of the looming deadline of EuroGP 1998, the First European Workshop on Genetic Programming held in Paris, France,[1] Grammatical Evolution started its move from a back-of-a-napkin design to an actual working prototype. We knew we had something special—an evolutionary algorithm that was so general purpose that one could use a grammar to describe phenotypes and yet still use the simplest possible representation underneath it all, a binary genetic algorithm.

The GA would keep it simple and fast, and the use of grammars would let us tackle all sorts of interesting, complex problems, even those with multiple types and massive amounts of constraints. It would even let us, as we claimed with some bravado in 2001,[2]

> ...use the weapons of the enemy against them.

meaning that we could use the grammars to encode all sorts of delicious domain-specific knowledge that would let us address problems, the complexity of which we had previously only dreamed.

Conor was less than a year in his first faculty position, Mike and JJ were fersh-faced young postgrads, all of us hungry for publications, and we figured GE would be good to us. It would give us at least half a dozen, we figured, and probably even a couple of journal publications before we moved onto the next big thing.

It *was* good to us. GE quickly became known in the field and our presentations were well attended; people liked what we were doing. Then something surprising happened: other GE publications that we weren't involved with started to appear. First, it was GE publications by authors we knew, applying GE to problems they were already familiar with, but soon after—Chap. 1 in this book describes some of these—papers with no connections to us began to appear. People were using GE

---

[1] EuroGP rapidly transformed itself into a full conference, co-located with other workshops and conferences on Evolutionary and Natural Computation.

[2] This was in the introduction to the 2003 book on Grammatical Evolution by Michael O'Neill and Conor Ryan.

in extremely creative and interesting ways on problems that we would either never have thought to address or didn't have enough background in to make a significant contribution to either GE or the problem. It was a very gratifying experience: *our tool was so good that other people wanted to use it.*

With the help of sponsorship from the Science Foundation of Ireland, we produced some bulletproof and easy-to-understand GE code and released it Open Source; we figured this might get even more people using it.

More people *were* using it, but not just for applications; people were trying to make it better. Fairly soon after the first application papers were published, papers began to appear that suggested extensions, or pointed out that by modifying certain parts, it could be improved; shortly after, different versions of GE appeared. Things went from us and a close cadre of colleagues promoting and designing our GE system to a true community effort, a living, breathing system that hundreds of people were working with and adapting.

Coming up on the 20th anniversary of GE, there are now thousands of GE papers, 20 different GE systems running in all sorts of environments. It has been used for everything from automatic program generation to financial trading to 3D design. In this volume, we are delighted to bring together some exciting examples of both research and applications, which have taken place over the past twenty years.

We debated what a state-of-the-art GE system would look like and eventually settled on the minimal system in Chap. 1. The magic in the genotype-to-phenotype mapping can be harnessed in all sorts of ways; if you are an experienced GE practitioner with your own system, keep doing what you're doing, but take a look at the other chapters; we've been doing this for twenty years and are still amazed at what people are producing. If you are a novice or a newcomer, read the first chapter for a flavour and then choose which chapters resonate most with your application, but read them all! Part of why GE has been so well embraced is that every part of it is configurable or open to redesign, and each of us has experienced the thrill of reading a paper about X only to take away some wonderful tips on Y.

The book is divided into two sections: analysis, which contains chapters looking at how best to configure GE, be it specifically looking at grammars, mapping, or semantics, among other issues, and applications, which contain a truly dizzying array of problems tackled with GE. Better equipped than ever to combat our enemy, we fully expect to be back for the 50th anniversary of GE, with an even more incredible line-up!

Limerick, Ireland   Conor Ryan
Dublin, Ireland   Michael O'Neill
Limerick, Ireland   JJ Collins

Contents

Introduction to 20 Years of Grammatical Evolution

Conor Ryan, Michael O'Neill, and JJ Collins

Abstract Grammatical Evolution (GE) is a Evolutionary Algorithm (EA) that takes inspiration from the biological evolutionary process to search for solutions to problems. This chapter gives a brief introduction to EAs, paying particular attention to those involved in automatic program generation. We then describe grammars, the core building blocks of programs, before detailing how GE's usage of them is one of the key differentiators between it and other EAs.

We give a brief overview of GE and its use, before looking at some of the key developments in the past 20 years, along with a detailed look at the chapters in this book.

1 Evolutionary Computation

Evolutionary Computation (EC) is a machine learning technique inspired by the manner in which the biological evolutionary process operates. Populations of *individuals*, that is, candidate solutions, are evaluated and their performance on a particular problem scored. The population is replaced with a new one created by probabilistically recombining the best performing individuals. In this way, the population slowly evolves towards an optimal or near optimal solution.

Two key factors that limit the sort of problems that can be tackled by EC and, indeed, any iterated machine learning technique, are *representation* and *fitness*. Representation is concerned with the complexity of the solutions that the system can evolve and manipulate. As individuals become more complex, it becomes increasingly more difficult to recombine them with each other.

C. Ryan (✉) · JJ Collins
Department of Computer Science and Information Systems, University of Limerick, Castletroy, Limerick, Ireland
e-mail: conor.ryan@ul.ie; j.j.collins@ul.ie

M. O'Neill
School of Business, University College Dublin, Dublin, Ireland
e-mail: m.oneill@ucd.ie

© Springer International Publishing AG, part of Springer Nature 2018
C. Ryan et al. (eds.), *Handbook of Grammatical Evolution*,
https://doi.org/10.1007/978-3-319-78717-6_1

Fitness is the ability to measure the quality of an individual, specifically its ability to solve the problem at hand. If no *fitness evaluator* exists, creating one can be prohibitively expensive, as unless they are quick and accurate, they will quickly become a bottleneck.

EC has been used with considerable success in areas as varied as Bioinformatics [15, 51], Automatic Circuit Generation [42, 94] and Fluid Dynamics [4]—as far back as the seventies!

Evolutionary Automatic Programming is specifically focused on evolving programs, and more recently has been referred to as the problem of program synthesis. The most commonly used approach, Genetic Programming (GP) [41–45] uses expression trees to represent individuals, as in Fig. 1.

These individuals are recombined with each other using *crossover*, an operation that swaps subtrees from the two parent individuals. The subtrees are selected at random and placed into the corresponding location in the other parent, resulting in two offspring as in Fig. 2.

GP has enjoyed much success and has been successfully applied to an enormous number of problem domains. There is, however, no simple way to deal with multiple types in GP, nor to handle constraints for the manner in which programs are put together. This is because all GP individuals must obey the *closure rule*, that is, all functions must take and return the same type. It is possible to use *Strongly Typed Genetic Programming* [50], in which multiple types can be maintained, but this

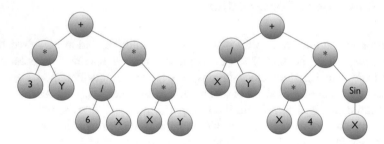

Fig. 1 GP individuals represented as syntax trees. The individual on the left corresponds to (+ (* 3 Y) (* (/ 6 X) (* X Y))) while the one on the right corresponds to (+ (/ X Y) (* (* X 4) (Sin X)))

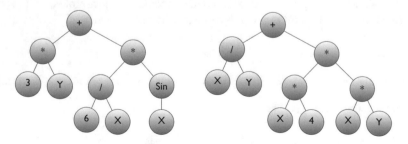

Fig. 2 The resulting offspring from crossing over the parents from Fig. 1

involves performing constrained crossover, with only those nodes of the same type being able to be swapped, which reduces the searching abilities of the system.

However, this constrains the search space, and becomes particularly problematic when dealing with dimensionally aware [37, 38] problems. Furthermore, it also doesn't facilitate the passing of information down through the trees as in Attribute Grammars (AG), which is necessary to generate dynamic types such as those required in matrix multiplication.

Most users do not use GP with multiple types, however, and standard GP has achieved extraordinary success across a very wide range of domains.

2 Grammatical Evolution

2.1 Grammars and Evolutionary Computation

All evolutionary systems that produce programs use grammars of one form or another whether explicitly [49] or implicitly [87]. Grammars describe how programs can be constructed from constituent parts, i.e. how variables and operators can be legally combined to create executable code. The sorts of languages that different kinds of grammars can produce is documented in Chomsky's well known Hierarchy of Grammars [7–9]. Most EC systems use Context Free Grammars (CFG), Type-2 grammars.

As noted above, most Evolutionary Automatic Programming (EAP) systems, including GP, generally considered to be one of the more advanced ones, exclusively use *Closed Grammars* [72, 73], which are a special, restricted form of CFGs that have a single type.

Sometimes these are implicit, as with GP and Gene Expression Programming [23], while other systems are more explicit, such as GE, G3P [95–98], etc. The main trade-off between implicit and explicit grammar usage is speed and expressiveness. We refer the interested reader to two relatively recent syntheses of grammars and genetic programming [49], and more broadly in the context of developmental systems [5].

GE, on the other hand, employs simple linear strings (typically binary or integer) as genotypes, using a mapping scheme to map them onto arbitrarily complex structures. The mapping scheme takes the form of a CFG, which specifies legal relationships between *terminals* (items which can appear in the final structure) and *non-terminals* (interim values to help link terminals together). CFGs enable one to evolve considerably more complex structures than standard GP, because they permit multiple types.

GE has a modular nature, see Fig. 3, meaning that everything from the problem being tackled to the language being used and even the search algorithm being employed can easily be swapped out. Section 4 describes how this modular nature has lead to a massive community effort in further developing GE.

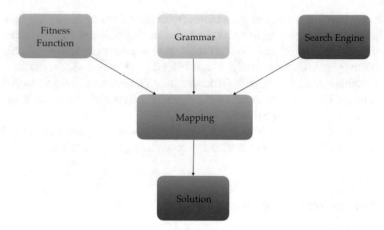

Fig. 3 The modular nature of Grammatical Evolution. Everything from the fitness function to the grammar and even the search engine can be modified or replaced

3 Crash Course in Grammatical Evolution

GE traditionally uses an evolutionary algorithm comprising a variable-length linear genome encoding of a computer program. The genotype-phenotype mapping (mapping) takes as input the linear genome and a grammar, and outputs a sentence in the language described by the grammar, with context-free grammars being the most often used. To drive search the quality of the each individual (that is, a sentence from the language) needs to be assigned a measure of quality.

GE individuals are usually executable entities, but can be any structure represented by a grammar; for example, Chapter 13, "Design, Architecture, and Engineering with Grammatical Evolution" in this book describes the GENR8 [30] system that uses GE and Autodesk's Maya CAD tool to evolve digital surfaces.

When the sentence is in the form of code, it is usually embedded in some wrapper code to manage its execution. The result of the execution of the code is used as its measure of fitness.

We illustrate the mapping process using a simple example grammar to generate strings of characters, vowels and consonants. We first specify the grammar of the output language, which describes all possible sentences that can be generated.

The sentences generated by the example grammar below are of type `string`, which are comprised of one or more `letter`'s. A `letter` is allowed to be one of our primitives, that is, either a `vowel`, `consonant` or `character`.

A convenient formal notation for grammars, often employed by GE, is Backus Naur Form (BNF). BNF is comprised of the tuple {N, T, P, S}, where N is the set of intermediary symbols called non-terminals, which are mapped to the set of terminal symbols (T) according to P, the set of production rules. The terminal set consists of items that can actually appear in legal sentences for the grammar. The final item, S, is a special non-terminal *start* symbol, from which all derivation sequences begin.

For example, in this particular grammar the terminals are neatly described by three types: `vowel`, `consonant` and other `character`. We use the following sets for N and P.

$N = \{$`<string>`, `<letter>`, `<vowel>`, `<consonant>`, `<character>`$\}$, and

$T = \{$a, b, c, d, e, f, g, h, i, j, k, l, m, n, o, p, q, r, s, t, u, v, w, x, y, z, ", ?, ',', ., ;, :, ' '$\}$.

That is, the terminal set consists of letters, spaces and punctuation symbols, while the non-terminal set consists of the three types noted above, along with `string`, the start symbol, and `letter`. `letter` is a non-terminal that will be used to help group various vowels, consonants and characters together. The production rules for this grammar can be specified as follows:

```
<string> ::= <letter>|<letter><string>
<letter> ::= <vowel>|<consonant>|<character>

<vowel>     ::= a|e|i|o|u
<consonant> ::= b|c|d|f|g|h|j|k|l|m|n|p|q|r|s|t|v|w|x|y|z
<character> ::= "|*|?|Ã|@|,|.|;|:|' '
```

Thus, the above grammar contains the set of all possible primitive symbols of the sentences, and the structural rules, which govern the generation of syntactically legal sentences. For example, the following is an example of a sentence generated by this grammar, with a partial derivation tree shown overleaf in Fig. 4:

to evolve or not to evolve, that is the question.

3.1 Mapping

GE individuals describe a derivation sequence through a grammar. They do so by selecting choices from the production rules at every derivation step, for example, whether to choose a `vowel`, `consonant` or `letter` from `letter`.

The linear genome is interpreted as 8 bit *codons*, i.e. the smallest functional unit in GE. Each time a choice needs to be made in the derivation sequence a codon is taken and the **mod** of the number of available rules calculated, which is then used to select the appropriate rule. If, for example, we were choosing a production rule for `letter` we would mod the codon by 3 because there are three production rules.

The process continues as described in Fig. 5, consuming a codon for each choice in the derivation sequence, until the full derivation tree has been produced. If there are unconsumed codons remaining, these are said to be the *tail* of an individual and do not contribute to the mapping. In the event that the individual has not fully mapped and all the codons are consumed, either the individual is simply abandoned and assigned the lowest possible fitness or is *wrapped*, meaning that the first codon is reused. In these cases, an upper limit is placed on the number of times an individual can be wrapped.

Although this can lead to more successful mappings, particularly early in runs, results have been mixed [89] and the ability for wrapping to help evolution is often

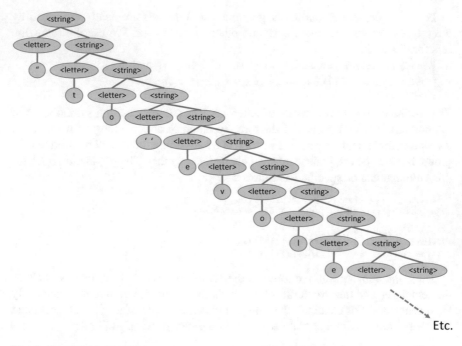

Fig. 4 Partial derivation of the sentence "to evolve or not to evolve, that is the question." from the example grammar

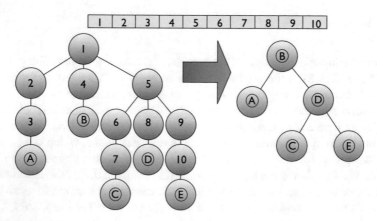

Fig. 5 GE generating a derivation and corresponding parse tree from a binary string. The numbers indicate the order of the mapping was done; circled nodes labelled with letters indicate terminals

dependent on the grammar being used. Many researchers have found that removing wrapping doesn't have a major detrimental effect.

3.2 Alternative Grammars

With the exceptions noted here, GE and, indeed, virtually all other grammar based systems, predominantly use CFGs which, although expressive enough for GE to be a very broadly applicable system [3, 24, 61, 71], is limited to regular and context free languages.

Alternative grammars, which have been employed with GE include Attribute Grammars (more details below in Sect. 3.2.1), Shape Grammars [77], L-Systems [66] and Map L-Systems [83], logic grammars [39], graph grammars [47], meta-grammars (albeit CFG) [63, 70] and Tree Adjoining Grammars [54, 56, 58].

3.2.1 Attribute Grammars

Attribute Grammars (AG) can be used to expand the expressive power of GE by attaching *attributes* (pieces of information) to the symbols in a grammar [10, 11, 35, 36, 75, 84]. These entities can interpret and generate attributes; attributes are generated either passed down (*inherited*) or passed up (*synthesized*), although *default* attributes can also be created and passed around as in Fig. 6. Attributes can take any form, from simple atomic forms to arrays or lists. These attributes can be used by a developing structure in AGE to pass information about various parts of the structure to other parts. AG facilitates the manipulation and exploitation of contextual information, which can be about other parts of the solution or the problem. For example, in the context circuit design, attributes could be used to pass information about which input pins have already been processed.

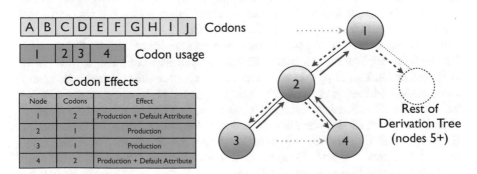

Inherited attributes ⋯⋯▶   Synthesized attributes ⟶   Default attributes ⋯⋯▷

Fig. 6 The GE mapping process augmented with AG. Individuals are mapped from simple binary strings (*codons*) to high level structures using arbitrarily complex grammars, including attribute grammars, which can pass contextual information around

4 Twenty Years of Grammatical Evolution

As shown in Fig. 3, the genotype-phenotype mapping of GE provides the advantage of a modular framework to approach Genetic Programming. The main components of this framework are the search engine, the mapper, the grammar, and the fitness evaluation. Activities over the past 20 years can be described in terms of these components, see Fig. 7 for an overview.

Research in the search engine revolves around understanding the impact of the genome encoding [34], initialisation [59, 86], modularity [29, 33, 82, 90–93], crossover [27, 48, 69, 72], the impact of dynamic environments [13, 79], the behaviour of search operators of crossover and mutation, proposing alternative search operators [6, 17, 25, 28, 52, 62, 76] to replacing the traditional evolutionary algorithm with alternatives such as Particle Swarm Optimisation [65, 74], Simulated Annealing [85], Differential Evolution [64] and even random search [85]. Continuing this vein of research Chapter 7, "Geometric Semantic Grammatical Evolution" outlines a geometric semantic search operator approach to GE, and in Chapter 3, "On the Non-uniform Redundancy of Representations for Grammatical Evolution: The Influence of Grammars" we see an emphasis on analysing the locality of the GE mapping and some of its genetic search operators.

The mapping process itself has been a target for investigation with a number of alternatives having been proposed in part to gain a deeper understanding of the generative process and in attempts to make improvements by, for example, complexifying the mapping by bringing it closer to its biological counterpart [1, 16, 40]. Chapter 4, "Mapping in Grammatical Evolution" provides an overview and highlights key studies in this area.

At the heart of GE is the grammar and while the majority of papers adopt CFGs, we noted earlier in this chapter (Sect. 3.2) the variety of grammars which have been adopted with a GE mapping is impressive, including shape, logic, attribute, meta, graph and tree adjunct grammars to prefix, infix and postfix encoding [31]. This line of research continues to this day, and Chapter 2, "Understanding Grammatical Evolution: Grammar Design" provides a critical analysis on the importance of grammar design in the successful application of GE.

Part of the attraction of genetic programming algorithms such as GE are their flexibility of application. As such, GE has enjoyed application to a wide set of problems areas. Part II of this book contains a selection of chapters highlighting some of these including Financial Modelling (Chapter 11, "Grammatical Evolution in Finance and Economics: A Survey"), Medicine and Bioinformatics (Chapter 15, "Identification of Models for Glucose Blood Values in Diabetics by Grammatical Evolution" and Chapter 16, "Grammatical Evolution Strategies for Bioinformatics and Systems Genomics"), Architecture and Design (Chapter 13, "Design, Architecture, and Engineering with Grammatical Evolution"), Business Analytics (Chapter 19, "Business Analytics and Grammatical Evolution for the Prediction of Patient Recruitment in Multicentre Clinical Trials"), Computational Creativity (Chapter 14, "Grammatical Evolution and Creativity") and Game Artificial

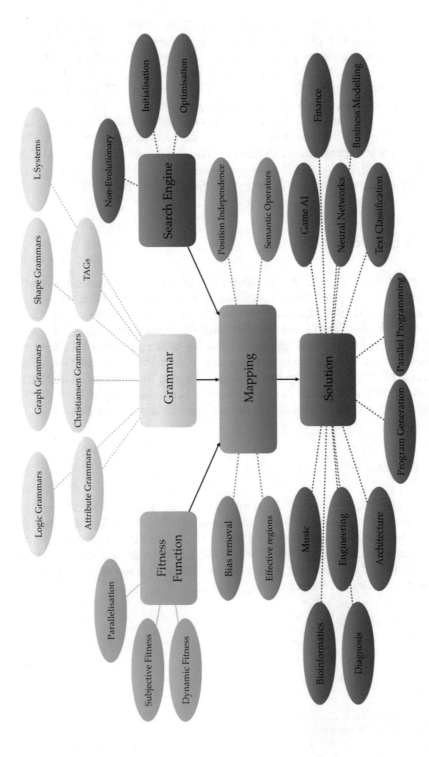

Fig. 7 Some of the key research areas in GE. New topics, especially applications are being added all the time

Intelligence (Chapter 18, "Evolving Behaviour Tree structures using Grammatical Evolution"). Other examples include communication networks [19, 20, 32], search-based software engineering [12] and program synthesis [67, 68, 80], sport analytics [81], eco-system modelling [14, 60], and animation [53, 55, 57].

Matlab[1] and more recently in Python with PonyGE2 [21, 22] with the majority of these employing an integer genome encoding as standard.

Finally, as noted in Sect. 5.4, a large number of variants of GE have appeared. These include position independent approaches such as Chorus and πGE [2, 16, 88], context-sensitive approaches such as Adaptive Logic Programming [39], TAGE [56] and DTAGE [58], to a novel 3D MAP L-system GENr8 [83], and exploiting meta-grammars for Grammatical Evolution by Grammatical Evolution [70].

5   The State of the Art

As noted in the foreword, as the authors of the original GE paper, one of the most rewarding things we have experienced is how it has been taken up by other researchers. The state of the art in 1998 was easy to articulate; there were only three researchers, three problem domains and one system. Twenty years of evolution have had their impact on the sort of applications that GE can be applied to. It is important to note that it isn't possible to definitively state what set up is the best GE, mainly because of the hugely broad spectrum of uses. Instead, we focus in this section on the sorts of choices that need to be considered when tackling a problem with GE, and discuss how various characteristics of problems influence these choices.

5.1   Grammars

AGs are more expressive than CFGs and can be used to enforce constraints and pass context information around derivation trees, as in Fig. 6. The key advantage for CFGs is their simplicity, and mappers using CFGs are generally faster than their AG counterparts, but at the cost of sacrificing expressiveness. Several chapters in this book look in detail at grammar design and our advice is to use the most powerful grammar necessary, but no more.

---

[1] http://ncra.ucd.ie/Software.html.

5.2 Genetic Operators

The genetic operators are generally inherited from whatever underlying GA or search engine is driving GE, but early work analysing the operation of single point crossover [72] showed that, when compared to other crossover operators, including highly tuned homologous[2] operators, actually performed surprisingly well, giving a very good performance-to-cost ratio. More recent work, such as Chapter 7, "Geometric Semantic Grammatical Evolution" in this book, has examined semantic crossover operators, and show some very promising results.

For a simple GE, set up we recommend what has become known as *effective crossover*, that is, to simply ensure that at least one crossover point is selected within the coding part of an individual as described in Fig. 8. This is simple to implement and dramatically increases the probability that at least one of the offspring will be phenotypically different from the parents.

5.2.1 Initialisation

Originally, we used random initialisation for the GE population. However, as noted in [18, 26, 86], random initialisation can lead to very heavily biased initial populations. Consider the simple grammar below:

$< S >::=< op >< v >< v > \mid < v >$
$< op >::= + \mid - \mid * \mid /$
$< v >::= x \mid y$

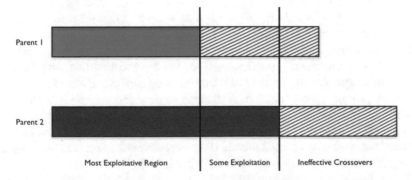

Fig. 8 The three distinct crossover regions for Grammatical Evolution. The solid area in each parent represents the coding regions, while the diagonal lines represent regions that were not used in the mapping. When each crossover point occurs within these regions, the operation will simply result in two offspring identical to the parents. When the points are in either of the other two regions, the crossover operation is said to be *effective*

---

[2]Crossover operators that attempt to swap functionally similar sections from parents.

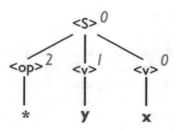

Fig. 9 Creating derivation trees in Sensible Initialisation. The production rule number at each step is noted and will subsequently be used in the following "umod" step. Each individual has a sequence of choices associated with it. In this case the sequence is 0210

Uniform random initialisation will create a population in which 50% of the individuals consist of just one item, due to the $< S >:==< v >$ production; of these, approximately half will be **x** and the rest **y**. Clearly this compromises the variation in the initial population, making evolution towards a useful product more difficult than it needs to be.

Thus, it is important to ensure a spread of individuals in the first generation. Sensible Initialisation [86] takes the *ramped-half-and-half* approach often used in GP and uses it for GE. Sensible initialisation operates by creating a population of derivation trees of various shapes and sizes and performing an "unmod" operation on them to generate linear strings that can subsequently be processed by GE.

When creating each individual in the initial population, first a derivation tree of a particular size is generated. Figure 9 gives an example of a derivation tree of depth 3. The choice made at each step is noted, for example, the initial step used the production rule $< S >::=< op >< v >< v >$, which is choice 0 from those available for $< S >$. Similarly, when mapping $< op >$, choice 2 is made from the available productions rules, that is, $< op >::= *$.

Each individual in the initial population has a list of these choices, which can be used to quickly identify duplicates. Once we are satisfied that the population consists of unique genotypes, the final "unmod" step can be performed.

Unmod produces the actual codons that will be used and essentially performs the opposite operation to mod, returning a number that, when divided by the number of choices available for the particular non-terminal, will return the choice made. In our example, we wish to perform 2 unmod 0 for the first production rule, meaning that we require a number that, when modded by 2 will yield 0.

This means that any even number between 0 and 255 will suffice. Similarly, in the second production rule, we perform 4 unmod 2 as there are four choices and our tree used the second one. Any number in the set {2, 6, 10..} will give the necessary number.

Clearly, unmod is a stochastic operator and, while its output doesn't impact the initial generation in any way, it is crucial to introduce variation so that when individuals from the first generation are crossed over with each other, codons that end up being used for different production rules than they originally were, will not bias the choices made.

More recent work on initialisation includes that of Nicolau, who demonstrated that across the problems examined in their study, a variant of Harper's PTC2 consistently outperforms other initialisations [59], as well as the work of Lourenco [46], which is further advanced in Chapter 6, "Structured Grammatical Evolution: A Dynamic Approach".

What is crucial though, is to put some effort into ensuring good variation in that initial population, and to avoid simple random initialisation.

5.3 Parameter Settings

As with all EAs, GE has a number of parameter settings, such as population size, mutation rates and the like. There is a vast amount of literature in the field about how to set these parameters, but suffice it to say that population size is the most sensitive, and that more difficult problems generally require larger populations. It is important to turn this knob carefully though, as grammars and initialisation also play a part.

5.4 Variants

As described earlier in Sect. 4, not only has there been considerable research into the use of GE and analysis into its operations, there have also been quite a number of variants. It would take a whole other book to exhaustively test these against each other on a broad enough range of problems to be able to make any sort of recommendations, but readers are encouraged to investigate these variants, particularly those that have been shown to outperform GE on problems related to their own.

6 Contents of This Book

The book is divided into two key sections, *Analysis* and *Applications*. Rather appropriately, we start in the applications section with two chapters on grammar design. In Chapter 2, "Understanding Grammatical Evolution: Grammar Design", Nicolau and Agapitos present some domain-independent guidelines for designing grammars, and, in Chapter 3, "On the Non-uniform Redundancy of Representations for Grammatical Evolution: The Influence of Grammars", Schweim, Thorhauer and Rothlauf present a fascinating study on the impact of grammar design and redundancy on the creation of biased trees.

These are followed up by a trio of chapters on mapping in GE. Starting with a comprehensive survey in Chapter 4, "Mapping in Grammatical Evolution" by Fagan and Murphy, we then move to a contribution by Hemberg, Chapter 5, "Theory of Disruption in GE" in which he formalizes and analyzes the mapping process. This leads nicely into Chapter 6, "Structured Grammatical Evolution: A Dynamic Approach" by Lourenco et al., in which they further develop their *Dynamic Structured Grammatical Evolution* (DSGE) system, a version of GE that employs a different mapping to improve the power of the genetic operators.

Similar motivations are evident in Chapter 7, "Geometric Semantic Grammatical Evolution" and Chapter 8, "GE and Semantics", by Moraglio et al. and Echeandia et al., respectively, the former which develops a semantic crossover operator for GE and the latter employs grammars to enable semantics, giving an excellent review of related work as it does so.

This section of the book is rounded out by two final chapters. Chapter 10, "Comparing Methods to Creating Constants in Grammatical Evolution" by Azad and Ryan tackles the issue of constant generation, highlighting the pros and cons of the more well-known methods, while Dufek et al. describe a parallel implementation of GE in Chapter 9, "Multi- and Many-Threaded Heterogeneous Parallel Grammatical Evolution", which yields hugely impressive results.

We then switch gear to applications and provide seven radically different problems that have been tackled by experts in the field. Starting with a survey of financial applications in GE in Chapter 11, "Grammatical Evolution in Finance and Economics: A Survey" by Brabazon, we move to parallel program generation in Chapter 12, "Synthesis of Parallel Programs on Multi-Cores" by Chennupati et al.

The creative side of GE is explored in the next two chapters, starting with Fenton et al. in Chapter 13, "Design, Architecture, and Engineering with Grammatical Evolution", who use GE to evolve physical designs, and then with Loughran in Chapter 14, "Grammatical Evolution and Creativity" who, in a very philosophical paper, uses GE to evolve music. There then follow two chapters from medical domains; first Hidalgo et al. use GE to generate models for glucose blood values in Diabetics in Chapter 15, "Identification of Models for Glucose Blood Values in Diabetics by Grammatical Evolution", while Moore and Sipper give a thorough review of the use of GE in bioinformatics and systems genomics.

7 Summary

We hope this book provides useful snapshots of research and applications in Grammatical Evolution which has taken place over the past 20 years since the original work was published in EuroGP 2008, and presents some of the state of the art and current thinking in this field. Grammatical Evolution as a form of Genetic Programming in particular in its application to automatic programming or program synthesis has still a lot of open issues to address [78] and we hope to witness and be involved in the continued development of this exciting field of research for some time to come.

References

1. R.M.A. Azad, A position independent evolutionary automatic programming algorithm - the Chorus system, in *Graduate Student Workshop*, New York, 8 July 2002, ed. by S. Luke, C. Ryan, U.-M. O'Reilly (AAAI, Menlo Park, 2002), pp. 260–263
2. R.M.A. Azad, A position independent representation for evolutionary automatic programming algorithms - the Chorus system. Ph.D. Thesis, University of Limerick, Ireland, Dec. 2003
3. R.M.A. Azad, A.R. Ansari, C. Ryan, M. Walsh, T. McGloughlin, An evolutionary approach to wall sheer stress prediction in a grafted artery. Appl. Soft Comput. **4**(2), 139–148 (2004)
4. H. Beyer, H. Schwefel, Evolution strategies - a comprehensive introduction. Nat. Comput. **1**(1), 3–52 (2002)
5. A. Brabazon, M. O'Neill, S. McGarraghy, *Natural Computing Algorithms* (Springer, Berlin, 2015)
6. J. Byrne, E. Hemberg, A. Brabazon, M. O'Neill, A local search interface for interactive evolutionary architectural design, in *Proceedings of the 1st International Conference on Evolutionary and Biologically Inspired Music, Sound, Art and Design, EvoMUSART 2012*, Malaga, Spain, 11–13 Apr. 2012, ed. by P. Machado, J. Romero, A. Carballal. Lecture Notes in Computer Science, vol. 7247 (Springer, Berlin, 2012), pp. 23–34
7. N. Chomsky, Three models for the description of language. IRE Trans. Inf. Theory **2**(3), (1956)
8. N. Chomsky, On certain formal properties of grammars. Inf. Control (2), 137–167 (1959)
9. N. Chomsky, M. Schutzenberger, On certain formal properties of grammars, in *Computer Programming and Formal Languages* (North Holland, Amsterdam, 1963)
10. R. Cleary, Extending grammatical evolution with attribute grammars: an application to knapsack problems. Master of science in computer science, University of Limerick, Ireland, 2005
11. R. Cleary, M. O'Neill, An attribute grammar decoder for the 01 multiconstrained Knapsack problem, in *Evolutionary Computation in Combinatorial Optimization – EvoCOP 2005*, Lausanne, Switzerland, 30 Mar.–1 Apr. 2005, ed. by G.R. Raidl, J. Gottlieb. Lecture Notes in Computer Science, vol. 3448 (Springer, Berlin, 2005), pp. 34–45
12. B. Cody-Kenny, M. Fenton, A. Ronayne, E. Considine, T. McGuire, M. O'Neill, A search for improved performance in regular expressions, in *Proceedings of the Genetic and Evolutionary Computation Conference, GECCO '17*, Berlin, Germany, 15–19 July 2017 (ACM, New York, 2017), pp. 1280–1287
13. I. Dempsey, M. O'Neill, A. Brabazon, *Foundations in Grammatical Evolution for Dynamic Environments*. Studies in Computational Intelligence, vol. 194 (Springer, Berlin, 2009)
14. S. Donne, M. Nicolau, C. Bean, M. O'Neill, Wave height quantification using land based seismic data with grammatical evolution, in *Proceedings of the 2014 IEEE Congress on Evolutionary Computation*, Beijing, China, 6–11 July 2014, ed. by C.A. Coello Coello, pp. 2909–2916
15. J.A. Driscoll, B. Worzel, D. MacLean, Classification of gene expression data with genetic programming, in *Genetic Programming Theory and Practice*, ed. by R.L. Riolo, B. Worzel, chap. 3 (Kluwer, Boston, 2003), pp. 25–42
16. D. Fagan, Analysing the genotype-phenotype map in grammatical evolution. Ph.D. Thesis, University College Dublin, Ireland, 30 Oct. 2013
17. D. Fagan, E. Hemberg, M. O'Neill, S. McGarraghy, Fitness reactive mutation in grammatical evolution, in *18th International Conference on Soft Computing, MENDEL 2012*, Brno, Czech Republic, 27–29 June 2012, ed. by R. Matousek (Brno University of Technology, Brno, 2012), pp. 144–149
18. D. Fagan, M. Fenton, M. O'Neill, Exploring position independent initialisation in grammatical evolution, in *Proceedings of 2016 IEEE Congress on Evolutionary Computation (CEC 2016)*, Vancouver, 24–29 July 2016, ed. by Y.-S. Ong (IEEE Press, New York, 2016), pp. 5060–5067

19. M. Fenton, D. Lynch, S. Kucera, H. Claussen, M. O'Neill, Multilayer optimization of heterogeneous networks using grammatical genetic programming. IEEE Trans. Cybern. **47**(9), 2938–2950 (2018)
20. M. Fenton, D. Lynch, S. Kucera, H. Claussen, M. O'Neill, Multilayer optimization of heterogeneous networks using grammatical genetic programming, in *Proceedings of the Genetic and Evolutionary Computation Conference Companion, GECCO '17*, Berlin, Germany, 15–19 July 2017 (ACM, New York, 2017), pp. 3–4
21. M. Fenton, J. McDermott, D. Fagan, S. Forstenlechner, E. Hemberg, M. O'Neill, Ponyge2: Grammatical evolution in python, in *Proceedings of the Genetic and Evolutionary Computation Conference Companion, GECCO'17*, Berlin, Germany, 15–19 July 2017 (ACM, New York, 2017), pp. 1194–1201
22. M. Fenton, J. McDermott, D. Fagan, S. Forstenlechner, M. O'Neill, E. Hemberg, Ponyge2: grammatical evolution in python. arXiv, 26 Apr. 2017
23. C. Ferreira, Gene expression programming and the automatic evolution of computer programs, in *Recent Developments in Biologically Inspired Computing*, ed. by L.N. de Castro, F.J. Von Zuben, chap. 6 (Idea Group Publishing, Boulder, 2004), pp. 82–103
24. D. Gavrilis, I.G. Tsoulos, E. Dermatas, Selecting and constructing features using grammatical evolution. Pattern Recogn. Lett. **29**(9), 1358–1365 (2008)
25. R.T.R. Harper, Enhancing grammatical evolution. Ph.D. Thesis, School of Computer Science and Engineering, The University of New South Wales, Sydney 2052, Australia, 2009
26. R. Harper, Ge, explosive grammars and the lasting legacy of bad initialisation, in *IEEE Congress on Evolutionary Computation (CEC 2010)*, Barcelona, Spain, 18–23 July 2010 (IEEE Press, New York, 2010)
27. R. Harper, A. Blair, A structure preserving crossover in grammatical evolution, in *Proceedings of the 2005 IEEE Congress on Evolutionary Computation*, Edinburgh, UK, 2–5 Sept. 2005, ed. by D. Corne, Z. Michalewicz, M. Dorigo, G. Eiben, D. Fogel, C. Fonseca, G. Greenwood, T. K. Chen, G. Raidl, A. Zalzala, S. Lucas, B. Paechter, J. Willies, J. J. M. Guervos, E. Eberbach, B. McKay, A. Channon, A. Tiwari, L. G. Volkert, D. Ashlock, M. Schoenauer, vol. 3 (IEEE Press, New York, 2005), pp. 2537–2544
28. R. Harper, A. Blair, A self-selecting crossover operator, in *Proceedings of the 2006 IEEE Congress on Evolutionary Computation*, Vancouver, 6–21 July 2006, ed. by G.G. Yen, L. Wang, P. Bonissone, S.M. Lucas (IEEE Press, New York, 2006), pp. 5569–5576
29. R. Harper, A. Blair, Dynamically defined functions in grammatical evolution, in *Proceedings of the 2006 IEEE Congress on Evolutionary Computation*, Vancouver (IEEE Press, 2006), pp. 9188–9195. https://doi.org/10.1109/CEC.2006.1688638
30. M. Hemberg, U.-M. O'Reilly, P. Nordin, GENR8 - a design tool for surface generation, in *2001 Genetic and Evolutionary Computation Conference Late Breaking Papers*, San Francisco, California, USA, 9–11 July 2001, ed. by E.D. Goodman, pp. 160–167
31. E. Hemberg, N. McPhee, M. O'Neill, A. Brabazon, Pre-, in- and postfix grammars for symbolic regression in grammatical evolution, in *IEEE Workshop and Summer School on Evolutionary Computing*, University of Ulster, Derry, Northern Ireland, 18–22 Aug. 2008, ed. by T.M. McGinnity, pp. 18–22
32. E. Hemberg, L. Ho, M. O'Neill, H. Claussen, A comparison of grammatical genetic programming grammars for controlling femtocell network coverage. Genet. Program. Evolvable Mach. **14**(1), 65–93 (2013)
33. E. Hemberg, C. Gilligan, M. O'Neill, A. Brabazon, A grammatical genetic programming approach to modularity in genetic algorithms, in *Proceedings of the 10th European Conference on Genetic Programming*, Valencia, Spain, ed. by M. Ebner, M. O'Neill, A. Ekárt, L. Vanneschi, A.I. Esparcia-Alcázar. Lecture Notes in Computer Science, vol. 4445 (Springer, Berlin, 2007), pp. 1–11. https://doi.org/10.1007/978-3-540-71605-1_1
34. J. Hugosson, E. Hemberg, A. Brabazon, M. O'Neill, Genotype representations in grammatical evolution. Appl. Soft Comput. **10**(1), 36–43 (2010) https://doi.org/10.1016/j.asoc.2009.05.003
35. M.R. Karim, C. Ryan, A new approach to solving 0-1 multiconstraint knapsack problems using attribute grammar with lookahead, in *Proceedings of the 14th European Conference*

on *Genetic Programming, EuroGP 2011*, Turin, Italy, 27–29 Apr. 2011, ed. by S. Silva, J.A. Foster, M. Nicolau, M. Giacobini, P. Machado. Lecture Notes in Computer Science, vol. 6621 (Springer, Berlin, 2011), pp. 250–261

36. M.R. Karim, C. Ryan, On improving grammatical evolution performance in symbolic regression with attribute grammar, in *GECCO Comp'14: Proceedings of the 2014 Conference Companion on Genetic and Evolutionary Computation Companion*, Vancouver, BC, Canada, 12–16 July 2014, ed. by C. Igel, D. V. Arnold, C. Gagne, E. Popovici, A. Auger, J. Bacardit, D. Brockhoff, S. Cagnoni, K. Deb, B. Doerr, J. Foster, T. Glasmachers, E. Hart, M.I. Heywood, H. Iba, C. Jacob, T. Jansen, Y. Jin, M. Kessentini, J.D. Knowles, W. B. Langdon, P. Larranaga, S. Luke, G. Luque, J.A.W. McCall, M.A. Montes de Oca, A. Motsinger-Reif, Y. S. Ong, M. Palmer, K.E. Parsopoulos, G. Raidl, S. Risi, G. Ruhe, T. Schaul, T. Schmickl, B. Sendhoff, K.O. Stanley, T. Stuetzle, D. Thierens, J. Togelius, C. Witt, C. Zarges (ACM, New York, 2014), pp. 139–140

37. M. Keijzer, Scientific discovery using genetic programming. Ph.D. Thesis, Danish Technical University, IMM, Institute for Mathematical Modelling, Digital Signal Processing group, DK-2800 Lyngby, Denmark, Mar. 2002

38. M. Keijzer, V. Babovic, Dimensionally aware genetic programming, in *Proceedings of the Genetic and Evolutionary Computation Conference*, Orlando, Florida, USA, 13–17 July 1999, ed. by W. Banzhaf, J. Daida, A.E. Eiben, M.H. Garzon, V. Honavar, M. Jakiela, R.E. Smith, vol. 2 (Morgan Kaufmann, Burlington, 1999), pp. 1069–1076

39. M. Keijzer, V. Babovic, C. Ryan, M. O'Neill, M. Cattolico, Adaptive logic programming, in *Proceedings of the Genetic and Evolutionary Computation Conference (GECCO-2001)*, San Francisco, California, USA, 7–11 July 2001, ed. by L. Spector, E. D. Goodman, A. Wu, W.B. Langdon, H.-M. Voigt, M. Gen, S. Sen, M. Dorigo, S. Pezeshk, M.H. Garzon, E. Burke (Morgan Kaufmann, Burlington, 2001), pp. 42–49

40. M. Keijzer, M. O'Neill, C. Ryan, M. Cattolico, Grammatical evolution rules: The mod and the bucket rule, in *Genetic Programming, Proceedings of the 5th European Conference, EuroGP 2002*, Kinsale, Ireland, 3–5 Apr. 2002, ed. by J.A. Foster, E. Lutton, J. Miller, C. Ryan, A.G.B. Tettamanzi. Lecture Notes in Computer Science, vol. 2278 (Springer, Berlin, 2002), pp. 123–130

41. J.R. Koza, *Genetic Programming: On the Programming of Computers by Means of Natural Selection* (MIT Press, Cambridge, MA, USA, 1992)

42. J.R. Koza, *Genetic Programming II: Automatic Discovery of Reusable Programs* (MIT Press, Cambridge MA, 1994)

43. J.R. Koza, D. Andre, F.H. Bennett III, M. Keane, *Genetic Programming III: Darwinian Invention and Problem Solving* (Morgan Kaufmann, San Francisco, 1999)

44. J.R. Koza, M.A. Keane, M.J. Streeter, W. Mydlowec, J. Yu, G. Lanza, *Genetic Programming IV: Routine Human-Competitive Machine Intelligence* (Kluwer Academic, Norwell, 2003)

45. W.B. Langdon, R. Poli, *Foundations of Genetic Programming* (Springer, Berlin, 2002)

46. N. Lourenco, F.B. Pereira, E. Costa, SGE: a structured representation for grammatical evolution, in *Artificial Evolution*, Lyon, France, 26–28 Oct. 2015, ed. by S. Bonnevay, P. Legrand, N. Monmarche, E. Lutton, M. Schoenauer, *Lecture Notes in Computer Science*, vol. 9554 (Springer, Cham, 2015), pp. 136–148

47. J. McDermott, Graph grammars for evolutionary 3D design. Genet. Program. Evolvable Mach. **14**(3), 369–393 (2013). Special issue on biologically inspired music, sound, art and design.

48. J. McDermott, M. O'Neill, A. Brabazon, Interactive interpolating crossover in grammatical evolution, in *2010 IEEE World Congress on Computational Intelligence*, Barcelona, Spain, 18–23 July 2010 (IEEE Computational Intelligence Society/IEEE Press, New York, 2010), pp. 3018–3025

49. R.I. McKay, N.X. Hoai, P.A. Whigham, Y. Shan, M. O'Neill, Grammar-based genetic programming: a survey. Genet. Program. Evolvable Mach. **11**(3/4), 365–396 (2010). Tenth Anniversary Issue: Progress in Genetic Programming and Evolvable Machines

50. D.J. Montana, Strongly typed genetic programming. Evol. Comput. **3**(2), 199–230 (1995)

51. J.H. Moore, J.S. Parker, L.W. Hahn, Symbolic discriminant analysis for mining gene expression patterns, in *Machine Learning: EMCL 2001, 12th European Conference on Machine Learning, Freiburg, Germany, September 5–7, 2001, Proceedings*, 2001, pp. 372–381

52. A. Moraglio, J. McDermott, M. O'Neill, Geometric semantic grammatical evolution, in *Semantic Methods in Genetic Programming*, Ljubljana, Slovenia, 13 Sept. 2014, ed. by C. Johnson, K. Krawiec, A. Moraglio, M. O'Neill. Workshop at Parallel Problem Solving from Nature 2014 conference.

53. J.E. Murphy, Applications of evolutionary computation to quadrupedal animal animation. Ph.D. Thesis, School of Computer Science and Informatics, University College Dublin, Ireland, Mar. 2011

54. E. Murphy, An exploration of tree-adjoining grammars for grammatical evolution. Ph.D. Thesis, University College Dublin, Ireland, 6 Dec. 2014

55. J. Murphy, M. O'Neill, H. Carr, Exploring grammatical evolution for horse gait optimisation, in *Proceedings of the 12th European Conference on Genetic Programming, EuroGP 2009*, Tuebingen, Apr. 15–17 2009, ed. by L. Vanneschi, S. Gustafson, A. Moraglio, I. De Falco, M. Ebner. Lecture Notes in Computer Science, vol. 5481 (Springer, Berlin, 2009), pp. 183–194

56. E. Murphy, M. O'Neill, E. Galvan-Lopez, A. Brabazon, Tree-adjunct grammatical evolution, in *2010 IEEE World Congress on Computational Intelligence*, Barcelona, Spain, 18–23 July 2010 (IEEE Computational Intelligence Society/IEEE Press, New York, 2010), pp. 4449–4456

57. J.E. Murphy, H. Carr, M. O'Neill, Animating horse gaits and transitions, in *Eighth Theory and Practice of Computer Graphics TPCG 2010*, Sheffield, UK, 6–8 Sept. 2010, ed. by J. Collomosse, I. Grimstead. Eurographics

58. E. Murphy, M. Nicolau, E. Hemberg, M. O'Neill, A. Brabazon, Differential gene expression with tree-adjunct grammars, in *Parallel Problem Solving from Nature, PPSN XII (part 1)*, Taormina, Italy, Sept. 1–5 2012, ed. by C.A. Coello Coello, V. Cutello, K. Deb, S. Forrest, G. Nicosia, M. Pavone. *Lecture Notes in Computer Science*, vol. 7491 (Springer, Berlin, 2012), pp. 377–386

59. M. Nicolau, Understanding grammatical evolution: initialisation. Genet. Program. Evolvable Mach. **18**(4), 467–507 (2017)

60. M. Nicolau, M. Saunders, M. O'Neill, B. Osborne, A. Brabazon, Evolving interpolating models of net ecosystem co2 exchange using grammatical evolution, in *Proceedings of the 15th European Conference on Genetic Programming, EuroGP 2012*, ed. by A. Moraglio, S. Silva, K. Krawiec, P. Machado, C. Cotta. Lecture Notes in Computer Science, vol. 7244, Malaga, Spain, 11–13 Apr. 2012 (Springer, Berlin, 2012), pp. 134–145

61. M. O'Driscoll, S. McKenna, J.J. Collins, Synthesising edge detectors with grammatical evolution, in *GECCO 2002: Proceedings of the Bird of a Feather Workshops, Genetic and Evolutionary Computation Conference*, New York, 8 July 2002, ed. by A.M. Barry (AAAI, Menlo Park, 2002), pp. 137–140

62. C. Oesch, D. Maringer, A neutral mutation operator in grammatical evolution, in *IEEE Conference on Intelligent Systems (1)*, ed. by P.P. Angelov, K.T. Atanassov, L. Doukovska, M. Hadjiski, V.S. Jotsov, J. Kacprzyk, N. Kasabov, S. Sotirov, E. Szmidt, S. Zadrozny. Advances in Intelligent Systems and Computing, vol. 322 (Springer, Berlin, 2014), pp. 439–449

63. M. O'Neill, A. Brabazon, mGGA: the meta-grammar genetic algorithm, in *Proceedings of the 8th European Conference on Genetic Programming*, Lausanne, Switzerland, 30 Mar.–1 Apr. 2005, ed. by M. Keijzer, A. Tettamanzi, P. Collet, J. I. van Hemert, M. Tomassini. Lecture Notes in Computer Science, vol. 3447 (Springer, Berlin, 2005), pp. 311–320

64. M. O'Neill, A. Brabazon, Grammatical differential evolution, in *Proceedings of the 2006 International Conference on Artificial Intelligence, ICAI 2006*, Las Vegas, Nevada, USA, June 26–29 2006, ed. by H.R. Arabnia, vol. 1 (CSREA Press, Athens, 2006), pp. 231–236

65. M. O'Neill, A. Brabazon, Grammatical swarm: the generation of programs by social programming. Nat. Comput. **5**(4), 443–462 (2006)

66. M. O'Neill, A. Brabazon, Evolving a logo design using Lindenmayer systems, postscript and grammatical evolution, in *2008 IEEE World Congress on Computational Intelligence*, Hong Kong, 1–6 June 2008, ed. by J. Wang (IEEE Computational Intelligence Society/IEEE Press, New York, 2008), pp. 3788–3794

67. M. O'Neill, C. Ryan, Automatic generation of caching algorithms, in *Evolutionary Algorithms in Engineering and Computer Science*, Jyväskylä, Finland, 30 May–3 June 1999, ed. by K. Miettinen, M.M. Mäkelä, P. Neittaanmäki, J. Periaux (Wiley, New York, 1999), pp. 127–134

68. M. O'Neill, C. Ryan, Evolving multi-line compilable C programs, in *Genetic Programming, Proceedings of EuroGP'99*, Goteborg, Sweden, 26–27 May 1999, ed. by R. Poli, P. Nordin, W.B. Langdon, T.C. Fogarty. Lecture Notes in Computer Science, vol. 1598 (Springer, Berlin, 1999), pp. 83–92

69. M. O'Neill, C. Ryan, Crossover in grammatical evolution: a smooth operator? in R. Poli, W. Banzhaf, W.B. Langdon, J.F. Miller, P. Nordin, T.C. Fogarty, *Genetic Programming, Proceedings of EuroGP'2000*, Edinburgh, 15–16 Apr. 2000. Lecture Notes in Computer Science, vol. 1802 (Springer, Berlin, 2000), pp. 149–162

70. M. O'Neill, C. Ryan, Grammatical evolution by grammatical evolution: The evolution of grammar and genetic code, in *Genetic Programming 7th European Conference, EuroGP 2004, Proceedings*, Coimbra, Portugal, 5–7 Apr. 2004, ed. by M. Keijzer, U.-M. O'Reilly, S.M. Lucas, E. Costa, T. Soule. Lecture Notes in Computer Science, vol. 3003 (Springer, Berlin, 2004), pp. 138–149

71. M. O'Neill, J.J. Collins, C. Ryan, Automatic generation of robot behaviours using grammatical evolution, in *Proceedings of the Fifth International Symposium on Artificial Life and Robotics*, Oita, Japan, 26–28 Jan. 2000, ed. by M. Sugisaka, H. Tanaka (2000), pp. 351–354

72. M. O'Neill, C. Ryan, M. Keijzer, M. Cattolico, Crossover in grammatical evolution: the search continues, in *Genetic Programming, Proceedings of EuroGP'2001*, Lake Como, Italy, 18–20 Apr. 2001, ed. by J.F. Miller, M. Tomassini, P.L. Lanzi, C. Ryan, A.G.B. Tettamanzi, W.B. Langdon. Lecture Notes in Computer Science, vol. 2038 (Springer, Berlin, 2001), pp. 337–347

73. M. O'Neill, C. Ryan, M. Keijzer, M. Cattolico, Crossover in grammatical evolution. Genet. Program. Evolvable Mach. **4**(1), 67–93 (2003)

74. M. O'Neill, A. Brabazon, C. Adley, The automatic generation of programs for classification problems with grammatical swarm, in *Proceedings of the 2004 IEEE Congress on Evolutionary Computation*, Portland, Oregon, 20–23 June 2004 (IEEE Press, New York, 2004), pp. 104–110

75. M. O'Neill, R. Cleary, N. Nikolov, Solving Knapsak problems with attribute grammars, in *GECCO 2004 Workshop Proceedings*, Seattle, Washington, USA, 26–30 June 2004, ed. by R. Poli, S. Cagnoni, M. Keijzer, E. Costa, F. Pereira, G. Raidl, S.C. Upton, D. Goldberg, H. Lipson, E. de Jong, J. Koza, H. Suzuki, H. Sawai, I. Parmee, M. Pelikan, K. Sastry, D. Thierens, W. Stolzmann, P.L. Lanzi, S.W. Wilson, M. O'Neill, C. Ryan, T. Yu, J.F. Miller, I. Garibay, G. Holifield, A.S. Wu, T. Riopka, M.M. Meysenburg, A.W. Wright, N. Richter, J.H. Moore, M.D. Ritchie, L. Davis, R. Roy, M. Jakiela (2004)

76. M. O'Neill, A. Brabazon, E. Hemberg, Subtree deactivation control with grammatical genetic programming in dynamic environments, in *2008 IEEE World Congress on Computational Intelligence*, Hong Kong, 1–6 June 2008, ed. by J. Wang (IEEE Computational Intelligence Society/IEEE Press, New York, 2008), pp. 3768–3774

77. M. O'Neill, J. McDermott, J.M. Swafford, J. Byrne, E. Hemberg, A. Brabazon, E. Shotton, C. McNally, M. Hemberg, Evolutionary design using grammatical evolution and shape grammars: Designing a shelter. Int. J. Des. Eng. **3**(1), 4–24 (2010)

78. M. O'Neill, L. Vanneschi, S. Gustafson, W. Banzhaf, Open issues in genetic programming. Genet. Program. Evolvable Mach. **11**(3/4), 339–363 (2010). Tenth Anniversary Issue: Progress in Genetic Programming and Evolvable Machines.

79. M. O'Neill, M. Nicolau, A. Brabazon, Dynamic environments can speed up evolution with genetic programming, in *GECCO'11: Proceedings of the 13th Annual Conference Companion on Genetic and Evolutionary Computation*, Dublin, Ireland, 12–16 July 2011, ed. by N. Krasnogor, P. L. Lanzi, A. Engelbrecht, D. Pelta, C. Gershenson, G. Squillero, A. Freitas, M. Ritchie, M. Preuss, C. Gagne, Y.S. Ong, G. Raidl, M. Gallager, J. Lozano, C. Coello-Coello, D.L. Silva, N. Hansen, S. Meyer-Nieberg, J. Smith, G. Eiben, E. Bernado-Mansilla,

W. Browne, L. Spector, T. Yu, J. Clune, G. Hornby, M.-L. Wong, P. Collet, S. Gustafson, J.-P. Watson, M. Sipper, S. Poulding, G. Ochoa, M. Schoenauer, C. Witt, A. Auger (ACM, New York, 2011), pp. 191–192

80. M. O'Neill, M. Nicolau, A. Agapitos, Experiments in program synthesis with grammatical evolution: a focus on integer sorting, in *Proceedings of the 2014 IEEE Congress on Evolutionary Computation*, Beijing, China, 6–11 July 2014, ed. by C.A. Coello Coello (2014), pp. 1504–1511

81. M. O'Neill, A. Brabazon, D. Fagan, An exploration of grammatical encodings to model six nations rugby match outcomes, in *Proceedings of 2016 IEEE Congress on Evolutionary Computation (CEC 2016)*, Vancouver, 24–29 July 2016, ed. by Y.-S. Ong (IEEE Press, New York, 2016), pp. 4429–4436

82. M. O'Neill, C. Ryan, Grammar based function definition in grammatical evolution, in *Proceedings of the Genetic and Evolutionary Computation Conference (GECCO-2000)*, Las Vegas, NV, ed. by D. Whitley, D. Goldberg, E. Cantu-Paz, L. Spector, I. Parmee, H.-G. Beyer (Morgan Kaufmann, San Francisco, 2000), pp. 485–490

83. U.-M. O'Reilly, M. Hemberg, Integrating generative growth and evolutionary computation for form exploration. Genet. Program. Evolvable Mach. **8**(2), 163–186 (2007). Special issue on developmental systems.

84. A. Ortega, M. de la Cruz, M. Alfonseca, Christiansen grammar evolution: grammatical evolution with semantics. IEEE Trans. Evol. Comput. **11**(1), 77–90 (2007)

85. J. O'Sullivan, C. Ryan, An investigation into the use of different search strategies with grammatical evolution, in *Genetic Programming, Proceedings of the 5th European Conference, EuroGP 2002*, Kinsale, Ireland, 3–5 Apr. 2002, ed. by J.A. Foster, E. Lutton, J. Miller, C. Ryan, A.G.B. Tettamanzi. Lecture Notes in Computer Science, vol. 2278 (Springer, Berlin, 2002), pp. 268–277

86. C. Ryan, R.M.A. Azad, Sensible initialisation in grammatical evolution, in *GECCO 2003: Proceedings of the Bird of a Feather Workshops, Genetic and Evolutionary Computation Conference*, Chicago, 11 July 2003, ed. by A.M. Barry (AAAI, Menlo Park, 2003), pp. 142–145

87. C. Ryan, M. O'Neill, How to do anything with grammars, in *GECCO 2002: Proceedings of the Bird of a Feather Workshops, Genetic and Evolutionary Computation Conference*, New York, 8 July 2002, ed. by A.M. Barry (AAAI, Menlo Park, 2002), pp. 116–119

88. C. Ryan, M. Nicolau, M. O'Neill, Genetic algorithms using grammatical evolution, in *Genetic Programming, Proceedings of the 5th European Conference, EuroGP 2002*, Kinsale, Ireland, 3–5 Apr. 2002, ed. by J.A. Foster, E. Lutton, J. Miller, C. Ryan, A.G.B. Tettamanzi. Lecture Notes in Computer Science, vol. 2278 (Springer, Berlin, 2002), pp. 278–287

89. C. Ryan, M. Keijzer, M. Nicolau, On the avoidance of fruitless wraps in grammatical evolution, in *Genetic and Evolutionary Computation – GECCO-2003*, Chicago, 12–16 July 2003, ed. by E. Cantú-Paz, J.A. Foster, K. Deb, D. Davis, R. Roy, U.-M. O'Reilly, H.-G. Beyer, R. Standish, G. Kendall, S. Wilson, M. Harman, J. Wegener, D. Dasgupta, M.A. Potter, A.C. Schultz, K. Dowsland, N. Jonoska, J. Miller. Lecture Notes in Computer Science, vol. 2724 (Springer, Berlin, 2003), pp. 1752–1763

90. J.M. Swafford, M. O'Neill, M. Nicolau, A. Brabazon, Exploring grammatical modification with modules in grammatical evolution, in *Proceedings of the 14th European Conference on Genetic Programming, EuroGP 2011*, Turin, Italy, ed. S. Silva, J.A. Foster, M. Nicolau, M. Giacobini, P. Machado. Lecture Notes in Computer Science, vol. 6621. (Springer, Berlin, 2011), pp. 310–321. https://doi.org/10.1007/978-3-642-20407-4_27

91. J.M. Swafford, E. Hemberg, M. O'Neill, A. Brabazon, Analyzing module usage in grammatical evolution, in *Parallel Problem Solving from Nature, PPSN XII (part 1)*, Taormina, Italy, ed. by C.A. Coello Coello, V. Cutello, K. Deb, S. Forrest, G. Nicosia, M. Pavone. Lecture Notes in Computer Science, vol. 7491 (Springer, Berlin, 2012), pp. 347–356. https://doi.org/10.1007/978-3-642-32937-1_35

92. J.M. Swafford, E. Hemberg, M. O'Neill, M. Nicolau, A. Brabazon, A non-destructive grammar modification approach to modularity in grammatical evolution, in *Gecco'11: Proceedings of*

the 13th Annual Conference on Genetic and Evolutionary Computation, Dublin, Ireland, ed. by N. Krasnogor, P.L. Lanzi, A. Engelbrecht, D. Pelta, C. Gershenson, G. Squillero, A. Freitas, M, Ritchie, M. Preuss, C. Gagne, Y.S. Ong, G. Raidl, M. Gallager, J. Lozano, C. Coello-Coello, D.L. Silva, N. Hansen, S. Meyer-Nieberg, J. Smith, G. Eiben, E. Bernado-Mansilla, W. Browne, L. Spector, T. Yu, J. Clune, G. Hornby, M.-L. Wong, P. Collet, S. Gustafson, J.-P. Watson, M. Sipper, S. Poulding, G. Ochoa, M. Schoenauer, C. Witt, A. Auger (ACM, New York, 2011), pp. 1411–1418. https://doi.org/10.1145/2001576.2001766

93. J. Swafford, M. Nicolau, E. Hemberg, M. O'Neill, A. Brabazon, Comparing methods for module identification in grammatical evolution, in *GECCO'12: Proceedings of the Fourteenth International Conference on Genetic and Evolutionary Computation Conference*, Philadelphia, PA, ed. by T. Soule, A. Auger, J. Moore, D. Pelta, C. Solnon, M. Preuss, A. Dorin, Y.-S. Ong, C. Blum, D.L. Silva, F. Neumann, T. Yu, A. Ekart, W. Browne, T. Kovacs, M.-L. Wong, C. Pizzuti, J. Rowe, T. Friedrich, G. Squillero, N. Bredeche, S.L. Smith, A. Motsinger-Reif, J. Lozano, M. Pelikan, S. Meyer-Nienberg, C. Igel, G. Hornby, R. Doursat, S. Gustafson, G. Olague, S. Yoo, J. Clark, G. Ochoa, G. Pappa, F. Lobo, D. Tauritz, J. Branke, K. Deb (ACM, New York, 2012), pp. 823–830. https://doi.org/10.1145/2330163.2330277

94. A. Thompson, Silicon evolution, in *Genetic Programming 1996: Proceedings of the First Annual Conference*, Stanford University, CA, USA, 28–31 July 1996, ed. by J.R. Koza, D.E. Goldberg, D.B. Fogel, R.L. Riolo (MIT Press, Cambridge, 1996), pp. 444–452

95. P.A. Whigham, Grammatically-based genetic programming, in *Proceedings of the Workshop on Genetic Programming: From Theory to Real-World Applications*, Tahoe City, California, USA, 9 July 1995, ed. by J.P. Rosca (1995), pp. 33–41

96. P.A. Whigham, A schema theorem for context-free grammars, in *1995 IEEE Conference on Evolutionary Computation*, Perth, Australia, 29 Nov.–1 Dec. 1995, vol. 1 (IEEE Press, New York, 1995), pp. 178–181

97. P.A. Whigham, Grammatical bias for evolutionary learning. Ph.D. Thesis, School of Computer Science, University College, University of New South Wales, Australian Defence Force Academy, Canberra, Australia, 14 Oct. 1996

98. P.A. Whigham, Search bias, language bias, and genetic programming, in *Genetic Programming 1996: Proceedings of the First Annual Conference*, Stanford University, CA, USA, 28–31 July 1996, ed. by J.R. Koza, D.E. Goldberg, D.B. Fogel, R.L. Riolo (MIT Press, Cambridge, 1996), pp. 230–237

Understanding Grammatical Evolution: Grammar Design

Miguel Nicolau and Alexandros Agapitos

Abstract A frequently overlooked consideration when using Grammatical Evolution (GE) is grammar design. This is because there is an infinite number of grammars that can specify the same syntax. There are, however, certain aspects of grammar design that greatly affect the speed of convergence and quality of solutions generated with GE. In this chapter, general guidelines for grammar design are presented. These are domain-independent, and can be used when applying GE to any problem. An extensive analysis of their effect and results across a large set of experiments are reported.

1 Introduction

One of the attractive aspects of Grammatical Evolution (GE) is how it can be easily applied to a multitude of problem domains: just design a grammar specifying the syntax of potential solutions, and supply a fitness function to evaluate them.

Easily and *just* are large over-simplifications. While specifying the syntax of solutions with a context-free grammar is a relatively simple task, depending on the problem domain (a multitude of grammars exist in the literature for symbolic regression applications, for example), there is an infinite number of grammars that can specify the same syntax. But not all of them are adequate for use with GE.

In fact, the effectiveness of a grammar is deeply tied to GE's mapping process, and its effect on the search operators. In this study, this effect is analysed, and general guidelines are provided, with the aim of improving GE's search process.

There are many aspects to consider, when designing a grammar for use with GE. Some of these include which and how many non-terminal symbols to use,

M. Nicolau (✉)
College of Business, University College Dublin, Dublin, Ireland
ORCiD: orcid.org/0000-0002-1981-1300
e-mail: Miguel.Nicolau@ucd.ie

A. Agapitos
School of Computer Science, University College Dublin, Dublin, Ireland

© Springer International Publishing AG, part of Springer Nature 2018
C. Ryan et al. (eds.), *Handbook of Grammatical Evolution*,
https://doi.org/10.1007/978-3-319-78717-6_2

recursiveness, mapping probabilities, symbol biases, length of derivation sequences, prefix vs. infix vs. postfix notation, readability/understandability/maintenance of grammars, and many more.

These topics are analysed in this chapter, in terms of initial search space sampling (i.e. their combined effect with initialisation), search effectiveness (combined effect with the search operators), and quality of final solutions (fitness and size of final solutions). A large set of experiments are also executed, for empirical evidence. The results obtained confirm and highlight just how much grammar design can affect the performance of GE.

Based on these findings, a set of general grammar design guidelines are proposed for GE with linear genome representations. Although the resulting grammars can be substantially larger and more complex, most of these transformations can be automatically applied to well-designed base grammars.

2 Previous Work

Although a large volume of work exists in the literature on grammar design, particularly in linguistics and computer science, it almost exclusively relates to their use in parsing applications, i.e. syntax verification, compiler design, text mining, etc. In GE, on the contrary, grammars are used in a constructive manner, which, when combined with linear numerical sequences (genotypes) to determine derivation sequences, creates a mostly unique role for grammars.

There is surprisingly little work in the literature on the design of grammars for GE. This is probably due to the remarkable resilient nature of the evolutionary search process: given a correct and reasonably designed grammar, GE tends to produce a working solution. This is not always ideal, however, both in terms of the search effort required, and also the quality of the final solutions produced.

One of the earliest studies of the influence of grammar design on the performance of GE [22] looked specifically at reducing the number of non-terminal symbols in grammars, and proposed an automatic process of achieving this. This resulted in a small increase in performance across all problems attempted.

Hemberg et al. [11] studied the design of grammars using prefix, infix and postfix notation, and their relative performance on a series of symbolic regression problems. The most relevant conclusion is indeed that "the choice of grammar can produce performance advantage".

One of the most comprehensive analysis of the influence of grammar design in the performance of GE is found in Hemberg's doctoral thesis [10]. By allowing the grammar to evolve at the same time as the linear genome structures, knowledge is uncovered about the influence of different grammars on the performance of GE. Not surprisingly, it was again concluded that the choice of grammar can influence the performance of GE, for the problems examined.

Byrne et al. [1] analysed two types of mutation events in GE, structural or nodal in nature, and showed how these can be related to exploration and exploitation, respectively. These mutation events are directly dependent on the design of the grammars used.

Harper [9] highlighted the problem of having more production rules adding non-terminal symbols to the mapping sequence than removing them, and the negative impact of this on the performance of GE, if using linear genomes. Nicolau et al. [26] also analysed the effect of grammar design, focusing on the issue of mapping termination. Both studies highlighted the importance of good grammar design.

Grammar design, and its corresponding effect in representational bias, can also greatly influence the size of the resulting solutions. In Genetic Programming (GP), a possible outcome of this is bloat, i.e. a substantial growth in solution size, with negligible effect in performance increase [20]. Although bloat in GE is not quite as prevalent, studies have shown how grammar design directly influence the generation of very small [25] or very large [9] solutions.

More recently, work has been made on the design of grammars for sorting networks [6] and automatic program synthesis [7], although the results obtained only apply to grammar-based genetic programming systems using derivation trees.

All these studies have a common theme, which is how grammar design in GE can greatly affect its performance. The following section takes this into account, and presents a series of grammar design guidelines, or transformations for existing grammars, aimed at improving the performance of GE in different levels.

3 Grammar Design

A series of grammar transformations are presented in this section. To illustrate their application, Grammar 0 (G0) is used as a starting point. This is a typical grammar for symbolic regression applications with GE, slightly simplified (no unary operators) to illustrate the design techniques presented.

```
<s> ::= <e>
<e> ::= <e> <o> <e>
      | ( <e> <o> <e> )
      | <f> ( <e> , <e> )
      | <v>
<o> ::= + | - | *
<f> ::= pdiv
<v> ::= x | 1.0
```

Grammar 0 Simple arithmetical expressions grammar. Division uses a protected implementation, termed pdiv (more details in Sect. 5.3)

3.1 Balanced Grammars

In order to generate variable-length, unbounded phenotype solutions for any problem, GE makes use of two components:

- Variable-length genotype structures[1];
- Recursively-defined grammar rules.

Both conditions are required, in order to generate phenotype solutions of any size. If genotypes are unbounded but the grammar has no recursively defined symbols, a phenotype solution is only as large as the largest sequence of terminal symbols generated by the longest derivation path through the grammar (some studies [18] use this as both a means to limit solution size, and also to ensure validity of mapping, by always using genotype strings sufficiently long to terminate any derivation sequence).

If on the other hand the grammar is recursive, but the genotype is a fixed-length structure (of length l), the maximum phenotype solution length is the longest derivation path through the grammar smaller or equal to l mapping steps (unless wrapping is used).

The use of recursiveness in grammars with GE appears right from its first publication [38], although some interesting GE applications make use of non-recursive grammars, defining either fixed-length solutions (such as the design of a genetic algorithm using GE [28]), or maximum-length bounded solutions (such as the design of an ant-colony optimisation algorithm using GE [40]).

Recursiveness should be applied with care, however. Single levels of recursiveness are easy to implement and understand (see e.g. the second line of G0), but multiple recursive symbols or multiple line recursiveness easily become hard to design and/or understand. See for example the history of attempts at solving the Santa Fe Ant Trail Problem [15] with GE, from the original incorrect grammar [29], to a first [35] and then second [9] correction, and its analysis [26]. And yet, recent publications [17, 18, 21, 42] still use incorrect grammars, not respecting the original problem syntax.

The influence of grammar recursiveness in the ability to terminate mapping, and thus in the effectiveness of GE, has been studied as early as 2003 [39], where productions were categorised based on whether they added, maintained or reduced the number of non-terminal symbols left to map, when applied.

A way to label productions as recursive or not was proposed by Ryan and Azad [37], within the context of initialisation. Subsequently, Harper [9] labelled grammars as *explosive* or *balanced*, depending on whether there is a higher probability of adding non-terminal symbols during mapping over adding terminal symbols.

---

[1]Technically, genotypes used with GE are length-bounded, in the sense that they cannot be smaller than zero, or larger than what the memory of the machine running the experiments can hold. This maximum size is, however, a technical limitation, rather than a conceptual bound.

```
<s> ::= <e>
<e> ::= <e> <o> <e> | <v>
        | ( <e> <o> <e> ) | <v>
        | <f> ( <e> , <e> ) | <v>
<o> ::= + | - | *
<f> ::= pdiv
<v> ::= x | 1.0
```

Grammar 1 Balanced recursion grammar

These analyses are all related. In this chapter, we define as *explosive* grammars where at least one symbol has more recursive productions than non-recursive. An example is grammar G0: the symbol <e> has three recursive productions associated, and a single non-recursive production. This kind of grammar is explosive, and has a low probability of generating a fully mapped phenotype string, when used in conjunction with a randomly-generated genotype string.

For a grammar to be *balanced*, each recursive production should have a corresponding "consuming" production. Grammar 1 (G1) achieves this, by having a non-recursive production for every recursive production associated with <e>.

Note that this does not alter any biases, other than that of replacing <e> using a recursive or non-recursive production. There is also a downside: G1 now has a 50% probability of generating expressions consisting solely of either x or 1.0.

3.2 Unlinked Productions

When using GE with a linear genome, if the grammar has several non-terminal symbols, the function of a codon (the production it will choose) is dependent on the non-terminal symbol to be mapped, at a given stage of the mapping process. This means that, when crossover occurs, the function of a codon might change.

The potential destructive nature of such changes is addressed in Sect. 3.3, by reducing the number of non-terminal symbols. But if several non-terminal symbols are needed, production rules associated with different symbols can be *functionally linked*, in the sense that all codon values that choose a specific production for a symbol, if used to make a choice for a different symbol, will always choose another specific production.

Take grammar G1 as an example. Symbol <e> has six associated productions, which is a multiple of both the number of productions associated with <o> (three) and <v> (two). So if codon values transforming <e> into <e> <o> <e> are used to choose a production for <o> or <v>, they will always transform them into + and x, respectively. Table 1 illustrates this.

This can introduce biases in the exploration of the search space. As individuals grow in size (only achievable in standard GE through the use of the crossover operator), a larger proportion of even codon values are required at the start of the genome (see Table 1), and a larger proportion of odd values towards the end (to

Table 1 Functionally-linked productions of grammar G1: codon values transforming `<e>` into `<e>` `<o>` `<e>` will always transform `<o>` into + and `<v>` into x; by contrast, `<o>` and `<v>` are unlinked, as codon values transforming `<o>` into + can transform `<v>` into either x or 1.0

Codon values	Parity	`<e>`	`<o>`	`<v>`
0,6,12,...	Even	`<e>` `<o>` `<e>`	+	x
1,7,13,...	Odd	`<v>`	-	1.0
2,8,14,...	Even	(`<e>` `<o>` `<e>`)	*	x
3,9,15,...	Odd	`<v>`	+	1.0
4,10,16,...	Even	`<f>` (`<e>` , `<e>`)	-	x
5,11,17,...	Odd	`<v>`	*	1.0

terminate the recursion of the `<e>` symbol). However, this will also result in a higher proportion of symbol x at the start of the genome, and of 1.0 towards the end. Only through later specific mutation events can suitable proportions of x and 1.0 be evolved, assuming the unbalanced solution will survive until then. In other words, the structural function of the `<e>` symbol, and the nodal content function of the `<v>` symbol are linked.

The link between `<e>` and `<o>` is less obvious, but biases also exist: a solution requiring only the use of the +, - and * operators will be biased towards + and *, when solutions grow in size (first and third productions associated with `<e>`).

Note that these biases can be either beneficial or detrimental, depending on the problem domain. But for a black-box approach, with no domain knowledge, it is desirable to explore the search space in the most unbiased way.

An example is the typical grammar used with GE for the Max problem [8]. Inconsistent results were obtained with different GE mapping orders [4], and further analysis [5] produced no clear explanations for this issue; it was subsequently shown [26] that the grammar used in those experiments suffered from functionally linked productions.

The problem of linked productions was identified as early as 2002 [13]. The solution proposed then was the adoption of a different mapping procedure, called the *Bucket Rule*. However, it was later shown [26] that these biases can also be removed without modifying the standard GE mapping process, through careful grammar design.

Grammar 2 (G2) illustrates how to achieve this, through production rule repetition. In this case, six copies of each production associated with `<o>` are introduced (for a total of $6 * 3 = 18$ productions), whereas 18 copies of each production associated with `<v>` are used, for a total of $18 * 2 = 36$ productions. Note that sufficiently large codon value ranges are required, when using this technique, to ensure minimal production choice biases, but this is good GE practice anyway [31].

```
<s> ::= <e>
<e> ::= <e> <o> <e> | <v>
        | ( <e> <o> <e> ) | <v>
        | <f> ( <e> , <e> ) | <v>
<o> ::= + | + | + | + | + | +
        | - | - | - | - | - | -
        | * | * | * | * | * | *
<f> ::= pdiv
<v> ::= x | x | x | x | x | x
        | x | x | x | x | x | x
        | x | x | x | x | x | x
        | 1.0 | 1.0 | 1.0 | 1.0 | 1.0 | 1.0
        | 1.0 | 1.0 | 1.0 | 1.0 | 1.0 | 1.0
        | 1.0 | 1.0 | 1.0 | 1.0 | 1.0 | 1.0
```

Grammar 2 Unlinked productions grammar

3.3 Reduced Non-terminals

The use of linear genomes and a one point crossover with GE leads to what has been termed the *ripple effect* [32]. This means that, when viewed at a derivation tree level, crossover removes several sub-trees from each parent, which are filled with genetic material from the other parent. Given that the exchanged genetic material consists of a numerical sequence, the actual phenotypic material received may or may not correspond to the original phenotypic material from the other parent: codons reinterpreted under different derivation tree nodes (i.e. non-terminal symbols) will generate different, potentially never-seen before phenotypic material.

This change of interpretation of genetic material can be very damaging to the already fragile locality of crossover in GE [36]. However, many grammars in the literature define more non-terminal symbols than strictly required, creating further cases of reinterpretation of exchanged genetic material.

A solution is thus to reduce the number of non-terminal symbols as much as possible [22]. In fact, for symbolic regression (the most common application domain of GP-like systems [43]), grammars with a single non-terminal symbol can be used (effectively single-type languages, corresponding to GP's closure requirement).

Grammar 3 (G3) shows a single non-terminal symbol version of G1 (using G1 or G2 as a base is irrelevant, given that a single non-terminal symbol remains, <e>, so no linked productions will occur). This process works by replacing non-recursively defined non-terminal symbols by all of their productions, wherever they are used, while keeping the biases of the original grammar. A more detailed description and step by step illustration can be found in the relevant publication [22].

```
<e> ::= <e> + <e> | <e> - <e> | <e> * <e>
      | <e> + <e> | <e> - <e> | <e> * <e>
      | x | x | x
      | 1.0 | 1.0 | 1.0
      | ( <e> + <e> ) | ( <e> - <e> ) | ( <e> * <e> )
      | ( <e> + <e> ) | ( <e> - <e> ) | ( <e> * <c> )
      | x | x | x
      | 1.0 | 1.0 | 1.0
      | pdiv ( <e> , <e> ) | pdiv ( <e> , <e> )
      | pdiv ( <e> , <e> )
      | pdiv ( <e> , <e> ) | pdiv ( <e> , <e> )
      | pdiv ( <e> , <e> )
      | x | x | x
      | 1.0 | 1.0 | 1.0
```

Grammar 3 Single non-terminal grammar

```
<e> ::= ( <e> + <e> )
      | <e> + <e>
      | ( <e> - <e> )
      | <e> - <e>
      | ( <e> * <e> )
      | <e> * <e>
      | <e> pdiv <e>
      | ( <e> pdiv <e> )
      | x | x | x | x
      | 1.0 | 1.0 | 1.0 | 1.0
```

Grammar 4 Corrected-biases grammar

3.4   Grammar Biases

Grammars such as G0 are common in the literature. However, it has a 66.666% bias towards the use of one of the operators (+, -, *), resulting in a 22% bias for each, and a 33.333% bias towards the use of pdiv, which may not be desired.

To ensure an unbiased exploration of the search space, all four operators should have the same biases. This also makes the search space more comparable to that of GP. Grammar 4 (G4) shows a transformation of G3 to take this into account.

3.5   Infix/Prefix Notation

From a mathematical point of view, using a single non-terminal symbol grammar, a prefix or postfix notation will essentially produce the same performance (subject to the stochastic nature of the search process), as they explore the same (inverted) syntax space. However, infix will not, if used both with and without parenthesised expressions. For example, a prefix expression *xx may become *x+xx, if the

```
<e> ::= + <e> <e>
      | - <e> <e>
      | * <e> <e>
      | pdiv <e> <e>
      | x | x
      | 1.0 | 1.0
```

Grammar 5 Prefix-notation grammar

```
<e> ::= + <e> <e>
      | - <e> <e>
      | * <e> <e>
      | pdiv <e> <e>
      | <v>
      | <v>
      | <v>
      | <v>
<v> ::= x | x | x | x | x | x | x | x
      | 1.0 | 1.0 | 1.0 | 1.0 | 1.0 | 1.0 | 1.0 | 1.0
```

Grammar 6 Compromise transformations for a compact, understandable grammar. Note that unlinking of productions associated with `<e>` and `<v>` was required

codon encoding the second argument is mutated; with infix notation, however, $x*x$ can become either $x*(x+x)$, which is equivalent, or $x*x+x$, which is not.

There is no obvious choice to make here. Infix provides a more connected search space, but at the expense of further loss of locality for the genetic operators; prefix/postfix do the opposite. They also provide a more comparable search space to that of tree-based GP. Grammar 5 (G5) shows a prefix version of G4.

3.6 Compromise Grammars

Although the transformations presented can be achieved through an algorithmic process (and thus automated), the resulting grammars can easily grow exponentially in both size and complexity, and become very hard to understand or modify. The addition of a carefully chosen single non-terminal symbol (`<v>` in this case) is often enough to maintain the readability of a grammar, at the expense of a slight worsening of crossover locality. Grammar 6 (G6) illustrates this. Although not apparent when compared to G5, in problems with large numbers of operators and variables, this can drastically reduce the number of productions in a grammar (see Table 5, grammars G5 (5625 productions) and G6 (17 productions)).

4 Transformations Analysis

A series of detailed experiments were performed, using grammars G0–G6, to analyse the effect of grammar design on search space biases, size, termination, repetition, and performance. Table 2 shows the experimental setup used.

Populations were initialised using Random Initialisation (RND) (random integer strings), or using a depth-less variant of Probabilistic Tree Creation 2 (PTC2) [19, 23]. These were chosen as many recent publications still use RND initialisation [17, 21], whereas PTC2 was chosen for its proven performance [23]. Depending on the grammar used, the specified number of codons/expansions for initialisation is sufficient to generate expressions of up to a corresponding syntax tree depth of 5.

4.1 Initialisation Biases

This first experiment analyses the initial populations generated using the two initialisation methods. The proportion of each phenotypic symbol (+, -, *, pdiv, 1.0 (const) and x (var)) in all successfully mapped individuals was recorded, along with measures related to the mapping process: average phenotype length, number of invalid (non-mapping) individuals generated, and number of repeated (valid) phenotypic solutions. Figure 1 shows the results obtained, for 100 independent runs.

The top half of the figure illustrates how grammar design affects the initial sampling of the search space. G0–G3 exhibit a bias towards the use of division. In the first three grammars, this is because 2/3 of the recursive definitions of the <e> symbol use a function of the set (+, -, *), whereas 1/3 use division; this results in a biased sampling of $2/3 \div 3 = 2/9$ for each of (+, -, *), and 3/9 for division. These biases are held with the reduction of non-terminal symbols used in G3.

Table 2 Experimental setup

Population size	500[a]
Number of generations	50
Random initialisation genome length	31
PTC2 max expansions	31
Maximum genome length	–
Selection tournament size	1%
Elitism (for generational replacement)	1%
Crossover ratio	50%
Average mutation events per individual	1
Max wrapping events	0

[a]200 for Shape Match (Easy and Medium) (see Sect. 5); 1000 for V4, K12, Housing, EPar5 and Mux11 (see Sect. 5); 2000 for Dow (see Sect. 5)

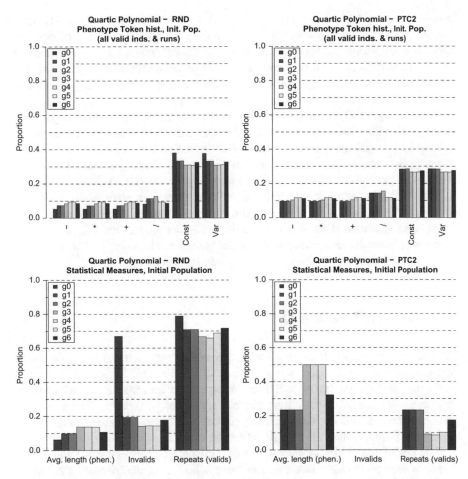

Fig. 1 Symbol frequency proportions (top) in the initial populations (measured over all successfully mapped solutions), and mapping process related statistics (bottom), using RND (left) and PTC2 (right). Results obtained from 100 independent runs

Other biases are seen in this figure. G0–G2 and G6, due to their larger number of non-terminal symbols, generate smaller expressions than the other grammars, when provided with the same number of genes (RND) or expansions (PTC2); this explains their slightly smaller frequency of functions, and higher frequency of terms (1.0 and x). In any case, all grammars exhibit a larger proportion of terms in their phenotypes, when using RND; this is due to the very high probability of transforming an <e> symbol into a term (1/4 for G0, and 1/2 for all the other grammars), meaning many solutions will consist of a single term. The use of PTC2 substantially reduces the appearance of such solutions.

The bottom half of the figure shows statistics related to the mapping process. The average length is a ratio of the average number of functions/terms in the generated phenotypes (e.g. `1.0 + x` and `(1.0 + x)` both have length 3) over 31. RND creates much shorter solutions than PTC2, due to the 50% probability of creating very short solutions. As for G0, although it is biased towards larger solutions, it usually cannot create such solutions, due to its reduced probability of terminating the mapping process. In any case, G0–G2 and G6 create shorter phenotypes, due to the intermediate symbols used during the mapping process.

When using RND, the proportion of non-mapping individuals is alarmingly high for explosive G0. Although far lower, G1, G2 and G6 also have some difficulty to map integer strings, due to the number of derivation steps required to terminate the mapping process (a problem shared with G0). G3–G5 map around 85% of the random integer strings. Naturally, all phenotypes generated by PTC2 are valid.

Within the successfully-mapped individuals, there is a very high proportion of repeated solutions with RND, again a consequence of the high probability of generating single term solutions. This is slightly higher for G0, due to the increasing difficulty in successfully mapping long individuals. PTC2, ramping by size, generates longer solutions, and thus generates less repetition.

4.2 Random Walk Biases

This second experiment tests the effect of recombination and mutation on the initial populations seen in the previous experiment. To this end, 50 generations were performed in each run, but all individuals (mapping or not) were assigned the same flat fitness. This effectively means random walks are performed, biased both by grammar design, and by the genetic operators used (linear crossover and integer mutation). Figure 2 shows the results obtained, at the last generation.

The top half of the figure shows no major differences between RND and PTC2. There is an even stronger bias towards using + and `1.0`, due to shorter solutions being generated. However, the biases introduced by grammar design are still quite present, particularly towards division, in G0–G3.

The bottom plot shows that grammar design affects the dissemination of illegal individuals by a large amount: by generation 50, over 90% of individuals in runs using G0 are invalid, due to its non-terminating bias. G1, G2 and G6 exhibit ≈ 70% invalids, suffering from their complex, many non-terminal symbols mapping (a problem shared with G0). G3–G5 have an expected 50% chance of generating mapping individuals under random search. This is the case using both RND and PTC2, which shows that this bias exists irrespective of the starting population.

Finally, there is a huge amount of repetition in the (valid) solutions generated. The majority are short, single term solutions, as they are more likely to survive unharmed (and unchanged) genetic operators applied with no fitness pressure.

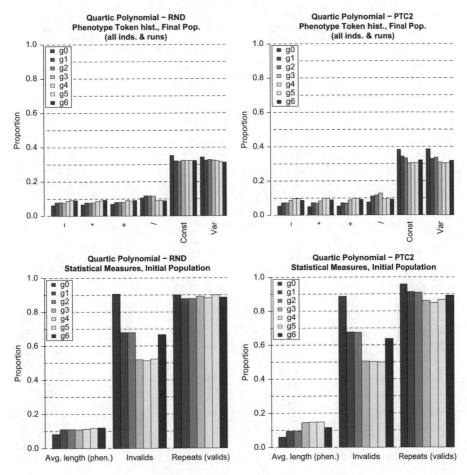

Fig. 2 Symbol frequency proportions (top) in the final populations (measured over all successfully mapped solutions), and mapping process related statistics (bottom), using RND (left) and PTC2 (right). Results obtained from 100 independent runs

4.3 Termination Biases

Mapping termination has always been a hotly debated topic in GE. This third experiment investigates how it is influenced by grammar design. The experimental setup is the same as in the previous sub-section, except that non-mapping individuals are assigned a very bad fitness score (the usual way of dealing with non-mapping solutions in GE [30]), whereas all others are assigned a fixed (good) fitness. The results obtained are shown in Fig. 3.

The top half of the figure shows once again that, irrespectively of using RND or PTC2, symbol biases are practically the same. The previously analysed bias towards division is still visible in G0–G3. Particularly worrying is the high bias of 1.0 over

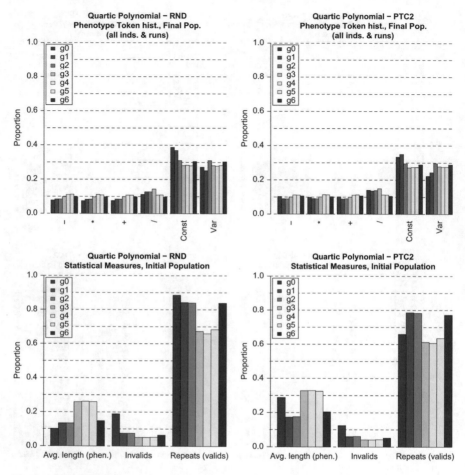

Fig. 3 Symbol frequency proportions (top) in the final populations (measured over all successfully mapped solutions), and mapping process related statistics (bottom), using RND (left) and PTC2 (right). Results obtained from 100 independent runs. Non-mapping solutions were assigned the worst possible fitness

x in G0 and G1. This is a direct reflection of the propagation and recombination of mapping individuals, in combination with linked grammar productions. In G0, a large amount of codons with a value $c_i \% 4 = 3$ are required, to choose the recursion stopping production "$<e>$ becomes $<v>$"; but those same codons, when interpreted under the context of $<v>$, will choose the term 1.0. The same effect is seen in G1: odd codon values are required to stop recursion of the $<e>$ symbol, but these will choose the symbol 1.0 over the symbol x (see Table 1). These problems are removed by unlinking production choices (grammars G2–G6).

The use of bad fitness for non-mapping individuals is effective at reducing the number of illegal solutions, without requiring the propagation of extremely small solutions. There is still a large proportion of repetition, driven in this case by genetic drift: similar individuals undergoing crossover are less likely to produce illegal offspring, leading to increased repetition in the final population. Finally, note the smaller difference between RND and PTC2 at the end of these runs.

4.4 Performance Biases

To test how these findings affect performance, a series of symbolic regression experiments were ran with all seven grammars, to solve the following problems:

1. Quartic Polynomial: $x^4 + x^3 + x^2 + x$;
2. Sextic Polynomial: $x^6 + x^5 + \cdots + x^2 + x$;
3. Octic Polynomial: $x^8 + x^7 + \cdots + x^2 + x$;
4. Dectic Polynomial: $x^{10} + x^8 + \cdots + x^2 + x$.

These problems are easy to solve, with a controlled degree of difficulty, and can be correlated to the effects of symbol biases. Note that fully configured GE runs were performed; this included the use of tails [26] at a 50% ratio at initialisation, for better mapping termination. Figure 4 shows the measured biases and statistics for the quartic and dectic polynomial, using PTC2 (RND results were similar).

There is a clear bias towards the use of multiplication (mostly), addition, and x, the symbols required to solve the problem. The smaller uses of division, subtraction, and 1.0 are mostly due to non-effective code (bloat). It is interesting to observe that a bias towards division is still found when using G3. Solution length is short, a reflection of GE's mapping process and also the easy nature of the problems, with the downside of still a large amount of repetition in the last generation (due both to genetic drift and to smaller solutions being generated). Finally, experiments using G0 still generate a large amount of illegal solutions.

Figure 5 plots the results obtained. Most configurations solve the easier problem on every run, but as the polynomial degree increases, performance slowly worsens. Results using PTC2 are better than those using RND, as expected [23].

The graphs also illustrate how grammar design can affect (or not) the performance of GE. The most obvious observation is that the reduction of grammar complexity and the associated termination biases can vastly improve performance: setups using G0–G2 are consistently worse than all other setups. Also interesting is how the bias of G2 and G3 towards the use of division has almost no effect on performance. This is because division can be used almost as effectively as multiplication to increase the degree of the polynomial ($x \times x$ versus $\frac{x}{1/x}$).

Finally, the relative differences between grammars are consistent across the two initialisers, apart from G0: the lack of invalid solutions in the initial population of PTC2, along with its larger initial solution size (see Fig. 1), substantially improve the final performance of runs using G0.

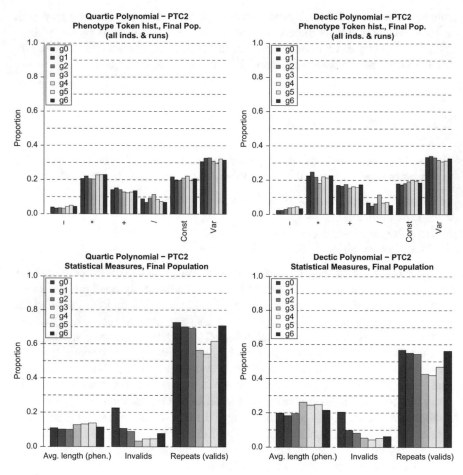

Fig. 4 Symbol frequency proportions (top) in the final populations (measured over all successfully mapped solutions), and mapping process related statistics (bottom), using PTC2, on quartic (left) and dectic (right) polynomial. Results obtained from 100 independent runs

5 Performance Analysis

5.1 Problems

To measure the effect of grammar design on the final outcome of GE's evolutionary process, a series of experiments were ran across several problem types. These include regression, classification and design problems, across several application domains and difficulty ranges. Table 3 lists all the problems attempted.

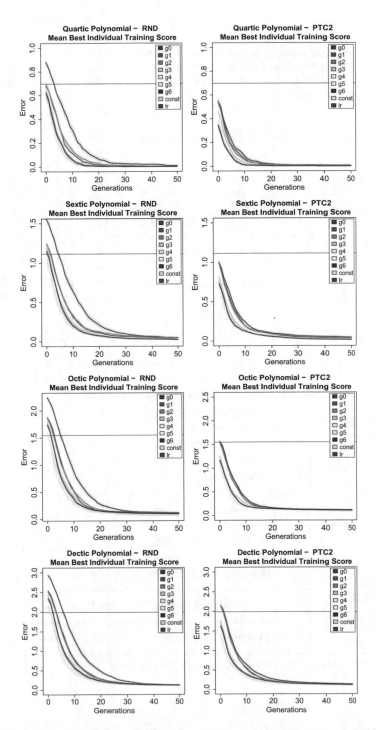

Fig. 5 Mean best individual fitness for the polynomial regression experiments, using RND (left) and PTC2 (right), averaged across 100 independent runs; error is measured as RMSE. Shades indicate 95% confidence intervals about the mean. Cyan and blue lines (where visible) show the RMSE of a constant predictor (mean of the train response variable) and a linear regression model of the training set, respectively

Table 3 Benchmark problems; if specified, $E[a, b, c]$ means a grid of points evenly spaced with an interval of c, from a to b inclusive, whereas $U[a, b, c]$ means c uniform random samples drawn from a to b inclusive; the specified type is regression (R), classification (C#) (# = number of classes), or image matching (IM)

Name	Vars.	Data source	Type	Training set Test Set
Keijzer-6 (K6) [12]	1	$y = \sum_i^x \frac{1}{i}$	R	$E[1, 50, 1]$ $E[1, 120, 1]$
Pagie-1 (P1) [34]	2	$y = \frac{1}{1+x_1^{-4}} + \frac{1}{1+x_2^{-4}}$	R	$E[-5, 5, 0.4]$ $E[-5, 5, 0.1]$
Vladislavleva-4 (V4) [41]	5	$y = \frac{10}{5+\sum_{i=1}^5 (x_i-3)^2}$	R	$U[0.05, 0.05, 1024]$ $U[-0.25, 6.35, 5k]$
Tower [41]	5	Gas chromatography data	R	4721 points 278 points
Korns-12 (K12) [14]	5	$y = 2 - 2.1cos(9.8x_1)sin(1.3x_5)$	R	$U[-50, 50, 10k]$ $U[-50, 50, 10k]$
Forest [2]	12	Forest Fires data	R	414 points 103 points
Housing [16]	13	Housing values	R	354 points 152 points
Dow Chemical (Dow)[a]	57	Chemical process data	R	747 points 319 points
Even-parity 5 (EPar5) [15]	5	Parity of boolean inputs	C2	32 points –
Multiplexer 11 (Mux11) [15]	11	Boolean multiplexer	C2	2048 points –
Breast Cancer Wisconsin [16]	9	Diagnostic data	C2	400 points 283 points
Wine Quality: red [3]	11	Physicochemical test data	C10	1000 points 599 points
Wine Quality: white [3]	11	Physicochemical test data	C10	3000 points 1898 points
Shape Match (Easy) [33]	–	Generated 250x250 shape	IM	– –
Shape Match (Medium) [33]	–	Generated 250x250 shape	IM	– –
Shape Match (Hard) [33]	–	Generated 250x250 shape	IM	– –

[a]Source: http://gpbenchmarks.org/symbolicregressioncompetition/

5.2   Grammars

For every problem attempted, seven grammar versions were designed, G0–G6, as detailed in Sect. 3. Each of the grammars respects as much as possible the original function and terminal sets as defined in their original publications; this is important for benchmarking purposes, as attempting to solve a problem using different functions can severely alter the difficulty of the benchmarks [27]. For all problems, constants were created using digit concatenation, with 100 possible values within the range [0.0 . . . 9.9], and a step of 0.1.

Each of the problems was attempted using both RND and PTC2, over 100 independent runs. To illustrate the grammar transformation process, and its impact on the search effectiveness of GE, three problems are examined in detail: Keijzer-6, Vladislavleva-4, and Shape Match (hard).

5.2.1   Keijzer-6

The Keijzer-6 (K6) problem [12], also known as the Harmonic function, is a single-variable problem, using only addition, multiplication and three unary functions. A typical GE grammar defining possible solutions for this problem is shown in Table 4, cell G0. The symbol `<e>` has more productions creating new `<e>` symbols rather than mapping them to something else, so the G1 version addresses this, by having a "`| <v>`" production for each production replacing one `<e>` symbol with two. There are two sets of non-terminal symbols with linked productions: `<o>` with `<v>`, and `<e>` with `<d>`. This is addressed in G2, through repetition of productions.

G3 reduces the number of non-terminal symbols to a single one, while maintaining the biases of G1 and G2. This results in a much larger grammar, with 3000 production rules. Grammar G4 addresses the slightly higher bias towards use of the operators $+$ and $*$ over the functions inv, neg and $sqrt$.

Grammar G5 is a conversion to prefix notation, which considerably reduces the complexity of the grammar, by removing bracketed versions of the $+$ and $*$ operators. Finally, G6 separates the definition of functions and terminals into two symbols (`<e>` and `<v>`), resulting in a very compact grammar, but without the extra complexity of grammars G0–G2.

5.2.2   Vladislavleva-4

The Vladislavleva-4 (V4) problem [41], also known as the UBall5D function, is a five-variable problem, and its function set, as defined in its original publication, is extensive:

- Functions: $+, -, *, /, square, x^{real}, x + real, x \cdot real$
- Terminals: $x0, x1, x2, x3, x4$

Table 4 Grammars used for the Keijzer-6 (K6) problem, versions G0–G6; a set of productions followed by {n} means they are repeated n times, whereas the notation $\alpha| \ldots |\delta$ is shorthand for a production for each of the elements in the sequence $[\alpha..\delta]$; constants in G6 are created using GECodonValue [24]

G0	G1	G2
`<e> ::= <e>`	`<e> ::= <e>`	`<e> ::= <e>`
`<e> ::= <op> <e> <e>`	`<e> ::= <op> <e> <e>`	`<e> ::= <op> <e> <e>`
`	(<e> <op> <e>)`	`	<v>`	`	<v>`
`	<f> (<e>)`	`	(<e> <op> <e>)`	`	(<e> <op> <e>)`
`	<v>`	`	<v>`	`	<v>`
`<op> ::= +	*`	`	<f> (<e>)`	`	<f> (<e>)`
`<f> ::= inv|neg|sqrt`	`<op> ::= +|*`	`<op> ::= +|+`
`<v> ::= <d>.<d>`	`<f> ::= inv	neg	sqrt`	`	*	*`
`  |x0`	`<v> ::= <d>.<d>`	`<f> ::= inv|neg|sqrt`
`<d> ::= 0|1|2|3|4|5|6|7|8|9`	`  |x0`	`<v> ::= <d>.<d>`
	`<d> ::= 0|1|2|3|4|5|6|7|8|9`	`	x0`
		`<d> ::= 0|0|0|0|0|1|1|1|1|1`
		`  |2|2|2|2|2|3|3|3|3|3`
		`  |4|4|4|4|4|5|5|5|5|5`
		`  |6|6|6|6|6|7|7|7|7|7`
		`  |8|8|8|8|8|9|9|9|9|9`

G3	G4	G5
`<e> ::= <e> + <e> {300}`	`<e> ::= <e> + <e> {300}`	`<e> ::= + <e> <e> {100}`
`	<e> * <e> {300}`	`	<e> * <e> {300}`	`	* <e> <e> {100}`
`	x0 {300}`	`	x0 {300}`	`	x0 {100}`
`	0.0| ... |9.9 {3}`	`	0.0| ... |9.9 {3}`	`	0.0| ... |9.9`
`	(<e> + <e>) {300}`	`	(<e> + <e>) {300}`	`	inv(<e>) {100}`
`	(<e> * <e>) {300}`	`	(<e> * <e>) {300}`	`	neg(<e>) {100}`
`	x0{300}`	`	x0{300}`	`	sqrt(<e>) {100}`
`	0.0| ... |9.9 {3}`	`	0.0| ... |9.9 {3}`	
`	inv(<e>) {200}`	`	inv(<e>) {300}`	
`	neg(<e>) {200}`	`	neg(<e>) {300}`	
`	sqrt(<e>) {200}`	`	sqrt(<e>) {300}`	

G6
`<e> ::= + <e> <e>	<v>`
`	* <e> <e>	<v>`
`  |inv <e> |neg <e> |sqrt <e>`
`<v> ::= x0| <GECodonValue{0.0 : 9.9 : 0.1}>`

This results in a complex base grammar, shown in Table 5, cell G0. The definition of the <e> symbol has a heavy bias towards growth, which is addressed in G1. It also has a more complex set of linked production, between the symbols <a> (five productions), <v> (five productions) and <d> (ten productions); G2 addresses this by introducing 10 copies of each original production associated with <a>, and 50 copies of each original production associated with <v>.

As before, G3 reduces the number of non-terminal symbols to just one, but to ensure the same bias choices as G1 and G2, and due to the required combinations of 5 variables and 100 constants for certain operators, it defines 17,498 production rules.[2] Grammar G4 balances the bias between all four binary operators (+, −, ∗, /), with 1250 productions using each (625 bracketed and 625 non-bracketed), and the single unary operator, *square* (625 productions); the resulting grammar, while smaller, still contains 10,625 productions.

---

[2]The required number of 2500/3 copies of each of the productions using the operators +, −, ∗ were rounded to 833, resulting in a negligible bias.

Table 5 Grammars used for the Vladislavleva-4 (V4) problem, versions G0–G6; a set of productions followed by {*n*} means they are repeated *n* times, whereas the notation $\alpha | \ldots | \delta$ is shorthand for a production for each of the elements in the sequence $[\alpha..\delta]$; constants in G6 are created using GECodonValue [24]

G0	G1	G2
`<e>::=<e>`	`<e>::=<e>`	`<e>::=<e>`
`<e>::=<e> <o> <e>`	`<e>::=<e> <o> <e>`	`<e>::=<e> <o> <e>`
`	(<e> <o> <e>)`	`	<v>`	`	<v>`
`	<f1> (<e>, <e>)`	`	(<e> <o> <e>)`	`	(<e> <o> <e>)`
`	<f2> (<e>, 2)`	`	<v>`	`	<v>`
`	<v>`	`	<f1> (<e>, <e>)`	`	<f1> (<e>, <e>)`
`<o>::= +| - |*`	`	<v>`	`	<v>`
`<f1>::= pdiv`	`	<f2> (<e>, 2)`	`	<f2> (<e>, 2)`
`<f2>::= pow`	`<o>::= +| - |*`	`<o>::= +| - |*`
`<e>::= pow(<v>, <d><d>)`	`<f1>::= pdiv`	`<f1>::= pdiv`
`   |(<v> + <d><d>)`	`<f2>::= pow`	`<f2>::= pow`
`   |(<v> * <d><d>)`	`<e>::= pow(<v>, <d><d>)`	`<e>::= pow(<v>, <d><d>){10}`
`	<v>`	`	(<v> + <d><d>)`	`	(<v> + <d><d>){10}`
`	<d><d>`	`	(<v> * <d><d>)`	`	(<v> * <d><d>){10}`
`<v>::= x0|x1|x2|x3|x4`	`	<v>`	`	<v> {10}`
`<d>::= 0|1|2|3|4|5|6|7|8|9`	`	<d><d>`	`	<d><d> {10}`
	`<v>::= x0|x1|x2|x3|x4`	`<v>::= x0|x1|x2|x3|x4{50}`
	`<d>::= 0|1|2|3|4|5|6|7|8|9`	`<d>::= 0|1|2|3|4|5|6|7|8|9`

G3	G4	G5
`<e>::=<e> + <e> {833}`	`<e>::=<e> + <e> {625}`	`<e>::= + <e> <e> {625}`
`	<e> - <e> {833}`	`	<e> - <e> {625}`	`   |- <e> <e> {625}`
`	<e> * <e> {833}`	`	<e> * <e> {625}`	`   |* <e> <e> {625}`
`   |(<e> + <e>) {833}`	`	<e> pdiv <e> {625}`	`   |pdiv <e> <e> {625}`
`   |(<e> - <e>) {833}`	`   |(<e> + <e>) {625}`	`   |pow <e> 2 {625}`
`   |(<e> * <e>) {833}`	`   |(<e> - <e>) {625}`	`   |pow x0 0.0|...|pow x0 9.9`
`   |pdiv(<e>, <e>) {2500}`	`   |(<e> * <e>) {625}`	`   |pow x1 0.0|...|pow x1 9.9`
`   |pow(<e>, 2) {2500}`	`   |(<e> pdiv <e>) {625}`	`   |pow x2 0.0|...|pow x2 9.9`
`   |pow(x0, 0.0)|...|pow(x0, 9.9) {3}`	`   |pow(<e>, 2) {2500}`	`   |pow x3 0.0|...|pow x3 9.9`
`   |pow(x1, 0.0)|...|pow(x1, 9.9) {3}`	`   |pow(x0, 0.0)|...|pow(x0, 9.9) {2}`	`   |pow x4 0.0|...|pow x4 9.9`
`   |pow(x2, 0.0)|...|pow(x2, 9.9) {3}`	`   |pow(x1, 0.0)|...|pow(x1, 9.9) {2}`	`   |+ x0 0.0|...|+ x0 9.9`
`   |pow(x3, 0.0)|...|pow(x3, 9.9) {3}`	`   |pow(x2, 0.0)|...|pow(x2, 9.9) {2}`	`   |+ x1 0.0|...|+ x1 9.9`
`   |pow(x4, 0.0)|...|pow(x4, 9.9) {3}`	`   |pow(x3, 0.0)|...|pow(x3, 9.9) {2}`	`   |+ x2 0.0|...|+ x2 9.9`
`   |(x0 + 0.0)|...|(x0 + 9.9) {3}`	`   |pow(x4, 0.0)|...|pow(x4, 9.9) {2}`	`   |+ x3 0.0|...|+ x3 9.9`
`   |(x1 + 0.0)|...|(x1 + 9.9) {3}`	`   |(x0 + 0.0)|...|(x0 + 9.9) {2}`	`   |+ x4 0.0|...|+ x4 9.9`
`   |(x2 + 0.0)|...|(x2 + 9.9) {3}`	`   |(x1 + 0.0)|...|(x1 + 9.9) {2}`	`   |* x0 0.0|...|* x0 9.9`
`   |(x3 + 0.0)|...|(x3 + 9.9) {3}`	`   |(x2 + 0.0)|...|(x2 + 9.9) {2}`	`   |* x1 0.0|...|* x1 9.9`
`   |(x4 + 0.0)|...|(x4 + 9.9) {3}`	`   |(x3 + 0.0)|...|(x3 + 9.9) {2}`	`   |* x2 0.0|...|* x2 9.9`
`   |(x0 * 0.0)|...|(x0 * 9.9) {3}`	`   |(x4 + 0.0)|...|(x4 + 9.9) {2}`	`   |* x3 0.0|...|* x3 9.9`
`   |(x1 * 0.0)|...|(x1 * 9.9) {3}`	`   |(x0 * 0.0)|...|(x0 * 9.9) {2}`	`   |* x4 0.0|...|* x4 9.9`
`   |(x2 * 0.0)|...|(x2 * 9.9) {3}`	`   |(x1 * 0.0)|...|(x1 * 9.9) {2}`	`   |x0|x1|x2|x3|x4 {100}`
`   |(x3 * 0.0)|...|(x3 * 9.9) {3}`	`   |(x2 * 0.0)|...|(x2 * 9.9) {2}`	`   |0.0|...|9.9 {5}`
`   |(x4 * 0.0)|...|(x4 * 9.9) {3}`	`   |(x3 * 0.0)|...|(x3 * 9.9) {2}`	
`   |x0|x1|x2|x3|x4 {300}`	`   |(x4 * 0.0)|...|(x4 * 9.9) {2}`	
`   |0.0|...|9.9 {15}`	`   |x0|x1|x2|x3|x4 {200}`	
	`   |0.0|...|9.9 {10}`	

G6

```
<e>::= + <e> <e>
   |- <e> <e>
   |* <e> <e>
   |pdiv <e> <e>
   |pow <e> 2
   |pow <v> <GECodonValue{0.0 : 9.9 : 0.1}>
   |+ <v> <GECodonValue{0.0 : 9.9 : 0.1}>
   |* <v> <GECodonValue{0.0 : 9.9 : 0.1}>
   | <v>
   | <v>
   | <GECodonValue{0.0 : 9.9 : 0.1}>
   | <GECodonValue{0.0 : 9.9 : 0.1}>
<v>::= x0|x1|x2|x3|x4
```

The conversion to a prefix notation in G5 further reduces complexity, but it still contains 5625 productions. Finally, the separation of variables to a different symbol (<v>) removes the complexity of variable and constant combination, and the resulting grammar is far more compact and understandable.

5.2.3 Shape Match (Hard)

The Shape Match problem [33] was setup as a demonstration of the use of shape grammars with GE. The objective is to match a pre-defined image, defined in a 250x250 binary pixel matrix, using a sequence of shape creation and manipulation instructions. It was defined using three variants, *easy*, *medium* and *hard*, with increasingly more complex target images. The drawing functions available are as follows: s0 moves the shape right 10 pixels; s1 moves the shape down 10 pixels; s2 moves the shape left 10 pixels; s3 moves the shape up 10 pixels; gro doubles the size of the shape; shrnk halves the size of the shape; [and] push and pop the pen's state (position where it will draw next) onto and off the stack. Finally, sqr draws a square, and crcl draws a circle.

Table 6 shows the original grammar [33] as G0, with a call to a Python interpreter. It has no recursively defined binary operators: a single call to <p>::=<e> stops recursion of symbol <p>, and likewise, a single call to <e>::=<v> terminates the recursion of <e>. As such, G1 is identical to G0. There are, however, two sets of non-terminal symbols with linked productions: <p> with <v>, and <e> with <o>. G2 addresses this, through the explained approach of repetition of productions.

G3 reduces the number of non-terminal symbols to three. Although the first symbol (<s>) is of minor importance (it has a single associated production, so no codon is used, and it appears only once, at the start), the recursive nature of symbols <p> and <e> in G0–G2 requires the presence of both. Also, after the incorporation of symbols <o> and <v> into <e>, the resulting number of productions is even, which links them with those associated with <p>, so the explained unlinking process was employed. G4 is similar, but reduces the bias of the [] operator to that of all other transformations.

G5 replaces [] with a prefix equivalent operator, *pushed*. This allows the definition of what is essentially a single non-terminal symbol grammar (not counting the <s> symbol, as explained above). The exact biases of G4 are impossible to keep, so a compromise was chosen. Finally, G6 uses three symbols, <p>, <o> and <v>, to create a compact and highly readable grammar.

5.3 Experimental Setup

The experimental setup used was the same as in Table 2, but using 50% non-coding tails at initialisation [26]. Also, as seen in Sect. 4.1, different grammars will generate different solution sizes at initialisation, with direct influence in their initial fitnesses. In order to properly analyse the effect of grammar design in the search capability

Table 6 Grammars used for the Shape Match (hard) problem, versions G0–G6; a set of productions followed by {n} means they are repeated n times, whereas the notation α| . . . |δ is shorthand for a production for each of the elements in the sequence [α..δ]; constants in G6 are created using GECodonValue [24]

G0	G1 (same as G0)	G2
<s>::= python hard.py <p>	<s>::= python hard.py <p>	<s>::= python hard.py <p>
<p>::=<e>	<p>::=<e>	<p>::=<e>
| <e> <p>	| <e> <p>	| <e> <p>
<e>::=<t>	<e>::=<t>	<e>::=<t>
| <t> <e>	| <t> <e>	| <t> <e>
| [<e>]	| [<e>]	| [<e>]
<t>::= s0	<t>::= s0	<t>::= s0|s0|s0
| s1	| s1	| s1|s1|s1
| s2	| s2	| s2|s2|s2
| s3	| s3	| s3|s3|s3
| gro	| gro	| gro|gro|gro
| shrnk	| shrnk	| shrnk|shrnk|shrnk
<d>::= sqr	<d>::= sqr	<d>::= sqr|sqr
| crcl	| crcl	| crcl|crcl

G3	G4	G5
<s>::= python hard.py <p>	<s>::= python hard.py <p>	<s>::= python hard.py <p>
<p>::=<e> {18}	<p>::=<e> {42}	<p>::= sqr {7}
| <e> <p> {18}	| <e> <p> {42}	| crcl {7}
<e>::= sqr {3}	<e>::= sqr {7}	| s0 <p> {2}
| crcl {3}	| crcl {7}	| s1 <p> {2}
| s0 <e>	| s0 <e>	| s2 <p> {2}
| s1 <e>	| s1 <e> {4}	| s3 <p> {2}
| s2 <e>	| s2 <e> {4}	| gro <p> {2}
| s3 <e>	| s3 <e> {4}	| shrnk <p> {2}
| gro <e>	| gro <e> {4}	| pushed <p> {2}
| shrnk <e>	| shrnk <e> {4}	| sqr <p> {7}
| [<e>] {6}	| [<e>] {4}	| crcl <p> {7}

G6
<s>::= python hard.py <p>
<p>::=<t> | <t> <p> | <t> <p>
<t>::= s0 | s1 | s2 | s3 | gro | shrnk | pushed
<d>::= sqr | crcl

Table 7 Genome length (for RND) and min/max derivation steps (for PTC2) used during initialisation, for the three problems analysed

Problem	Parameter	g0	g1	g2	g3	g4	g5	g6
Keijzer6	Genome length	30	30	30	15	15	15	23
	Min. der. steps	3	3	3	1	1	1	2
	Max. der. steps	31	31	31	15	15	15	23
Vladislavleva4	Genome length	54	54	54	15	15	15	31
	Min. der. steps	4	4	4	1	1	1	2
	Max. der. steps	55	55	55	15	15	15	31
Shape Match (hard)	Genome length	24	24	24	14	14	14	23
	Min. der. steps	4	4	4	3	3	2	3
	Max. der. steps	25	25	25	15	15	16	24

of GE, experiments using different grammars were setup such that they generate similarly sized phenotype solutions at initialisation. As such, RND and PTC2 were setup as shown in Table 7. Finally, protected versions of some operators were used, such as division (1.0 if divisor $< 1e - 5$), inversion (1.0 if argument $< 1e - 5$), and square root ($\sqrt{|x|}$).

5.4 Results

Figure 6 plots the mean best train results for the K6, V4 and Shape Match (hard) problem, using RND and PTC2 initialisation.[3] All grammar variants find similarly good solutions for the K6 experiment at the 50th generation, using PTC2, but much larger differences are found between the results obtained with grammars G0–G2 versus those with grammars G3–G6, when using RND. A similar result is observed for the V4 experiment, except that in this case, the difference between G0–G2 and G3–G6 is more evident when using PTC2.

Finally, the Shape Match (hard) experiments again show a large difference between both clusters of grammars, along with the positive effect in convergence of removing the high bias towards the [] operator in G4–G6 (applying it more than once has no practical effect). Although there is a very marked change in the speed of convergence towards an optimal solution, particularly with the reduction of non-terminal symbols, eventually all grammar solutions find similarly good solutions.

5.4.1 Significance and Test Results

In order to quantify the effect of each grammar design on the search effectiveness of GE, two-sample Mann-Whitney U-tests were calculated for final median best fit results, for all grammars. The results are shown in Table 8.

These are similar to what was observed in the K6, V4 and Shape Match problems. Overall, runs using G3–G5 are significantly better than all others. Small differences between G3–G5 are mostly problem domain specific. G0–G2 are often significantly better only amongst themselves, with the exception of a few noisy real-world datasets, such as Tower and Wine Quality. G6 seems to provide a compromise between performance and complexity of grammar. As before, G0 does particularly bad with RND initialisation, and differences between different grammars are less evident when using PTC2.

Regarding test performance, no validation or early-stopping approaches were employed in these experiments, so it is not unreasonable to expect some level of overfitting, particularly from approaches with very good training performance. The statistical significance results are shown in Table 9.

As expected, the test results are far less clear cut. Results are still better when using G3–G5, but are very problem-dependent. This mostly results from problems such as K12: it is such a hard problem to solve using the original function and terminal set [14] (which uses no trigonometric functions), that any small improvement in training performance invariably led to a degradation in test performance.

---

[3] As the focus of this study is on grammar design, no regression performance improving techniques such as linear scaling [12] or cross-validation were used.

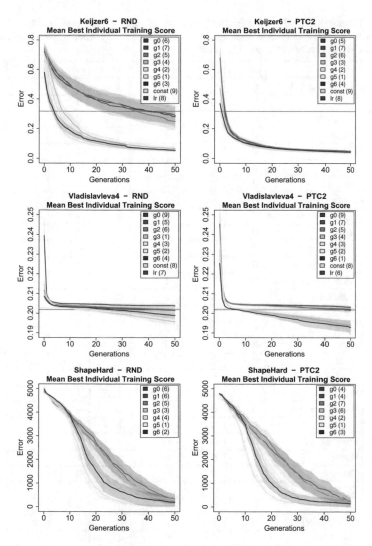

Fig. 6 Mean best train scores for the K6 (top), V4 (middle) and Shape match (hard) (bottom) experiments, using RND (left) or PTC2 (right), averaged across 100 independent runs; error is measured as the Root Mean Squared Error (RMSE) for K6 and V4, or the number of mismatched pixels for shape matching. Shades indicate 95% confidence intervals about the mean. Cyan and blue lines (where visible) indicate the RMSE of a constant predictor (mean of the train response variable) and a linear regression model of the training set, respectively

Table 8 Mann-Whitney U-tests of final median best training fit results, for all problems attempted; each number is a count of all grammars against which a significantly differently better performance was measured (results across 100 independent runs)

		G0	G1	G2	G3	G4	G5	G6
RND	BreastCancerW	0	0	0	5	3	0	0
	Dow	0	0	0	3	3	3	3
	EvenParity5	0	0	0	4	4	4	0
	Forest	0	1	1	4	4	5	1
	Housing	0	1	1	3	3	3	3
	Keijzer6	0	0	0	3	4	4	3
	Korns12	0	0	0	3	4	6	4
	Multiplexer11	0	1	1	3	3	1	4
	Pagie1	0	0	0	4	4	4	0
	Tower	0	2	2	4	5	2	1
	Vladislavleva4	0	0	0	4	0	4	3
	WineQualityRed	0	1	1	5	5	2	2
	WineQualityWhite	0	1	1	3	3	3	3
	ShapeEasy	0	0	0	0	0	0	0
	ShapeMedium	0	0	0	0	0	0	0
	ShapeHard	0	0	0	0	0	1	0
	Sum	0	7	7	48	45	42	27
	Mean	0	0.438	0.438	3	2.812	2.625	1.688
	Median	0	0	0	3	3	3	1.5
	Std. dev.	0	0.6292	0.6292	1.633	1.797	1.857	1.580
PTC2	BreastCancerW	0	0	0	4	4	1	0
	Dow	0	0	0	2	0	2	3
	EvenParity5	0	0	0	1	1	4	1
	Forest	0	0	0	2	4	1	0
	Housing	0	0	0	3	2	2	2
	Keijzer6	0	0	0	3	4	4	0
	Korns12	0	0	0	3	4	5	6
	Multiplexer11	0	1	0	0	0	0	4
	Pagie1	0	0	0	4	4	4	2
	Tower	0	0	1	1	3	1	1
	Vladislavleva4	0	0	0	3	3	3	3
	WineQualityRed	1	1	0	2	2	0	0
	WineQualityWhite	1	1	3	2	1	0	1
	ShapeEasy	0	0	0	0	0	0	0
	ShapeMedium	0	0	0	0	0	0	0
	ShapeHard	0	0	0	0	0	0	0
	Sum	2	3	4	30	32	27	23
	Mean	0.125	0.188	0.25	1.875	2	1.688	1.438
	Median	0	0	0	2	2	1	1
	Std. dev.	0.342	0.403	0.774	1.408	1.713	1.778	1.788

Table 9 Mann-Whitney U-tests of final median best test fit results (of best training solutions), for all problems with a test set; each number is a count of all grammars against which a significantly differently better performance was measured (results across 100 independent runs)

		G0	G1	G2	G3	G4	G5	G6
RND	BreastCancerW	0	0	0	0	0	1	0
	Dow	0	0	0	4	2	2	0
	Forest	6	2	1	0	0	0	3
	Housing	0	1	1	3	3	3	3
	Keijzer6	0	0	0	2	4	4	3
	Korns12	3	3	6	3	0	0	1
	Pagie1	0	0	0	4	4	4	0
	Tower	1	0	0	0	0	0	1
	Vladislavleva4	0	1	1	0	0	0	1
	WineQualityRed	0	1	1	5	5	2	2
	WineQualityWhite	5	0	0	0	0	0	0
	Sum	15	8	10	21	18	16	14
	Mean	1.364	0.727	0.909	1.909	1.636	1.455	1.273
	Median	0	0	0	2	0	1	1
	Std. dev.	2.248	1.009	1.758	1.973	2.014	1.635	1.272
PTC2	BreastCancerW	0	0	0	0	4	4	0
	Dow	0	0	0	1	2	0	0
	Forest	1	0	0	0	0	0	1
	Housing	0	0	0	3	2	2	2
	Keijzer6	1	0	0	1	2	2	0
	Korns12	4	3	3	3	2	0	0
	Pagie1	0	0	0	4	3	4	2
	Tower	1	0	0	0	0	0	1
	Vladislavleva4	1	1	0	0	0	0	1
	WineQualityRed	0	1	0	2	1	0	0
	WineQualityWhite	0	0	0	0	0	0	0
	Sum	8	5	3	14	16	12	7
	Mean	0.727	0.455	0.273	1.273	1.455	1.091	0.636
	Median	0	0	0	1	2	0	0
	Std. dev.	1.191	0.934	0.905	1.489	1.368	1.640	0.809

5.5   Analysis

The results obtained show just how much the design of a grammar can affect the search capability of GE. The most obvious performance improvements come from the construction of balanced grammars, and the reduction of the number of non-terminal symbols. These come at a price, however, particularly the latter: the complexity of the generated grammars can make them particularly hard to read and/or modify by hand. However, the application of these transformations is a deterministic process, meaning that they can be applied automatically: this allows manual grammar modifications to be applied to the simpler versions of the grammars, with subsequent application of automatic transformations. In any case, even a partial (manual) application of some of these modifications can be of use, as seen with the results for G6 variants.

The usefulness of some of these applications is problem-dependent. This is particularly the case of bias-related transformations, expressed in the results obtained with G2 and G4. For the problems attempted, the unlinking process employed with G2 grammars does not seem to confer any performance advantage when compared to G1 grammars. Likewise, the removal of biases towards certain operators employed in G4 grammars does not seem to confer any advantage, in the problems attempted. Finally, the switch from infix to prefix notation only makes a small difference for a few problems (for better or worse).

It is worth pointing out again that these results relate only to GE using a linear genome representation. Derivation tree based approaches make use of different search operators, and as such, the effect of grammar design is markedly different.

Another observation is the need to understand grammar design, when setting up any initialisation procedure (even something as simple as RND initialisation). The size of genotype structures required to generate certain solution (phenotype) size ranges needs to be adapted, depending on the grammar used.

6 Conclusions

Grammar design is one of the main tasks in GE: in order to write a good grammar, deep knowledge in both GE and the application domain are required. The experiments examined in this chapter, however, show that this is not necessarily always the case: there are specific grammar design principles that can be applied when attempting to solve any problem using GE, which do not require domain knowledge. Of the transformations analysed, the creation of recursion-balanced grammars and the reduction of the number of non-terminal symbols are particularly useful for improving the performance of GE, when using a linear genome representation.

Fixing symbol biases does not necessarily lead to better performance: this is completely problem dependent, and it can both degrade or improve performance. But it does affect search space exploration, as shown in the experiments conducted. This leads to two recommendations:

- When designing a GE grammar to compare its performance with systems such as GP, respect the symbol biases of the original system;
- When applying GE to a real-world problem, where symbol biases are known, use this knowledge to bias the exploration of the search space.

GE is like any other search algorithm, and in fact like any tool: it has its advantages and disadvantages, and will only provide its best performance if correctly used. There has been a recent surge of publications criticising GE's performance [17, 18, 21, 42], some even deeming that its performance "resembles that of random search" [42]. But most of the results provided were the result of using badly designed grammars, and poor experimental setup. The analysis and results presented in this chapter aim to provide another step towards achieving the goal of *Understanding Grammatical Evolution*.

References

1. J. Byrne, M. O'Neill, J. McDermott, A. Brabazon, An analysis of the behaviour of mutation in grammatical evolution, in *European Conference on Genetic Programming, EuroGP 2010*, ed. by A.I. Esparcia-Alcázar et al. Lecture Notes in Computer Science, vol. 6021 (Springer, Berlin, 2010), pp. 14–25
2. P. Cortez, A. Morais, A data mining approach to predict forest fires using meteorological data, in *Portuguese Conference on Artificial Intelligence, EPIA 2007*, ed. by J. Neves et al. (APPIA, Lisboa, 2007), pp. 512–523
3. P. Cortez, A. Cerdeira, F. Almeida, T. Matos, J. Reis, Modeling wine preferences by data mining from physicochemical properties. Decis. Support. Syst. **47**(4), 547–553 (2009)
4. D. Fagan, M. O'Neill, E. Galván-López, A. Brabazon, S. McGarraghy, An analysis of genotype-phenotype maps in grammatical evolution, in *European Conference on Genetic Programming, EuroGP 2010*, ed. by A.I. Esparcia-Alcázar et al. Lecture Notes in Computer Science, vol. 6021 (Springer, Berlin, 2010), pp. 62–73
5. D. Fagan, M. Nicolau, E. Hemberg, M. O'Neill, A. Brabazon, S. McGarraghy, Investigation of the performance of different mapping orders for GE on the max problem, in *European Conference on Genetic Programming, EuroGP 2011, Torino, Italy, April 27–29, 2011, Proceedings*, ed. by S. Silva et al. Lecture Notes in Computer Science, vol. 6621 (Springer, Berlin, 2011), pp. 286–297
6. S. Forstenlechner, M. Nicolau, D. Fagan, M. O'Neill, Grammar design for derivation tree based genetic programming systems, in *European Conference on Genetic Programming, EuroGP 2016*, ed. by M. Heywood et al. Lecture Notes in Computer Science, vol. 9594 (Springer, Cham, 2016), pp. 199–214
7. S. Forstenlechner, D. Fagan, M. Nicolau, M. O'Neill, A grammar design pattern for arbitrary program synthesis problems in genetic programming, in *European Conference on Genetic Programming, EuroGP 2017*, ed. by J. McDermott et al. Lecture Notes in Computer Science, vol. 10196 (Springer, Berlin, 2017), pp. 262–277
8. C. Gathercole, P. Ross, An adverse interaction between crossover and restricted tree depth in genetic programming, in *Genetic Programming 1996: First Annual Conference*, ed. by J.R. Koza et al. (MIT Press, Cambridge, 1996), pp. 291–296
9. R. Harper, GE, explosive grammars and the lasting legacy of bad initialisation, in *IEEE Congress on Evolutionary Computation, CEC 2010*, 2010, pp. 2602–2609
10. E. Hemberg, An exploration of grammars in grammatical evolution. Ph.D. Thesis, University College Dublin, University College Dublin, Ireland, 2010
11. E. Hemberg, N. McPhee, M. O'Neill, A. Brabazon, Pre-, in- and postfix grammars for symbolic regression in grammatical evolution, in *IEEE Workshop and Summer School on Evolutionary Computing, 2008*, 2008, pp. 18–22
12. M. Keijzer, Improving symbolic regression with interval arithmetic and linear scaling, in *European Conference on Genetic Programming, EuroGP 2003*, ed. by C. Ryan et al. Lecture Notes in Computer Science, vol. 2610 (Springer, Berlin, 2003), pp. 70–82
13. M. Keijzer, M. O'Neill, C. Ryan, M. Cattolico, Grammatical evolution rules: the mod and the bucket rule, in *European Conference on Genetic Programming, EuroGP 2002*, ed. by J.A. Foster et al. Lecture Notes in Computer Science, vol. 2278 (Springer, Berlin, 2002), pp. 123–130

14. M.F. Korns, Accuracy in symbolic regression, in *Genetic Programming Theory and Practice IX*, ed. by R. Riolo et al. Genetic and Evolutionary Computation (Springer, New York, 2011), pp. 129–151
15. J.R. Koza, *Genetic Programming: On the Programming of Computers by Means of Natural Selection* (MIT Press, Cambridge, 1992)
16. M. Lichman, UCI machine learning repository (2013), http://archive.ics.uci.edu/ml
17. N. Lourenço, J. Ferrer, F.B. Pereira, E. Costa, A comparative study of different grammar-based genetic programming approaches, in *European Conference on Genetic Programming, EuroGP 2017*, ed. by J. McDermott et al. Lecture Notes in Computer Science, vol. 10196 (Springer, Cham, 2017), pp. 311–325
18. N. Lourenço, F. B. Pereira, E. Costa, Unveiling the properties of structured grammatical evolution. Genet. Program. Evolvable Mach. **17**(3), 251–289 (2017)
19. S. Luke, Two fast tree-creation algorithms for genetic programming. IEEE Trans. Evol. Comput. **4**(3), 274–283 (2000)
20. S. Luke, L. Panait, A comparison of bloat control methods for genetic programming. Evol. Comput. **14**(3), 309–344 (2006)
21. E. Medvet, A comparative analysis of dynamic locality and redundancy in grammatical evolution, in *European Conference on Genetic Programming, EuroGP 2017*, ed. by J. McDermott et al. *Lecture Notes in Computer Science*, vol. 10196 (Springer, Cham, 2017), pp. 326–342
22. M. Nicolau, Automatic grammar complexity reduction in grammatical evolution, in *Genetic and Evolutionary Computation Conference, GECCO 2004*, ed. by R. Poli et al. (2004)
23. M. Nicolau, Understanding grammatical evolution: initialisation. Genet. Program. Evolvable Mach. **18**(4), 1–41 (2017)
24. M. Nicolau, I. Dempsey, Introducing grammar based extensions for grammatical evolution, in *IEEE Congress on Evolutionary Computation, CEC 2006* (2006), pp. 2663–2670
25. M. Nicolau, M. Fenton, Managing repetition in grammar-based genetic programming, in *Genetic and Evolutionary Computation Conference - GECCO 2016, Denver, CO, USA, July 20–24, 2016, Proceedings*, ed. by T. Friedrich (ACM, New York, 2016), pp. 765–772
26. M. Nicolau, M. O'Neill, A. Brabazon, Termination in grammatical evolution: grammar design, wrapping, and tails, in *IEEE Congress on Evolutionary Computation, CEC 2012* (2012), pp. 1–8
27. M. Nicolau, A. Agapitos, M. O'Neill, A. Brabazon, Guidelines for defining benchmark problems in genetic programming, in *IEEE Congress on Evolutionary Computation, CEC 2015* (2015)
28. M. O'Neill, A. Brabazon, mGGA: the meta-grammar genetic algorithm, in *European Conference on Genetic Programming, EuroGP 2005*, ed. by M. Keijzer et al. Lecture Notes in Computer Science, vol. 3447 (Springer, Berlin, 2005), pp. 311–320
29. M. O'Neill, C. Ryan, Evolving multi-line compilable c programs, in *European Workshop on Genetic Programming, EuroGP 99*, ed. by R. Poli et al. Lecture Notes in Computer Science, vol. 1598 (Springer, Berlin, 1999), pp. 83–92
30. M. O'Neill, C. Ryan, *Grammatical Evolution - Evolutionary Automatic Programming in an Arbitrary Language*. Genetic Programming, vol. 4 (Kluwer Academic, Dordrecht, 2003)
31. M. O'Neill, C. Ryan, M. Nicolau, Grammar defined introns: an investigation into grammars, introns, and bias in grammatical evolution, in *Genetic and Evolutionary Computation Conference, GECCO 2001*, ed. by L. Spector et al. (Morgan Kaufmann, Burlington, 2001), pp. 97–103
32. M. O'Neill, C. Ryan, M. Keijzer, M. Cattolico, Crossover in grammatical evolution. Genet. Program. Evolvable Mach. **4**(1), 67–93 (2003)
33. M. O'Neill, J.M. Swafford, J. McDermott, J. Byrne, A. Brabazon, E. Shotton, C. McNally, M. Hemberg, Shape grammars and grammatical evolution for evolutionary design, ed. by G. Raidl et al. *Genetic and Evolutionary Computation Conference, GECCO 2009* (ACM, New York, 2009), pp. 1035–1042
34. L. Pagie, P. Hogeweg, Evolutionary consequences of coevolving targets. Evol. Comput. **5**(4), 401–418 (1997)

35. D. Robilliard, S. Mahler, D. Verhaghe, C. Fonlupt, Santa fe trail hazards, in *International Conference on Evolution Artificielle, EA 2005*, ed. by E.-G. Talbi et al. Lecture Notes in Computer Science, vol. 3871 (Springer, Berlin, 2005), pp. 1–12
36. F. Rothlauf, M. Oetzel, On the locality of grammatical evolution, in *European Conference on Genetic Programming, EuroGP 2006*, ed. by P. Collet et al. Lecture Notes in Computer Science, vol. 3905 (Springer, Berlin, 2006), pp. 320–330
37. C. Ryan, A. Azad, Sensible initialisation in grammatical evolution, in *Genetic and Evolutionary Computation Conference, GECCO 2003*, ed. by E. Cantú-Paz et al. (AAAI, Menlo Park, 2003)
38. C. Ryan, J. Collins, M. O'Neill, Grammatical evolution: evolving programs for an arbitrary language, in *European Workshop on Genetic Programming, EuroGP 1998*, ed. by W. Banzhaf et al. Lecture Notes in Computer Science, vol. 1391 (Springer, Berlin, 1998), pp. 83–95
39. C. Ryan, M. Keijzer, M. Nicolau, On the avoidance of fruitless wraps in grammatical evolution, in *Genetic and Evolutionary Computation Conference, GECCO 2003*, ed. by E. Cantú-Paz et al. Lecture Notes in Computer Science, vol. 2724 (Springer, Berlin, 2003), pp. 1752–1763
40. J. Tavares, F. B. Pereira, Automatic design of ant algorithms with grammatical evolution, in *European Conference on Genetic Programming, EuroGP 2012*, ed. by A. Moraglio et al. Lecture Notes in Computer Science, vol. 7244 (Springer, Berlin, 2012), pp. 206–217
41. E.J. Vladislavleva, G.F. Smits, D. den Hertog, Order of nonlinearity as a complexity measure for models generated by symbolic regression via pareto genetic programming. IEEE Trans. Evol. Comput. 13(2), 333–349 (2009)
42. P.A. Whigham, G. Dick, J. Maclaurin, C.A. Owen, Examining the "best of both worlds" of grammatical evolution, in *Genetic and Evolutionary Computation Conference, GECCO 2015*, ed. by S. Silva (ACM, New York, 2015) pp. 1111–1118
43. D.R. White, J. McDermott, M. Castelli, L. Manzoni, B.W. Goldman, G. Kronberger, W. Jaśkowski, U.-M. O'Reilly, S. Luke, Better GP benchmarks: community survey results and proposals. Genet. Program. Evolvable Mach. 14(1), 3–29 (2013)

On the Non-uniform Redundancy of Representations for Grammatical Evolution: The Influence of Grammars

Dirk Schweim, Ann Thorhauer, and Franz Rothlauf

Abstract The representation used in grammatical evolution (GE) is non-uniformly redundant as some phenotypes are represented by more genotypes than others. This article studies how the non-uniform redundancy of the GE representation depends on various types of grammars. When constructing the phenotype tree from a genotype, the used grammar determines B_{avg}, the average branching factor. B_{avg} measures the expected number of non-terminals chosen when mapping one genotype codon to a phenotype tree node. First, the paper illustrates that the GE representation induces a bias towards small trees. This bias gets stronger with lower B_{avg}. For example, when using a grammar with $B_{avg} = 0.5$, 75% of all genotypes encode a phenotype tree of size one (codon length 10, two bits per codon, no wrapping, and random bit initialisation). Second, for $B_{avg} \geq 1$, the expected size of a phenotype tree is infinite. The resulting bias towards invalid trees increases with higher B_{avg}. For example, for a grammar with $B_{avg} = 2.25$, around 75% of all genotypes encode invalid trees. In summary, the GE encoding is strongly non-uniformly redundant and the bias depends on B_{avg}. As a compromise between the different biases, the results of this study suggest setting $B_{avg} \approx 1$.

1 Introduction

If a heuristic search procedure visits some solutions or solution structures more often than others, a bias exists [1, 20]. It is possible to distinguish desired bias from unwanted bias. Desired bias guides the search towards promising solutions, whereas unwanted bias does the contrary [1, 14]. For example, selection operators in evolutionary algorithms (EAs) lead to a desired bias, as they are intended to guide the search towards promising solutions. Hence, selective bias is used on purpose in various types of EAs, e.g., in grammatical evolution (GE) [17]. Other types of biases

D. Schweim (✉) · A. Thorhauer · F. Rothlauf
Dept. of Information Systems and Business Administration, University of Mainz, Mainz, Germany
e-mail: schweim@uni-mainz.de; thorhauer@uni-mainz.de; rothlauf@uni-mainz.de

© Springer International Publishing AG, part of Springer Nature 2018
C. Ryan et al. (eds.), *Handbook of Grammatical Evolution*,
https://doi.org/10.1007/978-3-319-78717-6_3

can also occur during the search process. Their occurrence is sometimes hidden in the sense that their cause is not transparent or that the user is not even aware of them [1]. This can be a problem if the biases hinder the search from finding better solutions. Thus, it is important to make different types of biases transparent and to measure their effects such that EA users can deliberately decide either to avoid them or to purposefully use them, in order to guide the search towards promising high-quality solutions.

Many empirical studies have also confirmed that the combination of representation and variation operator can be biased [1, 15]. A representation assigns genotypes to corresponding phenotypes and it is possible to distinguish direct representations from indirect representations [1, 13, 14]. Direct representations do not differentiate between genotypes and phenotypes. A prominent example is (standard tree-based) genetic programming (GP) [5], where phenotype solutions are encoded by trees. Variation operators are applied on these trees, which can often be directly interpreted as a phenotype, e.g., as mathematical expressions. On the contrary, an indirect representation explicitly distinguishes between genotypes and phenotypes, making an additional mapping between them necessary.

GE is an EA variant which uses an indirect representation [17], where genotypes are variable-length binary strings. A grammar in Backus-Naur form (BNF) is used to decode genotypes into their corresponding phenotypes [17]. The variation operators—like mutation and crossover—are applied to genotypes, but the actual effects of these operators are observed in the corresponding phenotypes [13, 14]. The used representation that maps genotypes to corresponding phenotypes is a source of search bias if the representation is non-uniformly redundant [1, 15].

An indirect representation is redundant if more than one genotype represents the same phenotype [15]. Furthermore, a representation is uniformly redundant if every phenotype is represented by the same number of genotypes; it is non-uniformly redundant if one or more phenotypes are represented by a larger number of genotypes than others. Hence, indirect representations can be biased. This could lead to unwanted bias if optimal solutions or parts of them are under-represented (compared to worse solutions), as optimal solutions will then probably be visited less often during search [15].

In this article, we analyse the decoding process from genotypes to phenotypes as a possible source for non-uniform redundancy in GE representations. We extend previous results [18] and analyse a diverse set of grammars. In addition, we provide a model explaining the number of invalid phenotypes in GE.

In our experiments, we created all possible genotype bit-strings for a fixed string length as well as the corresponding phenotype trees using various types of grammars. Since the decoding process in GE is deterministic and we considered all possible genotypes, we obtained frequencies (and not probabilities) for the number of genotypes mapped to phenotypes. When constructing the tree from a genotype, the used grammar determines the average branching factor B_{avg}, which measures the expected number of non-terminals chosen when mapping one genotype codon to a phenotype tree node. Thus, by using B_{avg}, we were able to compare different grammars. We confirmed previous results that GE representations are redundant, since the number of different genotypes strongly exceeds the number of different phenotypes. The redundancy is non-uniform because some phenotypes are encoded by genotypes with (much) higher frequencies.

We observed a strong bias towards short trees in the phenotype space. In fact, trees with a size of one were strongly over-represented (e.g., for a grammar with a low $B_{avg} = 0.5$, we observed trees with sizes of one or three with a frequency of 89%). This bias gets stronger with lower B_{avg}. In contrast, deeper and larger trees are encoded with much lower frequencies (e.g., for the same grammar with a low branching factor, trees with a size larger than three were observed with a frequency of 9%). We also found that the type of grammar has a strong effect on the frequencies of invalid phenotype trees. Grammars with a high branching factor (i.e., due to a high probability of choosing non-terminals during decoding) produce more invalid trees. In invalid trees, tree creation could not be completed. We show that the expected tree size resulting from GE's tree creation process (or more generally the decoding) can be modelled by using a geometric series. Thus, the expected tree size for grammars with $B_{avg} \geq 1$ tends to infinity. In summary, representations in GE are biased and the type of grammar has a strong impact on this bias as it influences the number of genotypes that encode one particular phenotype and the number of invalid phenotypes.

The article is structured as follows. In Sect. 2, we describe recent work on bias of GE representations. In Sect. 3, we describe a model to calculate the expected tree size resulting from GE's tree creation process. The model is based on previous work on types of grammars in GE and enabled us to analyse the tree creation process. Our experimental setup for this analysis is described in Sect. 4. The results of our experiments are presented in Sect. 5. The article ends with concluding remarks.

2 Bias of Representations in Grammatical Evolution

A variety of work studies how the chosen grammar affects GE performance. Hemberg et al. [4] considered three different grammars (postfix, prefix, infix) and examined their influence on GE performance for symbolic regression problems. They observed no differences between the grammars for small problem instances. However, for large problems, a postfix grammar was found to be advantageous. Fagan et al. [2] compared GE performance for four different genotype-phenotype mappings (depth-first, breadth-first, random, and πGE [10]) for four benchmark problems. The πGE mapping[1] outperformed the other mappings in three out of four problems [10]. Breadth-first mapping produced larger trees in three out of four problems compared to the other mappings. These studies indicate that the tree

---

[1]πGE uses a flexible mapping where the genome defines not only the application of rules as in standard GE, but also specifies which non-terminal is decoded next. This implies that the order of non-terminal expansions is itself evolved in πGE [10].

construction process and the grammar used in this process are both relevant to the design of a well-performing GE search heuristic.

Another study that analysed selecto-recombinative genetic algorithms (GAs) supported this finding. Rothlauf and Goldberg [15] examined the impact of redundant representations on the performance of GAs. If representations are uniformly redundant and the order of redundancy is low, the performance of the GA is not affected. On the contrary, GA performance can be increased or decreased if non-uniformly redundant representations are used. In their experiments, Rothlauf and Goldberg [15] illustrated that search performance can be increased when optimal solutions are over-represented and it can be decreased when optimal solutions are under-represented.

A number of other studies analysed the effect of bias in GE. Montes de Oca [7] focused on creating numerical values by concatenating digits and found that the most-commonly used GE grammar induces a bias towards short-length numbers. Harper [3] showed that standard GE random bit initialisation produces trees that are non-uniformly distributed since "80% of the trees have 90% of their nodes on one side of the tree or the other" [3]. Thus, trees are biased to be "tall and skinny" [3]. Thorhauer and Rothlauf [19] found that a random walk with GE using standard operators (one-point crossover, mutation and duplication) has a strong bias towards "sparse" trees. Murphy et al. [8] examined different types of biases which are introduced by using tree-adjoining grammars and found that this bias depends on the grammar and the problem.

Ryan and Azad [16] analysed standard random bit initialisation of genotypes in GE. They noted that "depending on the grammar employed, a significant proportion of individuals in the initial populations can consist of a single terminal" [16]. They propose "sensible initialisation", an initialisation scheme comparable to Kozas "ramped-half-and-half" [5], which results in a greater variety of trees in the initial population [16]. Similar to this, Nicolau [9] compared several initialisation routines. He found 73.5% of generated trees to be identical (with random bit initialisation and a symbolic regression single non-terminal, prefix notation grammar). A large number of these trees had a size of one. Also, trees were, in general, similar to each other when using random bit initialisation [9].

O'Neill and Ryan examined the effect of genetic code degeneracy [11, 12]. Genetic code degeneracy exists if codons consist of more bits than actually necessary to represent the number of choices within the production rules of a grammar. For example, the number of possible decisions encoded in a codon with a length of two bits is four (00, 01, 10 and 11). If the number of choices to substitute a non-terminal in the production rules of a grammar is smaller than four, the grammar is degenerated [11, 12]. O'Neill et al. [12] found that degeneracy leads to a mapping bias. The strength of this bias depends on both the number of choices in the production rules of the grammar to choose from and on how many different choices each codon can represent (determined by the number of bits of a codon) [12]. In most realistic grammars, degeneracy is common since the usual codon size is 8 bit, meaning that a codon can express $2^8 = 256$ different choices. However, in most GE applications, the number of decisions in production rules is usually much lower, which can lead to an unwanted bias. To circumvent this, O'Neill et al. suggested using grammar defined introns [12].

3 Balanced, Explosive, and Collapsing Grammars

We will first define the terms genotype space and phenotype space. Then, we will describe how grammars are used when decoding genotypes into phenotypes in GE. Following this, we will define the average branching factor and use this measure to distinguish between balanced, explosive, and collapsing grammars.

The genotype search space Φ_g is defined as the set of possible genotypes [15]. The phenotype space Φ_p is the set of all encoded valid and invalid phenotypes [15]. We assume that every phenotype can be assigned to at least one genotype and vice versa. If a phenotype is not represented by any of the genotypes, it is not an element of Φ_p and cannot be found by an optimisation algorithm [15].

In GE, a grammar in BNF determines how genotypes are decoded to their corresponding phenotypes [17]. A grammar can be defined by a tuple $\{N, T, P, S\}$. When starting the decoding from geno- to phenotype in GE, an appropriate start symbol S is used. S is usually a non-terminal in the finite set of non-terminals N ($S \in N$). Terminals are defined in the finite set of terminals T ($T \cap N = \emptyset$). During decoding, each non-terminal is substituted by terminals, non-terminals, or by sequences combining both. A finite set of production rules P defines how non-terminals can be substituted during decoding: For every non-terminal n ($n \in N$), one production rule p_n ($p_n \in P$) exists, which specifies the set of possible substitutions I_n ($|I_n| > 0$ for each p_n). A substitution i ($i \in I_n$) can be a terminal, a non-terminal or a function. In GE, functions can be defined by combining terminals and non-terminals in the form of a sequence (unlike GP, in GE no function set exists). If only one substitution i is defined in p_n ($|I_n| = 1$), n is always replaced by i during decoding without using codons from the genotype. If more than one sequence of symbols exists in p_n ($|I_n| > 1$), a decision is made by taking the modulo of the codons (integer) value and the number of possible decisions for n (given by $|I_n|$). The resulting number denotes the substitution j ($j \in I_n$), with which n will be replaced.

Figure 1 shows an example of the production rules of a grammar in BNF. The grammar has the start symbol "$< expr >$", which is also the single non-terminal n ($|N| = 1$). The grammar uses one production rule p_n ($|P| = 1$) that maps the non-terminal to one of two choices ($|I_n| = 2$): Either the non-terminal is replaced by a terminal symbol ("X"), or it is replaced by a sequence of symbols consisting

```
<start>  ::= <expr>
<expr>   ::= <expr> + <expr> | X
```

Fig. 1 Example of the production rules of a grammar in BNF

of a terminal (the operator "+") and two non-terminals ("$< expr >$"), representing a function in this case ("$< expr > + < expr >$"). The two possible choices are separated by "|" in the grammar.

Harper [3] introduced the notion of grammars being "balanced" or "explosive". He built upon previous work for GP by Luke [6], who found how the average size of a tree depends on the average branching factor B_{avg} of the functions in the GP function set. For GE, we define B_{avg} as the expected number of non-terminals in one decoding step. Unfortunately, it can be difficult to calculate B_{avg} for complex GE grammars since it depends on interdependencies between the decoding steps of multiple production rules in the grammar.

In the following paragraphs, we will focus on grammars with a single production rule ($|P| = 1$). This is only a minor limitation since more complex grammars with multiple non-terminals and production rules can lead to structurally identical trees like a grammar with a single production rule. This is the case if the number of substitutions per production rule as well as the arities between the two grammars match. In this case, the number of production rules could also differ and the resulting trees would only differ in the semantics of their nodes—not in their structures (size, depth and shape of the trees would be identical).

For a grammar with only one production rule ($|P| = 1$), the average branching factor is calculated as

$$B_{avg} = \sum_{i \in I_p} p(i) \times B(i), \tag{1}$$

where I_p denotes the set of possible substitutions for the single production rule p ($p \in P$) and $p(i)$ is the probability of choosing the substitution i. Furthermore, $B(i)$ is the branching factor of substitution i and denotes the number of non-terminals in i.

We will provide an example that uses the grammar defined in Fig. 1, which consists of only one production rule. To calculate B_{avg}, we need to know the probabilities for every substitution, which depend on the codon length. We assume a codon length of one (1 bit) and standard uniform-random bit assignment of genotypes. Thus, both possible substitutions are selected with an equal probability of 50% (Eq. (2a)). Because the function in the production rule includes two non-terminals, its branching factor is two (Eq. (2b)). For the terminal "X", the branching factor is zero (Eq. (2c)). Therefore, the average branching factor of the grammar is one (Eq. (2d)).

$$p(< expr > + < expr >) = p(X) = 50\% \tag{2a}$$

$$B(< expr > + < expr >) = 2 \tag{2b}$$

$$B(X) = 0 \tag{2c}$$

$$B_{avg} = (50\% \times 2) + (50\% \times 0) = 100\% = 1 \tag{2d}$$

B_{avg} allows us to distinguish between different forms of grammars based on their expected phenotype tree size. Luke [6] found that the expected number of nodes E_d at depth d ($d \geq 0$) in a tree can be calculated as

$$
E_d = \begin{cases} 1 & \text{if } d = 0 \\ E_{d-1} \times B_{\mathrm{avg}} & \text{if } d > 0 \end{cases} \tag{3}
$$

The expected size E_{tree} of a tree is calculated as the sum of E_d over all depths d in the tree, $E_{tree} = \sum_{d=0}^{\infty} E_d$. We can rewrite this expression [6] as

$$
E_{tree} = \sum_{d=0}^{\infty} (B_{\mathrm{avg}})^d . \tag{4}
$$

As this is a geometric series, the expected size of a tree with average branching factor $B_{\mathrm{avg}} > 0$ is

$$
E_{tree} = \sum_{d=0}^{\infty} (B_{\mathrm{avg}})^d = \begin{cases} \frac{1}{1-B_{\mathrm{avg}}} & \text{if } B_{\mathrm{avg}} < 1 \\ \infty & \text{if } B_{\mathrm{avg}} \geq 1 \end{cases} \tag{5}
$$

If $B_{\mathrm{avg}} < 1$, the encoded phenotype trees are finite with an expected size of $\frac{1}{1-B_{\mathrm{avg}}}$ (under the assumptions that the genotype string is long enough to finish decoding and that the bit assignment of the codons in the genotype is uniform-random). Consequently, we denote grammars with $B_{\mathrm{avg}} < 1$ as "collapsing grammars". In collapsing grammars, the probability to finish decoding is one (if the genotype is long enough). If the average branching factor of a grammar is only slightly lower than one ($B_{\mathrm{avg}} \lesssim 1$), the expected size of a tree E_{tree} becomes very large, which can lead to huge trees (for $B_{\mathrm{avg}} \to 1$, E_{tree} goes towards ∞). For a lower B_{avg}, the expected size E_{tree} of the trees gets lower fast, which often leads to unreasonably small trees (for $B_{\mathrm{avg}} \to 0$, E_{tree} goes towards 1).

If $B_{\mathrm{avg}} \geq 1$, the expected tree size E_{tree} is infinite, as the geometric series tends to infinity [6]. Thus, we denote a grammar to be "balanced" if the average branching factor $B_{\mathrm{avg}} = 1$ [3, 6]. For balanced grammars, the expected number of non-terminals in each decoding step is equal to one.

If $B_{\mathrm{avg}} > 1$, we follow the notion of Harper [3] and denote the grammar to be "explosive". For such grammars, non-terminal expansions are more likely to be chosen during decoding when deciding between terminals and non-terminals [3]. Thus, the decoding process substitutes non-terminals by other non-terminals with a higher probability than terminals. Consequently, the decoding process often does not finish since the probability of finishing the decoding tends to zero after a certain number of non-terminals have been chosen [3, 6]. Furthermore, like in balanced grammars, the expected tree size E_{tree} is infinite.

Luke notes that for GP it can be hard to define a combination of terminals and functions that results in a finite (and reasonable) tree size. Even small changes in the function and terminal sets can lead to either very small or infinite expected tree sizes [6]. The same holds true for GE, as small changes in the grammar can have a large impact on tree size. For most grammars, the phenotype trees are expected to be either very small or invalid.

4 Experimental Setup

We studied how the non-uniform redundancy of GE encodings depends on the used grammar. For all of our experiments, we used the same non-terminal set N, which consists of only a single non-terminal "$< expr >$". "$< expr >$" is also used as start symbol S. The terminal set T consists of two terminals: The terminal "X" represents a leaf in a phenotype tree and the terminal "$join$" is a function of arity k—it joins k different parameters. In our experiments, the join functions differ by their arity but not by their semantics. In a valid tree, the join function represents an internal node.

In our experiments, we changed the number and type of substitutions in the production rules of the grammars. The grammars were defined in BNF. All rule sets P consisted of a single production rule with different substitutions of the non-terminal "$< expr >$". We define different grammars which are either balanced (denoted as "Bal"), explosive (denoted as "Exp"), or collapsing (denoted as "Col"). An additional subscript indicates the arity of the function used in the grammar. For example, Bal_2 is a balanced grammar ($B_{avg} = 1$) with a binary join function of arity two ($k = 2$).

In our study, the number of codons was set to 10. Each codon consists of two bits, and we use no wrapping operator. Thus, the number of different genotypes is $2^{20} = 1,048,576$. Using more than two bits would only lead to a stronger degeneracy of the genetic code, and wouldn't change the types nor frequencies of encoded phenotypes. For our experiments, we created all possible genotypes and decoded them into the corresponding phenotype trees using standard depth-first mapping. For each phenotype tree, we determined the depth d, the tree size n (sum of all tree nodes) and the individual shape of a tree.

5 Results and Analysis

We studied how the non-uniform redundancy of the representation depends on various types of GE grammars. We examined grammars with binary join functions ("binary grammars", arity $k = 2$), unary join functions ("unary grammars", $k = 1$), trinary join functions ("trinary grammars", $k = 3$), and join functions with different arities ("mixed arity grammars", $k \in \{1, 2, 3\}$).

5.1 Binary Grammars

In this section, we will extend previous findings [18] on non-uniform redundancy by analysing one balanced grammar Bal_2 (Fig. 2), one explosive grammar Exp_2 (Fig. 3), and one collapsing grammar Col_2 (Fig. 4).

The production rule of the balanced grammar Bal_2 defines four possible substitutions for the single non-terminal "$< expr >$". Two of them are the terminal "X" and the other two are binary join functions. The grammar's average branching factor is $B_{avg} = 1$, resulting in an expected average tree size of $E_{tree} = \infty$.

Grammar Exp_2 (Fig. 3) defines one production rule, which substitutes a non-terminal in either one out of three binary join functions or one terminal node "X". Since $B_{avg} = 1.5$, the expected average tree size E_{tree} is also infinity.

Grammar Col_2 (Fig. 4) also defines one production rule, which substitutes a non-terminal in either one binary join function or one of three terminals "X". The grammar's average branching factor is $B_{avg} = 0.5$ and the expected tree size is $E_{tree} = 2$ (assuming enough codons to finish decoding).

We analysed the encoded phenotype trees for the three different grammars. Figure 5 plots the different phenotype trees over their depth d and size n. Valid trees were plotted using a circle, invalid ones using a cross. The dotted lines depict boundaries for valid binary trees. We do not show plots for the different grammars, as all grammars produced the same phenotype trees. With a genotype of 10 codons, all three grammars mapped the genotypes to the same seven valid and seven invalid phenotype structures. The maximum size of the valid trees was nine and the maximum depth is four. All invalid trees, which were the result of an unfinished decoding process, have the maximum number of ten nodes.

To analyse whether the representation is non-uniformly redundant, we examine the frequencies of the phenotype tree structures (that is, the number of genotypes that encode trees with the same size and depth divided by the number of all genotypes). Figure 6a–c shows the resulting frequencies of the phenotypes over their depth and size for the three grammars.

Fig. 2 Production rules of grammar Bal_2 ($B_{avg} = 1.0$)

```
<start>  ::= <expr>
<expr>   ::= join(<expr> ; <expr>)
         |  join(<expr> ; <expr>)
         |  X  |  X
```

Fig. 3 Production rules of grammar Exp_2 ($B_{avg} = 1.5$)

```
<start>  ::= <expr>
<expr>   ::= join(<expr> ; <expr>)
         |  join(<expr> ; <expr>)
         |  join(<expr> ; <expr>)
         |  X
```

Fig. 4 Production rules of grammar Col_2 ($B_{avg} = 0.5$)

```
<start>  ::= <expr>
<expr>   ::= join(<expr> ; <expr>)
         |  X  |  X  |  X
```

Fig. 5 Encoded trees over different sizes and depths (*circle* for valid, *cross* for invalid trees; results are identical for grammars Bal_2, Exp_2, and Col_2)

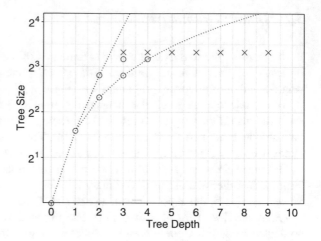

As expected, the frequency of invalid trees increases with B_{avg}. For Col_2 ($B_{avg} = 0.5$) it is relatively low (1.89%), for Bal_2 ($B_{avg} = 1$) about one fourth of the genotypes encode invalid trees (24.61%), and for Exp_2 ($B_{avg} = 2$) almost two thirds of all encoded trees are invalid (67.30%). We found that the GE decoding process creates some tree structures (defined by their size and depth) with much higher frequencies. For all three grammars, a large percentage of the encoded phenotypes consists of only a single terminal. These trees have a size of one and a depth of zero. For Bal_2, their ratio is 50% (Fig. 6a), for Exp_2 it is 25% (Fig. 6b), and for Col_2 it is 75% (Fig. 6c). This means for the three considered grammars that between 25% and 75% of all genotypes encode a phenotype tree with one node ("X"). All other phenotypes are encoded with much lower frequencies. Thus, the representation is strongly non-uniform redundant for all three grammars. Looking at large but still valid trees, the frequency of trees with a tree size $n > 3$ is highest for grammar Bal_2. The other two grammars map the genotypes to valid and large trees with lower frequency, as Col_2 has a strong bias towards very short trees of size one or three ($E_{tree} = 2$) and Exp_2 often does not allow the decoding process to be finished ($E_{tree} = \infty$), leading to a large proportion of invalid trees. This explains why most grammars used in the literature have an average branching factor of $B_{avg} \approx 1$.

Until now, we characterised trees only by their size and depth. However, in many applications the position of nodes in the tree can be important. Thus, in the following paragraphs, we study how many genotypes encode one particular tree. For the three grammars and a codon size of 10, we observe 23 different valid trees and 252 different invalid trees. Figure 7 plots the frequencies over the 23 valid trees. From left to right, the frequencies are in decreasing order. We added additional labels for each tree, indicating the size n and depth d of the corresponding tree.

As before, the representation is strongly non-uniform redundant. About one million different genotypes encode only 23 valid trees. For Bal_2 (Fig. 7a), the tree with a size of one and depth of zero is encoded by 50% of all genotypes; the full tree of depth one and size three is encoded by 12.5% of all genotypes. The remaining

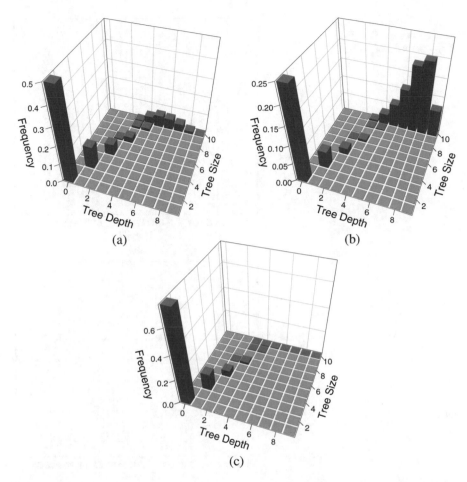

Fig. 6 Frequencies of (valid and invalid) trees over sizes and depths (grammars Bal_2 (**a**), Exp_2 (**b**) and Col_2 (**c**))

21 valid phenotype trees are encoded with an overall frequency of only 12.89%, ranging from about 0.2% to 3.13%. For Exp_2 (Fig. 7b), valid trees with $n > 3$ are encoded with frequencies between 0.03% and 0.88%. For Col_2 (Fig. 7c), trees with $n > 3$ are encoded with frequencies ranging from 0.09% to 2.64%.

With 252 invalid trees, there are about ten times more invalid trees than valid trees. The frequencies of invalid trees increase with B_{avg}. For Col_2, all frequencies of invalid trees are below 0.0232%, for Bal_2, each invalid tree is encoded with a frequency of about 0.098%, and for Exp_2, the frequencies of invalid trees are between 0.02% and 5.63%.

In summary, the GE encoding is strongly non-uniform redundant, independently of the used grammar. All studied binary grammars map genotypes to the same phenotype trees, but the frequencies of encoding a particular tree vary considerably

Fig. 7 Frequencies of valid trees (grammars Bal_2 (**a**), Exp_2 (**b**) and Col_2 (**c**))

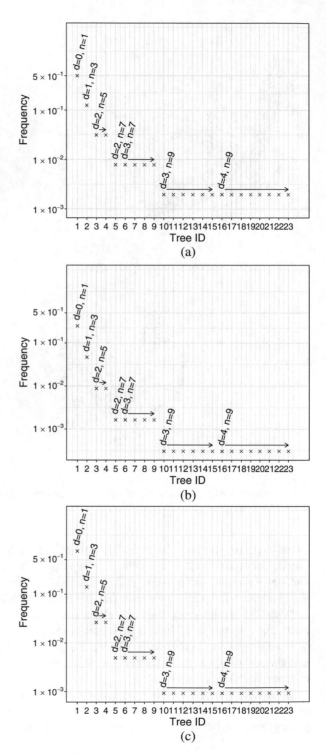

across the grammars. We observe a strong over-representation of short valid trees when using the collapsing grammar Col_2; with higher B_{avg}, the bias towards short trees gets lower, however, the percentage of invalid phenotypes strongly increases. For most real-world applications, a branching factor $B_{avg} \approx 1$ is a reasonable choice as it is a compromise between the two observed types of biases.

5.2 Unary Grammars

We studied the non-uniform redundancy of GE representations for grammars using only functions with arity one ("unary", $k = 1$). For unary grammars, balanced or explosive grammars can't be defined. Thus, unary grammars are always collapsing grammars. For our analysis, we used the grammar "Col_1", which substitutes a non-terminal with either one of two unary join functions or two terminals (Fig. 8). Thus, $B_{avg} = 0.5$ and $E_{tree} = 2$ (which are the same properties as Col_2).

As before, we examined the number of genotypes that encode trees characterised by n and d. Figure 9 plots the encoded phenotype trees over their depth and size. There were ten valid trees between $n = 1$ ($d = 0$) and $n = 10$ ($d = 9$) and only one type of invalid tree with $n = 10$ ($d = 9$). The invalid trees are the result of the limited number of genotype codons which lead to an unfinished decoding.

We examined whether the frequencies of tree structures (number of genotypes that encode a particular tree structure characterised by n and d divided by the number of all possible genotypes) are non-uniformly distributed. Figure 10 plots the frequencies for the valid and invalid trees over their depth and size. Analogously

Fig. 8 Production rules of grammar Col_1 ($B_{avg} = 0.5$)

```
<start> ::= <expr>
<expr>  ::= join(<expr>)
         |  join(<expr>)
         |  X | X
```

Fig. 9 Encoded trees over different sizes and depths (*circle* for valid, *cross* for invalid trees; grammar Col_1)

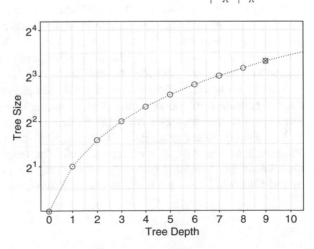

Fig. 10 Frequencies of (valid
and invalid) trees over sizes
and depths (grammar Col_1)

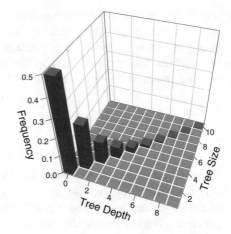

Fig. 11 Frequencies of valid
trees (grammar Col_1)

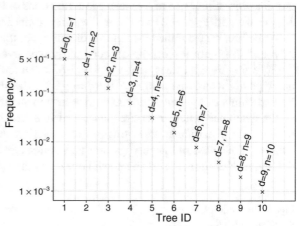

to binary grammars, there are large differences in the number of encoded trees. Short trees are strongly over-represented and the decoding process finishes for most genotypes (the frequency of invalid trees is only 0.1%). We find that both collapsing grammars (Col_2 as well as Col_1) have a low frequency of invalid trees and a strong bias to short trees (compare Figs. 6c and 10).

We also analysed the frequencies of valid trees in greater detail. Figure 11 plots the frequencies over the ten valid trees in decreasing order. We found that the frequency of a tree decreases with higher size.

In summary, unary grammars also result in a strongly non-uniform encoding, as short trees are strongly over-represented. The bias is comparable to the bias observed in the collapsing binary grammar Col_2, as also almost no genotypes are mapped to invalid trees due to the low average branching factor.

5.3   Trinary Grammars

We studied the non-uniform redundancy of GE representations using grammars
with arity three functions. We define two different grammars: Exp_3 (Fig. 12) with
a production rule that substitutes the non-terminal by either one of three arity three
join functions or one terminal, and Col_3 (Fig. 13) which substitutes the non-terminal
with either one arity three join function or one of three terminals. The average
branching factor of Exp_3 is $B_{avg} = 2.25$; for Col_3 it is $B_{avg} = 0.75$.

Figure 14 plots the encoded phenotype trees over their depth and size. Both
example grammars map the genotypes to the same five different valid trees and
eight different invalid trees (trees are characterised by their size and depth). The
lower number of different valid tree structures of five (in comparison to seven in
binary grammars) is a result of the high branching factor of the trinary function: It
requires that once a function is selected, at least three more non-terminals have to
be decoded (compared to only two more non-terminals in a binary function). Thus,
if one trinary function is chosen, at least three more codons are needed to finish the
decoding for this subtree.

Figure 15a, b plots the frequencies of all trees over their depth and size. Again,
the frequencies are strongly non-uniform and the encoding is strongly biased
towards short trees. There are only three valid tree types (characterised by n and

Fig. 12 Production rules of
grammar Exp_3 ($B_{avg} = 2.25$)

```
<start> ::= <expr>
<expr>  ::= join(<expr> ; <expr> ; <expr>)
          | join(<expr> ; <expr> ; <expr>)
          | join(<expr> ; <expr> ; <expr>)
          | X
```

Fig. 13 Production rules of
grammar Col_3 ($B_{avg} = 0.75$)

```
<start> ::= <expr>
<expr>  ::= join(<expr> ; <expr> ; <expr>)
          | X | X | X
```

Fig. 14 Encoded trees over
different sizes and depths
(*circle* for valid, *cross* for
invalid trees; grammars Exp_3
and Col_3)

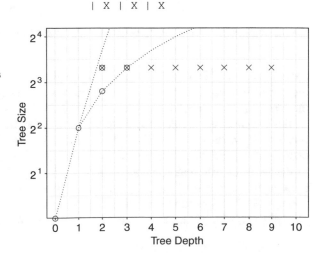

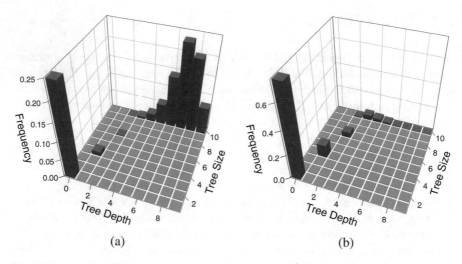

(a)   (b)

Fig. 15 Frequencies of (valid and invalid) trees over sizes and depths (grammars Exp_3 (a) and Col_3 (b))

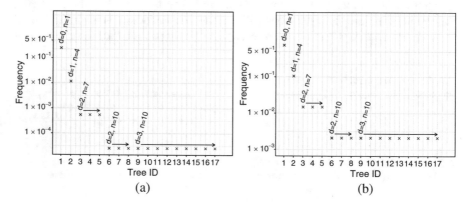

(a)   (b)

Fig. 16 Frequencies of valid trees (grammars Exp_3 (a) and Col_3 (b))

d) with a size smaller than ten (there are two valid tree structures with $n = 10$). For the two grammars, the differences in the frequencies are large. For Exp_3, 73.6% of the phenotypes are invalid, compared to only 7.5% for Col_3.

Furthermore, we studied the frequencies of valid trees, considering the exact position of nodes in a tree. We plotted the valid trees over their frequency in decreasing order from left to right (Fig. 16a, b). Both grammars map the genotypes to the same 17 different valid trees, however the tree frequencies strongly differ between the grammars. For Exp_3, the overall frequency of valid trees with $n > 1$ is only 1.37%, compared to 17.5% for grammar Col_3. This is a result of the lower B_{avg} of Col_3, which leads to a stronger bias towards short (and valid) trees.

In summary, the results for trinary grammars are similar to the results presented for unary and binary grammars: With increasing B_{avg}, the bias towards short trees decreases and the percentage of invalid trees increases.

5.4 Mixed Arity Grammars

Finally, we studied grammars containing functions with different arities between one and three. The production rule in grammar $Bal_{1,2}$ (Fig. 17) substitutes the non-terminal with either one of two unary join functions, one binary join function or one terminal. Grammar $Bal_{1,3}$ (Fig. 18) uses one unary join function, one trinary join function, and two terminals ("X"). The production rule in grammar $Exp_{1,2}$ (Fig. 19) substitutes the non-terminal with either one of two binary join functions, one unary join function, or one terminal. Grammar $Exp_{1,3}$ (Fig. 20) substitutes the non-terminal with either one of two unary functions, a trinary function, or one

Fig. 17 Production rules of grammar $Bal_{1,2}$ ($B_{avg} = 1.0$)

```
<start> ::= <expr>
<expr>  ::= join(<expr> ; <expr>)
          | join(<expr>)
          | join(<expr>)
          | X
```

Fig. 18 Production rules of grammar $Bal_{1,3}$ ($B_{avg} = 1.0$)

```
<start> ::= <expr>
<expr>  ::= join(<expr> ; <expr> ; <expr>)
          | join(<expr>)
          | X | X
```

Fig. 19 Production rules of grammar $Exp_{1,2}$ ($B_{avg} = 1.25$)

```
<start> ::= <expr>
<expr>  ::= join(<expr> ; <expr>)
          | join(<expr> ; <expr>)
          | join(<expr>)
          | X
```

Fig. 20 Production rules of grammar $Exp_{1,3}$ ($B_{avg} = 1.25$)

```
<start> ::= <expr>
<expr>  ::= join(<expr> ; <expr> ; <expr>)
          | join(<expr>)
          | join(<expr>)
          | X
```

Fig. 21 Production rules of grammar $Exp_{1,2,3}$ ($B_{avg} = 1.5$)

```
<start> ::= <expr>
<expr>  ::= join(<expr> ; <expr> ; <expr>)
          | join(<expr> ; <expr>)
          | join(<expr>)
          | X
```

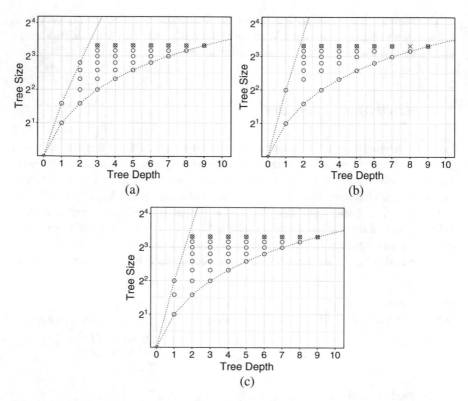

Fig. 22 Encoded trees over different sizes and depths (*circle* for valid, *cross* for invalid trees; grammars $Bal_{1,2}$, $Bal_{1,3}$, $Exp_{1,2}$, $Exp_{1,3}$, and $Exp_{1,2,3}$). (**a**) Grammars $Bal_{1,2}$ and $Exp_{1,2}$. (**b**) Grammars $Bal_{1,3}$ and $Exp_{1,3}$. (**c**) Grammars $Exp_{1,2,3}$

terminal. Grammar $Exp_{1,2,3}$ (Fig. 21) combines all possibilities and substitutes a non-terminal by either a terminal, a unary, a binary, or a trinary join function.

Figure 22 plots the encoded phenotype trees characterised by their depth and size. We found that all grammars map the genotypes to a wide variety of phenotype trees, since they can create many different types of structures due to multiple function arities used in the grammars. Grammar $Exp_{1,2,3}$ contains the highest number of functions with different arities, allowing us to construct 40 valid and 8 invalid tree structures. This is also the highest number of different resulting tree structures we observed (Fig. 22c). Grammars $Bal_{1,2}$ and $Exp_{1,2}$ map the genotypes to the same 36 valid and 7 invalid tree structures (Fig. 22a). Grammars $Bal_{1,3}$ and $Exp_{1,3}$ map the genotypes to the same 32 valid and 8 invalid tree structures (Fig. 22b).

Again, we examine the frequencies of the trees characterised by their size and depth. Figure 23 plots the fractions of valid and invalid trees over their depth and size. Analogously to the previous results, short trees are strongly over-represented. With a higher average branching factor, the number of invalid trees increases and the bias towards short trees decreases.

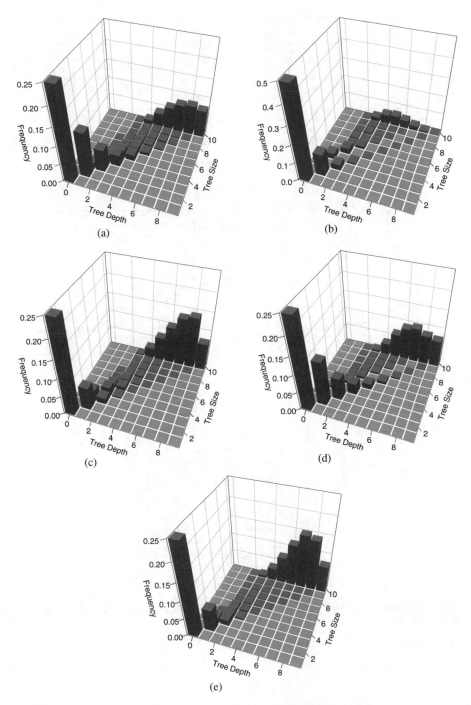

Fig. 23 Frequencies of (valid and invalid) trees over sizes and depths (grammars $Bal_{1,2}$ (**a**), $Bal_{1,3}$ (**b**), $Exp_{1,2}$ (**c**), $Exp_{1,3}$ (**d**), and $Exp_{1,2,3}$ (**e**))

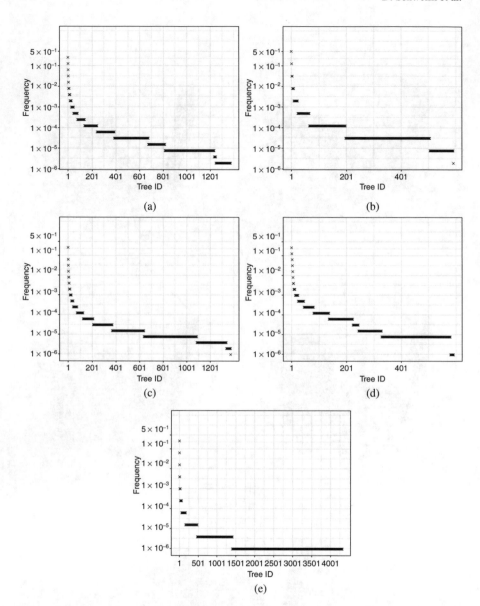

Fig. 24 Frequencies of valid trees (grammars $Bal_{1,2}$ (**a**), $Bal_{1,3}$ (**b**), $Exp_{1,2}$ (**c**), $Exp_{1,3}$ (**d**), and $Exp_{1,2,3}$ (**e**))

Figure 24 plots the frequencies of valid trees over their depth and size in decreasing order from left to right. Due to the high number of different trees, we left out tree depths and sizes. In general, the number of different trees is high. Grammars $Bal_{1,3}$ and $Exp_{1,3}$ map the genotypes to 592 valid trees and 125,121 invalid trees. Grammars $Bal_{1,2}$ and $Exp_{1,2}$ map the genotypes to 1374 valid and 17,303 invalid trees. Grammar $Exp_{1,2,3}$ maps the genotypes to the highest number of different trees (4315 valid and 626,859 invalid).

6 Conclusions

In this paper, we studied how different types of grammars affect the non-uniform redundancy of GE. After a brief overview of recent work on the bias of GE representations and grammars in GE, we illustrated how the expected tree size E_{tree} of a phenotype tree depends on the average branching factor B_{avg}, which is determined by the used BNF grammar. In GE, grammars define production rules which describe how non-terminals are substituted by either functions of various arities k or terminal nodes. The average branching factor B_{avg} sums up the branching factor of each substitution, which is the number of non-terminals of the substitution, multiplied by the probability of choosing the particular substitution.

We distinguished between collapsing grammars ($B_{\text{avg}} < 1$), balanced grammars ($B_{\text{avg}} = 1$), and explosive grammars ($B_{\text{avg}} > 1$). For collapsing grammars, the expected size E_{tree} of the encoded phenotype tree is finite, whereas for balanced and explosive grammars $E_{\text{tree}} \to \infty$. For $B_{\text{avg}} \to 0$, the expected phenotype tree size becomes 1. With increasing B_{avg}, this strong bias towards short trees gets lower, however, the number of GE genotypes that encode an invalid tree increases. For practical GE applications, the average branching factor should be $B_{\text{avg}} \approx 1$, as otherwise large phenotype trees could hardly be encoded. The experimental study presented in Sect. 5 supports this finding for a variety of different grammars.

Table 1 summarises some of these findings. For each grammar, we listed the average branching factor B_{avg}, the number of different valid $|\Phi_p^{valid}|$ and invalid $|\Phi_p^{invalid}|$ phenotype trees, the percentage $|\Phi_p^{valid}| / |\Phi_p|$ of valid trees over all trees, and the percentage f_p^{valid} of genotypes that encode a valid phenotype. For all results, the genotypes had 10 codons and we did not use wrapping. The results confirmed previous findings that GE representations are strongly redundant, as the number of genotypes ($2^{20} \approx 1.05 \times 10^6$) strongly exceeds the number of phenotypes. The numbers of valid phenotypes are between 10 and 4315; the numbers of invalid phenotypes range from 1 to 626,859.

Also, we found that the representation is non-uniformly redundant. The mapping has a large bias towards short trees. This bias gets stronger with lower B_{avg}. For example, when using a balanced grammar with $B_{\text{avg}} = 1$ (Bal_2), 50% of the genotypes encode a phenotype tree of size 1. For a collapsing grammar with $B_{\text{avg}} = 0.5$ (Col_2), the bias is stronger since 75% of all genotypes encode a tree of

Table 1 Properties of GE representations for various explosive, balanced, and collapsing grammars

Grammar name	B_{avg}	$|\Phi_p^{valid}|$	$|\Phi_p^{invalid}|$	$|\Phi_p^{valid}| / |\Phi_p|$	f_p^{valid}
Exp_3	2.25	17	412	3.96%	26.37%
Exp_2	1.50	23	252	8.36%	32.70%
$Exp_{1,2,3}$	1.50	4315	626,859	0.68%	40.22%
$Exp_{1,2}$	1.25	1374	17,303	7.36%	45.66%
$Exp_{1,3}$	1.25	592	25,121	2.30%	55.53%
$Bal_{1,2}$	1.00	1374	17,303	7.36%	66.36%
Bal_2	1.00	23	252	8.36%	75.39%
$Bal_{1,3}$	1.00	592	25,121	2.30%	80.06%
Col_3	0.75	17	412	3.96%	92.50%
Col_2	0.50	23	252	8.36%	98.11%
Col_1	0.50	10	1	90.91%	99.90%

size one. For balanced and explosive grammars ($B_{avg} \geq 1$), E_{tree} is infinite, resulting in a bias towards invalid trees. For example, for the explosive grammar Exp_3, we found that around 75% of all genotypes encode invalid trees (Table 1, results are for a codon length of 10 and no wrapping).

The results can help practitioners choose the right grammar when applying GE to problems of practical relevance. If too many of the genotypes encode invalid phenotypes or the encoded trees are too large, we recommend reducing the average branching factor. This can be done for example by adding more terminals to a grammar, reducing the number of functions, or reducing the arity of the functions. In general, we recommend that $B_{avg} \approx 1$. If B_{avg} is too small ($0 \geq B_{avg} \ll 1$), then the bias towards short trees is too strong and the percentage of genotypes that encode larger trees is too low. We believe that proper values of B_{avg} depend on the problem instance, as larger branching factors reduce the bias towards small trees and encode larger tree structures more often. The question of how a change on the average branching factor (by adapting the grammar) might affect search performance remains open and should be answered by future studies.

References

1. R.A. Caruana, J.D. Schaffer, Representation and hidden bias: gray vs. binary coding for genetic algorithms, in *Proceedings of the Fifth International Conference on Machine Learning*, ed. by J. Laird (Morgan Kaufmann, San Mateo, CA, 1988), pp. 153–161
2. D. Fagan, M. O'Neill, E. Galván-López, A. Brabazon, S. McGarraghy, An analysis of genotype-phenotype maps in grammatical evolution, in *Proceedings of the 13th European Conference on Genetic Programming, EuroGP 2010*, ed. by A.I. Esparcia-Alcázar, A. Ekárt, S. Silva, S. Dignum, A.B. Uyar. Lecture Notes in Computer Science, vol. 6021 (Springer, Berlin, 2010), pp. 62–73

3. R. Harper, GE, explosive grammars and the lasting legacy of bad initialisation, in *Proceedings of the IEEE Congress on Evolutionary Computation 2010, CEC 2010* (IEEE Press, New York, 2010), pp. 1–8

4. E. Hemberg, N. McPhee, M. O'Neill, A. Brabazon, Pre-, in- and postfix grammars for symbolic regression in grammatical evolution, in *IEEE Workshop and Summer School on Evolutionary Computing*, ed. by T.M. McGinnity. (IEEE, New York, 2008), pp. 18–22

5. J.R. Koza, *Genetic Programming: On the Programming of Computers by Means of Natural Selection* (MIT Press, Cambridge, MA, 1992)

6. S. Luke, Two fast tree-creation algorithms for genetic programming. IEEE Trans. Evol. Comput. **4**(3), 274–283 (2000)

7. M.A. Montes de Oca, Exposing a bias toward short-length numbers in grammatical evolution, in *Proceedings of the 11th European Conference on Genetic Programming, EuroGP 2008*, ed. by M. O'Neill, L. Vanneschi, S. Gustafson, A.I. Esparcia Alcázar, I. De Falco, A. Della Cioppa, E. Tarantino. Lecture Notes in Computer Science, vol. 4971 (Springer, Berlin, 2008), pp. 278–288

8. E. Murphy, E. Hemberg, M. Nicolau, M. O'Neill, A. Brabazon, Grammar bias and initialisation in grammar based genetic programming, in *Proceedings of the 15th European Conference on Genetic Programming, EuroGP 2012*, ed. by A. Moraglio, S. Silva, K. Krawiec, P. Machado, C. Cotta. Lecture Notes in Computer Science, vol. 7244 (Springer, Berlin, 2012), pp. 85–96

9. M. Nicolau, Understanding grammatical evolution: initialisation. Genet. Program. Evolvable Mach. **18**(4), 467–507 (2017)

10. M. O'Neill, A. Brabazon, M. Nicolau, S. Mc Garraghy, P. Keenan, π Grammatical evolution, in *Proceedings of the Genetic and Evolutionary Computation Conference, GECCO 2004*, ed. by K. Deb, R. Poli, W. Banzhaf, H.G. Beyer, E. Burke, P. Darwen, D. Dasgupta, D. Floreano, J. Foster, M. Harman, O. Holland, P. Lanzi, L. Spector, A. Tettamanzi, D. Thierens, A. Tyrrell. Lecture Notes in Computer Science, vol. 3103 (Springer, Berlin, 2004), pp. 617–629

11. M. O'Neill, C. Ryan, Genetic code degeneracy: implications for grammatical evolution and beyond, in *Advances in Artificial Life: 5th European Conference, ECAL 1999*, ed. by D. Floreano, J.D. Nicoud, F. Mondada. Lecture Notes in Computer Science, vol. 1674 (Springer, Berlin, 1999), pp. 149–153

12. M. O'Neill, C. Ryan, M. Nicolau, Grammar defined introns: an investigation into grammars, introns, and bias in grammatical evolution, in *Proceedings of the Genetic and Evolutionary Computation Conference, GECCO 2001*, ed. by L. Spector, E.D. Goodman, A. Wu, W. Langdon, H.M. Voigt, M. Gen, S. Sen, M. Dorigo, S. Pezeshk, M.H. Garzon, E. Burke (Morgan Kaufmann, San Francisco, CA, 2001), pp. 97–103

13. F. Rothlauf, *Representations for Genetic and Evolutionary Algorithms*, 2 edn. (Springer, Berlin, 2006)

14. F. Rothlauf, *Design of Modern Heuristics: Principles and Application*. Natural Computing Series (Springer, Heidelberg, 2011)

15. F. Rothlauf, D.E. Goldberg, Redundant representations in evolutionary computation. Evol. Comput. **11**(4), 381–415 (2003)

16. C. Ryan, R.M.A. Azad, Sensible initialisation in grammatical evolution, in *Proceedings of the Bird of a Feather Workshops, Genetic and Evolutionary Computation Conference, GECCO 2003*, ed. by A.M. Barry (AAAI, Chicago, 2003), pp. 142–145

17. C. Ryan, J.J. Collins, M.O. Neill, Grammatical evolution: evolving programs for an arbitrary language, in *Proceedings of the First European Workshop on Genetic Programming, EuroGP 1998*, ed. by W. Banzhaf, R. Poli, M. Schoenauer, T.C. Fogarty (Springer, Berlin, 1998), pp. 83–96

18. A. Thorhauer, On the non-uniform redundancy in grammatical evolution, in *Parallel Problem Solving from Nature – PPSN XIV: 14th International Conference*, ed. by J. Handl, E. Hart, P.R. Lewis, M. López-Ibáñez, G. Ochoa, B. Paechter. Lecture Notes in Computer Science, vol. 9921 (Springer, Cham, 2016), pp. 292–302

19. A. Thorhauer, F. Rothlauf, Structural difficulty in grammatical evolution versus genetic programming, in *Proceedings of the 15th Annual Conference Companion on Genetic and Evolutionary Computation, GECCO 2013*, ed. by C. Blum (ACM Press, New York, NY, 2013), pp. 997–1004
20. P.A. Whigham, Search bias, language bias and genetic programming, in *Genetic Programming 1996: Proceedings of the First Annual Conference on Genetic Programming*, ed. by J.R. Koza, D.E. Goldberg, D.B. Fogel, R.L. Riolo (MIT Press, Cambridge, MA, 1996), pp. 230–237

Mapping in Grammatical Evolution

David Fagan and Eoin Murphy

Abstract The act of going from genotype to phenotype in Grammatical Evolution requires the application of a mapping process. This mapping process works in conjunction with a grammar, to transform an ordinary string of integers into a possible solution to a problem. In this chapter, the reader is exposed to the rich vein of research exploring mappings in Grammatical Evolution. A comprehensive survey of the field of Mapping in GE is presented before the chapter focuses on the main theme, Position Independent Mappings. Firstly πGE is presented outlining some of the benefits of the approach, before the reader is presented with a position independent mapping that utilises advances in mappings and grammars to present a very powerful variant of GE, TAGE. The chapter concludes by briefly exploring a highly complex developmental variant of the TAGE mapping.

1 Introduction

Grammatical Evolution (GE) uses Neo-Darwinian principles of evolution to evolve automatically generated solutions to problems. GE is commonly referred to as a grammar-based form of Genetic Programming (GP) [31]. However, this description can prove over-simplistic [4] once the inner workings of GE are examined. Genetic Algorithms (GA) [15] and Genetic Programming (GP) [28] are two of the most popular forms of EC. A GA uses a population of bit string individuals and evolves this population of strings until the desired solution is found. The bit strings of a GA can represent a multitude of solutions depending on the encoding used. GP, on the other hand, uses a population of parse tree individuals. At their core, both

D. Fagan (✉)
UCD, Dublin, Ireland
e-mail: david.fagan@ucd.ie

E. Murphy
FanDuel, Edinburgh, Scotland, UK
e-mail: eoin@murph.ie

algorithms share similar workings. GE [43] takes inspiration from both these classic EC algorithms, while also harnessing the added power of grammars.

Whereas GP has a one-to-one mapping between parse tree and solution (although it could be argued that the genotype and phenotype are essentially the same thing in canonical GP), GE gains a many-to-one mapping by adopting the genotype-phenotype map. In this many-to-one mapping, many chromosomes will map to the same program. The usage of grammars in GE allows for the evolution of problems in a domain representable by a grammar, unlike canonical GP and its implicit grammar, where limitations such as the closure property have to be dealt with.

The mapping process in GE, which is a simple abstraction of the expression of DNA, is the conversion of a chromosome (genotype) to a solution (phenotype). In canonical GE this is done by taking a chromosome and a BNF context-free grammar and using the mod rule (Eq. (1)) a derivation tree is constructed. From this derivation tree, the solution can be extracted for evaluation.

$$New\ Node\ =\ Codon\ value\ \%\ Number\ of\ rules\ for\ Non\ Terminal \qquad (1)$$

There has been much debate recently [48, 49] as to the merits of the usage of a genotype to phenotype mapping in GE. One side argues for the removal of such mappings, while others, such as O'Neill and Nicolau [41], point towards the large amount of inspiration that can be taken from nature and its mapping processes, and their potential benefits to the GE representation. The issue of good representations is also of importance to the wider EC/GP community [31]. This chapter presents several approaches to exploring and enhancing the GE mapping process. While the approaches have not gained widespread usage within the GE community, this chapter moves to rectify this by providing researchers with an overview of some of these advances, before focusing in-depth at the position independent vein of GPM research.

Much work has been done to date with regards to the mapping process in GE. Some of the earliest work focused on a replacement for the mod rule. The bucket rule [25] looked to remove inherent biases in the traditional mod rule. This approach did not gain widespread use and many of the advantages of the method can be achieved by simply using a balanced and well-designed grammar. Another interesting vein of research that was carried out looked to enhance the mapping of GE, by exploring other factors that impact the successful mapping of individuals. Nicolau et al. [39] performed an in-depth investigation into termination in GE, noting a link between poor grammar design and termination issues in GE, and also the benefits of tail usage.

Several variants of GE have also come to be over the years since the first introduction of GE. These variants all use unique approaches to the genotype-phenotype mapping process. Chorus [2] is a position independent encoding system for grammar-based EA's. In Chorus the reading of codons from the chromosome is subject to positional change. Chorus uses a modified mod rule, where every production choice is considered, unlike GE where only the relevant production choices are considered. The modified mod rule, in conjunction with a concentration table, is used to construct derivation trees. The derivation is performed in a depth-first manner, similar to GE, using the concentration table to jump around the chromosome selecting codons as needed. The concentration table allows for Chorus to not leave any unused genetic introns in the chromosome that would occur if using the modified mod rule exclusively. Genetic Algorithms using Grammatical Evolution (GAuGE) [5] uses GE and attribute grammars to evolve what each gene positions in the GA codes for. The system features position independent genetic algorithms and uses the mod operation on codon values allowing for redundant coding, to mention but a few features. Recently we have seen the introduction of Structured Grammatical Evolution [30] to the field. SGE adapts the grammar and mapping process to provide GE with a more structured representation that allows for increased locality and reduces the ripple effect of traditional GE.

The chapter that follows first explores Position Independent Mapping in Sect. 2. This is then followed by an overview of a more complex mapping process, Tree Adjunct Grammatical Evolution, in Sect. 3. Finally, the chapter concludes with a summary in Sect. 4.

2 π GE: Position Independent Mapping in GE

π GE first proposed by O'Neill et al. [42] looks to enhance the GE GPM by removing the linear dependency of the genome in the traditional mapping process by giving control of the order of derivation to evolutionary search. The following section first presents the idea of position independent mapping, before examining the inner workings of the approach and highlighting desirable features. This work draws heavily from [8] and the associated publications that made up that volume of research [9–14].

2.1   Position Independent Mapping

The π GE GPM differs from the traditional GE mapping in one way. While the expansion of the NTs is performed identically in both approaches the order in which these expansions take place is different. GE adopts a fixed order mapping, while π GE uses evolution to control the order of NT expansions.

Before any mapping can be done in π GE, there are some changes that need to be made to the chromosome. π GE's mapping process differs from that of GE in that each expansion of a NT requires two codons. The standard GE chromosome is essentially split into a chromosome of pair values. The first codon of the pair (The Order Codon), is used to choose which NT to expand and the second (The Content Codon), is used to choose what the production, based on the rules available for a NT of that type, just like in GE. The chromosome shown in Fig. 1 can be viewed as a list of paired values such as $((2,12),(7,9)\ldots)$.

```
<e> ::= <e> <o> <e> | <v>
<o> ::= + | -
<v> ::= X | Y
```

Chromosome = 2,12,7,9,3,15,23,1,11,4,6,13,2,7,8,3,35,19,2,6

Fig. 1 An example grammar and chromosome

2.1.1 π GE Mapping Example

The mapping process begins from the embryonic start symbol of the grammar. Taking the simple grammar provided in Fig. 1 this is $< e >$. $< e >$ is then added to the list of possible expansions, $[< e >]$. Selecting the first π GE codon from the chromosome (Fig. 1) yields the codon (2, 12). The order codon, 2 is then passed to Eq. (2), that results in selecting the NT to be expanded from the NT list, $[(< e >)]$ as $2\%1 = 0$. Now for the second half of the π GE expansion we have to perform the standard GE expansion on the selected NT. In this case there are two possible transformations which can be applied to $< e >$. Either it will be replaced with $< e >< o >< e >_0$ or with $< v >_1$. To decide what rule is taken, the content codon 12 and the number of choices available are used in conjunction with Eq. (3). In this case $12\%2 = 0$ so $< e >$ will be transformed into $< e >< o >< e >$, and the NT list will be updated, $[< e >, < o >, < e >]$.

$$NT\ to\ expand\ =\ Order\ Codon\ \%\ |NT\ list| \qquad (2)$$

$$Expansion\ Choice\ =\ Content\ Codon\ \%\ Number\ of\ rules\ for\ NT \qquad (3)$$

The second expansion of the π GE derivation tree follows a similar process, first the next π GE codon is read, (7, 9). The order codon of the pair is used to select the next NT to expand, $< o >$ is chosen as $7\%3 = 1$. Next the content codon is used to select what the expansion becomes. Similarly to the first expansion $< o >$ has two possible productions, $+_0$ or $-_1$, and $-$ is chosen in this case as $9\%2 = 1$. As $-$ is a terminal it is not added to the NT list and so the list now consists of $[< e >, < e >]$. When a NT production results in the generation of new NTs, these NTs are placed at the same location in the NT list of possible expansions, that the initial NT was selected from.

This expansion process is repeated until the tree is completed or the derivation process reaches the end of the chromosome. If all the codons have been used the mapper will either return an invalid individual or else wrap around to the start of the chromosome and continues mapping (if wrapping is enabled). Figure 2 provides the complete derivation example, with Fig. 2a showing the NT list at each step of the derivation, and Fig. 2b showing the completed derivation tree. The number associated with each branch of the tree is a reference to the numbered steps shown in Fig. 2a, which show how each choice of NT to expand comes about. A pseudo-code outline of the π GE mapping process is also shown in Algorithm 1.

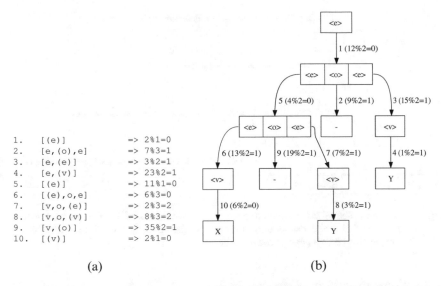

```
1.    [(e)]           => 2%1=0
2.    [e,(o),e]       => 7%3=1
3.    [e,(e)]         => 3%2=1
4.    [e,(v)]         => 23%2=1
5.    [(e)]           => 11%1=0
6.    [(e),o,e]       => 6%3=0
7.    [v,o,(e)]       => 2%3=2
8.    [v,o,(v)]       => 8%3=2
9.    [v,(o)]         => 35%2=1
10.   [(v)]           => 2%1=0
```

             (a)   (b)

Fig. 2 Example of the πGE mapping process. The derivation tree is expanded in the order that is dictated by the chromosome and Eq. (2). This process is outlined in (**a**). In this figure the expansion order is indicated on the arrowed edges between the tree nodes. 5(4%2 = 0), indicates that this was the fifth expansion in the mapping and that 4%2 = 0 dictates what the fifth expansion will entail. (**a**) πGE order choice list. (**b**) πGE derivation tree example

---

Algorithm 1: πGE Genotype-Phenotype Map Algorithm. The addition of the order codons are highlighted. It can now be seen how the order codons are used to pick an index in the NT list. It is also worth noting how the new productions are then added to the index where the parent NT was taken from originally, this preserves the ordering of the derivation string

---

$listNT$ {List to store NT's seen}
Add start symbol from grammar to $listNT$
$wraps = 0$
while $listNT$ is not empty **do**
    if reached end of chromosome **then**
        $wraps$++
        if $wraps$ > max wraps allowed **then**
            return false
        reset chromosome iterator
    {This is where the πGE order comes in}
    $currentOrderCodon$ = get next codon value
    $nextProductionIndex = currentOrderCodon$ % size of $listNT$
    $currentNT =$ get $listNT[nextProductionIndex]$
    $currentContentCodon$ = get next codon value
    $newProduction = currentCodon$ % number of productions for $currentNT$
    set $currentNT's$ children = $newProduction$
    {The new NT's are added where the parent NT was removed from}
    insert $newProduction$ at $listNT[nextProductionIndex]$ {Only adds NTs}
Generate Phenotype by traversing the leaf nodes of the derivation tree.
return true

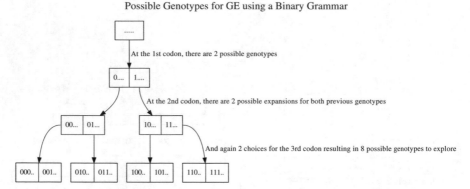

Fig. 3 This figure shows the minimum possible genotypes needed by GE, to map to every possibility for the first 3 expansions of a grammar, consisting of the rule $E ::= EE|EE$. Note that with 3 expansions 8 (2^3) genotypes are needed

2.2   Connectivity of Representation

πGE has been shown to be comparable and in many cases exceed the performance of GE. The addition of the evolvable ordering of πGE increases the possible number of genotypes to be searched substantially. How does πGE effectively search this space without any addition in search effort. Does the addition of the evolvable order also carry with it some benefits not available to GE's fixed order mapping?

2.2.1   GE Versus πGE Genotypes

Consider a simple demonstration: a GE derivation tree that starts off with three expansions. At each of these expansions, a grammar allows for two possible expansion choices, and each choice produces two NT's and consumes one NT, e.g., $E ::= EE|EE$. This results in a branching factor (the number of possible expansions at a tree node) at each expansion of two for GE, that leads to a requirement of 2^3 genotypes that map to the trees needed to fully explore the first three expansions, as shown in Fig. 3.

πGE for these same three expansions presents a different situation. The first expansion has a single NT so πGE has a choice of one NT to expand. This NT then presents two possible choices for the grammar exactly like GE. This choice results in the consumption of one NT and the creation of two new NTs. Now for the second expansion πGE has the choice of two NTs, and from this it will then have two choices from the grammar for whichever NT it selected. The second expansion consumed one NT but produced two new ones so there is now three NTs. The final of the three expansions for πGE results in a choice between the three unexpanded NT's. Finally, the expansion of the NT results in a choice of two from the grammar. To model these three expansions πGE has to cover 48 ($1*2*2*2*3*2$) possible combinations of genotypes that can generate the eight possible derivation trees, as

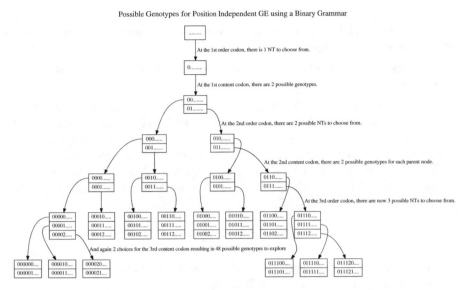

Possible Genotypes for Position Independent GE using a Binary Grammar

Fig. 4 This figure shows the minimum number of genotypes needed by πGE to cover all possible mapping sequences for the first 3 expansions of a grammar, consisting of the rule $E := EE|EE$. Note that the grammar consumes 1 NT and produces 2 NTs to the possible locations πGE can choose for expansion. This leads to the NT list increasing by 1 per expansion. Due to this, 48 $(1 * 2 * 2 * 2 * 3 * 2)$ genotypes are needed to model the first 3 expansions. This results in only 8 derivation trees, but πGE has 48 possible paths to these trees

demonstrated in Fig. 4. πGE has 40 more genotype combinations than GE, and if we were to carry this on to a fourth expansion GE would have 16 (2^4) possible trees that requires 16 genotypes, while πGE is facing 384 $(1 * 2 * 2 * 2 * 3 * 2 * 4 * 2)$ possible genotypes to generate the same 16 trees.

Given that GE and πGE share a common grammar, the phenotypes that can be derived from both systems are identical, given the same amount of codons, where a πGE codon is a pair. This shared phenotypic space, called the phenotypic landscape, allows for the direct comparison of how each respective system can search the landscape. Modelling each algorithm's interaction with this landscape may shed light on how πGE can overcome the massive overhead of order search. Koza and Poli [29] noted that understanding how an algorithm operates can be aided by visualising the program space, i.e., the phenotype space in GE and πGE.

2.2.2 Search Landscapes

Landscapes are an idea that can be employed to aid in the understanding of complex systems [22, 29]. Good visualisation of a landscape can facilitate the study of an aspect of interest in the system. This visualisation may allow the user to gain an increased understanding of the process in question, thus allowing for the deduction of solutions to observed behaviours in the system being examined. The doctoral thesis of Jones [21], focused on trying to understand and define landscapes in terms of EC methods. Jones stated:

> A landscape is a metaphor by which we hope to imagine some aspect of the behaviour of an algorithm [21].

He put forward the idea that an algorithm contains many landscapes dependent upon the operator performing search, such as mutation, and crossover in EC. Jones hypothesised that there was not one landscape, but rather a combination of these individual landscapes that provides a complete model of the system [22].

The landscape model, as outlined in detail in Jones' thesis [21], was employed for this study. What follows is a brief description. In the model, a landscape can be described as a five tuple (Eq. (4)).

$$L = (R, \phi, f, F, >_F) \tag{4}$$

- R denotes the representation space of the search algorithm.
- ϕ denotes the operator acting on the landscape.
- f a function that maps a multiset of R $(M(R))$ to F, the fitness space, $f : M(R) \rightarrow F$.
- F the fitness space
- $>_F$ represent a partial ordering over the fitness space.

The landscape L can be visualised as a labelled directed graph $G_L = (V, E)$, where the vertices V are a subset of $M(R)$, $V \subseteq M(R)$, and the edges E are a subset of the cross product of V, $E \subseteq V \times V$. An edge E between two vertices, v and w, can be said to exist if and only if there is a connection between v and w via an application of ϕ, $(v, w) \exists E \iff \phi(v, w) > 0$.

This model was further defined by Murphy et al. [36] for usage in a comparison of grammars in GE, and a similar definition is used for this experiment. The landscapes to be examined in this study are defined by the representation space R, that combines the chromosome space, and a GE GPM or πGE GPM resulting in the phenotype space. The phenotype space represents all the valid phenotypes that can be derived from the grammar within a given chromosome length, this is the object space O. Single int-flip mutation represents ϕ, and f is the GE fitness function. For this landscape, the graph $G_L = (V, E)$ can be viewed as having set of vertices V, where $V \subseteq M(R)$ and $V \subseteq O$, meaning the vertices are genotypes, but also valid phenotypes. Given that GE and πGE share the same phenotype space, V will be the same regardless of what GPM is used. The edges between the vertices may differ, due to how ϕ interacts with the representation space R. Through these differences in E, GE and πGE will be compared.

2.2.3 Mutate and Store

Mutate and Store (MS), originally introduced by Murphy et al. [36], and modified to meet the requirements of this study, allows for exploration and mapping of any grammar's phenotypic landscape. MS maps the phenotypic landscape via single int flip mutation events, whereby exactly one codon is mutated per mutation event. MS requires a fixed length chromosome of all zero codons. MS then takes the desired grammar and this initial chromosome and builds the phenotypic landscape. MS does this by starting at the first codon and finding all the possible choices for that codon, by checking the grammar. Once all the possible choices for the codon are known, MS generates new genotypes for each choice and stores them in a neighbourhood. Having stored all possible neighbours, MS evaluates these neighbours and records what mutations resulted in chromosomes with valid phenotypes. These valid phenotypes are then added to the population for mutation at the next codon index. This process is repeated until all codon indices in the genotype have been fully explored. Once this process is done, all the individual neighbourhoods of valid phenotypes are compressed into a single neighbourhood of phenotype connections. This final neighbourhood is then represented as a graph for analysis.

MS removes all degeneracy in the genotypes by only allowing the codon values at each point of the chromosome to represent the choices available thus removing the degeneracy and neutral mutations that GE can take advantage of. Degeneracy in GE is provided by the mod rule. Consider the following: a GE codon valued 62 is mutated to 64. When this codon is applied to a binary grammar rule, the mutation results in no change to the expansion of the tree. Removing the degeneracy is important as it significantly limits the number of possible phenotypes. If MS allowed codons values between 0 and 255, and a chromosome was limited to a size of just 3 codons, that would result in over 16 million possible genotypes that would need to be explored regardless of the arity of the grammar. MS when investigating a grammar with an arity of 2, leads to only 8 possible genotypes to explore 3 codons.

πGE presented an extra layer of exploration that needed to be added to MS, for the mapping of πGE phenotypes. In the above explanation, at each codon of the genotype, the grammar was consulted for the possible expansion choices, for that codon. For πGE this process took place at every even valued codon index. πGE required that for every odd codon index the NT list size was consulted so that every possible expansion point in the partial πGE derivation tree be explored. This resulted in an increase in the number of possible genotypes and restricted the size of genotype that could be explored in this study. The degeneracy for the expansion order codons was removed, as it was for standard GE codons.

2.3   *Phenotypic Landscape Visualisations*

This section visualises the phenotypic landscapes of both GE and πGE. The graphs of the phenotypic landscapes for both are displayed and discussed. The graph representation allows for visualisation of multiple connections between phenotypes, e.g., where a pair of phenotypes are connected via both order, and content codon mutation events in πGE.

The visualisations produced are limited by several constraints. Beyond the limitations of printed media, initial tests highlighted a computational constraint for grammar usage with πGE. Usage of grammars with high arity production rules resulted in MS not being able to model the phenotype landscape of πGE. This was due to the increase in possible genotypes that πGE has to explore, as explained in Sect. 2.2.1.

A simple grammar was designed to enable modelling to take place. This grammar (Fig. 5) is a binary grammar that has two choices for every rule. The grammar shares the same core rules as the commonly used symbolic regression grammars (Fig. 6).

Figure 7 shows all possible phenotypes for πGE on the binary grammar. The common connects for GE and πGE are displayed in blue, while the unique πGE connections are in red. The addition of position independence in the mapping can clearly be seen. Position independence allows for a pure neutral mutation that cannot be seen in GE without the use of degeneracy in the mod rule. The neutral mutation as indicated with a loop edge on the states.

Phenotypes of a single variable, such as $(x1)$, cannot exhibit neutral mutations other than via the mod rule, eliminated earlier. This is due to the NT list for such a tree never exceeding a size of one, thus the left-most non-terminal is always picked. When the tree sizes of individuals grow to permit a varied ordering in πGE, it is seen that a mutation in the order codons results in neutral mutations.

Fig. 5 Example grammar 1, binary grammar

```
<expr> ::= <op> <expr> <expr>    (0)
         | <var>                 (1)

<op> ::= +                       (0)
       | *                       (1)

<var> ::= x0                     (0)
        | 1.0                    (1)
```

Fig. 6 Example grammar 2, 3 variable variant

```
<expr> ::= <op> <expr> <expr>    (0)
         | <var>                 (1)

<op> ::= +                       (0)
       | *                       (1)

<var> ::= x0                     (0)
        | x1                     (1)
        | 1.0                    (2)
```

Fig. 7 The connectivity of GE and π GE using the grammar in Fig. 5 is shown. Each vertex represents a phenotype and each edge represent the ability to move from one phenotype to another in a single mutation. The blue edges are common paths shared by π GE and GE. The edges in red represent connections only available to π GE. These extra connections are a direct result of the π GE GPM, who's evolvable order allows the same phenotypes being connected in multiple ways

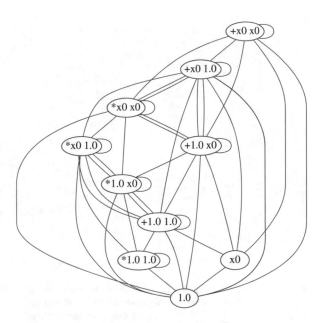

Table 1 Table outlining features of the connectivity graphs shown for both experiments

Graph features	GE grammar 1	π GE grammar 1	GE grammar 2	π GE grammar 2
# Vertices	10	10	21	21
$\sum_{i=1}^{n} DegreeVertex(i)$	42	90	98	198
# Edges	21	45	49	99
VertexDegree	4.2	9.0	4.67	9.43

The table notes the total number of vertices and edges, the total degree of the graph and the average degree for a vertex for each GPM approach on both grammars used

The red edges show the mutations that are a direct result of order mutations. It can be seen how π GE allows for transitions in the search space that are not possible with GE. Table 1 provides a numerical overview of this increase in connectivity through a numerical summary of the individual graphs of GE and π GE. It is interesting to note that an algorithm whose phenotype space has a densely connected search space will have a greater amount of freedom moving from phenotype to phenotype. This freedom can aid in increasing the search performance.

In order to provide an understanding of how the landscapes scale, an enhanced version of the initial grammar is applied (Fig. 6). The second examination of the connectivity of π GE versus GE was performed using the three variable version of the binary grammar (Fig. 6). This grammar variant was used to show how the landscapes scale. The addition of just one extra variable, increasing the total number of variables from two to three, results in a 110% increase in the number of vertices needed to represent the phenotypic landscape (from 10 to 21).

Figure 8 shows the phenotypic landscape graph for GE and π GE on the expanded grammar. Each vertex represents a valid phenotype and each edge represents a

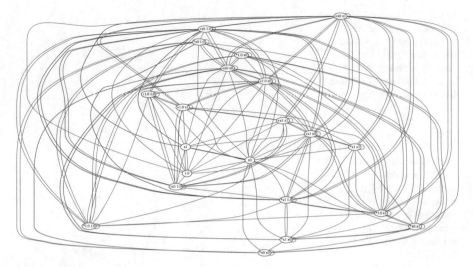

Fig. 8 The connectivity of GE and πGE using the grammar in Fig. 6 is displayed. Each vertex represents a phenotype and the edges represent the ability to move from one phenotype to another in a single mutation. The edges in red represent the connections that are only available to πGE. The blue edges shown the common paths shared by πGE and GE. The graph once again displays the increase in connectivity that the variable order GPM in πGE provides

connection between the phenotypes via a single mutation event. From examining Table 1 it can be seen that the two setups still produce a vastly different number of edges between vertices. The neutral mutations and multiple paths between the same vertices also remain present as expected.

This comparison is summarised in Table 1 and also compared against the initial setup. The table shows that the addition of position independence to the mapping process increases the connections between phenotypes in the landscape. With both the grammars there is slightly more than a 100% increase in the number of connections between phenotypes. The average degree of a vertex in the graph doesn't quite match the increase in nodes, indicating that some nodes get more than a doubling of edges.

2.3.1 Limitations

The connectivity studies [8, 14] where limited to the exploration of the phenotypic connectivity in terms of the mutation operation due to certain factors. The massive amount of possible derivation trees that πGE can produce consumed massive resources. Once the complexity of crossover would have been added this would have just exacerbated the problem of possible combinations of trees. The reason for simple grammars being used is a similar issue in that any increase in arity of the grammar's rules resulted in a combinatorial explosion of possible trees.

2.3.2 Discussion

Visualising of the GE and πGElandscapes was done with the intention of gaining further insight into how the πGE algorithm works. πGE introduces an increase to the search space of genotypes with its variable ordered GPM. With this increase in the search space, how can πGE still maintain good search performance? πGE and GE was compared using a simple grammar. From this comparison certain aspects of the πGE algorithm became evident. πGE has a much more connected phenotypic landscape, that allows for a better ability to explore the search space. πGE also introduces pure neutral mutations via the varying of the expansion order of the GPM. These neutral mutations are not possible with GE except via codon degeneracy.

πGE increases the genotypic search space that it must navigate by introducing an evolvable expansion order as shown in Sect. 2.2.1. This evolvable expansion order also brings with it some unforeseen benefits. The addition of the variable order to the GPM has resulted in an algorithm that exhibits far more connectivity in the phenotypic space than standard GE. πGE's variable order GPM allows for phenotypes to neutrally mutate back to themselves. Neutral mutations of this nature are only seen in GE through the degeneracy gained via the use of codon values and the mod rule in the GPM. πGE will not only enjoy the benefit of standard GE's degeneracy, but will also gain additional degeneracy via the use of a mod rule to control the variable order GPM, and the natural neutral mutations it gains from the usage of the variable order GPM.

Redundancy, neutral mutation, and degeneracy can have a drastic effect on the performance of an EA [3, 26, 27, 40, 44, 45]. This may provide more insight into how πGE can maintain performance under the strain of order search. πGE presents a very redundant GPM, with order redundancy, and the codon redundancy on both the NT choice and tree expansion choice. Ebner et al. [7] have shown that a GPM that exhibits high redundancy increases evolvability (the ability for random variation to produce a fitness improvement). The added redundancy in the πGE GPM also leads to a substantial amount of neutral mutation, as seen in the number of potential genotypes that MS explored to generate the phenotypic landscapes. This explosion of genotypes is the reason why πGE could only be modelled on such a limited landscape.

Kimura [26, 27] argued that in the neutral theory of evolution, most mutation events are neutral mutations and that only a small number of non-neutral mutations are actually beneficial. Kimura also studied neutral networks in nature and noted how most mutations simply navigate this neutral network until a beneficial mutation occurs. Ebner et al. [6] examined the idea of neutral mutations and neutral networks in GPM. Shackleton et al. [46] and Shipman [47] also explored this avenue of research into redundancy and neutral mutations, highlighting again how a many to one GPM was beneficial over a one to one mapping due to redundancy.

Many others have investigated redundancy in GPM and found it to be a key component to driving evolution. Kargupta [24] provided a theoretical examination of a simple redundant mapping in a search space, that underpins a lot of the research in this area. Rothlauf [44, 45] has also undertaken significant research in the area as have Banzhaf [3] and O'Neill [40]. Rothlauf believed that redundancy was a good this only if the optimum solution is over-represented in the search space. This represents a sampling of research in the area, and in the majority of cases, redundancy and neutral mutation are viewed as a beneficial property in a mapping from genotype to phenotype. πGE has a larger search space than GE to explore, and the added connectivity, redundancy and neutral mutations that the evolvable ordering of the GPM provided πGE is the only difference between the two algorithms. Therefore it is argued that the increased connectivity and redundancy in πGE, must be responsible for πGE's ability to achieve comparable performance to GE.

2.4   Expansion Order in πGE

What happens within πGE with regards to the expansion orders used in the algorithm. Does πGE effectively search the order space and in doing so does the population converge to a specific ordering. In [14], two metrics were developed and used to monitor how far a πGE population was away from depth-first and breadth-first orders. The orders of πGE individuals during evolution were recorded, from a random order initialisation and a fixed order initialisation, on a range of setups and problems. It was shown that πGE drifts towards a distribution of orders rather than one particular order. The effect that grammar complexity has on the distribution of orders was discussed and it was found that more complex grammars lead to a wider distribution of orders. Crossover was examined and found to have limited impact on the orders observed within πGE. The orders discovered during evolution were examined to verify that πGE continued to search the order space, and encountered new orders during evolution. Derivation tree bias was also examined and it was found that the addition of the variable expansion order in πGE did not change the bias in the initial population.

2.5 πGE Summary

The previous sections have outlined position independent mapping and provided a discussion on the advantages of adopting the approach within GE. The addition of the variable mapping introduces an increase in the genotype space to be searched. This increase in search also provides a more connected search space which allows for an increase in ability to mutate between possible solutions, and also introduces a significant amount of neutral mutations. The following section will expand on this idea of position independent mapping by using Tree Adjunct Grammars and a position independent mapping to enhance GE further.

3   TAGE: Tree Adjunct Grammatical Evolution

Tree Adjunct GE(TAGE) is a system designed by Murphy et al. [33, 35–37]. TAGE uses Tree Adjunct Grammars(TAG) instead of canonical GE's context-free grammars to construct solutions to problems. The usage of TAGs and requires the adopting of a GPM that extends on from that used in πGE. This section outlines the incorporation of Tree Adjunct Grammars (TAGs) into the standard GE algorithm and goes on to highlight some of the advantages of using TAGs in GE. This work is an overview of the work performed by Murphy in [32] and its associated publications [33, 35–37]. While it has been shown explicitly in the publication by Murphy et al. that TAGE provides a performance increase over GE, this section will look to outline how TAGE works as well as highlight some of the benefits of adopting this approach to GE.

3.1   Tree Adjunct Grammars

TAGs, have been used previously in GP in the form of TAG3P by Hoai and McKay [17] and later TAG3P+ [16, 18]. They have also been used for incremental and developmental evaluation [19, 20] and ant colony optimisation [1]. GE uses context-free grammars, that offer users with a way to easily create grammars. TAGE takes advantage of the ease of construction that CFGs offer and automatically converts CFGs to TAGs, as TAGs are not very intuitive to create.

3.1.1   From CFG to TAG

A lexicalised TAG (LTAG) is a special instance of a TAG. A lexicalised grammar has two defining properties. Firstly the grammar consists of a finite set of structures, each structure with at least one terminal symbol, known as the anchor. Secondly, it has at least one operation for composing these structures together.

The TAGs used in TAGE are LTAGs, as all leaf nodes of the elementary trees, with the exception of foot nodes, are labelled with terminal symbols. The terms TAG and LTAG will be synonymous throughout and will both refer to lexicalised TAGs. Joshi [23] stated that for a *"finitely ambiguous CFG[1] which does not generate the empty string, there is a lexicalised TAG generating the same language and tree set as that CFG"*. Joshi and Schabes also provided an algorithm for generating such a TAG. This algorithm, presented in Algorithm 2, as well as being outlined below, allows existing CFGs used by GE to be transformed into TAGs. It also enables TAGs to be created by designing new CFGs. This is beneficial as CFGs can be more

---

[1] A grammar is said to be *finitely ambiguous* if all finite length sentences produced by that grammar cannot be analysed in an infinite number of ways.

Algorithm 2: Generating a TAG from a CFG

Require: $G = \{N, T, P, S\}$ {A CFG}
   $g \leftarrow$ createDiGraph(G)
   $c \leftarrow$ findBaseCycles(g)
   $R \leftarrow$ getRecursiveProductions(P, g)
   $NR \leftarrow P - R$;
   $I \leftarrow$ generateTreesByExpansionEnumeration(S, NR)
   $A \leftarrow \emptyset$
   for all c_i in c **do**
      for all n_j in c_i **do**
         $E \leftarrow I \cup A$
         if a tree in E has a node labelled the same as n_j **then**
            $A \leftarrow A \cup$ generateTreesByExpansionEnumeration(n_j, c_i, NR)

Fig. 9 An example CFG

```
<e> ::= <e> <o> <e> | <v>
<o> ::= * | + | -
<v> ::= X | Y
```

trivially designed by hand. Figure 10 provides an example of a TAG produced by this algorithm.

The algorithm proceeds as follows. Given a finitely ambiguous CFG,

$$G = \{N, \Sigma, P, S\}$$

where N is the set of non-terminal symbols, Σ is the set of terminal symbols, P is the set of production rules, and S is the start symbol:

1. Construct a directed graph, g, from G. The nodes of g are labelled with symbols from N and the edges of g are labelled with the productions from P which map between them;
2. Find the set of minimal cycles, c, in g such that they contain no other cycles within them;
3. The productions in P are then divided into two separate sets, R is the set of recursive productions, and NR is the set of non-recursive productions in the grammar. A production is recursive if it is part of a cycle, c_i;
4. Using S as the root node, create the set of all possible derivation trees using only the productions in NR. This is the set of initial trees, I;
5. Create A, the set of auxiliary trees, as an empty set. $A = \emptyset$;
6. For each node n_j, in each of the cycles c_i, if there is a tree in $I \cup A$ that contains a node which has the same label as n_j, then create the set of all possible derivation trees using only the productions in NR and the current cycle where the n_j is the root node and the foot node is the node with the same label as n_j. Add this set of trees to A;
7. This continues until all cycles have been processed.

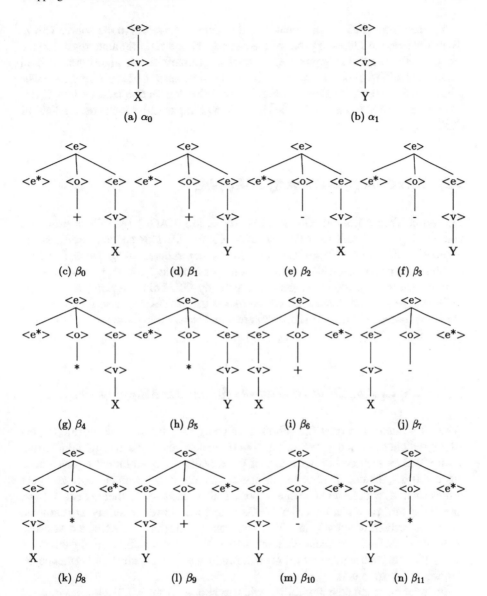

Fig. 10 The set of initial trees, $I = \{\alpha_0, \alpha_1\}$, and the set of auxiliary trees, $A = \{\beta_0, \beta_1, \ldots, \beta_{11}\}$, generated by the transformation of the CFG shown in Fig. 9 into a TAG using Algorithm 2

The resulting TAG is both weakly and strongly equivalent to the source CFGs. That is to say, the TAG can produce the same language and the same tree set as the source CFG. Algorithm 2 provides a concise summary of this algorithm, with an example of a TAG produced by the algorithm can be seen in Fig. 10. This TAG was generated from the CFG shown in Fig. 9. The following section outlines how TAGs have been applied to date in the field of EC, with a particular focus on the field of GBGP.

3.2 TAG Genotype-Phenotype Mapping

The novel Tree-Adjoining Grammatical Evolution (TAGE) [34–37] is proposed and developed in order to make use of TAGs in GE. This section describes the required modifications to the GE algorithm in order to make use of TAGs. Firstly, a discussion is provided on TAG composition operations and how they might be used in conjunction with the linear genotype used by GE. Following this, a genotype to phenotype mapping algorithm which makes use of TAGs is described in detail. Other components of the GE algorithm are then discussed in the context of their use in TAGE.

3.3 Tree Composition Operations for Linear Mapping

While TAGs can construct derivation trees using two different composition operations, adjunction, and substitution, TAGE makes exclusive use of adjunction. While TAGs which do not make use of the substitution operator are equivalent to those that do, the use of substitution operations allows for a much more compact representation, with fewer elementary trees. This is discussed further in Sect. 3.6. An interesting and powerful feature of TAGs is that they have the ability to guarantee complete derivation trees from which valid phenotypes may be extracted at every stage of the derivation process. This property is known as feasibility, and guarantees that a TAG derivation tree of *any size* will produce a syntactically valid sentence, as defined by the grammar.

In order to guarantee feasibility when mapping from a GE chromosome of finite length using a TAG, the use of the substitution operation must be excised. If both composition operations are to be used, the chromosome would require partitioning, with the first partition mapping adjunction operations and the second mapping substitution operations. The amount of substitution operations required to complete the tree is dependent upon the number of adjunction operations applied. As there is a finite number of codons in the chromosome, no guarantee can be made that the second partition will be of a sufficient length to map the required amount of substitution operations to complete the tree. Alternatively, a quasi-diploid chromosome approach could be used, where a second chromosome is used for the sole purpose of mapping substitution operations. While this approach removes the need for a chromosomal partitioning scheme, it remains impossible to guarantee that there will be sufficient codons to map the requisite number of substitution operations to complete the tree, and hence, impossible to ensure feasibility.

The exclusive use of the adjunction operation requires the TAGs utilised in this thesis to be fully anchored LTAGs. That is to say that, with the exception of the foot node, all branches of the generated auxiliary trees are fully expanded with terminal symbols labelling all leaf nodes. In doing so, this allows the adjunction operation to take a complete tree as input, and return a complete tree as output. The output tree is composed of an auxiliary tree adjoined to the input tree. This approach guarantees complete derivation trees before and after each adjunction operation, without the use of the substitution operation, ensuring feasibility. For example, initial and auxiliary trees can be seen in the sample grammar presented in Fig. 10. This design decision introduces some limitations to the system which are discussed in Sect. 3.6.

3.4 Genotype-Phenotype Mapping

TAGs make use of tree composition operations, combining partial or elementary trees together in the construction of their structured sentences. TAGs differentiate between the derivation and derived tree. While the resulting TAG derived tree (Fig. 11) is equivalent to the CFG derivation tree, TAG derivation can be more

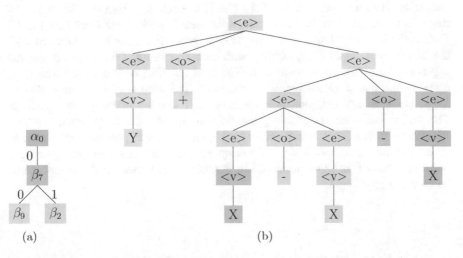

Fig. 11 An example of a TAG derivation tree and its respective derived tree. The derivation tree (**a**) defines the adjunction operations which produce the derived tree (**b**). The nodes in (**a**) are labelled with elementary trees with each edge declaring an adjunction operation between parent and child. Each edge is labelled with the address of a node in the parent tree where the adjunction will occur

compactly described by using a TAG derivation tree (Fig. 11). The nodes of a TAG derivation tree are labelled with elementary trees, and each of the edges between derivation nodes is labelled with an address. This address provides the location of a particular node within the elementary tree labelling the parent derivation node of that edge. It is at this location that the auxiliary tree labelling the child node of the edge is to be applied using a composition operator. Applying each of these composition operations creates the TAG derived tree.

In TAGE, the genotype is the same as that in GE. However, while the codons are applied to the same general mapping rule, $codonValue \% c = choice$. c no longer represents the number of available production choices. Rather, in place of c there is either the number of possible locations throughout the entire derivation tree where adjunction might be applied, $codonValue \% \|adjoinableAdresses\| = choice$ or the number of auxiliary trees, one of which, may be adjoined to a particular location, $codonValue \% \|A'\| = choice$. Another important difference from GE is that mapping from genotype to phenotype in TAGE will only terminate when the end of the chromosome is reached. While mapping in GE may expand all non-terminal nodes before reaching the end of the chromosome, there are always adjoinable nodes available in TAGE derivation trees.

To begin mapping, a genotype to phenotype in TAGE an initial tree is required and is chosen from the set of initial trees, I. A list of addresses of adjoinable nodes in the tree is then created. A node address is that node's index in a breadth-first traversal of the elementary tree it is contained in. An adjoinable node is any node which has not already been adjoined to and is labelled with a symbol which is also the label of the root node of an auxiliary tree in A. Adjunction is restricted from occurring on foot nodes. An auxiliary tree is then chosen from A. This auxiliary tree will be adjoined to the initial tree at the chosen node. Both trees now form a TAG derivation tree of size two. With an edge going from root node, labelled with the initial tree, to child node, labelled with the auxiliary tree. This edge denotes the adjunction operation to be performed. The trees labelling each node are traversed, updating the list of adjoinable node addresses. The used address is removed and the addresses of any additional adjoinable nodes in the new auxiliary tree are added. The next node address and auxiliary tree are chosen and added to the derivation tree. All choices in this example consume a codon, and the above process continues until all codons are consumed. A worked example is presented in the following section, with each step of mapping portrayed in Fig. 12. Pseudo-code for the mapping can be seen in Algorithm 3.

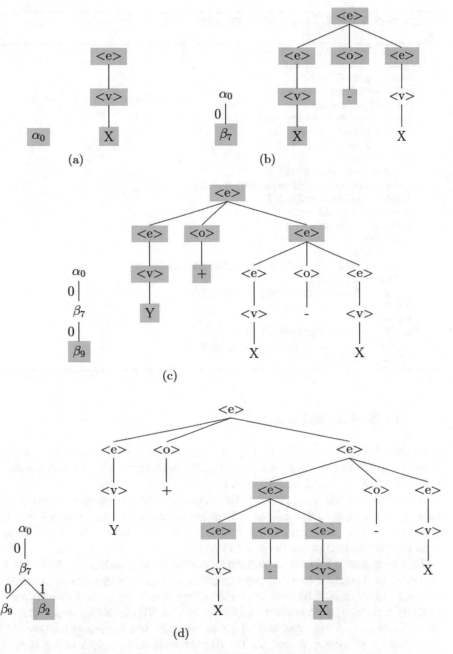

Fig. 12 The derivation tree (left) and derived tree (right) throughout TAGE derivation. The shaded nodes indicate new content added at each step. (**a**) Initial tree α_0. (**b**) β_7 adjoined to α_0 at node address 0. (**c**) β_9 adjoined to β_7 at node address 0. (**d**) β_2 adjoined to β_7 at node address 1

Algorithm 3: TAGE Derivation: GPM using a TAG, G, and a chromosome, C

Require: $G = \{N, \Sigma, I, A, S\}$ {A TAG}
Require: C {A chromosome}
$addresses \leftarrow \emptyset$
$codon \leftarrow C$.removeFirst
$root \leftarrow I$.get($codon$)
$nodeAddresses \leftarrow root$.getAdjoinableAddresses
for all a_i in $nodeAddresses$ **do**
  $addresses$.add$((root, a_i))$
while C.size> 1 **do**
  $codon \leftarrow C$.removeFirst
  $node, address \leftarrow addresses$.remove($codon$)
  $type \leftarrow address$.getSymbol
  $trees \leftarrow A$.getAll($type$)
  $codon \leftarrow C$.removeFirst
  $auxTree \leftarrow trees$.get($codon$)
  $node$.adjoin($auxTree, address$)
  $nodeAddresses \leftarrow node$.getAdjoinableAddresses
  for all a_i in $nodeAddresses$ **do**
    $addresses$.add$((node, a_i))$
$tree \leftarrow root$.getDerivedTree
$phenotype \leftarrow \epsilon$
for all $node_i$ in $tree$.getLeafNodes **do**
  $phenotype \leftarrow phenotype + node_i$.getSymbol
return $phenotype$

3.4.1 TAGE Mapping Example

Given the TAG G, where $\Sigma = \{$X, Y, +, -, $*\}$, $N = \{$<e>, <o>, <v>$\}$, $S =$<e> and I and A are as shown in Fig. 10, derivation using the chromosome $(12, 3, 7, 14, 9, 36, 14)$ proceeds as follows.

The first codon value, 12, is read. This is used to select an initial tree from I, by using $||I||$, which is in this case is 2. Utilising the same mapping function as GE, 12 mod 2 = 0, the zeroth tree from I is chosen, α_0. This tree is set as the root node of t, the derivation tree (as seen in Fig. 12).

Following this, a location to perform adjunction must be selected. The vector V is created of the adjoinable addresses available within all nodes (trees) contained within t. An adjoinable address in an elementary tree is the breadth-first traversal index of a node. The node must be labelled with a NT symbol of which there is an auxiliary tree of that type, and where no auxiliary tree is currently adjoined at that index. In this case, $V = \{\alpha_0[0]\}$ (the zeroth node of α_0). A codon is read, 3, and an address is selected from V using $||V||$, 3 mod 1 = 0 indicating which address to choose, $V[0]$. Adjunction will be performed at $\alpha_0[0]$, or node index 0 of tree α_0, <e>. Next, an auxiliary tree is chosen from A that is of the type T, i.e., the label of root node of the auxiliary tree is T, where T is the label of the node at which adjunction is being performed. In this case $\mathtt{T} = \mathtt{<e>}$. There are 12 such trees in A. Reading the next codon, 7, and using $||A||$, $7 \bmod 12 = 7$, β_7 is chosen. This is added to t as a child of the tree being adjoined to, labelling the edge with the address 0 from $\alpha_0[0]$, see Fig. 12. The adjoinable addresses in β_7 are added to V for the next pass of the algorithm, $V = \{\beta_7[0], \beta_7[1]\}$. A codon is used to select an address, followed by another codon to select an auxiliary tree of the correct type, adding a new node and edge to the derivation tree with each pair of codons read. This process is repeated, consuming two codons with each iteration until all remaining codons have been read. If the chromosome has an even number of codons, there will be a single codon remaining, unread, as an intron at the end of the chromosome. The resulting derivation and derived trees at each stage of this process can be seen in Fig. 12.

3.5 Operators

This section describes the standard GE components and how they are applied in TAGE. Basic initialisation used for TAGE is the same as that for GE. As both representations are based upon linear integer genomes, random initialisation, can be used without any change. Further discussion regarding initialisation in TAGE is explored in [36]. Both selection and replacement in TAGE are the same as those used in GE. As TAGE and GE share the same genotype, variation operations used by canonical GE, such as integer-flip mutation and one-point crossover, can be utilised by TAGE. However, due to the genotype to phenotype mapping used by TAGE, these operations can generate different effects when used. It is also worth noting that subtree style operations remain unexplored in TAGE.

In standard GE, the modification of a single codon in the encoding region of a GE chromosome can have multiple effects. These effects include: no change due to the use of the mod rule; changing a single terminal symbol; affecting the entire course of expansion in the derivation tree from the expansion encoded by that codon onward, through the right side of the derivation tree, due to the ripple effect. Whereas in TAGE, the same modification can bring about a different range of effects. Small effects similar to those of GE can occur: with no changes to the phenotype occurring, due to the redundancy of the mod mapping rule; the modification of a single terminal symbol by replacing an auxiliary tree with similar tree; or the modification of many terminal symbols by replacing the auxiliary with a very different tree. However, as codons in the TAGE genotype encode both for location (adjoinable addresses) and content (auxiliary trees), a modification to the chromosome which affects the number of adjunction addresses available for the next adjunction operation can induce a ripple effect. Unlike GE, there is no directional dependence inherent in the TAGE genotype-phenotype mapping. As such, adjunctions may occur in any part of the tree at any stage of derivation. This causes the ripple effect to occur throughout the entire tree, rather than just at the non-terminal expansions which follow the affected expansion as seen in GE.

One feature of the use of these operators with the TAGE representation is that only crossover, a highly destructive operator in TAGE, can affect the size of a TAGE individual. With canonical GE, where only a portion of the genotype might be used to encode the phenotype, mutation can introduce additional non-terminals into the derivation sequence requiring the use of additional codons to terminate mapping, resulting in a larger phenotype. With TAGE, the entire genotype is used to encode the phenotype, and as such, mutation has no effect on the size of the derivation tree. Mutation can only affect the size of the phenotype if elementary trees of varying size are mutated into the derivation tree. It is only through crossover that TAGE genotypes and derivation trees can change in size.

3.6 Limitations of TAGE

As substitution allows for a more compact representation [23], making sole use of the adjunction operation can result in the grammar becoming very large. CFGs containing non-terminal symbols which can be expanded using many different production rules can result in the TAGE representation becoming unfeasible. As Algorithm 2 creates all auxiliary trees from an enumeration of all possible expansions of the non-terminal symbols from root to leaf, a small increase in the number of possible expansions for any symbol can result in a large increase in the number of trees in the representation. As an example, rules from the relatively simple grammar in Fig. 9 are modified, adding extra production choices for the <o> and <v> symbols. When Algorithm 2 is applied to the modified grammar, the number of auxiliary trees in the grammar increases to from the original 12, as seen in Fig. 10, to 30. As the grammar complexity increases the number of trees also increases.

To partially address this limitation, Murphy put forward the idea of Tree Stubs(TS). The idea behind TS is that the sets of initial and auxiliary trees in TAGE are not generated at the beginning of the algorithm, but rather sets of elementary tree *stubs* are generated. This can greatly reduce the amount of memory needed to store the grammar. An elementary tree stub is an almost fully expanded elementary tree, with the terminal symbol leaf nodes excluded. In their place is a number representing the total number of different terminal nodes (variations) that can be attached at that point to complete the tree. For example, continuing with the sample grammar from Fig. 10, the original 12 auxiliary trees can be reduced to two auxiliary tree stubs. The modified version of the grammar presented above which originally had 30 auxiliary trees is also reduced to just two auxiliary stubs.

3.6.1   Generating TAGE Tree Stubs

When choosing a tree in TAGE, the modulus operation is performed on the codon value and the number of trees available for selection. This results in a number, c,

---

Algorithm 4: Selecting a complete elementary tree from stubs

Require: *graph* {the symbol/production graph used in TAG creation}
Require: *symbol* {root symbol for stubs}
Require: *stubs* {a nonempty set of stubs rooted with *symbol*}
Require: *choice* {the codon value}
  {Get *choice* in the correct range}
  choice ← *choice* mod *stubs*.sumVariations
  {Find which stub to expand}
  sum ← 0
  while *sum* ≤ *choice* **do**
    sum ← *sum*+ getNextStub.variations
  stub ← getCurrentStub
  {While there are still nodes to expand get the next node and count its variations}
  product ← 1
  while *stub*.hasNTLeafNodes **do**
    node ← *stub*.getNextNTLeafNode
    vars ← *node*.getVariations
    {Graph edges are labelled with productions}
    nrprods ← *graph*.getNonRecursiveEdges(node.label)
    {Get the productions with only terminal symbols}
    tprods ← *nrprods*.getTerminalProductions
    {Divide by *products* to discard information for already expanded nodes then mod by the
    number of variations at that node}
    production ← *tprods*.get((*choice*/*product*) mod *vars*)
    {Add the new production to the tree}
    node.addChildren(*production*)
    {Multiply so the next node will discard the correct information}
    product ← *product* ∗ *vars*

---

between zero and the total number of trees less one. If c has been used before, the correct tree is retrieved directly from a map of previously constructed trees. Alternatively, if c has not been seen before, then in order to find the correct stub to expand, each stub's total number of variations are summed, in order, until the sum is greater than c. Following this, the stub is completed by visiting each NT leaf node of that last stub in a depth-first manner, dividing c by the product of the variations of all the NT leaves visited so far while expanding that stub. Performing the modulus operation on this product and the number of possible variations at the current NT node results in a number between zero and the total variations possible at that node. This allows the selection of the correct terminal production to expand the current node with. The process continues until there are no additional NT nodes to expand, and the complete tree is stored in a map for later use before being returned. This process is further explained in Algorithm 4.

This process addresses the problem of transforming CFGs which contain many terminal production rules for the same symbol into TAGs. It does not, however, fully solve the problem of transforming highly complex CFGs into TAGs. If a CFG has a large number of non-terminal production rules for the same symbol, regardless of the number of terminal productions then the size of the generated tree sets will remain large.

3.7 Connectivity

Having displayed how to create a TAG from a CFG and outlining the mapping process that exhibits position independence, it would stand to argue that TAGE will also exhibit the same increase in connectivity as πGE. Murphy et al. [36] examined the mutation landscape of TAGE and GE in depth. The findings of this study showed that TAGE not only gained connections from the addition of the position independent mapping, but that the usage of TAGs provided a far more expressive landscape with far fewer codons than GE. To fully grasp the magnitude of the difference that TAGs add, in terms of expressiveness, and connectivity, the authors refer you to [32, 36]. The images presented in both show just how much TAGs add to the GE representation.

3.8 Summary

The previous sections have outlined what a TAG is, how to convert a CFG to a TAG, and described the benefits and limitation of the algorithm TAGE. TAGE present a highly expressive form of GE, that is evaluable at each step of the derivation process. TAGE can do a lot more with a lot less genetic material. TAGE has been shown to outperform GE in many cases. However, there are some drawbacks to TAGE when a high arity grammar is used. This may or may not hinder future developments with TAGE in domains such as program synthesis. However, as storage and ram increase the inability to use these tree building grammars will be negated. TAGE has been extended further to incorporate a Gene Regulatory Network (GRN) to guide the construction of TAGE solutions and allow for a developmental approach to TAGE, DTAGE [32, 38].

4 Conclusions

The chapter presented the current state of the art in the GE Genotype-Phenotype Mapping. A comprehensive overview of previous studies was presented before the chapter focused on a particular vein of research in position independent mappings.

πGE was presented and examined and found to provide GE with much-increased connectivity. It was argued that this allowed for GE to better move through the phenotype space during variation operations.

Following this TAGE was presented and showed how position independence could be further enhanced by using a more complex grammar. TAG exhibited the same increased connectivity of πGE be also presented a GE variant that was evaluable at any stage of the derivation process. This fact remains an open issue to be exploited in the current world of semantic GE. Some drawback to TAG were also stated and methods to overcome them examined.

In closing the authors find that the added power and performance of TAGE present the best approach going forward in the mapping domain. It truly provides GE with a best of both worlds approaches to GE whilst also providing excellent performance and fully evaluable trees during derivation.

Acknowledgements This research is based upon works supported by the Science Foundation Ireland under grant 13/IA/1850 and previously grant 08/IN.1/I1868.

References

1. H. Abbass, N.X. Hoai, R.I.B. McKay, AntTAG: a new method to compose computer programs using colonies of ants, in *Proceedings, 2002 World Congress on Computational Intelligence*, vol. 2 (IEEE Press, New York, 2002), pp. 1654–1666. https://doi.org/10.1109/CEC.2002. 1004490
2. R.M.A. Azad, A position independent representation for evolutionary automatic programming algorithms - the chorus system. Ph.D. Thesis, University of Limerick, Ireland, 2003
3. W. Banzhaf, A. Leier, Evolution on neutral networks in genetic programming, in *Genetic Programming Theory and Practice III*, ed. by T. Yu, R.L. Riolo, B. Worzel. Genetic Programming, vol. 9, chap. 14 (Springer, Ann Arbor, 2005), pp. 207–221. https://doi.org/10. 1007/0-387-28111-8_14
4. A. Brabazon, M. O'Neill, S. McGarraghy, *Natural Computing Algorithms, Part V* (Springer, Berlin, 2015)
5. M.N.F. dos Santos Nicolau, Genetic algorithms using grammatical evolution. Ph.D. Thesis, University of Limerick, 2006
6. M. Ebner, M. Shackleton, R. Shipman, How neutral networks influence evolvability. Complexity **7**(2), 19–33 (2001). https://doi.org/10.1002/cplx.10021
7. M. Ebner, P. Langguth, J. Albert, M. Shackleton, R. Shipman, On neutral networks and evolvability, in *Proceedings of the 2001 Congress on Evolutionary Computation CEC2001*, Seoul, Korea (IEEE Press, New York, 2001), pp. 1–8
8. D. Fagan, Analysing the genotype-phenotype map in grammatical evolution. Ph.D. Thesis, University College Dublin, Ireland, 2013. http://ncra.ucd.ie/papers/ DavidFaganPhDThesis2014.pdf
9. D. Fagan, M. O'Neill, E. Galván-López, A. Brabazon, S. McGarraghy, An analysis of genotype-phenotype maps in grammatical evolution, in *Proceedings of the 13th European Conference on Genetic Programming, EuroGP 2010*, Istanbul, ed. by A.I. Esparcia-Alcazar, A. Ekárt, S. Silva, S. Dignum, A.S. Uyar. Lecture Notes in Computer Science, vol. 6021 (Springer, Berlin, 2010), pp. 62–73. https://doi.org/10.1007/978-3-642-12148-7_6
10. D. Fagan, M. Nicolau, M. O'Neill, E. Galván-López, A. Brabazon, S. McGarraghy, Investigating mapping order in πGE, in *2010 IEEE World Congress on Computational Intelligence, pp. 3058–3064*, Barcelona, Spain (IEEE Computational Intelligence Society/IEEE Press, New York, 2010). https://doi.org/10.1109/CEC.2010.5586204
11. D. Fagan, M. Nicolau, E. Hemberg, M. O'Neill, A. Brabazon, S. McGarraghy, Investigation of the performance of different mapping orders for GE on the Max problem, in *Proceedings of the 14th European Conference on Genetic Programming, EuroGP 2011*, Turin, Italy, ed. by S. Silva, J.A. Foster, M. Nicolau, M. Giacobini, P. Machado. Lecture Notes in Computer Science, vol. 6621 (Springer, Berlin, 2011), pp. 286–297. https://doi.org/10.1007/978-3-642-20407-4_25

12. D. Fagan, E. Hemberg, M. O'Neill, S. McGarraghy, Fitness reactive mutation in grammatical evolution, in *18th International Conference on Soft Computing, MENDEL 2012*, ed. by R. Matousek (Brno University of Technology, Brno, 2012), pp. 144–149

13. D. Fagan, E. Hemberg, M. Nicolau, M. O'Neill, S. McGarraghy, Towards adaptive mutation in grammatical evolution, in *GECCO Companion '12: Proceedings of the Fourteenth International Conference on Genetic and Evolutionary Computation Conference Companion*, Philadelphia, Pennsylvania, USA, ed. by T. Soule, A. Auger, J. Moore, D. Pelta, C. Solnon, M. Preuss, A. Dorin, Y.S. Ong, C. Blum, D.L. Silva, F. Neumann, T. Yu, A. Ekart, W. Browne, T. Kovacs, M.L. Wong, C. Pizzuti, J. Rowe, T. Friedrich, G. Squillero, N. Bredeche, S. Smith, A. Motsinger-Rei, J. Lozano, M. Pelikan, S. Meyer-Nienber, C. Igel, G. Hornby, R. Doursat, S. Gustafson, G. Olague, S. Yoo, J. Clark, G. Ochoa, G. Pappa, F. Lobo, D. Tauritz, J. Branke, K. Debpp (ACM, New York, 2012), pp. 1481–1482. https://doi.org/10.1145/2330784.2331002

14. D. Fagan, E. Hemberg, M. O'Neill, S. McGarraghy, Understanding expansion order and phenotypic connectivity in πGE, in *Proceedings of the 16th European Conference on Genetic Programming, EuroGP 2013*, Vienna, Austria, ed. by K. Krawiec, A. Moraglio, T. Hu, A.S. Uyar, B. Hu. Lecture Notes in Computer Science, vol. 7831 (Springer, Berlin, 2013), pp. 37–48. https://doi.org/10.1007/978-3-642-37207-0_4

15. D.E. Goldberg, *Genetic Algorithms in Search, Optimization and Machine Learning*, 1st edn. (Addison-Wesley Longman, Boston, 1989)

16. N.X. Hoai, A flexible representation for genetic programming from natural language processing. Ph.D. Thesis, Australian Defence force Academy, University of New South Wales, Australia, 2004

17. N. Hoai, R. McKay, A framework for tree adjunct grammar guided genetic programming, in *Proceedings of the Post-graduate ADFA Conference on Computer Science* (ADFA, Campbell, 2001), pp. 93–99. https://doi.org/10.1.1.79.4037

18. N.X. Hoai, R.I. McKay, H.A. Abbass, Tree adjoining grammars, language bias, and genetic programming, in *Genetic Programming, Proceedings of EuroGP'2003*, Essex, ed. by C. Ryan, T. Soule, M. Keijzer, E. Tsang, R. Poli, E. Costa. Lecture Notes in Computer Science, vol. 2610 (Springer, Berlin, 2003), pp. 335–344

19. T.H. Hoang, Evolutionary developmental evaluation : the interplay between evolution and development. Ph.D. Thesis, Information Technology & Electrical Engineering, Australian Defence Force Academy, University of New South Wales, Australia, 2008

20. T.H. Hoang, D. Essam, R.I.B. McKay, N.X. Hoai, Developmental evaluation in genetic programming: the TAG-based frame work. Int. J. Knowl Based Intelligent Eng. Syst. **12**(1), 69–82 (2008)

21. T. Jones, Evolutionary algorithms, fitness landscapes, and search. Ph.D. Thesis, University of New Mexico, 1995

22. T. Jones, One operator, one landscape. Santa Fe Institute Technical Report, 1995, pp. 95–02

23. A.K. Joshi, Y. Schabes, *Tree-Adjoining Grammars* (Springer, Berlin,1997), pp. 69–123. https://doi.org/10.1007/978-3-642-59126-6_2

24. H. Kargupta, Gene expression: the missing link in evolutionary computation. Technical Report, Los Alamos National Lab., NM (United States), 1997

25. M. Keijzer, M. O'Neill, C. Ryan, M. Cattolico, Grammatical evolution rules: the mod and the bucket rule, in A.G.B.T. J. A. Foster, E. Lutton, J. Miller, C. Ryan (ed.) *Proceedings of the Fifth European Conference on Genetic Programming (EuroGP-2002)*, Kinsale, Ireland. Lecture Notes in Computer Science, vol. 2278, pp. 123–130 (Springer, Berlin, 2002)

26. M. Kimura, *The Neutral Theory of Molecular Evolution* (Cambridge University Press, Cambridge, 1985)

27. M. Kimura, *Population Genetics, Molecular Evolution, and the Neutral Theory: Selected Papers* (University of Chicago Press, Chicago, 1995)

28. J.R. Koza, *Genetic Programming: On the Programming of Computers by Means of Natural Selection* (MIT Press, Cambridge, MA, 1992)

29. J.R. Koza, R. Poli, Genetic programming, in *Search Methodologies: Introductory Tutorials in Optimization and Decision Support Techniques*, chap. 5 (Springer, Berlin, 2005), pp. 127–164

30. N. Lourenco, F.B. Pereira, E. Costa, SGE: a structured representation for grammatical evolution, in *Artificial Evolution*, Lyon, France, ed. by S. Bonnevay, P. Legrand, N. Monmarche, E. Lutton, M. Schoenauer. Lecture Notes in Computer Science, vol. 9554 (Springer, Cham, 2015), pp. 136–148. https://doi.org/10.1007/978-3-319-31471-6_11

31. R.I. McKay, N.X. Hoai, P.A. Whigham, Y. Shan, M. O'Neill, Grammar-based genetic programming: a survey. Genet. Program. Evolvable Mach. **11**(3/4), 365–396 (2010). https://doi.org/10.1007/s10710-010-9109-y. Tenth Anniversary Issue: Progress in Genetic Programming and Evolvable Machines

32. E. Murphy, An exploration of tree-adjoining grammars for grammatical evolution. Ph.D. Thesis, University College Dublin, Ireland, 2014. http://ncra.ucd.ie/papers/EoinMurphy_thesis.pdf

33. E. Murphy, M. O'Neill, E. Galván-López, A. Brabazon, Tree-adjunct grammatical evolution, in *2010 IEEE World Congress on Computational Intelligence*, Barcelona, Spain (IEEE Computational Intelligence Society/IEEE Press, New York, 2010), pp. 4449–4456. https://doi.org/10.1109/CEC.2010.5586497

34. E. Murphy, M. O'Neill, E. Galvan-Lopez, A. Brabazon, Tree-adjunct grammatical evolution, in *2010 IEEE World Congress on Computational Intelligence*, Barcelona, Spain (IEEE Computational Intelligence Society/IEEE Press, New York, 2010), pp. 4449–4456. https://doi.org/10.1109/CEC.2010.5586497

35. E. Murphy, M. O'Neill, A. Brabazon, A comparison of GE and TAGE in dynamic environments, in *GECCO'11: Proceedings of the 13th Annual Conference on Genetic and Evolutionary Computation*, Dublin, Ireland, ed. by N.K. Krasnogor et al. (ACM, New York, 2011), pp. 1387–1394. https://doi.org/10.1145/2001576.2001763

36. E. Murphy, M. O'Neill, A. Brabazon, Examining mutation landscapes in grammar based genetic programming, in *Proceedings of the 14th European Conference on Genetic Programming, EuroGP 2011*, Turin, Italy, ed. by S. Silva, J.A. Foster, M. Nicolau, M. Giacobini, P. Machado. Lecture Notes in Computer Science, vol. 6621 (Springer, Berlin, 2011), pp. 130–141. https://doi.org/10.1007/978-3-642-20407-4_12 Best paper

37. E. Murphy, E. Hemberg, M. Nicolau, M. O'Neill, A. Brabazon, Grammar bias and initialisation in grammar based genetic programming, in *Proceedings of the 15th European Conference on Genetic Programming, EuroGP 2012*, Malaga, Spain, ed. by A. Moraglio, S. Silva, K. Krawiec, P. Machado, C. Cotta. Lecture Notes in Computer Science, vol. 7244, pp. 85–96 (Springer, Berlin, 2012). https://doi.org/10.1007/978-3-642-29139-5_8

38. E. Murphy, M. Nicolau, E. Hemberg, M. O'Neill, A. Brabazon, Differential gene expression with tree-adjunct grammars, in *Parallel Problem Solving from Nature, PPSN XII (part 1)*, Taormina, Italy, ed. by C.A. Coello Coello, V. Cutello, K. Deb, S. Forrest, G. Nicosia, M. Pavone. Lecture Notes in Computer Science, vol. 7491 (Springer, Berlin, 2012), pp. 377–386. https://doi.org/10.1007/978-3-642-32937-1_38

39. M. Nicolau, M. O'Neill, A. Brabazon, Termination in grammatical evolution: grammar design, wrapping, and tails, in *Proceedings of the 2012 IEEE Congress on Evolutionary Computation*, Brisbane, Australia, ed. by X. Li (2012), pp. 2381–2388. https://doi.org/10.1109/CEC.2012.6256563

40. M. O'Neill, Automatic programming in an arbitrary language: Evolving programs with grammatical evolution. Ph.D. Thesis, University Of Limerick, Ireland, 2001

41. M. O'Neill, M. Nicolau, Distilling the salient features of natural systems: Commentary on "on the mapping of genotype to phenotype in evolutionary algorithms" by Whigham, Dick and Maclaurin. Genet. Program. Evolvable Mach. **18**(3), 379–383 (2017). https://doi.org/10.1007/s10710-017-9293-0

42. M. O'Neill, A. Brabazon, M. Nicolau, S.M. Garraghy, P. Keenan, π grammatical evolution, in *Genetic and Evolutionary Computation – GECCO-2004, Part II*, Seattle, WA, USA. Lecture Notes in Computer Science, vol. 3103 (Springer, Heidelberg, 2004), pp. 617–629

43. M. O'Neill, E. Hemberg, C. Gilligan, E. Bartley, J. McDermott, A. Brabazon, GEVA: grammatical evolution in java. SIGEVOlution **3**(2), 17–22 (2008)

44. F. Rothlauf, *Representations for Genetic and Evolutionary Algorithms*, 2nd edn. (Springer, Berlin, 2006)
45. F. Rothlauf, M. Oetzel, On the locality of grammatical evolution, in *Proceedings of the 9th European Conference on Genetic Programming*, Budapest, Hungary, ed. by P. Collet, M. Tomassini, M. Ebner, S. Gustafson, A. Ekárt. Lecture Notes in Computer Science, vol. 3905 (Springer, Berlin, 2006), pp. 320–330
46. M. Shackleton, R. Shipman, M. Ebner, An investigation of redundant genotype-phenotype mappings and their role in evolutionary search, in *Proceedings of the 2000 Congress on Evolutionary Computation CEC00* (IEEE Press, New York, 2000), pp. 493–500
47. R. Shipman, M. Shackleton, M. Ebner, R. Watson, Neutral search spaces for artificial evolution: a lesson from life. Artif. Life **7**, 162–169 (2000)
48. L. Spector, P.A. Whigham, G. Dick, J. Maclaurin, L. Altenberg, A. Ekárt, P.R. Lewis, D.B. Kell, M. O'Neill, M. Nicolau, C. Ryan, G. Squillero, A. Tonda, J.A. Foster, Peer commentary special section on "on the mapping of genotype to phenotype in evolutionary algorithms" by Peter A. Whigham, Grant Dick, and James Maclaurin. Genet. Program. Evolvable Mach. **18**(3), 351–405 (2017). https://doi.org/10.1007/s10710-017-9287-y
49. P.A. Whigham, G. Dick, J. Maclaurin, On the mapping of genotype to phenotype in evolutionary algorithms. Genet. Program. Evolvable Mach. **18**(3), 353–361 (2017). https://doi.org/10.1007/s10710-017-9288-x

Theory of Disruption in GE

Erik Hemberg

Abstract We formalize and describe the mapping process of integer input (genotype) to an output sentence (phenotype) in Grammatical Evolution (GE). The aim
is to study the grammatical and search bias which is produced by the mapping. We
investigate changes in input and the effect on output and analyze the neighboring
solutions as well as the effect of changes and bias in representation. Different types
of changes are defined to allow classification of the effects that input changes
(operators) have. The changes are a part of identifying what the neighborhood
for GE search looks like. We call this disruption in GE. Furthermore, a schema
theorem is introduced for investigating preservation of material during application
of variation operators, an attempt to identify the population effects.

1 Introduction

In this chapter we ask the question: *what happens to the output (phenotype) when
there is a change in the input (genotype) and a Context Free Grammar mapping
is used in Grammatical Evolution (GE)?* The aim is to extend the studies of
the genotype-to-phenotype mapping and investigate the effect on derivations and
output resulting from one single change in input as well as from multiple changes
in input [9]. The mapping of GE introduces redundancies and dependencies on
previous input and the parent in the derivation tree, as well as the design of the
grammar. These properties have effects on the preservation of the derivation; often
the changes can be quite large, something which in GE is called a "ripple", for
the multiple changes that can occur during e.g. mutation or crossover [13]. When
the locality of the mapping in GE was investigated, the study concluded that some
operators in GE had low locality, i.e. genotypic neighbors did not correspond to
phenotypic neighbors [16].

E. Hemberg (✉)
Computer Science and Artificial Intelligence Lab (CSAIL), MIT, Boston, MA, USA
e-mail: hembergerik@csail.mit.edu

© Springer International Publishing AG, part of Springer Nature 2018   109
C. Ryan et al. (eds.), *Handbook of Grammatical Evolution*,
https://doi.org/10.1007/978-3-319-78717-6_5

An intuitive description of a grammar is that of a mechanism for producing sets of strings [3, 8]. The use of a grammar in GE is to rewrite or generate sentences. A grammar in Evolutionary Computation (EC) is an indirect form of representation, inducing bias to the search. Bias are all the factors that influence the form of each solution [24]. For a successful search, a proper representation of the problem and of the appropriate search operators is needed [15]. GE is approached with a more formal description with inspiration from previous works on grammars and mapping in EC [19, 24, 25].

The contribution is analysis and insight regarding the use of grammars in EC, more specifically, the use of grammars with the GE algorithm. We formally describe GE to clearly show the different representations within the algorithm and theoretically analyze the impact of change on GE input. We show how an indirect representation from a linear input sequence reacts to changes, and the conclusion is that the fewer non-terminals there are in the grammar, the less susceptible it will be to disruption. Finally, we introduce a GE schema were operators were examined in relation to how sequences of the individual genotype are propagated over a generation.

The structure of the chapter is the following. Background is in Sect. 2. In Sect. 3 we formalize and describe the mapping process in order to break down the grammatical and search bias which is produced by the mapping. Section 4 investigates changes in input and the effect on output and analyze the neighboring solutions and the effect of changes (and bias in representation), of both single and multiple changes. Section 5 has a discussion, and conclusions are in Sect. 6.

2 Background

Grammatical Evolution (GE) is a grammar-based form of Genetic Programming (GP). The GE system is flexible and allows the use of alternative search strategies, whether evolutionary, deterministic or of some other approach. This system also includes the ability to bias the search by changing the grammar used. Editing the grammar modifies the output structures. The genotype-phenotype, i.e. input-output, mapping means that GE allows search operators to be performed on any representation in the algorithm, e.g. on the genotype (integer or binary), as well as on partially generated phenotypes, and on the completely generated derivation trees or phenotypes.

The representation, i.e. the encoding, as well as the operators can be changed in an attempt to make the search smoother [2]. However, some studies claim that complex gene interactions are advantageous for the chance of exploring new, functionally advantageous phenotypes, i.e. evolvability as a mechanism of stabilization [20]. Another investigation study neutral diversity and claim that if the number of phenotypes accessible to an individual by mutation is smaller than the total number of phenotypes in the fitness landscape then mutational robustness can facilitate adaptation [5].

The bias in GE mapping that occurs when a production is selected from a rule with respect to the design of different grammars and grammar-defined introns has been studied [12]. Further studies look at search, neutral evolution and mapping in evolutionary computation [25]. The analysis is done by grouping the GE codons into quotient sets and showing their adjacencies regarding the mapping, this is then used to explain the population's movements on neutral landscapes [25]. The equivalence relation of the quotient sets is linked to the search neutrality of the codons, i.e. neutrality (many-to-one mappings) related to codons being indistinguishable on applying the mutation part of the evolutionary process. The locality of a genotype-phenotype mapping describes how well genotypic neighbors correspond to phenotypic neighbors [17]. Some operators in GE have low locality.

In this chapter we further study change, disruption and schemas in GE. The following definitions needed for this. In a Context-Free Grammar the generation of a word is not dependent on the surroundings, see [3].

Definition 1 (Context-Free Grammar (CFG)) A CFG is a four tuple $G = \langle N, \Sigma, R, S \rangle$, where:

- N is a finite non-empty set of non-terminal symbols.
- Σ is a finite non-empty set of terminal symbols and $N \cap \Sigma = \emptyset$.
- R is a finite set of production rules of the form $R : N \mapsto V^* : A \mapsto \alpha$ or (A, α) where $A \in N$ and $\alpha \in V^*$. V^* is the set of all strings constructed from $N \cup \Sigma$ and $R \subseteq N \times V^*$, $R \neq \emptyset$.
- S is the start symbol, $S \in N$.   □

"Context-Free" means that for a rule $A \rightarrow \alpha$, A can always be replaced by α, regardless of context [8]. A grammar generates a language $L(G)$, see [21]. The following definition of rewriting or generation is used, see [8]

Definition 2 (Generation) Let $G = \langle N, \Sigma, R, S \rangle$ be a context-free grammar and let $\alpha', \beta' \in V^*$. α' directly generates β', written as $\alpha' \Rightarrow \beta'$ if there exist $\alpha_1, \alpha_2, \alpha, \beta \in V^*$, such that $\alpha' = \alpha_1 \alpha \alpha_2$, $\beta' = \alpha_1 \beta \alpha_2$ and $\alpha \rightarrow \beta$ is in R.   □

Note that the multiple-step generation, $\stackrel{*}{\Rightarrow}$ is the reflexive-transitive closure of $\Rightarrow$. A set is closed under some operation if application of that operation on members of the set always produces a member of the set. A set that is closed under an operation satisfies a closure property [8].

A *sentential form* of G is $S(G) = \{x : S \stackrel{*}{\Rightarrow} \alpha, \alpha \in V^*\}$. If $\alpha \in \Sigma$ then it is called a sentence.

Σ^* denotes the set of all finite length Σ sequences [8].

Definition 3 (Language) The language generated by G is $L(G) = S(G) \cap \Sigma^* = \{x : S \stackrel{*}{\Rightarrow} x, x \in \Sigma^*\}$.   □

The CFG can be expanded to a Probabilistic Context-Free Grammar, where each rule has an associated probability, see [21].

Definition 4 (Probabilistic Context-Free Grammar (PCFG)) The Probabilistic CFG is the tuple $\langle G, P \rangle$, where G is a CFG and P is an ordered set of probabilities $\{p_{ij}\}$, i is the index for the non-terminal left-hand side and j is the index for the productions with the same left-hand side.

- For all $r_{ij} \in R$ there exists one probability $p_{ij} \in P$.
- For each $p_{ij} \in P, 0 \le p_{ij} \le 1$. If $p_{ij} = 0$ then r_{ij} can be eliminated from the grammar.
- For all $r_{i*} \subseteq R$, i.e. $*$ is a wildcard and r_i is the restriction $R\big|_{\{n_i\}}$, $\{n_i\} \in N$, $\sum_{0 \le j \le |r_{i*}|} p_{ij} = 1$. $|r_{i*}|$ is the number of productions with the same non-terminal left-hand side. Let $n_i \in N$ be the non-terminal with index i; then

$$r_{i*} = \{(n_i, r(n_i)) : r \in R\} \subseteq R \tag{1}$$

□

Now it is possible to look at derivations from the PCFG, where expansion of the grammar generates sentences in the language. That is, first the start symbol is expanded, and then each non-terminal, to create a sentential form. The derivation is finished when there are only terminal symbols in the string, a sentence in the language, from [21].

Definition 5 (Derivation) A derivation Δ in a grammar G is a sequence of production numbers, $\langle i_0, \ldots i_n \rangle$, such that

1. For $0 \le k \le n$, P_{i_k} is a production of G.
2. For each k there exists a sentence $\delta_k = \alpha_k A_k \beta_k$, $A_k \in R$, $\alpha_k, \beta_k \in V^*$.
3. There is a string $\delta_{n+1} \in V^*$.
4. $\delta_0 = S$ (i.e. $\alpha_1 = \beta_1 = \Lambda$)
5. For each $0 \le k \le n$, $P_{i_k} = A_k \to \gamma_k$.
6. For each $0 \le k \le nk$, $\delta_k = \alpha_k A_k \beta_k \Rightarrow \alpha_k \gamma_k \beta_k = \delta_{k+1}$. □

From Definition 5 it is possible to give a probability to a word, see [21].

Definition 6 (Word Probability) The probability of a word $w \in \Sigma^*$ is

$$p(w) = \prod_{1 \le k \le |\Delta|} p_k \tag{2}$$

where $|\Delta|$ is the length of the derivation. □

Here, we define a derivation tree as multiple derivation steps, see [22].

Definition 7 (Derivation Tree) The derivation tree from the start symbol is denoted by $D := \{S \overset{*}{\Rightarrow} \alpha, \alpha \in \Sigma^*\}$. □

In the derivation tree a branch is defined as

Definition 8 (Branch) The branch is denoted $D(A)$, from the non-terminal A, therefore $D(A) = \{A \overset{*}{\Rightarrow} \alpha, \alpha \in \Sigma^*, A \in N\}$, $D(A) \subset D$ □

Within the input sequence and derivation tree there are partial derivation trees called subtrees, see [23].

Definition 9 (Derivation Subtree) A subtree is $D_N = \{x \overset{*}{\Rightarrow} \alpha, x \in N, \alpha \in V^*\}$.

$\square$

Differences in derivations are distinguished by their derivation trees, see [21].

Definition 10 (Derivation Difference) Two derivations, δ and δ' are different if their derivation trees are different. $\square$

3 Formal Description of GE

This section provide complementary insights into the GE algorithms. GE is approached with a more formal description with inspiration from works on grammars and mapping in EC [18, 23, 25]. We aim to understand how changes in input are translated to alterations in output, see Fig. 1. In GE the grammar maps the input (genotype) to the output (phenotype) which is evaluated. During this process several mappings between different spaces are made. Different grammars which impose different mapping orders have different search behaviors. When understanding and expanding GE it can be useful to see where explicit bias and different impacts of change in one space will occur and how these relate to the space they are mapped to and also which operators should be used.

In GE there is redundancy in more than one of the mappings, i.e. a many-to-one mapping between input and output. The grammar has an impact on both the derivation of the output (phenotype) and the final phenotype, e.g. on non-terminals and rules, and on the language that the terminals can generate. The GE evaluation, consisting of genotype-phenotype (input-output) mapping and fitness assignment. The structure of this section consists of a formal description of the components of GE in Sect. 3.1, while we defer a discussion on the implications of this description to Sect. 5.

3.1 GE Components

We start by describing the components of GE mapping more formally, in order to illustrate the mapping bias mediated by the CFG from input to output. The input sequence (genotype) consists of chromosomes which are comprised of codons. In GE a chromosome is a sequence of integers.[1,2]

---

[1]Canonical GE has a binary chromosome that will be transcribed to integers, $f : \mathbb{Z}_2 \rightarrow \mathbb{Z}_{2^m}$, $f(C_2) = C$ where m is the codon size and C_2 the binary representation of the chromosome. Here we simplify and skip the transcription step, binary-to-integer, and use a sequence of integers instead.

[2]$\mathbb{N}$ refers to the natural numbers, $\mathbb{Z}$ denotes integers, and $\mathbb{Z}_n$ integers modulo n.

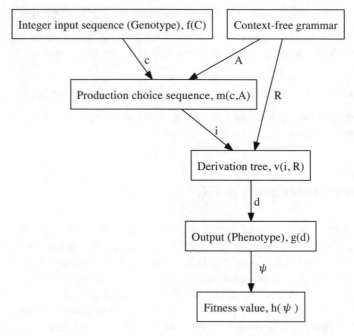

Fig. 1 Grammatical Evolution spaces. In GE the grammar maps the input (genotype) to the output (phenotype) which is evaluated. During this process several mappings between different spaces are made. The arrow labels indicate the mapping from one space to another

Definition 11 (Individual in GE) An individual in GE is a single chromosome C, a sequence of codons. Each codon uses m bits to encode an integer: this gives codon values in the range $[0, 2^m - 1]$:

$$C = \langle c_0, \dots, c_n \rangle, \; c_i \in \mathbb{Z}_{2^m}, \; 0 \leq i \leq n, \; m, n \in \mathbb{N}$$

□

3.1.1 Chromosome to Production Choice Sequence

In the mapping, the leftmost non-terminal is expanded and the value of the current codon decides which production to choose for the expansion of the rule. A Context-Free Grammar is denoted by G (Definition 1 on page 111) and a Probabilistic Context-Free Grammar is the tuple $\langle G, P \rangle$ (Definition 4 on page 112). We denote the space of Probabilistic Context-Free Grammars as $\langle G, P \rangle \in \mathcal{G}$. The first step of the mapping in the GE system can be described as a chromosome C and a grammar $\langle G, P \rangle$ generating a production choice sequence of production choices $I = \langle i_0, \dots, i_n \rangle, n \in \mathbb{N}$. Alternatively, there is a mapping between two integer spaces, lists of integers to lists of integers with max value being the maximum number of production choices of all the rules in the grammar.

Table 1 Codon change and production choice type change

Type	Codon (c)	Production choice (i)
Unchanged	$c = c'$	$i = i'$
Redundant	$c \neq c'$	$i = i'$
Change	$c \neq c'$	$i \neq i'$

These are the impacts from a redundant deterministic mapping

$$f : \langle \mathbb{Z}_{2^m}, \ldots, \mathbb{Z}_{2^m} \rangle \times \mathcal{G} \to \langle \mathbb{Z}_{r_{max}} \rangle, f(\langle G, P \rangle, C) = I \qquad (3)$$

For the integer input sequence $r_{max} = |R|$ we use unique identifiers for each production choice up to the number of productions in the grammar[3] and I can also be written as a derivation tree D.

The types of changes that are possible from the mapping from codon sequence to input sequence, $f(C) = I$ are shown in Table 1. The cases $c = c'$ and $i \neq i'$ are not possible when using a deterministic mapping. ($'$ denotes the next time step, not only change)

To ensure that a correct production is chosen the modulo of the codon value is used to decide the corresponding production. The integer value of the codon is mapped to an integer value in the range of the number of production choices for the rule, $[0, |A_k|]$. In other words, the mapping decides which production choice to use, given the derivation step $k, 0 \leq k$ for index of the current rule (non-terminal to expand) and j for the index of the codons c_j. There is a many-to-one mapping from codon integer value and non-terminal to an integer representing the production choice

$$m : \mathbb{Z}_{2^m} \times N \to \mathbb{Z}_{r_{max}}, m(c, A) = i \qquad (4)$$

denoting $i_{k_a} = m(c_j, A_k)$ with

$$m(c_j, A_k) = c_j \bmod |A_k| \qquad A_k \in N, c_j \in C \qquad (5)$$

where $|A_k|$ is the number of productions corresponding to non-terminal A_k. To get a unique identification for i_k then

$$u : \mathbb{Z}_{|A_k|} \times \mathcal{G} \times \mathcal{G} \to \mathbb{Z}_{r_{max}}, u(i_{k_a}, G, A_k) = i_k \qquad (6)$$

The point of the following equation is to clarify the derivation order in which the phenotype is generated by the grammar. In canonical GE the derivation sequence

---

[3]In canonical GE the maximum number of production choices is $r_{max} = max_{r_{i*} \in R}(|r_{i*}|)$. If r_{max} uses unique identifiers the analysis can be facilitated. The context and analysis should make it obvious when the integer inputs are unique or ambiguous.

is read from left-to-right. A_k is the leftmost non-terminal in the derivation δ_k. The sequence of non-terminals in derivation δ_k is denoted δ_k^N and the index i is written $\delta_{k,i}^N$

$$A_{k+1} = \delta_{k,0}^N \tag{7}$$

$$\delta_k^N = \{x : x \in \delta_k, \ x \in N\}$$

and the initial derivation starts with the start symbol, $\delta_0 = S \Rightarrow A_0 = S$.

The purpose of this paragraph is to show the discrepancy in codons used and integer input length. The derivation step k indicates the current index in I as well as the number of times the genotype C is wrapped and reread from the beginning, $0 \le k \le |C|w, \ w \in \mathbb{N}$. The wrapping is expressed as the modulo of the genotype length taken from the derivation step counter, k and gives the chromosome index j,

$$j = k \bmod |C| \tag{8}$$

Moreover, note that a new input from codon c_j is only read when the current rule, A_k, is non-deterministic, i.e.

$$j := \begin{cases} j, & \text{if } |A_k| = 1 \\ j+1, & \text{if } |A_k| > 1 \end{cases} \tag{9}$$

This gives the relation between the used codon sequence and the input sequence, i.e. the index for codon c_j and integer input i_k has $j \le k$, as shown in Eqs. (8) and (9).

In order to avoid too much bias from the production choice mapping in Eq. (5) a large enough difference between the max codon value and the number of production rules is required, $2^m \gg r_{max}$. With this assumption the modulo operation in the Eq. (5) makes all the probabilities uniform for the current rule $p_{ij} = 1/|A_k|$, $p_{ij} \in P$, with the probability to be selected $1/|A_j|$. Otherwise there is a bias when the modulo rule is applied to the codon which makes some i_j more probable than others [10, 25].[4]

The following analysis describes very generally what types of changes occur when the chromosome changes, and how the grammar impacts them. The mapping introduced the grammar by Eq. (5) increases the number of parameters from the basic case described in Table 1. The mapping from codon to input is first extended with a dependency on the current rule i.e the parent, which comes from the grammar. If the current rule changes we call this a change of derivation context. Basic types of

---

[4]GE can be seen as a PCFG (Definition 4 on page 112), where all the probabilities are uniform, i.e. the probabilities are determined by the number of production choices for each non-terminal, $p_{ij} = 1/|r_{i*}|$. A bias towards productions r_{ij} can be achieved by multiple identical production choices in the solution grammar rules.

Table 2 Codon change, current rule and production choice type change

Type	Production choice (i)	Codon (c)	Parent (A)
Change/redundant	$i \neq i'$	$c \neq c'$	$A \neq A'$
Change/redundant	$i \neq i'$	$c = c'$	$A \neq A'$
Change/redundant	$i \neq i'$	$c \neq c'$	$A = A'$
Redundant	$i = i'$	$c \neq c'$	$A = A'$
No change	$i = i'$	$c = c'$	$A = A'$

Deterministic neutral mapping and dependency impact. The input i denotes production choices, c the codon value and A the current rule. Change can occur, depending on the grammar

change to the production choice are shown in Table 2. The dependency introduced by the current rule sets the input in a context where the position of the integer value is important, which makes the table itself not directly applicable to GE. Change/redundant represents the types that occur due to the position dependency. Furthermore, in BNF form the grammar can have duplicated rules. This leads to the possibility of change occurring, depending on the grammar, in three of the five cases. The number of cases where change can be directly caused by a codon change is two. An example of a grammar that would have a maximum probability of change would be one without duplicated rules or production choices, since then there would be no redundant changes.

3.1.2 Genotype to Phenotype: Integer Sequence to Word

For GE, one defining aspect is the redundancy in the mapping (many-to-one). With the grammar mapping in GE it is not guaranteed that the language the grammar produces will be able to produce all possible solutions. The mapping $\zeta : \langle \mathbb{Z}_{2^m}, \ldots, \mathbb{Z}_{2^m} \rangle \to \Psi$ from the chromosome in genotype space to the sentence in the solution space generates a solution (sentence) in the language generated by the grammar $\psi \in L(G) \subseteq \Sigma^*$. This is a property of the grammar and allows declarative bias to parts of the solution space. Ideally the grammar biases to a subset of the solution space, $V^* \subseteq \Psi$ where an optimal solution exists. If there is no knowledge of which solutions should be constrained the grammar can cover the entire solution space, $V^* = \Psi$. Of course, it should be avoided to constrain the grammar to a region without optimal solutions. Finally, the mapping ζ of GE $\zeta : \langle \mathbb{Z}_{2^m}, \ldots, \mathbb{Z}_{2^m} \rangle \to \Psi$ is many-to-one (depending on Ψ).

The space of derivation trees is denoted $\mathcal{D}$. The input sequence can be written as a derivation tree D

$$v : \langle \mathbb{Z}_r \rangle \times \mathcal{G} \to \mathcal{D}, v(I, \langle G, P \rangle) = D \qquad (10)$$

where v is one-to-many if regarded out of the context dependency. In graph theory a tree D is a directed graph without cycles and is the ordered triple of a set of vertexes (or nodes), a set of edges and a mapping from the set of edges to ordered

Table 3 Codon change, production choice, current rule and next rule type change

Type	Rule (A_{k+1})	Codon (c_j)	Parent (A_k)	Production choice (i)
Change	$A_{k+1} \neq A'_{k+1}$	$c_j \neq c'_j$	$A_k \neq A'_k$	$i \neq i'$
Delayed/redundant	$A_{k+1} = A'_{k+1}$	$c_j \neq c'_j$	$A_k \neq A'_k$	$i \neq i'$
Change	$A_{k+1} \neq A'_{k+1}$	$c_j = c'_j$	$A_k \neq A'_k$	$i \neq i'$
Delayed/redundant	$A_{k+1} = A'_{k+1}$	$c_j = c'_j$	$A_k \neq A'_k$	$i \neq i'$
Change	$A_{k+1} \neq A'_{k+1}$	$c_j \neq c'_j$	$A_k = A'_k$	$i \neq i'$
Delayed/redundant	$A_{k+1} = A'_{k+1}$	$c_j \neq c'_j$	$A_k = A'_k$	$i \neq i'$
Redundant	$A_{k+1} = A'_{k+1}$	$c_j \neq c'_j$	$A_k = A'_k$	$i = i'$
No change	$A_{k+1} = A'_{k+1}$	$c_j = c'_j$	$A_k = A'_k$	$i = i'$

The table shows the deterministic neutral mapping and dependency impact. The interval for change for the eight cases is between three cases and six cases. Delayed/redundant implies that the change might be delayed since the expanded non-terminal is the same

pairs of vertexes $D = \langle \gamma, \epsilon, \upsilon \rangle$. The transformation from input to production rule, $\upsilon(I, \langle G, P \rangle) = D$. When studying how a grammar reacts to changes in Table 3 the change in a codon and how it is related to the production choice are shown. The interval for change for the eight cases is between three and six cases. Delayed/redundant is indirect since it implies that the change might be delayed since the expanded non-terminal is the same. When reading from left to right a delayed change occurs in right recursive grammars $A \rightarrow A\alpha$. Delayed implies that the change in output (phenotype) might be delayed since the expanded non-terminal is the same.

Preservation from a delay or shift should occur when the parent is not the same, but the rule A_{k+1} is, i.e. when there has been a previous change but the output at this point stays the same.

The derivation tree D generates a derivation δ_T via a many-to-one mapping g (depending on the grammar g it can be one-to-one), i.e. the derivation tree is collapsed and the leaves read from left to right give the phenotype, or the derivation at the last step T, δ_T. The space of grammar symbols is V^*

$$g : D \rightarrow V^*, g(D) = \delta_T \tag{11}$$

The mapping from g has the same properties as in Table 1. In the step from the final derivation to a solution (phenotype) $k : V^* \rightarrow \Psi, k(\delta_T) = \psi$

$$\psi = \begin{cases} \delta_T, & \text{if } \delta_T \in \Sigma^* \\ \text{Undefined}, & \text{otherwise} \end{cases} \tag{12}$$

Note that we assume that the sentences that are created by the grammar are defined in the solution space $\Sigma^* \subseteq \Psi$.

3.1.3 Output to Fitness Value

The phenotype, ψ is assigned a real value by evaluating it with a fitness function, $h : \Psi \rightarrow \mathbb{R}, h(\psi) = \phi$. It is difficult to generalize the properties of a fitness function; the mapping is often many-to-one, but ideally the fitness function should map from the phenotype space to the real values one-to-one and onto.

$$h(\psi) = \begin{cases} \phi, & \text{if } \psi \in \Psi \\ \phi_{min}, & \text{if } \Psi \text{ is Undefined} \end{cases} \tag{13}$$

This gives individuals that were not mapped completely minimum fitness, ϕ_{min}. The entire process in this section is shown in Fig. 1 on page 114.

Combining Eqs. (3), (11) and (13) for each input codon sequence gives the following expression for mapping and evaluating GE, see Fig. 1 on page 114. Given a grammar, and probabilities of production choices in the grammar and codons, a fitness value ϕ is calculated as

$$\phi = h(k(g(v(m(f(C), \langle G, P \rangle), \langle G, P \rangle)))) \tag{14}$$

3.2 Representation Spaces in GE

The GE evaluation, consisting of input-output mapping and fitness assignment, can be described with the following spaces for the individual, showing that there is a redundant (many-to-one) mapping between more than one pair of spaces. Changed values are denoted by $'$, e.g. after a change to chromosome C the new chromosome is C'. $\Delta(x, x') = y$, $y \in \mathbb{R}$ denotes a function measuring a difference. The spaces in GE where changes are examined are:

1. The chromosome which has chromosome changes, $0 < \Delta_C(C, C')$
2. The production choice sequence of integers has changes, $0 \leq \Delta_I(I, I')$
3. The derivation tree has changes, which are grammar dependent, $0 \leq \Delta_D$ (D, D') i.e. there are grammars that generate identical derivation trees
4. The phenotype changes are the changes in the derivation tree leaves $0 \leq \Delta_\Psi$ $(\Psi, \Psi'))$. In other words, there are grammars where different derivations give the same phenotype.
5. The fitness changes, which are $\Delta_\phi(\phi, \phi') \in \mathbb{R}$, different phenotypes can have the same fitness.

In GE, there is redundancy in more than one of the mappings; one point clearly shown is the impact of the grammar both on the input and the derivation, i.e. N and R, and on possible phenotypes $\psi \in \Sigma^*$.

A canonical EA is presented in [2]: one addition here is the mapping part, Eq. (11). A population is a vector of individuals, where the individuals are defined by their chromosomes C, $\Omega = [C_0, C_1, \dots]$. The difference between populations $\Delta(\Omega, \Omega')$ is created by the different operators, where each is operating on either a single individual, on pairs or on the entire population. Replacement of individuals in a population is denoted by ρ, when two populations, Ω, Ω' are joined and a population, Ω'' is returned:

$$\rho : \langle \mathbb{Z}_{2^m}, \dots, \mathbb{Z}_{2^m} \rangle \times \langle \mathbb{Z}_{2^m}, \dots, \mathbb{Z}_{2^m} \rangle \to \langle \mathbb{Z}_{2^m}, \dots, \mathbb{Z}_{2^m} \rangle, \rho(\Omega, \Omega') = \Omega'' \tag{15}$$

Selection in the population is denoted ς and operates on the fitness values ϕ. This value is used to set the selection probability of the individual. The fitness values belonging to individuals are operated on by ς which takes a fitness value and returns a selected individual.

$$\varsigma : \langle \mathbb{R}, \langle \mathbb{Z}_{2^m}, \dots, \mathbb{Z}_{2^m} \rangle \rangle^M \to \langle \mathbb{Z}_{2^m}, \dots, \mathbb{Z}_{2^m} \rangle, \varsigma(x) = C \tag{16}$$

From other GE operators are mutation, μ, which takes a codon and returns a codon:

$$\mu : \langle \mathbb{Z}_{2^m}, \dots, \mathbb{Z}_{2^m} \rangle \to \langle \mathbb{Z}_{2^m}, \dots, \mathbb{Z}_{2^m} \rangle, \mu(C) = C' \tag{17}$$

and crossover, ξ which takes a pair of individuals and returns a pair,[5] $\xi(C_0, C_1) = [C_0', C_1']$

$$\xi : \langle \mathbb{Z}_{2^m}, \dots, \mathbb{Z}_{2^m} \rangle \times \langle \mathbb{Z}_{2^m}, \dots, \mathbb{Z}_{2^m} \rangle \to [\langle \mathbb{Z}_{2^m}, \dots, \mathbb{Z}_{2^m} \rangle, \langle \mathbb{Z}_{2^m}, \dots, \mathbb{Z}_{2^m} \rangle] \tag{18}$$

The full canonical GE with all the components in the system is created by combining mapping equation (14), crossover equation (18), mutation equation (17), selection equation (16) and replacement equation (15).

4 Theory of Disruption in GE

In this section we ask the question: what happens to the output (phenotype) when there is a change in the input (genotype) and a CFG mapping is used in GE? The mapping of GE introduces redundancies by Eq. (5) and dependencies on previous input and the parent in the derivation tree, as well as the design of the grammar. These properties have effects on the preservation of the derivation; often the changes can be quite large, something which in GE is called a "ripple", for the multiple changes that can occur during e.g. mutation or crossover [13].

---

[5]It is possible to create crossover operators that only return a single individual.

In Sect. 4.1 change in the input to the grammar is examined. The question of change as an expansion from the new start symbol in the sub-derivation tree, for all unexpanded non-terminals in the derivation, is also raised in Sect. 4.2. Finally, in Sect. 4.3 an attempt is made to formulate a schema theorem to quantify disruptions, inspired by [23].

4.1 Change in the Chromosome

The key to understanding changes in GE are the dependencies that occur due to the sequential use of the chromosome and mapping. Here we will examine changes in the different stages of the GE mapping.

4.1.1 Codon Change

Consider a single change that could be performed by integer flip mutation of a codon in the codon input sequence and where X is a discreet random variable, $c'_j = X$, $X \in [0, 2^m - 1]$. This would change the old chromosome C into the new chromosome $C' = \langle c_1, \ldots, c'_j, c_{j+1}, \ldots, c_n \rangle, n = |C|$.

Let Y be a continuous random variable in $[0, 1]$ and p_{mut} the probability to change per codon. The events of codon change and mutation are two separate events. First a mutation event occurs and then the codon value change event, depending on the mutation event. The probability that mutation will happen is $p_{mut} = p(Y \leq p_{mut}), \ 0 \leq p_{mut} \leq 1$.

Definition 12 (Codon Change) The event that the codon changes when mutation occurs, is the probability of the codon changing multiplied by the mutation probability:

$$p(\text{codon change}) = p(c \neq c') \, p_{mut}$$

□

The uniform probability for a codon to be different can be written as $p(c \neq c') = \frac{2^m - 1}{2^m}$, since there are 2^m integer values for X and $2^m - 1$ are different. When looking at the entire chromosome the probability of a chromosome to not change is dependent on the chromosome size, the mutation rate and the possible codon values. This probability can be written as:

$$p(C = C') = \prod_{j=0}^{|C|-1} (1 - p_{mut} \, p(c_j \neq c'_j))$$

4.1.2 Integer Production Choice Change

For the integer production choice sequence we get the following.

Definition 13 (Integer Production Choice Change) The event that the derivation changes when mutation occurs and the changed codon changes the production choice in the input, is the probability of input changing multiplied by the mutation probability:

$$p(\text{production choice change}) = p(i \neq i')\, p(c \neq c')\, p_{mut}$$

□

This states the fact that the probability of not changing is the product of the mutation probability and the number of productions in the rule: $p(i \neq i') = p_{mut} \frac{|A_k|-1}{|A_k|} \frac{2^m-1}{2^m}$.

The probability $\mu(n)$ for an integer production choice sequence of length $n \leq |I|$ to not change ($I = I'$) when a uniform mutation rate p_{mut} is applied to the chromosome is the probability of the mutated codon c'_j selecting the same production. Using Definition 13,

$$\mu = \prod_{j=0}^{n}(1 - p(\text{production choice change})) = \prod_{j=0}^{n}(1 - p_{mut}\, p(i_j \neq i'_j)\, p(c \neq c'))$$

(19)

The mapping dependency creates the possibility of context changes, i.e. the current rule in the tree changes, which means that the codons are not choosing the same production choices. It is the dependency on previous choices and on the size of the sub-sequence which gives the possible multiple output changes given a single input change. In CFGs the choice of production is only dependent on the current rule. With a grammar the probability of maintaining a sub derivation beginning at zero given a change is $p(i_j = i'_j | i_0 = i'_0, \ldots, i_{j-1} = i'_{j-1}) = \prod_{k=0}^{j} p(i_k = i'_k)$, taken from Definition 5.

Definition 14 (Context Change) In a grammar without duplicate rules the context changes if the parent (non-terminal) changes.   □

A context change in our notation is $A_k \neq A'_k$. The codon selecting the parent is influenced by the sizes of previous subtrees in the derivation, since changes in subtree sizes will change the codon used for mapping.

Furthermore, Definition 13 gives only an upper bound for no change in the phenotype via mutation, since there are grammars which give the same phenotype even though the production choice sequence has changed. This is an example of redundancy created by the grammar. The probability for the phenotype of the individual not to change when a mutation event has occurred is $0 \leq p(\psi = \psi') \leq \mu$.

```
<S>::=<A>|<B>|<C><B><C>
<A>::=a|b
<B>::=c|<D><E>|d
<C>::=g|h
<D>::=i|j
<E>::=k|l|m
```

Grammar 1 Grammar for Example 1

One question that has been raised several times regarding GE is that the sequential input and deterministic mapping will create multiple changes in production choice sequence from one single change in the genome, i.e. a ripple [13, 17] as empirically investigated by [4]. The following section helps to show that each element in the derivation has a higher probability of change the further the point of genotypic change is from the root of the derivation tree, since there is a dependency on previous choices and parents.

4.1.3 Derivation Change

The probability for no change to occur in an integer production choice sub-sequence decreases as the index of the codons, j, increases. That is, the longer the sequence the higher the probability of change. Where $\mu(n)$ is the probability for an integer production choice sequence of length $n \leq |I|$ to not change. This can be written as $\mu(j-1) \geq \mu(j)$, $1 \leq j \leq |I|$. First, from Eq. (19) the probability of changing the sequence is:

$$\mu(j) = \prod_{k=0}^{j} (1 - p_{mut} \, p(i_k \neq i'_k) \, p(c_k \neq c'_k)) \tag{20}$$

This gives $\mu(0) \geq \mu(1)$. we can induce that $\mu(j-1) \geq \mu(j)$ from $p(c_k \neq c'_k)$ and $p(i_j \neq i'_j) \leq 1$, $j \leq |I|$.

Note that for simplicity the deterministic choices in the grammar are collapsed.

In Example 1 on page 123 the effect on input with higher index in the sequence I is shown.

Example 1 (GE Derivation Change) For the input codon sequence $C = \langle 44, 666, 13, 49, 606, 303 \rangle$ and mutation rate $p_{mut} = 0.1$ and Grammar 1 $f(\langle G, P \rangle, C) = \langle 2, 0, 1, 0, 0, 1 \rangle$. Then the probability for i_0 to change, from Eq. (20), is $\mu(1) = 1 - 0.1 \cdot 0.66 = 0.93$ and for i_3 it is:

$$\mu(3) = (1 - 0.1 \cdot 0.66)(1 - 0.1 \cdot 0.5)(1 - 0.1 \cdot 0.66)(1 - 0.1 \cdot 0.5)$$

$$= 0.79$$

The probability for the derivation tree root to change, from Eq. (20), in δ_0 is 0 and for δ_3:

$$\mu(3) = (1 - 0.1 \cdot 0.66)(1 - 0.1 \cdot 0.66)$$
$$= 0.90$$

□

Another example is the probability to change the symbol corresponding to the root which is lower than the i_j corresponding to any succeeding input, if the selected production i_j has the same number of productions as other non-terminals. Thus, there exists a possibility to reach anywhere in the search space which is less or equal to p_{mut} at the first codon.

To summarize, the linear input sequence and the CFG make a change at the end of the derivation more probable than changes in the beginning. This section has established how changes in the genotype affect the phenotype for GE and has also given bounds for the disruptions of the derivation.

4.1.4 Change Grammar Design

This section studies design of grammars that reduce ripple changes by a analysing derivation trees and their probability to change the context of the mapping. We extend previous work on grammar design and how it should be informed by a theory of change. First we define a term in a GE derivation regarding unexpanded non-terminals in the derivation sequence or tree and call them ripple sites.

Definition 15 (Ripple Site) Ripple sites are unexpanded non-terminals in the derivation after the current non-terminal. If the derivation $\delta_k = \alpha A \beta, \alpha \in \Sigma^*$, $A \in N, \beta \in V_{N>0}^*$, where a set containing at least one non-terminal is $V_{N>0}^* = \{x : \exists x \in N, x \in V^*\}$, it contains at least one ripple site. □

We denote the number of ripple sites for derivation $\delta_k = \alpha A \beta$ as $|\beta_N|$, $\beta_N = \{x : x \in N, x \in \beta\}$

A previous study describe disruptions and the possibility to reduce the number of non-terminals and rules, in order to facilitate schema propagation in Grammatical Genetic Programming [23]. This is also discussed in a paper where the aim is to reduce the number of such ripple sites in the derivation tree by limiting the number of non-terminals in the grammar, although it is not general and it should be noted that not all grammars are reducible in this way [11]. The use of recursive rules prevents generalization for grammars to produce the same language with a reduced grammar.

For GE the disruption to the input I from terminals and non-terminals can be given a lower bound. The lower bound is related to the number of edges in the derivation tree, which is the number of input production choices. Let $|R_\Sigma(D)|$ be the number of inputs in a derivation subtree coming from I. Then the number of non-terminal productions, $|n|$, choosing productions with only terminals in the derivation tree is:

$$|n| = |I| - |R_\Sigma(D)| \tag{21}$$

In Example 2 there is an example of different grammars for the same language building different derivation trees, thus affecting the degree of change in the derivation tree if the input codon sequence is changed.

Example 2 (CFG Designs) This example shows the effect of different numbers of non-terminals. Note that the probabilities for the words generated by the grammar will not be the same in the different grammars. First we have the grammar

```
<S>::=<A><C>|<C><C>
<A>::=<B>|<C>
<B>::=c|d
<C>::=e|f|g
```

with $C = \langle 0, 1, 1, 0 \rangle$, $I = \langle 0, 1, 1, 0 \rangle$, $|n| = 2$, $|I| = 4$, $|R_\Sigma(D)| = 2$. This can be rewritten as

```
<S>::=ce|cf|cg|de|df|dg|ee|ef|eg|fe|ff|fg|ge|gf|gg
```

with $C = \langle 6 \rangle$, $I = \langle 6 \rangle$, $|n| = 1$, $|I| = 1$, $|R_\Sigma(D)| = 0$.

```
<S>::=<A><C>|<C><C>
<A>::=c|d
<C>::=e|f|g
```

with $C = \langle 1, 1, 0 \rangle$, $I = \langle 1, 1, 0 \rangle$, $|n| = 1$, $|I| = 3$, $|R_\Sigma(D)| = 2$. Figure 2 shows that it is the length of the input that is affected by the grammar.   □

The Eq. (21) gives us a lower bound for the probability to change if there is a change in the chromosome and if a rule with non-terminals in the productions is changed. The probability of changing a non-terminal such that the derivation tree length $|D(i_j)|$ changes is $p(i_j \neq i'_j)(|I| - |R_\Sigma(D)|)$. For GE 1/2 is the highest production choice probability, since if there is only one production it is deterministically chosen. Moreover, a lower bound is given if there are no mixed rules, a rule with production choices that are not only terminal. Thus, a grammar that is as compressed as possible, and which allows for a language with the desired sentences will be the least susceptible to disruption. A caveat is that such a grammar might not be the most intuitive to write.

4.1.5 Multiple Changes in the Chromosome

The single disruption analysis in Sect. 4.1 is used as a basis for analysis of multiple disruptions. This helps us to understand crossover. A single point crossover can be considered as multiple changes occur in the codons after the crossover point.

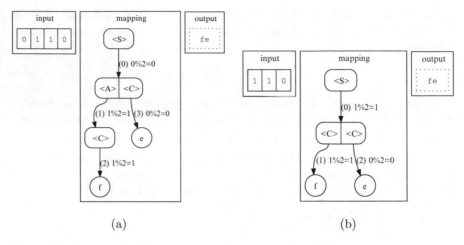

Fig. 2 Grammars with different numbers of rules. (**a**) Original. (**b**) Reduced

A single point crossover at point xo in the input codon sequence, $1 \leq xo \leq min$ $(|C|, |C'|)$ results in $C = \langle c_1, \ldots, c_{xo-1}, c'_{xo}, \ldots, c'_n \rangle$ and $n = |C'|, C' = \langle c'_1, \ldots, c'_{xo-1}, c_{xo}, \ldots, c_n \rangle$ and $n = |C|$. Here, only one child from the crossover is considered. Change is considering the parent which contributed with the beginning of the chromosome.

Definition 16 (Crossover Change) The probability for a crossover event on the input to change the output can be written as $1 - \xi(xo, n)$:

$$\xi = p_{xo} \prod_{j=xo}^{n} p(i_j = i'_j) \tag{22}$$

□

Crossover behavior is similar to mutation but from the crossover point xo to the end of the chromosome C, as regards Eq. (22), a longer chromosome makes disruptions more probable. Note the similarity to $p(i_j = i'_j | i_0 = i'_0, \ldots, i_{j-1} = i'_{j-1})$ crossover generating the same sequence as one parent.

4.2 Input Change and Output Preservation

It is known that one change in input can change the order of expansion in the grammar completely, leading to multiple changes in output by changing the size of the subtree rooted in the expansion. Two types of input changes have been mentioned, single and multiple. The questions we now pose are: can our understanding of the preservation of the derivation after a change be analyzed and classified further than the insight of the "intrinsic polymorphism"[13] of GE? If one codon changes, how much does the context for the succeeding codons change? To begin with we investigate those types of change on the input as shown in Sect. 3.1 on page 113 and the change effects that originate from them.

4.2.1   Change Effects

Given the redundant mapping and parent dependency in GE, a change to the input will be one of two types: change or redundant.

Definition 17 (Redundant Change) Redundant changes occur when a change in the codon does not result in a change in derivation $i_j = i'_j, c_i \neq c'_i, I = I', C \neq C'$.

$\square$

Of course this also gives $D = D'$.

The change can be direct, the change in input is reflected in the corresponding output, or dependent on the previous mappings. Here it is the grammar and the mapping that determine the degree of redundancy after a change in the chromosome. A preservation occurs when the input is the same, the codon is the same, but the context (the previous derivations, i.e. the parents) is changed. Thus, a return to the same output with the same input is preservation. This is different from when preservation of output occurs from different input. Table 3 presents an overview of the types of changes. The point is that each of the indirect or extended changes are artifacts of the GE indirect mapping from a sequence, i.e. from the grammar. Changes to the chromosome are all direct. The indirect encoding of GE allows for indirect changes, i.e. parts not directly connected with the change in the original output are affected by the mapping to the new representation. Both the indirect and direct changes are deterministic, being properties of the encoding.

When any of the changes occur there will be a change effect. See Table 4 for an overview of the effects of change. The definitions of change effects are based on subtree size $|D(A_k)|$ from where the change occurs and the number of ripple sites $|\beta_N|$ at that point in time (derivation) when we are reading the changed codon. The argument for this definition comes from the fact that changes are based on codon changes and/or parent change. Therefore, if a subtree size changes the codons used to determine the other subtrees at the potential ripple sites, the new derivation subtree size will have changed from the original tree. Thus, this will lead to the possibility of different codons for deciding production choices from the unexpanded non-terminals at the ripple sites.

Some change effects can occur in sequence since the derivation tree has maintained some of its original structure. The change effect occurs as soon as there is a change which is not redundant. A branch effect can be followed by another branch effect. As seen in the definition a branch effect can also be followed by the special case of a branch terminal effect. Within a change effect there can be other change effects. The ripple tail effect is when the tail end of the tree changes. This includes the special case where the root node changes. The effect in ripple

Table 4 Derivation tree change effects for the derivation $\delta = \alpha A \beta, \alpha, \beta \in V^*$ with derivation tree $D(A)$

Effect	Subtree size ($|D|$)	Ripple sites (β_N)
Ripple (R)	$|D| \neq |D'|, |\beta_N^{RC}| = 0$	$|\beta_N| > 0$
Ripple ripple (RR)	$|D| \neq |D'|, |\beta_N^{RC}| = 0$	$|\beta_N| = 1$
Ripple contained (RC)	$|D| \neq |D'|, |\beta_N^{RC}| > 0$	$|\beta_N| > 1$
Ripple tail (RT)	$|D| \neq |D'|$	$|\beta_N| = 0$
Branch (B)	$|D| = |D'|$	
Branch terminal (BT)	$|D| = |D'|, |D| = 1$	

The change effects are dependent on if the subtree changes size, then it is either a ripple or a branch

```
<S>::=<A>|<B>|<S><C>
<A>::=<B>|<C>
<B>::=c|d
<C>::=e|f|g
```

Grammar 2 Grammar for demonstrating branch change in Fig. 3 the change is from Fig. 3a to b

contained is the case when a ripple can be limited by canceling out the change in subtree size on the first ripple site by the same size from preceding ripple sites, thus leaving the next site unchanged. That creates a possibility to isolate ripples to subtrees, if they occur at a position with more than 1 ripple site. When the number of ripple sites is less than 2 the ripple cannot be contained, as with the ripple tail effect. $|\beta_N^{RC}|$ denotes the number of subtrees which cancel each other out, $\beta_N^{RC} = \{\exists n \in [2, |c|] : \sum_{i=1}^{n} |D_i| = \sum_{i=1}^{n} |D_i'|\}$.

These definitions allow some sequences of change effects to be classified. If a branch effect or a branch terminal effect occurs, all of the other change effects can occur afterwards. If a contained ripple effect occurs and the difference in subtree sizes for the ripple sites is 0 and there are ripple sites left, all of the other types of changes can occur.

Preservation of output can occur from two sources, either the context of the input is preserved or a different input generates the same output as was found in the original. To identify the other type of preservation the grammar must be examined.

First, what happens when the derivation changes? Since the sequence is known some inferences about what is preserved can be made. The preservation from the root can be shifted from the site of the initial change before the expansion of the start symbol $S = A_k$, for all the unexpanded non-terminals. A shift refers to when the input has been changed but the output only changes at a subsequent position. The shift can occur with more than one step from where the codon changed. The same applies for crossover but the codons are also changed, which makes preservation less probable. An example of branch changes is shown in Fig. 3a, the original individual, which use Grammar 2, can be rewritten after a branch change to Fig. 3b.

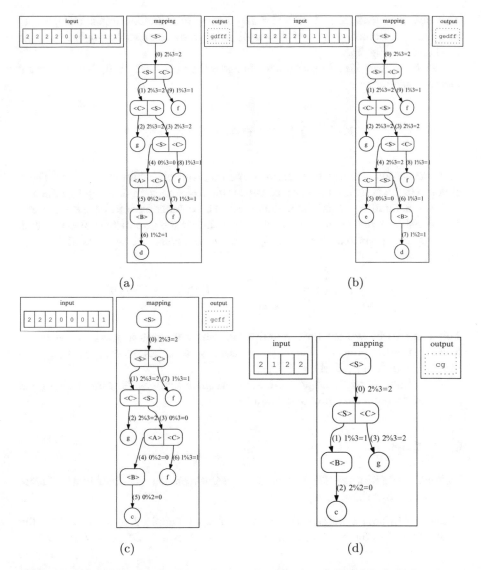

Fig. 3 Example individual and different changes, given Grammar 2 (**a**) Original. (**b**) Branch. (**c**) Ripple with preservation. (**d**) Ripple

4.2.2 Branch Change

Subtree sizes are also important for how much the context will change.

Definition 18 (Branch) The change can be contained to a branch. If the change affects $D(A_j)$ and the size is maintained $|D(A_j)| = |D(A'_j)|$. $\qquad\square$

This definition leads to all terminal changes being classified as branch changes. An example of a branch change is shown with the grammar from Example 2 is begin used again in Fig. 3b.

The probability for a branch not to change is the same as Eq. (19), but at different intervals and indices:

$$p_m^{|D(i_j)|} \prod_{j=k}^{|D(i_j)|} p(i_k = i_k'), 0 \le j \le k, k \le n$$

The branch changes can be described and be given probabilities to occur. These changes in the derivation interval can occur multiple times, thus changing branches but still maintaining subsequent sequences. The parents have to be the same and the preceding branches must be of the same size. If the size of the subtree is one, $l = 1$ the change is in a terminal. $\pi(i_j)$ is the set of parents for j. Probabilities for a branch are:

$$\prod_{k \in \pi(i_j)} p(i_k = i_k') \prod_{k \notin \pi(i_j) \cap k < j} p(|D(i_k)| = |D(i_k')|) \tag{23}$$

This can also be written for the derivation, where there is a non-terminal in the derivation at the point of change, $\delta_k = \alpha A \beta, \alpha \in \Sigma^*, A \in N, \beta \in V_{N>0}^*$ and $|D(A_k)| = |D'(A_k)|, D(A) \ne D'(A)$.

Apart from changes that preserve the subsequent subtrees there are changes that can ripple through the entire derivation tree.

4.2.3 Ripple

Definition 19 (Ripple) The context changes if the branch size changes and if there is more than one ripple site.   □

Example 3 (Ripple Change) The grammar from Example 2 is used to show the change from Fig. 3a–d. Or with e.g. $\delta_k = \alpha_0 A_0 \alpha_1 A_1 \beta, \alpha \in \Sigma^*, A \in N, \beta \in \Sigma^*$.   □

Thus, the codons change mapping in the new context if $c_j \ne c_j'$ and $|D(A_j)| \ne |D(A_j')|$, where $D(A_j)$ is the sub derivation tree starting with i_j.

For ripple a shift can occur due to the input codon sequence and the grammar. The preserved subtrees appear from each non-terminal expansion of the input codon sequence; it is difficult to speak of a preservation of subtrees since these effects could be purely random.

Example 4 (Ripple Contained) The grammar from Example 2 is used to show the change from Fig. 3a–c. There is a preservation of the output after a ripple site, even though the subtree where the change occurred has a different size.   □

The number of productions can guarantee or prevent context change, with the order of the productions being important. The derivation context comes from the parent $A_k = A'_k$ and will be unchanged as long as $i_j = i'_j$. For $i_j \notin \pi(i_j)$ only $|D(i_j)| = |D(i'_j)|$ needs to hold, meaning there can be a shift even if $|D(i_j)| \neq |D(i'_j)|$. For $|D(i_j)| \neq |D(i'_j)|$ a branch is maintained if $|c_j - c'_j|$ $\mathrm{mod}|A_k| = 0$ or $c_j = c'_j$, and $|A_k| = |A'_k|$, or has a probability to not change $|c_j - c'_j| \neq 0$ and $|A_k| \neq |A'_k|$. Take into account $p(|c_i - c'_i| \mathrm{mod}|A_k| = 0) = 1/|A_k|$.

The grammar reduction technique from [11] can be further analyzed from the defined change properties. An example of how a grammar used for low disruption for crossover might be more sensitive to mutation is shown in Example 5.

Example 5 (Reduced Grammar) The following grammar will exchange material in the same context from crossover events and create a branch change from the crossover point.

```
<R>::=a|b|<R>a|<R>c
```

And mutation will always only change one production, thus using Eq. (21) the change is either single terminal change (subtree size 1), expansion or contraction.

□

4.3   Disruption in a GE Population

It is often argued, supported by a schema theorem, that the reason why GAs work is that small fit parts of the genotype are propagated during the evolutionary process [6]. The GA schema theorem has been studied for many different EA systems. For example, one study aims to generalize the building block hypothesis for variable-length strings and program trees [14]. Further, another investigates a schema theorem for CFGs [23].

Evolvability is the ability of the genetic operator/representation to produce offspring fitter than their parents [1]. There have been studies to generalize the GA schema theorem with Price's theorem [2]. Price's theorem regards the covariance between parental fitness and offspring traits for informing how selection drives evolution.

4.3.1   GE Schema

A schema is a template containing zero or more non-terminals, matching multiple valid individuals. Following [23], an attempt to describe how schemas are propagated during evolution is made in this section. When a derivation δ represents a schema, a "do not care" symbol, often *, used in GA and GP schemata, is not needed, since a sentential form is a valid derivation [24]. The derivation string is expressive enough, where non-terminals denote unexpanded subtrees. From [23]:

Definition 20 (Schema in CFG) A schema H for a Context-Free Grammar is the sub derivation tree $H = \{x \xrightarrow{*} \beta\}, x \in N, \beta \in V^*$ □

In the schema, $|H|$ is the length of the schema i.e. subderivation tree. H is rooted in a non-terminal and the schema H can occur more than once in the derivation D. Also worth noting is that the individuals that match the schema can differ in size. The number of fixed symbols in a schema is called the order of the schema. We investigate the probability of a schema to not be disrupted during a generation. This means that the probability of crossover and mutation to change the schema are studied, as well as the probability of selecting a schema using fitness proportional selection.

Schema Disruption Due to Crossover The probability of a derivation tree D containing H to not change due to crossover is:

$$p(H = H') = \prod_{j=xo}^{h_e} p(i_j = i'_j) \tag{24}$$

where h_e is the index in D where H ends and the crossover point $xo, 0 \le xo \le |H|$. The probability to change the schema is $\kappa = 1 - p(H = H'), 0 \le \kappa \le 1$, see Eq. (22). The comparison is made with the parent that contains the start of the chromosome.

Note that cases of redundant grammars are ignored here. Moreover, with the change effect "branch" where the change occurs in the unexpanded non-terminal region the schema will still be maintained.

Schema Disruption Due to Mutation The probability of a derivation tree D containing H to not change due to mutation is:

$$p(H = H') = \prod_{j=m_s}^{h_e} p(i_j = i'_j) \tag{25}$$

With m the point of mutation and $0 \le m \le |H|$. The probability to change is $\varpi = 1 - p(H = H'), 0 \le \varpi \le 1$, see Eq. (19).

We define $|D_H|$ as the number of occurrences of schema H in the derivation tree D and the average disruption due to crossover $\overline{K}$ and mutation $\overline{M}$, i.e. the number of schema in each individual in the population times the probability of disruption due to crossover or mutation divided by the total number of schema in the population. This can be written as: (where Ω is the population)

$$\overline{K} = \frac{\sum_{D \in \Omega} \kappa |D_H|}{\sum_{D \in \Omega} |D_H|}, 0 \le \overline{K} \le 1 \tag{26}$$

$$\overline{M} = \frac{\sum_{D \in \Omega} \varpi |D_H|}{\sum_{D \in \Omega} |D_H|}, 0 \le \overline{M} \le 1 \tag{27}$$

The fitness of derivation D is f_D and the average schema fitness for fitness proportional selection and replacement ρ is:

$$\rho = \frac{\overline{f}_H}{\overline{f}} \tag{28}$$

$$\overline{f}_H = \frac{\sum_{D \in \Omega} f_D |D_H|}{\sum_{D \in \Omega} |D_H|} \tag{29}$$

$$\overline{f} = \frac{\sum_{D \in \Omega} f_D}{|\Omega|} \tag{30}$$

Where $\overline{f}_H$ is average fitness of a schema in a population and $\overline{f}$ is the average fitness of the entire population.

Combining Eqs. (27), (26) and (28) it is possible to set up bounds for the propagation of schema H due to crossover, mutation, and replacement and selection over time. That is, a schema is propagated if it is not disrupted by mutation and crossover and fit enough to be selected by proportional selection. We use p_{xo} as the probability of crossover and p_{mut} as the probability of mutation. $(1 - (1 - p_{mut})^{|H|})$ denotes the probability that a mutation occurs within the derivation tree needed to describe the schema.

Theorem 1 *The number $n(H, t)$ of schema H to be found at time t:*

$$n(H, t) \geq n(H, t - 1) \cdot \rho \cdot (1 - p_{xo}\overline{K}) \cdot (1 - (1 - (1 - p_{mut})^{|H|})\overline{M}) \tag{31}$$

$\square$

Proof From combining Eqs. (28), (26) and (27).

$$n(H, t) = n(H, t - 1) \cdot \rho \tag{32}$$

$$n(H, t) \geq n(H, t - 1) \cdot \rho \cdot (1 - p_{xo}\overline{K}) \cdot (1 - (1 - (1 - p_{mut})^{|H|})\overline{M}) \tag{33}$$

∎

Note that a lower bound for schema disruption is the probability that a random derivation gives the schema $p(H) = \prod_{i=0}^{|H|} p(H_i)$, thus reoccurring by random chance. That is a crossover or mutation reintroduces the schema. This is important since it shows the impact of the grammar for allowing schema.

5 Discussion

The regularity of the grammar can have obvious effects on the change impacts, by guaranteeing, delaying or making the change redundant. Mixed rules, i.e. rules with both non-terminal and terminal productions, will make the analysis more difficult.

Moreover, mixed production choices, i.e. productions with both terminal and non-terminal symbols, further complicate analysis. Therefore, the use of normal forms, e.g. those of Chomsky or Greibach [8], could facilitate the analysis.

From the definitions of change effects we see that the non-terminal distribution of I is important, especially for one-point-crossover. With this terminology a context-sensitive operator [7] would guarantee a branch change and insert or replace a subtree so that everything in I' would be within the same context as in I. From experiments regarding the positional effect of crossover and mutation in GE there is support for the idea that events occurring in the first position of the genotype are more destructive, but they can also be the most constructive, regarding fitness [4]. The ripple effect means that a few changes to the chromosome can be propagated to multiple changes to the phenotype. This affects the local search capabilities of GE and the causality principle.

The propagation of schemas is bounded by the operators and the expansion of non-terminals. One view of GE is that the integer sequence I tends to converge from left to right, since the schemas are most likely kept at the beginning of the derivation. Another part is the probability of derivations from N which can contain schemas. This means the re-introduction of schemas due to the bias in the grammar.

6 Conclusions and Future Work

A formal description of GE is proposed and this provides us with the tools to analyze the impact of changes on the genotype-phenotype mapping of GE. With an improved understanding of how the algorithm works, more efficient search operators can be designed. The study of changes has revealed a lower bound for the disruption probability in a grammar and thus given some pointers for grammar design. In other words, the fewer non-terminals it contains, the less susceptible it will be to disruption. The effects of a change on the input were labeled. Furthermore a schema theorem for canonical GE has been formulated.

Future work will investigate the availability of sequences in the population and the availability of the bias in the search, even if the sequences are not directly preserved there will be a bias from the genetic material available. Here the grammar should affect the search, as discussed in the mod and bucket [10].

References

1. L. Altenberg, The evolution of evolvability in genetic programming. Adv. Genet. Program. **3**, 47–74, (1994)
2. L. Altenberg, The schema theorem and Price's theorem. Found. Genet. Algorithms **3**, 23–49 (1995)
3. T.L. Booth, *Sequential Machines and Automata Theory* (Wiley, New York, 1967)
4. T. Castle, C.G. Johnson, Positional effect of crossover and mutation in grammatical evolution, in *European Conference on Genetic Programming*. LNCS (Springer, Berlin, 2010)

5. J.A. Draghi, T.L. Parsons, G.P. Wagner, J.B. Plotkin, Mutational robustness can facilitate adaptation. Nature, **463**(7279), 353–355 (2010)
6. D.E. Goldberg, *Genetic Algorithms in Search, Optimization, and Machine Learning* (Addison-Wesley, Boston, 1989)
7. R. Harper, A. Blair, A structure preserving crossover in grammatical evolution, in *The 2005 IEEE Congress on Evolutionary Computation*, vol. 3, 2005.
8. M.A. Harrison, *Introduction to Formal Language Theory* (Addison-Wesley Longman, Boston, 1978)
9. E.A.P. Hemberg, An exploration of grammars in grammatical evolution. PhD thesis, University College Dublin, 2010
10. M. Keijzer, M. O'Neill, C. Ryan, M. Cattolico, Grammatical evolution rules: the mod and the bucket rule, in *EuroGP*, vol. 2278 (Springer, Berlin, 2002), pp. 123–130
11. M. Nicolau, Automatic grammar complexity reduction in grammatical evolution, in *GECCO 2004 Workshop Proceedings*, Seattle, Washington, 26–30 June 2004, ed. by R. Poli et al. (2004)
12. M. O'Neill, C. Ryan, M. Nicolau, Grammar defined introns: an investigation into grammars, introns, and bias in grammatical evolution, in *Proceedings of the 3rd Annual Conference on Genetic and Evolutionary Computation* (Morgan Kaufmann, San Francisco, 2001), pp. 97–103
13. M. O'Neill, C. Ryan, M. Keijzer, M. Cattolico, Crossover in grammatical evolution. Genet. Program. Evolvable Mach. **4**(1), 67–93 (2003)
14. R. Poli, C.R. Stephens, The building block basis for genetic programming and variable-length genetic algorithms. Int. J. Comput. Intell. Res. **1**(1–2), 183–197 (2005)
15. F. Rothlauf, *Representations for Genetic and Evolutionary Algorithms* (Springer, Berlin, 2006)
16. F. Rothlauf, M. Oetzel, On the locality of grammatical evolution, in *European Conference on Genetic Programming* (Springer, Berlin, 2006), pp. 320–330
17. F. Rothlauf, M. Oetzel, On the locality of grammatical evolution, in *EuroGP*, ed. by P. Collet, M. Tomassini, M. Ebner, S. Gustafson, A. Ekrt. Lecture Notes in Computer Science, vol. 3905 (Springer, Berlin, 2006), pp. 320–330
18. M. Toussaint, The evolution of genetic representations and modular neural adaptation. PhD thesis, Ruhr-Universität Bochum, 2003
19. M. Toussaint, The evolution of genetic representations and modular adaptation. PhD thesis, 2003
20. G.P. Wagner, L. Altenberg, Complex adaptations and the evolution of evolvability. Evolution **50**(3), 967–976 (1996)
21. C.S. Wetherell, Probabilistic languages: a review and some open questions. ACM Comput. Surv. **12**(4), 361–379 (1980)
22. P.A. Whigham, Grammatically-based genetic programming, in *Proceedings of the Workshop on Genetic Programming: From Theory to Real-World Applications*, Tahoe City, 9 July 1995, ed. by J.P. Rosca (1995), pp. 33–41
23. P.A. Whigham, A schema theorem for context-free grammars, in *1995 IEEE Conference on Evolutionary Computation* (IEEE Press, Piscataway, 1995), pp. 178–181
24. P.A. Whigham, Grammatical bias for evolutionary learning. PhD thesis, School of Computer Science, University College, University of New South Wales, Australian Defence Force Academy, Canberra, 14 October 1996
25. D. Wilson, D. Kaur, Search, neutral evolution, and mapping in evolutionary computing: a case study of grammatical evolution. IEEE Trans. Evol. Comput. **13**(3), 566–590 (2009)

Structured Grammatical Evolution: A Dynamic Approach

Nuno Lourenço, Filipe Assunção, Francisco B. Pereira, Ernesto Costa, and Penousal Machado

Abstract Grammars have attracted the attention of researchers within the Evolutionary Computation field, specially from the Genetic Programming community. The most successful example of the use of grammars by GP is Grammatical Evolution (GE). In spite of being widely used by practitioners of different fields, GE is not free from drawbacks. The ones that are most commonly pointed out are those linked with redundancy and locality of the representation. To address these limitations Structured Grammatical Evolution (SGE) was proposed, which introduces a one-to-one mapping between the genotype and the non-terminals. In SGE the input grammar must be pre-processed so that recursion is removed, and the maximum number of expansion possibilities for each symbol determined. This has been pointed out as a drawback of SGE and to tackle it we introduce Dynamic Structured Grammatical Evolution (DSGE). In DSGE there is no need to pre-process the grammar, as it is expanded on the fly during the evolutionary process, and thus we only need to define the maximum tree depth. Additionally, it only encodes the integers that are used in the genotype to phenotype mapping, and grows as needed during evolution. Experiments comparing DSGE with SGE show that DSGE performance is never worse than SGE, being statistically superior in a considerable number of the tested problems.

1 Introduction

Grammars are widely used by computer scientists and researchers to represent complex structures by specifying restrictions on general domains, thus limiting the number of expressions that can be generated. The most common application

N. Lourenço (✉) · F. Assunção · E. Costa · P. Machado
CISUC, Department of Informatics Engineering, University of Coimbra, Coimbra, Portugal
e-mail: naml@dei.uc.pt; fga@dei.uc.pt; ernesto@dei.uc.pt; machado@dei.uc.pt

F. B. Pereira
CISUC, Department of Informatics Engineering, University of Coimbra, Coimbra, Portugal
Polytechnic Institute of Coimbra, Quinta da Nora, Coimbra, Portugal
e-mail: xico@dei.uc.pt

© Springer International Publishing AG, part of Springer Nature 2018   137
C. Ryan et al. (eds.), *Handbook of Grammatical Evolution*,
https://doi.org/10.1007/978-3-319-78717-6_6

is perhaps on the specification of the syntax of a programming language to define things such as type restrictions and operators precedence. Grammars are also useful to represent and describe interaction constraints between the different components of a system. As such, it is not a surprise that grammars captivated the attention of Evolutionary Computation (EC) researchers to help in the specification of problem restrictions and constraints that guide the evolutionary process, specifically in Genetic Programming (GP) [10].

One of the first GP proposals that used grammars to define the syntax and control the search bias was introduced by Whigham with his Context-Free-Grammar GP [22]. The introduction of grammars limited the form of possible solutions, allowing the definition of an explicit structure through the use of the productions of a grammar, and enabled the definition of constraints, ensuring that different components of solutions are not mixed together.

The main achievement in Grammar-Based Genetic Programming (GBGP) came with the introduction of Grammatical Evolution (GE) by Ryan et al. [15, 19], which since then has become one of the most popular and widespread GP methods. The main difference between CFG-GP and GE is related with how individual solutions are represented. While the former relies on a derivation-tree based representation, the latter uses a variable length linear integer string and a grammar to map individuals from the search space into the problem space. This separation between genotype and phenotype is usually seen as an advantage of GE over other techniques, since it is possible to decouple the search method from the problem we are solving, simplifying its application to different domains.

Despite the popularity of GE, some studies have shown that it has some drawbacks. Firstly, GE suffers from high levels of redundancy. A representation is said to be redundant when several different genotypes map in the same phenotype. Secondly, GE has a low locality [18], i.e., how variations at the genotype level reflect on differences at the phenotype level [6]. In a representation with high locality, a small modification on the genotype usually results in a small modification on the phenotype, nurturing the conditions for an effective sampling of the search space. If this condition is not satisfied, the search performed by an Evolutionary Algorithm (EA) tends to resemble that of a random search [17].

Over the years several modifications have been made to the original GE proposal in order to overcome its limitations. The most recent one is called Structured Grammatical Evolution (SGE), proposed by the authors in [12]. Its most noticeable characteristic is having a one-to-one relationship between genes and the non-terminals of the grammar being used. In order to allow a valid mapping, each gene encodes a list of integers that represent the possible derivation choices for the corresponding non-terminal. The structured representation of SGE, in which a gene is explicitly linked to a non-terminal of the grammar, ensures that changes in a single genotypic position do not affect the derivation options of other non-terminals. In the aforementioned work we analysed and compared the properties of both SGE and GE, and concluded that the new representation not only increases locality but also reduces redundancy. These results justify the increased performance of SGE over the traditional GE representation.

Nevertheless, SGE has been criticised because we need to specify beforehand the maximum levels of recursion in order to remove it from the grammar. In this work, we introduce a new version of the SGE, called Dynamic Structured Grammatical Evolution (DSGE), which addresses this main criticism. In this new version we specify the maximum tree-depth (similarly to what happens in standard tree-based GP), and the algorithm add the mapping numbers as required during the evolutionary search. Thus, we do not need to pre-process the grammar to remove the recursive productions. Additionally, we provide mechanisms to make sure that the generated trees are always within the allowed limits. We show that the DSGE version performs as good as the initial SGE algorithm, and in some cases it even surpasses its performance.

This chapter is organised as follows: in Sect. 2 we present the background. Next, in Sect. 3 we detail our new method: DSGE. In Sect. 4 we evaluate and compare the performance of the new method with the vanilla version of SGE in classical GP benchmarks, followed by a comparison of the two approaches in the domain of NeuroEvolution (Sect. 5). Finally, Sect. 6 gathers the main conclusions.

2 Background

Context-Free-Grammars (CFGs) have been widely used to represent and control the search bias of EAs [14]. Formally, a CFG is a tuple $G = (N, T, S, P)$, where N is a non-empty set of non-terminal symbols, T is a non-empty set of terminal symbols, S is an element of N called the axiom, and P is a set of production rules of the form $A ::= \alpha$, with $A \in N$ and $\alpha \in (N \cup T)^*$. N and T are disjoint. Each grammar G defines a language $L(G)$ composed by all sequences of terminal symbols (the words) that can be derived from the axiom: $L(G) = \{w : S \stackrel{*}{\Rightarrow} w, w \in T^*\}$. An example of a CFG is presented in Fig. 1. In this section we describe the GE and SGE approaches. For an in-depth review of the developments related with grammar-based evolutionary methods the reader might refer to [14].

Fig. 1 Example of a Context-Free-Grammar in the Backus-Naur Form (BNF)

$$
\begin{array}{lll}
<\text{start}> & ::= <\text{expr}><\text{op}><\text{expr}> & (0) \\
& \mid\quad <\text{expr}> & (1) \\
<\text{expr}> & ::= <\text{term}><\text{op}><\text{term}> & (0) \\
& \mid\quad (<\text{term}><\text{op}><\text{term}>) & (1) \\
<\text{op}> & ::= + \quad (0) \\
& \mid\quad - \quad (1) \\
& \mid\quad / \quad (2) \\
& \mid\quad * \quad (3) \\
<\text{term}> & ::= x_1 \quad (0) \\
& \mid\quad 0.5 \quad (1)
\end{array}
$$

2.1 Grammatical Evolution

In Grammatical Evolution (GE) there is a separation between the genotype, i.e., a linear string of integers, and the phenotype, i.e., a program in the form of a tree expression. As a consequence, a mapping process is required to map the string into an executable program, using the production rules of a CFG. The translation of the genotype into the phenotype is done by simulating a leftmost derivation from the axiom of the grammar. This process scans the linear sequence from left to right and each integer (i.e., each codon) is used to determine the grammar rule that expands the leftmost non-terminal symbol of the current partial derivation tree. Consider the set of production rules defined in Fig. 1, where there are two options to rewrite the left-hand side symbol <start>. In the beginning we have a sentential form equal to the axiom <start>. To rewrite the axiom one must choose which alternative will be used by taking the first integer of the genotype and dividing it by the number of options in which we can derive <start>. The remainder of that operation will indicate the option to be used. In the example above, assuming that the first integer is 23, it follows that 23%2 = 1 and the axiom is rewritten as <expr><op><expr>. Then the second integer is read, and the same method is used to the left most non-terminal of the derivation. The complete mapping of an individual is showed in Table 1. Sometimes the length of the genotype is not enough to complete the mapping. When that happens the sequence is repeatedly reused in a process known as *wrapping*. If the mapping exceeds a pre-determined number of wrappings, the process stops and the worst possible fitness value is assigned to the individual.

The separation between the search space and the problem space is usually seen as one of the biggest advantages of GE, allowing it to be easily used in different problem domains. These characteristics is also appealing to practitioners of various scientific domains, since they can easily use GE to solve their problems.

Table 1 GE mapping procedure that translates the genotype of an individual into a polynomial expression (phenotype)

Derivation step	Integers left
<start>	[23, 7, 55, 22, 3, 4, 30, 16, 203, 24]
<expr><op><expr>	[7, 55, 22, 3, 4, 30, 16, 203, 24]
(<term><op><term>)<op><expr>	[55, 22, 3, 4, 30, 16, 203, 24]
(0.5 <op><term>)<op><expr>	[22, 3, 4, 30, 16, 203, 24]
(0.5 / <term>)<op><expr>	[3, 4, 30, 16, 203, 24]
(0.5 / 0.5)<op><expr>	[4, 30, 16, 203, 24]
(0.5 / 1) + <expr>	[30, 16, 203, 24]
(0.5 / 1) + <term><op><term>	[15, 203, 24]
(0.5 / 1) + x_1 <op><term>	[203, 24]
(0.5 / 1) + x_1 * <term>	[24]
(0.5 / 1) + x_1 * x_1	[]

Each row represents a derivation step. The used grammar is represented in Fig. 1

GE it is not exempted from criticisms. One is concerned with its initialisation procedure, which makes it difficult to create populations with valid individuals [16]. To overcome the initialisation problem, GE adopted a method similar to the one proposed in GP [10]. Another criticism pointed at GE is concerned with its high redundancy and its low locality. Rothlauf et al. in [18] showed that in approximately 90% of the time a change in the genotype does not change the phenotype. A second important result of this work is related with the remaining 10% of the modifications. Specifically, when the genotype suffers one mutation, changes of more than one unit occur at the phenotypic level. This means that many genotypic neighbours originate highly dissimilar phenotypes. One of the first proposals to increase the locality of GE was by Byrne et al. [3, 4]. They proposed new mutation operators that worked on the phenotypic level, which only changed the labels of the nodes in the derivation tree.

2.2 Structured Grammatical Evolution

Structured Grammatical Evolution (SGE) is a recent genotypic representation aimed at overcoming the locality and redundancy issues of GE. In SGE each gene is linked to a specific non-terminal, and it is composed by a list of integers used to select the expansion option. The length of each list is determined by computing the maximum possible number of expansions of the corresponding non-terminal. This structure ensures that the modification of a gene does not affect the derivation options of other non-terminals, thus limiting the number of changes that can occur at the phenotypic level, which result in a higher locality. The values inside each list are bounded by the number of possible expansion options of the corresponding non-terminal. Therefore, the mapping procedure does not rely on the modulo rule, avoiding the redundancy associated with it.

As an example consider the grammar depicted in Fig. 1. The non-terminals set is {<start>, <expr>, <term>, <op>}. Therefore, the SGE genotype is composed by four genes, each one linked to one specific non-terminal. To determine the length of the gene's lists we calculate the maximum number of expansions of each non-terminal. The <start> symbol is expanded only once, as it is the grammar axiom. The <expr> symbol is expanded, at most, twice, because of the rule <expr><op><expr>. The computation of the list size for <term> establishes a direct dependence between this non-terminal and <expr>: each time <expr> is expanded, <term> is expanded twice (in the two possible expansion options). As the grammar allows a maximum of two <expr> expansions, it immediately follows that the list size for the <term> gene is four. Following the same line of reasoning, the list size for the <op> gene is 3. Thus, the list sizes for each gene are: <start> : 1, <expr> : 2, <term> : 4, <op> : 3. To complete the list inside each gene we take the number of derivation options c_N of the corresponding non-terminal, and assign a random value from the interval $[0, c_N - 1]$ to every position. The <start>, <expr> and <term> symbols have $c_N = 2$, whereas <op> has

Fig. 2 Example of a SGE genotype for the grammar showed in Fig. 1

| <start> | <expr> | <op> | <term> |

| Genotype | | | |
| [0] | [0,1] | [2,0,3] | [1,1,0,0] |

Table 2 SGE mapping procedure that converts a SGE individual into a polynomial expression

Derivation step	Integers left
<start>	[[0], [0, 1], [2, 0, 3], [1, 1, 0, 0]]
<expr><op><expr>	[[], [1, 0], [2, 0, 3], [1, 1, 0, 0]]
(<value><op><value>)<op><expr>	[[], [0], [2, 0, 3], [1, 1, 0, 0]]
(0.5 <op><value>)<op><expr>	[[], [0], [2, 0, 3], [1, 0, 0]]
(0.5 / <value>)<op><expr>	[[], [0], [0, 3], [1, 0, 0]]
(0.5 / 1)<op><expr>	[[], [0], [0, 3], [0, 1]]
(0.5 / 1) + <expr>	[[], [0], [3], [0, 1]]
(0.5 / 1) + <value><op><value>	[[], [], [3], [0, 0]]
(0.5 / 1) + x_1 <op><value>	[[], [], [3], [0]]
(0.5 / 1) + x_1 * <value>	[[], [], [], [0]]
(0.5 / 1) + x_1 * x_1	[[], [], [], []]

Each row represents a derivation step. The used grammar is represented in Fig. 1. The list of codons represents the integers needed for expanding <start>, <expr>, <op> and <value>, respectively

$c_N = 4$. Figure 2 shows an example of the genotype of a SGE individual. The complete mapping of this same individual into a polynomial expression is depicted in Table 2.

3 Dynamic Structured Grammatical Evolution

Dynamic Structured Grammatical Evolution (DSGE) is our novel GBGP approach. It derives from SGE, and addresses its common criticism of having to remove the recursion from the grammar beforehand. In this new version there is no need to pre-process the grammar in order to compute the maximum tree-sizes of each non-terminal symbol, so that intermediate grammar derivation rules are created to mimic the recursion process. Another advantage of the new proposal is that all of the genotype is used. Whilst in GE and SGE the genotype encodes the largest allowed sequence, in DSGE the genotype grows as needed. In the next sections we describe in detail the procedures needed to implement the DSGE.

Algorithm 1: Random candidate solution generation

```
 1: procedure CREATE_INDIVIDUAL(grammar, max_depth, genotype, symbol, depth)
 2:     expansion = randint(0, len(grammar[symbol])-1)
 3:     if is_recursive(symbol) then
 4:         if expansion in grammar.recursive(symbol) then
 5:             if depth ≥ max_depth then:
 6:                 non_rec = grammar.non_recursive(symbol)
 7:                 expansion = choice(non_rec)
 8:     if symbol in genotype then
 9:         genotype[symbol].append(expansion)
10:     else
11:         genotype[symbol] = [expansion]
12:     expansion_symbols = grammar[symbol][expansion]
13:     for sym in expansion_symbols do
14:         if not is_terminal(sym) then
15:             create_individual(grammar, max_depth, genotype, sym, depth+1)
```

3.1 Representation

Each candidate solution encodes an ordered sequence of the derivation steps of the used grammar that are needed to generate a specific solution for the problem at hand. The representation is similar to the one used in SGE, with one main difference: instead of computing and generating the maximum number of derivations for each of the grammar's non-terminal symbols, a variable length representation is used, where just the number of needed derivations are encoded. Consequently, there is no need to create intermediate symbols to deal with recursive rules.

To limit the genotype size, a maximum tree-depth needs to be defined. This means that the trees that are being generated will grow until a certain limit. To ensure that valid individuals are generated we need to change the initialisation and mapping procedures. These modifications are detailed in the following sections.

3.2 Initialisation

Algorithm 1 details the recursive function that is used to generate each initial solution. This procedure takes as input the following parameters: the grammar that describes the domain of the problem; the maximum tree-depth; the genotype (which is initially empty); the non-terminal symbol that we want to expand (initially the axiom is used); and the current tree-depth (initialised to 0). Then, for the non-terminal symbol given as input, one of its possible derivation rules is selected (lines 2–11) and the non-terminal symbols of the chosen derivation rule are recursively expanded (lines 12–15) following a depth-first approach. However, when selecting

---

Algorithm 2: Genotype to phenotype mapping procedure

```
 1:  procedure MAPPING(genotype, grammar, max_depth, read_integers, symbol, depth)
 2:      phenotype = ""
 3:      if symbol not in read_integers then
 4:          read_integers[symbol] = 0
 5:      if symbol not in genotype then
 6:          genotype[symbol] = []
 7:      if read_integers[symbol] ≥ len(genotype[symbol]) then
 8:          if depth ≥ max_depth then
 9:              generate_terminal_expansion(genotype, symbol)
10:          else
11:              generate_expansion(genotype, symbol)
12:      gen_int = genotype[symbol][read_integer[symbol]]
13:      expansion = grammar[symbol][gen_int]
14:      read_integers[symbol] += 1
15:      for sym in expansion do
16:          if is_terminal(sym) then
17:              phenotype += sym
18:          else
19:              phenotype += mapping(genotype, grammar, max_depth, read_integers, sym,
                 depth+1)
20:      return phenotype
```

---

the expansion rule there is the need to check whether or not the maximum tree-depth has already been reached (lines 3–5). If that happens, only non-recursive derivation rules can be selected for expanding the current non-terminal symbol (lines 6–7). This procedure is repeated until an initial population with the desired size is created.

3.3 Mapping Function

To map the candidate solutions genotype into the phenotype we use Algorithm 2. This procedure is similar to the one used to generate the initial population but, instead of randomly selecting the derivation rule to use in the expansion of the non-terminal symbol, we use the choice that is encoded in the individual's genotype (lines 12–19). During evolution, the genetic operators might change the genotype in a way that more integers will be necessary than the ones that we have available. When this happens new derivation rules are selected randomly and added to the genotype of the individual (lines 3–11).

3.4 Genetic Operators

To explore the problem's domain and therefore promote evolution EAs usually rely on recombination and mutation operators to explore the search space, looking for promising solutions for the problem being solved.

3.4.1 Mutation

The mutation operator is restricted to integers that are used in the genotype to phenotype mapping and changes a randomly selected expansion option (encoded as an integer) to another valid one, constrained to the restrictions imposed by the maximum tree-depth. To do so, we first select one gene. Then, we randomly select one of its integers and replace it with another valid possibility. Note that genes where there is just one possibility for expansion are not considered for mutation purposes. Figure 3 shows the application of the mutation operator.

3.4.2 Recombination

Recombination is used to recombine two parents to generate two offspring. The crossover is the same introduced by [12]. It starts by creating a random binary mask and the offspring are created by selecting the parents genes' based on the mask values. Recombination does not modify the lists inside the genes. This is

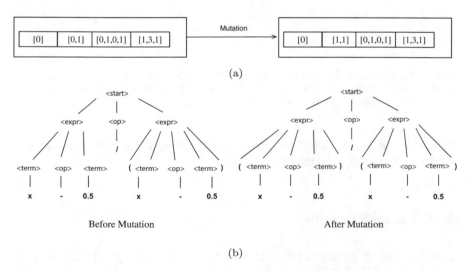

Fig. 3 Application of the mutation operator. Panel (**a**) details the application at the genotypic level, whereas panel (**b**) illustrates changes in the corresponding derivation trees. (**a**) Mutation application. (**b**) Derivation trees

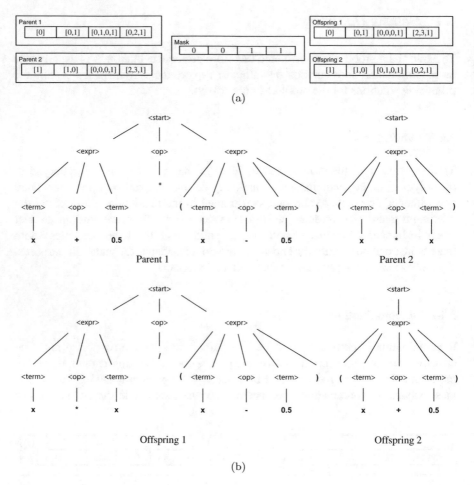

Fig. 4 Application of the recombination operator. Panel (**a**) details the application at the genotypic level, whereas panel (**b**) illustrates the changes in the corresponding derivation trees. (**a**) Crossover application. (**b**) Derivation trees

similar to what happens with uniform crossover for binary representations. Figure 4 demonstrates the application of this operator.

4 Classical Problems

In this section we present the experimental results that we conducted to assess the performance of the DSGE, conducting a relative comparison with its ancestor. We rely on the version of SGE described in [12].

Table 3 Experimental parameters used in the analysis for SGE and DSGE

Parameter	Value
Num. runs	30
Population size	1000
Generations	50
Crossover rate	95%
Mutation rate	$\dfrac{1}{\text{code size}}$
Tournament size	3
Elite size	1%
SGE parameter	Value
Recursion level	6
DSGE parameter	Value
Max. Initialisation depth	6
Max. depth	17

4.1 Experimental Setup

All the results reported are averages of 30 evolutionary runs, to allow for a sound statistical analysis. Considering that we are performing comparisons with only two groups, we do not assume anything about the distribution of the data, and because the initial populations of each method are different we rely on the Mann-Whitney non-parametric test with a significance level $\alpha = 0.05$. Since that we are performing comparisons between only two groups, no $p - value$ correction is needed. Note that when statistical differences are found, we also report the effect size [5] of the differences.

The numerical parameters used for the experiments performed with SGE and DSGE are presented in Table 3.[1] The *codon size* parameter stands for the number of integers in the DSGE genotype.

4.2 Benchmark Description

The problems that were considered in the experiments are the Boston housing symbolic regression, quartic symbolic regression, the 5-bit even parity, the 11-bit Boolean multiplexer and the Santa Fe Ant Trail. All the problems consider the minimisation of an error. For the regression problems, i.e., the Boston housing and quartic, we used the Root Relative Squared Error (RRSE) which is 0 for a model with a perfect fit. For the 5-bit parity and the 11-bit Boolean multiplexer we count the number of test cases that were incorrectly predicted. Finally, for the Santa Fe

---

[1] The implementations of SGE and DSGE are available at: SGE—https://github.com/nunolourenco/sge and DSGE—https://github.com/nunolourenco/dsge.

Ant Trail we consider the number of food pellets left after the maximum number of steps has been achieved.

4.2.1 Quartic Symbolic Regression

The relevance of this problem as a GP benchmark is highly debated [13], but we included it mostly for historical reasons. The aim is to approximate the function defined by:

$$f(x) = x^4 + x^3 + x^2 + x + 1 \tag{1}$$

where x is sampled in the interval $[-1, 1]$ with a step $s = 0.1$ The set of production rules considered for this problem is:

$$<\text{start}> ::= <\text{expr}>$$

$$<\text{expr}> ::= <\text{expr}><\text{op}><\text{expr}>$$

$$| (<\text{expr}><\text{op}><\text{expr}>)$$

$$| <\text{pre\_op}>(<\text{expr}>)$$

$$| <\text{var}>$$

$$<\text{op}> ::= + | - | * | /$$

$$<\text{pre\_op}> ::= \sin | \cos | \exp | \text{inv} | \log$$

$$<\text{var}> ::= x | 1.0$$

where *inv* is $\frac{1}{f(x)}$. Moreover, we considered that the division, and the logarithm functions are protected, i.e., $\frac{1}{0} = 1$ and $log(f(x)) = 0$ *iff* $f(x) \leq 0$.

4.2.2 Boston Housing Problem

This is a regression dataset from the UCI repository [11]. The dataset is composed by the housing prices from the suburbs of Boston, and the aim is to create a regression model that predicts the median house price, given a set of demographic features. The dataset is composed by 506 examples, each one composed by 13 features (12 continuous, 1 binary), and one continuous output variable in the range [0, 50]. This problem corresponds to a typical machine learning task and we need to measure the ability of the evolved models to work with unseen instances. Following the guidelines from [23], the dataset is partitioned into 2 disjoint sets: (1) 90% of the examples are used as the training set to learn a model; (2) the remaining 10% are used as the test set, to assess the performance of the model. The set of production rules is extended from the quartic problem, with the inclusion of the additional descriptive variables used for predicting house prices to the non-terminal <var>.

4.2.3 Pagie Polynomial Regression

The objective is to approximate the polynomial function defined by:

$$\frac{1}{1+x^{-4}} + \frac{1}{1+y^{-4}}. \tag{2}$$

The function is sampled in the $[-5, 5]$ interval, with a step $s = 0.4$. For this regression problem we use the following production set:

$$<start> ::= <expr>$$

$$<expr> ::= <expr><op><expr>$$

$$| (<expr>)$$

$$| <pre\_op>(<expr>)$$

$$| <var>$$

$$<op> ::= + | - | * | /$$

$$<pre\_op> ::= \sin | \cos | \exp | \log$$

$$<var> ::= x | y$$

Even though it defines a smooth search space, the Pagie polynomial has the reputation for being difficult [9, 13].

4.2.4 Harmonic Curve Regression

The purpose is to approximate the series defined by:

$$\sum_i^x \frac{1}{i}, \tag{3}$$

where x is in the $[1, 50]$ interval, with a step $s = 1.0$. This problem is interesting as it complements the standard interpolation task with a generalisation step. In this second stage, the interval $x \in [51, 120]$ with $s = 1.0$ is considered. For the harmonic curve regression problem we use the following production set:

$$<\text{start}> ::= <\text{expr}>$$

$$<\text{expr}> ::= <\text{expr}><\text{op}><\text{expr}>$$

$$| (<\text{expr}>)$$

$$| <\text{pre\_op}>(<\text{expr}>)$$

$$| <\text{var}>$$

$$<\text{op}> ::= + | *$$

$$<\text{pre\_op}> ::= + | * | \text{inv} | \text{sqrt}$$

$$<\text{var}> ::= x$$

4.2.5 5-Bit Parity

The aim of this problem is to evolve a Boolean function that takes a binary string of length 5 as input and returns a value that indicates whether the number of 1s in the string is even (0) or odd (1). The production set for this problem is:

$$<\text{start}> ::= <\text{B}>$$

$$<\text{B}> ::= <\text{B}> \text{ and } <\text{B}>$$

$$| <\text{B}> \text{ or } <\text{B}>$$

$$| \text{not}(<\text{B}> \text{ and } <\text{B}>)$$

$$| \text{not}(<\text{B}> \text{ or } <\text{B}>)$$

$$| <\text{var}>$$

$$<\text{var}> ::= b_0 | b_1 | b_2 | b_3 | b_4$$

where b_0, b_1, b_2, b_3, b_4 are the input bits.

4.2.6 11-Bit Boolean Multiplexer

The task of the 11-bit Boolean multiplexer is to decode a 3-bit address and return the value of the corresponding data register (d0, d1, d2, d3, d4, d5, d6, d7). The Boolean 11-multiplexer is a function of 11 arguments: three, s_0 to s_2 which correspond to the addresses and eight data registers, i_0 to i_7. The production set for this problem is defined as:

$$<start> ::= <B>$$
$$<B> ::= <B> \text{ and } <B>$$
$$| <B> \text{ or } <B>$$
$$| \text{not}(<B>)$$
$$| \text{not}(<B>\text{or}<B>)$$
$$| (<B>) \text{ if } (<B>) \text{ else } (<B>)$$
$$| <var>$$
$$<var> ::= s_0 | s_1 | s_2 | i_0 | i_1 | i_2 | i_3 | i_4 | i_5 | i_6 | i_7$$

4.2.7 Santa Fe Ant Trail

The goal of the Santa Fe Ant Trail problem is to evolve a set of instructions for an artificial agent so that it can collect a certain number of food pellets in a limited number of steps (650). The trail consists of 89 food pellets distributed in a 32×32 toroidal grid. The agent starts in the top-left corner of the grid facing east, and it can turn left, right, move one square forward, and check if the square ahead contains food. The production set for this problem is:

$$<start> ::= <code>$$
$$<code> ::= <line>$$
$$| <code>$$
$$<line>$$
$$<line> ::= \text{if ant.sense\_food():}$$
$$<line>$$
$$\text{else:}$$
$$<line>$$
$$| <op>$$
$$<op> ::= \text{ant.turn\_left()}$$
$$| \text{ant.turn\_right()}$$
$$| \text{ant.move\_forward()}$$

Like the Quartic Polynomial problem, it was included for historical reasons, in spite of the debate surrounding its utility as a GP benchmark.

4.3 Experimental Results

The experimental results described below are reported in terms of the mean best fitness value obtained at each generation, over the 30 independent runs.

The results for the Boston housing problem are shown in Fig. 5. Looking at the training results (left panel) it is possible to see that in the first 8 generations the performance of the two approaches is very similar. In the next two generations the SGE version seems to discover solutions that have a smaller error. However, at generation 12, the quality of the solutions found by DSGE surpasses the quality of the ones found by SGE. From this point onwards it seems that the former method has an advantage, resulting in solutions with a smaller error. This behaviour is observable until the end of the evolutionary search. The test results (right panel) exhibit a similar behaviour. Although for the first 7 generations DSGE generates worse quality solutions, its error rapidly decreases, and after about 12 generations is already smaller than the error showed by SGE. Regarding the statistical differences, the tests show no evidence of significant differences between the approaches on both the train and test phases.

Figure 6 shows the results of the harmonic curve regression problem; similarly to the previous problem the experimentation is divided into two stages: train and test. Regarding the train phase (left panel) the figure reveals that both SGE variants gradually discover better approximations as evolution progresses. However, DSGE seems to exhibit an increased effectiveness, since it discovers solutions with a lower error, in less time. In the test results (right panel), approximately from generation 10, the performance of DSGE starts decreasing (higher fitness values), indicating that it may be overfitting. Nonetheless, the test results reported by DSGE are slightly superior to the SGE ones (not statistically).

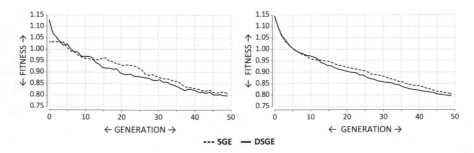

Fig. 5 Evolutionary results for the Boston Housing Problem. The panel on the left shows the results for training, and the panel on the right corresponds to the test results

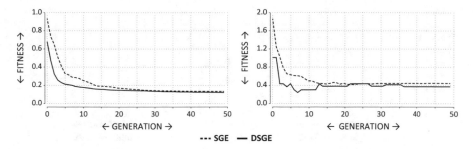

Fig. 6 Evolutionary results for the Harmonic Curve Regression. The panel on the left shows the results for training, and the panel on the right corresponds to the test results

Concerning the quartic problem, the results are depicted in Fig. 7a. It is possible to see that in both approaches the error gradually decreases over time, being almost 0 by the end of the evolutionary process. For this problem it is possible to see that there are no clear differences between DSGE and SGE. This apparent result is confirmed by the statistical analysis, which shows that there are no meaningful differences between the approaches. Looking at the Pagie polynomial, the optimization results follow a trend similar to the one identified in the previous problem (Fig. 7b). The individuals of the initial population of SGE and DSGE have comparable fitness, with the DSGE one being slightly worse. Then, as optimisation advances, DSGE gradually and consistently obtains low error solutions without stagnating. On the contrary, the vanilla version of SGE has a slower gradient, which prevents it from reaching better solutions within the allocated evolutionary time. Looking at the quality obtained by the two variants in the end of the evolutionary run, there is a noticeable difference between the methods, with DSGE obtaining solutions with considerable lower error. We applied a statistical test to look for meaningful differences, and the results showed that there are statistical significant differences between the approaches.

For the 5-bit even parity problem the results are shown in Fig. 7c. In this problem it is possible to see that having a less tightened algorithm such as DSGE is advantageous. Although in the first 8 generations SGE finds solutions with a smaller error, DSGE rapidly catches up with it, surpassing the quality of the solutions being found by the former method. This trend is visible throughout the entire evolutionary process. Statistical tests do not reveal any differences between the methods for this particular problem.

The 11-bit Boolean multiplexer results are shown in Fig. 7d. The plot shows that for this problem the DSGE clearly outperforms the vanilla version of SGE. Together with the 5-bit problem, the results seem to indicate that for Boolean problems with grammars similar to the ones described above it is advantageous to use the dynamic version of SGE. The statistical tests show that for the multiplexer problem there are meaningful differences between the two approaches, and that the effect size of the differences is large ($r > 0.5$).

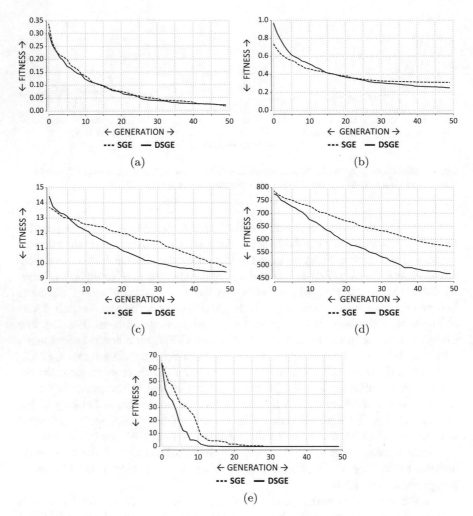

Fig. 7 Evolutionary results for the (**a**) quartic regression, (**b**) pagie polynomial regression, (**c**) 5-bit parity, (**d**) 11-bit Boolean multiplexer and (**e**) Santa Fe Ant Trail

Finally, Fig. 7e shows the results for the Santa Fe Ant problem. The figure shows that for this problem, at the end of the evolutionary search, there are no differences between the two methods. However it is possible to see that the DSGE is more efficient since it needs less generations to reach a optimal solution for the problem. The statistical tests corroborated the fact that there are no significant differences between the two methods.

5 NeuroEvolution

In addition to testing DSGE with the above classical problems we also investigate its capacity of automatically searching for the topology and weights of Artificial Neural Networks (ANNs) (also known as NeuroEvolution). This problem is deemed as a more complex task, since we have to simultaneously search for both the structure of the model, i.e., the network topology, and its real parameterisation, i.e., the synaptic weights. Our goal is to show that for this type of problems DSGE is a good alternative, able to find effective neural network architectures.

5.1 Experimental Setup

The experiments described in this section follow a setup similar to the one described in Table 3, where only the population size, number of generations and maximum depth parameters differ. We use a population size of 100 individuals, which are evolved throughout 500 generations, totalling 50,000 evaluations per evolutionary run.

The grammar used for the conducted experiments is detailed in Fig. 8. The grammar is capable of representing one-hidden-layered networks with a single output neuron. The sequence of hidden-nodes is encoded in the <sigexpr> non-terminal symbol. Each hidden-node is the result of an activation function (in this case the sigmoid function) that receives as input the connections to input nodes and a bias value. The output of the activation function is then multiplied by a weight that encodes the synaptic weight between that specific neuron and the output neuron.

Fig. 8 Grammar used for the NeuroEvolution experiments

$$
\begin{aligned}
<\text{sigexpr}> &::= <\text{node}> \\
&\quad | <\text{node}> + <\text{sigexpr}> \\
<\text{node}> &::= \text{sig}(<\text{sum}> + <\text{bias}>) * <\text{weight}> \\
<\text{sum}> &::= <\text{weight}> * <\text{features}> \\
&\quad | <\text{sum}> + <\text{sum}> \\
<\text{features}> &::= x_1 \\
&\quad | \ldots \\
&\quad | x_n \\
<\text{weight}> &::= <\text{number}> \\
<\text{bias}> &::= <\text{number}> \\
<\text{number}> &::= <\text{digit}>.<\text{digit}><\text{digit}> \\
&\quad | - <\text{digit}>.<\text{digit}><\text{digit}> \\
<\text{digit}> &::= 0 | 1 | 2 | 3 | 4 \\
&\quad | 5 | 6 | 7 | 8 | 9
\end{aligned}
$$

While in the previous experiments we defined a maximum depth that was counted from the root node, in the following experiments we consider the depth at the sub-tree level, and define maximum depths for each non-terminal symbol. This way, we are able to set the upper bounds on the number of nodes and connections. For the following experiment we define for the <sigexpr> and <sum> non-terminal symbols a maximum depth of 6 and 3, respectively.

To evolve effective ANNs, apart from defining a grammar to encode the topology and weights of the ANNs, we also need to choose a fitness function suitable to measure the performance of the candidate solutions. For the tasks described in this section we use the exponential Root Mean Squared Error (RMSE) per class, which is defined as:

$$\prod_{c=1}^{m} exp\left(\sqrt{\frac{\sum_{i=1}^{n_c}(o_i - t_i)^2}{n_c}}\right),$$

where m is the number of classes of the problem, n_c is the number of instances of the problem that belong to class c, o_i is the confidence value predicted by the evolved network, and t_i is the target value. This way, on the one hand we are able to deal with unbalanced datasets because the error is computed at a class level; on the other hand we avoid overfitting by penalising more higher errors than lower ones.

5.2   Benchmark Description

We selected four classification problems, all of them binary because of the constraints imposed by the used grammar-based approaches, that do not allow the reuse of previously created neurons (further discussed in [1]). The problems have an increasing number of features, and thus increasing complexity in terms of the classification task to be solved. The following paragraphs present a brief description of each of the used benchmarks.

Flame [7]   Gathers 240 instances, each with two attributes, and the goal is to separate between two different classes: one containing 87 instances and the other with 153 instances. Typically used for clustering purposes.

Wisconsin Breast Cancer Detection (WDBC) [11, 21]   Comprises 30 features that are extracted from digitalised images of breast masses. The dataset has 569 instances, where 212 are malign and 357 are benign.

Ionosphere [11, 20]   Collects ionosphere radar returns, that are to be separated into good (if the returns evidences of structure, 300 instances) and bad (other-wise, 126 instances). For each instance 34 properties are given.

Sonar [8, 11]   Contains 60 features of sonar signals that allow a classification model to separate between signals that are bounced off a metal cylinder (111 instances) or a rock cylinder (97 instances).

5.3   Experimental Results

Figure 9 shows the evolution of the fitness of the best individuals across generations for SGE and DSGE for the flame, WDBC, ionosphere and sonar datasets. Results are averages of 30 independent runs. Despite the similar results during the initial generations, it is perceptible that in the long term DSGE outperforms SGE on all tested problems, indicating that the new representation, where no mutation is silent, promotes locality and the efficient exploration of the search space.

Apart from analysing the fitness evolution we have also recorded several other metrics related with the performance of the generated networks, namely: RMSE, Area Under the ROC Curve (AUROC) and f-measure. These metrics are recorded for both the train and test sets; recall that only the train set is used for the evolutionary process. Table 4 reports the results that are obtained with SGE and DSGE. Results are averages of the best network (in terms of fitness) of each of the 30 evolutionary runs; each cell is formatted as: mean $\pm$ standard deviation. Moreover we also report the number of neurons and number of used features, which allow us to better understand the structure and complexity of the evolved networks.

A perusal analysis of the results confirms that DSGE outperforms SGE on all tested benchmarks, and on all recorded performance metrics, i.e., RMSE DSGE values are inferior to those reported by SGE, and accuracy, AUROC and f-measure are superior on the experiments conducted using DSGE. In addition, the standard deviation values are lower when using DSGE, which indicates that it consistently discovers effective solutions.

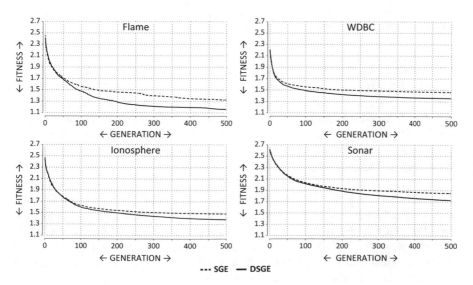

Fig. 9   Fitness evolution of the best individuals across generations for the flame, WDBC, ionosphere and sonar datasets

Table 4 Evolution of one-hidden-layered ANNs

			Flame	WDBC	Ionosphere	Sonar
Fitness		SGE	1.32 ± 0.25	1.46 ± 0.08	1.48 ± 0.18	1.85 ± 0.18
		DSGE	$1.16 \pm 0.13^{+++}$	$1.36 \pm 0.06^{+++}$	$1.38 \pm 0.13^{+++}$	$1.73 \pm 0.12^{+++}$
Train	RMSE	SGE	0.16 ± 0.13	0.19 ± 0.03	0.21 ± 0.07	0.34 ± 0.06
		DSGE	$0.08 \pm 0.06^{+++}$	$0.15 \pm 0.03^{+++}$	$0.17 \pm 0.05^{++}$	$0.30 \pm 0.05^{++}$
	Accuracy	SGE	0.96 ± 0.08	0.95 ± 0.02	0.93 ± 0.11	0.84 ± 0.12
		DSGE	$0.99 \pm 0.03^{+++}$	$0.97 \pm 0.01^{+++}$	$0.97 \pm 0.03^{+++}$	$0.90 \pm 0.04^{++}$
	AUROC	SGE	0.98 ± 0.04	0.99 ± 0.01	0.94 ± 0.04	0.91 ± 0.04
		DSGE	$0.99 \pm 0.01^{+++}$	$0.99 \pm 0.00^{+++}$	$0.96 \pm 0.03^{+++}$	$0.93 \pm 0.04^{\sim}$
	F-measure	SGE	0.96 ± 0.08	0.93 ± 0.03	0.93 ± 0.18	0.78 ± 0.23
		DSGE	$0.99 \pm 0.02^{+++}$	$0.96 \pm 0.02^{+++}$	$0.98 \pm 0.02^{+++}$	$0.88 \pm 0.05^{++}$
Test	RMSE	SGE	0.22 ± 0.13	0.23 ± 0.04	0.32 ± 0.05	0.44 ± 0.04
		DSGE	$0.14 \pm 0.08^{++}$	$0.20 \pm 0.03^{++}$	$0.28 \pm 0.04^{+++}$	$0.43 \pm 0.04^{\sim}$
	Accuracy	SGE	0.93 ± 0.09	0.93 ± 0.02	0.87 ± 0.10	0.73 ± 0.09
		DSGE	$0.97 \pm 0.05^{+++}$	$0.95 \pm 0.02^{+++}$	$0.90 \pm 0.03^{++}$	$0.76 \pm 0.05^{\sim}$
	AUROC	SGE	0.96 ± 0.08	0.98 ± 0.02	0.90 ± 0.05	0.82 ± 0.05
		DSGE	$0.99 \pm 0.03^{++}$	$0.98 \pm 0.01^{++}$	$0.93 \pm 0.04^{++}$	$0.83 \pm 0.04^{\sim}$
	F-measure	SGE	0.94 ± 0.09	0.91 ± 0.03	0.89 ± 0.17	0.64 ± 0.20
		DSGE	$0.98 \pm 0.04^{+++}$	$0.93 \pm 0.03^{+++}$	$0.93 \pm 0.02^{++}$	$0.72 \pm 0.06^{\sim}$
Num. neurons		SGE	4.87 ± 1.83	3.73 ± 1.53	3.53 ± 1.36	3.07 ± 1.39
		DSGE	6.47 ± 1.20	6.23 ± 1.58	5.97 ± 1.78	6.13 ± 1.69
Num. features		SGE	2.00 ± 0.00	12.0 ± 6.51	12.1 ± 5.79	13.3 ± 6.42
		DSGE	2.00 ± 0.00	14.5 ± 3.52	13.3 ± 4.74	17.6 ± 4.66

Comparison between DSGE and other grammar-based approaches. Results are averages of 30 independent runs. $+$ and $\sim$ represent the result of statistical tests (see text)

To analyse the tendency of evolution to overfit we measure the difference between the train and test performances, which for SGE are, on average, 0.08, 0.06, 0.04 and 0.06, for the RMSE, accuracy, AUROC and f-measure, respectively. For DSGE the differences are, on average, 0.09, 0.06, 0.04 and 0.06, for the same metrics. However the difference in the accuracy in slightly superior when using DSGE, it is our understanding that this is a result of the DSGE greater performance, rather than an indicator of overfitting.

To verify if the differences between DSGE and SGE are significant we perform a statistical analysis. First, we use the Kolmogorov-Smirnov and Shapiro-Wilk tests, with a significance level of $\alpha = 0.05$, where it is possible to acknowledge that the data does not follow any distribution, and as such, the Mann-Whitney U test (non-parametric), with $\alpha = 0.05$ is used to perform the pairwise comparison. The results of the statistical tests are reported in Table 4 using a graphical overview, where: $\sim$ indicates no statistical difference between the compared methods and $+$ signals that DSGE is statistically superior to SGE. The effect size is denoted by the number of

+ signals, where +, ++ and + + + correspond respectively to low ($0.1 \leq r < 0.3$), medium ($0.3 \leq r < 0.5$) and large ($r \geq 0.5$) effect sizes.

For those searching a comparison between SGE and GE on the same benchmarks, and using the same grammar, refer to [2]. It has already been demonstrated that evolving both the structure and weights of ANNs using SGE was the path to follow, in the sense that the found weights directly impact the learning of the network. Moreover, it was demonstrated that SGE was able to discover better results than GE. Consequently, as DSGE performs better than SGE we indirectly conclude that DSGE performs better than GE for these specific class of problems.

6 Conclusions

Since the early days of GP that researchers have been using grammars to specify restrictions on problem domains and guide the evolutionary process. Amongst the most successful proposals is GE, which is used by practitioners from different backgrounds, due to its simplicity and for being a plug-and-play approach. Consequently, to deal with the evolution of solutions for different problem domains, only the grammar needs to be changed. Nevertheless, GE has been target of some criticisms concerning the way in which it searches the space of solutions. Amidst these criticisms, the most infamous are concerned with the high levels of redundancy and the low locality of the representation, which arguably make it less effective [23].

SGE is a new GE variant, with its most distinctive feature being the one-to-one correspondence between genes and non-terminals of the used grammar. In spite of the good results obtained by SGE, it was perceptible that it still had some drawbacks, namely the fact that we needed to pre-process the grammar in order to remove any recursive rules. This was done by adding intermediate symbols that resemble the recursive expansions of the grammar.

In this work we introduce a new version of SGE called DSGE, which removes the need to pre-process the grammar. In concrete we define the maximum depth that each expression tree can have, and we stop the trees from growing beyond that limit (as in traditional tree-based GP). We presented the procedures needed to create and map solutions from the genotype to the phenotype, and conducted a wide and systematic set of experiments to assess the effectiveness of the new approach. We selected classical benchmark problems from the literature, and a more challenging set of problems from the NeuroEvolution area.

The results show that the performance of the new method, DSGE, is never inferior to the vanilla version of SGE, being superior in a vast set of the used benchmarks, obtaining solutions with a better quality.

Acknowledgements This research is partially funded by: Fundação para a Ciência e Tecnologia (FCT), Portugal, under the grant SFRH/BD/114865/2016. We gratefully acknowledge the support of NVIDIA Corporation for the donation of a Titan X GPU. We would also like to thank Tiago Martins for all the patience making the charts herein presented.

References

1. F. Assunção, N. Lourenço, P. Machado, B. Ribeiro, Towards the evolution of multi-layered neural networks: a dynamic structured grammatical evolution approach, in *Proceedings of the Genetic and Evolutionary Computation Conference, GECCO '17* (ACM, New York, 2017), pp. 393–400. https://doi.org/10.1145/3071178.3071286
2. F. Assunção, N. Lourenço, P. Machado, B. Ribeiro, Automatic generation of neural networks with structured grammatical evolution, in *2017 IEEE Congress on Evolutionary Computation (CEC)* (2017), pp. 1557–1564. https://doi.org/10.1109/CEC.2017.7969488
3. J. Byrne, M. O'Neill, A. Brabazon, Structural and nodal mutation in grammatical evolution, in *Proceedings of the 11th Annual Conference on Genetic and Evolutionary Computation*, New York, 2009, pp. 1881–1882
4. J. Byrne, M. O'Neill, J. McDermott, A. Brabazon, An analysis of the behaviour of mutation in grammatical evolution, in *Genetic Programming*. Lecture Notes in Computer Science, vol. 6021 (Springer, Berlin, 2010), pp. 14–25
5. A. Field, *Discovering Statistics Using IBM SPSS Statistics* (Sage, Los Angeles, 2013)
6. R. Franz, *Representations for Genetic and Evolutionary Algorithms* (Springer, Berlin, 2006)
7. L. Fu, E. Medico, FLAME, a novel fuzzy clustering method for the analysis of DNA microarray data. BMC Bioinf. **8**(1), 1 (2007)
8. R.P. Gorman, T.J. Sejnowski, Analysis of hidden units in a layered network trained to classify sonar targets. Neural Netw. **1**(1), 75–89 (1988)
9. R. Harper, Spatial co-evolution: quicker, fitter and less bloated, in *Proceedings of the 14th Annual Conference on Genetic and Evolutionary Computation* (ACM, New York, 2012), pp. 759–766
10. J.R. Koza, *Genetic Programming: On the Programming of Computers by Means of Natural Selection*, vol. 1 (MIT Press, Cambridge, 1992)
11. M. Lichman, UCI machine learning repository (2013). http://archive.ics.uci.edu/ml
12. N. Lourenço, F.B. Pereira, E. Costa, Unveiling the properties of structured grammatical evolution. Genet. Program. Evolvable Mach. **17**(3), 251–289 (2016)
13. J. McDermott, D.R. White, S. Luke, L. Manzoni, M. Castelli, L. Vanneschi, W. Jaskowski, K. Krawiec, R. Harper, K. De Jong, U.M. O'Reilly, Genetic programming needs better benchmarks, in *Proceedings of the 14th Annual Conference on Genetic and Evolutionary Computation* (ACM, New York, 2012), pp. 791–798
14. R.I. Mckay, N.X. Hoai, P.A. Whigham, Y. Shan, M. O'Neill, Grammar-based genetic programming: a survey. Genet. Program. Evolvable Mach. **11**(3–4), 365–396 (2010)
15. M. O'Neill, C. Ryan, Grammatical evolution. IEEE Trans. Evol. Comput. **5**(4), 349–358 (2001)
16. M. O'Neill, C. Ryan, *Grammatical Evolution: Evolutionary Automatic Programming in a Arbitrary Language*. Genetic Programming, vol. 4 (Kluwer Academic, Boston, 2003)
17. F. Rothlauf, On the locality of representations, in *Genetic and Evolutionary Computation Conference*. Lecture Notes in Computer Science (2003), pp. 1608–1609
18. F. Rothlauf, M. Oetzel, On the locality of grammatical evolution, in *European Conference on Genetic Programming* (Springer, Berlin, 2006), pp. 320–330
19. C. Ryan, J. Collins, M.O. Neill, Grammatical evolution: evolving programs for an arbitrary language, in *European Conference on Genetic Programming* (Springer, Berlin, 1998), pp. 83–96

20. V.G. Sigillito, S.P. Wing, L.V. Hutton, K.B. Baker, Classification of radar returns from the ionosphere using neural networks. Johns Hopkins APL Tech. Dig. **10**(3), 262–266 (1989)
21. W.N. Street, W.H. Wolberg, O.L. Mangasarian, Nuclear feature extraction for breast tumor diagnosis, in *IS&T/SPIE's Symposium on Electronic Imaging: Science and Technology* (International Society for Optics and Photonics, Bellingham, 1993), pp. 861–870
22. P.A. Whigham, et al.: Grammatically-based genetic programming, in *Proceedings of the Workshop on Genetic Programming: From Theory to Real-World Applications*, vol. 16 (1995), pp. 33–41
23. P.A. Whigham, G. Dick, J. Maclaurin, C.A. Owen, Examining the best of both worlds of grammatical evolution, in *Proceedings of the 2015 Annual Conference on Genetic and Evolutionary Computation* (ACM, New York, 2015), pp. 1111–1118

Geometric Semantic Grammatical Evolution

Alberto Moraglio, James McDermott, and Michael O'Neill

Abstract Geometric Semantic Genetic Programming (GSGP) is a novel form of
Genetic Programming (GP), based on a geometric theory of evolutionary algorithms, which directly searches the semantic space of programs. In this chapter, we
extend this framework to Grammatical Evolution (GE) and refer to the new method
as Geometric Semantic Grammatical Evolution (GSGE). We formally derive new
mutation and crossover operators for GE which are guaranteed to see a simple
unimodal fitness landscape. This surprising result shows that the GE genotype-
phenotype mapping does not necessarily imply low genotype-fitness locality. To
complement the theory, we present extensive experimental results on three standard
domains (Boolean, Arithmetic and Classifier).

1 Introduction

Geometric Semantic Genetic Programming (GSGP) is a novel form of Genetic
Programming (GP), introduced by Moraglio et al. [1]. In GSGP, search operators
act on the syntax of the programs but can be understood as acting directly on the
underlying semantics of programs: mutation and crossover produce offspring which
are, respectively, semantically close to and semantically intermediate between
their parents. Specific GSGP operators for Boolean, Regression and Classification
domains have been derived [1] and have a simple form. This is possible because
the mapping from genotypes to semantics in these GP domains is simple, not
complex as was widely believed before GSGP. Furthermore, the fitness landscape
seen by GSGP is *always* a simple unimodal landscape, and its search performance
is provably good on large classes of problems [2–4].

A. Moraglio (✉)
University of Exeter, Exeter, UK
e-mail: A.Moraglio@exeter.ac.uk

J. McDermott · M. O'Neill
University College Dublin, Dublin, Ireland
e-mail: james.mcdermott2@ucd.ie; m.oneill@ucd.ie

© Springer International Publishing AG, part of Springer Nature 2018   163
C. Ryan et al. (eds.), *Handbook of Grammatical Evolution*,
https://doi.org/10.1007/978-3-319-78717-6_7

GE [5] is a successful form of GP that represents programs indirectly as integer lists. Phenotypes are obtained by using the integers of the genotype to select among alternatives in the grammatical rules. One benefit of this indirect encoding is that it simplifies the application of search to different programming languages and constrained structures. A common criticism of GE is that because of the rather complex developmental genotype-phenotype mapping, search operators can be disruptive to both syntax and semantics, e.g. low locality of the genotype-phenotype mapping [6].

The purpose of the current chapter is to extend the ideas of GSGP to GE, giving Geometric Semantic Grammatical Evolution (GSGE). The remainder of the chapter is organised as follows. In Sect. 2, GSGP itself is reviewed. In Sect. 3, we describe theoretical requirements for translating GSGP concepts to GE, and in Sect. 4 we use these to derive new geometric semantic search operators for GE, and prove their properties for three domains (Boolean, Arithmetic, and Classifier). We give also a general recipe to derive GSGE operators from GSGP operators for any domain. In Sect. 5, we present an efficient implementation of GSGE (the size of the solutions grows only linearly even when using crossover). In Sect. 6, we present extensive experimental results and analysis. In Sect. 7, we provide a discussion, and in Sect. 8 a summary of the chapter.

2   Geometric Semantic Genetic Programming

Traditional genetic programming ignores the *meaning* of programs, as the search operators it employs act on their syntactic representations, regardless of their semantics. E.g., subtree swap crossover is used to recombine functions represented as parse trees, regardless of whether trees represent Boolean expressions, arithmetical functions, or classifier programs. While this guarantees the production of syntactically well-formed expressions, why should such a *blind* syntactic search work well for different problems and across domains? In the end, it is the meaning of programs that determines how successful search is at solving the problem.

The semantics of a program can be formally defined in a number of ways. It can be a canonical representation, so that any two programs with the same semantics or behaviour have the same canonical representation (e.g., Binary Decision Diagrams for Boolean expressions). It can instead be a description of program behaviour in a logical formalism, as used in formal methods. In the context of black-box search, it may be argued that the semantics of a program is just its fitness. Finally, semantics can be defined as the mathematical function computed by a program, i.e., the set of all possible input-output pairs making up the computed function. In practice, in GP, it is calculated over a restricted set of input-output pairs, and this is the definition we use in this paper.

In the literature, there are a number of works using the semantics of programs to improve GP. As many GP individuals may encode the same function, some researchers use canonical representations of functions to enforce semantic diversity by discarding individuals of duplicate semantics, in initialization [7, 8], crossover, and mutation [9, 10]. Nguyen et al. [11] measure semantic distance between individuals as distance between their outputs for the same set of inputs. This distance is used to semantically bias the search operators: mutation rejects offspring that are not sufficiently semantically similar to the parent, and crossover swaps only semantically similar subtrees between parents. Krawiec et al. [12, 13] have also used semantic distance to propose a crossover for GP trees that is approximately geometric [14, 15] in the semantic space. Interestingly, the fitness landscape induced by this operator has perfect fitness-distance correlation. The operator was implemented approximately by using a traditional crossover, generating a large number of offspring, and accepting only offspring semantically intermediate to their parents.

While the semantically aware methods above produce overall superior performance to traditional methods, they are *indirect*: search operators are implemented by acting on the syntax of the parents to produce offspring, which are accepted only if some semantic criterion is satisfied. This has two drawbacks: (1) these implementations are very wasteful, as they are heavily reliant on trial and error; (2) they do not provide insights on how syntactic and semantic searches relate to each other. Would it then be possible to *directly* search the semantic space of programs? More precisely, would it be possible to build search operators that, acting on the syntax of the parent programs, produce offspring that are *guaranteed* by construction to respect some semantic criterion or specification? Krawiec et al. [12, 13] argued that due to the complexity of the genotype-phenotype mapping in GP, a direct implementation of exact semantic operators is probably impossible.

However, GSGP [1] shows that the genotype-phenotype (syntax to semantics) map of commonly considered GP domains is, in an important sense, easy — not complex. GSGP gives *exact* geometric semantic crossovers and mutations for different problem domains (Boolean, Arithmetic, Classifier). By construction these search operators see a simple unimodal fitness landscape for any problem in these domains [1].

2.1 Geometric Semantic Operators

A search operator $CX : S \times S \rightarrow S$ for a search space S is a *geometric crossover* [14, 15] w.r.t. the metric d if for any choice of parents $T1, T2 \in S$, each offspring $T3 = CX(T1, T2)$ is in the d-metric segment between parents, that is $d(T1, T3) + d(T3, T2) = d(T1, T2)$. A search operator $M : S \rightarrow S$ is a *geometric ϵ-mutation* w.r.t. the metric d if for any choice of the parent $T1$, each offspring $T2 = M(T1)$ is in the d-metric ball of radius ϵ centered in the parent, that is $d(T1, T2) \leq \epsilon$. Suppose (as is typical) that the fitness function can be written as a distance $F(T) = d(O(T), t)$ between the output vector $O(T)$ of the program $T \in S$ on a fixed vector of inputs, and a target output vector t on the same inputs. Then the *semantic distance* SD between two programs $T1, T2 \in S$ is defined as the distance between their corresponding output vectors $O(T1)$, $O(T2)$, measured with the metric d. That is, $SD(T1, T2) = d(O(T1), O(T2))$. *Geometric semantic operators* are operators on the space of functions which are geometric with respect to metric SD. E.g., geometric semantic crossover on Boolean functions returns offspring Boolean functions such that the output vectors of the offspring are in the Hamming segment between the output vectors of the parents.

This is however only an abstract specification of geometric semantic search operators. We require an algorithmic characterization. Note that there is a different type of geometric semantic crossover for each choice of space S and distance d. Consequently, there are different semantic crossovers for different GP domains. In the following, we provide algorithmic definitions of geometric semantic operators for Boolean, Arithmetic and Classification domains. A formal treatment and explicit derivations have been previously given [1].

Boolean Crossover Given two parent Boolean functions $T1, T2$, the geometric semantic crossover is the recombination that returns the offspring Boolean function $T3 = (T1 \wedge TR) \vee (\overline{TR} \wedge T2)$ where TR is a randomly generated Boolean function (see Fig. 1). TR is effectively a crossover mask, choosing a point in the semantic space intermediate to T1 and T2.

Boolean Mutation Given a parent function T, the mutation returns the offspring $TM = T \vee M$ with probability 0.5 and $TM = T \wedge \overline{M}$ with probability 0.5 where M is a random *minterm* of all input variables. (A minterm is a term consisting of the product of all variables, each either negated or non-negated.)

Arithmetic Crossover Given two parent functions $T1, T2$, the geometric semantic crossover is the recombination that returns the real function $T3 = (T1 \cdot TR) + ((1 - TR) \cdot T2)$ where TR is a random real constant in $[0, 1]$.

Arithmetic Mutation Given a parent function T, the mutation with mutation step ms returns the real function $TM = T + ms \cdot (TR1 - TR2)$ where $TR1$ and $TR2$ are random real functions.

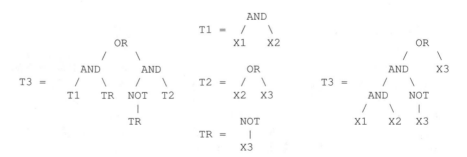

Fig. 1 Left: Semantic Crossover scheme for Boolean Functions; Centre: Example of parents (T1 and T2) and random mask (TR); Right: Offspring (T3) obtained by substituting T1, T2 and TR in the crossover scheme and simplifying

Classifier Crossover Given two parent classifiers T1, T2, with symbols as inputs (IS) and outputs (OS), the geometric semantic crossover is the recombination that returns the offspring classifier T3 = IF CONDR THEN T1 ELSE T2 where CONDR is a random condition (e.g. of the form $X_i == s$ where $s \in IS$).

Classifier Mutation Given a parent classifier T, the mutation returns the offspring classifier TM = IF CONDR THEN OUTR ELSE T where CONDR is a condition which is true only for a single random setting of all input parameters, and OUTR is a random output symbol. The offspring can be expressed as nested IF-THEN-ELSE statements with simple conditions of a single input parameter each.

3 Foundations for Geometric Semantic Operators for GE

In this section, we first introduce the concept of *compositional semantics*, then we show that the GE mapping is compositional, and finally equipped with this we provide a formal recipe to derive geometric semantic operators for the GE encoding.

3.1 Compositional Semantics

In both linguistics—the study of natural languages—and theory of programming languages, *compositional semantics* refers to a relation between syntax of the sentences in a language and their semantics. The principle of compositional semantics states that the meaning (semantics) of a sentence (syntax) can be derived by combining the meanings of its sub-sentences. For example, the meaning of the sentence S = A and B is $[S]$ = [A and B] = [and]([A], [B]), where [] is a function that maps a syntactic element to its meaning. This is a natural relation that holds for most languages, natural or artificial.

The relation between syntax and semantics in GSGP is compositional. Syntactically, geometric semantic crossovers plug parent trees T1 and T2 into a recombination tree XT to obtain an offspring tree T3. We are allowed to write this operation as T3 = XT(T1, T2) and interpret it as a functional composition because the syntactic operation of plugging the structures T1 and T2 in the structure XT is mirrored by the semantic operation of function composition of the function XT on the functions $T1$ and $T2$ producing the function $T3$, i.e., $[T3] =$ [XT(T1, T2)] = [XT]([T1], [T2]). That is, geometric semantic crossovers are compositional. In contrast, traditional subtree swap crossover is not compositional. Formally this crossover could be similarly written as T3 = XO(T1, T2) denoting that the offspring structure T3 can be obtained by some syntactic operation XO on the structures T1 and T2. However, this time the semantics of T3 cannot be written as [T3] = [XO]([T1], [T2]) as the semantics of the operation XO (swapping two subtrees) is inherently linked to the syntactic representation of T1 and T2, and cannot be defined solely on their semantics.

An immediate consequence of the semantic compositionality of GSGP is that, as the semantics of the offspring depend solely on the semantics of their parents, and not on their syntactic representations, functions and geometric semantic operators acting on these can also be equivalently represented in a form or language other than trees, *if it respects semantic compositionality*.

We will show that the genotype-phenotype mapping in GE is compositional, i.e., by stringing together linear representations of parents, we get the corresponding linear representations of the offspring.

3.2   Compositionality of the GE Mapping

In Sect. 4, we will introduce simple GE search operators for several domains which are semantically geometric, i.e. perfectly well-behaved in terms of semantic effects. Given the non-trivial developmental encoding of GE, it is surprising that these operators are at all possible, especially in a simple form. In this section, we present a theory that explains rigorously how this is possible. The gist of the argument is as follows. We will observe that the GE developmental process mapping naturally preserves (compositional) modularity: phenotypic modules (derivation subtrees) correspond to genotypic modules (sublists). Together with a compositional interpretation of the geometric semantic operators, this implies the existence of a *genotypic* crossover/mutation scheme (on integer lists) equivalent to a *phenotypic* crossover/mutation scheme (on derivation trees), which is in turn equivalent to the GSGP crossover/mutation scheme (on GP trees): that is, an implementation of GSGP geometric semantic operators for GE. These considerations apply to the domains for which GSGP operators were derived by Moraglio et al. [1] (Boolean, Regression and Classification) and may extend to GSGP operators in other domains [16].

Let us now briefly review the GE genotype-phenotype mapping. Figure 2 illustrates the mapping. The genotype encoding a solution is the vector at the top. The corresponding derivation tree (not shown) is obtained through depth-first traversal of the grammar, using the genotype to select among multiple alternatives in the rules. The derivation tree is produced incrementally: at each step, the next gene (integer) in the genome is used to select the expansion for the left-most non-terminal node in the developing derivation tree. The value of each gene is taken modulo the number of available choices in the grammar for this non-terminal. When there are no non-terminal nodes left to expand, the derivation tree is complete. (In early versions of GE, a "wrapping" method was used, that is if the genotype has been exhausted and derivation is not finished, then indexing "wraps around" to the beginning of the genotype. Alternatively, it may be the case that derivation is completed before the genotype is exhausted. In this case, extra genes are simply ignored. The operators presented in the next section avoid these complications by

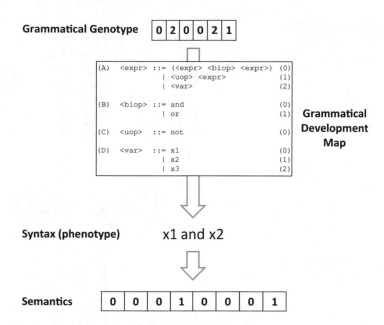

Fig. 2 Grammatical evolution genotype-phenotype mapping

design.) The phenotype (a string representing a program) is then extracted from the derivation tree by reading the derivation tree leaf nodes from left to right. Finally, the vector at the bottom of Fig. 2 is the semantics of the phenotype, that is the vector of the outputs of the program for all possible combinations of inputs (or for some subset, depending on the domain).

To show that the GE mapping is semantically compositional, we will look more closely at several derivation trees. Figures 3, 4 and 5 show the derivation trees and the genotypes (bottom) for the expressions x1 and x2, x2 or x3 and not x3 respectively, obtained using the grammar in Fig. 2. The number annotating each non-terminal node of the derivation tree identifies the grammatical production that was used to generate its child nodes out of the available applicable productions. For example, the number (0) annotating the root node (expr) of the derivation tree in Fig. 3 signifies that its child nodes (expr, biop and expr) were obtained by selecting production rule 0 in the grammar in Fig. 2, out of those whose LHS is expr. The choice of production rule 0 for the root node is dictated by the 0 as first entry of the genotype. The phenotype x1 and x2 is just the terminal nodes of the derivation tree, read from left to right.

Let us now make three observations that together will show the semantic compositionality of the GE mapping, and provide a formal recipe to derive search operators for the grammatical genotype equivalent to the geometric semantic operators.

Fig. 3 Derivation tree for the expression `x1 and x2`

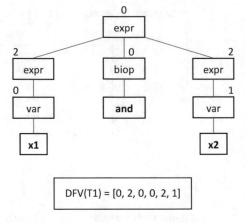

DFV(T1) = [0, 2, 0, 0, 2, 1]

Fig. 4 Derivation tree for the expression `x2 or x3`

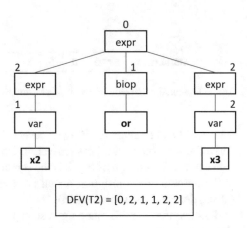

DFV(T2) = [0, 2, 1, 1, 2, 2]

Fig. 5 Derivation tree for the expression `not x3`. The quotation marks ("0") indicate that a codon is not strictly required, since only one production for the `uop` non-terminal exists; in some GE systems the codon is consumed regardless, and we follow this practice

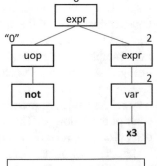

DFV(TR) = [1, "0", 2, 2]

Observation 1 The derivation tree is effectively the *parse tree* of the given expression w.r.t. the given grammar. The *parsing* of a sentence w.r.t. a given grammar is the inverse operation of generating (or deriving) a valid sentence of the grammar. This observation leads to an algorithmic recipe to *invert the GE genotype-to-phenotype mapping*, i.e., a mechanical way to compute the GE representation of any grammatically valid phenotypic expression: (1) using a standard parsing algorithm, parse the given phenotypic expression (sentence) w.r.t. the grammar; the obtained parse tree is the derivation tree of the phenotypic expression; (2) use the numbering of the production rules in the grammar to annotate each non-terminal node of the derivation tree with the choice of production rule consistent with its child nodes (similar to GE Sensible Initialisation "unmodding" [17]); (3) visit the derivation tree using depth-first traversal and collect the sequence of choices on the nodes. The resulting sequence is a genotype (one among many) of the given expression. For example, looking again at Fig. 3 but from the bottom to the top this time, given the phenotypic expression x1 and x2 and the grammar in Fig. 2, a standard parsing algorithm can be used to obtain its (unannotated) parse tree, which is the same as the derivation tree. This can then be annotated by looking at the numbering of the grammatical productions in Fig. 2, obtaining the same annotations. Then the genotype can be obtained by traversing depth-first the annotated tree obtaining the sequence $[0, 2, 0, 0, 2, 1]$, which is the same as the original genotype.

Observation 2 The use of depth-first expansion of the parse tree makes the genotype-to-phenotype mapping *modular* in the following sense. As noted in the previous point, we can obtain the genotype associated with a parse tree by traversing depth-first the annotated tree (T) and collecting the numbers in sequential order obtaining the sequence S, i.e., $S = DFV(T)$. If we 'hide' any subtree of the derivation tree by replacing the subtree with a node X encapsulating the subtree and compute the genotype by depth-first traversal, we obtain that $DFV(T) = S1, DFV(X), S2$, which means that the depth-first visit of T is a sequence of the form: uninterrupted sequence $S1$, followed by the (unknown) uninterrupted sequence obtained by depth-first visit of the hidden tree X, followed by a second uninterrupted sequence $S2$. This holds for depth-first traversal because of its prioritisation of visit of the nodes in a tree, which has the property that when the traversal enters a subtree, it will then visit all its nodes before leaving it, and then it will not return to it anymore. This property does not hold for other tree traversal strategies. For example, it does not hold for breadth-first traversal of the tree. This is because breadth-first traversal could enter and leave any given subtree several times (more precisely, a number of times equal to the depth of the subtree) with the effect of interleaving the nodes of the subtree with the nodes of the rest of the tree in the output sequence. The modularity of the genotype-phenotype mapping is illustrated in Fig. 6. The nodes with gray background are nodes encapsulating subtrees. The dash-line is the order of visit of the nodes of the depth-first traversal strategy. The genotype sequence contains the number associated to the non-terminal nodes, and when a hidden subtree is encountered (a gray node), its genotype sequence is included as a self-contained subsequence. A similar concept of modularity in the

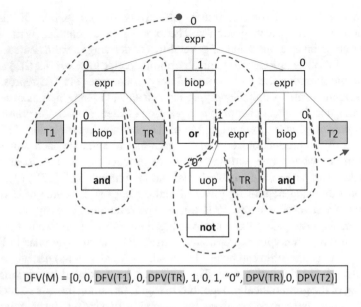

DFV(M) = [0, 0, DFV(T1), 0, DPV(TR), 1, 0, 1, "0", DPV(TR),0, DPV(T2)]

Fig. 6 Derivation tree of crossover mask. The dash-line is the order of visit of the nodes of the depth-first traversal strategy

genotype-phenotype mapping is implicit in the work of Hemberg [18] (p. 176) on the classification of operator behaviours in GE.

Observation 3 A geometric semantic operator is a function (i.e., recombination scheme) that when applied to input functions (parents) returns an output function (offspring). We observe that when viewed as a 'sentence' generated by a grammar, a geometric semantic operator is a syntactical expression representing the recombination scheme with 'holes' in which to plug the syntactical expressions representing the input functions. For example, geometric semantic crossover for Boolean functions, $T3 = (T1 \wedge TR) \vee (\overline{TR} \wedge T2)$, can be seen syntactically as a sentence of the grammar for Boolean expressions in Fig. 2 where the unspecified input functions $T1$, $T2$ and TR (i.e., formal parameters of the recombination scheme) can be seen syntactically as 'holes' or 'hidden sub-sentences'. The corresponding syntax of the output function $T3$ can then be obtained by plugging in the syntactic expressions of $T1$, $T2$ and TR in the 'holes' of the syntactic representation of the recombination scheme.

From these observations it follows that we can obtain the GE genotypic representation corresponding to the recombination scheme, by applying the procedure outlined in observation 1 to invert the genotype-to-phenotype mapping to the syntactic representation of the recombination scheme (interpreted as in observation 3) i.e., parsing it, annotating the parse tree, and visiting the annotations depth-first. The 'holes' in the sentence correspond to 'hidden subtrees' in the parse tree of the sentence, which as argued in observation 2 correspond to self-contained subsequences in the genotype sequence. Figure 6 shows the parse tree of the

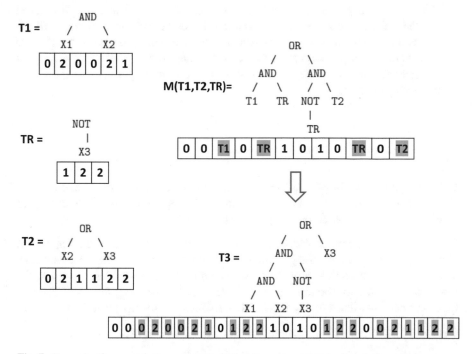

Fig. 7 Example of geometric semantic search operators on grammatical evolution genotype

syntactic representation of the recombination scheme $T3 = (T1 \wedge TR) \vee (\overline{TR} \wedge T2)$ and the corresponding GE genotype. Given the GE genotypes of the functions $T1$, $T2$ and TR in Figs. 3, 4 and 5 respectively, the GE genotype of the function $T3$ is then obtained by simply placing them in their places in the GE genotype of the recombination scheme (see Fig. 7). This by construction is equivalent to the functional composition of the recombination scheme to generic functions $T1$, $T2$ and TR, hence it is the geometric semantic crossover for Boolean functions expressed using the GE representation.

4 Derivation of Geometric Semantic Operators for GE

The theory developed in the previous section is applied here to derive a complete set of geometric semantic operators for the GE genotype for Boolean, Arithmetic and Classifier domains. In particular, we aim at deriving crossover, mutation and initialisation operators acting *solely* on GE genotypes and being *guaranteed* by construction to be equivalent to geometric semantic operators acting on the corresponding expressed phenotypes. This allows an evolutionary process on GE genotypes exactly equivalent to an evolutionary process on the corresponding phenotypes. Note that the design of the search operators is inextricably dependent on the specific grammar used for each domain. The grammar however is used only in the design phase of the search operators. We do not allow it to be used during the search to e.g., repair the offspring generated by the operators. All the operators *by design* must be guaranteed to produce genotypes corresponding to grammatically valid phenotypic expressions. Furthermore, the offspring genotypes will be guaranteed to be perfectly formed without requiring genome "wrapping" or ignoring surplus genes.

4.1 Operators for Boolean Domains

In the following, we first introduce the grammar we use for Boolean expressions. We then derive crossover, mutation and initialisation operators on GE genotypes for Boolean expressions based on this grammar.

Grammar The grammar for Boolean expressions considered is in Fig. 8. For simplicity of illustration, this grammar has only three variables (x1, x2 and x3). This grammar can express any Boolean function of three variables. However, the grammar and the corresponding geometric semantic search operators on GE genotypes can be generalised to any number of variables and to expanded function sets.

Crossover The geometric semantic crossover for Boolean expressions is

$$T3 = (T1 \wedge TR) \vee (\overline{TR} \wedge T2)$$

where $T1$ and $T2$ are the parent Boolean expressions, TR is a random Boolean expression, and $T3$ is the offspring Boolean expression.

The geometric semantic crossover for GE is an operation on the genotype of parents that generates the genotype of the offspring such that the developmental process via the grammar produces the offspring whose expression is given above.

```
(A)   <expr> ::= (<expr> <biop> <expr>)   (0)
              |  <uop> <expr>             (1)
              |  <var>                    (2)

(B)   <biop> ::= and                      (0)
              |  or                       (1)

(C)   <uop>  ::= not                      (0)

(D)   <var>  ::= x1                       (0)
              |  x2                       (1)
              |  x3                       (2)
```

Fig. 8 Grammar for Boolean expressions

```
0:              (<expr> <biop> <expr>)
0:              (<expr> <biop> <expr>)
g(T1):          T1
0:              and
g(TR):          TR
1:              or
0:              (<expr> <biop> <expr>)
1:              <uop> <expr>
0:              not
g(TR):          TR
0:              and
g(T2):          T2
```

Fig. 9 Derivation of phenotype for geometric semantic crossover for Boolean expressions

The corresponding geometric semantic crossover for this grammar is

$$g(T3) = [0, 0, g(T1), 0, g(TR), 1, 0, 1, 0, g(TR), 0, g(T2)]$$

where $g(.)$ returns the genotype of its argument. The genotype $g(T3)$ of the offspring $T3$ is the sequence obtained by inserting the sequences $g(T1)$, $g(TR)$, and $g(T2)$ in the specified positions. Note that the genotypes of the parents ($g(T1)$ and $g(T2)$) are readily available from the previous stage of the evolutionary process. The genotype of the random expression ($g(TR)$) is generated using the initialisation procedure described below.

Figure 9 shows that expanding the expression $g(T3)$ using the grammar while considering $T1$, TR, and $T2$ as parameter expressions we obtain the geometric semantic crossover scheme on phenotypes.

Mutation The geometric semantic mutation for Boolean expressions returns the offspring Boolean expression $TM = T \vee M$ with probability 0.5 and $TM = T \wedge \overline{M}$ with probability 0.5 where T is the Boolean expression undergoing mutation, M is a random minterm of all input variables, and TM is the mutated Boolean expression.

The corresponding geometric semantic mutation for this grammar is $g(TM) = [0, g(T), 1, g(M)]$ with probability 0.5 and $g(TM) = [0, g(T), 0, 1, g(M)]$ with probability 0.5. The genotype of the parent ($g(T)$) is readily available from the previous stage of the evolutionary process. The genotype of the random minterm ($g(M)$) is generated using the procedure in Fig. 10, which illustrates it for three variables.

Figure 11 shows that expanding the expression $g(TM)$ using the grammar while considering T and M as parameter expressions we obtain the geometric semantic mutation scheme on phenotypes.

Initialisation We aim at creating a random genotype that corresponds to a valid grammatical expression, i.e. a valid phenotype, without using wrapping or leaving unused codons or using modulus of the gene values. This would be easy to do by traversing the grammar to generate the genotypes. We however do not allow explicit

```
def generate_mintermgeno(3 variables):
    result = [0] # <expr> <biop> <expr>

    result += random.choice([[], [1]]) # do-nothing, or negate
    result += [2, 0] # <var>, x1
    result += [0, 0] # and, <expr> <biop> <expr>

    result += random.choice([[], [1]]) # do-nothing, or negate
    result += [2, 1] # <var>, x2
    result += [0] # and

    result += random.choice([[], [1]]) # do-nothing, or negate
    result += [2, 2] # <var>, x3
    return result
```

Fig. 10 Procedure to build the genotype of a random minterm of three variables

```
# T or M
0:          (<expr> <biop> <expr>)
g(T):       T
1:          or
g(M):       M

# T and not M
0:          (<expr> <biop> <expr>)
g(T):       T
0:          and
1:          (<uop> <expr>)
'0':        not
g(M):       M
```

Fig. 11 Derivation of phenotype for geometric semantic mutation for Boolean expressions

use of the grammar *at runtime* (apart from during fitness evaluation of genotypes, for which it is unavoidable), as we want the complete evolutionary process to happen on the genotypes only, i.e., all search operators, including initialisation, must not 'peep' through the genotype-phenotype mapping at runtime. We want the search operators, including initialisation, to work solely at genotype level, and induce via the genotype-phenotype map their intended effect at phenotype level, *entirely by design*. The design of these search operators naturally is inextricably grounded in the used grammar.

For Boolean expressions, the initialisation procedure used in GSGP is in Algorithm 1. We can design an initialisation operator acting entirely on genotypes inducing at the phenotype level the same behaviour by simply mapping each phenotypic sub-component to the corresponding genotypic sub-sequence, as illustrated in Algorithm 2.

Algorithm 1: Initialisation: Generate a random Boolean phenotype

```
1  Function RandomBoolean (depth)
2  │  if depth = 1 or probability < 2^(-depth) then
3  │  │     return random.choice(x1, x2, ...)
4  │  else
5  │  │     with probability 1/3: return (not RandomBoolean(depth-1))
6  │  │     with probability 1/3: return ( RandomBoolean(depth-1) and
   │  │        RandomBoolean(depth-1))
7  │  │     with probability 1/3: return ( RandomBoolean(depth-1) or
   │  │        RandomBoolean(depth-1))
```

Algorithm 2: Initialisation: Generate a valid random Boolean genotype

```
1  Function RandomBoolean (depth)
2  │  if depth = 1 or probability < 2^(-depth) then
3  │  │     return [2] + [RndInt(numvar)]
4  │  │     (phenotype = x1 / x2 / etc)
5  │  else
6  │  │     with probability 1/3: return [1] + RandomBoolean(depth-1)
7  │  │     (phenotype = not < expr >)
8  │  │     with probability 1/3: return [0] + RandomBoolean(depth-1) + [0]
   │  │        + RandomBoolean(depth-1)
9  │  │     (phenotype = < expr > and < expr >)
10 │  │     with probability 1/3: return [0] + RandomBoolean(depth-1) + [1]
   │  │        + RandomBoolean(depth-1)
11 │  │     (phenotype = < expr > or < expr >)
```

4.2 Operators for Arithmetic Domains

In the following, we first introduce the grammar we use for arithmetic expressions. We then derive crossover, mutation and initialisation operators on GE genotypes for arithmetic expressions based on this grammar.

Grammar the grammar for arithmetic expressions considered is in Fig. 12. This grammar can express any polynomial of three variables. However, the grammar and the corresponding geometric semantic search operators on GE genotypes can be readily generalised to any number of variables and other function sets.

Crossover The geometric semantic crossover for arithmetic expressions is

$$T3 = (T1 \cdot TR) + ((1 - TR) \cdot T2)$$

where $T1$ and $T2$ are the parent arithmetic expressions, TR is a random real constant in $[0, 1]$, and $T3$ is the offspring arithmetic expression.

```
(A) <expr>  ::= (<expr> <biop> <expr>)    (0)
              | <var>                       (1)
              | <const>                     (2)

(B) <biop>  ::= +                           (0)
              | -                           (1)
              | *                           (2)

(C) <var>   ::= x1                          (0)
              | x2                          (1)
              | X3                          (2)

(D) <const> ::= 0.0                         (0)
              | 0.1                         (1)
              ...                          ...
              | 1.0                        (10)
```

Fig. 12 Grammar for Arithmetic expressions

The corresponding geometric semantic crossover for this grammar is

$$g(T3) = [0, 0, 2, g(TR), 2, g(T1), 0, 0, 0, 2, 10, 1, 2, g(TR), 2, g(T2)]$$

where $g(.)$ returns the genotype of its argument. The offspring $T3$ has the genotype formed by substituting the genotypes of $T1$, $T2$ and TR ($g(T1)$, $g(T2)$ and $g(TR)$) in the above pattern. For simplicity of illustration, we assume TR takes only values 0.0, 0.1, ..., 1.0, so that $g(TR)$ is a random integer between 0 and 10, producing floating-point values through use of the <const> non-terminal in Fig. 12.

Mutation The geometric semantic mutation for arithmetic expressions returns the offspring $TM = T + ms \cdot (TR1 - TR2)$ where T is the Boolean expression undergoing mutation, $TR1$ and $TR2$ are random arithmetic expressions, and ms is the mutation step, which is a constant real value.

The corresponding geometric semantic mutation for this grammar is $g(TM) = [0, g(T), 0, 0, g(ms), 2, 0, g(TR1), 1, g(TR2)]$. The genotypes of the random arithmetic expressions ($g(TR1)$ and $g(TR2)$) are generated using the initialisation procedure for arithmetic expressions presented below. The genotype of the parameter ms can be obtained by factoring the parameter appropriately as a valid sentence of the grammar, and then deriving its genotype by parsing this sentence. For example, $ms = 0.001$ can be factored into $ms = 0.1 * 0.1 * 0.1$ which is a valid expression in the given grammar, and so its genotype can be derived, in this case obtaining $g(ms) = [0, 0, 2, 1, 2, 2, 1, 2, 2, 1]$.

Initialisation We can design an initialisation operator acting entirely on genotypes inducing at the phenotype level the same behaviour as the initialisation procedure used in GSGP. It works by mapping each phenotypic sub-component to the corresponding genotypic sub-sequence, as illustrated in Algorithm 3.

Algorithm 3: Initialisation: Generate a valid random Arithmetic genotype

---

1 **Function** *RandomArithmetic (depth)*
2   **if** $depth = 1$ *or* $probability < 2^{-depth}$ **then**
3   with probability $1/2$: **return** `[1] + [RndInt(numvar)]`
4   (phenotype = $< var >$, x1 / x2 / etc)
5   with probability $1/2$: **return** `[2] + [RndInt(numconst)]`
6   (phenotype = $< const >$, 0.0 / 0.1 / etc)
7   **else**
8   **return** `[0] + RandomArithmetic(depth-1) + [RndInt(numop)]`
         `+ RandomArithmetic(depth-1)`
9   (phenotype = $< expr >$, $(+/-/*)$, $< expr >$)

4.3 Operators for Classifier Domains

In the following, we first introduce the grammar we use for classifiers i.e., nested `if`-expressions. We then derive crossover, mutation and initialisation operators on GE genotypes for classifiers based on this grammar.

Grammar The grammar for classifiers considered is in Fig. 13. For simplicity of illustration, this grammar has only three variables (`x1`, `x2` and `x3`), three input symbols (`is1`, `is2` and `is3`), and two output symbols (`os1` and `os2`). This grammar can express any classifier of three variables with three input classes and two output classes. However, the grammar and the corresponding geometric semantic search operators can be generalised to any number of variables, input symbols, and output symbols.

Crossover The geometric semantic crossover for classifiers is

$$T3 = T1 \text{ IF } CONDR \text{ ELSE } T2$$

where $T1$ and $T2$ are the parent classifiers, $CONDR$ is a random condition depending on one or more input variables, and $T3$ is the offspring classifier.[1]

The corresponding geometric semantic crossover for this grammar is

$$g(T3) = [0, g(T1), 0, g(Rvar), g(Ris), g(T2)]$$

---

[1]Implementation note: The unusual IF-ELSE syntax here means that (in Python) the code is a single expression—which can be evaluated using Python's `eval()`—rather than a statement, which cannot.

```
(A) <cf> ::= (<cf> if <cond> else <cf>) (0)
             | <os>                       (1)

(B) <cond> ::= <var> == <is>             (0)
               | <cond> and <var> == <is> (1)

(C) <is> ::= is1                         (0)
             | is2                        (1)
             | is3                        (2)

(D) <os> ::= os1                         (0)
             | os2                        (1)

(E) <var> ::= x1                         (0)
              | x2                        (1)
              | x3                        (2)
```

Fig. 13 Grammar for classifiers

where $g(.)$ returns the genotype of its argument. For simplicity of illustration, the random condition $CONDR$ is of the form $Rvar == Ris$, where $Rvar$ is a random variable and Ris is a random input symbol. The offspring $T3$ has the genotype formed by substituting the genotypes of $T1$, $T2$, $Rvar$ and Ris, $(g(T1), g(T2), g(Rvar)$ and $g(Ris))$ in the above pattern. The genotype of the random variable and the random input symbol $(g(Rvar)$ and $g(Ris))$ are both integers randomly chosen from $\{0, 1, 2\}$, since in the grammar there are three input variables and three input symbols.

Mutation The geometric semantic mutation for classifiers returns the offspring classifier TM = IF CONDR THEN OUTR ELSE T where T is the parent classifier undergoing mutation, CONDR is a condition which is true only for a single random setting of all input parameters, and OUTR is a random output symbol. The offspring can be expressed as nested IF-THEN-ELSE statements with simple conditions of a single input parameter each.

The corresponding geometric semantic mutation for this grammar is $g(TM) = [0, 1, g(OUTR), g(CONDR), g(T)]$. The genotype of the parent $(g(T))$ is readily available from the previous stage of the evolutionary process. The genotype of the random output symbol $(g(OUTR))$ is an integer randomly chosen from $\{0, 1\}$, since in the grammar there are two output symbols. The genotype of the random condition $(g(CONDR))$ is generated using the procedure in Fig. 14, which illustrates it for three variables where each can take on n possible values.

Initialisation We design an initialisation operator acting entirely on genotypes inducing at the phenotype level the same behaviour as the initialisation procedure used in GSGP by simply mapping each phenotypic sub-component to the corresponding genotypic sub-sequence, as illustrated in Algorithm 4.

```
def generate_conjunction(3 variables):
    result = []

    result += [1, 1, 0]
    # <cond> ->
    # <cond> and <var> == <is> ->
    # <cond> and <var> == <is> and <var> == <is> ->
    # <var> == <is> and <var> == <is> and <var> == is

    result += [0, random.rangrange(n)]
    # <var> == <is> -> x1 == i3 (eg)

    result += [1, random.rangrange(n)]
    # <var> == <is> -> x2 == i2 (eg)

    result += [2, random.rangrange(n)]
    # <var> == <is> -> x3 == i2 (eg)

    return result
```

Fig. 14 Procedure to build the genotype of a random condition of three variables

---

Algorithm 4: Initialisation: Generate a valid random classifier genotype

---

1 **Function** *RandomClassifier (depth)*
2   **if** $depth = 1$ *or* $probability < 2^{-depth}$ **then**
3   **return** *[1] + [RndInt (numos)]*
4   (phenotype = $< os >$, o1 / o2 / o3 etc (output symbols))
5   **else**
6   **return** *[0] + RandomClassifier(depth-1) + [0,*
            RndInt(numvar), RndInt(numis)] +
            RandomClassifier(depth-1)
7   (phenotype = $(< cf >$ if $< cond >$ else $< cf >$), $< expr >$, $< var > ==$
        $< is >$, (x1 / x2 / x3 etc), (i1 / i2 / i3 etc), $< expr >$)

---

5 An Efficient Implementation of GSGE

A drawback of GSGP with crossover is the exponential growth of individuals due to the fact that the offspring tree contains both parent trees, hence individuals double their size at each generation. This problem applies to GSGE also. One solution, proposed in [1], is to keep program size manageable using automated simplification during the run.

Castelli et al. [19] proposed an implementation of GSGP that avoids exponential growth by referring via pointers to a trace of the ancestry of individuals, rather than storing them directly. We propose a new implementation of GSGP and GSGE also based on tracing the ancestry of individuals, that however does not explicitly build and maintain a new data structure, but uses higher-order functions and memoization to achieve the same effect, leaving the burden of book-keeping to the compiler. The resulting implementation is fast, elegant and concise. A Python implementation of GSGP with this feature (under 100 lines without comments) is on GitHub at https://github.com/amoraglio/GSGP, while the GSGE code used in this paper is available at https://github.com/jmmcd/GSGE.

Solution Representation We represent solutions directly using functions of the programming language used to program the GSGP system. E.g., in a GSGP to evolve Boolean expressions written in Python, the representation of a Boolean expression is a Python (anonymous) function computing that Boolean expression, and not a data structure (e.g., a tree) representing the Boolean expression.

Search Operators Geometric semantic crossover and mutation can be interpreted as higher-order functions. We implement them directly as such: they do not manipulate data structures representing solutions, but take directly as inputs the (anonymous) parent functions and return (anonymous) offspring functions. The returned offspring function *calls* the parent functions in its definition. In particular, the parent function definitions *are not substituted* in the offspring definition, hence there is no growth of the offspring function. The function calls to the parents in the offspring implicitly build the data structure that relates offspring to parents all the way up the ancestry without the need to use pointers, manage memory and maintain an archive of past solutions.

Fitness Evaluation Even if individuals do not grow, evaluating them takes exponential time, as querying a function for some input requires calling both its parents on that input, which in turn need to call their parents on it and so forth, doubling the number of calls at each generation. The complexity of queries on training data can be reduced from exponential to constant time by memoization (i.e., caching the output values of a function of previously encountered inputs rather than recomputing them) of all individuals generated in the course of evolution. This works because each individual caches its outputs on the training examples the first time its fitness is computed, and later re-uses them when its descendants call it. This reduces the number of calls needed to compute the fitness of an individual from exponential to the number of parents, i.e. two, constant. Memoization is easily implemented as a higher-order wrapping function (it is a standard library function in Python 3.2+).

Display of Best Individual As solutions are represented directly as compiled Python functions, displaying them (in particular the best-of-run individual) would require decompilation, which is not very practical. The technique we have used to display functions that avoids both decompilation and direct representations of functions during evolution consists of adding an extra implicit call structure in individuals, where the extra structure implicitly keeps track of how to reconstruct the final genotype of the individual (its source code) mirroring the first call structure (its semantics) interpreting subroutine calls as function body substitutions (i.e. asking the parents to return their source code to embed in the offspring source code). Then individuals can be asked to display themselves by calling their associated 'source code' function. This can be implemented with minor additions to the code. Naturally displaying the best individual after evolution takes exponential time as its genotype is exponentially long. However, querying the final solution on unseen values (i.e. making predictions) takes only time linear in the number of distinct ancestors thanks to the memoization of individuals. The number of distinct ancestors grows linearly with the number of generations (not exponentially, in the long term, because the population size is fixed).

6 Computational Experiments

We next present extensive experimental results. Our goal is to compare GE and GSGE representations. For comparison with previous work, we will include the GSGP representation also. As the fitness landscape is unimodal, we expect a semantic stochastic hill-climber to find the optimal solution efficiently. Therefore, we will test both hill-climbing and evolutionary search algorithms. Finally, our choice of test problems mimics that of [1]. Thus, we will compare:

- GE, GSGE, and GSGP representations;
- stochastic hill-climbing and evolutionary search algorithms;
- symbolic regression, Boolean, and classifier problems.

Based on theory, we expect that GSGE will obtain the same very good performance as GSGP in these experiments, as the two systems perform an equivalent search: the search done by GSGE on genotypes projected through the genotype-phenotype mapping coincides with the search done by GSGP on phenotypes.

The training data in the symbolic regression problems is synthesized from polynomials with coefficients uniformly sampled in $[-1, 1]$. The degree of the polynomials is varied from 3 to 10, in order to scale problem difficulty. The test data is resampled independently in the same way.

The Boolean problems are True, n-Parity, Comparator, Multiplexer, and Random. True is the Boolean function which returns True for any input. Random is a Boolean function whose truth table is randomly generated. Again, each problem is tested in several sizes in order to scale problem difficulty. The training data consists of all possible cases, and the test data is the same.

The classifier problems are synthetic. Each problem is characterised by its number of input variables n_v, number of possible values of these variables n_i, and number of possible output values n_o. Each input variable may take integer values in the range $[0, n_i - 1]$. The output is an integer in the range $[0, n_o - 1]$. It is a simple synthetic function of the input variables, $(x_0 + x_1) \bmod n_o$. For example, with $n_v = n_i = n_o = 2$, the classifier is equivalent to Boolean addition.

To facilitate easy comparison, we will report the *percentage of hits* and the standard deviation in this figure, for each problem, each representation, and each search algorithm. A hit is a test case correctly solved by the best individual of the run. On Boolean and classifier problems, a hit means the correct answer. On symbolic regression problems, a hit means an output value within 0.01 of the correct value.

Table 1 shows results. The GSGP results effectively replicate those reported by Moraglio et al. [1], with very strong performance using both search algorithms, often slightly better using hill-climbing versus evolutionary search. As expected, the GSGE results are effectively identical to the GSGP results, confirming that GSGE operators "see" the cone landscape characteristic of GSGP.

In contrast, GE itself does poorly, especially on the symbolic regression and n-Parity problems. With GE, evolutionary search tends to work better than hill-climbing. Note that the comparison to GE may be called unfair for two reasons. Our implementations of both GE and GSGE do not use a feature which has come to be common in GE implementations, *sensible initialisation* [17]; and in our implementations of both GE and GSGE, non-coding tails have been cut. Recent work has suggested that non-coding tails can improve performance in GE [20].

7 Discussion

This work had a two-fold motivation. The first was to extend the GSGP framework to a new representation. The second was to show how to design provably good search operators for GE. In the following we discuss these two perspectives in the light of the work presented in this chapter.

Why Apply GSGP to GE? On one hand, GSGE has provably good performance. On the other hand, the search on GE genotypes is exactly equivalent to the search done by GSGP on phenotypes. If they are equivalent, why bother using GSGE instead of GSGP? Expressing geometric semantic search operators in the various GP representations (GE, Cartesian GP, PushGP, etc.) and more generally for evolutionary approaches to evolving functions (e.g., evolving neural networks, finite state machines, etc.) is a good thing for three reasons: (1) it allows for unification and direct comparison of very different representations; (2) it unveils the specific properties of a representation that are ultimately linked to good performance (unimodal landscapes); and (3) it allows us to understand GSGP ideas in more detail.

The ideas of GSGP have transferred successfully to the GE representation. GE search operators that see a unimodal landscape can be built for any problem, and they can be built mechanically for any new grammar. By transferring GSGP ideas to GE, we have learned that the GE map is *modular*, with compositional semantics, and that this is a requirement for any new representation for GSGP. We have also seen that GSGE solutions grow exponentially, but that their growth can be reduced to linear.

Some of the specific benefits of GE are:

Constrained The grammar in GE can be used to enforce regularities and other constraints to solutions.

Linearity The linear genotype allows for simple search operators.

Table 1 Results with GE, GSGE, and GSGP representations on various problems, at various sizes, using hill-climbing (HC) and evolutionary (Evo) search

Problem	Size	GE/HC		GE/Evo		GSGE/HC		GSGE/Evo		GSGP/HC		GSGP/Evo	
		avg	sd	avg	sd	avg	sd	avg	sd	avg	sd	avg	sd
Polynomial	3	4.2	8.4	21.0	25.5	100.0	0.0	100.0	0.0	100.0	0.0	100.0	0.0
	4	4.5	7.0	10.8	18.5	100.0	0.0	100.0	0.0	100.0	0.0	100.0	0.0
	5	3.0	5.9	10.0	12.8	100.0	0.0	100.0	0.0	100.0	0.0	100.0	0.0
	6	3.2	5.8	10.0	8.0	99.8	0.9	99.3	2.8	100.0	0.0	99.5	2.0
	7	3.2	5.4	5.5	4.9	100.0	0.0	91.5	16.0	100.0	0.0	93.3	12.6
	8	2.0	3.8	10.2	11.6	99.5	2.0	84.5	14.9	99.5	2.0	86.8	13.8
	9	2.2	4.9	7.5	7.8	91.2	14.0	69.3	25.8	94.7	8.0	70.3	25.5
	10	2.3	5.4	5.2	6.4	87.2	16.3	64.5	22.9	88.8	14.8	67.5	22.9
Boolean true	5	89.0	17.4	98.3	5.1	99.1	1.6	99.5	1.4	99.7	0.9	99.0	1.5
	6	88.5	19.9	100.0	0.0	99.7	0.6	99.2	1.0	99.8	0.5	99.1	1.1
	7	87.5	21.2	100.0	0.0	99.9	0.2	99.8	0.4	99.9	0.3	99.9	0.2
	8	84.2	22.8	100.0	0.0	100.0	0.1	100.0	0.1	100.0	0.1	99.9	0.2
nparity	5	50.2	0.8	50.3	0.9	99.4	1.5	94.6	3.2	99.7	0.9	95.1	3.3
	6	50.0	0.0	50.0	0.0	99.9	0.4	96.9	1.9	99.9	0.4	97.5	1.7
	7	50.0	0.0	50.0	0.0	100.0	0.1	98.9	0.7	100.0	0.0	99.0	1.0
	8	50.0	0.0	50.0	0.0	100.0	0.1	98.6	0.9	100.0	0.1	98.6	0.6
	9	50.0	0.0	50.0	0.0	100.0	0.0	98.8	0.5	100.0	0.0	98.9	0.4
	10	50.0	0.0	50.0	0.0	100.0	0.0	98.8	0.3	100.0	0.0	98.7	0.3
Comparator	6	75.6	1.9	73.8	4.7	99.9	0.4	98.8	1.2	99.9	0.4	98.4	1.8
	8	75.5	1.2	78.9	3.9	100.0	0.1	99.6	0.4	100.0	0.1	99.6	0.4
	10	75.3	1.0	79.3	3.2	100.0	0.0	99.9	0.1	100.0	0.0	99.9	0.1
Multiplexer	6	64.5	2.5	64.3	2.6	99.9	0.4	98.5	1.4	99.8	0.5	98.2	1.8
	11	57.8	1.8	63.2	2.5	100.0	0.0	99.8	0.1	100.0	0.0	99.8	0.1
Random boolean	5	66.5	4.5	64.2	4.6	99.7	0.9	96.8	3.4	99.6	1.1	96.6	2.9
	6	61.5	4.3	61.6	4.2	99.9	0.4	97.9	1.6	99.8	0.5	97.9	2.0
	7	58.0	3.1	60.5	2.6	99.9	0.4	99.2	0.8	99.9	0.3	99.2	0.7
	8	56.7	2.3	58.3	2.0	100.0	0.1	99.2	0.5	100.0	0.1	99.1	0.5
	9	55.1	1.3	56.7	1.3	100.0	0.0	99.3	0.3	100.0	0.0	99.3	0.4
	10	53.6	1.2	55.0	0.9	100.0	0.0	99.4	0.2	100.0	0.0	99.3	0.2
	11	52.6	0.8	53.8	0.8	100.0	0.0	99.1	0.2	100.0	0.0	99.2	0.2
Classifier	3,3,2	55.6	0.0	55.4	0.7	55.3	0.9	55.6	0.0	55.6	0.0	55.6	0.0
	3,3,4	34.2	2.8	34.1	4.7	77.5	0.9	74.9	3.9	77.4	1.1	74.3	3.6
	3,3,8	34.6	3.4	35.8	8.1	99.6	1.1	84.9	5.0	99.5	1.3	85.1	4.6
	3,4,2	50.0	0.0	49.7	1.0	49.9	0.4	49.8	0.5	50.0	0.0	50.0	0.0
	3,4,4	29.1	3.2	27.3	3.0	74.9	0.3	73.0	1.6	74.8	0.5	71.9	1.6
	3,4,8	25.7	1.9	27.9	4.5	99.9	0.4	86.0	2.8	99.9	0.3	84.1	3.7
	4,3,2	55.6	0.0	53.7	10.0	55.6	0.0	55.6	0.0	55.6	0.0	55.6	0.0
	4,3,4	35.8	4.2	38.2	9.9	77.7	0.2	76.7	1.0	77.8	0.0	75.9	1.1
	4,3,8	34.8	3.8	41.7	6.8	100.0	0.2	88.0	2.6	100.0	0.0	87.9	2.6
	4,4,2	50.0	0.0	50.0	0.0	50.0	0.1	50.0	0.0	50.0	0.0	50.0	0.0
	4,4,4	28.7	3.0	35.2	6.4	75.0	0.0	74.3	0.5	75.0	0.1	74.5	0.5
	4,4,8	25.3	1.2	37.3	6.3	100.0	0.0	94.7	0.9	100.0	0.1	94.9	1.1

For classifier problems, problem size is given as n_v, n_i, n_o

Developmental   In GE a small genotype can express a large phenotype (via wrapping). Even without wrapping, developmental effects can come in to play, such as a greater importance of the earliest genes in the genotype.

Neutrality   Unused codons can function as a "memory" of previous solutions.

How do these beneficial aspects of GE transfer to GSGE?

Constrained   This property is linked to using grammars to enforce constraints, and has been used at a phenotypic level with GSGE, i.e., grammars can be used directly in GSGP, see e.g. [16].

Linearity   The GSGE operators are not as simple as those in GE.

Developmental   In GSGE, the developmental mapping is of less importance. The size of the phenotype is directly proportional to the size of the genotype.

Neutrality   Unused codons do not occur in GSGE. However, because GSGE individuals functionally incorporate all ancestors, there is a type of "memory".

From this analysis, it seems that GSGE uses the GE language to express a fundamentally different search than that done by GE itself. When two different perspectives are presented in a common language, it is often the case that their features can be fruitfully combined to produce unexpected novel ideas and results. This is where we are at the moment! In a broader sense, GSGE "completes" GE as it makes a link with semantics and the unimodal landscape. All of these seem to be ingredients necessary for evolving programs, the holy grail of GE. It would be interesting to investigate how different ways of including semantics in GE (e.g. attribute grammars) can be linked to GSGE.

8   Summary

In this chapter, we have recalled that GSGP sees a unimodal fitness landscapes for any problem. Geometric semantic search operators are purely functional operators that do not depend on the underlying representation. In principle, any representation could be used if sufficiently expressive to describe these operators algorithmically.

In practice, geometric semantic search operators are naturally expressed in functional languages as higher order functions. Even if in principle possible, it could be practically impossible to express these operators in a language or representation which does not naturally express functional relations and operations.

The GE encoding is rather complex, especially when using wrapping. It has been shown to have low locality [21]: small changes of the genotype may correspond to large changes on the phenotype, leading to highly disruptive operators (i.e., ripple effect) and highly discontinuous fitness landscapes. We have thus asked the question: can we express geometric semantic search operators using the GE encoding?

Expressing geometric semantic search operators on GE genotypes that act equivalently to geometric semantic operators on expressions (phenotypes) requires an understanding of how to invert the GE genotype-phenotype map, and project through this mapping search operators on the phenotype space to corresponding search operators on the genotype space. Given the complexity of the GE mapping, determining such operators rigorously may seem hopeless. Surprisingly, in this chapter this goal has been achieved.

The key property of the GE mapping that allows this is its modularity: a subexpression in the phenotype corresponds to an uninterrupted subsequence in the genotype. This allows functional composition (at the phenotypic level) to be expressed as plugging a subsequence into a sequence schema (at the genotypic level). Geometric semantic operators are then expressed at a genotypic level as specific sequence schema.

The genotypic definitions of geometric semantic search operators depend inextricably on the specific grammar used, as they are designed around the genotype-phenotype mapping. However, these operators can be derived mechanically by parsing their phenotypic expression using the grammar, and then linearizing the parse tree by depth-first traversal. We have put this methodology into practice, deriving geometric semantic crossover, mutation and initialisation for GE, equivalent to existing GSGP operators for Boolean, Arithmetic and Classifier domains.

The new GSGE operators produce exponentially large solutions, similar to GSGP. However, we have provided an elegant implementation of these operators based on interpreting the operators as higher-order functions and making use of memoization, which reduces the growth from exponential to linear (in the number of ancestors).

Finally, we have reflected that GSGE, even if phrased using the same representation, is fundamentally quite different from standard GE.

References

1. A. Moraglio, K. Krawiec, C. Johnson, Geometric semantic genetic programming, in *Proc. PPSN XII* (Springer, Berlin, 2012), pp. 21–31
2. A. Moraglio, A. Mambrini, L. Manzoni, Runtime analysis of mutation-based geometric semantic genetic programming on boolean functions, in *Proceedings of the Twelfth Workshop on Foundations of Genetic Algorithms XII. FOGA XII '13* (ACM, New York, 2013), pp. 119–132
3. A. Moraglio, A. Mambrini, Runtime analysis of mutation-based geometric semantic genetic programming for basis functions regression, in *Proceedings of the 15th Annual Conference on Genetic and Evolutionary Computation. GECCO '13* (ACM, New York, 2013), pp. 989–996
4. A. Mambrini, L. Manzoni, A. Moraglio, Theory-laden design of mutation-based geometric semantic genetic programming for learning classification trees, in *2013 IEEE Congress on Evolutionary Computation* (June 2013), pp. 416–423
5. M. O'Neill, C. Ryan, *Grammatical Evolution: Evolutionary Automatic Programming in a Arbitrary Language*. Genetic Programming (Kluwer Academic Publishers, Boston, 2003)
6. F. Rothlauf, M. Oetzel, On the locality of grammatical evolution, in *EuroGP*, ed. by P. Collet, et al. LNCS, vol. 3905, 10–12 April 2006 (Springer, Budapest, 2006), pp. 320–330
7. L. Beadle, C.G. Johnson, Semantic analysis of program initialisation in genetic programming. Genet. Program. Evolvable Mach. **10**(3), 307–337 (2009)

8. D. Jackson, Phenotypic diversity in initial genetic programming populations, in *Proceedings of EuroGP* (2010), pp. 98–109
9. L. Beadle, C.G. Johnson, Semantically driven mutation in genetic programming, in *Proceedings of IEEE CEC '09* (2009), pp. 1336–1342
10. L. Beadle, C.G. Johnson, Sematically driven crossover in genetic programming, in *Proceedings of IEEE WCCI '08* (2008), pp. 111–116
11. N.Q. Uy, N.X. Hoai, M. O'Neill, R. McKay, F. Galván-López, Semantically-based crossover in genetic programming: application to real-valued symbolic regression. Genet. Program. Evolvable Mach. **12**(2), 91–119 (2011)
12. K. Krawiec, P. Lichocki, Approximating geometric crossover in semantic space, in *Proceedings of GECCO '09* (2009), pp. 987–994
13. K. Krawiec, B. Wieloch, Analysis of semantic modularity for genetic programming. Found. Comput. Decis. Sci. **34**(4), 265–285 (2009)
14. A. Moraglio, R. Poli, Topological interpretation of crossover, in *Proceedings of GECCO '04* (2004), pp. 1377–1388
15. A. Moraglio, Towards a geometric unification of evolutionary algorithms. PhD thesis, University of Essex (2007)
16. A. Moraglio, K. Krawiec, Geometric semantic genetic programming for recursive boolean programs, in *Proceedings of the Genetic and Evolutionary Computation Conference* (ACM, New York, 2017), pp. 993–1000
17. C. Ryan, A. Azad, Sensible initialisation in grammatical evolution, in A.M. Barry, ed.: *GECCO Bird of a Feather Workshops*, Chicago, IL (2003), pp. 142–145
18. E.A.P. Hemberg, an exploration of grammars in grammatical evolution. PhD thesis, University College Dublin (2010)
19. M. Castelli, S. Silva, L. Vanneschi, A C++ framework for geometric semantic genetic programming. Genet. Program. Evolvable Mach. **16**(1), 73–81 (2015)
20. M. Nicolau, M. O'Neill, A. Brabazon, Termination in grammatical evolution: Grammar design, wrapping, and tails, in *2012 IEEE Congress on Evolutionary Computation (CEC)* (IEEE, Piscataway, 2012) 1–8
21. F. Rothlauf, M. Oetzel, On the locality of grammatical evolution, in *EuroGP*, ed. by P. Collet, M. Tomassini, M. Ebner, S. Gustafson, A. Ekárt. LNCS, vol. 3905 (Springer, Berlin, 2006), pp. 320–330

GE and Semantics

**Marina de la Cruz Echeandía, Younis R. SH. Elhaddad, Suzan Awinat,
and Alfonso Ortega**

Abstract The main goal of this chapter is to explain in a comprehensible way the semantic context in formal language theory. This is necessary to properly understand the attempts to extend Grammatical Evolution (GE) to include semantics. Several approaches from different researchers to handle *semantics*, both directly and indirectly, will be briefly introduced. Finally, previous works by the authors will be described in depth.

1 A Comprehensible Introduction to Semantics in Formal Languages

1.1 Syntax vs. Semantics

Most people, in their daily life, have an intuitive idea about the differences between syntax and semantics: the structure or *shape* of the sentences is the syntax, while their actual meaning, the message that the speaker is trying to convey, is the semantics. Nevertheless, semantics of formal languages is a rather difficult concept, perhaps due to the fact that, from a formal viewpoint, semantics do not exist. It is thus reasonable that non-experts try to apply their previous common ideas to formal domains. We'll take a detailed look at this question, even though this look must review most of the history of computers. Every computer scientist knows that formal language theory is structured around the concepts of machines, grammars, and (obviously) languages.

M. de la Cruz Echeandía · Y. R. SH. Elhaddad · S. Awinat · A. Ortega (✉)
UAM, Computer Engineering Department, Madrid, Spain
e-mail: marina.cruz@uam.es; alfonso.ortega@uam.es

© Springer International Publishing AG, part of Springer Nature 2018   189
C. Ryan et al. (eds.), *Handbook of Grammatical Evolution*,
https://doi.org/10.1007/978-3-319-78717-6_8

1.2   Machines and Computability

In these first paragraphs we'll provide an intuitive summary of a complex question that connects Mathematics and the basis of theoretical computer science. The most popular formal results applicable to this topic are the works by Kurt Gödel, Alan Turing and Alonzo Church. In [16] Gödel proved the existence of undecidable propositions in Arithmetics if one starts from the Peano axioms, a result that can be extended to many formal systems. This opened the door to the existence of uncomputable tasks, as computability can be considered a counterpart to decidability. On the other hand, almost simultaneously, Alan Turing [31] and Alonzo Church [9] introduced what is known as the *Turing-Church's thesis* about the equivalence between algorithms (computable tasks) and universal computational models (such as Turing machines and Church λ-calculus). This thesis is a conjecture that nobody has been able to prove or to reject, up to now.

At this point, these complex concepts are impossible to understand informally. The difficult goal of the following paragraphs is simplifying these concepts without introducing misunderstandings. For the formal and complete details, we refer the reader to the references.

The Turing machine is the most powerful and expressive machine. It is, in fact, the mathematical model for von Neumann's architecture. That means that our *conventional* computers (those we use on a daily basis) more or less implement the Turing machine. The relationship between computability and the Turing machine is very tight; any task solvable by a Turing machine is considered to be *computable*, and we call an *algorithm* the way in which computable tasks are actually solved, in terms of the instructions of a Turing machine.

There is, of course, an intuitive way of figuring out what the word *computable* means. Computability implies algorithms and these could be naively considered as some kind of *general purpose recipes*, that is, procedures that describe how to perform computable tasks. Algorithms ensure that anyone that executes all their steps, from the beginning to the end, will complete the task, even without understanding what is being done. It is very important for correct algorithms designed for computable tasks *to perform each step* and *to complete all of them from the beginning to the end*. If just one step cannot be completed, or if all the steps in the algorithm cannot be performed, either the algorithm is incorrect, or we are facing an uncomputable task. There are different reasons why a task can be uncomputable; in other words, it is impossible to device an algorithm that will execute that task. Without going into technical details, consider the following two tasks: make someone fall in love with you, and write all the natural numbers. Can you describe your first love in detail? Do you think this task is computable? On the other hand, how many natural numbers must you write to be sure you have completed the task? Do you think one can design a procedure that, after having executed all its steps, completes the task? Do you think this is a computable task? Lots of tasks, like those, do not fit with any *well written* algorithm and, hence, are uncomputable.

Computer science links the expressive power of machines with the complexity of the problems they can solve. In fact, there is a parallel hierarchy that relates problems and machines, according to their complexity and power.

All types of computing machines share the same kind of elements:

- A way to represent all the different situations in which the machine can be. These elements are called *states*;
- A way for the machine to change from one state to another. These elements are named *transitions*;
- A way to store additional information needed to perform the task under consideration. More sophisticated storage devices result in more powerful machines.

We can informally characterize machines by their additional storage devices as follows:

- A Turing machine has a random access storage device implemented by a bidirectional tape that can be accessed randomly. In every computing step, the tape head can move forward or backwards, after possibly changing the contents of its current position in the tape. A random access memory can be seen as a matrix, each of whose cells can be accessed by its position. It is easy to figure out how this can be implemented with a bidirectional tape. This kind of storage is the most sophisticated we will consider and is, in fact, the kind of memory you can find in the RAM of your PC.
- The simplest interesting computing devices are called *finite automata*. They can be found all around: the software for controlling vending devices for soft drinks or snacks, for instance, have such a simple logic that it can be described by means of finite automata. Finite automata have no additional storage devices.
- The last type of computing machines we are interested in are named *push down automata*. Their additional storage device is a stack of cells. Stacks are *LIFO* (**L**ast **I**n-**F**irst **O**ut) devices. Inserting and extracting information is only allowed at just one of the ends of a stack. Thus, the stored information is pushed-down when a new bit of data enters the stack, and it is popped-out when a bit of data is extracted. It is easy to see that stacks are less sophisticated than random access memories.

  Stacks can seem a rather artificial mechanism to be included in a computing device. Push-down automata were introduced while looking for computing devices specifically designed to analyse the syntax of the high-level programming languages invented since the 1950s.

  Ignoring technical details, try to figure out how a stack would help to check if the two kinds of parentheses (and) are balanced in an arithmetic expression. One can, for example, push down each left parenthesis (into the stack and pop one whenever a) is found. It is easy to see that, based on this mechanism, sequences of paired elements can be checked in reverse order, or *something* counted and checked later against *some other thing* that should occur the same number of times, or a related number of times. These conditions are the basic syntactic constraints one must check while analyzing the syntax of programming languages. Think, for instance, about checking if every *else* clause comes after a corresponding *then* clause.

How can these machines be linked to formal languages, including programming languages? From our viewpoint, everything in this domain is expressed by means of symbols that play the role of *words* in natural languages, plus sequences of words that play the role of *sentences*. A *language* is just a set of words. In general, all the machines we have mentioned can be described in abstract form as *language processors*, which means that a computation performed by anyone of them will take a word as input, start from its first symbol and perform a sequence of actions until reaching the last symbol, or until it cannot go on and stops. These machines have mechanisms to determine if a given string is accepted or rejected, thus they can also be considered as *language recognizers*.

But how can we relate tasks of different degrees of complexity, with languages and machines? Any problem can be expressed as a question that can be answered in different words. The set of these words conforms the language of the solutions for the problem. Any possible solution is represented by a word in this language, and every word in the language represents a solution to the problem. From this perspective, a machine is able to solve a problem if it only recognizes words that correspond with the solutions to the problem. It is easy to imagine that the structure of the words that are solutions to difficult or complex problems is much more sophisticated than the structure of the solutions to simpler problems.

But why are we talking about computability and machines? Because *problems*, *tasks*, and their characteristics, such as their *complexity*, or *the kind of machine that is needed to tackle each type of task* are informally considered *semantic* questions.

1.3   Grammars and Languages

Grammars can be considered the formal counterpart associated with syntax in formal language theory, as their rules fully describe the form and structure of the words belonging to the language they generate. It is worth mentioning that linguistics and theoretic computer science are quite close, both intrinsically linked to algebra. Formal grammar theory was proposed and studied in the late fifties and the early sixties by Noam Chomsky and Schützenberger [5–7]. Marcel-Paul Schützenberger was a Doctor in Mathematics and Medicine. As a mathematician, he was interested in formal languages, information theory and their relationship, and also in linguistics. Noam Chomsky is one of the most relevant linguists in modern history. He introduced the idea of a formal grammar to explain the construction of correct sentences in natural languages. They shared the same historical period with the first relevant developments of modern computer science. Their ideas were easily and quickly used as tools to define formal languages, where algorithms programmed in computers are specified.

There are several types of grammars in the Chomsky (or the Chomsky-Schützenberger) hierarchy, such as linear, regular, context-free or unrestricted (type 0) grammars. As with natural languages, formal grammars are devices able to generate sets of correct strings (*languages*). Rather than generating natural languages, they generate formal languages, but the mechanisms are the same. Grammars form a hierarchy based on their expressiveness, in such a way that the less expressive grammars are included in the more expressive, while the latter can generate strings that comply with more sophisticated constraints. Each family has its own mechanisms to generate strings:

- Regular grammars can generate strings that grow from just one end (always the same) of the string. Notice that this is the simplest way to make strings grow (the simplest *growth pattern*): one starts from a symbol and adds new symbols, always at the same end.
- Context-free grammars use more complex growth patterns. Roughly speaking, they add two main new mechanisms:
  - Strings can grow from both ends at the same time and in the same (or related) way, i.e. symbols can be added simultaneously to both ends of the string. Thus, balanced parenthesis in arithmetic expressions can be generated like this: (), (()), ... , (...(())....).
  - Strings can grow at any position, not just at the ends of the string. This is a straightforward mechanism to describe the structure of a string as a sequence of patterns that can be handled separately. It is possible to do something similar with regular grammars, but in a slightly more tedious way.

  Context-free grammars are very important for this chapter. They have been designed to express the *syntax* of high level programming languages.
- Unrestricted grammars can make their strings grow without any restrictions. They are the most expressive grammars.

The Chomsky hierarchy also gives rise to a correspondence among machines and grammars. Thus, regular grammars and finite automata, context-free grammars and pushdown automata, are two couples of equivalent models. To study these equivalences, machines are usually considered as language recognisers and a machine is supposed to recognise the language generated by a grammar (conversely, a grammar generates the language recognised by a machine).

From this point of view, Turing machines are equivalent to unrestricted grammars (or type 0 grammars). Given that these machines are able to execute any algorithm, this equivalence implies that unrestricted grammars can express any algorithm designed to execute any computable task.

This conclusion is very relevant: there exists a kind of grammar able to express every detail of whatever algorithm, and every step needed to solve any computable task. Remember that computer science informally binds grammars and syntax, so that everything in an algorithm can be considered syntactic. This eliminates the gap in natural language between the message carried by a sentence and the actual form and structure of the sentence itself, which means that there is no need for semantics in formal language theory... if you are willing to cope with type 0 grammars, of course.

1.3.1 Let Us Try to Formalize

Formal Notations for Grammars

In this chapter we are working with formal models and objects. In every section we will introduce first the notation we use. Every formal grammar has:

- Two disjoint *alphabets* or non empty sets of symbols: *non terminals* (the set of symbols that can be changed while generating strings) and *terminals* (the symbols that cannot be changed further). Valid strings derived by the grammar are made exclusively of terminal symbols. These two sets will be respectively denoted as N and T.
- A set of derivation rules that establishes how non terminal symbols can be changed into other strings of symbols. The shape of these rules determines the class of the grammar. Let us analyze those of interest for this chapter:

  1. A **context-free** derivation rule has only a non terminal symbol at its left hand side. The right hand side is unrestricted, i.e. it belongs to the set $(N \cup T)^*$. The *star operator* $(^*)$ indicates that the string to its left can be repeated any number of times (also zero). We will use λ to represent a string without any symbols.
  2. A **type 0 (unrestricted)** derivation rule only has one constraint: its left hand side must contain at least one non-terminal symbol.

- Grammars generate languages by applying their derivation rules successively, starting from a specific non terminal symbol, called the *axiom* of the grammar, until just terminal symbols are obtained.

As an example, we'll show the formal notation for a context-free grammar which generates the language $L_{(^n)^n}$ of balanced parentheses. This representation is made of the two alphabets (N and T), the axiom, and the rules:

$$G_{(^n)^n} = \{\{S\}; \{(,)\}; S; \{S \rightarrow (S), S \rightarrow \lambda\}\}$$

Given that λ has 0 symbols, it seems clear that, when used as the right hand side of a derivation rule for a non-terminal (in our example S) it just removes the non-terminal symbol in the current string. In our example, if this λ rule is applied to the axiom, the *empty string* is generated, i.e. the axiom is removed and a string with no symbols is generated.

Using the same notation, the following *type-0* set of derivation rules can be written:

$$\{S \rightarrow \lambda, S \rightarrow SAB, AB \rightarrow BA\}$$

Fig. 1 Derivation tree for the string $((()))$, generated by $G_{(n)^n}$. The axiom is placed on the top, as the root of the tree. The axiom is always the root of all derivation trees derived by a grammar. Notice that the derivation tree hides the order in which rules are applied. Each possible choice is a different derivation. In this case there is only one possibility: the derivation represented in short as $S \Rightarrow *((()))$ and in detail as $S \Rightarrow (S) \Rightarrow ((S)) \Rightarrow (((S))) \Rightarrow ((()))$

Where the only type 0 rule is the last one $AB \rightarrow BA$ that indicates that the two symbols AB can be exchanged, generating BA. We will revisit this idea in following sections.

Derivation Trees

Another important object related to grammars and languages is a *derivation tree*. Derivation trees are graphical representations of the derivation processes. They make it possible to see a complete derivation at a single glance. Look at Fig. 1 to see how derivation trees are built.

Figure 2 shows an example of type-0 derivation tree.

In the remainder of this paper we will introduce the problem of breaking the expressive power of context-free grammars, specially when used in GE. We will try to summarize different approaches by other authors, and explain how we do it: through Evolution with Attribute Grammars and Evolution with Christiansen Grammars. In addition, in the remaining sections, we will complete our reflections about the questions we have highlighted so far: the meaning of semantics in formal models; the balance between expressive power and comfort when designing solutions to real problems; the different techniques to design each different formal model; and so forth.

Fig. 2 Derivation tree for the string $a^n b^n$, generated by $G_{0a^n b^n} = \{\{S, A, B\}; \{a, b\}; S; \{S \to SAB, AB \to BA, A \to a, B \to b\}\}$. Notice that the positions of non-terminals symbols A and B must be properly exchanged before they can derive the terminal symbols a and b. Otherwise a string could be generated with an a to the right of a b. We will revisit this idea in next section when talking about *synchronization* processes with type-0 grammars

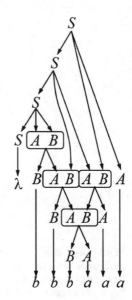

2 Breaking the Expressive Limits of Context-Free Models with a Semantic Approach

In previous sections we have introduced the equivalence between Chomsky's type-0 grammars and Turing machines. Let's look at this in more detail. The most relevant feature of unrestricted grammars, which gives them their expressive power, is the ability to take into account the context during the process of string deriving. This capability can be briefly described as the ability of expressing different derivations for the same symbol, depending on the substrings around it. It is easy to realize that this fact implies that *computation* is based on *signal propagation* implemented by context sensitivity; in other words, changes in strings needed to properly express their structure are made by sending signals that will provoke the change when they arrive at the proper place. Readers familiar with programming Turing machines will realize that this is the same mechanism which must be used to change the contents of the tape, to make the computation progress. It is a rather mechanical, but boring procedure, somewhat similar to programming in assembler languages. Computer engineers have developed a bevy of higher level programming languages and tools to hide these details and ease the programming process.

This evolution has been mimicked in the history of the design of programming languages and their compilers. The first compiler, developed in the fifties by the FORTRAN team, led by John W. Backus, took 18 man years during 2 years. Nowadays, computer engineering students develop their own compilers for similar programming languages in just one semester. This has been made possible because of advances in the tools developed to standardize and automatize this task. One of the milestones was structuring compilers around a context-free kernel. In this way, a beautiful theoretical paradox arises: unrestricted grammars are the only family of grammars able to *express* any algorithm; nevertheless, context-free grammars, less expressive and able to embody only context-free constructions, are the chosen family to develop compilers for high level programming languages, whose goal is easing the writing of algorithms, so that the computer can solve any computable task whatever.

Once this scenario has been properly introduced and depicted, we can define *semantics*. In our opinion, and from the point of view of formal language theory, the *semantics* of a programming language can more easily be defined as something that is missing. Let us assume a given programming language and the context free grammars for its syntax. We can informally conclude that the semantics (of this language) is what is missing in context-free grammars before it can be completely described. We can also conclude that this name (*semantics*) originates by opposition to the term *syntax*, usually bound to grammatical constructions.

2.1   GE and Semantics

Grammar Evolution (GE) uses context-free grammars (CFGs) to control the mapping process from the genotype of every possible solution in the population into its corresponding phenotype. This ensures the syntactical correctness of the phenotypes that, in fact, are frequently programs.

Once we have set semantics in its context, this section intends to introduce briefly different attempts to extend the expressive power of context-free grammars when used in GE, before describing in detail our own proposals, based on attribute grammars and Christiansen grammars. Some of the attempts have proposed the use of tree-adjoining grammars; a formal model whose expressive power is close to that of mildly context-sensitive grammars [19, 24, 25, 33–35]. Others add semantics indirectly, back-propagating information from the phenotypes; these ideas have also been developed in other domains [3, 15, 18, 28, 29, 32]. A few incorporate semantic information by means of probabilities. That this is actually a semantic approach is not so easy to see, for probabilistic context-free grammars are a subfamily of the context-free grammars initially included in the classical Chomsky hierarchy [4, 20, 21, 23].

Our own extensions focus specifically on semantics in the way previously described. In the remainder of this chapter we will describe in more detail the two models used in our proposals (Attribute Grammar Evolution and Christiansen Grammar Evolution [13, 27]), from a perspective focused on their expressive power, programming techniques, etc. Then we describe our proposals themselves, before ending up with some conclusions and future research lines. These proposals continue previous attempts to extend GE with attributes in specific domains [10, 11, 26].

2.2 Attribute Grammars

2.2.1 Introducing Attribute Grammars

Donald Ervin Knuth coined the term *attribute grammar* [22] to refer to a model specifically devised to be used as the core of compilers for high level programming languages. As previously mentioned, attribute grammars fill the semantic gap between context-free grammars and unrestricted Chomsky grammars, so that the former become computationally complete models, by adding to them what is called an *attribute system* that includes the following components:

- To each symbol in the context-free grammar, we add a set of variables (considered as names linked to a domain, in the same way as variables are declared in high level programming languages). For instance, int a; or float b; or complexNumber c1;, although in the last case one must previously define which domain is represented by the name complexNumber;. These attributes are considered as local variables belonging to the symbols with which they are associated. They store *semantic information* about them. While deriving words from the grammar, whenever a derivation rule is applied to a symbol, that symbol will also store in its variables the associated semantic information. In this way, after a derivation is completed, the attribute grammar will have computed the semantic information for all the symbols involved in the derivation.
- A set of *global variables* (or *name-domain* links) called *global information* is accessible at any moment from any point of the grammar. They are used to store useful intermediate information during the derivation process.
- Each derivation rule is associated to an arbitrary algorithm that contains a set of operations called *semantic actions*. This algorithm computes the value of the attributes of some symbols as a function of the values of the attributes of other symbols. As will be explained in further sections, these semantic actions can be divided into two groups, depending on whether the computed attributes belong to symbols on the left or on the right side of the context-free rule.

Derivations of attribute grammars produce two different results:

- The same string that the context-free kernel would derive.
- The results of the computation associated with the algorithms spread across the semantic actions. The fact that any algorithm can be used, implies that attribute grammars are computationally complete. Given any algorithm Ψ, there is a trivial procedure to find an attribute grammar that runs this algorithm: its context-free kernel has just one symbol (the axiom) and just one rule, which generates λ from the axiom. The associated semantic action runs Ψ. The eventual inputs and outputs for Ψ can be implemented as global variables.

2.2.2 Propagation Mechanisms in Attribute Grammars

The name *propagation* is given to the process that computes the value of the attributes of the symbols in the derivation trees generated by an attribute grammar. Propagation is the main *programming technique* in attribute grammars. While designing an attribute grammar, one must decide how to propagate attributes in the derivation trees from one node to another (technically, from the values of the attributes of the symbols contained in the first node, to those in the second). This is a graphical way of programming, for one actually draws arrows between the nodes to assign values to the attributes of the symbols. Propagation is specifically added to the grammar in the semantic actions of each derivation rule. Propagation can be split into two groups:

- *Synthesis*, when the values of the attributes of the non-terminal symbol on the left of the rule are computed from the values of the attributes belonging to the symbols on the right. Synthesis is graphically represented by means of *ascending arrows* in the derivation tree.
- *Inheritance*, when the attributes of the symbols on the right of the rule are computed as functions of the attributes of the symbol on the left of the rule, or of the symbols preceding the right hand side symbol under consideration. Inheritance is graphically represented as *descending* or *horizontal left to right* arrows.

This classification is extended to attributes. An attribute computed by means of synthesis (or inheritance) is called *synthesized* (*or inherited*).

2.2.3 Attribute Grammar Examples

We have previously mentioned that attribute grammars are computationally complete models. To compare the programming techniques of context-free and attribute grammars, it could be interesting to show an example of an attribute grammar that solves a simple problem (a context-free problem). This example will also be used to show a possible *formal notation* to describe attribute grammars.

We shall design an attribute grammar for generating language $L_{a^n b^n} = \{a^n b^n, , n \geq 0\}$ from a context-free kernel that generates the language $L_{a^n b^m} = \{a^n b^m, , n, m \geq 0\}$, which is actually a regular language. It is easy to see that the context-free grammar induced by the following set of derivation rules (where S is the axiom and λ, as previously stated, represents the empty word) generates $L_{a^n b^m}$. $G_{a^n b^m} = \{S \rightarrow AB, A \rightarrow aA, A \rightarrow \lambda, B \rightarrow bB, B \rightarrow \lambda\}$. The shortest word generated by $G_{a^n b^m}$ is λ, and this grammar can generate any word containing any number of a symbols (including 0) followed by any number of b symbols (including 0 and not necessarily the same). The following are a few examples of words generated by $G_{a^n b^m}$: *abb, bbb, aaaa, aaa, aaaaab*.

Let us describe how we could design the attribute grammar:

1. First we will compute the number of symbols a generated. Attribute n_a will be associated to symbol A and used for that purpose. This could be easily done by synthesis, taking into account that

   (a) $n_a = 0$ for λ, the word generated by the rule $A \rightarrow \lambda$;
   (b) If a derivation adds a new a by means of the rule $A \rightarrow aA$, the value of n_a is increased by 1. That is, the A in the left hand side computes the value of its n_a by adding 1 to the value of the same attribute associated to A at the right hand side.

2. Then, the root of the subtree for the B block, that contains the first B symbol, inherits the total number of a symbols and decreases it by 1 each time a symbol b is generated by means of the rule $B \rightarrow bB$.
3. Correct words must be finished by using the rule $B \rightarrow \lambda$ if and only if the current value of n_a is 0. It is easy to see that attribute n_a associated to B is given its initial value through inheritance.

Now we will formally describe this attribute grammar. The following notation enumerates the initial attributes of the grammar: $\{A\{int\ n_a\}, B\{int\ n_a\}\}$. Semantic actions should be added in the proper place of the derivation rules, using, for example, a notation similar to language C. Action number $1.a$ from above, for example, could be written like this: $A \rightarrow \lambda\{A.n_a = 0; \}$ The complete attribute grammar is shown below:

$$Ga_{a^n b^n} = \{$$
$$\quad \{A\{int\ n_a\}, B\{int\ n_a\}\};$$
$$\quad S;$$
$$\quad \{$$
$$\qquad A \rightarrow \lambda\{A.n_a = 0; \}$$
$$\qquad A_1 \rightarrow aA_2\{A_1.n_a = A_2.n_a + 1; \}$$
$$\qquad S \rightarrow AB\{B.n_a = A.n_a; \}$$
$$\qquad B_1 \rightarrow bB_2\{B_2.n_a = B_1.n_a - 1; \}$$
$$\qquad B \rightarrow \lambda\{if(B.n_a\ != 0)error(); \}$$
$$\quad \}$$
$$\}$$

In the next sections we will review examples related to this problem.

Consider the following language: $L_{\sharp_a = \sharp_b} = \{w \in \{a, b\}^* | \sharp_a(w) = \sharp_b(w)\}$. This way of defining the language uses two new operators:

- A new use for the $*$ operator: when applied to an alphabet it refers to the set of all the possible strings that can be built with symbols taken from the alphabet.
- $\sharp_{symbol}(string)$ indicates the number of times the *symbol* occurs in the *string*.

The following attribute grammar generates $L_{\sharp_a = \sharp_b}$.

$$Ga_{\sharp_a = \sharp_b} = \{$$
$$\quad \{S', S\{int\ n_a;\ int\ n_b; \}, X\{int\ n_a;\ int\ n_b; \}\};$$
$$\quad \{a, b\};$$

```
{
        S' → S{if (S.n_a! = S.n_b) error (); }
        S_1 → X S_2{S_1.n_a = S_2.n_a + X.n_a; S_1.n_b = S_2.n_b + X.n_b; }
        S → λ{S.n_a = 0; S.n_b = 0; }
        X → a{X.n_a = 1; X.n_b = 0; }
        X → b{X.n_a = 0; X.n_b = 1; }
}

}
```

Notice that symbol X represents either an a or a b. Only two attributes are needed (n_a and n_b) and both are synthesized in the same way:

- For symbol X, they are initialized whenever X derives an a ($n_a = 1$ and $n_b = 0$) or a b ($n_a = 0$ and $n_b = 1$);
- For symbol S, they are initialized to 0 in the $λ$ rule;
- They are incremented in the recursive rule for S;
- The rule for the axiom checks that $n_a = n_b$.

Theoretical Expressive Power vs. Comfort

We can now pose the following question: Can we easily design a context-free grammar that generates the language $L_{\sharp_a = \sharp_b}$? or would it be too complex and time-consuming?

The complete answer requires answering a previous question: can we prove that this language is context-free? A formal proof for a positive answer would require showing a context-free grammar that generates the language, or a push-down automaton that accepts it. In our opinion, this problem is easier to solve by means of a stack than with a grammar. The formal definition of push-down automata is out of the scope of this chapter, but it is easy to see that a stack is enough:

- The shortest word is $λ$, and it is always trivial to accept $λ$ (there is an standard technique for this, when designing push-down automata, by means of a specific *final state* which is accessed when $λ$ must be accepted).
- Excluding $λ$, in any intermediate step the automaton could face either a or b symbols. Both can be handled in the same way:
  - The stack can be used to store the *unbalanced* symbols; that is, symbols a without their corresponding b and the opposite. This implies that the stack can contain
    Nothing, when $\sharp_a(w) = \sharp_b(w)$ where w is the current portion of string having been processed;
    n symbols a; when $\sharp_a(w) - \sharp_b(x) = n$;
    n symbols b; when $\sharp_b(w) - \sharp_a(w) = n$.
  - If the next symbol is a (b) and the stack contains as (bs), push a (b) into the stack.

- If the next symbol is a (b) and the stack contains bs (as), pop the top of the stack.
- It is obvious that, after processing a correct string with the same numbers of a and b symbols, the stack will be empty.

Although this is just an informal guide to design a push-down automaton that recognizes $L_{\sharp_a=\sharp_b}$, it outlines a formal proof that this language is context-free. Once we are *reasonably* sure that $L_{\sharp_a=\sharp_b}$ is context-free, we should be able to design a context-free grammar to generate it. Let us look at a possible approach. Perhaps you remember Bolzano's theorem for continuous real functions. You can find it in any Calculus book [1, 2, 17].

Theorem 1 *If a continuous function defined on an interval is sometimes positive and sometimes negative, it must be 0 at some point.*

Keep this idea in mind and try to apply a similar theorem in the following informal explanation that outlines the formal design of our context free grammar: Let us try to imagine all the possible structures of a word w that belongs to $L_{\sharp_a=\sharp_b}$. It can start and end by different symbols (either a or b)?, as in *aabb*, *bbbaaa*; or it may start and end by the same symbol, as in *abba*, *baab*.

We will denote $|w|$ to represent the length of word w (the number of its symbols). Let us consider the following integer function that takes a string as a parameter: $f(w) = \sharp_a(w) - \sharp_b(w)$. It is obvious that this function is defined on the integer interval $[0, |w|]$, and that it is sometimes positive and sometimes negative. Figures 3, 4 and 5 show the values taken by f for all the subsequent substrings of the following three words belonging to the language, that will be important in the descriptions below: *aaabbb*, *aaabbbbbaa* and *aaabbbbbaaabbbaa*.

In the grammar we are discussing, we will represent any valid string by the non-terminal symbol S, which also represents the axiom. In Fig. 3 you can see a very simple case: string *aaabbb* starts and ends by different symbols. It is simple,

Fig. 3
$\sharp_a(aaabbb) - \sharp_b(aaabbb)$. *aaabbb* is an example of a string that belongs to $L_{\sharp_a=\sharp_b}$ and starts and ends with different symbols

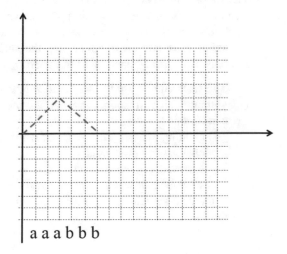

a a a b b b

Fig. 4 $\sharp_a(aaabbbbbaa) -$
$\sharp_b(aaabbbbbaa)$.
aaabbbbbaa is an example
of a string that belongs to
$L_{\sharp_a=\sharp_b}$ and starts and ends by
the same symbol (a). It shows
that in similar cases there is a
point where f equals 0. This
point splits the string in two
substrings that also belong to
$L_{\sharp_a=\sharp_b}$ and in this case they
start and end by different
symbols, as in Fig. 3.
In this case
$f(aaabbb) = f(bbaa) = 0$

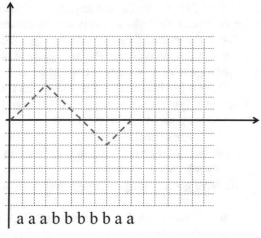

a a a b b b b b a a

Fig. 5
$\sharp_a(aaabbbbbaaabbbaa) -$
$\sharp_b(aaabbbbbaaabbbaa)$.
aaabbbbbaaabbbaa is
another example of a string
that belongs to $L_{\sharp_a=\sharp_b}$ and
starts and ends by the same
symbol (a). This case is more
complex, for the string can be
split in two ways: *aaabbb*
and *bbaaabbbaa*; or
aaabbbbbaa and *abbbaa*

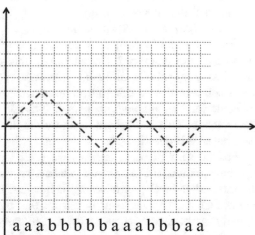

a a a b b b b b a a a b b b a a

because the *a*s cannot be balanced until the string ends at the last *b*. This means that
f just takes the value 0 at the beginning and end of the string.

An important characteristic of this kind of strings is that, if the first and the last
symbol are removed, one gets a valid string that also belongs to $L_{\sharp_a=\sharp_b}$. In our
example, both *aaabbb* and *aabb* belong to the language. This is a general fact that
can be coded by a derivation rule for our grammar: $S \rightarrow aSb$ (together with the
symmetric rule $S \rightarrow bSa$).

All the strings that start and end by the same symbol have a more complex
structure. For all of them, f must take the value 0 at least in one intermediate point.
This happens because, if a string w starts by a, f starts being positive, and if w ends
also by a, the last-but-one value of f must be negative (-1, in fact). You can see
this situation if Fig. 4. A similar situation happens for words starting and ending in

symbol b: $f(w)$ starts getting negative and ends positive (1) just before the last b symbol. Recall Theorem 1: a very similar theorem is applicable here.[1]

This is the second relevant and important factor that will help us understand the structure of the strings belonging to $L_{\sharp_a=\sharp_b}$. It has been suggested informally that if you put together two strings belonging to the language, the result will also belong to it. These substrings can be of any kind. So, if we have a string starting and ending by the same symbol, it can be split into two substrings, each with the same number of as and bs, precisely at the intermediate point where function f goes through the value 0. We can code this amazing fact by means of the rule $S \rightarrow SS$.

Additionally, we must take into account the shortest string in $L_{\sharp_a=\sharp_b}$: λ that obviously satisfies $f(\lambda) = 0$.

We have given strong, although informal evidence that the set of rules $\{S \rightarrow SS, S \rightarrow aSb, S \rightarrow bSa, S \rightarrow \lambda\}$ always generates strings in $L_{\sharp_a=\sharp_b}$. The additional needed complete formal proof that no string in $L_{\sharp_a=\sharp_b}$ requires different rules than those discussed above, is out of the scope of this chapter. We can thus assume that the context free grammar $Gcf_{\sharp_a=\sharp_b} = \{\{S\}; \{a, b\}; S; \{S \rightarrow \lambda, S \rightarrow aSb, S \rightarrow bSa, S \rightarrow SS\}\}$ generates $L_{\sharp_a=\sharp_b}$.

What is easier to design? A context-free grammar that represents a language, or an attribute grammar? The answer to this question is subjective and depends on a subtle magnitude, difficult to measure, that we could call *comfort*. We think most software developers and programmers will feel more comfortable with the attribute version, although mathematicians and algebraists may prefer the context-free version. This is what we mean by the title *expressive power vs. comfort*. We will revisit this question later in this chapter.

For the sake of completeness, we shall look at a typical problem solved by attribute grammars in computer science, specifically when developing compilers. In most high level programming languages, one must declare variables before using them. Compilers usually ensure this by means of a global *symbol table*, usually implemented by means of a *dictionary*. A *dictionary* is an abstract data type that makes it possible to store and retrieve information associated to a key. High level programming languages usually need lots of *semantic information* about the symbols defined in the program, to properly check all the *semantic constrains* a correct program has to comply with, and also to generate successfully the equivalent low level code (usually in machine language). The names of the variables are usually considered to be their keys. The semantic information includes: the basic type of the

---

[1] Let's consider f as $f : [0, |w|] \rightarrow [-|w|, |w|]$ so that $f(i) = \sharp_a(w[0, i]) - \sharp_b(|w[0, i])$ and where $w[0, i]$ is the subsequence of w respectively starting and ending in 0 and i. It is clear that $|f(i + 1) - f(i)| = 1 \forall i$. For this step of the proof, it is easy to consider either a version of Bonzano's theorem for this kind of functions; or to define a function to which Bolzano's result could be applied. In the first case, notice that for every zero of f ($\forall i | f(i) = 0$); the sequence of points $\{(i, -1), (i, 0), (i, 1)\}$ (or $\{(i, 1), (i, 0), (i, -1)\}$) always belongs to f. In the last case, one could consider the continuous function f' that can be drawn connecting consecutive points of f or even a polynomial interpolation that preserves its points (all of them or at least the most relevant, around its zeros).

variable; whether it is a structure or a simple variable; or the types of the arguments and the return variable of a function, among others.

The syntax of high level programming languages is represented by huge grammars, sometimes with hundreds of rules. A simple example will show how to solve the declaration problem. Most programming languages include rules for declaring identifiers similar to the following:

{

$\ldots$

$program \rightarrow declarations\,sentences$
$declarations \rightarrow declaration \ldots$
$declaration \rightarrow type\,\textbf{identifier}$

$\ldots$

}

When an identifier is declared using this set of rules, it is easy to imagine the set of attributes and semantic actions needed to propagate the semantic information of the identifier (for example its type) in such a way that it can be inserted in the symbol table after the last rule is applied. When the compiler is analyzing the *sentences*, rules similar to the following make it possible to test arithmetic expressions involving variables as operands.

{

$\ldots$

$sentences \rightarrow sentence$
$sentence \rightarrow assignment$
$assignment \rightarrow identifier = expression;$
$expression \rightarrow expression + expression$

$\ldots$

$expression \rightarrow \textbf{numericConstant}$
$expression \rightarrow \textbf{identifier}$

$\ldots$

}

These rules can be used to generate assignments like the following:

{

$\ldots$

$x = y + 3;$

$\ldots$

}

Where x and y are identifiers and 3 is a numeric constant. Whenever an identifier is used, the corresponding rule can access the symbol table to recover the information associated with the variable (using its name as the key). So, in the rule $assignment \rightarrow \textbf{identifier} = expression;$ the compiler will recover first the information about the variable at the left side of the assignment (x in the example) to test, for instance, that x has been previously declared. In a similar way, in the rule $expression \rightarrow \textbf{identifier}$ the symbol table is accessed to get the semantic information about y. This is a standard use of attribute grammars, together with global information.

2.2.4 Comparison with Chomsky Type-0 Grammars

This section try to show in a comprehensible way the most common techniques to design Chomsky type-0 grammars. We have previously introduced type-0 derivation rules by means of this simple example:

$$\{S \rightarrow \lambda, S \rightarrow SAB, AB \rightarrow BA\}$$

It is easy to complete these rules to design a grammar that generates the previously described language $L_{\sharp_a = \sharp_b}$. Notice that the following type-0 grammar $G_{0\sharp_a = \sharp_b} = \{\{S, A, B\}; \{a, b\}; S; \{S \rightarrow \lambda, S \rightarrow SAB, AB \rightarrow BA, A \rightarrow a, B \rightarrow b\}\}$ generates $L_{\sharp_a = \sharp_b}$.

After all the As and Bs are in their proper positions, one can remove S (applying the λ rule) and translate upper case letters into lower case (by means of $A \rightarrow a$ and $B \rightarrow b$).

- The shortest string λ is generated by the rule $S \rightarrow \lambda$.
- The rule $S \rightarrow SAB$ generates A and B couples.
- The context dependent rule $AB \rightarrow BA$ can be used as many times as needed to place each symbol in its proper position, as in the following derivations:
  $SABABABABABAB \Rightarrow \star SAAAAAABBBBBB$;
  $SABABABABABAB \Rightarrow \star SBBBBBBAAAAAA$;
  $SABABABABABAB \Rightarrow \star SBBAAAABABAABB$.
- Once all the As and Bs are in their proper positions, one can remove S (applying the λ rule) and translate the upper case letters into the lower case equivalents by means of rules $A \rightarrow a$ and $B \rightarrow b$.

It is worth devoting a couple of minutes to think about what can be concluded from the context dependent rule in this example, compared to the way in which the symbols are generated using context-free grammars. In the latter case, one must ensure that every correct combination of the symbols in the language will be generated by means of *explicit* rules. This means that, if one wants to generate independent blocks of as and bs, one must do so by means of explicit derivation rules (as, for instance, $S \rightarrow aSb$). Remember, nevertheless, the different approach needed to ensure that we can generate $L_{\sharp_a = \sharp_b}$ with context-free resources and by using additional mathematical tools, such as Bolzano's theorem. With type-0 rules, it is enough to generate the proper number of symbols of each type, and then use the *standard* context-dependent mechanism to exchange their positions. At this point, it is interesting to compare strictly syntactic models that generate $L_{\sharp_a = \sharp_b}$ (context-free and type-0 grammars) with semantic models (such as attribute grammars). We will revisit this question later: *exactly where are the semantics?*

We complete our examples of how to design Chomsky type-0 grammars with one generating the other previously described language: $L_{a^n b^n}$. This example hides a basic, absolutely relevant computing problem: *synchronization*, usually solved by a feature inherent in different models of computation (not just grammars): *signals*.

The previous type-0 example generates the desired structure (SA^nB^n), among many others. So, our main concern will be to avoid generating strings with just terminal symbols from wrong structures (for example, from $SAAABABBB$). In our opinion, the key to solve this problem is to express it in terms of synchronization in the following way: *we cannot generate terminal symbols (as and bs) until after having finished exchanging A's and B's, attaining the right structure A^nB^n.* It seems clear that if we wait until this point, we'll only get strings belonging to $L_{a^nb^n}$. Chomsky type-0 grammars provide different powerful techniques to solve this issue. One can take advantage of context dependent rules to synchronize processes implementing *signals*. In computer science, a signal is just some information that moves across some spatial structure. The use of signals to convey information at a distance is as old as man, in the form of noise (whistles, tom toms), visual signals (smoke or fire, naval flags) or electric signals (telegraph, telephone).

Consider the following type 0 derivations rules that implement signals to ensure synchronization in the generation of $L_{a^nb^n}$ (these rules should be added to some of the rules in $G_{0\#_a=\#_b}$ above): $\{S \to \alpha, \alpha A \to a\alpha, \alpha B \to b\beta, \beta B \to b\beta, \beta \to \lambda\}$.

Let us study them informally by means of the following relevant examples: what happens when you start from $SAAABBB$? And, what happens when you start from $SAABABB$?

1. There is just one derivation that generates a string with only terminals:
   $SAAABBB \Rightarrow \alpha AAABBB \Rightarrow a\alpha AABBB \Rightarrow aa\alpha ABBB \Rightarrow aaa\alpha BBB$
   $\Rightarrow aaab\beta BB \Rightarrow aaabb\beta B \Rightarrow aaabbb\beta \Rightarrow aaabbb$. Notice that if you change
   a capital A (a B) by a (by b) before receiving the signals, you won't get a correct
   string made only of terminal symbols. In fact, the rules $A \to a$ and $B \to b$
   are not needed any longer and will be removed in the final set of rules of the
   grammar.
2. Check that, if we try to apply these rules to the second case ($SAABABB$),
   where the structure is wrong, the signals make it impossible to generate a string
   made only of terminal symbols. Let us look at one initially promising derivation,
   later ruined because not all the non-terminals can be transformed into terminals:
   $SAABABB \Rightarrow \alpha AABABB \Rightarrow a\alpha ABABB \Rightarrow aa\alpha BABB \Rightarrow aab\beta ABB$
   $\Rightarrow \ldots$

In the previous rules, two signals have been used: α, to tell the non-terminal symbol A at its right that it can safely derive its terminal counterpart a, for it is located in the initial block of As (without a previous B), and to the non-terminal symbol B that this is the first B after the initial block of As. β is a signal that tells the non-terminal symbol B at its right that it can safely derive its terminal counterpart b, for it is located inside the block of Bs that follows the only allowed block of As.

The complete Chomsky type-0 grammar for this language consists of the following derivation rules:

$\{S \to \lambda, S \to SAB, AB \to BA, S \to \alpha, \alpha A \to a\alpha, \alpha B \to b\beta, \beta B \to b\beta, \beta \to \lambda\}$.

This toy example has demonstrated the two most powerful techniques to program Chomsky type-0 grammars to solve specific problems: moving parts of the derived strings using the context, and synchronizing processes by means of signals.

2.3 Christiansen Grammars

2.3.1 A Short Historical and Academic Introduction

The last grammatical model that we will introduce in this chapter are *Christiansen grammars* (CGs). They were first introduced by Henning Christiansen in [8] as a model related to the *Generative Grammars*, introduced by Shutt in [30] in 1985. These grammars are an extension of attribute grammars that includes them as a special case. Therefore they also are computationally complete,the same as attribute grammars. From a taxonomic viewpoint, CGs are an adaptable version of attribute grammars. *Adaptability* is usually understood as the ability to change and adjust to new conditions. For computational formal models, *adaptability* is the capacity of the model to modify itself while it is being used. No grammar we have mentioned so far is adaptable, for once defined they never change.

Christiansen first proposed his grammars as a practical Prolog *data structure*. Prolog is a logic programming language, i.e. it implements the logic programming paradigm, an automatic deduction system based on the Robinson's resolution inference system. Prolog has the following useful characteristics:

1. Prolog programs are *first order logic theories* written in a normal form called *clauses*. The specific structure of these theories and the characteristics of these clauses are out of the scope of this chapter.
2. First order logic can be considered a formal way to describe the knowledge about a domain using the following mechanisms:
   (a) Relevant individuals can be represented by means of so called *terms* that in Prolog notation can be divided into the following groups:
      (i) *Constants*, as 0, 34, *john*.
      (ii) *Variables*, whose value can be any other term,as X, Y or even unnamed (_).
      (iii) Individuals described by means of *functions* that refers to other individuals. For instance, $father(john)$, $arm(mary)$, $double(X)$.
   (b) Relationships between individuals can also be formalized by means of so called *predicates*, which are defined in a *recursive* (*inductive*) way:
      (i) First, basic true facts are included. They are called *atomic predicates* or *atoms*). For example, $natural(0)$ (asserts that 0 is a natural number); $father(john, mary)$, $mother(ann, mary)$ (they assert that John is Mary's father and Ann is Mary's mother).
      (ii) Plus *recursive* or *inductive* rules, defining logical conditions that must hold to deduce that something is true, as in the following examples:

- *parent*(*X*, *Y*) : − *father*(*X*, *Y*); *parent*(*X*, *Y*) : −*mother*(*X*, *Y*); these two rules define *X* as the *parent* of *Y* if *X* is the father of *Y* or the mother of *Y*.
- *natural*(*successor*(*X*)) : −*natural*(*X*). This rule, together with the atom *natural*(0), declares that the predicate *natural* is true for any natural number, i.e. 0, *successor*(0), *successor*(*successor*(0)), and so on.

3. As in any inference system, one declares a priori knowledge about the domain under consideration by means or an *initial theory* (a Prolog program), and there are built in *inference rules* (*resolution* and *unification*) that make it possible to infer (or deduce) new knowledge from previous knowledge, which is then incorporated to the current theory, becoming undistinguishable from the original theory.

In Prolog there is no distinction between *data structures* and *executable* code. Prolog programmers working on formal languages use a special data structure called *Definite Clause Grammar* (DCG), the Prolog way of defining attribute grammars. This notation is slightly different to that of clauses, to highlight the similarity with formal grammars. The following example makes clear these similarities with clauses and grammars. It defines a grammar for a small kind of English sentences taken from http://www.cs.uni-potsdam.de/wv/lehre/Material/Prolog/Eclipse-Doc/userman/node68.html.

```
sentence --> noun_phrase(Number), verb_phrase(Number).

noun_phrase(Number) --> determiner, noun(Number).
noun_phrase(Number) --> pronom(Number).

verb_phrase(Number) --> verb(Number).
verb_phrase(Number) --> verb(Number), noun_phrase(_).

determiner --> [the].

noun(singular) --> [man].
noun(singular) --> [apple].
noun(plural) --> [men].
noun(plural) --> [apples].

verb(singular) --> [eats].
verb(singular) --> [sings].
verb(plural) --> [eat].
verb(plural) --> [sing].
pronom(plural) --> [you]
```

This grammar can generate, among others, the following sentences, written as Prolog lists: [*the, man, eats, the, apple*], [*the, men, eat*], [*the, men, eats*], [*eat, the, apples*].

After this brief outline from first order logic to Prolog DCGs we can highlight the following conclusions:

- The Prolog clause structure is quite similar to derivation rules for context-free grammars.
- Prolog features to attach variables to predicate names provide a natural and native way to add semantic information to a symbol of a grammar. The Prolog inference rules (resolution and unification, specially unification) include the propagation mechanisms of attribute grammars when the grammar is expressed as DCGs.

Starting from this context, it is easy to understand the question posed by H. Christiansen, to be solved by CGs: how can attribute grammars take advantage of the fact that Prolog can modify the initial program with new proven facts?

This is a good point to describe briefly the mechanisms by means of which Prolog programs can *self*-change while they are running. To write a Prolog program, you open your preferred text editor and write your predicates exactly in the same way as in most programming languages. But there are a couple of families of built in predicates that make it possible to change your theory by adding and removing clauses when they are executed:

1. The *assert*(*Clause*) adds a new clause (*Clause*) to the theory, which the Prolog inference rule will be able to use in the future, together with the remainder of the program. (In the following simplified examples, you can get compilation errors if you write this in a Prolog environment). Assume your program contains this clause instead of the one mentioned before: $natural(successor(X))$: $-natural(X), assert(natural(successor(X)))$. If the system executes this for $X = sucessor(0)$, your theory will now have an explicit atom declaring $natural(sucessor(sucessor(0)))$.
2. There is also a family of predicates (namely *retract*) that does the opposite. If your program, for example, after explicitly asserting several natural numbers (such as $successor(0)$, $successor(successor(0))$ and $successor(successor(successor(0)))$) retracts the recursive clause for the predicate *natural* the system will only consider correct natural numbers the first four: 0, 1, 2 and 3.

It is easy, then, to understand how a Prolog version of the attribute grammars can easily become adaptable. If *assert* or *retract* clauses are added in your DCG derivation rules can be added or removed. This is the technique used by Christiansen to define his CGs.

2.3.2 Partial Formalization for CG

Informally CGs extend attribute grammars with the following two mechanisms (although the second one is actually a consequence of the first):

- Rather than considering just one global set of derivation rules, each non terminal symbol is provided with a local copy of the rules that can be used to generate derivations from that symbol.
- This is implemented by providing each symbol in the grammar with an inherited first attribute containing its CG. Additional attributes can also contain CGs that will be used to change and propagate the grammar to other symbols, while deriving strings.

Thus the same notation will be used for CGs as was used for attribute grammars. As an example, we will handle by means of Christiansen grammars the same kind of constraints as in the attribute grammar that used a symbol table. Figure 6 shows a similar grammar for a similar language. It has been slightly changed, so that the figure is the proper size. This figure shows the complete grammar. Let us describe its main characteristics and differences with the previous one:

- The context-free kernel considers as the only valid identifier names strings with just one letter.
- Valid sentences are reduced to assignments among variables (this is just a toy language, complex enough to show the use of CG).
- The non-terminal that refers to the name of the variables while they are being declared is called *string*, because it represents a string of symbols.
- The non-terminal that refers to the name of the variables when they are used in sentences is *identifier*.
- There are no rules to derive from the non-terminal symbol *identifier*. This is important, for a context-free grammar with this set of derivation rules is incomplete, as it contains non-terminal symbols unable to generate terminal symbols.

In addition to the set of derivation rules and the derivation tree for the string $\{int\ i, j; i = j; \}$. Figure 6 graphically shows the propagation process, distinguishing between synthesis (red arrows) and inheritance (blue ones). It also adds, as extra information, a numeric sequence that follows a possible order in which semantic actions, and hence propagation occurs. Let us analyze the example in detail:

- The first relevant topic is that CGs allow incomplete sets of derivation rules, as they are supposed to be completed while deriving strings. In our example, rules for *identifier* should be added to the current grammar before the non-terminal is derived in the right subtree of Fig. 6.
- The propagation process graphically highlighted focus on the way in which the current grammar for each symbol is computed.
- We will explain the sequence of this process because the order followed is the most powerful one, which makes it possible to build the derivation tree at the same time than both kind of attributes (synthesized and inherited) are computed.

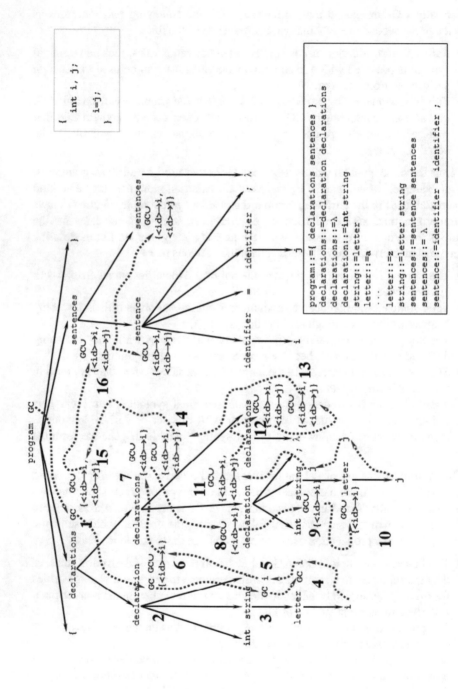

Fig. 6 Derivation tree for a CG that avoids a global symbol table to check that only previously declared variables are used in executable sentences

This order is known as *in depth, left-most with backtracking*, because it goes deeper and deeper through the left-most sons until finding a leaf. At this point, it backtracks to the deepest next option to the right. This order corresponds with the sequence of numbers added to the tree:

1 Initially, the axiom passes to its first left child (*declarations*), as its current set of derivation rules, those shown in the figure.

2,3 In these steps the process is the same: the subsequent parents (*declarations*, *declaration* and *string*) just pass the initial grammar to their children.

4 After reaching the leaf containing the terminal symbol **i**, we know a possible right hand side for the non-terminal *identifier*, so the rule *identifier* → **i** is added to the initial set of rules, and a second CG attribute (this time synthesized) is computed.

5,6 The synthesized grammar is sent back, up to node *declaration*, previously visited in step 2.

7 At this point, the grammar is inherited by the right sibling *declarations*, with all the names of the different variables declared up to this point accumulated in the grammar.

8,...,15 A similar propagation is followed to add the rule *identifier* → **j** to the grammar, which is finally inherited by the right sibling *sentences*.

16, etc. From this point, no additional changes are made to the current grammar, which is now complete and hence will be inherited from parent to children.

2.3.3   Conclusions

It is time to try to extract some useful conclusions of these examples. The first one is specific to the last example: adaptability could simplify the attribute system. In this way, the use of a global symbol table could be avoided by using two different non-terminal symbols (*string* and *identifier*) for the names of variables being declared and used, respectively; leaving initially undefined the rules for *identifier*, and adding them during the propagation of the current grammar. But we must keep in mind that adaptability does not add expressive power to CGs, for they just extend the attribute grammars and these grammars are the most expressive. So we must conclude again that choosing between these two types of grammars (or, as in our example, using or not a symbol table) is a question of taste for the developers; thence, again, a *comfort* question.

2.4   AGE and CGE

2.4.1   How We Extend GE

We extend GE using both attribute grammars or Christiansen grammars, explicitly building the derivation tree while attributes are propagated across the tree with the *in depth, left-most with backtracking* order. In this way we can ensure the *semantic* correctness of phenotypes and include in the grammar as many semantic constraints as we consider appropriate for all our candidate solutions. As previously discussed, the choice between attribute grammars and Christiansen grammars is a comfort question for the designer of the experiment.

2.4.2   Previous Works

We first proposed AGE in [13]. In this paper we tested the viability of this approach by replicating previously published GE experiments to solve the *symbolic regression* problem: how to get a symbolic expression for points sampled among the values of $f(x) = x^4 + x^3 + x^2 + x$ when $x \in [-1, 1]$. In this work we performed different experiments from which we have drawn the following conclusions:

- GE and AGE show a similar performance to get similar results in terms of number of fitness functions evaluated. In our first experiment we discarded, by means of the attribute system, candidate solutions undefined in some of the input points. This condition is in some *ad hoc* way also checked using GE, by means of the fitness function, which gave rise to a significant increase in the time needed by the mapping function.
- We performed a second experiment to compare GE and AGE performance when a very simple constraint was added to all the candidate solutions: that all the phenotypes should match the goal at least in one of the three input points $-1, 0$ of 1. In this case, there was a clear improvement in the performance of AGE.

We proposed CGE in a later paper, [27], where we posed for the first time that the choice between AGE and CGE is rather a comfort than a performance question. We made an exhaustive comparison between GE and CGE in the *logical regression* domain. This is a special case of symbolic regression, where the goal function is boolean. We started by a clearly context-free language and then added a few conditions not as easy to implement by context-free rules, such as forcing the use of logical operators from the same complete set: either $\{and, or, not\}$, or $\{nand\}$ or $\{nor\}$. We got the following conclusions:

- CGE is too sophisticated for simple problems: GE performance is better that CGE for the simplest cases.
- CGE could be a more comfortable way for the designer to express some restrictions: in our CG, we just removed those operators incompatible with the first generated one, for example, if *nand* is the first generated operator, from that

point the other operands are removed as valid right hand sides for the derivation rules that generate operands.

In further papers [12, 14] we have explored different questions related with the performance and the possibility of using AGE and CGE as a kind of *software engineering tool* when trying to solve real problems by programming new bio-inspired models of computation.

3 Most Relevant Conclusions

3.1 In General

We have tried to introduce in a comprehensible way every question necessary to understand not just the context, but also the type of tasks related with the solution of problems by means of AGE and CGE. We can highlight the following general conclusions:

- *Roughly speaking*, semantics seems to be everything that we cannot express by means of context-free grammars. *Formally speaking*, everything is syntax. Although something similar could be said about semantics... everything can be expressed as semantics.
- Type-0 grammars should only be used if the implementor is comfortable designing signals to synchronize processes, and expressing global behaviours in terms of local interactions.
- Attribute grammars should be used when the implementor is more comfortable graphically describing global behaviours (such as propagation on derivations trees represented by means of arrows) and writing algorithms, rather than developing inductive algebraic proofs.
- Context-free grammars should be used to represent strings whose structure can be split into independent parts, each part exhibiting a pattern that grows simultaneously at both ends, or of similar complexity.
- A subtle magnitude that can be called *comfort* could be the key to choose between all these different models. Comfort could be more relevant for making these decisions than the theoretical expressive power of the model under consideration.

3.2 AGE and CGE

There is a significant difference between GE and our semantic approaches (AGE and CGE). The designer must decide between two alternatives: expressing some conditions of the solutions to the problem either in the fitness function, or in the attribute system of the grammar. In the first case, individuals violating those conditions will sometimes be generated and must be punished by the fitness function, while in the second case those bad individuals will never be generated. This could be considered as a new parameter to be tuned: *the amount of semantics* explicitly expressed.

We have concluded from our experiments that:

- The advantages provided by CGE and AGE can only be seen when tackling *difficult problems*, meaning those with huge search spaces.
- *Too much semantics* does not necessarily imply better results. We have previously explained in this chapter that both attribute grammars and CGs are computationally complete models. This means that the solutions can be completely described by means of semantic constraints. It is clear that, in this case, all the population generated would consist of correct solutions to the problem, therefore the evolutive side of the system would not be used at all in the search. It would be just a random search.
- The more constraints the attribute system includes, the less diversity in the population. But the fewer constraints in each individual, the less solutions will be found by the evolutionary computation.
- Sometimes just a few semantics are enough, for the increase in performance will be clear even with weak or trivial semantic conditions.

Acknowledgements This work has been supported by several research grants: Spanish Ministry of Science and Education under Project Code TIN2014-56494-C4-4-P (ephemeCH) and TIN2017-85727-C4-3-P (DeepBio). We thank also Manuel Alfonseca's help to improve this work.

References

1. T.M. Apostol, *Calculus*, 2nd edn. One-Variable Calculus, With an Introduction to Linear Algebra, vol. 1 (Blaisdell, Waltham, MA, 1967), p. 143
2. B. Bolzano, Rein analytischer Beweis des Lehrsatzes dass zwischen je zwey Werthen, die ein entgegengesetztes Resultat gewaehren, wenigstens eine reele Wurzel der Gleichung liege. Prague, 1817. English translation in Russ, S. B. A Translation of Bolzano's Paper on the Intermediate Value Theorem. Hist. Math. **7**, 156–185 (1980)
3. P.A.N. Bosman, E.D. de Jong, Learning probabilistic tree grammars for genetic programming, in Proceedings of *8th International Conference, Parallel Problem Solving from Nature - PPSN VIII*, Birmingham, UK, September 18-22, 2004, pp. 192–201. https://doi.org/10.1007/978-3-540-30217-9_20
4. Z. Chi, Statistical properties of context-free grammars. Comput. Linguist. **25**(1), 131–160 (1999)
5. N. Chomsky, Three models for the description of language. IRE Trans. Inform. Theory (2), 113–124 (1956). https://doi.org/10.1109/TIT.1956.1056813
6. N. Chomsky, On certain formal properties of grammars. Inform. Control **2**(2), 137–167 (1959). https://doi.org/10.1016/S0019-9958(59)90362-6
7. N. Chomsky, M.P. Schötzenberger, The algebraic theory of context free languages, in *Computer Programming and Formal Languages*, ed. by P. Braffort, D. Hirschberg (North Holland, Amsterdam, 1963), pp. 118–161

8. H. Christiansen, Syntax, semantics, and implementation strategies for programming languages with powerful abstraction mechanisms, in *Proceedings of the 18th Hawaii International Conference on System Sciences*, vol. 2 (1985), pp. 57–66
9. A. Church, An unsolvable problem of elementary number theory. Am. J. Math. **58**(2), 345 (1936). ISSN 0002-9327. JSTOR 2371045. https://doi.org/10.2307/2371045
10. R. Cleary, Extending grammatical evolution with attribute grammars: an application to knapsack problems. Masters Thesis, University of Limerick (2005). http://ncra.ucd.ie/papers/thesisExtGEwithAGs-CRC.pdf
11. R. Cleary, M. O'Neill, An attribute grammar decode for the 0/1 multiconstrained knapsack problem, in *European Conference on Evolutionary Combinatorial Optimisation EvoCOP 2005*, ed. by G.R. Raidl, G.J. Lausanne. Lecture Notes in Computer Science, vol. 3448 (Springer, Cham, 2005), pp. 34–45. http://ncra.ucd.ie/papers/evocop2005.pdf
12. M. de la Cruz Echeandía, A. Ortega de la Puente, A Christiansen grammar for universal splicing systems, in *IWINAC (1)* (2009), pp. 336–345
13. A. Ortega, M. de la Cruz, M. Alfonseca, Christiansen grammar evolution: grammatical evolution with semantics. IEEE Trans. Evol. Comput. **11**(1), 77–90 (2007). https://doi.org/10.1109/TEVC.2006.880327
14. M. de la Cruz Echeandía, A. Martín Lázaro, A. Ortega de la Puente, J. Luis Montaña, C. Luis Alonso, The role of keeping "semantic blocks" invariant - effects in linear genetic programming performance, in *IJCCI (ICEC)* (2010), pp. 365–368
15. A. Ganatra, Y.P. Kosta, G. Panchal, C. Gajjar, Initial classification through back propagation in a neural network following optimization through GA to evaluate the fitness of an algorithm. Int. J. Comput. Sci. Inf. Technol. **3**(1), 98–116 (2011)
16. K. Gödel, Über formal unentscheidbare Sätze der Principia Mathematica und verwandter Systeme, I. Monatshefte für Mathematik und Physik **38**, 173–198 (1931). https://doi.org/10.1007/BF01700692
17. J.V. Grabiner, Who gave you the epsilon? Cauchy and the origins of rigorous calculus. Am. Math. Mon. **90**, 185–194 (1983)
18. J.M. Guo, X.F. Yuan, Z.X. Xiong, Force finding of suspended-domes using back propagation (BP) algorithm. Adv. Steel Constr. **12**(1), 17–31 (2016)
19. A.K. Joshi, Y. Schabes, Tree-adjoining grammars, in *Handbook of Formal Languages* (Springer, Berlin, Heidelberg, 1997), pp. 69–123
20. G. Katsirelos, N. Narodytska, T. Walsh, The weighted CFG constraint. CoRR (2009). abs/0909.4456
21. H.T. Kim, C.W. Ahn, A new grammatical evolution based on probabilistic context-free grammar, in *Proceedings of the 18th Asia Pacific Symposium on Intelligent and Evolutionary Systems - Volume 2*, ed. by H. Handa, H. Ishibuchi, Y.S. Ong, K.C. Tan. Proceedings in Adaptation, Learning and Optimization, vol. 2 (Springer, Cham, 2015)
22. D.E. Knuth, Semantics of context-free languages. Math. Syst. Theory **2**, 127 (1968). Springer. https://doi.org/10.1007/BF01692511. ISSN 0025-5661
23. M. Mohri, F.C.N. Pereira, Dynamic compilation of weighted context-free grammars, in *COLING-ACL* (1998), pp. 891–897
24. E. Murphy, An exploration of tree-adjoining grammars for grammatical evolution. Ph.D. thesis, University College Dublin, D.S.o.C.S.I., University College (2013)
25. E. Murphy, M. O'Neill, E. Galván-López, A. Brabazon, Tree-adjunct grammatical evolution, in *2010 IEEE Congress on Evolutionary Computation (CEC)* (IEEE, New York, July 2010), pp. 1–8
26. M. O'Neill, R. Cleary, N. Nikolov, Solving knapsack problems with attribute grammars, in *Proceedings of the Third Grammatical Evolution Workshop GEWS 2004 ISGEC*, Seattle, WA, ed. by M. O'Neill, C. Ryan. http://ncra.ucd.ie/papers/WGEW003.pdf
27. A. Ortega de la Puente, M. de la Cruz Echeandía, M. Alfonseca Moreno, Christiansen grammar evolution: grammatical evolution with semantics. IEEE Trans. Evol. Comput. **11**(1), 77–90 (2007)

28. H. Sato, Y. Hasegawa, D. Bollegala, H. Iba, Probabilistic model building GP with belief propagation, in *IEEE Congress on Evolutionary Computation* (2012), pp. 1–8
29. H. Sato, Y. Hasegawa, D. Bollegala, H. Iba, Improved sampling using loopy belief propagation for probabilistic model building genetic programming. Swarm Evol. Comput. **23**, 1–10 (2015). ISSN 2210-6502
30. J.N. Shutt, Imperative adaptive grammars. Web page dated 28 March 2001. http://web.cs.wpi. edu/~jshutt/adapt/imperative.html
31. A. Turing, On computable numbers, with an application to the Entscheidungs problem. Proc. Lond. Math. Soc. Ser. **2**(42), 230–265 (1936–1937). Online versions: from journal website, from Turing Digital Archive, from abelard.org. Errata appeared in Series **2**(43), 544–546 (1937)
32. S.D. Turner, S.M. Dudek, M.D. Ritchie, ATHENA: a knowledge-based hybrid backpropagation-grammatical evolution neural network algorithm for discovering epistasis among quantitative trait Loci. BioData Min. **3**(1), 5 (2010)
33. K. Vijayashanker, A.K. Joshi, *A Study of Tree Adjoining Grammars* (University of Pennsylvania, Philadelphia, 1988)
34. K. Vijay-Shanker, D.J. Weir, A.K. Joshi, Tree adjoining and head wrapping, in *Proceedings of the 11th Conference on Computational Linguistics* (Association for Computational Linguistics, New York, August 1986), pp. 202–207
35. D.J. Weir, K. Vijay-Shanker, A.K. Joshi, The relationship between tree adjoining grammars and head grammars, in *Proceedings of the 24th Annual Meeting on Association for Computational Linguistics* (Association for Computational Linguistics, New York, July 1986), pp. 67–74

Multi- and Many-Threaded Heterogeneous Parallel Grammatical Evolution

Amanda Sabatini Dufek, Douglas Adriano Augusto, Helio José Corrêa Barbosa, and Pedro Leite da Silva Dias

Abstract There are some algorithms suited for inference of human-interpretable models for classification and regression tasks in machine learning, but it is hard to compete with Grammatical Evolution (GE) when it comes to powerfulness, model expressiveness and ease of implementation. On the other hand, algorithms that iteratively optimize a set of programs of arbitrary complexity—which is the case of GE—may take an inconceivable amount of running time when tackling complex problems. Fortunately, GE may scale to such problems by carefully harnessing the parallel processing of modern heterogeneous systems, taking advantage of traditional multi-core processors and many-core accelerators to speed up the execution by orders of magnitude. This chapter covers the subject of parallel GE, focusing on heterogeneous multi- and many-threaded decomposition in order to achieve a fully parallel implementation, where both the breeding and evaluation are parallelized. In the studied benchmarks, the overall parallel implementation runtime was 68 times faster than the sequential version, with the program evaluation kernel alone hitting an acceleration of 350 times. Details on how to efficiently accomplish that are given in the context of two well-established open standards for parallel computing: OpenMP and OpenCL. Decomposition strategies, optimization techniques and parallel benchmarks followed by analyses are presented in the chapter.

A. S. Dufek (✉) · H. J. C. Barbosa
National Laboratory for Scientific Computing, Rio de Janeiro, Brazil
e-mail: amandasd@lncc.br; hcbm@lncc.br

D. A. Augusto
Oswaldo Cruz Foundation, Rio de Janeiro, Brazil
e-mail: daa@fiocruz.br

P. L. da Silva Dias
Institute of Astronomy, Geophysics and Atmospheric Sciences, University of São Paulo, São Paulo, Brazil
e-mail: pedro.dias@iag.usp.br

© Springer International Publishing AG, part of Springer Nature 2018
C. Ryan et al. (eds.), *Handbook of Grammatical Evolution*,
https://doi.org/10.1007/978-3-319-78717-6_9

1 Introduction

The field of machine learning has gained a lot of momentum recently and its applications have become ubiquitous across many domains. Most these applications, though, employ some variation of artificial neural network, for instance, Deep Neural Network and Recurrent Neural Network [5, 6]. However, there are classes of problems in machine learning that do not fit well black-box techniques, which is the case of artificial neural network and its derivatives. For example, the important class of knowledge extraction is in most cases better approached by means of symbolic-based techniques, where the model is itself the representation of the knowledge. Sophisticated symbolic-based methods allow for precisely defining the structure of the models or, in other words, defining their language, which in turn establishes the optimization's search space. Grammatical evolution is a symbolic-based technique that allows specifying the language of the models via formal grammars such as context-free grammars. Not only this, but all that can be easily implemented through a simple linear-based mechanism, which maps binary arrays into actual program/models.

Genetic programming algorithms—which includes GE—are known for their high computational demand, especially for population-based ones. This is particularly critical when dealing with complex large-scale regression problems which contain at least one of: (1) high-dimensional datasets; (2) difficult landscapes, which demands several number of generations; (3) complex and/or large number of candidate solutions. Unfortunately, in real-world problems it is rare to not have at least one of the listed characteristics. Indeed, frequently several of them will be simultaneously present for real-world problems.

Here is where parallelism takes place. GE, like evolutionary algorithms in general, is embarrassingly parallel, which means it can be decomposed efficiently thereby enabling it to scale to complex problems. In shared-memory systems, the more usual and straightforward strategy to parallelize GE is by decomposing the population and performing the breeding and evaluation tasks on multiple individuals simultaneously. However, it is well known that the evaluation procedure, which boils down to iterated program interpretation/execution over a dataset, accounts for the majority of computational time, due mainly to complex candidate solutions and/or high-dimensional datasets. Fortunately, as the evaluation phase is pretty regular in terms of instructions and memory access, it is possible to efficiently harness the computing power of general purpose accelerators to speed up even further this phase.

That is where heterogeneous computing fits in. Virtually all computational systems nowadays come with different processors where each one is more efficient at a certain workload. For instance, a typical modern system contains a conventional CPU, which deals well with irregular workloads (multiple divergent instructions, random memory accesses), and one or more accelerators, which are optimized for high computational intensity and regular workloads (single instruction, coalesced memory accesses). CPU designs consist of multiple high-frequency and complex processor cores that efficiently access data through the intensive use of large cache memories. As opposed to CPU's latency-oriented design, accelerators are characterized by a large number of relatively simple cores and a high-bandwidth memory in order to maximize throughput at the expense of increasing latency, with a low-power consumption. Of course, the most efficient way of utilizing a processor is assigning to it the workload for which the architecture was optimized for. This chapter will present an efficient heterogeneous scheme to fully parallelize the GE algorithm, taking advantage of both CPUs and accelerators, and is organized as follows: Sect. 2 shows how the breeding phase of GE can be decomposed into multiple threads in a coarse-grained fashion. In Sect. 3, the evaluation phase is addressed and some strategies are detailed on how this phase can be properly parallelized through fine-grained decomposition. Performance analyses are presented in Sect. 4, where several experiments followed by discussions are conducted on two benchmark setups.

2 Multi-Threaded Parallel GE

Massively parallel many-core accelerators have become increasingly popular in high-performance computing, mainly because of their huge theoretical raw performance, which actually brings impressive speed-ups to many algorithms across domains. They are not a panacea, though. Every processor architecture has compromises, usually meaning being either extremely efficient at a certain workload pattern or designed towards a more balanced efficiency over different workloads—it all boils down to what the transistors on a chip are devoted to, either to actual processing (ALU) or to some higher-level purpose such as multi-level cache hierarchy, speculative and out-of-order execution [13]. GPUs are more like specialized processors—thus very efficient but sensitive to the processing pattern—whereas conventional CPUs are more general—that is, do not excel at specific tasks but are robust and provide satisfactory performance regardless of the workload.

Algorithm 1 outlines the pseudo-code of a basic GE algorithm. The initialization of the population of binary genomes (`generate`), the decoding of genomes into phenotypes/programs (`decode`) and the derivation of new individuals from fit ones (`derive`) are here collectively referred to as *breeding*. The fitness evaluation of the programs is computed by `evaluate`, whose parallel decomposition is presented in Sect. 3. We use the term *evolutionary tasks* to refer to breeding and evaluation-related tasks all together.

Technically speaking, there is nothing that prevents the parallelization of the GE's breeding phase on accelerators, as proposed for instance in [14] and [16]. However, there are compelling arguments why multi-core CPUs are well suited

---

Algorithm 1: Basic GE algorithm

$P \leftarrow$ generate (); $\quad$ // initialize population of genomes P with random bits
$P' \leftarrow$ decode (P); $\quad$ // decode binary genomes in P according to a grammar
evaluate (P'); // transfer P' to accelerator, evaluate and calculate best
while *stop criteria not met* **do**
    $P_{tmp} \leftarrow$ derive (P); $\quad$ // select, crossover and mutate from P into P_{tmp}
    $P' \leftarrow$ decode (P_{tmp});
    evaluate (P');
    $P \leftrightarrows P_{tmp}$; $\quad\quad\quad\quad$ // swap P_{tmp} with P (no actual copy is needed)
return the *best program* found

---

for the task: (1) CPUs are designed to be smarter and predicable on irregular workloads which typically show up when generating random numbers, traversing the grammar during the decoding, and deriving new individuals; (2) heterogeneous computing aims at efficiently adding together the power of multiple processors, that is, harnessing all of them properly while minimizing their idleness; (3) finally, low-level programming models for accelerators lead to considerable more code complexity, especially when compared with directive-based models on CPUs.

With that being said, we will show how a very simple yet efficient directive-based OpenMP [4] parallelism is introduced to the breeding phase. OpenMP is an open directive-based specification designed for thread-based parallelism models to be executed on shared memory multiprocessors, with guaranteed portability across architectures from multiple vendors. The most prominent feature of directive-based parallel programming models is how little code has to be introduced in order to parallelize a routine. As seen in Algorithms 2, 3 and 4, only a simple *pragma* directive per routine was necessary.

Algorithm 2: [generate]

#pragma omp parallel for
for $p \leftarrow 0$ **to** *population$_{size}$* $- 1$ **do**
    for $i \leftarrow 0$ **to** *genome$_{size}$* $- 1$ **do**
        $genome_p^i \leftarrow$ RandomBit();

Algorithm 3: [decode]

#pragma omp parallel for
for $p \leftarrow 0$ **to** *population$_{size}$* $- 1$ **do**
    $program_p \leftarrow$ decode($genome_p$);

Algorithm 4: [derive]

#pragma omp parallel for

for $p \leftarrow 0$ **to** $population_{size} - 1$ **do**

    Select from P two fit programs, g_1 and g_2;

    if *[probabilistically] crossover* **then**

        | Recombine g_1 and g_2 into P_{tmp};

    else Clone g_1 and g_2 into P_{tmp};

    if *[probabilistically] mutation* **then**

        | Mutate the recently inserted programs in P_{tmp};

    $p \leftarrow p + 2$;

The directive `parallel for` instructs OpenMP to parallelize the loop that follows it, effectively distributing the effort among threads. As usually the population size surpasses the number of available CPU threads (cores), what will happen at runtime is that each thread will process roughly $\frac{population_{size}}{|threads|}$ genomes sequentially, where by the default OpenMP scheduling means chunks of adjacent genomes.

2.1 Startup Tasks

Although not mentioned in Algorithm 1, before the actual evolution there are some startup tasks that take place. In particular, two are related to this multi-threaded decomposition: the pseudo random number generation (`rng init`) and the memory allocate for the main and temporary populations (`evolution init`). They are small and quick tasks, but implementing them incorrectly may cause performance degradation to the whole evolutionary phase.

What `rng init` does is basically allocating storage for the seed of each instance of a pseudo random number generator—in multi-threaded applications there is an RNG instance for each thread with its own seed in order to not interfere with the other instances. Analogously, `evolution init` performs the allocation of genome arrays.

There are two important optimizations to care about: (1) minimizing the data path length between a CPU thread and the memory region that it accesses; and (2) preventing that multiple CPU threads invalidate the cached data of one another.

The first issue occurs on computers that feature *Non-Uniform Memory Access* (NUMA) memory topology, typically found in modern high-performance systems, and is handled by following the so-called *first touch policy* [12]. What it says is that upon the first memory allocation the processor tries to allocate the space on the nearest memory to the thread that issued the allocation. Therefore, if only one thread performs the whole allocation—be it genomes or seeds—all that region would be closest to that single thread, implying that other threads would probably have to struggle over a longer data path to access this region afterwards. Fortunately, the solution is as simple as decomposing the population into individual genomes (seeds) and making sure that every thread allocates its own range of genomes (or seeds). In order to allow for deterministic reproducibility and ensure different seeds across RNGs, each RNG instance will have its seed expressed by $seed_{global} \veebar thread_{id}$, where $\veebar$ is the bitwise `exclusive or` binary operator.

The second issue affects nearly all multi-core machines because of their cache-based memory architecture, and is known as *false sharing* [3]. This occurs when two or more threads access distinct memory locations in the same cache line.[1] When a thread writes to a cache line required by another thread for reading or writing, it invalidates the cache line and forces an update—which results in access to the much slower main memory—leading to performance degradation. Thankfully, a positive side effect of the data decomposition introduced to tackle the first issue is that it also distributes the data on the memory thereby minimizing the likelihood of multiple threads operating on the same cache line.

3 Many-Threaded Parallel GE

While multi-core CPUs are well-suited for the type of workload involved in the breeding phase, most of the architectural design that make CPUs so robust are useless for the well-behaved processing pattern of program evaluation, resulting in a low performance per transistors count ratio. This is especially true for strategies that optimize workload regularity, in which accelerators genuinely shine.

Three well-known strategies were examined for the parallel implementation of the evaluation process; they are: *Program-level Parallelism* (PP), *Data-level Parallelism* (DP) and *Program- and Data-level Parallelism* (PDP) [2, 15]. The first strategy explores the iteration-level parallelism; the second one addresses the solution-level parallelism; and the last one is the most complete strategy as it explores both iteration- and solution-level parallel models. The evaluation phase of GE is parallelized via the OpenCL programming language [11], an open standard managed by the Khronos Group for the development of portable parallel applications on heterogeneous computing systems. An advantage of OpenCL is that it supports a wide range of parallel devices from multiple vendors as well as many different hardware platforms. Sections 3.1–3.3 describe the three evaluation kernels. The OpenCL kernel designed to compute the best program at each iteration is presented in Sect. 3.4.

---

[1] Put simply, cache is a very fast but small memory that stores the most recently/commonly accessed data. When a requested data is not in cache, a fixed size block of data—which contains not only the requested data, but also the nearby ones—is copied from main memory into the cache, which is known as *cache line* or *cache block* [10].

3.1 Program-Level Parallelism: PP

A general scheme of OpenCL kernel for the *Program-level Parallelism* (PP) strategy in pseudo-code is outlined in Algorithm 5. The iteration-level parallel model is achieved by distributing the programs among the processing elements of a compute device. For this strategy, the programs are partitioned into work-groups of size $local_{size}$, where $local_{size}$ represents the number of work-items in a work-group. A work-item—globally identified by $global_{id}$—corresponds to a single program, and $global_{size}$ denotes the total number of work-items, which in this case is the population size. The $local_{size}$ and the $global_{size}$ were defined as follows:

$$local_{size} = \min(local_{max\_size}, \lceil population_{size}/cu \rceil), \qquad (1)$$

$$global_{size} = \lceil population_{size}/local_{size} \rceil \times local_{size}, \qquad (2)$$

ensuring that $global_{size}$ is divisible by $local_{size}$, as required by the OpenCL specification, such that $number_{groups} = \frac{global_{size}}{local_{size}} = \lceil population_{size}/local_{size} \rceil$. Equation 1 ensures that the maximum number of work-items per work-group, $local_{max\_size}$, is not exceeded, and also that the distribution of the programs among the cu compute units is balanced even though the population size, $population_{size}$, is smaller than the total number of device's processing elements. In Eq. 2, if $population_{size}/local_{size}$ is not evenly divisible, the rounding up implies $global_{size} > population_{size}$. Thus, the checking at the line 2 in Algorithm 5 is required to avoid accessing invalid elements.

Algorithm 5: PP OpenCL kernel— [evaluate]

$global_{id} \leftarrow$ get_global_id();

2 **if** $global_{id} < population_{size}$ **then**

  $program \leftarrow$ nthprogram($global_{id}$);

  $P \leftarrow 0.0$;

5 **for** $n \leftarrow 0$ **to** $dataset_{size} - 1$ **do**

6   $\lfloor$ $P \leftarrow P +$ error(interpreter($program, n$), $Y[n]$);

  $E[global_{id}] \leftarrow P/dataset_{size}$;

For each register n of the dataset, the error() function returns an accuracy measure for the problem in question, according to the fitness function predefined by the user. Error() requires two arguments: the expected value $Y[n]$ and the one returned by interpreter() (line 6), a function that executes *program* on the n-th register of the dataset. Note that a single work-item within a work-group computes the sum of partial errors of *program* over the $dataset_{size}$ registers of the dataset, and stores it into variable P, allocated in the work-item's private memory.

At the end of for loop (line 5), the error of the program indexed by $global_{id}$ is stored into array E of size $population_{size}$, allocated in the device's global memory.

3.2 Data-Level Parallelism: DP

Algorithm 6 shows a pseudo-code of the *Data-level Parallelism* (DP) strategy. The solution-level parallel model is achieved by partitioning the whole dataset among the processing elements of a compute device. For this strategy, the registers of the dataset are partitioned into work-groups of size $local_{size}$, while the programs are evaluated sequentially, i.e. only one program is evaluated at a time. A work-item—globally identified by $global_{id}$—is a register of the dataset, and $global_{size}$ is equivalent to the dataset size. By following the same reasoning as in the PP strategy, the $local_{size}$ and the $global_{size}$ were defined as follows:

$$local_{size} = \min(local_{max\_size}, \lceil dataset_{size}/cu \rceil), \tag{3}$$

$$global_{size} = \lceil dataset_{size}/local_{size} \rceil \times local_{size}, \tag{4}$$

such that $number_{groups} = \lceil dataset_{size}/local_{size} \rceil$.

Algorithm 6: DP OpenCL kernel— [evaluate]

$local_{id} \leftarrow$ get_local_id();
$global_{id} \leftarrow$ get_global_id();
$group_{id} \leftarrow$ get_group_id();

4 for $p \leftarrow 0$ **to** $population_{size} - 1$ **do**
5   barrier();
    $P[local_{id}] \leftarrow 0.0$;
7   **if** $global_{id} < dataset_{size}$ **then**
       $program \leftarrow$ nthprogram(p);
9 $P[local_{id}] \leftarrow$ error(interpreter($program, global_{id}$), $Y[global_{id}]$);

10 $s \leftarrow 2^{\lceil \log_2(local_{size}) \rceil}/2$;
11   **while** $s > 0$ **do**
12   barrier();
13   **if** $local_{id} < s$ **and** $local_{id} + s < local_{size}$ **then**
          $P[local_{id}] \leftarrow P[local_{id}] + P[local_{id} + s]$;
15 $s \leftarrow s/2$;

    if $local_{id} = 0$ **then**
       $E[p \times number_{groups} + group_{id}] \leftarrow P[0]$;

For each program indexed by p, $local_{size}$ registers of the dataset are simultaneously evaluated by each work-group, indexed by $group_{id}$. For a given $global_{id}$ register, error takes the expected value $Y[global_{id}]$ and the one returned by `interpreter()`, and calculates an accuracy measure (line 9). Thus, each work-group measures the accuracy of *program* over $local_{size}$ registers of the dataset, and stores the values returned by `error()` into array P of size $local_{size}$, allocated in the work-group's local memory.

The parallel reduction procedure [7] for sum operation takes place between the lines 11 and 15, in which the partial errors of the $local_{size}$ work-items are added up. At the end of parallel sum, the first element of P contains the sum of $local_{size}$ errors of *program* from $group_{id}$. It is stored into array E of size $number_{groups} \times population_{size}$, allocated in the device's global memory. `Barrier()`, at line 12, consists of a synchronization barrier for work-items within the same group. It guarantees the consistency of the local memory since $P[local_{id} + s]$ refers to a memory region modified by a neighbor of the current $local_{id}$ work-item. For the correct use of the parallel reduction, $local_{size}$ should be a power of 2. If $local_{size}$ is not a power of 2, the rounding to the next power of 2 in s calculation (line 10) implies $local_{id} + s > local_{size}$ for some ($local_{id}$, s) tuples. Thus, the checking at the line 13 is required to avoid accessing invalid elements. Finally, the $number_{groups}$ partial errors from each program indexed by p, stored in array E, are added up on the host processor, thus providing the fitness of the program.[2] Upon entering the next iteration, the `barrier()` function (line 5) will ensure that all work-items of the just ended iteration have finished their processing.

3.3 Program- and Data-Level Parallelism: PDP

A general pseudo-code of OpenCL kernel for the *Program- and Data-level Parallelism* (PDP) strategy is outlined in Algorithm 7. For this strategy, each work-group is responsible for evaluating one program, indexed by $group_{id}$, whose work-items—locally identified by $local_{id}$—collectively take care of all registers of the dataset. The $local_{size}$ and $global_{size}$ were calculated as follows:

$$local_{size} = \begin{cases} dataset_{size} & \text{if } dataset_{size} < local_{max\_size} \\ local_{max\_size} & \text{otherwise} \end{cases} \tag{5}$$

$$global_{size} = population_{size} \times local_{size}, \tag{6}$$

ensuring that $global_{size}$ is divisible by $local_{size}$. According to Eq. 5, $local_{size}$ can be less than $dataset_{size}$. In this case, a given $local_{id}$ may cover multiple registers of the dataset through an iterative procedure (line 5), whose stopping criterion is given by $\lceil dataset_{size} / local_{size} \rceil$.

---

[2]Due to accelerator device constraints, the OpenCL programming model forbids synchronization among work-groups which precludes gathering the partial errors within the evaluation kernel. Since only a fraction of partial errors remains at the end of the kernel execution, it is preferred to reduce them directly on the host processor (CPU).

Algorithm 7: PDP OpenCL kernel—[evaluate]

$local_{id} \leftarrow \texttt{get\_local\_id}();$
$group_{id} \leftarrow \texttt{get\_group\_id}();$
$program \leftarrow \texttt{nthprogram}(group_{id});$

$P[local_{id}] \leftarrow 0.0;$
5 **for** $i \leftarrow 0$ **to** $\lceil dataset_{size}/local_{size}\rceil - 1$ **do**
    $n \leftarrow i \times local_{size} + local_{id};$
7   **if** $n < dataset_{size}$ **then**
8      $\lfloor\ P[local_{id}] \leftarrow P[local_{id}] + \texttt{error}(\texttt{interpreter}(program, n), Y[n]);$

9 $s \leftarrow 2^{\lceil \log_2(local_{size})\rceil}/2;$
10 **while** $s > 0$ **do**
11   $\texttt{barrier}();$
12   **if** $local_{id} < s$ **and** $local_{id} + s < local_{size}$ **then**
    $\lfloor\ P[local_{id}] \leftarrow P[local_{id}] + P[local_{id} + s];$
14   $\lfloor\ s \leftarrow s/2;$

  if $local_{id} = 0$ **then**
    $\lfloor\ E[group_{id}] \leftarrow P[0]/dataset_{size};$

At each iteration i of for loop (line 5), $local_{size}$ registers—identified by the variable n—are simultaneously evaluated by each work-group. The line 7 guarantees access to only the valid elements. For a given n register, error() takes the expected value $Y[n]$ and the one returned by interpreter(), and calculates an accuracy measure (line 8). Thus, each work-group measures the error of a single program over the $dataset_{size}$ registers of the dataset, and stores the values returned by error() into array P of size $local_{size}$, allocated in the work-group's local memory.

The parallel reduction procedure takes place between the lines 10 and 14, in which the partial errors of the $local_{size}$ work-items are added up. At the end of parallel sum, the first element of P contains the sum of the $dataset_{size}$ errors of the program indexed by $group_{id}$. It is stored in array E of size $population_{size}$, allocated in the global memory of the device.

3.4 Iteration's Best Program

A pseudo-code of OpenCL kernel developed to find the best program at each iteration is outlined in Algorithm 8. The $local_{size}$ and the $global_{size}$ are the same as defined in the PP strategy (see Sect. 3.1).

Let E be an array of size $population_{size}$, allocated in the device's global memory, where $E[global_{id}]$ represents the error of program $global_{id}$. The errors are partitioned into work-group of size $local_{size}$ and stored into array PB of size $local_{size}$, allocated in the work-group's local memory (line 4). Note that the positions associated with the errors in the array E are stored into array PI for a future identification of the best program.

Algorithm 8: Iteration's best program— [best]

$local_{id} \leftarrow$ get_local_id();
$global_{id} \leftarrow$ get_global_id();

3 **if** $global_{id} < population_{size}$ **then**
4 | $PB[local_{id}] \leftarrow E[global_{id}]$;
   | $PI[local_{id}] \leftarrow global_{id}$;

6 $s \leftarrow 2^{\lceil \log_2(local_{size}) \rceil}/2$;
7 **while** $s > 0$ **do**
8 | barrier();
9 | **if** $local_{id} < s$ **and** $local_{id} + s < local_{size}$ **then**
10 | | **if** $PB[local_{id}] > PB[local_{id} + s]$ **then**
   | | | $PB[local_{id}] \leftarrow PB[local_{id} + s]$;
   | | | $PI[local_{id}] \leftarrow PI[local_{id} + s]$;

13 | $s \leftarrow s/2$;

   if $local_{id} = 0$ **then**
   | $B[group_{id}] \leftarrow PB[0]$;
   | $I[group_{id}] \leftarrow PI[0]$;

The parallel reduction procedure for minimum operation takes place between the lines 6 and 13. At each iteration of *while* loop (line 7), $local_{size}$ work-items are simultaneously executed by each work-group. However, only the work-items identified by $local_{id} = 0, \ldots, \min(local_{size} - s, s)$ execute the line 10 which compares the errors of the programs indexed by $local_{id}$ and $local_{id}+s$, and store the best one in the $local_{id}$-th position of the array PB. At the end of parallel comparison, the first element of PB contains the smallest value from the $local_{size}$ errors of $group_{id}$. It is stored into array B of size $number_{groups}$, allocated in the device's global memory. The first element of PI contains the position associated with the best program in the array E. Finally, the host processor finds the n minor values from the $number_{groups}$ errors retained in the array B, which will be used by the next iteration.

4 Performance Analysis

In this section we first present a case study to analyze the individual impact of each parallel optimization on GE performance as well as its dependence on parallel strategy and architecture. The set of experiments discussed in Sect. 4.1.1 take into account only the OpenMP evolutionary tasks, while the ones reported in Sect. 4.1.2 consider only the OpenCL kernels. Both OpenMP and OpenCL evolutionary tasks are added together to the GE algorithm in Sect. 4.1.3.

Thereafter, a controlled experiment is conducted in Sect. 4.2 to provide an in-depth performance analysis of the three evaluation kernels as a function of population and dataset size.

Computational Environment All the experiments were conducted on (1) a 4-core Intel i7-2600k CPU with *Hyper-Threading* enabled (4 physical + 4 logical cores = 8 threads), featuring 4 compute units (CU), 8 processing elements (PE) per CU, maximum local size of 4096 and 32GB of global memory; (2) an NVIDIA Geforce GTX-580 GPU accelerator with 16 CUs, 32 PEs per CU, maximum local size of 1024 and 3GB of global memory. The host was running Ubuntu 16.04 64-bit GNU/Linux, GNU Compiler Collection version 5.4, and two OpenCL platforms: pocl 0.14, providing support for the CPU [9], and NVIDIA 367.57 for the GPU.

The heterogeneous parallel GE implementation used is dubbed *Parallel Program Induction* (ppi),[3] a Free Software written in C/C++, OpenMP and OpenCL.

Data Layout Depending on how the input dataset is arranged in the memory, either a *coalesced* or *strided* memory access pattern take effect during the concurrent execution of the interpreter [17]. Coalesced means that while a work-item accesses an array position, its neighbors are accessing adjacent positions, resulting in a contiguous memory region being accessed at a given time; for strided, there is always a gap between the access positions of two adjacent work-items, typically meaning that each work-item processes a chunk of adjacent elements, one at a time. In general, cache-based architectures such as CPUs prefer the non-coalesced strided access to avoid cache interference because when an array element is accessed from global memory, the processor automatically caches many other elements in advance for the work-item that requested the data. On the other hand, GPUs take advantage of many work-items accessing a neighbor memory region by combining various independent data requests into a single memory transaction. In the context of the evaluation kernels discussed in Sect. 3, transposing the dataset—each variable column becomes a row in memory—leads to coalescence whereas the natural arrangement leads to the strided pattern. That being so, transposition was applied when executing the kernels on GPU.

Maximum Local Size As stated in Eqs. 1, 3 and 5, the evaluation kernels calculate their $local_{size}$ based on the $local_{max\_size}$ provided by the compute device, which in our case is 4096 for the CPU and 1024 for the GPU. However, using the maximum value not necessarily leads to the optimal performance: too much work-items within a single work-group may overload the hardware capacity whereas too few work-items may underutilize it. This is why for every experiment configuration we first calibrate the $local_{max\_size}$ parameter to maximize performance.

4.1 Case Study

Problem GE was applied to the symbolic regression problem given by 10^3 pairs (x_i, y_i), where $x_i = 0.015i$, $i = 1, 2, \ldots, 10^3$, are fixed points and $y_i = f(x_i) =$

---

[3]ppi is freely available at http://github.com/daaugusto/ppi.

$\min\left\{\frac{2}{x_i}, \sin(x_i) + 1\right\}$ are the target function values at specific points x_i. This problem is the same as addressed by [1], except for the total number of pairs.

Parameters and Methodology Since we are interested in GE's performance analyses instead of actually finding a solution to a given problem, the GE's fixed parameters were set as follows: population of 10^3 programs, 2 generations,[4] crossover rate of 90%, per-bit mutation rate of 0.5%, tournament size of 100 programs, genome size of 10^3 bits, gene size of 8 bits, and 16-bit ephemeral constant precision. The fitness function was defined as the Mean Squared Error (MSE) on the dataset. The number of OpenMP threads vary from 1 to 10, according to the purpose of the experiment. Five hundred independent runs of each version of the GE algorithm were performed. The performance analysis is conducted in terms of median execution time over 500 runs as well as their median speedup[5] and improvement percentage.[6] It will be placed more emphasis on evolutionary tasks which are the core of the algorithm, since the startup tasks run only once at the beginning of the algorithm. The grammar defines a language of mathematical expressions that contains sine, cosine, arithmetic operations, numerical constants and the variable x.

4.1.1 Multi-Threaded + Sequential

This section focuses on the multi-threaded parallel GE, where the following evolutionary tasks are executed on the multi-core CPU via OpenMP: `generate`, `decode` and `derive`. The `evaluate` and `best` events are executed on the CPU in a serial way.

Given that the experiments were run on a multi-core CPU processor, it is expected that the parallel execution time of loop iterations regarding the OpenMP-accelerated breeding phase—`generate`, `decode` and `derive`—decreases as the number of threads increases, particularly up to four threads, as we can see in Fig. 1a. Indeed, their speedup increases up to eight threads, with the highest values obtained by `generate`, followed by `derive`, and `decode` with the worst performance, as shown in Fig. 1b. For eight threads, the speedup was 6.1, 4.4 and 2.4, respectively. One may speculate that `decode`'s scalability was probably impaired by its rather irregular workload in terms of instructions and memory accesses which, although to a much less extent, impacts CPUs too; fortunately, it is the lightest weight workload among the three and thus does not contribute much to the overall time. The relative

---

[4]Note that a single generation would suffice to estimate the execution time of the tasks of the GE algorithm, however, we used two generations in order to make the timeline visualization more appealing.

[5]Speedup is the ratio between the execution time of the algorithm before and after improvement.

[6]Improvement percentage is the difference between the execution time of the algorithm before and after improvement over the execution time of the unimproved version, and multiplying by 100.

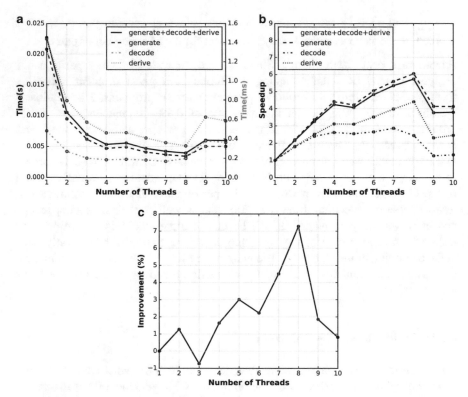

Fig. 1 (**a**) Median execution time and (**b**) median speedup corresponding to the three OpenMP evolutionary tasks—generate, decode and derive—as a function of the number of threads. (**c**) Improvement percentage that compares the median execution time of the sequential GE (thread equal to one) with that obtained by the multi-threaded parallel GE using two or more threads. The startup tasks were not taken into account for calculating the execution time of the algorithm

decline in speedup of the three OpenMP evolutionary tasks with five threads can be seen as a persistent anomalous behavior (see Fig. 1b). On the other hand, the relative worsening in parallel performance when using more OpenMP threads than the number of available CPU threads is attributed to a classic multi-threaded problem known as oversubscription [8], in which the OpenMP threads compete for resources.

The generate event takes roughly 6–9 times more time to run in parallel mode than the other two events together—derive and decode. On the other hand, the generate runtime is negligible when compared to the evaluate runtime, about 28 times slower than the former. By consequence, the improvement percentage in the execution time of the multi-threaded parallel GE with respect to that obtained by the sequential GE is very small (see Fig. 1c). For instance, the reduction from 0.70 s with one thread to 0.65 s with eight threads represents an improvement of 0.05 s in 0.70, or a reduction of just 7% in total execution time of the evolutionary tasks. The anomalous worsening in runtime with three and six threads is probably due

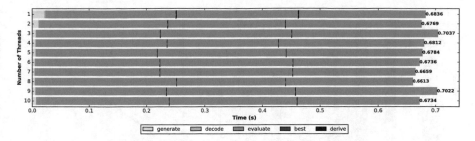

Fig. 2 Execution timeline visualization of the five main evolutionary tasks of the multi-threaded parallel GE with numbers of OpenMP threads ranging from one to ten. Vertical dashed lines indicate the beginning of a generation. Total execution time (in seconds) of the evolutionary tasks is displayed at the right of the graph, which does not take into account the startup tasks

to a higher `evaluate` runtime since the three OpenMP evolutionary tasks reduce their respective runtime on three and six threads (see Fig. 1a). Figure 2 illustrates an execution timeline of the five main evolutionary tasks of the multi-threaded parallel GE with numbers of OpenMP threads ranging from one to ten, and highlights the importance of parallelizing the evaluation of programs which is clearly the most time-consuming hotspot. The representative run over a sample of 500 runs was obtained from the calculation of the medoid using a fractional distance metric $L_{\frac{1}{d}}$ in a d-dimensional space:

$$L_{\frac{1}{d}}(\mathbf{u}, \mathbf{v}) = \left(\sum_{i=1}^{d} |u^i - v^i|^{\frac{1}{d}} \right)^d, \tag{7}$$

where vectors $\mathbf{u}$ and $\mathbf{v}$ of size $d = 30$ are composed of the start and end time of each startup and evolutionary tasks.

4.1.2 Sequential + Many-Threaded

In this next batch of experiments OpenMP is switched off temporarily, allowing us to focus on the many-threaded parallel execution of two events: `evaluate`, accelerated by three parallel strategies (PP, DP and PDP), and `best`, on both the multi-core CPU and many-core GPU via OpenCL. Thus, the breeding phase is now executed with only one thread, i.e. in sequential mode. Hereafter, this setup will be referred to as many-threaded parallel GE.

Figure 3a provides a performance analysis of the OpenCL kernels—`evaluate` and `best`, with their respective data transfer between host and device memories, which is called `data transfer`—for each parallel strategy on each architecture. According to that figure, the PDP OpenCL kernel was the most efficient strategy for running `evaluate` on the GPU, followed by GPU/DP configuration, roughly three times slower than the former. On the other hand, the PP OpenCL kernel

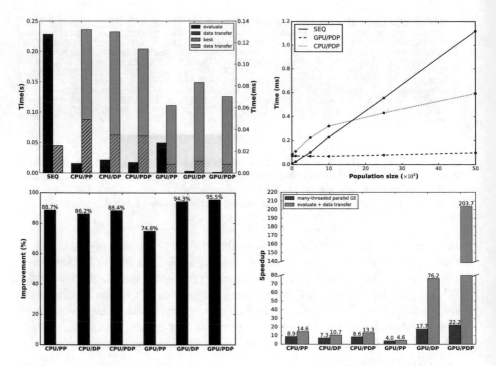

Fig. 3 (**a**) Median execution time corresponding to the two OpenCL evolutionary tasks—evaluate and best, with their respective data transfer between host and device memories—for each of the six combinations between parallel strategies (PP, DP and PDP) and architectures (CPU and GPU), besides the sequential version (SEQ). (**b**) Median execution time of best and data transfer together over 30 runs as a function of the population size for the SEQ, GPU/PDP and CPU/PDP configurations. Population size varied from 10^2 to 5×10^4. (**c**) Improvement percentage that compares the median execution time of the sequential GE with that obtained by the many-threaded parallel GE under each of the six configurations. (**d**) Median speedup corresponding to evaluate and data transfer together, and to the many-threaded parallel GE under each of the six configurations

turned out to be the best strategy for the evaluation task on the CPU, which is about 20 times slower than the GPU/PDP configuration. The evaluate runtime in sequential mode (SEQ) takes approximately 228 ms, whereas the GPU/PDP configuration takes only 0.76 ms, about 300 times faster than the former. The data transfer runtime relative to the evaluation process takes 0.34–0.37 ms for the CPU, which tends to increase as population size increases. Fortunately, it is too small when compared to kernel execution time, as shown in Fig. 3a. On the other hand, it takes 0.37–0.64 ms for the GPU which requires an explicit data transfer. Although it also seems too small, it is equivalent to the evaluate runtime for the GPU/PDP configuration. The execution time of evaluate and data transfer together achieves a speedup varying from 4.6 to 203.7 compared to its sequential execution time, with the highest value obtained by GPU/PDP, followed by GPU/DP with 76.2 (see Fig. 3d). All other configurations obtained speedup values below 15.

In theory, the `best` runtime depends only on the compute device in which it runs in a parallel way, i.e. it is independent of the strategy. The same goes for its respective `data transfer`, except for the DP strategy which is a bit different from the other two strategies, as discussed below. In fact, the differences observed in `best` runtime between the three strategies belonging to the same compute device can be attributed to statistical fluctuations, whose values are 0.03–0.05 and 0.008–0.011 ms for the CPU and GPU devices, respectively, i.e. the GPU was on average four times faster than the CPU. Their respective `data transfer` take 0.08–0.09 and 0.05–0.07 ms, whose maximum values came from the DP strategy due to the additional step of transferring back the error values from the host memory to the device memory—the fitness calculation initialized by the DP OpenCL kernel is completed on the host (see Sect. 3.2). An intuitive explanation for the equivalence between the CPU's and GPU's `data transfer` values is that the best kernel and the parameter settings of the regression problem are very simple; thus, time cost of the explicit transfer made by the GPU of the two tiny arrays B and I (which in the case contain just eight elements each, see Sect. 3.4) is negligible. On top of that, the overhead of the pocl CPU OpenCL implementation was estimated at approximately 0.08 ms; thus, the effective time spent on transferring data relative to best kernel was on the order of microseconds for the CPU device. Adding the execution time of `best` and `data transfer`, the CPU was on average almost two times slower than the GPU, which in turn was nearly three times slower than the sequential mode, as we can see in Fig. 3a. However, it does not impair the overall speedup since the aforementioned runtime is two to three orders of magnitude smaller than the `evaluate` runtime. According to Fig. 3b, the execution time of `best` and `data transfer` together increases linearly with population size in sequential mode while it remains almost constant for GPU/PDP configuration. From a population size of 5×10^3, GPU/PDP was faster than sequential mode, being 11 times faster when set up with a population of 5×10^4 programs. In the case of CPU/PDP, it was better than sequential mode from a population size of 2.5×10^4. The CPU/PDP curve moves further away from GPU/PDP as the population size increases, reaching a speedup of 6 when set up with a population of 5×10^4 programs.

Regarding the sequential GE, the many-threaded parallel GE equipped with the GPU/PDP configuration achieved a speedup of 22.2, going from 0.70 s to 31 ms (see Fig. 3d). It corresponds to an improvement of 0.67 s in 0.70, or an impressive reduction of 95.5% in total execution time of the evolutionary tasks, as shown in Fig. 3c. The second better configuration, GPU/DP, achieved a speedup of 17.7. All others obtained speedup values below 9.

4.1.3 Multi-Threaded + Many-Threaded

The multi- and many-threaded parallel GE arises from the combination of the three OpenMP evolutionary tasks—`generate`, `decode` and `derive`—with the two OpenCL evolutionary tasks—`evaluate` and `best`—in order to achieve a fully parallel implementation, where both the breeding and evaluation are parallelized.

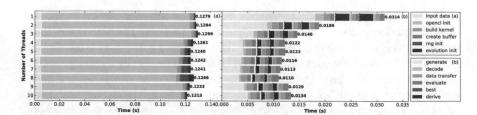

Fig. 4 Execution timeline visualization of the multi- and many-threaded parallel GE with numbers of OpenMP threads ranging from one to ten. The `evaluate` coupled with the PDP strategy and `best` kernels were executed on the GPU. All the startup tasks were executed on the CPU. Total execution time (in seconds) of the startup and evolutionary tasks is displayed at the right of each graph. Vertical dashed lines indicate the beginning of a generation. The representative run over a sample of 500 runs was obtained from Eq. 7, with $d = 54$

Although all six configurations will be considered here, the following discussion emphasizes the GPU/PDP configuration as it is clearly the most power efficient one, as shown in the previous section.

Figure 4 depicts an execution timeline of the heterogeneous parallel GE with numbers of OpenMP threads ranging from one to ten. The `evaluate` coupled with the PDP strategy and `best` kernels were executed on the GPU. Besides the two events described in Sect. 2.1—`rng init` and `evolution init`—the following four events also belong to startup tasks: `input data`, the loading of the input dataset from disk; `opencl init`, which includes the process of defining the platform and devices and configuring an abstract environment for managing communication between host and device; `build kernel`, the creation and compilation of kernels from source code; and `create buffer`, the allocation of memory buffers for holding data. The last event also includes setting the buffers as kernels arguments and initializing the input data buffer. Although the total execution time of the startup tasks is roughly 4–10 times higher than that of the evolutionary tasks, it is worth noting that only the first two generations were taken into accounted for calculating the total execution time of the evolutionary tasks. In practice, the algorithm iterates for thousands or more of generations, whereas the startup tasks run only once; therefore, the startup tasks runtime becomes irrelevant in regard to the total execution time of the algorithm.

From Fig. 4, it can be observed that the behavior of the total execution time of the evolutionary tasks relative to the number of threads is similar to that obtained from Fig. 1a—that is, it decreases up to eight threads and thereafter it increases— as expected since the number of threads for the execution of the three OpenMP evolutionary tasks is the only variant of the problem. However, note that `evaluate` is clearly not a hotspot anymore, and other events can now be identified as hotspots, such as `generate`, `decode` and `derive`. Therefore, the performance gain in parallelizing them through OpenMP becomes quite expressive, as we can see in Fig. 5a. For instance, the parallel heterogeneous GE with the GPU/PDP configuration takes three times less time to run with eight threads than with only one, going from 31 ms to 10 ms, i.e. an improvement of 68%.

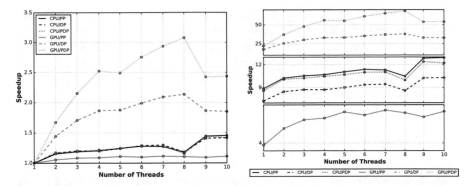

Fig. 5 Median speedup of the multi- and many-threaded parallel GE as a function of the number of OpenMP threads when compared to (**a**) the many-threaded parallel GE and (**b**) the sequential GE for each parallel strategy (PP, DP and PDP) on each architecture (CPU and GPU). The startup tasks were not taken into account for calculating the execution time of the algorithm

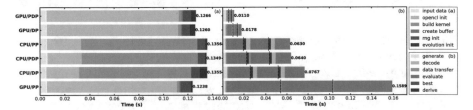

Fig. 6 Execution timeline visualization of the multi- and many-threaded parallel GE for each parallel strategy (PP, DP, and PDP) on each architecture (CPU and GPU) with eight threads. The y-axis is in ascending order of total execution time of the evolutionary tasks. Total execution time (in seconds) of the startup and evolutionary tasks is displayed at the right of each graph. Vertical dashed lines indicate the beginning of a generation. The representative run over a sample of 500 runs was obtained from Eq. 7, with $d = 54$ for all strategies, except for DP that assumes $d = 60$

Figure 6 shows an execution timeline of the parallel heterogeneous GE for each parallel strategy on each architecture with eight threads, displayed in ascending order of total execution time of the evolutionary tasks. It reveals that `evaluate` is still a hotspot for configurations other than GPU/PDP. By consequence, their peak speedup values was 1.1–2.1, with the highest one obtained by GPU/DP with eight threads (see Fig. 5a). Among the startup tasks, the `opencl init` event is the most computationally costly one when the two OpenCL kernels run on the GPU. However, it is not true for the CPU, whose the most costly event is `build kernel`. Moreover, the total execution time of startup tasks on the CPU is about 10% higher than that obtained by the GPU.

The parallel heterogeneous GE combines two major parallel decompositions: breeding phase and evaluation of programs, besides the identification of iteration's best program. The parallel GE coupled with GPU/PDP configuration was 3.1 times faster with eight threads than with one thread (see Fig. 5a), which in turn achieved a speedup of 22.2 when compared to the sequential GE (see Fig. 3d). Therefore, the overall speedup of the former was given by the product of the two individually attained speedups, that is $3.1 \times 22.2 \cong 68.3$ times faster than the sequential GE, going from 0.70 s to 10 ms (see Fig. 5b). It represents an improvement of 0.69 s in 0.70, or an impressive reduction of 98.5% in total execution time of the evolutionary tasks. The second better configuration, GPU/DP, achieved a speedup of $2.1 \times 17.7 \cong 37.7$ with eight threads. All others obtained speedup values below 13.

4.2   In-Depth Kernel Analysis

The experiments presented in this section are an extension adapted to GE of the work done by [2] and aim at providing an in-depth performance analysis of (1) evaluation kernels and (2) data transfer between host and device memories as a function of two parameters: population and dataset size.

Problem A controlled experiment that simulates a typical symbolic regression problem.

Parameters and Methodology Population and dataset size varied from 10^2 to 5×10^4. For each combination, a total of thirty independent runs were performed, and the resulting median GPop/s[7] over them was used as the estimated performance per configuration. The GE fixed parameters were: 1 generation, crossover rate of 90%, per-bit mutation rate of 0.5%, tournament size of 1 program (no selection pressure), genome size of 10^3 bits, gene size of 8 bits, and 16-bit ephemeral constant precision. The grammar was adjusted in such a way that the size of all programs is 50 nodes, which contains sine, cosine, arithmetic operations, numerical constants, and ten randomly sampled input variables uniformly distributed over the interval $[-1, 1]$. The fitness function was defined as the Mean Average Error (MAE) on the dataset.

4.2.1   Results

Figure 7 shows a three-dimensional plot of the evaluation kernel's performance in terms of billion GPop/s as a function of population and dataset size for each of the three parallel strategies (PP, DP and PDP) executed on the CPU. Figure 8 is similar to Fig. 7 for the GPU.

The four 3-D surface-shapes of Fig. 7 are all quite similar, particularly for the CPU/PP and CPU/PDP configurations, which have equivalent mean, maximum and minimum performance values. The difference in peak performance between them is about 10%. Therefore, any of the three strategies can be used on CPUs in practice. As mentioned earlier, this is a result of the CPU design which packs

---

[7]GPop/s stands for *genetic programming operations per second* and is equivalent to the number of program "symbols" processed per second.

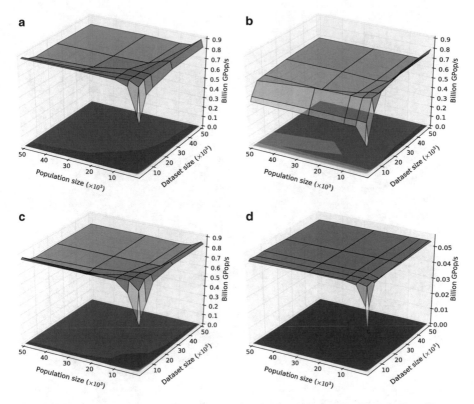

Fig. 7 Performance in terms of billion GPop/s of evaluation kernel on the CPU via OpenCL as a function of two parameters: population and dataset size for each of the three parallel strategies (PP, DP and PDP), besides the sequential version. (**a**) CPU/PP. (**b**) CPU/DP. (**c**) CPU/PDP. (**d**) CPU sequential mode

sophisticated control logic units dedicated to branch prediction, speculative, out-of-order execution [13, 18], making its performance independent of parallelisation strategy. On the other hand, GPU designs are characterized by a substantial compute power as a result of the increase in the ratio of arithmetic to control logic units. This makes GPUs very sensitive to the strategy, as we can see in Fig. 8. From Fig. 7, it is observed that the performance does not vary greatly with population and dataset size and quickly stabilizes at a level beneath the peaks. It is not evident, but this might be due to cache misses, i.e. the effective cache size not being large enough to fully accommodate the data. The DP strategy (Figs. 7b and 8b) as well as the GPU/PP configuration (Fig. 8a) are highly dependent, respectively, on dataset and population size, making them inefficient for low-workload applications.

Although the CPU/PP and CPU/PDP configurations are equivalent to each other, the PP OpenCL kernel was the most efficient strategy running in parallel on the CPU, with a mean performance of 0.82 billion GPop/s, which is about 16 times greater than the sequential mode (see Fig. 7a, d). Given the four physical cores

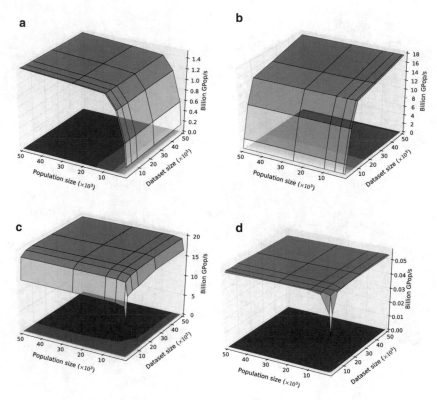

Fig. 8 As Fig. 7, but for the GPU. (**a**) GPU/PP. (**b**) GPU/DP. (**c**) GPU/PDP. (**d**) CPU sequential mode

present on the tested CPU device, with 8 SIMD[8] lanes each one, a speedup of 16 corresponds to half the theoretical maximum speedup ($4 \times 8 = 32$), which may seem disappointing but is in fact an achievement. Although the values belonging to the aforementioned peak region vary little between them, the CPU/PP's peak performance was 0.89 billion GPop/s when set up with a population of 5×10^3 programs evaluated on a dataset of 10^3 registers, apparently without any obvious or reasonable explanation for this.

As described in Sect. 3.3, in the PDP strategy each work-group evaluates a different program while all its work-items execute the same instruction on different registers of the dataset. Such a strategy fits well the GPU architecture, which supports the SPMD[9] model among compute units and SIMD model among processing

---

[8]SIMD stands for *Single Instruction Multiple Data* and means that a single instruction is executed on multiple data simultaneously.

[9]SPMD stands for *Single Program Multiple Data* and means that different compute units of a compute device are able to execute different instructions simultaneously from the same kernel.

elements within a compute unit [2]. The GPU/PDP performance increases rapidly until reaching a quasi-plateau region, in which the improvement rate is much slower (see Fig. 8c). In other words, the accelerator's capacity has been saturated with respect to this kernel and therefore no further gains are possible. Unlike GPU/DP and GPU/PP, the GPU/PDP strategy does not require a large dataset or population size to achieve optimal performance (see Fig. 8a–c). GPU/PDP obtained a mean performance of 17.54 billion GPop/s, in contrast to just 0.05 billion GPop/s for the sequential mode, which is about 350 times slower than the former (see Fig. 8c, d). The highest peak performance was achieved by the GPU/PDP configuration with 19.65 billion GPop/s (population: 5×10^4; dataset: 5×10^4), followed by GPU/DP with 17.64 billion GPop/s (population: 10^3; dataset: 5×10^4).

According to Sect. 3.2, in the DP strategy all the processing elements execute the same instructions on different registers of the dataset for a single program, and thus it is well suited to heavy SIMD-based architectures like GPU [2]. The GPU/DP configuration produces a 3-D surface-shape invariant to population size, whose performance increases as dataset size increases, with a more pronounced slope for dataset size between 10^2 and 10^4 (see Fig. 8b). The larger the dataset, the lower the idleness of thousands of processing elements available on the accelerator device. On the other hand, the PP strategy is not well suited to the GPU architecture since each processing element evaluates a different program and, by consequence, the instructions within a compute unit likely diverge most of the time, degrading the performance [2]. Although the GPU/PP's performance increases as population size increases, the overall performance is weak, just 1 billion GPop/s (see Fig. 8a).

When the data transfer time between host and device memories is also taken into account for calculating the median GPop/s, the GPU/PDP performance becomes more dependent on dataset size, with a clear performance loss as the dataset size decreases, worsening up to 70–85% for dataset size equal to 100 (see Fig. 9). As a result, the overall performance reduces from 17.54 billion GPop/s to 14.62 billion GPop/s, but the peak performance of 19.50 billion GPop/s (population:

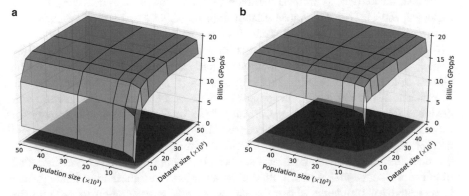

Fig. 9 Performance in terms of billion GPop/s of evaluation kernel (**a**) taking and (**b**) not taking into account the data transfer between host and device memories for GPU/PDP configuration

5×10^4; dataset: 5×10^4) did not change much. All the other five configurations obtained a relative performance loss of maximum 21% (not shown). Note that the GPU/PDP's 3-D surface-shape now resembles the GPU/FP's one in Fig. 8b, although the throughput of the former is still better than that of the last one.

5   Conclusions

This chapter presented a heterogeneous parallel model for the GE algorithm through OpenMP and OpenCL, in which the evolutionary tasks are decomposed into multi- and many-threads, matching respectively the speciality of multi- and many-core processors. The goal is to bring together the best of each computing device in order to provide a fast, efficient and scalable GE. In this token, the many-threaded OpenCL kernels are responsible for evaluating the programs and finding the best ones at each iteration, while the multi-threaded OpenMP tackles the breeding phase. Three well-known parallel strategies were proposed for the evaluation of programs and were assessed on a GPU and multi-core CPU, totaling six different configurations: PP/CPU, DP/CPU, PDP/CPU, PP/GPU, DP/GPU and PDP/GPU.

In the case-study experiments consisting of a relatively small population and dataset, PDP/GPU was by far the most performant strategy for running the evaluation, followed by DP/GPU, CPU/PP, CPU/PDP, CPU/DP, and GPU/PP far behind with the worst performance. The parallel heterogeneous GE accelerated by the GPU/PDP configuration was 68 times faster than the sequential GE, resulting from the combination of two individual speedups, that is $22.2 \times 3.1 \cong 68.3$. The first one is attributed to the OpenCL kernels, while the second one to the OpenMP evolutionary tasks with eight threads. It shows the importance of fully parallelizing the GE algorithm to obtain better performances.

A controlled experiment that simulates a typical regression problem made it possible to analyze the effects of varying population and dataset size on the performance of evaluation kernels as well as estimate the potential of each configuration. As expected, the GPU is far more efficient than the CPU for the parallel execution of evaluation kernels. The three strategies are very similar with respect to the 3-D surface-shape and performance when run on the CPU. Despite the fact that any strategy can be run on the CPU without much performance loss, it would not be chosen over the GPU to perform the evaluation phase in practice—the principle of efficiency is to assign to a processor the type of workload its architecture was designed for. On the GPU device, in turn, PDP was the best overall strategy for running evaluation kernel mainly because (1) it does not require a population and dataset size as large as GPU/PP and GPU/DP to maximize throughput, and (2) still provides the highest mean performance, which is about 350 times faster than that obtained by sequential mode. GPU/DP is an interesting alternative strategy that is indicated for problems whose the dataset size is large enough to saturate the accelerator.

Altogether, the performance analysis highlighted the importance of carefully decomposing both the breeding and evaluation phases of GE into heterogeneous multi- and many-threaded systems when dealing with large-scale real-world problems.

Acknowledgements The authors would like to thank the support provided by CNPq (grants 310778/2013-1, 502836/2014-8 and 300458/2017-7), FAPEMIG (grant APQ-03414-15), EU H2020 Programme and MCTI/RNP–Brazil under the HPC4E Project (grant 689772).

References

1. D.A. Augusto, H.J.C. Barbosa, Symbolic regression via genetic programming, in *Proceedings. Vol. 1 Sixth Brazilian Symposium on Neural Networks* (2000), pp. 173–178
2. D.A. Augusto, H.J.C. Barbosa, Accelerated parallel genetic programming tree evaluation with OpenCL. J. Parallel Distrib. Comput. **73**(1), 86–100 (2013)
3. W.J. Bolosky, M.L. Scott, False sharing and its effect on shared memory performance, in *USENIX Systems on USENIX Experiences with Distributed and Multiprocessor Systems - Volume 4*. Sedms'93, Berkeley, CA (USENIX Association, Berkeley, CA, 1993), pp. 3–3
4. R. Chandra, L. Dagum, D. Kohr, D. Maydan, J. McDonald, R. Menon, *Parallel Programming in OpenMP* (Morgan Kaufmann, San Francisco, CA, 2001)
5. L. Deng, D. Yu, Deep learning: methods and applications. Technical Report (2014)
6. S.S. Haykin, *Neural Networks and Learning Machines*, 3rd edn. (Pearson Education, Upper Saddle River, NJ, 2009)
7. W.D. Hillis, G.L. Steele Jr., Data parallel algorithms. Commun. ACM **29**, 1170–1183 (1986)
8. C. Iancu, S. Hofmeyr, F. Blagojević, Y. Zheng, Oversubscription on multicore processors, in *2010 IEEE International Symposium on Parallel Distributed Processing (IPDPS)* (April 2010), pp. 1–11
9. P. Jääskeläinen, C.S. de La Lama, E. Schnetter, K. Raiskila, J. Takala, H. Berg, pocl: A performance-portable OpenCL implementation. Int. J. Parallel Program. **43**(5), 752–785 (2015)
10. B. Jacob, S. Ng, D. Wang, *Memory Systems: Cache, DRAM, Disk* (Morgan Kaufmann, San Francisco, CA, 2007)
11. D. Kaeli, P. Mistry, D. Schaa, D.P. Zhang (eds.), *Heterogeneous Computing with OpenCL 2.0*, 3rd edn. (Morgan Kaufmann, Boston, 2015)
12. C. Lameter, Numa (non-uniform memory access): an overview. Queue **11**(7), 40:40–40:51 (2013)
13. B.W. Lampson, Lazy and speculative execution in computer systems, in *OPODIS*, ed. by A. A. Shvartsman, vol. 4305. Lecture Notes in Computer Science, pp. 1–2 (Springer, Berlin, 2006)
14. P. Pospichal, E. Murphy, M. O'Neill, J. Schwarz, J. Jaros, Acceleration of grammatical evolution using graphics processing units: computational intelligence on consumer games and graphics hardware, in *Proceedings of the 13th Annual Conference Companion on Genetic and Evolutionary Computation*, GECCO '11, New York, NY (ACM, New York, 2011), pp. 431–438
15. D. Robilliard, V. Marion-Poty, C. Fonlupt, Genetic programming on graphics processing units. Genet. Program Evolvable Mach. **10**(4), 447 (2009)
16. I.L.S. Russo, H.S. Bernardino, H.J.C. Barbosa, A massively parallel grammatical evolution technique with OpenCL. J. Parallel Distrib. Comput. **109**, 333–349 (2017)
17. J. Shen, J. Fang, H.J. Sips, A.L. Varbanescu, Performance traps in OpenCL for CPUs, in *PDP* (IEEE Computer Society, 2013), pp. 38–45

18. J.E. Smith,   A study of branch prediction strategies,   in *Proceedings of the 8th Annual Symposium on Computer Architecture, ISCA '81*, Los Alamitos, CA (IEEE Computer Society Press, Los Alamitos, CA, 1981), pp. 135–148

Comparing Methods to Creating Constants in Grammatical Evolution

R. Muhammad Atif Azad and Conor Ryan

Abstract This chapter evaluates the performance of various methods to constant creation in Grammatical Evolution (GE), and validates the results by comparing against those from a reasonably standard Genetic Programming (GP) setup. Specifically, the chapter compares a standard GE method to constant creation termed *digit concatenation* with what this chapter calls *compact methods* to constant creation. Constant creation in GE is an important issue due to the disruptive nature of *ripple crossover*, which can radically remap multiple terminals in an individual, and we investigate if more compact methods, which are more similar to the GP style of constant creation (*Ephemeral Random Constants* (ERCs), perform better. The results are surprising. Against common wisdom, a standard GE approach of digit concatenation does not produce individuals that are any larger than those from methods which are designed to use less genetic material. In fact, while GP characteristically evolves increasingly larger individuals, GE—after an initial growth or drop in sizes—tends to keep individual sizes stable despite no explicit mechanisms to control size growth. Furthermore, various GE setups perform acceptably well on unseen test data and typically outperform GP. Overall, these results encourage a belief that standard GE methods to symbolic regression are relatively resistant to pathogenic evolutionary tendencies of code bloat and overfitting.

1 Introduction

Typically in statistics and Machine Learning [15], regression involves finding optimal (at least in a local sense) values of parameters of a given function to explain a given data set. Therefore, Machine Learning methods like Artificial

R. M. A. Azad (✉)
School of Computing and Digital Technology, Birmingham City University, Birmingham, UK
e-mail: atif.azad@bcu.ac.uk

C. Ryan
Department of Computer Science and Information Systems, University of Limerick, Castletroy, Limerick, Ireland
e-mail: conor.ryan@ul.ie

© Springer International Publishing AG, part of Springer Nature 2018
C. Ryan et al. (eds.), *Handbook of Grammatical Evolution*,
https://doi.org/10.1007/978-3-319-78717-6_10

Neural Network (ANN), and Support Vector Machine (SVM) work efficiently partly because, with a known target function, they only explore the parameter space to minimise the error between expected and predicted outputs: for example, although, an SVM employs a kernel function to project a low dimensional feature space on to a high dimensional feature space (even an infinite feature space, depending upon the choice of the kernel function), the choice of the kernel function is pre-determined; thereafter, optimisation tunes parameters of the SVM to maximise margins between training instances and a separating hyperplane. Likewise, before the so called *Deep Neural Networks* (which actively employ feature engineering methods) became popular, *learning* in early ANNs simply optimised a set of weights via backpropagation.

Genetic Programming (GP) takes regression to another level: it simultaneously explores spaces of both possible functions and their associated parameters (constants); hence, regression with GP is commonly referred to as *Symbolic Regression*. Therefore, finding suitable numeric constants is essential to how GP performs. However, GP typically does not involve specialised mechanisms for optimising numeric constants. Instead, GP uses *ephemeral random constants (ERCs)* [12], that randomly initialise numeric terminal nodes in a GP population. Thereafter, genetic operators recombine and filter out (possibly erroneously) these ERCs. The combined tasks of optimising structure and constants can be very difficult: for example Keijzer [10] noted that given a target function of $100 + x^2$ such that $x \in [-1, 1]$, GP approximated the numeric constant 100 but lost the genetic material to encode x^2. To combat this, Keijzer proposed *linear scaling*, a form of linear regression to optimise the slope and intercept of evolving GP functions to assist GP. Other proposals include numerical methods [14, 23] as well as specialised mutation operators [9, 22].

This chapter compares methods for evolving constants in Grammatical Evolution (GE) [18] on a number of problems from the symbolic regression domain. GE is a genetic programming system that maps a genotype, a linear string of 8 bit integers termed *codons*, to a functional expression from a language of choice, which is defined by a context free grammar (CFG). Usually, GE uses *digit concatenation* [4] to evolve constants. In this method, a string of GE codons select the constant defining rules from a grammar to yield the desired constant.

Since digit concatenation uses several codons to produce a number, that number can change when passed onto offspring, unlike a number encoded in a more compact way, i.e. as in GP. This is due to the so-called *ripple effect* of GE crossover, [19] which propagates changes to genetic material from left to right. We compare digit concatenation to two other *compact* methods that do not require several codons to encode a constant: these are, a GE version of ERCs called *persistent random constants (PRCs)* [4] and a *codon injection* method that directly converts a GE codon into a floating point value.

In order to compare digit concatenation with the compact methods, we take the following measures. First, much like in [4, 8], we compare the performance results on a suite of symbolic regression problems where error minimisation is a function of both finding a suitable mathematical expression **and** optimising constants therein. This (optimising constants alongside finding expressions) differs from some earlier comparisons of constant creating methods in GE which optimised constants given a fixed mathematical expression [1, 2, 7]; after all, as [22] notes, optimising constants alongside mathematical functions is a different challenge and, we believe, more relevant to the GP community. Furthermore, we compare different methods both with and without linear scaling and also compare against the benchmark results from GP because GP is commonly used for symbolic regression. Moreover, previous work solely compared **training** results; instead, we also consider unseen **test** data. Finally, this works compares lengths of genomes evolved by various constant creating methods to see if any method evolves more parsimonious solutions.

The results show that GP consistently outperforms GE on training data; however, on the test data, GE, regardless of the constant creating method, does better. However, among themselves, the various GE methods perform equally well on all the criteria. Notably, the genome lengths with digit concatenation are no greater than those with the compact methods. Moreover, using GP-like PRCs does not bridge the gap in training results of GP and GE, which suggests that the key difference between GP and GE is how the respective genetic operators behave. We also conclude that the compact methods are not *effectively* compact, give our reasons for that and give directions for further work.

The rest of the chapter is organised as follows: Sect. 2 gives a background to constant creating methods in GE and builds a motivation to this study; Sect. 3 describes the experimental setup, presents the results and discusses the lessons we can learn from these results; finally, Sect. 4 concludes the chapter.

2 Background

Digit concatenation with GE [4, 7] requires a CFG with appropriate rules for generating numeric constants. For example, with the grammars below and a rule `<expr> ::= <const> | -<const>`, cat-UnLtd can, in theory, encode any real constant, whereas cat-0-to-5 limits the values to the domain $(-5, 5)$.

```
cat-UnLtd:

<const> ::= <cat>.<cat>
<cat>   ::= <cat><digit>
          | <digit>
<digit>::= 0 | 1 | 2 | 3 | 4
         | 5 | 6 | 7 | 8 | 9

cat-0-to-5:

<const>::= <fdig>.<cat>
<cat>   ::= <cat><digit>
          | <digit>
<fdig> ::= 0 | 1 | 2 | 3 | 4
<digit> ::= 0 | 1 | 2 | ... | 9
```

This approach has some side effects. First, the number of codons GE takes to encode a constant is equal to the number of digits in it. Later, crossover can break the constant so that it does not pass on to the offspring intact. This is unlike as in GP, where an ERC is atomic. Thus, a stronger *causality* exists in GP, where offspring are likelier to resemble their parents. In fact, as noted in [22], a small number of ERCs quickly dominate the population, with many appearing multiple times in later generations. This is what initially motivated us to ask if GE can benefit from a more GP-like approach, as it appears as though GP first settles on the constants and then builds structure (functions) around them. Second, GE is free to encode a greater number of digits than that allowed by the underlying machine architecture, and as the machine ignores these additional digits, they provide a bloating opportunity. After all, concatenation of additional digits does not affect the fitness of the corresponding individual, and if a GE individual benefits from bloating in the manner that GP individuals do [13], then digit concatenation should, on average, produce individuals of increasingly larger sizes. Thus, the next question is: does digit concatenation produce longer genomes than those with an ERC type approach with GP or its counterparts in GE? If the answer is yes especially while digit concatenation performs *at most* as good as the ERC-styled constants, then a GE practitioner should discard the former in favour of the latter to avoid bloat.

To answer these questions we consider two *compact* representations for GE constants. The first, termed *persistent random constants* (PRCs) [7] embeds randomly generated constants (from a given range) inside the grammar as alternative choices. A single codon can pick a constant by selecting the corresponding rule. Previously digit concatenation outperformed PRCs when the objective was to evolve a single constant [7]. As the second method, we consider a *codon injection* method [16, 17], whereby when the non-terminal <const> is read, the following 8 bit codon value is converted into a floating point value in a given range. As in [1, 2], only a single codon produces a numeric constant.

The above set up investigates if compact representations are *effectively* more compact: that is, whether these methods produce higher fitness *and* smaller genomes. We also note results on unseen data to see if any method produces better predictive models.

3 Experiments

For the *best fit* individual we note: score on training data (best fitness); score on unseen (test) data; and genome length. We record genome lengths to compare which method requires more genetic material. Digit concatenation takes multiple codons to create a single constant (unless the constant has just a single digit); likewise, multiple PRCs may combine to create a constant. We record these statistics every generation and present their mean values over 100 independent runs. Moreover, we also record all the statistics with linear scaling, which we introduce in some detail below.

Linear scaling deterministically optimises two linear parameters to minimise the sum of squared errors between target values ($t(\mathbf{x})$) and approximate values ($y(\mathbf{x})$), where $\mathbf{x}$ represents a vector of independent variables. The *linearly scaled* sum of squared errors (SSE) is calculated as:

$$SSE(t(\mathbf{x}), a + by(\mathbf{x})) = \sum_{i=1}^{N}(t(\mathbf{x_i}) - (a + by(\mathbf{x_i})))^2$$

where

$$b = \frac{\sum_{i=1}^{N}(t(\mathbf{x_i}) - \bar{t})(y(\mathbf{x_i}) - \bar{y})}{\sum_{i=1}^{N}(y(\mathbf{x_i}) - \bar{y})^2}, a = \bar{t} - b\bar{y}.$$

Keijzer [10] has shown that linear scaling significantly boosts the performance of GP on *training cases*; results on test cases were not presented. Due to the simplicity and widespread usage of linear scaling, we employ it in this study.

Note, we use results for GP as a benchmark. Clearly, GP differs from GE in many ways: the genetic representation and genetic operators differ; consequently, we expect some difference in performance. However, since GP is more widely used for symbolic regression, we consider its results to validate the performance of GE. We want to see if the difference in performance is consistent (GP is always better or worse than GE), and whether using a relatively more GP-like approach with PRCs bridges the gap in performances of GP and GE.

We consider five different constant creating methods for GE. These are (legends in brackets): digit concatenation with constants from an infinite real domain (cat-UnLtd); digit concatenation with *absolute values* of constants limited to (0, 5) (cat-0-to-5); 50 and 25 persistent random constants embedded in the grammar (50-PRC-0-to-5 and 25-PRC-0-to-5) also derived from (0, 5); and the codon injection method that directly decodes a GE codon into a numeric value (codon-0-to-5). All these methods can also generate negative numbers.

The grammars incorporate problem specific input variables and arithmetic operators in a prefix notation as below.

```
<expr> ::=  mul( <expr> , <expr> )
          | sub( <expr> , <expr> )
          | add( <expr> , <expr> )
          | div( <expr> , <expr> )
          | ( <expr> )
          | <var> | <const> | -<const>
<var> ::= X1 | .... | XN
<const> ::= "the respective constant creating
            method"
```

Here <var> contains as many variables as the problem requires. Also, note that the grammar allows for both positive and negative constants. <const> expands to a set of rules defining the corresponding constant creating method as exemplified in Sect. 2.

3.1   Grammars Used for Experiments

We now describe the respective grammar fragments expanding the non-terminal <const> for each constant creating method with GE. Digit concatenation methods cat-UnLtd and cat-0-to-5 are designed as described in Sect. 2. Below we describe the ERC-styled approaches in GE.

```
N-PRC-startval-to-endval:
```

```
<const> ::= "N constants in interval (start, end)"
```

The following grammar fragment reads the next unread eight bit codon value and converts it into a floating point value in the given domain: f:-0+5 implies a floating point domain of [0, 5]. This is slightly different from the other setups in that the endpoints of the domain 0 and 5 are also part of the domain. The converted floating point value gets embedded into the phenotype.

```
codon-0-to-5:
```

```
<const> ::= <GECodonValue:f-0+5>
```

3.2   Problem Suite and Evolutionary Parameters

All experiments use a population size of 500, roulette wheel selection, steady state replacement and crossover with a probability of 0.9. For GE, we use the conventional [18, 21] bit wise mutation with a probability of 0.01, while for GP, we use point mutation with a standard probability value of 0.1 [12]. We use ramped half and half initialisation for GP with an initial maximum tree depth of 4; for GE we use the grammatical counterpart of this initialisation termed *sensible initialisation* [21]. Sensible initialisation uses a context free grammar to generate derivation trees for GE using a ramped half and half approach. We use a maximum initial depth of derivation trees of 10 (which is larger than 4 for GP) since a big derivation tree can still yield a small abstract syntax tree and GE grows trees at a slower rate than with standard GP [4].

Although we do not constrain tree sizes or maximum depth for GP (and GE), in the experiments reported here the average tree size for GP never exceeds 250; this is well below the maximum size allowed by a commonly used maximum tree depth of 17 for binary trees. A useful side effect, though, of imposing a maximum tree depth is that this imposition can prohibit emergence of extremely deep *skinny* trees, which can result if the functions set contains unary functions (those requiring a single argument). Prohibiting deep skinny trees that utilise unary functions can be useful because often these unary functions are transcendental (for example, sin, cos, exp, log) that encode a particularly non-linear behaviour which, although flexible enough to hug a response surface, can also overfit the training data [24]. In this study, however, we only use binary arithmetic functions; therefore, omitting a depth limit does not disadvantage GP.

We use six different problems from the symbolic regression domain here. As Keijzer [10] notes, choosing a good set of problems for testing symbolic regression is difficult in the absence of an established set of benchmarks. Like Keijzer, we use the following problems from previous work on symbolic regression.

$$f(x) = 0.3x sin(2\pi x) \tag{1}$$

$$f(x) = 1 + 3x + 3x^2 + x^3 \tag{2}$$

$$f(x, y) = 8/(2 + x^2 + y^2) \tag{3}$$

$$f(x, y) = x^4 - x^3 + y^2/2 - y \tag{4}$$

$$f(x, y) = x^3/5 + y^3/2 - y - x \tag{5}$$

$$f(x_1, \cdots, x_{10}) = 10.59x_1x_2 + 100.5967x_3x_4 - 50.59x_5x_6$$
$$+ 20x_1x_7x_9 + 5x_3x_6x_{10} \tag{6}$$

(1) comes from [11]; (2), also termed as *Binomial-3*, is a scalably difficult problem for GP [6] and has been investigated with GE [4]; (3), (4) and (5) come from [23]; and (6), referred to as *Poly-10* in the figures in this chapter, is a version of a difficult problem described in [20]. The dimensionality of these problems varies between 1 and 10 and their difficulty to GP type approaches also varies as is visible from the scales of the best fitness plotted in Fig. 1.

We use a variant of the standard one point crossover for GE termed *effective crossover* [17]. Since the entire lengths of GE chromosomes may not be used for mapping, the non-mapping regions in GE chromosomes can grow larger and larger; this transforms crossover into a duplication operator as crossing over in the non-mapping regions does not innovate in the phenotype space. Therefore, the effective crossover restricts the crossover point to within the mapping regions.

As noted in [10], protected division (and protected operators in general) can lead GP to producing models that do not generalise well to unseen data; therefore, we do not use protected division. Instead, in the case of a division by zero, we penalise the offending individual by assigning it the worst fitness value of 0.0.

All the GE experiments use libGE [17], while the GP experiments use TinyGP.[1] Evolutionary runs terminate after completing 50 generations. GP uses 50 constants from the domain $(-5, 5)$ and like GE, only uses arithmetic operators.

For each problem, we randomly initialise input variables between -1.5 and 1.5 and generate 100 data points. We randomly choose 50 data points for training and an equal number of data points for testing on unseen data (test data).

---

[1]http://cswww.essex.ac.uk/staff/rpoli/TinyGP/.

3.3 Results

Figures 1, 2, 3, 4, 5, 6 plot the results of the experiments. The x-axis consistently corresponds to 50 generations. The training and test scores are sums of squared errors (SSE) normalised between 0.0 and 1.0 (1.0 being the ideal score) as follows:

$$score = \frac{1}{1 + SSE}.$$

Each sampled point in the plots depicts an average over 100 independent runs. As in [5], the 95% confidence limits of the error bars at each point are computed as follows:

$$\overline{X} \pm 1.96 \frac{\sigma}{\sqrt{n}},$$

where $\overline{X}$ and σ are the mean and standard deviation of n observations; $n = 100$ represents the number of runs in this case. We can be 95% confident that the statistical population lies within these limits, and that a lack of overlap with another error bar means that the corresponding populations are different.

Figures 1–3 plot the results for experiments without using linear scaling. Figure 1 plots the best fitness on *training* data and shows that none of the GE constant creating setups stands out consistently. In fact, various GE methods do quite similarly. Moreover, GP does at least as well as GE (and usually better). Also, using the PRCs does not bring GE any closer to GP.

Of particular interest is cat-UnLtd: unlike all other methods, GE chooses from an infinite domain of constants. Except for problem (6), a domain of [−5,5] is suitable and even advantageous. However, cat_UnLtd does no worse than the other GE methods, suggesting that the larger range of constants available (and the correspondingly larger search space) poses no extra difficulty.

For problem (6) we also tried a domain of [−49,49] to assist methods other than cat-UnLtd in approximating important constants of 100 and 50 but even that did not improve the results; therefore, we do not further discuss those experiments in this chapter. Results also do not show that the brittle nature of constants with digit concatenation when facing crossover is a disadvantage any more than that with compact methods: both cat_UnLtd and cat-0-to-5 perform competitively with respect to the compact methods.

Figure 2 plots the results for the same individuals as in Fig. 1 on the unseen data. Again, no single GE method stands out. GP, however, changes behaviour on the unseen data: unlike on the training data where GP performed at *least* as well as GE methods, it now performs only at *most* as well as GE methods, and some times significantly worse. Again, using PRCs does not affect GE significantly. Let us also consider results on growth of genome lengths before further commenting on this difference in performance on the unseen data.

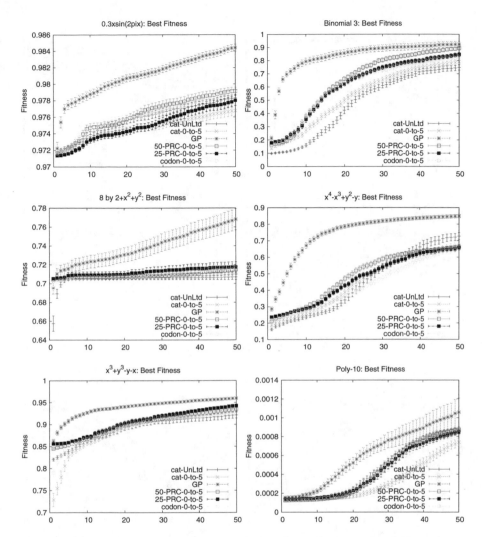

Fig. 1 This figure plots mean of best fitness achieved per generation for all the problems. No GE setup wins or loses consistently. On four problems, GP is significantly better than any GE method

Next, we check if digit concatenation costs more by requiring longer genomes. Figure 3 plots the genome lengths for the best fit individuals and shows that again digit concatenation is no worse than the compact methods. Moreover, while GP genomes clearly grow towards the end of the runs, the lengths of GE genomes remain relatively stable after an initial growth or drop. Note that GE genomes encode derivation trees instead of abstract syntax trees (ASTs) in GP. However, the set of leaves of a GE derivation tree can be interpreted as an AST and this AST can be much smaller than the corresponding derivation tree; hence, at the end of the

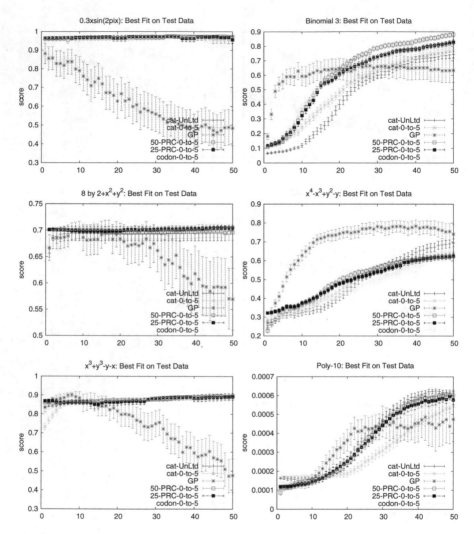

Fig. 2 This figure plots mean of Test Score per generation corresponding to Best-Fit individuals reported in Fig. 1. No GE setup wins or loses consistently. On three problems, performance consistently degrades for GP

runs the ASTs encoded by GE derivation trees are significantly smaller than those produced by GP even when the genome lengths are similar.

Although a deeper investigation into the exact nature of functions evolved by GP and GE may clearly explain the difference in their respective performances on unseen data, at this stage, a correlation between genome growth (or lack thereof in GE) and corresponding performance on the unseen data is visible. Although, we can not claim a causal relationship just yet, it is possible that by restraining genome growth, genetic operators in GE prevent overfitting.

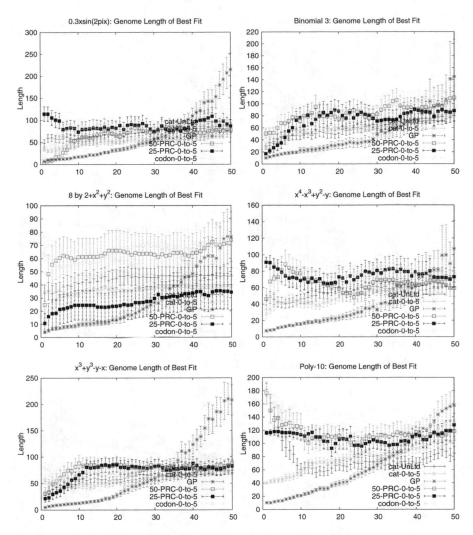

Fig. 3 This figure plots the mean genome lengths of the best fit individuals reported in Fig. 1. No GE setup maintains significantly different lengths

Next, we consider results with linear scaling.

While, as expected, linear scaling helps improve best fitness for all the setups during training, the relative performances of various GE methods remain mutually competitive. Also, with linear scaling, the gap in the performance of GP and GE narrows towards the end of the run; however, again, none of the compact GE methods performs consistently better or worse than digit concatenation.

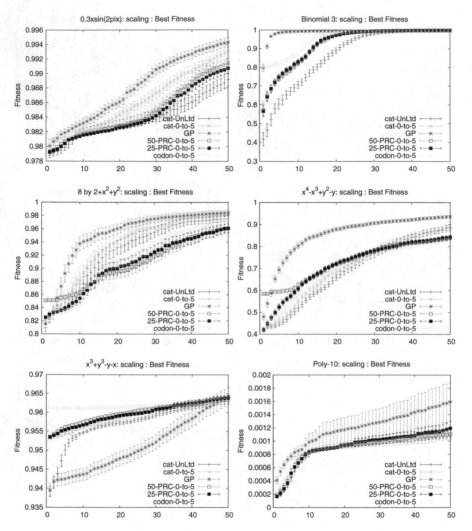

Fig. 4 (With Linear Scaling): this figure plots mean of best fitness on training data achieved per generation for all the problems. 0-to-5 in the legends means that the constants ranged between 0 and ± 5. None of the GE setups wins or loses consistently. Generally, GP is quicker than GE to reach better fitness; however, results converge towards the end of the runs

The scores on test data in Fig. 5 are also similar to those without linear scaling: again, all of the various GE setups perform competitively; similarly, GP performs at most as well as GE on the unseen data.

Finally, the results on genome lengths with linear scaling again show that GE methods show no tendency to grow consistently while GP clearly shows an increasing trend.

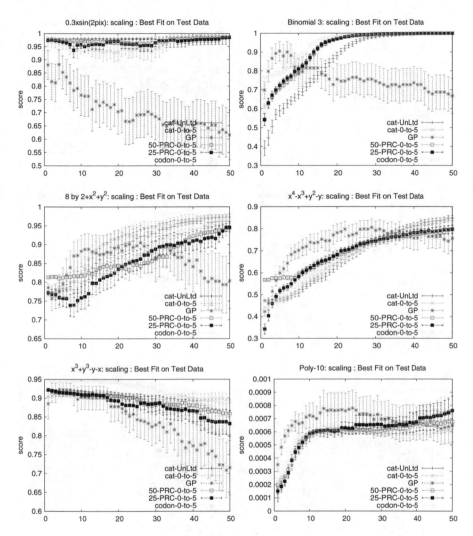

Fig. 5 (With Linear Scaling): this figure plots mean of Test Score per generation for the Best-Fit individuals. No GE setup wins or loses consistently. On all but one problem GE does not indicate overfitting, whereas GP does so on at least four occasions

3.4 Discussion

The results from Sect. 3.3 show that with the given evolutionary parameters and data sets, GE performs equally well with a variety of constant creating methods; however, GE differs significantly from GP. Notice, we only used standard configuration parameters for the respective algorithms to see if performances differ significantly when these various algorithms are used *off the shelf*; therefore, we did not attempt

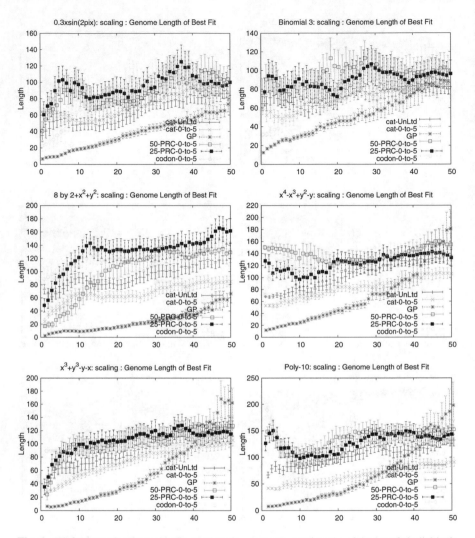

Fig. 6 (With Linear Scaling): this figure plots the mean genome lengths of the best fit individuals reported in Figure 4. 0-to-5 in the legends means that the constants ranged between 0 and ± 5. None of the GE setups maintains significantly different lengths

optimising the configuration parameters to individual problems. The best fitness results, particularly without linear scaling, show that GP *trains* better than GE; however, it does so at the cost of degrading test set results. This is not altogether surprising given the growing GP literature which aims to improve performance on unseen data [11, 24]. What is surprising, however, is that GE does so much better, at least on these problems.

The real focus of this work, however, is on comparing various constant creating methods with GE. Digit concatenation is natural and easy to implement with GE;

however, it can take many codons to encode a single constant. As a result, GE has to find a right sequence of codons and then ensure that crossover does not break that sequence. Moreover, with the ripple crossover [19] in GE, constants can not always transfer intact from the parent to offspring. However, the results here show that the compact methods (PRCs and codon injection) do not *train* better than digit concatenation; this agrees with results in [4, 7]. However, on a greater set of problems, we additionally find that compact methods produce neither smaller genomes (surprisingly) nor better test set results.

The question then is: why does digit concatenation work as well as the other methods? There can be two reasons. First, even with the compact methods if the desired constant is not available, evolution combines various constants to get the right one. Thus, PRCs, or ERCs in GP, are not always less *breakable* with crossover. Moreover, breakability with digit concatenation is not always bad, because it also brings *tunability* whereby genetic operators modify only a part of a constant. In fact, when the constant is reasonably long the chances of modifying its less significant part automatically increase, thereby decreasing both the chances and magnitude of an unfavourable change to the constant, and—by extension—to the overall fitness of the corresponding individual.

Secondly, [3] showed for a symbolic regression problem that crossover mostly produces offspring with significantly worse fitness values. Also, [22] showed that even with a careful numeric mutation that only slightly changes the constants in a GP tree, crossover does no better than with random mutation that uniformly replaces a constant from within a given range. Despite that GP trains well in this chapter. This suggests that passing constants from the parents to offspring is not crucial to GP: after all, even a constant ideal for a parent may be totally unsuitable for the offspring.

Genetic operators in GP and GE, by design, are disruptive and rely on chance and genetic convergence to ensure causality; in fact, a genetic and phenotypic change is the norm and not an exception, especially in the early (exploratory) phase of evolution. Therefore, in the light of the discussion above, an effort solely to make constants compact appears misplaced while the overall genetic and phenotypic structure remains fragile. In fact, the apparently more disruptive ripple crossover in GE generally performs better on the unseen test data, and therefore, perhaps such a disruption is good news. Thus, to further improve the accuracy of symbolic regression, GP/GE should use external methods that can tune the constants to suite whatever structure genetic operators have produced; these external methods can be numerical (such as in [10, 14, 23]) or evolutionary (mutation operators specifically for tuning constants, evolution strategies or real coded genetic algorithms). In the mean time, and especially due to an absence of performance differential across various GE methods, digit concatenation can stay as a default method of choice because it requires no problem specific information.

4 Conclusions

This chapter compares the so-called digit concatenation method of creating constants in Grammatical Evolution with what this chapter calls the compact methods to creating constants. The chapter raises two questions: first, whether the constants with digit concatenation are so brittle against crossover that taking a more GP-like approach to constants with compact methods improves the performance of GE; and second, whether digit concatenation breeds longer genomes than those with compact methods. The results from the problems considered in this chapter suggest that the answer to both the aforementioned questions is a resounding no. Because compact representations may also have to *synthesise* a constant when a suitable one is not available, we hypothesise that these constants are also not robust enough to outperform digit concatenation.

A fascinating result is that, although GP outperforms GE on training data, GE actually does substantially better on unseen test data.

The next steps in this research will be to do further critical evaluation of the performance of GE on test data, as well as its ability to generalise. In particular, work such as [11, 24] can be added to GE to ascertain if GE enjoys the same benefits that GP does from them. Finally, we observe that the disruptive nature of the ripple crossover in GE potentially produces better results on the unseen data. While overfitting on training data is a concern shared by the entire machine learning community, and code growth generally afflicts GP, GE appears inherently resistant to these undesirable behaviours.

References

1. D.A. Augusto, H.J.C. Barbosa, A. da Motta Salles Barreto, H.S. Bernardino, Evolving numerical constants in grammatical evolution with the ephemeral constant method, in *Proceedings 15th Portuguese Conference on Artificial Intelligence, EPIA 2011*, Lisbon, 10–13 Oct 2011, ed. by L. Antunes, H.S. Pinto. Lecture Notes in Computer Science, vol. 7026 (2011), pp. 110–124
2. D.A. Augusto, H.J.C. Barbosa, A.M.S. Barreto, H.S. Bernardino, A new approach for generating numerical constants in grammatical evolution, in *GECCO '11: Proceedings of the 13th Annual Conference Companion on Genetic and Evolutionary Computation*, Dublin, 12–16 July 2011, ed. by N. Krasnogor, P.L. Lanzi, A. Engelbrecht, D. Pelta, C. Gershenson, G. Squillero, A. Freitas, M. Ritchie, M. Preuss, C. Gagne, Y.S. Ong, G. Raidl, M. Gallager, J. Lozano, C. Coello-Coello, D.L. Silva, N. Hansen, S. Meyer-Nieberg, J. Smith, G. Eiben, E. Bernado-Mansilla, W. Browne, L. Spector, T. Yu, J. Clune, G. Hornby, M.L. Wong, P. Collet, S. Gustafson, J.P. Watson, M. Sipper, S. Poulding, G. Ochoa, M. Schoenauer, C. Witt, A. Auger (ACM, New York, 2011), pp. 193–194
3. W. Banzhaf, P. Nordin, R.E. Keller, F.D. Francone, *Genetic Programming – An Introduction; On the Automatic Evolution of Computer Programs and Its Applications* (Morgan Kaufmann, San Francisco, 1998)
4. J. Byrne, M. O'Neill, E. Hemberg, A. Brabazon, Analysis of constant creation techniques on the binomial-3 problem with grammatical evolution, in *2009 IEEE Congress on Evolutionary Computation*, Trondheim, 18–21 May 2009, ed. by A. Tyrrell (IEEE Computational Intelligence Society, IEEE Press, Piscataway, 2009), pp. 568–573

5. D. Costelloe, C. Ryan, On improving generalisation in genetic programming, in *Proceedings of the 12th European Conference on Genetic Programming, EuroGP 2009*, Tuebingen, 15–17 Apr 2009, ed. by L. Vanneschi, S. Gustafson, A. Moraglio, I. De Falco, M. Ebner. LNCS, vol .5481 (Springer, Berlin, 2009), pp. 61–72
6. J.M. Daida, R.R. Bertram, S.A. Stanhope, J.C. Khoo, S.A. Chaudhary, O.A. Chaudhri, J.A. Polito II, What makes a problem GP-hard? Analysis of a tunably difficult problem in genetic programming. Genet. Program. Evolvable Mach. **2**(2), 165–191 (2001)
7. I. Dempsey, M. O'Neill, A. Brabazon, Constant creation in grammatical evolution. Int. J. Innovative Comput. Appl. **1**(1), 23–38 (2007)
8. I. Dempsey, M. O'Neill, A. Brabazon, *Foundations in Grammatical Evolution for Dynamic Environments*. Studies in Computational Intelligence, vol. 194 (Springer, Berlin, 2009)
9. M. Evett, T. Fernandez, Numeric mutation improves the discovery of numeric constants in genetic programming, in *Genetic Programming 1998: Proceedings of the Third Annual Conference*, University of Wisconsin, Madison, 22–25 July 1998, ed. by J.R. Koza, W. Banzhaf, K. Chellapilla, K. Deb, M. Dorigo, D.B. Fogel, M.H. Garzon, D.E. Goldberg, H. Iba, R. Riolo (Morgan Kaufmann, San Francisco, 1998), pp. 66–71
10. M. Keijzer, Improving symbolic regression with interval arithmetic and linear scaling, in *Genetic Programming, Proceedings of EuroGP'2003*, Essex, 14–16 April 2003, ed. by C. Ryan, T. Soule, M. Keijzer, E. Tsang, R. Poli, E. Costa. LNCS, vol. 2610 (Springer, Berlin, 2003), pp. 70–82
11. M. Keijzer, V. Babovic, Genetic programming, ensemble methods and the bias/variance tradeoff – introductory investigations, in *Genetic Programming, Proceedings of EuroGP'2000*, Edinburgh, 15–16 Apr 2000, ed. by R. Poli, W. Banzhaf, W.B. Langdon, J.F. Miller, P. Nordin, T.C. Fogarty. LNCS, vol. 1802 (Springer, Berlin, 2000), pp. 76–90
12. J.R. Koza, *Genetic Programming: On the Programming of Computers by Means of Natural Selection* (MIT Press, Cambridge, 1992)
13. S. Luke, L. Panait, A comparison of bloat control methods for genetic programming. Evol. Comput. **14**(3), 309–344 (2006)
14. B. McKay, M. Willis, D. Searson, G. Montague, Non-linear continuum regression using genetic programming, in *Proceedings of the Genetic and Evolutionary Computation Conference*, Orlando, 13–17 July 1999, ed. by W. Banzhaf, J. Daida, A.E. Eiben, M.H. Garzon, V. Honavar, M. Jakiela, R.E. Smith, vol. 2 (Morgan Kaufmann, San Francisco, 1999), pp. 1106–1111
15. T.M. Mitchell, *Machine Learning*, 1st edn. (McGraw-Hill, New York, 1997)
16. M. Nicolau, I. Dempsey, Introducing grammar based extensions for grammatical evolution, in *Proceedings of the 2006 IEEE Congress on Evolutionary Computation*, Vancouver, 6–21 July 2006, ed. by G.G. Yen, L. Wang, P. Bonissone, S.M. Lucas (IEEE Press, Piscataway, 2006), pp. 2663–2670
17. M. Nicolau, D. Slattery, libGE. Grammatical Evolution Library for version 0.27alpha1, 14 September 2006
18. M. O'Neill, C. Ryan, *Grammatical Evolution: Evolutionary Automatic Programming in a Arbitrary Language*. Genetic Programming, vol. 4 (Kluwer Academic Publishers, Boston, 2003)
19. M. O'Neill, C. Ryan, M. Keijzer, M. Cattolico, Crossover in grammatical evolution. Genet. Program. Evolvable Mach. **4**(1), 67–93 (2003)
20. R. Poli, A simple but theoretically-motivated method to control bloat in genetic programming, in *Genetic Programming, Proceedings of EuroGP'2003*, Essex, 14–16 Apr 2003, ed. by C. Ryan, T. Soule, M. Keijzer, E. Tsang, R. Poli, E. Costa. LNCS, vol. 2610 (Springer, Berlin, 2003), pp. 204–217

21. C. Ryan, R.M.A. Azad, Sensible initialisation in grammatical evolution, in *GECCO 2003: Proceedings of the Bird of a Feather Workshops, Genetic and Evolutionary Computation Conference*, Chicago, 11 July 2003, ed. by A.M. Barry (AAAI, New York, 2003), pp. 142–145

22. C. Ryan, M. Keijzer, An analysis of diversity of constants of genetic programming, in *Genetic Programming, Proceedings of EuroGP'2003*, Essex, 14–16 April 2003, ed. by C. Ryan, T. Soule, M. Keijzer, E. Tsang, R. Poli, E. Costa. LNCS, vol. 2610 (Springer, Berlin, 2003), pp. 404–413

23. A. Topchy, W.F. Punch, Faster genetic programming based on local gradient search of numeric leaf values, in *Proceedings of the Genetic and Evolutionary Computation Conference (GECCO-2001)*, San Francisco, 7–11 July 2001, ed. by L. Spector, E.D. Goodman, A. Wu, W.B. Langdon, H.M. Voigt, M. Gen, S. Sen, M. Dorigo, S. Pezeshk, M.H. Garzon, E. Burke (Morgan Kaufmann, San Francisco, 2001), pp. 155–162

24. E.J. Vladislavleva, G.F. Smits, D. den Hertog, Order of nonlinearity as a complexity measure for models generated by symbolic regression via pareto genetic programming. IEEE Trans. Evol. Comput. **13**(2), 333–349 (2009)

Grammatical Evolution in Finance and Economics: A Survey

Anthony Brabazon

Abstract Finance was one of the earliest application domains for Grammatical Evolution (GE). Since the first such study in 2001, well in excess of 100 studies have been published employing GE for a diverse range of purposes encompassing financial trading, credit-risk modelling, supply chain management, detection of tax non-compliance, and corporate strategy modelling. This chapter surveys a sample of this work and in doing so, suggests some future directions for the application of GE in finance and economics.

1 Introduction

The application of computational algorithms whose design is metaphorically derived from phenomena in the natural world [11, 30] to finance and economics has providence dating back some 30 years. A huge literature running to thousands of papers has resulted. Previous survey articles spanning these contributions include [26, 29]. There have also been several edited volumes covering this area [20, 21, 27, 28, 34, 35, 37]. A good introduction to the application of biologically inspired algorithms to various aspects of financial modelling is provided in [18].

The late 1980s and early 1990s saw a plethora of studies applying (initially) neural networks for financial forecasting purposes and (slightly later) evolutionary approaches, particularly genetic algorithms (GAs). In the latter case, attention was primarily focused on the application of GAs for model parameter optimisation and variable selection [8, 45]. As Evolutionary Automatic Programming (EAP) methodologies such as Genetic Programming (GP) were introduced [59, 61] they too were applied by practitioners and researchers for economic modelling, financial forecasting [57], and trading system induction [5]. A significant feature of these

A. Brabazon (✉)
Natural Computing Research and Applications Group, School of Business, University College Dublin, Dublin, Ireland
e-mail: anthony.brabazon@ucd.ie

© Springer International Publishing AG, part of Springer Nature 2018
C. Ryan et al. (eds.), *Handbook of Grammatical Evolution*,
https://doi.org/10.1007/978-3-319-78717-6_11

methods was that, unlike neural networks, EAP approaches held out the potential to easily incorporate domain knowledge and to generate human-readable models.

It is an interesting footnote in the history of GP that one of the earliest exemplar applications of the methodology by John Koza was to recover the well-known *exchange equation* $M = PQ/V$ which relates the money supply (M), price level (P), gross national product (Q), and velocity of money (V) in an economy [59, 60]. Somewhat quaintly, the paper notes that a then state-of-the-art Apple Macintosh II PC was used to access the training data for the study!

The first finance-related papers which employed a Grammatical Evolution (GE) methodology were published in 2001 arising quite shortly after GE's introduction in 1998 [78]. With the benefit of hindsight it is perhaps unsurprising that finance was one of the early application domains for GE given the stream of related research which was arising in GP around the same time. In common with GP, much of the early GE research in finance was proof of concept in nature, being constrained by the availability of computing power and data (relative to the abundance of both resources today). Nonetheless, this work laid the foundation for more comprehensive subsequent studies which also took advantage of the increasing maturity of GP and GE methodologies. By the current day, application of GP and GE approaches in finance have moved beyond academic studies to include implementation in multiple instances by industry practitioners.

1.1 Structure of Chapter

In this chapter a survey of the literature which has applied GE to finance and economics since 2001 is provided, along with some suggestions for future research. As with any survey, there are difficult choices in deciding which research contributions to include and which to omit. By design, a broad coverage of the relevant literature is provided and this precludes detailed discussion of individual studies.

The rest of this chapter is organised as follows. In the following sections we introduce the application of GE across a range of financial applications including financial trading (Sect. 2), credit-risk modelling (Sect. 3), supply chain management (Sect. 4.1), detection of tax non-compliance (Sect. 4.2), and corporate strategy modelling (Sect. 4.3). Section 5 concludes this chapter, outlining some opportunities for future work.

2 Financial Trading

The earliest financial applications of GE were for the purposes of financial trading [22, 68, 69]. A variety of trading approaches are seen in practice and we outline three of these below in order to place the relevant GE literature into context.

2.1   Fundamental Analysis

Taking the example of investing in a share, investment using a fundamental analysis approach concentrates on the use of accounting and other information about a company, as well as industry and macro-economic data, in order to identify companies which are mispriced by the market. In other words, the object is to identify shares which are good value (underpriced by the market), or shares which are overpriced by the market (and therefore are candidates for 'shorting').

To apply this approach, the investor needs to develop stock screening rules in order to decide which shares to select. The utility of these rules can be tested using historical data, with the best rule (or set of rules) then being used for investment purposes. EAP methods such as GP or GE can be applied to evolve the actual structure of the filter rules. In spite of the widespread use of fundamental analysis (including the application of EAP methods) by actively-managed investment funds, few academic studies have explored the application of EAP for the task of filter rule development.

2.2   Technical Analysis

Under a technical analysis approach, investors attempt to identify imbalances in the supply and demand for a financial asset using information from the time-series of the asset's trading price and volume [64]. Technical indicators (pre-processed price and volume time series data about a financial asset) can be used in isolation, or combined, in order to produce a 'trading signal'. For example, one technical indicator that technical analysts could consider is the *moving average convergence-divergence (MACD) oscillator*, calculated by taking the difference of a short-run and a long-run moving average. If the difference is positive, it is taken as a signal that the market is trending upward, with a buy signal being generated when the shorter moving average crosses the longer moving average in an upward direction [64]. A sell signal is generated in a reverse case. Therefore, a sample MACD trading rule is:

$$IF\ x\text{-day MA of price} \geq y\text{-day MA of price}$$

$$THEN\ Go\ Long\ ELSE\ Go\ Short$$

where $x < y$ (for example $x = 10$ and $y = 50$). The MACD oscillator is a crude band-pass filter, removing both high-frequency price movements and certain low-frequency price movements, depending on the precise moving average lags selected.

A trader who wishes to construct a trading system using technical indicators as inputs faces several decisions, namely:

1. Which indicators will be used?
2. What parameter values (lag periods used to calculate the indicator and threshold values for the indicator to trigger a trading action) should be used?
3. How should the indicators be combined to produce a trading signal?

This results in a high-dimensional search space which is suitable for EAP methodologies.

2.3   Arbitrage

Arbitrage approaches to trading aim to profit by exploiting price differences between financial instruments, trading on different markets or trading in different forms. For example, suppose a share traded on one stock exchange for $23.78 and on another for $23.82, an investor could arbitrage by buying at the lower price and selling simultaneously at the higher price. As would be expected, such a simple arbitrage opportunity would tend to be closed very quickly and transactions costs of buying and selling can negate apparent arbitrage possibilities.

There are a plethora of arbitrage trading strategies employed in financial markets. One exemplar, based on *Put-Call Parity*, is illustrated in [86]. The concept underlying this trade is that the price of a 'long' position on an asset and an associated put (the right to sell that asset in the future at a specified price) must be equal to the price of a long call on the same asset and a long position in a risk-free bond. If either the put or call option are mispriced the investor can, in theory, make a risk-free gain by constructing a portfolio of the four financial instruments. The above example, describes an arbitrage opportunity between the cash market (for the asset) and the options market. Arbitrage opportunities can also exist between cash and futures markets and between futures and options markets.

2.4   GE and Trading

From the above discussion it is evident that there are a variety of trading approaches to which model induction approaches could be applied. Thus far, the bulk of applications of GE, and indeed other model induction methodologies, have adopted a technical analysis perspective. Within this perspective, the trading time horizon can be varied from inter-day to high-frequency trading, with the choice of trading horizon impacting on the temporal resolution of input data required by the trading system. A multiplicity of factors come into play in operationalising trading systems in the real-world including market microstructure, market structure, money management, the risk appetite of the investor and their trading 'style'. Academic contributions rarely consider all of these factors in detail.

2.4.1 Applications of GE for Trading System Design

The earliest study applying GE for trading system design, O'Neill et al. [68], focussed on the UK FTSE 100 index from the period 26/4/1984 to 4/12/1997. Initially, attention was restricted to the generation of a moving average inter-day trading system.

The grammar used to create the trading systems in this study included function definitions for moving average, momentum and trading range, permitting the inclusion of technical indicators using these functions in the generated trading systems. The grammar is outlined in Fig. 1, and includes the set of terminals (T), non-terminals (NT), the start symbol (S), and the set of production rules (P).

In addition to the technical indicators the grammar also allows the use of the binary operators f_and, f_or returning the minimum and maximum of two arguments respectively, the standard arithmetic operators, the unary operator f_not which returns 1-the argument, and the current day's index value day. The daily signals generated by the trading system are postprocessed using the rule in Fig. 2.

The evolved system produced a buy, sell or 'do nothing' signal with trades being left open for a pre-defined, fixed period of 10 days. The fitness function was defined as trading profit less maximum drawdown in order to encourage the

```
N={<code>,<expr>,<fopbi>,<fopun>,<matbi>,<relbi>,<var>,<int>}
T={p,=,(,),f_and,f_or,f_not,+,-,*,>,<,>=,<=,scale,ma,day,1,2,3,4,5,10}
S=<code>
P={
<code> ::=  p = <expr> ;

<expr> ::= <fopbi> (<expr>, <expr>) | <fopun> (<expr>)
         | <expr><matbi><expr> | <expr><relbi><expr> | <var>

<fopbi> ::= f_and | f_or

<fopun> ::= f_not

<matbi> ::= + | - | *

<relbi> ::= > | < | >= | <=

<var> ::= <int> | day | ma(<int>,day) | momentum(<int>,day)
        | trb(<int>,day)

<int> ::= 1 | 2 | 3 | 4 | 5 | 10
}
```

Fig. 1 Sample trading system grammar

Fig. 2 Postprocessing rules

$$Buy = Value < 0.33$$
$$DoNothing = 0.33 >= Value < 0.66$$
$$Sell = 0.66 >= Value$$

generation of trading rules with monotonic equity curves. Allowance was made in the calculation of fitness for both trading cost and slippage. Despite the simplicity of the trading system specification, it outperformed a naive buy-and-hold benchmark whilst maintaining a smaller 'at risk' average investment in the market. Follow on studies extended the approach to encompass an extended range of technical indicators [22] and an extended range of markets (DAX, ISEQ, Madrid stock exchange and NIKKEI) [39, 69, 70].

In Dempsey et al. [46], a number of methodological improvements to the canonical trading system of [68] were implemented. Instead of implementing a hard 'all or nothing' investment threshold, the trading system was allowed to invest a variable amount depending on the strength of the generated trading signal. A variety of population replacement strategies were also implemented in order to assess the impact of varying these on system performance. Changing this parameter in the GE implementation altered the importance of memory in the evolutionary process by impacting on the speed of convergence of the population. The resulting trading systems generated quite stable performance between in/out of sample periods and outperformed the original system when tested on US market data. After taking account of trade costs the system did not outperform a buy-and-hold benchmark however.

When applying an evolutionary approach to generate trading rules it is important to embed as much useful domain knowledge as possible in order to bias the generation process towards syntactically correct, well-formed, trading rules. For example, it would not be sensible to directly compare technical indicators of differing types (consider a moving average value for price which could assume a large or small value and a stochastic indicator which by definition is limited to values between 0 and 100) in constructing a trading rule. Certain indicators are also only validly parameterised within defined ranges. These issues require careful grammar design and an exemplar of this is provided in the GE implementation of [32].

A key aspect of financial markets is that they are dynamic. Consequently, trading systems need to be adaptive to changing conditions. In the early applications of GE for financial trading, a fixed in sample training, out of sample testing, approach was adopted. An obvious limitation of this approach is that trading rules will have a 'shelf life', with their performance deteriorating over time during the out of sample period. This problem was addressed in Dempsey et al. [47], implementing a 'live trading' system which updated its trading rules in real-time as new information became available. An initial training period is set aside on which the population of proto-trading rules is trained, with the aim that a competent population is evolved after a certain number of generations, G. The system then goes 'live'. The trading system takes the best performing rule from the initial training period, and uses this rule to trade for each of the following x days. After x days have elapsed, the training window moves forward in the time series by x days, and the population is retrained over the new data window for a number of generations g, where $g < G$. This embeds both a memory and an adaptive potential in the trading system, as knowledge of good past trading rules is not completely lost, rather it serves as a starting point for their subsequent adaptation. The size of g is crucial. A small value of g means that memory is emphasised over adaptation, as the new data has relatively less chance to influence the trading rules. This could be considered a tuning parameter that could be used to alter the adaptive characteristics of the system. In [48] the performance of an adaptive trading system based on the above approach was compared with that of a system which is periodically retrained ab initio, with the adaptive system demonstrating better results.

The bulk of trading systems using an EAP methodology have employed a technical analysis approach to trading. One notable exception to this is provided by Contreras et al. [40] who combine technical, fundamental and macro-economic analysis in a hybrid, top-down, paradigm. Initially, prospective investments are screened using macro-economic and corporate data, with the final invest decision in selected companies being made based on technical analysis. GE is used to create both the stock selection and trading rules respectively, thereby implementing a dual-layer version of GE. The system is found to produce better results with lower drawdown than benchmark systems including a GE approach which solely relies on technical indicators as inputs [40, 41].

2.5 Intraday Data

High-frequency financial data corresponds to data that is sampled at small time intervals (i.e., at high-frequency) during the trading day. Therefore, high-frequency financial data, in the limit, can contain every single event on an order book during a trading day. Traditionally, high-frequency data was difficult, and costly, to obtain so most early research examining the application of various computational intelligence techniques for trading used end of day data (i.e., a single data point for each trading day).

The first application of GE to high-frequency financial data was that of Brabazon et al. [25] which applied a technical analysis approach to price and volume data for Ford and IBM, sampled on a 5-min frame. Each data vector included the opening and closing prices, the high and low price, and the volume traded, for that 5-min interval. All open positions were closed out before the end of each day, with no inventory of stock being carried overnight.

In a complete implementation of a technical analysis trading system, the value of technical indicators are used to determine when to enter and exit a trade (the exit strategy can also incorporate a stop loss trigger in order to manage downside risk). Earlier implementations of technical analysis trading systems usually adopted a simpler design, such as having a fixed exit horizon with no stop loss trigger, and therefore only in effect evolving an entry point.

In addition to evolving the entry strategy for investment, [25] also assessed the performance of three different exit strategies namely, *standard close*, *extended close* and *stop-loss, take-profit close*. In the standard close, the evolved systems automatically close out trading positions 30 min after they are opened. In the extended close, the system rechecks after 30 min whether the prediction is unchanged from the initial prediction, and if it is, the trade is extended for a further 30 min. In the stop-loss, take-profit close, the position is initially held for 30 min, and thereafter, if the position generates a loss of 0.1% it is closed immediately, and profit is automatically taken on any position which makes a profit of 0.8% by closing the position once the take-profit trigger is hit.

In both the training and test periods, the extended close exit strategy was found to outperform the standard close strategy and the stop-loss, take-profit strategy, with all three strategies significantly outperforming a buy and hold benchmark, albeit that trading costs were ignored in this study. This highlights the impact that the choice of exit strategy can have on the returns produced by a trading system.

Adamu and Phelps [2], building on earlier related work by the same authors [1], take a more comprehensive approach, using GE to coevolve technical rules for entry/exit (for both long and short positions) and also implements a stop loss mechanism, using data based on 5-min bars, for a stock listed on the London stock exchange. An earlier paper by Sax and Maringer [79] had employed a similarly sophisticated approach in evolving trading strategies using GP on high-frequency tick data of the USD/EUR exchange rate.

Other studies to evolve both entry and exit rules include that of Gabrielsson et al. [52] which applied GE to develop a trading system for the S&P 500 E-mini index futures contract. This future is traded on the CME. The system used a simple moving average and a relative strength indicator. A moving window approach was applied to train, validate and test the trading strategies in order to create a method suitable for an online trading system. The authors noted the ease with which domain knowledge could be incorporated into the grammar in order to evolve targeted trading strategies, resulting in relatively transparent trading rules which were capable of human interpretation.

One notable feature of the literature applying computational intelligence approaches (including EAP methodologies) to develop trading systems is an increasing integration between the fields of finance and computer science. In particular, some recent contributions have exhibited a stronger input from the domain of finance, drawing much more deeply on finance theory. A good exemplar of this work is provided by Oesch and Maringer [66] which develops a high frequency trading system using GE and applies this to NASDAQ limit order book data (rebuild order book data). The trading system is motivated by a theoretical liquidity asymmetry theorem from the market microstructure literature, with GE being used to exploit volume inefficiencies at the bid-ask spread. GE evolves a condition which describes volume distributions in the order book. If the condition is violated, the system places a limit order on the side of the market where the volume is too small, expecting the temporary price impact to be reversed. In this study, attention is focussed on long-strategies only (i.e., the trading system aims to exploit liquidity undersupply on the bid side of the market). The resulting system is found to be able to generate profitable and robust strategies.

2.6 Foreign Exchange Markets

The use of technical analysis for trading spot foreign exchange markets is also common so an obvious extension of the early work applying GE for trading purposes was to apply it to these markets. The initial pilot study Brabazon et al. [23] applied the canonical approach of [22] to daily Daily US $—STG exchange rates for the period 9/3/93 to 13/10/97. This work was extended to include the US $—DM and US $—Yen exchange pairs with results indicating that the developed rules earned positive returns in hold-out sample test periods after allowing for trading and slippage costs [13, 17]. Subsequent studies focussing on foreign-exchange markets include [79], already discussed above.

2.7 Sentiment Analysis

Traditionally, stock trading models only incorporated quantitative data, drawn from the market, financial statements or macro-economic data. One source of information which has attracted increasing attention as an input into trading models in recent years is text data drawn from either internet message boards, social media or the financial press.

While initial studies such as Thomas and Sycara [84] looked at raw message count information, the next step was to consider the content or 'sentiment' of these messages in order to assess whether investors are (un)favorably disposed towards a stock. Sentiment analysis has become a major area of research covering natural language processing, computational linguistics and text mining.

Using text data in quantitative models has been made easier by the commercial availability of 'tagged' databases of financial news. One example of these is the Dow Jones Elementised News Feed which places discrete pieces of news—keywords, timestamps, symbols and other crucial data—into XML-tagged fields for easy parsing and direct embedding into trading programs.

Larkin and Ryan [62] used a post-processed version of this data (where the stories were classed as positive, negative or neutral, in essence a metric of market sentiment, with respect to a particular market), combined with a GP methodology, to predict intraday price jumps on the S&P 500 up to an hour before they occur. The results indicated that the system was successfully able to predict stock price movement using the news stories alone, without access to market price or volume data. Future work using text data will doubtless seek to extract more detailed semantic meaning from news stories as inputs to trading systems.

2.8   Fitness Function Design

One of the critical decisions in applying GE, or indeed any EAP approach, to trading system generation is the choice of fitness function. Poor choices will produce poor trading systems. For example, selection of raw profit as a fitness metric is quite likely to lead to the generation of trading systems with undesirable risk characteristics, in terms of the variance or skewness of trading returns, as the simple fitness metric contains no penalty against trading systems which produce volatile returns [18, 31].

A trading strategy will generate a corresponding distribution of payoffs (returns) if implemented repetitively, with the shape of the distribution depending on the nature of the strategy. The first moment of the underlying probability density function corresponds to the expected payoff to the strategy per trade with the higher moments of the distribution (variance, skewness, and kurtosis etc.) describing how payoffs vary around this value. In other words, the higher moments assess the risk that returns may vary from expected.

In most implementations of EAP to trading system design, attention is focussed on the first and second moments of the distribution (i.e., the mean and variance of returns) with the aim being to maximise the former and minimise the latter. However, there are clear limitations to this approach. It implicitly assumes constant risk aversion as it treats positive and negative outcomes symmetrically. Of course, the design of the fitness function can be much more nuanced than merely maximising a metric such as the *Stirling ratio*:

$$\frac{\text{Return}}{\text{Drawdown}} \tag{1}$$

and can be specified so as to bias the generated trading system towards systems with a desired distribution of returns.

Another problem with traditional approaches to fitness function selection is that risk metrics such as variance do not take account of the temporal ordering of returns. A sequence of negative returns can lead to large drawdowns which can have detrimental consequences if an individual investor or fund runs out of capital, suggesting an important role for consideration of all aspects of the shape of the produced equity curve in assessing trading systems.

Bradley et al. [31] examined the behavior of GE generated trading models evolved using different choices of fitness functions, finding that these choices have a very significant impact. This study forms a useful starting point for future work concerning fitness function design.

One issue which impacts on all trading system induction methods is that of data snooping. In essence, when a dataset is used multiple times for model selection an apparently good model could occur due to chance alone rather than representing a truly robust model of the data-generating process [89]. In these cases, the trading system will likely perform poorly out of sample. Data snooping is a particular concern in powerful methodologies such as EAP approaches due to the very large number of trading systems that can be generated and tested against the same dataset during training.

Agapitos et al. [3] addressed this point, aiming to investigate the profitability of evolved trading rules, having controlled for data-mining bias. The approach taken implements a multi-criterion fitness function that in addition to a measure of profitability, takes into account Hansen's Superior Predictive Ability test, which can directly quantify the effect of data-mining bias, by testing the performance of the best mined rule in the context of the full universe of technical trading rules. Another study addressing this issue, in the context of a for-ex trading system, is [80] which constructs a framework for trading rule selection using a-priori robustness strategies, where robustness is gauged on the basis of time-series bootstrap and multi-objective criteria.

2.8.1 Trade Execution

As noted above, most academic contributions on trading systems omit detailed consideration of implementation issues. In real-world trading, especially high-frequency trading, careful attention must be paid to the structure of the market being traded and the different ways in which investors can interact with this market.

2.9 Market Structure

Most large financial markets now operate as an electronic double auction limit order book on which investors can post buy or sell orders at a specific, desired, price. These orders are known as limit orders and are visible to market participants. Limit orders can be cancelled at any time prior to their execution. Alternatively, an investor may submit a market order which is executed immediately at current prices. The choice between use of a limit or a market order depends on the sensitivity of the investor to the probability of order execution versus the price paid.

As limit orders are visible when placed on the order book, investors wishing to buy or sell a large quantity of stock will usually seek to manage the trade in order to minimise its price impact. If an investor places a large 'buy' order, potential sellers will mark up prices. An obvious strategy in response is to attempt to break up the order into smaller pieces and push it out to the market a bit at a time. The potential drawback of this is that the market may move against the buyer, hence design of an execution strategy tries to balance market impact versus the risk of not filling the order. An efficient trade execution strategy seeks to address the following:

- Timing—when should the order be placed and/or what interval of time should there be between orders (what is the schedule?)
- Type—should the order be a market, limit, reserve, hidden order?
- Sizing—what size order should be sent to the market?

- Pricing—at what price should the order be, aggressive or passive?
- Destination—there are many market destinations and types. Which one will provide the best conditions of execution for the order?
- Management—if a limit order has been submitted, how should this order be managed post submission?

A variety of fitness functions could be designed to drive the evolution of the execution strategy but a common metric of trade execution performance is its *Volume Weighted Average Price* (VWAP):

$$VWAP = \frac{\sum(Price \cdot Volume)}{\sum(Volume)} \tag{2}$$

The VWAP of a strategy can be calculated and benchmarked against (for example) the overall VWAP for that share during the period of the trading strategy's execution. The aim is to evolve a strategy which produces as competitive a VWAP as possible.

In essence, the VWAP for a defined time period (say a day) is calculated by adding up the dollar value of every trade during the day, divided by the total shares traded during the day. If the VWAP obtained by a trading strategy is better (i.e., lower for a purchase of an equity position) than the market VWAP over the same period, the trade execution is considered to be good.

2.10 GE and Trade Execution

A novel approach was taken by Cui et al. [42, 43] where GE was used to evolve a dynamic trade execution strategy, with the resulting rule adapting to changing market conditions. Based on the finance literature analysing the relationship between order placement and the information content of limit order books, six order book metrics were selected as potential inputs for an execution strategy (Table 1).

The grammar adopted in our experiments is outlined in Fig. 3.

Table 1 Selected order book metrics

Variables	Definitions
BidDepth	Number of shares at the best bid
AskDepth	Number of shares at the best ask
RelativeDepth	Total number of shares at the best five ask prices divided by total number of shares at the best five bid and ask prices
Spread	Difference between the best bid price and best ask price
Volatility	Standard deviation of the most recent 20 mid-quotes
PriceChange	Number of positive price changes within the past 10 min divided by the total number of quotes submitted within the past 10 min

```
<lc> ::= if (<stamt>)
                class = "CrossingSpread"
        else
                class = "NotCrossingSpread"
<stamt> ::= <cond1><op><cond2><op><cond3><op><cond4>
            <op><cond5><op><cond6>
<op> ::= and | or
<cond1> ::= (BidDepth>AvgBidDepth) is <boolean>
<cond2> ::= (AskDepth>AvgAskDepth) is <boolean>
<cond3> ::= (RelativeDepth>AvgRelativeDepth) is <boolean>
<cond4> ::= (Spread>AvgSpread) is <boolean>
<cond5> ::= (Volatility>AvgVolatility) is <boolean>
<cond6> ::= (PriceChange>AvgPriceChange) is <boolean>
<boolean> ::= True | False
```

Fig. 3 Grammar used in trade execution studies of [42, 43]

```
if ( (BidDepth>AvgBidDepth) is True  or  (AskDepth>AvgAskDepth) is False
     and  (Spread>AvgSpread) is True  )   class = "CrossingSpread"
else         class = "NotCrossingSpread"
```

Fig. 4 Exemplar dynamic trade execution strategy

In the grammar, $AvgBidDepth$ represents the average bid depth of the market, $AvgAskDepth$ represents the average ask depth of the market, $AvgRelativeDepth$ represents the average relative depth of the market, $AvgSpread$ represents the average spread of the market, $AvgVolatility$ represents the average volatility of the market and $AvgPriceChange$ represents the average price change of the market. The six financial variables are observed at the time of order amendment. An example of an evolved dynamic strategy using three financial variables is provided in Fig. 4.

In this strategy, if the market condition satisfies

```
(BidDepth>AvgBidDepth) is True and (Spread>AvgSpread)
is True
```

or satisfies

```
(AskDepth>AvgAskDepth) is False and (Spread>AvgSpread)
is True
```

the uncompleted limit order will be crossed over the bid-ask spread. Otherwise, its limit price will be amended to the best price.

A practical issue arises in the assessment of potential execution strategies, in that they cannot be easily backtested using historical data as it is very difficult to assess the impact that an execution strategy would have produced ex ante. Apart from this issue, another practical problem is that historical order book information only represents a single sample path through time and hence, using this information to estimate the likely future utility of any specific execution strategy is problematic.

In [42, 43] the training and evaluation of all trade execution strategies was implemented in an artificial limit order market, simulated using an agent-based model, parameterised using data drawn from real-world financial markets. By implementing an artificial stock market environment, it is possible to create a closed world which allows the testing of new execution strategies over multiple runs, potentially allowing us to develop robust execution strategies.

In the implementation, GE was found to be able to evolve quality trade execution strategies and its results proved highly competitive against two basic benchmark execution strategies. A detailed discussion of the application and the relevant background finance literature is provided in [44].

There is notable scope for further research utilising GE for trade execution. One obvious route is to widen the number of market variables which can be included in the evolved execution strategies.

The above are not the only studies which have applied GE in an artificial stock market setting. Whigham and Withanawasam [88] implemented a Maslov limit-order model which can be parameterised to generate controlled cyclic behaviour in the price signal. A trader, whose strategy is evolved via GE using a range of technical indicators, interacts with this market and may place limit or market orders. The objective of the study is to gain insight into the evolved trader behaviour and discover how this alters with changes in the cyclic behaviour of the market. Potentially such understanding could provide insights into how best to generate trading strategies which need to generalise to a market with a range of cyclic behaviours. In essence, the study uses the artificial stock market as a tunable model in order to provide a closed environment for the testing of trading strategies.

3 Credit Risk Modelling

The assessment of credit risk plays an important role in lending decisions. While the precise nature of credit facilities can vary depending on the agreement between the borrower and lender, in all cases lenders need to assess the capability of a borrower to make both interest and capital repayments over the lifetime of the loan. The decision as to whether to extend a loan and if so extended, its pricing, will depend on this assessment of credit risk.

In the case of consumers, a credit risk model could consider factors such as current income, age, occupation, current employment status, past borrowing record and so on [87, 90]. Corporate risk models could include factors such as data drawn from the financial statements of the firm, data drawn from financial markets (such as share price), general macro-economic data, and non-financial firm-specific information. The development of these risk assessment models requires the discovery of suitable explanatory variables and model form, with model output being a metric of credit/default risk.

3.1 Bankruptcy Prediction

A closely related research topic is that of bankruptcy prediction where the objective is to predict whether a firm will declare bankruptcy within a predetermined forecast horizon. This is typically styled as a classification problem, the object being to correctly predict the classification of a firm out of sample, as being solvent or bankrupt. The pioneering study in this domain was that of Altman [6] in which five accounting ratios were selected and then combined to produce a linear discriminant classification model for corporate bankruptcy. A Z score was calculated for each company with this value determining whether the company was classified as being likely to go bankrupt or likely to remain solvent. The original Altman classifier had the form:

$$Z=0.012X_1+0.014X_2+0.033X_3+0.006X_4+0.999X_5$$

where:
$X_1 =$ working capital to total assets
$X_2 =$ retained earnings to total assets
$X_3 =$ earnings before interest and taxes to total assets
$X_4 =$ market value of equity to book value of total debt
$X_5 =$ sales to total assets
Subsequently, more sophisticated statistical approaches including logit and probit regression [67, 94] were utilised. As the range of computational intelligence techniques for classification have expanded, each new technique has been applied in turn to credit scoring and corporate failure prediction with model induction methodologies such as artificial neural networks and support vector machines producing good results. A drawback of these approaches is that the resulting classifiers are generally not human-readable which can preclude their use in practice as some jurisdictions require lenders to justify decisions not to grant loans. Hence, EAP methodologies can be useful.

The earliest application of GE for the purposes of corporate failure prediction was O'Neill et al. [71] which explored the potential of GE to uncover rules to assist in predicting corporate failure using information drawn from financial statements of 178 publicly quoted US firms, drawn from the period 1991–2000. Twenty two financial ratios, drawn from prior finance literature on corporate failure prediction, were supplied as potential explanatory variables. In the initial study, the grammar was restricted to generate linear classifiers. The results obtained were competitive against other classification methods with good classification accuracies being obtained out of sample. The best classifiers evolved for each period are outlined in Fig. 5.

Although the evolved models were free to select from 22 potential explanatory variables, it is notable that each model only employed a small subset of these. This lends support to the proposition that many financial ratios have similar information

One Year Prior to Failure:

```
Output = -3*Financial leverage -5*Return on Assets
+3*Inventory/Working Capital-20*Retained Earnings/Total Assets
+4*Total Liabilities/Total Assets
```

Two Years Prior to Failure:

```
Output = -2*Return on Assets+10*Sales/Total Assets-10*Fixed
Assets/Total Assets-2*varEBIT/Interest
```

Three Years Prior to Failure:

```
Output= -4*Return on Assets+20*Sales/ Total Assets-72.9*Cash from
Operations/Sales-10*EBIT/Interest
```

Fig. 5 Best evolved classifiers for one, two and three years prior to failure

Table 2 The accuracies reported for each of the 3 years prior to failure based on best evolved GE classifier

Years prior to failure	In sample	Out of sample
1	85.9%	80%
2	82.8%	80%
3	75.8%	70%

content and that classification accuracy is not enhanced through the construction of models with a large number of these ratios.

The risk factors suggested by each model differ somewhat but contain plausible findings. Examining the best classifier evolved for 1 year prior to failure suggests that risk factors include low return on assets, low retained earnings and a high ratio of total liabilities to total assets, which concords with financial intuition. Less obviously, a high ratio of inventory to net liquid assets (inventory+receivables+cash-payables) is also a risk factor, possibly resulting from depletion of cash or build-up of inventories as failure approaches.

Risk factors for firms 2 years prior to failure include low return on assets and a low ratio of earnings to interest costs. Less intuitive risk factors indicated are a low ratio of fixed assets to total assets and a high ratio of sales to total assets. The former could indicate firms with a lower safety cushion of saleable resources which could be sold to stave off collapse, the latter could be serving as a proxy variable for firms with rapid sales growth. Over-rapid sales growth can be a danger signal, indicating that management resources are being spread too thinly.

Finally, risk factors indicated for firms at 3 years prior to failure include low return on assets, a low ratio of profit to interest charge, a low level of cash generated from operations and, as for T2, a high ratio of sales to total assets.

Hence, the evolved classifiers for each prediction horizon, indicate a clear 'trajectory towards failure', with low profits and high interest payments as a percentage of profits being particular risk factors 2 and 3 years prior to failure, with short-term liquidity issues arising as a key risk factor in the final year before a firm's demise (Table 2).

A key assumption in the above study (and in all other literature on corporate failure prediction) is that the selected financial ratios provide the optimal pre-processing of raw numbers from the financial statements of corporates. The GE methodology provides an easy way to address this issue as raw data drawn from the financial statements can be provided as inputs instead of pre-processed financial ratios, with the grammar allowing GE to create classifiers consisting of 'self-evolved' ratios. This approach was adopted in [12]. In essence therefore, the human domain knowledge that was supplied in [71] in the form of pre-selected financial ratios, was omitted in this study.

The out of sample predictive accuracies obtained were similar to those in [71] indicating that not alone could GE generate quality linear classifiers for the problem at hand but it could also recover the domain knowledge embedded in the finance literature concerning financial ratios with good information content for prediction of bankruptcy. An expanded version of this study was subsequently presented in [14]. Other relevant work is that of Alfaro-Cid et al. [4] which considers the issues of unbalanced datasets, a particular feature of bankruptcy prediction modelling, as the number of failing companies is typically relatively small in comparison with the number of solvent companies.

While the above studies did not make use of non-financial information about the firms, or general macro-economic data, it would not be difficult to extend the approach to include such information.

3.2 Bond Rating Prediction

When large corporates wish to raise debt which is tradable on a recognised financial market, they need to obtain a bond rating from an independent rating firm such as Standard & Poor's (S&P) or Moody's. The bond rating firms undertake an assessment of either the proposed lender's general credit-worthiness (an issuer credit rating) or an assessment of the credit-worthiness of a specific bond issue they propose to make (a bond issue credit rating). Therefore the ratings serve as a surrogate measure of the risk of non-payment of interest or capital. These ratings impact on the borrowing cost and the marketability of issued bonds.

The ratings are revised periodically as the circumstances of the borrower change. Being able to anticipate bond rating changes could potentially provide a useful input into a stock or bond trading model. It would also provide useful information for pricing of credit-risk derivatives concerning that borrower.

Following some initial work in the 1960s, there was increased research interest in attempting to predict corporate bond ratings from the 1980s [50, 51, 53]. In common with corporate failure prediction a feature of bond rating prediction is that there is no unambiguous theoretical framework for guiding the choice of explanatory variables, or model form. Rating agencies assert that their credit rating process involves consideration of both financial and non-financial information about the firm and its industry, but the precise factors utilised, and the related weighting of these factors, are not publicly disclosed by the agencies. In the absence of an underlying theory, most published work on bond rating prediction employs a data-inductive modelling approach, using firm-specific financial data as explanatory variables, in an attempt to recover the model used by the rating agencies. This produces a high-dimensional combinatorial problem.

The initial application of GE to bond rating prediction focussed on issuer-credit ratings and aimed to predict whether a rating would fall into investment-grade or junk category Brabazon and O'Neill [15], followed by Brabazon and O'Neill [16, 19]. Financial data, and the associated Standard & Poor's issuer-credit ratings of 600 public US firms, drawn from the years 1999/2000 were used to train and test the model.

The best developed model was found to be able to discriminate in-sample (out-of-sample) between investment-grade and junk bond ratings with an average accuracy of 87.59 (84.92)% across a fivefold cross validation, producing very similar results to a Multi-Layer Perceptrons (MLP) applied to the same data. In contrast to the MLP models, the GE classification model was reasonably compact and produced a human-readable classification rule which concorded with domain knowledge. Given that GE was restricted to evolve linear classification rules, the comparability of its results with those from application of an MLP would indicate that the relationships between financial data and resulting bond ratings are not, in fact, highly non-linear.

3.3   Other Related Problems in Finance

There are several other areas of research in finance which seek to predict a corporate outcome using financial and other information about a firm and its industry. A significant stream of work involves the prediction of targets for merger or takeover. Obviously, being able to accurately predict which firms may be a target in advance of the market generally, could provide useful trading information. A wide a variety of methodologies have been applied in an attempt to forecast takeover and merger targets, including univariate analysis [76], Multivariate Discriminant Analysis (MDA) [7, 82], probit/logit analysis [63, 75], MLPs [33] and self-organising maps [56].

Another related stream of work is the prediction of an auditor's 'going-concern' qualification of the financial statements of a company. As this qualification states that the auditor does not believe that the company will continue in existence, the issuing of such a qualification will typically have a major impact on the decisions of investors, bank lenders, creditors and employees. When an entity receives a going concern qualification they will usually suffer serious repercussions including restrictions on trade credit, constraints on the raising of further finance/capital, and the possibility of a share price collapse. This domain has attracted research attention over the past three decades. A wide variety of methodologies have been applied in an attempt to predict going concern qualification including univariate analysis, Linear Discriminant Analysis (LDA) [65], logit [9], probit [49] and MLPs [85]. Most studies have relied heavily on the use of company accounting data as modelling inputs. As yet, GE has not been applied to either of these areas.

4 Other Finance and Economics Applications of GE

Over the years, GE has been introduced to a variety of application areas in finance and economics outside of the areas already discussed in this chapter. In this section we briefly overview a few of these.

4.1 Supply Chain Management

Supply chain management concerns the management of the flow of goods and services from point of origin to point of consumption. It encompasses flows of raw materials, work-in-process, and finished goods. Efficient and effective management of these flows is crucial in order to ensure the requisite availability of products/services to each customer as needed, and in order to control the costs of the supply chain as a whole. Modern supply chains can be very complex ranging over multiple countries and encompassing many different organisations.

A particular challenge in managing supply chains is that unexpected events can occur such as unanticipated changes in final customer demand, unexpected events in production systems (for example, closure of a factory), or changes in legislation impacting on the flow of some product. Such unexpected events can result in a 'bullwhip effect' with the initial impact being magnified at other stages in the supply chain, producing inefficiencies and high costs. In the worst-case scenario, customer service declines, lead-times increase, sales are lost, costs go up and capacity is adjusted [73]. A common example of the bullwhip effect is where orders to a supplier in the supply chain have a larger variance than sales to the buyer in the same supply chain, referred to as demand distortion. This can occur when suppliers do not have good information on final sales and over-respond to small fluctuations in these.

A traditional problem in supply chain management is to derive the optimal ordering policy for an individual firm, given the information available to it. Many approaches have been taken in the literature to derivation of this policy with Phelan and McGarraghy [73] novelly applying GE in an attempt to derive an optimal ordering policy for agents in a multi-tier supply chain. In this study, GE is implemented in a simulation environment where artificial agents are playing the Beer Game [81]. In this game, shipments arrive from upstream players, orders arrive from downstream players, orders are filled and shipped where possible, affecting the inventory and backorders of a player, the player in each step of the game (i.e., each time period) decides how much to order to replenish their inventory, and finally inventory holding costs and backorder costs are calculated for each player every week [73]. Different scenarios can be generated, depending on whether the final demand from customers is deterministic or stochastic. The GE grammar is defined so as to allow the generation of a valid ordering policy and the costs of a specific policy can be estimated by running a simulation of final demands and actions of each agent in the supply chain. The results indicated that GE was capable of producing effective ordering policies. Developments on this initial study are discussed in [72] and [74].

4.2 Tax Non-Compliance Detection

The setting of tax evasion can be considered as a co-evolutionary arms race in which the tax evader is attempting to outwit the rules as enforced by the tax authority. The latter is attempting to catch evaders via tax audits and to close off loopholes in tax regulation. A novel application of GE was implemented by Hemberg et al. [54] in the simulation modelling of this setting. In the study, a search heuristic called STEALTH is implemented that can simulate the co-evolution of abusive tax avoidance schemes and audit scores, where GE is applied to generate a series of transactions for the purposes of this simulation. The system has potential use in guiding policy formulation as it allows the exploration of the likely forms of (new) tax schemes in response to changes in audit policies of tax authorities. Obviously, if policy makers can anticipate potentially abusive tax avoidance schemes, they can implement novel audit procedures in order to counteract them. The developed system is quite complex and fuller details are provided in [55] and [77]. On a broader level, this work provides another exemplar of the application of GE in an agent-based setting.

4.3 Corporate Strategy

An enduring research question is whether organisational strategy matters in terms of explaining corporate performance, and if so, how much does it matter. While it appears self-evident at first glance that corporate decisions regarding firm scope and resource allocation would affect firm performance, the empirical evidence is not so clear cut, with studies of the performance of diversification and retrenchment strategies producing varying results [10, 83]. The strategy domain is characterised by a lack of strong theoretical frameworks. It is also notable that unlike areas such as financial market prediction, there have been virtually no applications of EAP methodologies to questions in the strategy domain.

Brabazon et al. [24] introduced GE to this domain, modelling the relationship between corporate strategy and shareholder wealth. A shareholder perspective is adopted in the study and it is assumed that the success of corporate strategy decisions is judged by equity markets. To allow for exogenous factors which could impact on stock market values generally, a relative performance metric, a market-value-added (MVA) rank is utilised. MVA is defined as: Market Value of Firm—Original Value of Capital Invested. The performance of the firm is determined by whether it improved its MVA ranking in the Stern-Stewart 1000 listing (published in Fortune magazine) over a 4 year period.

A total of 430 US firms were selected from the Stern-Stewart Performance 1000 list for the study and sixteen potential explanatory variables, which can proxy strategic intent [83], drawn from their financial statements are collected from the Compustat database for each firm. The best classifier correctly categorised the direction of performance ranking change in 66% of the firms in the training set and 65% in the out-of-sample validation set providing support for a hypothesis that changes in corporate strategy are linked to changes in corporate performance. A detailed discussion of the results and the form of the evolved classifiers can be found in [24]. Scope exists to further extend the application of GE into this domain beyond this pilot study.

5   The Future

GE has found a variety of applications in finance and economics since its introduction in 1998. It is notable that the sophistication of the studies employing the methodology has increased over the years moving from initial proof of concept studies to much more robust, industry-strength, applications. This process has been facilitated by the dissemination of knowledge about GE beyond computer science to include domain experts from finance and economics. A key selling point for many finance academics and practitioners concerning GE is its ability to encapsulate domain knowledge in the grammar. This helps reassure users that the resulting models are plausible. Hence, the areas with greatest potential for the application of GE are those where we have good data concerning the phenomenon of interest but only a partial understanding of how this data might fit together.

Financial trading will continue to be an important area of application for GE given its natural fit with this application. We can expect to see increasing sophistication in these application with fuller implementation of smart entry and exit strategies, and greater attention being paid to market structure. There is also substantial opportunity to undertake work concerning the design of appropriate fitness functions for trading applications. We can expect to see greater integration of non-financial information, such as that from social media or official news wires into trading systems.

The range of financial instruments traded on markets has expanded enormously over the past 20 years, moving far beyond the trading of shares and debt instruments to encompass a wide variety of financial derivatives. A key issue for investors wishing to trade in derivatives for speculative or hedging purposes is the determination of a fair price for the derivative. While GP has been applied for the purposes of reverse-engineering pricing models ([36, 38, 58, 91, 93] is a sampling of this work) and to develop hedging strategies [92], the relative ease with which domain knowledge and user-preferred bias in the structure of output models, can be incorporated into a grammar in GE makes these promising areas for future work.

Another area with significant potential for the application of GE is that of agent-based modelling (ABM). Although there have already been a number of studies applying GE in an ABM framework ([42–44, 54, 55, 88] being a sampling of these), it is perhaps surprising that GE has not gained greater traction as a tool for ABM. The nature of GE makes it particularly amenable for application in ABM as it is relatively easy for modellers to place a desired structure via the grammar definition on the strategies that agents can employ, while still allowing considerable room for agents to adapt their strategies. In addition to modelling of agents in financial markets, there are a multiplicity of opportunities for policy-focussed research via application of a GE methodology to ABM in economics.

The application of GE to finance and economics is nearly 'fiche bliain ag fás'.[1] It will be fascinating to see the continued development of this work over the next 20 years.

References

1. K. Adamu, S. Phelps, Modelling financial time series using grammatical evolution, in *Proceedings of the Workshop on Advances in Machine Learning for Computational Finance*, London, UK (2009)
2. K. Adamu, S. Phelps, Coevolution of technical trading rules for high frequency trading, in *Electrical Engineering and Applied Computing*. Lecture Notes in Electrical Engineering, vol. 90 (Springer, Berlin, 2011), pp. 311–322
3. A. Agapitos, M. O'Neill, A. Brabazon, Evolutionary learning of technical trading rules without data-mining bias, in *International Conference on Parallel Problem Solving from Nature (PPSN 2010)*. Lecture Notes in Computer Science, vol. 6238 (Springer, Berlin, 2010), pp. 294–303
4. E. Alfaro-Cid, A. Cuesta-Canada, K. Sharman, A. Esparcia-Alcazar, Stong typing, variable reduction and bloat control for solving the bankruptcy prediction problem using genetic programming, in *Natural Computing in Computational Finance* (Springer, Berlin, 2008), pp. 161–186
5. F. Allen, R. Karjalainen, Using genetic algorithms to find technical trading rules. J. Financ. Econ. **51**, 245–271 (1999)
6. E. Altman, Financial ratios, discriminant analysis and the prediction of corporate bankruptcy. J. Financ. **23**, 589–609 (1968)
7. P. Barnes, The prediction of takeover targets in the U.K. by means of multiple discriminant analysis. J. Bus. Financ. Account. **17**(1), 73–84 (1990)
8. R. Bauer, *Genetic Algorithms and Investment Strategies* (Wiley, New York, 1994)

---

[1]Fiche bliain ag fás, or translated from Irish into English—'Twenty Years A-Growing', is the title of a famous autobiographical book written by Muiris Ó Súilleabháin the Irish language. The book is set in the Great Blasket Island which lies off the south west coast of Ireland, part of a group of islands inhabited until 1953 by a completely Irish-speaking population. The book forms part of an 'island literature' which details the end of a Gaelic way of life in the early twentieth century.

9. T.B. Bell, R.H. Tabor, Empirical analysis of audit uncertainty qualifications. J. Account. Res. **29**(2), 350–370 (1991)
10. E. Bowman, C. Helfat, Does corporate strategy matter? Strateg. Manag. J. **22**, 1–23 (2001)
11. A. Brabazon, S. McGarraghy, *Foraging-Inspired Optimisation Algorithms* (Springer, Berlin, 2018)
12. A. Brabazon, M. O'Neill, Anticipating bankruptcy reorganisation from raw financial data using grammatical evolution, in *Proceedings of EvoIASP 2003: Applications of Evolutionary Computing*. Lecture Notes in Computer Science, vol. 2611 (Springer, Berlin, 2003), pp. 368–378
13. A. Brabazon, M. O'Neill, A Grammar model for foreign-exchange trading, in *Proceedings of the International Conference on Artificial Intelligence 2003 (ICAI '03)* (CSEA Press, San Jose, 2003), pp. 492–499
14. A. Brabazon, M. O'Neill, Diagnosing corporate stability using grammatical evolution. Int. J. Appl. Math. Comput. Sci. **14**(3), 363–374 (2004)
15. A. Brabazon, M. O'Neill, Bond-issuer credit rating with grammatical evolution, in *Proceedings of EvoIASP 2004: Applications of Evolutionary Computing*, ed. by G. Raidl, S. Cagnoni, et al. Lecture Notes in Computer Science, vol. 3005 (Springer, Berlin, 2004), pp. 268–277
16. A. Brabazon, M. O'Neill, A grammatical approach to bond-issuer credit rating, in *Proceedings of OR 2004*, Tilburg, 1–3 September 2004
17. A. Brabazon, M. O'Neill, Evolving technical trading rules for foreign-exchange markets. Comput. Manag. Sci. **1**(3–4), 311–327 (2004)
18. A. Brabazon, M. O'Neill, *Biologically Inspired Algorithms for Financial Modelling* (Springer, Berlin, 2006)
19. A. Brabazon, M. O'Neill, Credit classification using grammatical evolution. Informatica **30**(3), 325–335 (2006)
20. A. Brabazon, M. O'Neill (eds.), *Natural Computing in Computational Finance* (Springer, Berlin, 2008)
21. A. Brabazon, M. O'Neill (eds.), *Natural Computing in Computational Finance (Volume II)* (Springer, Berlin, 2009)
22. A. Brabazon, M. O'Neill, C. Ryan, J. Collins, Developing a market timing system using grammatical evolution, in *Proceedings of AAANZ 2001*, Auckland, 1–3 July 2001
23. A. Brabazon, M. O'Neill, C. Ryan, Trading foreign exchange markets using evolutionary automatic programing, in *Proceedings of the First Workshop on Grammatical Evolution: GECCO 2002*, New York, 9–13 July 2002, pp. 133–137
24. A. Brabazon, M. O'Neill, C. Ryan, R. Matthews, Evolving classifiers to model the relationship between strategy and corporate performance using grammatical evolution, in *Proceedings of EuroGP 2002, Genetic Programming*. Lecture Notes in Computer Science, vol. 2278 (Springer, Berlin, 2002), pp. 103–113
25. A. Brabazon, K. Meagher, E. Carty, M. O'Neill, P. Keenan, Grammar-mediated time-series prediction, J. Intell. Syst. **14**(2–3), 123–143 (2005)
26. A. Brabazon, M. O'Neill, I. Dempsey, An introduction to evolutionary computation in finance. IEEE Comput. Intell. Mag. **3**(4), 42–55 (2008)
27. A. Brabazon, M. O'Neill, D. Maringer (eds.), *Natural Computing in Computational Finance (Volume III)* (Springer, Berlin, 2010)
28. A. Brabazon, M. O'Neill, D. Maringer (eds.), *Natural Computation in Computational Finance (Volume IV)* (Springer, Berlin, 2011)
29. A. Brabazon, J. Dang, I. Dempsey, M. O'Neill, in *Natural Computing in Finance: A Review*, ed. by G. Rozenberg, T. Baeck, J. Kok. Handbook of Natural Computing: Theory, Experiments and Applications (Springer, Berlin, 2011), pp. 1707–1735
30. A. Brabazon, M. O'Neill, S. McGarraghy. *Natural Computing Algorithms* (Springer, Berlin, 2015)
31. R. Bradley, A. Brabazon, M. O'Neill, Objective function design in a grammatical evolutionary trading system, in *Proceedings of the 2010 IEEE Congress On Evolutionary Computation* (IEEE Press, New York, 2010), pp. 3487–3494

32. R. Bradley, A. Brabazon, M. O'Neill, Evolving trading-rule based policies, in *Proceedings of EvoFin 2010, Applications of Evolutionary Computation*. Lecture Notes in Computer Science, vol. 6025 (Springer, Berlin, 2010), pp. 250–259

33. J.J. Cheh, A. Weinberg, K.C. Yook, An application of an artificial neural network investment system to predict takeover targets. J. Appl. Bus. Res. **15**(4), 33–44 (1999)

34. S.-H. Chen (ed.), *Genetic Algorithms and Genetic Programming in Computational Finance* (Kluwer Academic Publishers, Dordrecht, 2002)

35. S.-H. Chen (ed.), *Evolutionary Computation in Economics and Finance* (Physica-Verlag, Wien, 2002)

36. S.-H. Chen, W.-C. Lee, C.-H. Yeh, Hedging derivative securities with genetic programming. Int. J. Intell. Syst. Account. Financ. Manag. **8**(4), 237–251 (1999)

37. S.-H. Chen, P. Wang, T.-W. Kuo (eds.), *Computational Intelligence in Economics and Finance (Volume II)* (Springer, Berlin, 2007)

38. N. Chidambaran, C. Lee, J. Trigueros, Adapting Black-Scholes to a non-Black-Scholes environment via genetic programming, in *Proceedings of the IEEE/IAFE/INFORMS 1998 Conference on Computational Intelligence for Financial Engineering (CIFEr)* (IEEE Press, New York, 1998), pp. 197–211

39. I. Contreras, J.I. Hidalgo, L. Núñez-Letamendia, Combining technical analysis and grammatical evolution in a trading system, in *Applications of Evolutionary Computation. EvoApplications 2013*. Lecture Notes in Computer Science, vol. 7835 (Springer, Berlin, 2013), pp. 244–253

40. I. Contreras, J.I. Hidalgo, L. Núñez-Letamendia, A hybrid automated trading system based on multi-objective grammatical evolution. J. Intell. Fuzzy Syst. **32**(3), 2461–2475 (2017)

41. I. Contreras, J.I. Hidalgo, L. Núñez-Letamendia, J. Manuel Velasco, A meta-grammatical evolutionary process for portfolio selection and trading. Genet. Program Evolvable Mach. **18**, 411–431 (2017). https://doi.org/10.1007/s10710-017-9304-1

42. W. Cui, A. Brabazon, M. O'Neill, Evolving dynamic trade execution strategies using grammatical evolution, in *Proceedings of EvoFin 2010, Applications of Evolutionary Computation*. Lecture Notes in Computer Science, vol. 6025 (Springer, Berlin, 2010), pp. 191–200

43. W. Cui, A. Brabazon, M. O'Neill, Evolving efficient limit order strategy using grammatical evolution, *Proceedings of the 2010 IEEE Congress On Evolutionary Computation* (IEEE Press, New York, 2010), pp. 2408–2413

44. W. Cui, A. Brabazon, M. O'Neill, Adaptive trade execution using a grammatical evolution approach. Int. J. Financ. Mark. Deriv. **2**(1/2), 4–31 (2011)

45. G. Deboeck, *Trading on the Edge: Neural, Genetic, and Fuzzy Systems for Chaotic Financial Markets* (Wiley, New York, 1994)

46. I. Dempsey, M. O'Neill, A. Brabazon, Investigations into market index trading models using evolutionary automatic programming, in *Proceedings of AICS 2002*. Lecture Notes in Artificial Intelligence, vol. 2464 (Springer, Berlin, 2002), pp. 165–170

47. I. Dempsey, M. O'Neill, A. Brabazon, Live trading with grammatical evolution, in *Proceedings of the Third Workshop on Grammatical Evolution: GECCO 2004*, Seattle, 26–30 June 2004

48. I. Dempsey, M. O'Neill, A. Brabazon, Adaptive trading with grammatical evolution, in *Proceedings of the Congress on Evolutionary Computation (CEC 2006)*, Vancouver, 16–21 July 2006 (IEEE Press, New Jersey, 2006), pp. 9137–9172

49. N. Dopuch, R.W. Holthausen, R.W. Leftwich, predicting audit qualifications with financial and market variables. Account. Rev. **LXII**(3), 431–454 (1987)

50. S. Dutta, S. Shekhar, Bond rating: a non-conservative application of neural networks, in *Proceedings of IEEE International Conference on Neural Networks, II* (IEEE Press, New York, 1988), pp. 443–450

51. H. Ederington, Classification models and bond ratings. Financ. Rev. **20**(4), 237–262 (1985)

52. P. Gabrielsson, U. Johansson, R. König, Co-evolving online high-frequency trading strategies using grammatical evolution, in *Proceedings of the 2014 IEEE Conference on Computational Intelligence for Financial Engineering and Economics (CIFEr 2014)* (IEEE Press, New York, 2014), pp.1–8

53. J. Gentry, D. Whitford, P. Newbold, Predicting industrial bond ratings with a probit model and funds flow components. Financ. Rev. **23**(3), 269–286 (1988)
54. E. Hemberg, J. Rosen, G. Warner, U.-M. O'Reilly, Tax non-compliance detection using co-evolution of tax evasion risk and audit likelihood, in *Proceedings of the 15th International Conference on AI and Law (ICAIL 2015)* (ACM, New York, 2015), pp. 79–88
55. E. Hemberg, J. Rosen, G. Warner, et al., Detecting tax evasion: a co-evolutionary approach. Artif. Intell. Law **24**(2), 149–182 (2016)
56. R. Hickey, E. Little, A. Brabazon, Identifying merger and takeover targets using a self-organising map, in *Proceedings of the 2006 International Conference on Artificial Intelligence (ICAI 06)*, Las Vegas, 26–29 June 2006, vol. 1 (CSEA Press, San Jose, 2006), pp. 408–413
57. H. Iba, N. Nikolaev, Genetic programming polynomial models of financial data series, in *Proceedings of CEC 2000* (IEEE Press, New York, 2000), pp. 1459–1466
58. C. Keber, Option valuation with the genetic programming approach, in *Proceedings of the Sixth International Conference* (MIT Press, Cambridge, MA, 2000), pp. 689–703
59. J.R. Koza, Genetic Programming: A Paradigm for Genetically Breeding Populations of Computer Programs to Solve Problems. Stanford University Computer Science Department Technical Report STAN-CS-90-1314, June 1990
60. J.R. Koza, A genetic approach to econometric modeling. Paper presented at Sixth World Congress of the Econometric Society, Barcelona, Spain, 27 August 1990
61. J. Koza, *Genetic Programming* (MIT Press, Cambridge, MA, 1992)
62. F. Larkin, C. Ryan, Good news: using news feeds with genetic programming to predict stock prices, in *Proceedings of the 11th European Conference on Genetic Programming (EuroGP 2008)*, ed. by M. O'Neill, et al. Lecture Notes in Computer Science, vol. 4971 (Springer, berlin, 2008), pp. 49–60
63. A. Meador, P. Church, L. Rayburn, Development of prediction models for horizontal and vertical mergers. J. Financ. Strateg. Decis. **9**(1), 11–23 (1996)
64. J.J. Murphy, *Technical Analysis of the Financial Markets* (New York Institute of Finance, New York, 1999)
65. J.F. Mutchler, A multivariate analysis of the auditor's going-concern opinion decision. J. Account. Res. **23**(2), 668–682 (1985)
66. C. Oesch, D. Maringer, Low-latency liquidity inefficiency strategies. Quant. Finan. **17**(5), 717–727 (2016)
67. J. Ohlson, Financial ratios and the probabilistic prediction of bankruptcy. J. Account. Res. **18**(1), 109–131 (1980)
68. M. O'Neill, A. Brabazon, C. Ryan, J. Collins, Evolving market index trading rules using grammatical evolution, in *Proceedings of EvoIASP 2001, Applications of Evolutionary Computing*. Lecture Notes in Computer Science (Springer, Berlin, 2001), pp. 343–353
69. M. O'Neill, A. Brabazon, C. Ryan, J. Collins, Developing a market timing system using grammatical evolution, in *Proceedings of the Genetic and Evolutionary Computation Conference (GECCO 2001)*, San Francisco, USA, 7–11 July 2001 (Morgan Kaufmann, Los Altos, 2001), pp. 1375–1381
70. M. O'Neill, A. Brabazon, C. Ryan, Forecasting market indices using evolutionary automatic programming: a case study, in *Genetic Algorithms and Genetic Programming in Economics and Finance*, ed. by S.-H. Chen (Kluwer Academic Publishers, Dordrecht, 2002), pp. 174–195
71. M. O'Neill, A. Brabazon, C. Ryan, R. Matthews, Grammatical evolution and corporate failure prediction, in *Proceedings of the Genetic and Evolutionary Computation Conference (GECCO 2002)*, New York, USA, 9–13 July 2002 (Morgan Kaufmann, Los Altos, 2002), pp. 1011–1019
72. M. Phelan, Bullwhips & beer: grammatical evolution in supply chains! ACM SIGEVOlution **9**(4), 3–8 (2016)
73. M. Phelan, S. McGarraghy, Mitigating the bullwhip effect in supply chains using grammatical evolution, in *System Dynamics Society Conference*, Boston, Massachusetts, USA, ed. by System Dynamics Society (2007)
74. M. Phelan, S. McGarraghy, Grammatical evolution in developing optimal inventory policies for serial and distribution supply chains. Int. J. Prod. Res. **54**(1), 336–364 (2016)

75. R. Powell, Modelling takeover likelihood. J. Bus. Financ. Account. **24**(7&8), 1009–1030 (1997)
76. U. Rege, Accounting ratios to locate take-over targets. J. Bus. Financ. Account. **11**(3), 301–311 (1984)
77. J. Rosen, E. Hemberg, U.-M. O'Reilly, Dynamics of adversarial co-evolution in tax non-compliance detection, in *Proceedings of the Genetic and Evolutionary Computation Conference (GECCO 2016)* (ACM, New York, 2016), pp. 1087–1094
78. C. Ryan, J.J. Collins, M. O'Neill, Grammatical evolution: evolving programs for an arbitrary language. in *Proceedings of the First European Workshop on GP* (Springer, Berlin, 1998), pp. 83–95
79. P. Saks, D. Maringer, Evolutionary money management, in *Natural Computing in Computational Finance*. Studies in Computational Intelligence, vol. 293 (Springer, Berlin, 2009), pp. 169–190
80. H. Schmidbauer, A. Rösch, T. Sezer, et al., Robust trading rule selection and forecasting accuracy. J. Syst. Sci. Complex. **27**, 169–180 (2014)
81. J. Sterman, Modeling managerial behavior - misperceptions of feedback in a dynamic decision-making experiment. Manag. Sci. **35**(3), 321–339 (1989)
82. D. Stevens, Financial characteristics of merged firms: a multivariate analysis. J. Financ. Quant. Anal. **8**(2), 149–159 (1973)
83. C. St. John, N. Balakrishnan, O. Fiet, Modelling the relationship between corporate strategy and wealth creation using neural networks. Comput. Oper. Res. **27**, 1077–1092 (2000)
84. J. Thomas, K. Sycara, GP and the predictive power of internet message traffic, in *Genetic Algorithms and Genetic Programming in Computational Finance*, ed. by S.-H. Chen (Kluwer Academic Publishers, Dordrecht, 2002), pp. 81–102
85. D. Thompson, S. Thompson, A. Brabazon, Predicting going concern audit qualification using neural networks, in *Proceedings of the 2007 International Conference on Artificial Intelligence (ICAI 07)*, Las Vegas, 25–28 June 2007, vol. 1 (CSEA Press, San Jose, 2007), pp. 199–204
86. W. Tung, C. Quek, GenSoOPATS: a brain-inspired dynamically evolving option pricing model and arbitrage system, in *Proceedings of the IEEE International Conference on Evolutionary Computation (CEC 2005)* (IEEE Press, New York, 2005), pp. 1722–1729
87. D. West, Neural network credit scoring models. Comput. Oper. Res. **27**, 1131–1152 (2000)
88. P. Whigham, R. Withanawasam, Evolving a robust trader in a cyclic double auction market, in *Proceedings of the 13th annual Conference on Genetic and Evolutionary Computation (GECCO 2011)* (ACM, New York, 2011), pp. 1451–1458
89. H. White, A reality check for data snooping. Econometrica **68**, 1097–1126 (2000)
90. M. Yobas, J. Crook, P. Ross, Credit scoring using neural and evolutionary techniques. IMA J. Math. Appl. Bus. Ind. **11**, 111–125 (2000)
91. Z. Yin, A. Brabazon, C. O'Sullivan, Adaptive genetic programming for option pricing, in *Proceedings of the Genetic and Evolutionary Computation Conference (GECCO 2007)* (ACM Press, New York, 2007), pp. 2588–2594
92. Z. Yin, A. Brabazon, C. O'Sullivan, M. O'Neill, A genetic programming approach for delta hedging, in *IEEE Congress on Evolutionary Computing*, Sendai, Japan (IEEE Press, New York, 2015), pp. 3312–3318
93. Z. Yin, C. O'Sullivan, A. Brabazon, An analysis of the performance of genetic programming for realised volatility forecasting. J. Artif. Intell. Soft Comput. Res. **6**(3), 155–172 (2016)
94. M. Zmijewski, Methodological issues related to the estimation of financial distress prediction models. J. Account. Res. **22**(Supplement), 59–82 (1984)

Synthesis of Parallel Programs on Multi-Cores

Gopinath Chennupati, R. Muhammad Atif Azad, Conor Ryan,
Stephan Eidenbenz, and Nandakishore Santhi

Abstract Multi-cores offer higher processing power than single core processors. However, as the number of cores available on a single processor increases, efficiently programming them becomes increasingly more complex, often to the point where the limiting factor in speeding up tasks is the software.

We present *Grammatical Automatic Parallel Programming* (GAPP), a system that synthesizes parallel code on multi-cores using OpenMP parallelization primitives in problem-specific grammars. As a result, GAPP obviates the need for programmers to think parallel while still letting them produce parallel code.

The performance of GAPP on a number of difficult proof of concept benchmarks informs further optimization of both the design of grammars and fitness function to extract further parallelism. We demonstrate an improved performance of evolving programs with controlled degree of parallelism. These programs adapt to the number of cores on which they are scheduled to execute.

1 Introduction

As the *multi-core* processors become the norm, researchers fabricate thousands of cores on a single chip [6, 28, 32]. As the number of cores on a chip increase, efficiently programming them becomes increasingly complex, often to the point where the limiting factor in speeding up tasks is the software. Contrarily, high

G. Chennupati (✉) · S. Eidenbenz · N. Santhi
Los Alamos National Laboratory, Los Alamos, NM, USA
e-mail: gchennupati@lanl.gov; eidenben@lanl.gov; nsanthi@lanl.gov

R. M. A. Azad
School of Computing and Digital Technology, Birmingham City University, Birmingham, UK
e-mail: atif.azad@bcu.ac.uk

C. Ryan
Department of Computer Science and Information Systems, University of Limerick, Castletroy, Limerick, Ireland
e-mail: conor.ryan@ul.ie

© Springer International Publishing AG, part of Springer Nature 2018   289
C. Ryan et al. (eds.), *Handbook of Grammatical Evolution*,
https://doi.org/10.1007/978-3-319-78717-6_12

performance computing developers [37, 46, 49] have identified that the software is trailing behind the rise of multi-cores. The inability of sequential software to scale with multi-cores initiates the necessity for the programmers to write parallel programs that exploit multi-cores.

Parallel programming APIs such as MPI [30] and OpenMP [26] help in exploiting the higher processing power of multi-cores. OpenMP exploits processing power on the shared memory architectures. Writing parallel programs using either of the above two standards is challenging compared to sequential programming [41]. Challenges include identifying the available parallelism, configuring the shared data, use of locks for mutual exclusion in order to guarantee correctness of the code, synchronizing and balancing the workload among multiple processors.

Alternatively, *automatic parallelization*, transforms a sequential program into a semantically equivalent parallel code. Some automatic parallelization compilers include Polaris [8], SUIF [5], and Vienna Fortran Compiler [7]. Automatic parallelization is still difficult, where the burden moves from the software developer to a compiler engineer. Later, engineers' efforts were augmented and in some cases replaced with machine learning [53]. Clearly, we need better tools to fully exploit the multi-cores.

We introduce an automatic parallel programming tool, *Grammatical Automatic Parallel Programming* (GAPP) to reduce the gap between traditional parallel programming and the human difficulties. GAPP combines Grammatical Evolution (GE) together with the design of parallel context-free grammars (CFGs). GAPP predominantly addresses the parallel programming concerns on shared memory architectures thereby, we use OpenMP parallelization constructs in order to guarantee parallelism. OpenMP primitives are an integral part of the grammars, GE together with these primitives creates a feasible solution space of parallel programs.

We examine GAPP in synthesizing parallel programs in both *recursion* and *iterative sorting* domains. We study the performance, measured in terms of speed-up and the amount of effort required to synthesize, measured in terms of the number of generations. The results indicate that GAPP generates correct and efficient parallel programs. We extend GAPP, and as a result we witness a slight improvement in the performance of the resultant parallel programs. At this stage, as a result of the improvements, we encounter a peculiar behaviour in the execution of the synthesized parallel programs. This characteristic behaviour is different in both the problem domains, where recursive parallel programs exhibit *excessive parallelism* while iterative sorting programs suffer with the concept of *false sharing*. In order to address these challenges, we further extend GAPP—slightly modify the design of the grammars. The enhancements resolve these hurdles while improving the performance of the synthesized parallel programs.

We organize the rest of the paper as follows: Sect. 2 describes the existing work; Sect. 3 describes GAPP on both the problem domains; Sect. 4 presents the experimental parameters; Sect. 5 demonstrates the experimental results; and Sect. 6 analyses and extends GAPP; finally, Sect. 7 concludes.

2   Related Research

2.1   Evolutionary Techniques for Recursion

Some of the earliest work on evolving recursion is from Koza [36, Chapter-18] which evolved a Fibonacci sequence; this work cached previously computed recursive calls for efficiency. Brave [10] used *Automatically Defined Functions* (ADFs) to evolve recursive tree search. In this, recursion terminated upon reaching the tree depth. Then, [55] concluded that infinite recursions was a major obstacle to evolve recursive programs. However, Wong and Mun [57] successfully used an adaptive grammar to evolve recursive programs; the grammar adjusted the production rule weights in evolving solutions.

Spector et al. [48] evolved recursive programs using PushGP by explicitly manipulating its execution stack. The evolved programs were of $O\left(n^2\right)$ complexity, which became $O\left(nlog(n)\right)$ with an efficiency component in fitness evaluation. Recently, Moraglio et al. [38] used a non-recursive scaffolding method to evolve recursive programs with a CFG based GP. Recently, Agapitos et al. [4] presented a review of GP for recursion.

2.2   Evolutionary Techniques for Sorting

In evolving sorting networks, Hillis [31] evolved a minimal 16-input network for the sorting network problem. O'Reilly and Oppacher [44] initially failed to evolve sorting with genetic programming (GP); however, they succeeded in [45] with a *swap* primitive. Later, Kinnear [33, 34] generated a bubble sort by swapping the disordered adjacent elements. Abbott [1] used Object Oriented Genetic Programming (OOGP) for insertion and bubble sorts. Spector et al., [48] used PushGP for recursive sorting that had an $O\left(n^2\right)$ complexity and enhanced to $O\left(nlog(n)\right)$ by adding efficiency.

Recently, Agapitos and Lucas [2, 3] evolved efficient recursive quicksort using OOGP in Java. The evolved programs were of $O\left(nlogn\right)$ complexity. Then, O'Neill et al. [43] applied GE for program synthesis by evolving an iterative bubble sort in Python; the evolved programs had quadratic $O\left(n^2\right)$ complexity. Most of these attempts belong to quadratic complexity $O\left(n^2\right)$, while the attempts in [2, 48] belongs to $O\left(nlogn\right)$.

2.3 Automatic Evolution of Parallel Programs

In general, automatic generation of parallel programs can be divided into two types: *auto-parallelization of serial code* and the *generation of native parallel code*.

Auto-parallelization requires a serial program. Using GP, [47, Chapter-5] proposed *Paragen* which had initial success, however, the execution of candidate solutions for fitness evaluation ran into difficulties with complex and time consuming loops. Later, *Paragen-II* [47, Chapter-7] dealt with loop inter-dependencies relying on a rough estimate of time. Then, [47] extended *Paragen-II* to merge independent tasks of loops.

Similarly, genetic algorithms evolved *transformations*; [40] and [56] proposed *GAPS* (Genetic Algorithm Parallelization System) and *Revolver* respectively. GAPS evolved sequence restructuring, while *Revolver* transformed the loops and programs, both optimized the execution time. On the other hand, *native parallel code generation* produces a working program that is also parallel. With multitree GP, [51] concurrently executed autonomous agents for automatic design of controllers.

Unlike PARAGEN-II [47], GAPP does not utilize dependency analysis; instead, GE works the data interdependencies out by selecting pragmas that guarantee program correctness. Recently, Chennupati et al., [15, 17] evolved natively parallel regression programs. Thereafter, MCGE-II in [20] evolved task parallel recursive programs. The minimal execution time of the synthesized programs was merely due to the presence of OpenMP pragmas which automatically map threads to cores. However, use of a different OpenMP pragma alters the performance of a parallel program, and skilled parallel programmers carefully choose the pragmas when writing code. To that end, in this paper, we extend MCGE-II in two ways: we re-structure the grammars so task and data level parallelism is separate, and we explicitly penalize long executions.

3 Grammatical Automatic Parallel Programming

Grammatical Automatic Parallel Programming (GAPP) presents the first instance of using grammars for the task of automatic parallel programming. GAPP provides an alternative to the *craftsman* approach of parallel programming. This is significantly different from other parallel EC approaches, because not only do we produce individuals that, in their *final form*, can exploit parallel architectures, we also exploit the same parallel architecture during evolution to reduce the execution time.

Figure 1 presents an overview of GAPP that operates on a string of codons which separate the search and the solution spaces. Like any application of GE, GAPP uses the typical search process, genetic operations and genotype-phenotype mapping. However, the major contribution of GAPP is the design of grammars that produce parallel programs, in which, OpenMP primitives are an integral part of the grammars

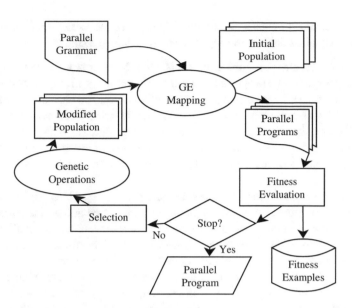

Fig. 1 An overview of GAPP parallel program synthesis

and creates a feasible solution space of parallel programs. The GE search process helps to find the [near] optimal parallel programs in that space. These programs are evaluated on a number of fitness cases such that the best among them is identified as a parallel program. We now discuss the parallelization strategy of the end programs.

3.1 GAPP for Parallel Recursion

GAPP relies on the grammars designed to produce parallel recursive programs [20]. We discuss the design of parallel recursive grammars for *Fibonacci*.

OpenMP Pragmas OpenMP is a portable, scalable, directive based specification to write parallel programs on shared memory systems. It consists of compiler directives, environment variables and run time libraries that are used to designate parallelism in C/C++ and Fortran. These directives are special preprocessor instructions termed as `pragmas` that follow the fork-join parallelism.

Some OpenMP pragmas are—`parallel for` is a loop construct that distributes the iterations of a loop among the threads. The use of a *parallel for* construct is limited to a for loop that has defined boundaries, that is a loop with a terminating condition. Another pragma, `parallel sections` defines a parallel region, in which, each task is handled independently. If there are more number of threads than the independent blocks, the remaining threads will be idle, otherwise, all the threads execute multiple code blocks. `parallel task` is another work-sharing pragma that works similar to section construct. Notice that the use of omp task is not optional. A detailed description of OpenMP API can be found in [12].

Design of Grammars Figure 2 presents GAPP grammars for the synthesis of Fibonacci program. The program begins at <program>, which derives the symbols <condition> and <parcode>. The symbols <omptask> and <ompdata> represent the task and data parallel pragmas, while <omppragma> selects one of the two options, therefore, a clear separation between task and data parallelism. This helps to accelerates the evolution of solutions because of the grammatical bias [54]. This design constrains the search to explore data or task parallel space rather both spaces.

The grammar has shared (<shared>) and private (<private>) clauses. The input (<input>) and two variables (*temp, res*) are shared among the threads. Input represents the *n*th Fibonacci number, while variable *res* returns the result of parallel execution. The local variables (*temp, a*) store the auxiliary results of recursive calls.

The variable "a" is thread private. OpenMP has private (<private>) clauses: private(a) makes a variable thread-specific, such that any changes on the variable are invisible outside the parallel region; firstprivate(a) maintains a constant value throughout the program; lastprivate(a) keeps the changes of last thread in the parallel region. Evolution selects one of the three private clauses depending on the problem.

The non-terminal <parblocks> produces parallel code blocks that are mapped through <blocks>. The non-terminal <blocks> generates a sequence of parallel blocks with each block containing an independent recursive call. The parallel code blocks ensure task level parallel execution. The non-terminal <stmt> depicts the recursive call of the Fibonacci program, while the symbols <bop> and <lop> refer to the binary arithmetic and logical operators respectively. The symbol <const> maps to integer constants. The base case is generated from the input variable, logical operators and constants generating non-terminals: <line1> and <line2>. The non-terminal <expr>, expresses the recursive calls, that is called in <parcode> and <blocks>.

Performance Optimization We encourage parallelism with the inclusion of execution time in the fitness function. The run time exerts external selection pressure, which helps in selecting an appropriate parallelization primitive. Therefore, the fitness function is a product of two factors: execution time and the mean absolute error, both are normalized in the range [0, 1]—a maximization function. The following equation computes the fitness of evolving parallel recursive program (f_{rprog}):

$$f_{rprog} = \frac{1}{(1+t)} * \frac{1}{\left(1 + \frac{1}{N}\sum_{i=1}^{N}|y_i - \hat{y}_i|\right)} \tag{1}$$

⟨program⟩	::=	⟨condition⟩ ⟨parcode⟩
⟨ompdata⟩	::=	#pragma omp parallel | #pragma omp single | #pragma omp parallel for
⟨omptask⟩	::=	#pragma omp parallel sections | #pragma omp task
⟨shared⟩	::=	shared(⟨input⟩,temp,res) ⟨nl⟩ {
⟨private⟩	::=	private(a) | firstprivate(a) | lastprivate(a)
⟨condition⟩	::=	if(⟨input⟩⟨lop⟩⟨const⟩) { ⟨nl⟩ ⟨line1⟩; ⟨nl⟩⟨line2⟩; ⟨nl⟩ }
⟨parcode⟩	::=	else{ ⟨nl⟩⟨omppragma⟩⟨private⟩⟨shared⟩ ⟨blocks⟩⟨nl⟩ } ⟨nl⟩ } ⟨nl⟩ ⟨result⟩
⟨omppragma⟩	::=	⟨ompdata⟩ | ⟨omptask⟩
⟨blocks⟩	::=	⟨parblocks⟩ | ⟨blocks⟩⟨nl⟩⟨blocks⟩
⟨parblocks⟩	::=	⟨secblocks⟩ | ⟨taskblocks⟩
⟨secblocks⟩	::=	#pragma omp section ⟨nl⟩ { ⟨nl⟩⟨line1⟩; ⟨nl⟩ ⟨atomic⟩ ⟨nl⟩ ⟨line2⟩ ⟨bop⟩ a; ⟨nl⟩ }
⟨taskblocks⟩	::=	#pragma omp task ⟨nl⟩ { ⟨nl⟩ ⟨line1⟩;⟨nl⟩ ⟨atomic⟩⟨line2⟩ ⟨bop⟩ a; ⟨nl⟩ }
⟨atomic⟩	::=	#pragma omp atomic
⟨line1⟩	::=	temp = ⟨expr⟩ | a = ⟨expr⟩;
⟨line2⟩	::=	res ⟨bop⟩= temp
⟨expr⟩	::=	⟨input⟩ | ⟨stmt⟩ | ⟨stmt⟩⟨bop⟩⟨stmt⟩
⟨result⟩	::=	return res; ⟨input⟩ ::= n ⟨nl⟩ ::= \n
⟨stmt⟩	::=	fib(⟨input⟩ ⟨bop⟩ ⟨const⟩);
⟨lop⟩	::=	'>=' | '<=' | '<' | '>'
⟨bop⟩	::=	+ | - | * | /
⟨const⟩	::=	0 | 1 | 2 | 3 | 4 | 5 | 6 | 7 | 8 | 9

Fig. 2 Design of GAPP grammar to synthesize parallel recursive Fibonacci programs

where, t is the execution time of a program; y_i and $\hat{y}_i$ are the actual and evolved outputs respectively. The choice of an OpenMP pragma can significantly impact the execution time of a program. The presence of an incorrect pragma in the end program will have an adverse effect on fitness evaluation. In limiting such effects, the first term, *normalized execution time* in Eq. (1) helps to select the correct pragma. That is, the changes in time component influence the performance of resultant programs, whereby, those with minimum execution time become the best parallel programs. Meanwhile, the second term, *normalized mean absolute error* enforces program correctness. Together, the twin objectives push for a correct and efficient parallel program.

3.2 GAPP for Parallel Iterative Sorting

Design of Grammars We describe the design of grammars for the synthesis of parallel *odd-even sort* programs [21]. Similar to recursive grammars, *Odd-Even sort* grammars are in [13, Appendix B]. The generation of an end program starts with `<program>` symbol, which derives to `<for_out>` and `<condition>` symbols. The non-terminal `<for_out>` maps to an outer "*for loop*". Note that GE fails to generate correct loop structures [43], hence, we preserve the loops in synthesizing the iterative sorts. The non-terminal `<condition>` derives problem specific base/termination conditions.

The symbols `<schedule>` and `<type>` derive the type of scheduling strategy. In scheduling a parallel for loop, OpenMP offers three clauses: *static*, *dynamic* and, *guided*; *static* divides the work among threads before the loop execution and *dynamic* allocates the work during the execution. The third type, *guided*, divides work in the execution but the allocation begins with the given *chunk size* ($CHUNK$) and decreases.

We include the mechanism of swapping the adjacent elements in two phases (odd and even). The input, index (`<index>`), and the size of the array are shared among all the cores. The temporary variable (*temp* in `<index>`) is private to the thread. We use absolute values (*abs* in `<for_in_line>` and `<swap>`) to avoid negative indexes.

Performance Optimization As with recursion (Eq. (1)), the time in fitness evaluation of parallel iterative sorting helps to choose an appropriate pragma. The accuracy is defined as mean *inversions*. For example, if $a_1a_2a_3\ldots a_n$ is a permutation of the set $1, 2,\ldots, n$ then the pair (a_i, a_j) is an *inversion* of the permutation iff $i < j$ and $a_i > a_j$ [35]. The fitness function (f_{sprog}) is shown in Eq. (2).

$$f_{pprog} = \frac{1}{(1+t)} * \frac{1}{\left(1 + \dfrac{\displaystyle\sum_{i=1}^{N} n(I(A_i))}{TP}\right)} \tag{2}$$

where, t stands for the execution time of the evolved parallel program over all the fitness cases (N); $n(I(A_i))$ is the number of inversions in the ith array $(A_i$; total, N arrays); and TP is the total number of pairs in all the fitness cases (N).

4 Experiments

We evaluate GAPP on six recursive and four iterative sorting benchmark problems. Table 1 presents all the benchmarks with their properties. Of the six recursive problems: first three (Sum-of-N, Factorial, Fibonacci) accept a positive integer as input; for *Sum-of-N*, it is randomly generated from the range [1, 1000] while, for *Factorial* and *Fibonacci* problems, it is in the range [1, 60] due to the limitations of data types in C; the remaining three problems (Binary-Sum, Reverse, Quicksort) accept an array of integers with their start and end indexes as input, for which, an array of 1000 elements are randomly generated from the range [1, 1000]. For the four iterative sorting benchmarks, 100 training cases with each array containing 1000 elements are randomly generated from the range [1, 1000]. The end programs of these four benchmarks use conditional (*if*), iterative (*for*) and variable indexing structures.

Table 1 Summary of both the recursive and iterative sorting benchmarks under investigation with their properties used in the experiments

#	Problem	Type		Local variables	Range
		Input	Return		
Recursion					
1	Sum-of-N	int	int	3	[1,1000]
2	Factorial	int	unsigned long long	3	[1,60]
3	Fibonacci	int	unsigned long long	3	[1,60]
4	Binary-Sum	int [ ], int, int	int	2	[1,1000]
5	Reverse	int [ ], int, int	void	2	[1,1000]
6	Quicksort	int [ ], int, int	void	3	[1,1000]
Iterative sorting					
1	Bubble sort	int [ ], int	void	4	[1:1000]
2	Quick sort	int [ ], int, int	void	5	[1:1000]
3	Odd-Even sort	int[ ], int	void	4	[1:1000]
4	Rank sort	int [ ], int	void	4	[1:1000]

Table 2 Parameters and experimental environment

GE parameters		Experimental environment	
Point mutation	0.1	CPU	Intel (R) Xeon (R) E7-4820,
One point crossover	0.9		16 cores
Selection	Roulette Wheel	OS	Debian Linux v 2.6.32, 64-bit
Replacement strategy	Steady state	C++	GNU GCC v 4.4.5
Initialization	Sensible		libGE [39] v 0.26
Depth	{9, 25}	OpenMP	libgomp v 3.0
Wrapping	Disabled	Timer utility	$omp\_get\_wtime()$
Population	500		
Generations, runs	{100, 50}		

Table 2 describes the algorithmic and hardware parameters. The grammars are general enough except for a few minor changes with respect to the problem at hand.

Generality of Grammars Grammars for the benchmarks Fibonacci (Fig. 2) and Odd-Even sort represent both the experimental domains. The grammars for other benchmarks are 90% similar, where all of them have common OpenMP pragmas while they differ in some domain specific knowledge. Grammars for all the benchmarks are presented in [13, Appendix B]. We evolve programs in C; however, GAPP is general enough to apply to the programming languages that offer OpenMP like parallelism. JOMP [11] is an OpenMP API for JAVA and can synthesize parallel programs in JAVA.

4.1 GAPP Variants

With the two different features (design of grammars and performance optimization) of GAPP, we study their influence in the synthesizability and fitness evaluation of the parallel programs. The study contains four GAPP variations: first variant, named as GAPP (Unoptimized), does not use both the separation of task and data parallel primitives as well as the time component of performance optimization (shown in Eqs. (1) and (2)). Second variant, named as *GAPP (Grammar)*, uses the design of grammars with parallel primitives and does not use the time component of performance optimization. Third variant, *GAPP (Time)*, neglects the separation of task and data parallel primitives, but uses the time in performance optimization. Finally, the fourth variant, *GAPP (Combined)*, uses both the design of grammars and the performance optimization.

5 Results

We present experimental results of GAPP for both recursion and iterative sorting domains. The results report two measures: *speed-up* and *mean best generation* (MBG), where the speed-up informs performance of the synthesized parallel programs while MBG shows the time taken to synthesize a best of run program in terms of generations.

Speed-Up The speed-up is defined as the ratio of *mean best execution time (MBT)* of synthesizing parallel programs on 1-core to n-cores and is shown in Eq. (3):

$$\text{Speed-up} = \frac{T_{MBT-1-core}}{T_{MBT-n-cores}} \tag{3}$$

where, $T_{MBT-1-core}$ is the *mean best execution time* on a single core, while $T_{MBT-n-cores}$ is that of n-cores of a processor. *Mean best execution time* (MBT) is defined as the mean of all the execution times of the average best-of-generation programs across all the experimental runs of GAPP, and is given as shown in Eq. (4):

$$T_{MBT} = \frac{\sum_{r=1}^{R} \sum_{g=1}^{G} T_{bprog}(g)}{R \times G} \tag{4}$$

where $T_{bprog}(g)$ is the execution time of the best program in a given generation g, G is the number of generations, r is a run, and R is the number of runs.

Mean Best Generation (MBG) *Mean best generation* (MBG) is defined as the number of generations required to converge to the best fitness, with a pre-condition that the program under consideration must be *correct*, averaged across R runs. MBG helps to investigate the effect of restructuring grammars on the synthesizability (ease of evolving) of the correct parallel programs.

5.1 Recursion

Figure 3 presents the speed-up of each of the four GAPP (*Unoptimized, Grammar, Time, Combined*) variants at different cores for all the six recursive benchmarks. The results indicate that the performance of GAPP improves as the number of cores increase. Non-parametric Friedman tests [27] are used to show the significance of these results.

Table 3 shows the non-parametric Friedman tests with Hommel's post-hoc [29] analysis on the speed-up of GAPP for recursive problems at $\alpha = 0.05$. The first column shows the number of cores. The second column shows the GAPP variant, while the third column presents the average rank. The fourth and the fifth columns show the p-value and p-Hommel. The lowest average rank shows the best (GAPP

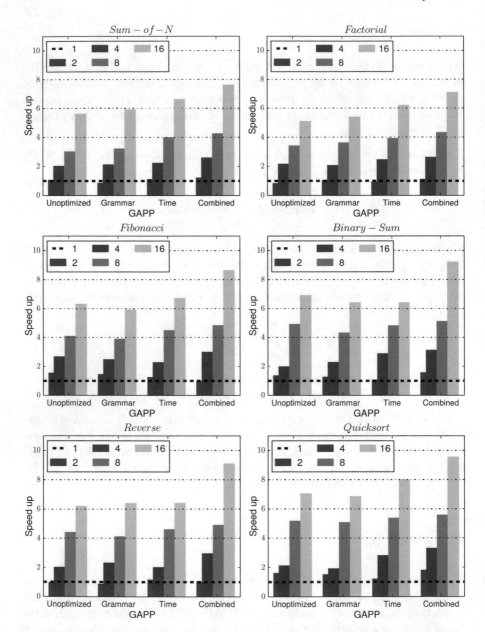

Fig. 3 The speed-up of *GAPP (Unoptimized, Grammar, Time, Combined)* variants for all the six experimental problems. The number of cores vary as 2, 4, 8 and 16. The horizontal dashed (- -) line represents the speed-up of 1 and acts as a reference for the remaining results

Table 3 Friedman statistical tests with Hommel's *post-hoc* analysis on speed-up of all the four GAPP variants

Cores	GAPP variant	Average	p-Value	p-Hommel
16	Unoptimized	**3.4999**	**7.96E-4**	**0.0167**
	Grammar	**3.4999**	**7.96E-4**	**0.025**
	Time	1.9999	0.1797	0.05
	Combined*	1.0	–	–

The boldface shows the significance at $\alpha = 0.05$, while asterisk (*) shows the best variant. These results are on 16 cores only due to space constraints

Table 4 The mean best generation (MBG ± [standard deviation]) of all the four GAPP (Unoptimized, Grammar, Time, Combined) variants on 16 cores and the lowest MBG is in boldface

	GAPP			
	Unoptimized	Grammar	Time	Combined
Problem	MBG	MBG	MBG	MBG
1	59.14 ± [4.96]	45.38 ± [2.81]	51.63 ± [6.19]	**43.27 ± [5.37]**
2	38.43 ± [2.85]	**31.19 ± [4.73]**	39.35 ± [3.19]	36.51 ± [3.67]
3	77.36 ± [5.58]	**44.73 ± [5.26]**	65.19 ± [6.43]	59.89 ±[4.15]
4	71.83 ± [6.37]	**59.14 ± [5.34]**	68.88 ± [4.51]	61.43 ± [5.19]
5	56.68 ± [2.19]	47.53 ± [2.19]	51.09 ± [2.39]	**45.32 ± [4.92]**
6	49.25 ± [4.57]	**40.49 ± [5.23]**	52.49 ± [2.58]	47.28 ± [3.15]

Friedman tests with Hommel's post-hoc analysis. Boldface shows the significance at $\alpha = 0.05$, while asterisk (*) shows the best variant.

GAPP variant	Average rank	p-Value	p-Hommel
Unoptimized	**3.0**	**5.3205E-4**	**0.001596**
Grammar*	1.16666	–	–
Time	**2.33333**	**0.0321438**	**0.042**
Combined	**1.99999**	**0.0024787**	**0.02**

(Combined)) variant, and is marked with an asterisk (*). A variant is significantly different from the best variant if *p*-value is less than *p*-Hommel at $\alpha = 0.05$, and is in boldface. A value is in *boldface* if it is significantly different from the best variant. The *p-value* of the corresponding method is less than the critical *p-Hommel* at $\alpha = 0.05$.

The performance on 2 cores is insignificant as the cost of thread overheads offset the performance gains. For 4 cores, GAPP (Combined) significantly outperforms the remaining three variants. For 8 and 16 cores, GAPP (Combined) outperforms the two GAPP (Unoptimized, Grammar) variants, and the difference with GAPP (Time) is insignificant due to the presence of execution time in their fitness evaluation.

Table 4 shows MBG of the four GAPP variants and statistical tests. GAPP (Grammar) outperforms GAPP (Unoptimized, Time, Combined), which requires a less number of generations over the remaining variants in synthesizing the best programs.

Although GAPP (Grammar) takes a few generations to synthesize parallel recursive programs, performance results (Fig. 3) show that GAPP (Time, Combined)

outperform GAPP (Grammar), where GAPP (Grammar) synthesized programs are not as efficient as that of GAPP (Time, Combined). However, GAPP (Combined) outperforms GAPP (Time) in terms of MBG (Table 4), where GAPP (Combined) is quick to synthesize efficient parallel recursive programs. Therefore, GAPP (Combined) is the best variant that reports an average (on the recursive problems) speed-up of 8.13 on 16 cores, an improvement of 23.86% over GAPP (Unoptimized) that reports 6.19 speed-up.

5.2 Iterative Sorting

Figure 4 shows the speed-up of GAPP (Unoptimized, Grammar, Time, Combined) on the four iterative sorting benchmarks for 2, 4, 8 and 16 cores. Table 5 shows the Friedman tests with Hommel's post-hoc analysis on speed-up of GAPP (Unoptimized, Grammar, Time, Combined) for 16 cores. A variant with the lowest rank is the best variant (GAPP(Combined)) and marked with an asterisk (*).

For 4 cores, GAPP (Combined) outperforms GAPP (Unoptimized) while it is insignificant from GAPP (Grammar, Time). For 8 and 16 cores, GAPP (Combined) outperforms GAPP (Unoptimized, Grammar) and is insignificant over GAPP

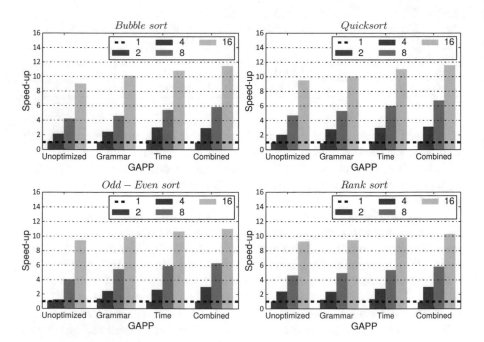

Fig. 4 The speed-up of all the four GAPP (Unoptimized, Grammar, Time, Combined) variants on the four iterative sorting problems for 2, 4, 8, and 16 cores

Table 5 Statistical tests on speed-up of GAPP for recursion with 16 cores

Cores	GAPP variant	Average rank	p-Value	p-Hommel
16	Unoptimized	**4.0**	**0.001015**	**0.0166**
	Grammar	**3.0**	**0.0204597**	**0.025**
	Time	2.0	0.2733216	0.05
	Combined*	1.0	–	–

Table 6 The mean best generation (MBG ± [standard deviation]) of all the GAPP (Unoptimized, Grammar, Time, Combined) variants (The lowest generation is in boldface)

Problem	GAPP			
	Unoptimized	Grammar	Time	Combined
	MBG	MBG	MBG	MBG
1	67.19 ± [4.16]	**37.63 ± [3.19]**	73.27 ± [3.31]	41.27 ± [0.81]
2	47.61 ± [3.51]	**31.35 ± [3.65]**	51.51 ± [3.67]	33.49 ± [2.95]
3	58.69 ± [5.86]	44.19 ± [6.43]	62.89 ±[4.15]	**35.27 ± [3.46]**
4	54.11 ± [3.43]	**29.88 ± [4.51]**	61.43 ± [5.19]	31.14 ± [3.17]

Friedman statistical tests with Hommel's post-hoc analysis. Boldface represents the significance at $\alpha = 0.05$, while asterisk (*) shows the best variant among all the four GAPP variants.

GAPP variant	Average rank	p-Value	p-Hommel
Unoptimized	**3.25**	**0.0284597**	**0.025**
Grammar*	1.25	–	–
Time	**3.75**	**0.0061698**	**0.0166**
Combined	1.75	0.5838824	0.05

(Time). GAPP (Combined) shows an average speed-up of 11.03, an improvement of 15.75% over GAPP (Unoptimized), which has an average speed-up of 9.29.

Table 6 compares the MBG of GAPP (Unoptimized, Grammar, Time, Combined) and their statistical significance. GAPP (Grammar) outperforms GAPP (Unoptimized, Time) while it is insignificant over GAPP (Combined). GAPP (Grammar) produces parallel iterative sorting programs in a less number of generations over GAPP (Time). It is because of the variation in the design of grammars among GAPP variants, which in fact impacts the evolution of programs. However, GAPP (Combined) evolves efficient programs over GAPP (Grammar) (see Fig. 4). Therefore, GAPP (Combined) is the best variant for the evolution of efficient parallel iterative sorting programs.

6 Enhancements in GAPP

We analyze the effect of *OpenMP thread scheduling* on performance of the GAPP evolved parallel programs, both in recursion and iterative sorting domains. We find that code growth in GAPP is surprisingly insignificant [19, 22, 23], therefore it does not affect the program execution. We found that the thread scheduling has a distinct influence on both the problem domains.

6.1 Recursion

The quality of parallel code is difficult to quantify as execution time often depends on the ability of OS to efficiently schedule the tasks. This job itself is complicated by other parallel threads (from other programs) running at the same time. OpenMP abstracts away much of these concerns from programmers, which makes it easier at the cost of some fine control. We compensate this through adapting a program to the hardware.

Excessive Parallelism Hardware caps the maximum number of threads; however, in the grammars each recursive call spawns a new thread. OS factors, specifically for the Linux kernels, eventually fail to scale in scheduling a high number of threads [9]. Moreover, when a parent thread spawns a child thread, it sleeps until all the child threads have finished. This process is expensive, when a large number of threads are involved. Memory access restrictions over shared and private variables can add to the complexity of the executing code. Complexity in this instance comes from the vagaries of scheduling what can be a high number of threads. We extend GAPP to overcome these limitations.

Extending GAPP for Recursion Armed with the knowledge of excessive parallelism, we constrain the system so as to optimize the degree of parallelism. We combine parallel and serial implementations of the evolved programs, which, further improves the performance. This reduces the overhead caused due to excessive parallelism as the top level recursive calls distribute load across a number of threads, whereas the lower level calls appropriately carry out the work instead of merely invoking more threads. Evolution detects the exact *level* at which recursion switches from parallel to serial. The intermediate results are saved temporarily in an auxiliary variable and are shared amongst all the threads under execution. This ceases the creation of exponential number of threads thereby reduces the overhead caused due to excessive parallelism.

The GAPP grammars used for recursive benchmarks (Sect. 3.1) are modified as shown in Fig. 5, termed as *GAPP (Scaled)*, hereafter. We alter the non-terminal `<condition>` to synthesize nested *if-else* condition blocks. The changes generate a program that reduces the execution time of the final programs, which evolve a two digit *thread limiting constant*, at which, the program starts to execute sequentially.

Figure 6 shows an example of the GAPP (Scaled) generated Fibonacci program. It evolves a thread limiting constant for a given problem and the computational environment; this constant, arrests the further creation of threads and continues to execute serially. The intermediate result (*temp* in *else if*) is shared among the threads, thus, further optimizes the execution time, thereby, efficiently exploits the power of multi-cores.

⟨*condition*⟩   ::= if(⟨*input*⟩⟨*lop*⟩⟨*const*⟩) { ⟨*nl*⟩ ⟨*line1*⟩; ⟨*nl*⟩ ⟨*line2*⟩; ⟨*nl*⟩ }

is altered to appear as

⟨*condition*⟩   ::= if(⟨*input*⟩⟨*lop*⟩⟨*const*⟩) { ⟨*nl*⟩⟨*line1*⟩; ⟨*nl*⟩⟨*line2*⟩; } ⟨*nl*⟩ else if
                              (⟨*input*⟩⟨*lop*⟩⟨*const*⟩⟨*const*⟩) { ⟨*nl*⟩⟨*line1*⟩; ⟨*nl*⟩ ⟨*line2*⟩; ⟨*nl*⟩ }

Fig. 5 The enhanced GAPP grammars to synthesize parallel recursive Fibonacci program

```
if (n <= 2) {
    temp = n; res += temp;
}
else if (n <= 39) {
    temp=fib(n-1)+fib(n-2); res +=temp;
}
else {
    #pragma omp parallel sections private(a) shared(n, temp, res) {
        #pragma omp section {
            a = fib(n-1);
            #pragma omp atomic
                res += temp+a;
        }
        #pragma omp section {
            a = fib(n-2);
            #pragma omp atomic
                res += temp+a;
} } }
return res;
```

Fig. 6 GAPP (Scaled) evolved program that combines both parallel and serial execution

The constant (39) in the *else if* (in Fig. 6) condition is the thread limiting constant for 16 cores. Figure 7 shows the thread limiting constants (standard deviation) with respect to the number of cores for the six benchmarks. These constants adapt to the underlying hardware architectures. For example, the constant (39), which, at a large input (say, a 1000000 element array) may not be an optimal value, that can be a bigger constant. This is addressed with digit concatenation grammars [42, Chapter 5].

Figure 8 shows the speed-up of GAPP (Scaled) over all the six benchmarks for 2, 4, 8, and 16 cores. Like the other GAPP variants, the speed-up of GAPP (Scaled) improves with an increase in the number of cores. Especially, the speed-up of GAPP (Scaled) can be better seen, where the performance is much better than its counterparts.

Table 7 presents the *mean best generation* (MBG) of GAPP (Unoptimized, Grammar, Time, Combined, Scaled) variants. The results show that GAPP (Gram-

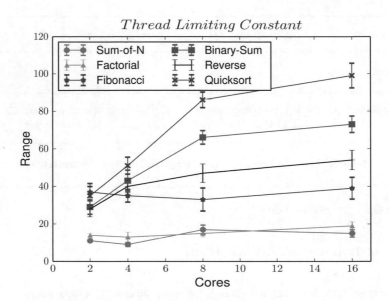

Fig. 7 GAPP (Scaled) evolved *thread limiting constants* of the six recursive benchmarks

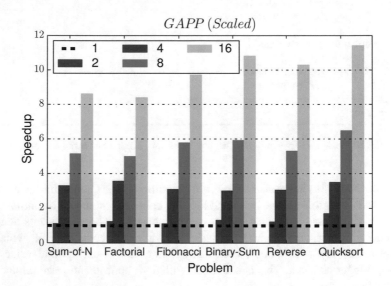

Fig. 8 The performance of GAPP (Scaled) programs for all the six recursive benchmarks

Table 7 The mean best generation (MBG ± [standard deviation]) of GAPP (Grammar, Combined, Scaled)

	GAPP				
	Unoptimized	Grammar	Time	Combined	Scaled
Problem	MBG	MBG	MBG	MBG	MBG
1	59.14 ± [4.96]	45.38 ± [2.81]	51.63 ± [6.19]	**43.27 ± [5.37]**	44.38 ± [2.81]
2	38.43 ± [2.85]	**31.19 ± [4.73]**	39.35 ± [3.19]	36.51 ± [3.67]	39.11 ± [4.73]
3	77.36 ± [5.58]	**44.73 ± [5.26]**	65.19 ± [6.43]	59.89 ± [4.15]	52.17 ± [4.45]
4	71.83 ± [6.37]	**59.14 ± [5.34]**	68.88 ± [4.51]	61.43 ± [5.19]	64.88 ± [3.51]
5	56.68 ± [2.19]	47.53 ± [2.19]	51.09 ± [2.39]	45.32 ± [4.92]	**44.53 ± [2.19]**
6	49.25 ± [4.57]	**40.49 ± [5.23]**	52.49 ± [2.58]	47.28 ± [3.15]	42.49 ± [5.23]

The lowest value is in boldface

Table 8 Friedman statistical tests with Hommel's post-hoc analysis on *speed-up* and *MBG* of GAPP (Unoptimized, Grammar, Time, Combined, Scaled)

GAPP variant	Average rank	p-Value	p-Hommel
Speed-up			
Unoptimized	**4.5**	**1.2604E-4**	**0.0125**
Grammar	**4.5**	**1.2604E-4**	**0.0166**
Time	**3.0**	**0.0284597**	**0.025**
Combined	**1.9998**	**0.0347332**	**0.05**
Scaled*	0.99999	–	–
Mean best generation			
Unoptimized	**4.333333**	**0.0019107**	**0.0125**
Grammar*	1.5	–	–
Time	**3.833333**	**0.0105871**	**0.01667**
Combined	**2.49998**	**0.0355132**	**0.05**
Scaled	**3.666667**	**0.0176221**	**0.025**

Boldface shows the significance (at $\alpha = 0.05$) and asterisk (*) shows the best variant

mar) generates a program faster than the two GAPP (Combined, Scaled) variants because of the grammatical bias. However, the last two GAPP (Combined, Scaled) variants use execution time in fitness evaluation. Thus, the evolution becomes hard, nevertheless, GAPP(Scaled) generates the efficient task parallel recursive programs.

Table 8 shows the non-parametric Friedman tests with Hommel's post-hoc analysis on speed-up and MBG of GAPP variants. The best variant with the lowest rank is marked with an asterisk (*), and significantly different variants are in boldface.

For *speed-up*, GAPP (Scaled) outperforms the remaining four GAPP variants. Note, these results are for 16 cores of a processor, and are similar for 8 cores, while they are insignificant with 4 cores and below. On average, for 16 cores, GAPP (Scaled) speeds up by a factor of 9.97, which improves over GAPP (Combined) and GAPP (Unoptimized) by 17.45% and 37.91% respectively. On an average, for 16 cores, GAPP (Scaled) shows a speed-up of 9.97, a significant improvement of

17.45% over GAPP (Combined). Similarly, a significant improvement of 37.91% over GAPP (Unoptimized).

For MBG, GAPP (Grammar) outperforms the other four GAPP variants. These results are for 16 cores, while they are similar for 8 and below. Although GAPP (Scaled) requires slightly more generations over other variants, GAPP (Scaled) is the best amongst all the GAPP variants in this paper, as it generates efficient parallel recursive programs.

However, a similar solution is to keep a table that records the result of a recursive call in its first evaluation, then, refer the table for the repeated recursive calls, similar to Koza [36]. However, that approach has often been criticized [38] for not being an exact recursion. We now analyze and extend GAPP for iterative sorting domain.

6.2 Iterative Sorting

In contrast to excessive parallelism in recursion, factors such as OpenMP work load scheduling plays a vital role in optimizing the performance of synthesized iterative sorting programs. Interestingly, OpenMP hides these details from the developer, which makes it easy to use, at the same time hard to realize their full potential. Load balancing by parallel threads is a serious concern on shared memory processors. OpenMP scheduling strategies (*static*, *dynamic*, *guided*) solve these performance issues effectively. However, optimally assigning the optional *chunk size* (*chunk*) explicitly is difficult, as the ideal value often requires the problem specific knowledge. The input chunk size changes with respect to the loop iterations, number of cores, and the threads under execution. On the other hand, smaller chunks of data leads to a well known parallel programming challenge of *false sharing*.

False Sharing False sharing is a performance challenge that occurs when threads on different cores modify variables that reside on the same cache line [50], which invalidates the cache line and forces a memory update, thereby reduces the performance. Precisely, if one core tries to load the same cache line loaded by another core, that line is marked as "shared" access. If this core stores shared cache line, then that line is marked as "modified" and all the remaining cores will receive a cache line "invalid" message. Herein, if any core tries to access the cache line marked with *modified*, that line will be written back to the memory and marks it as "shared". The other cores that try to access the same cache line will incur a cache miss. This frequent coordination among the cores, cache lines and memory that caused due to false sharing significantly degrades the performance of an application.

False sharing can be avoided by placing the variables far apart in the memory (using some compiler directives) so that they do not align in the same cache line. In the case of arrays, it can be avoided by aligning the array of elements on the cache line boundary. If this is impossible, we can set the array size to double the cache line, which is possible when dynamically allocating the array sizes. Our extensions

$\langle schedule \rangle$	$::=$ schedule($\langle type \rangle$, CHUNK)

is altered to appear as

$\langle schedule \rangle$	$::=$ schedule($\langle type \rangle$, $\langle const1 \rangle$)
$\langle const1 \rangle$	$::=$ 0 | 1 | 2 | 3 | 4 | 5 | 6 | 7 | 8 | 9 | $\langle const1 \rangle \langle const1 \rangle$

Fig. 9 The enhanced GAPP grammars to synthesize parallel recursive *Fibonacci* program

```
for(i=0; i < length; i++) {
 if (i%2 == 0) { //start of even phase
  #pragma omp parallel for shared(A,length) private(j,temp)
      schedule(dynamic, 89) {
    for(j=1; j < length-1; j+=2) {
       if(A[abs(j-1)]<A[abs(j-0)]) {
         temp=A[abs(j-1)]; A[abs(j-1)]=A[abs(j-0)]; A[abs(j-0)]=temp;
 } } } }
  else {          //start of odd phase
  #pragma omp parallel for shared(A,length) private(j,temp)
      schedule(dynamic, 87) {
    for(j=1; j < length-1; j+=2) {
      if(A[abs(j)] > A[abs(j+1)]) {
         temp=A[abs(j+1)]; A[abs(j+1)]=A[abs(j+0)]; A[abs(j+0)] = temp;
 } } } }
} // end for loop
```

Fig. 10 Evolved *Odd-Even* program that shows efficient performance

of GAPP ensure that controlling the array sizes helps to deal with false sharing in improving the performance of the evolving programs.

Extending GAPP for Iterative Sorting This section proposes to solve the false sharing that further extends GAPP to evolve more efficient parallel iterative sorting programs. We overcome the problem of ideal load balancing by evolving an appropriate *chunk size* that is independent of the problem and the number of cores that it executes. We adopt the digit concatenation grammars [42] for symbolic regression.

Figure 9 shows the modified GAPP grammar that automatically generates a sequence of digits. The evolved *chunk size* adapts to the number of cores, amount of load, and the number of threads. The proposed enhancements evolve more efficient programs.

Figure 10 presents the successfully evolved parallel iterative *Odd-Even* sort program using GAPP (Scaled) grammars. Note, the program contains two constants (89, 87) as it operates in two phases (odd and even).

Table 9 GAPP (Scaled) evolved *chunk size* (mean ± [standard deviation]), averaged across 50 runs for all the four experimental problems on 8 and 16 cores respectively

| | *chunk size* (CHUNK) | |
Problem	8 cores	16 cores
Bubble sort	135.17 ± [18.39]	55.43 ± [10.62]
Quicksort	159.34 ± [22.71]	67.91 ± [13.37]
Odd-Even sort	166.81 ± [17.33]	80.15 ± [12.59]
Rank sort	142.53 ± [21.45]	74.58 ± [11.11]

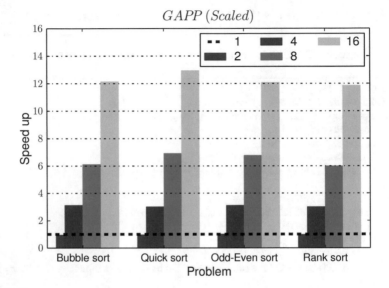

Fig. 11 Performance of *GAPP (Scaled)* on four iterative sorting benchmarks

Table 9 shows the GAPP (Scaled) evolved constants (*chunk size*). These are averaged from the evolved best of run programs across 50 runs. The *chunk* results are reported for 8, and 16 cores. They showed significant performance optimization while, 2 and 4 are insignificant, hence, neglected. As a result, the evolved constants balance the load effectively. These *chunk sizes* created larger data arrays as opposed to the arrays with a default chunk size of 10. Creation of larger chunks of data helped in controlling *false sharing*, is evident at the higher number of cores, thus, the performance improves.

Figure 11 shows the *speed-up* of GAPP (Scaled) evolved programs. The results indicate that the performance improves with an increase in the number of cores. It shows an average speed-up of 12.52 for 16 cores, a better improvement of 11.91% over GAPP (Combined), an improvement of 25.79% over GAPP (Unoptimized).

Table 10 represents the Wilcoxon Signed Rank Sum significance tests between GAPP (Scaled) and GAPP (Combined) at $\alpha = 0.05$. It contains the p-value for the corresponding problem while "☑" indicates that the difference between the results of both the methods is significant; that is, $p < 0.05$.

Table 10 Significance tests (at α = 0.05) show that GAPP (Scaled) outperforms GAPP (Combined) for 8 and 16 cores

| Cores | Problem | Wilcoxon signed rank sum test | | | |
		Rank sum	p-Value	Significant	A-measure
8	1	2089	0.00632	☑	0.6183
	2	2798	0.03183	☑	0.3917
	3	3321	0.01119	☑	0.7392
	4	2479	0.04178	☑	0.2851
16	1	2250	0.04261	☑	0.3545
	2	2701	0.00018	☑	0.8751
	3	3253	0.00461	☑	0.6559
	4	2221	0.03516	☑	0.5215

Note that "☑" states that the results are significant (p-value < 0.05). A measure shows the probability at which, GAPP (Scaled) is better over GAPP (Combined)

Vargha and Delaney [52] *A-measure* states how often that GAPP (Scaled) outperforms GAPP (Combined). A-measure lies in between 0 and 1: when it is above 0.5, GAPP (Scaled) is better than GAPP (Combined); when it is 0.5, then both are equal; when it is less than 0.5 GAPP (Combined) is better than GAPP (Scaled); if it is close to 0.5, the difference is small, otherwise the difference is large. For example, on *Bubble sort* with 16 cores, 35% of the time, GAPP (Scaled) performs better than GAPP (Combined). In other words, 65% of the time, GAPP (Combined) performs better than GAPP (Scaled). Overall, GAPP (Scaled) performs better than GAPP (Combined). Similarly for MBG, GAPP (Grammar) takes a less number of generations to evolve a parallel program. However, GAPP (Scaled) exhibits better performance with a few extra generations.

7 Conclusion

We presented GAPP to automatically generate efficient task parallel recursive and data parallel iterative sorting programs. GAPP offered a separation between the task and data parallelism in the design of the grammars along with the execution time in fitness evaluation. The modifications in the grammar favored quick generation of programs, while the execution time helped in optimizing their performance. We then analyzed the effect of OpenMP thread scheduling on performance of both the problem domains. We ceased the excessive parallelism, while restricting the degree of parallelism in the evolving programs. We limited this behavior with the evolution of programs that run both in serial (for lower level recursive calls) and parallel, thus, further optimized the performance. The most interesting contribution is the automatic load balancing that adapts to the experimental hardware environment, with which, the system has further improved the performance of the evolving sorting programs. The limiting constants for iterative sorting programs produce larger or smaller constants with the help of digit concatenation grammars. GAPP can further be extended to synthesize lock-free parallel programs, like in [24], applicable in gaming industry. Moreover, the synthesizability of GAPP can be further leveraged as in [14, 16, 18] that further improves the performance of the evolving parallel programs in less number of generations. Similarly, probabilistic approaches [25] for performance prediction help to further optimize the execution time.

References

1. R. Abbott, J.G.B. Parviz, Guided genetic programming, in *Proceedings of the International Conference on Machine Learning; Models, Technologies and Applications*, ed. by H.R. Arabnia, E.B. Kozerenko (CSREA Press, Las Vegas, 2003), pp. 28–34
2. A. Agapitos, S.M. Lucas, Evolving efficient recursive sorting algorithms, in *IEEE Congress on Evolutionary Computation* (IEEE, New York, 2006), pp. 2677–2684
3. A. Agapitos, S.M. Lucas, Evolving modular recursive sorting algorithms, in *Genetic Programming*, ed. by M. Ebner, M. O'Neill, A. Ekárt, L. Vanneschi, A.I. Esparcia-Alcázar. Lecture Notes in Computer Science, vol. 4445 (Springer, Berlin, 2007), pp. 301–310
4. A. Agapitos, M. O'Neill, A. Kattan, S.M. Lucas, Recursion in tree-based genetic programming. Genet. Program Evolvable Mach. **18**(2), 149–183 (2017)
5. S.P. Amarasinghe, J.-A.M. Anderson, M.S. Lam, C.-W. Tseng, An overview of the SUIF compiler for scalable parallel machines, in *Proceedings of the 7th SIAM Conference on Parallel Processing for Scientific Computing* (1995), pp. 662–667
6. S. Bell, B. Edwards, J. Amann, R. Conlin, K. Joyce, V. Leung, J. MacKay, M. Reif, L. Bao, J. Brown, M. Mattina, C.-C. Miao, C. Ramey, D. Wentzlaff, W. Anderson, E. Berger, N. Fairbanks, D. Khan, F. Montenegro, J. Stickney, J. Zook, Tile64 - processor: a 64-core soc with mesh interconnect, in *Proceedings of the 14th International Solid-State Circuits Conference, ISSCC '08* (IEEE, New York, 2008), pp. 88–598
7. S. Benkner, VFC: the vienna fortran compiler. Sci. Program. **7**(1), 67–81 (1999)
8. B. Blume, R. Eigenmann, K. Faigin, J. Grout, J. Hoeflinger, D. Padua, P. Petersen, B. Pottenger, L. Rauchwerger, P. Tu, S. Weatherford, Polaris: the next generation in parallelizing compilers, in *Proceedings of the Workshop on Languages and Compilers for Parallel Computing* (Springer, Berlin, 1994), pp. 10.1–10.18
9. S. Boyd-Wickizer, A.T. Clements, Y. Mao, A. Pesterev, M.F. Kaashoek, R. Morris, N. Zeldovich, An analysis of linux scalability to many cores, in *Proceedings of the 9th USENIX Conference on Operating Systems Design and Implementation, OSDI '10* (USENIX Association, Berkeley, 2010), pp. 1–8
10. S. Brave, Evolving recursive programs for tree search, in *Advances in Genetic Programming*, vol. 2 (MIT Press, Cambridge, MA, 1996), pp. 203–220
11. J.M. Bull, M.E. Kambites, Jomp–an openmp-like interface for java, in *Proceedings of the ACM 2000 Conference on Java Grande, JAVA'00* (ACM, New York, 2000), pp. 44–53
12. B. Chapman, G. Jost, R. van der Pas, *Using OpenMP: Portable Shared Memory Parallel Programming*. Scientific and Engineering Computation (The MIT Press, Cambridge, MA, 2007)
13. G. Chennupati, Grammatical evolution + multi-cores = automatic parallel programming!, PhD thesis, University of Limerick, Limerick, Ireland, 2015
14. G. Chennupati, C. Ryan, R.M.A. Azad, An empirical analysis through the time complexity of GE problems, in *19th International Conference on Soft Computing, MENDEL'13*, Brno, Czech Republic, ed. by R. Matousek (2013), pp. 37–44

15. G. Chennupati, J. Fitzgerald, C. Ryan, On the efficiency of multi-core grammatical evolution (MCGE) evolving multi-core parallel programs, in *Proceedings of the Sixth World Congress on Nature and Biologically Inspired Computing* (IEEE, New York, 2014), pp. 238–243
16. G. Chennupati, C. Ryan, R.M.A. Azad, Predict the success or failure of an evolutionary algorithm run, in *Proceedings of the Annual Conference on Genetic and Evolutionary Computation Companion, GECCO Comp '14* (ACM, New York, 2014), pp. 131–132
17. G. Chennupati, R.M.A. Azad, C. Ryan, Multi-core GE: automatic evolution of CPU based multi-core parallel programs, in *Proceedings of the Genetic and Evolutionary Computation Conference Companion* (ACM, New York, 2014), pp. 1041–1044
18. G. Chennupati, R.M.A. Azad, C. Ryan, Predict the performance of GE with an ACO based machine learning algorithm, in *Proceedings of the Genetic and Evolutionary Computation Conference Companion*, ed. by D.V. Arnold, E. Alba (ACM, New York, 2014), pp. 1353–1360
19. G. Chennpati, R.M.A. Azad, C. Ryan, On the automatic generation of efficient parallel iterative sorting algorithms, in *Proceedings of the Genetic and Evolutionary Computation Conference Companion, GECCO Companion '15* (ACM, New York, 2015), pp. 1369–1370
20. G. Chennupati, R.M.A. Azad, C. Ryan, Automatic evolution of parallel recursive programs, in *Proceedings of the 18th European Conference on Genetic Programming, EuroGP'15*, ed. by P. Machado, M.I. Heywood, J. McDermott, M. Castelli, P. García-Sánchez, P. Burelli, S. Risi, K. Sim (Springer, Berlin, 2015), pp. 167–178
21. G. Chennupati, R.M.A. Azad, C. Ryan, Automatic evolution of parallel sorting programs on multi-cores, in *Proceedings of the 18th European Conference on Applications of Evolutionary Computation, EvoApplications'15*, ed. by A.M. Mora, G. Squillero (Springer, Berlin, 2015), pp. 706–717
22. G. Chennupati, R.M.A. Azad, C. Ryan, Performance optimization of multi-core grammatical evolution generated parallel recursive programs, in *Proceedings of Genetic and Evolutionary Computation Conference, GECCO'15* (ACM, New York, 2015), pp. 1007–1014
23. G. Chennupati, R.M.A. Azad, C. Ryan, Synthesis of parallel iterative sorts with multi-core grammatical evolution, in *Proceedings of the Genetic and Evolutionary Computation Conference Companion, GECCO Companion '15* (ACM, New York, 2015), pp. 1059–1066
24. G. Chennupati, R.M.A. Azad, C. Ryan, Automatic lock-free parallel programming on multi-core processors, in *Proceedings of the IEEE Congress on Evolutionary Computation, CEC '16* (IEEE, New York, 2016), pp. 4143–4150
25. G. Chennupati, N. Santhi, S. Eidenbenz, S. Thulasidasan, AMM: scalable memory reuse model to predict the performance of physics codes, in *International Conference on Cluster Computing (CLUSTER)* (2017), pp. 649–650
26. L. Dagum, R. Menon, Openmp: an industry-standard api for shared-memory programming. IEEE Comput. Sci. Eng. **5**(1), 46–55 (1998)
27. J. Demšar, Statistical comparisons of classifiers over multiple data sets. J. Mach. Learn. Res. **7**, 1–30 (2006)
28. H. Esmaeilzadeh, E. Blem, R. St. Amant, K. Sankaralingam, D. Burger, Dark silicon and the end of multicore scaling. SIGARCH Comput. Archit. News **39**(3), 365–376 (2011)
29. S. García, F. Herrera, An extension on "statistical comparisons of classifiers over multiple data sets" for all pairwise comparisons. J. Mach. Learn. Res. **9**, 2677–2694 (2008)
30. W. Gropp, E. Lusk, N. Doss, A. Skjellum, A high-performance, portable implementation of the MPI message passing interface standard. Parallel Comput. **22**(6), 789–828 (1996)
31. W.D. Hillis, Co-evolving parasites improve simulated evolution as an optimization procedure. Phys. D Nonlinear Phenom. **42**(1), 228–234 (1990)
32. J. Howard, S. Dighe, Y. Hoskote, S. Vangal, D. Finan, G. Ruhl, D. Jenkins, H. Wilson, N. Borkar, G. Schrom, F. Pailet, S. Jain, T. Jacob, S. Yada, S. Marella, P. Salihundam, V. Erraguntla, M. Konow, M. Riepen, G. Droege, J. Lindemann, M. Gries, T. Apel, K. Henriss, T. Lund-Larsen, S. Steibl, S. Borkar, V. De, R. Van Der Wijngaart, T. Mattson, A 48-core ia-32 message-passing processor with dvfs in 45nm cmos, in *Proceedings of the 16th International Solid-State Circuits Conference, ISSCC '10* (IEEE, New York, 2010), pp. 108–109

33. K.E.J. Kinnear, Evolving a sort: lessons in genetic programming, in *IEEE International Conference on Neural Networks* (IEEE, New York, 1993), pp. 881–888
34. K.E.J. Kinnear, Generality and difficulty in genetic programming: evolving a sort, in *Proceedings of the 5th International Conference on Genetic Algorithms*, ed. by S. Forrest (Morgan Kaufmann, Los Altos, 1993), pp. 287–294
35. D.E. Knuth, *The Art of Computer Programming, Volume 3: Sorting and Searching*, 2nd edn. (Addison Wesley Longman Publishing, Redwood City, 1998)
36. J.R. Koza, *Genetic Programming: On the Programming of Computers by Means of Natural Selection* (MIT Press, Cambridge, MA, 1992)
37. T. Mattson, M. Wrinn, Parallel programming: can we PLEASE get it right this time?, in *45th Design Automation Conference* (IEEE, New York, 2008), pp. 7–11
38. A. Moraglio, F.E.B. Otero, C.G. Johnson, S. Thompson, A.A. Freitas, Evolving recursive programs using non-recursive scaffolding, in *IEEE Congress on Evolutionary Computation* (IEEE, New York, 2012), pp. 1–8
39. M. Nicolau, D. Slattery, Libge - grammatical evolution library (2006), http://bds.ul.ie/libGE/index.html
40. A. Nisbet, GAPS: a compiler framework for genetic algorithm (GA) optimised parallelisation. in *High-Performance Computing and Networking*, ed. by P. Sloot, M. Bubak, B. Hertzberger. Lecture Notes in Computer Science, vol. 1401 (Springer, Berlin, 1998), pp. 987–989
41. M.F.P. O'Boyle, J.M. Bull, Expert programmer versus parallelizing compiler: a comparative study of two approaches for distributed shared memory. Sci. Program. Parallel Comput. Proj. Swiss Prior. Programme **5**(1), 63–88 (1996)
42. M. O'Neill, C. Ryan, *Grammatical Evolution: Evolutionary Automatic Programming in an Arbitrary Language* (Kluwer Academic Publishers, Norwell, 2003)
43. M. O'Neill, M. Nicolau, A. Agapitos, Experiments in program synthesis with grammatical evolution: a focus on integer sorting, in *IEEE Congress on Evolutionary Computation* (IEEE, New York, 2014), pp. 1504–1511
44. U.-M. O'Reilly, F. Oppacher, An experimental perspective on genetic programming, in *Parallel Problem Solving from Nature*, ed. by R. Manner, B. Manderick, vol. 2 (Elsevier Science, Amsterdam, 1992), pp. 331–340
45. U.-M. O'Reilly, F. Oppacher, Chapter 2: A comparative analysis of genetic programming, in *Advances in Genetic Programming*, ed. by P.J. Angeline, J. Kenneth, E. Kinnear, vol. 2 (MIT Press, Cambridge, MA, 1996), pp. 23–44
46. D. Patterson, The trouble with multi-core. IEEE Spectr. **47**(7), 28–32, 53 (2010)
47. C. Ryan, *Automatic Re-engineering of Software Using Genetic Programming*. Genetic Programming, vol. 2 (Springer, Berlin, 1999)
48. L. Spector, J. Klein, M. Keijzer, The push3 execution stack and the evolution of control, in *Proceedings of the Genetic and Evolutionary Computation Conference* (ACM, New York, 2005), pp. 1689–1696
49. C. Stephen, Multicore processors create software headaches, Technical report, MIT Technology Review, April 2010
50. J. Torrellas, M. Lam, J.L. Hennessy, False sharing and spatial locality in multiprocessor caches. IEEE Trans. Comput. **43**(6), 651–663 (1994)
51. A. Trenaman, Concurrent genetic programming, tartarus and dancing agents, in *Genetic Programming*, ed. by R. Poli, P. Nordin, W.B. Langdon, T.C. Fogarty. Lecture Notes in Computer Science, vol. 1598 (Springer, Berlin, 1999), pp. 270–282
52. A. Vargha, H.D. Delaney, A critique and improvement of the "cl" common language effect size statistics of mcgraw and wong. J. Educ. Behav. Stat. **25**(2), 101–132 (2000)
53. Z. Wang, M.F. O'Boyle, Mapping parallelism to multi-cores: A machine learning based approach, in *Proceedings of the 14th ACM SIGPLAN Symposium on Principles and Practice of Parallel Programming, PPoPP '09* (ACM, New York, 2009), pp. 75–84
54. P.A. Whigham, Grammatical bias for evolutionary learning, PhD thesis, University of New South Wales, New South Wales, Australia, 1996

55. P.A. Whigham, R.I. McKay, Genetic approaches to learning recursive relations, in *Progess in Evolutionary Computation*, ed. by X. Yao. Lecture Notes in Artificial Intelligence (Springer, Berlin, 1995), pp. 17–27
56. K.P. Williams, Evolutionary algorithms for automatic parallelization, PhD thesis, University of Reading, 1998
57. M.L. Wong, T. Mun, Evolving recursive programs by using adaptive grammar based genetic programming. Genet. Program Evolvable Mach. **6**(4), 421–455 (2005)

Design, Architecture, and Engineering with Grammatical Evolution

Michael Fenton, Jonathan Byrne, and Erik Hemberg

Abstract Since its inception, Grammatical Evolution has had a rich history with design applications. The use of a formal grammar provides a convenient platform with which users can specify rules for design. Two main aspects of design evolution are the grammatical representation and the objective fitness evaluation.

The field of design representation has many strands, each with its own strengths and weaknesses for particular applications. An overview is given of four popular grammatical representations for design: Lindenmayer Systems, Shape Grammars, Higher Order Functions, and Graph Grammars, with examples of each.

The field of design is dominated by two often conflicting objectives: form and function. The disparity between the two is discussed: Interactive Evolutionary Design is examined in its capacity to provide a truly subjective fitness function for aesthetic form, while engineering applications of GE provide a basis for objective mathematically-based fitness evaluations. Finally, these two techniques can be combined to allow the designer to decide exactly how balance the optimisation and exploration of the process.

1 Introduction

Over the years, Grammatical Evolution has proved to be a prominent choice for design applications. The use of a formal grammar for describing the representational search space provides a convenient and powerful platform with which users can specify rules for design, and has proved to be extremely popular.

M. Fenton (✉)
Data Science and Machine Learning Group, Corvil Ltd, Dublin, Ireland

J. Byrne
Computer Vision Research Group, Intel Ltd, Leixlip, County Kildare, Ireland
e-mail: jonathan.byrne@intel.com

E. Hemberg
Computer Science and Artificial Intelligence Lab (CSAIL), MIT, Boston, MA, USA

© Springer International Publishing AG, part of Springer Nature 2018   317
C. Ryan et al. (eds.), *Handbook of Grammatical Evolution*,
https://doi.org/10.1007/978-3-319-78717-6_13

The automation process in evolutionary design can be used to stimulate and compliment the creativity process for many designers [23]. Population-based evolutionary algorithms are particularly fitting in this regard, as a range of potential solutions can be presented to designers, rather than a single option. As many facets of design are subjective, the aspect of choice resultant from a population of candidate solutions is a key asset intrinsic in evolutionary algorithms.

As with any application of an evolutionary algorithm, there are two main aspects to address in evolutionary design:

1. The encoding of the representation, and
2. The fitness evaluation of the phenotype.

1.1 Grammatical Representations for Evolutionary Design

With evolutionary algorithms, the representational encoding of the problem is one of the most important elements of the entire system. The representation defines the permissible space of problems through which the evolutionary process can search. With grammatically-based systems, the grammar essentially defines the representation space: the full range of solutions that are capable of being represented by the grammar itself. The representation space is a subset of the wider search space, which includes the universe of all possible solutions (viable or otherwise) to the problem.

When considering the basic components of a solution which are required to solve any given problem, many have somewhat constrained representational prospects. For example, symbolic regression problems are typically composed of problem variables (i.e. x[0], x[1], etc.) and an array of mathematical operators that can be combined to form an evaluable symbolic expression; program synthesis problems are typically composed of code snippets that can be combined to form an executable piece of code. Without these essential components, these various representations are incomplete, and individual problems cannot be solved. Design, on the other hand, is far more open-ended.

Consider an image of a simple square shown on the left in Fig. 1. Suppose this square was the output of a grammatical representation that has been designed to generate simple geometrical objects. This representation can be defined in numerous different ways, a small number of which are shown on the right of Fig. 1:

1. Solutions can be composed of angled sections in various states of rotation,
2. Solutions can be composed of straight lines,
3. Solutions can be the exterior perimeter of a composition of smaller geometrical objects, or
4. Solutions could use a form of vector or turtle graphics, with distances and angles dictating the form of the solution.

This relative freedom in representational ability makes grammatical systems extremely suitable for design applications.

Fig. 1 Example visual representation options for a simple square (left), with solutions (right) comprised of angled sections, straight lines, multiple smaller geometrical shapes, and turtle graphics

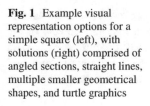 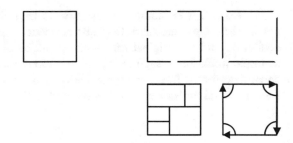

While there are a very high number of different representational encodings for design using grammatical systems, a select few of the most popular variants are described in detail in this chapter:

1. Lindenmayer Systems (L-Systems);
2. Shape Grammars;
3. Other representations (including Higher Order Functions and Graph Grammars).

1.2 Evaluation in Evolutionary Design

Automating any design process represents somewhat of a dilemma for those seeking to implement such a system. Assuming the objective functionality of the basic design criteria has been met (i.e. at its basest level the design can be considered "fit for purpose", regardless of *how* fit that may be), many aspects of design are purely subjective. However, this subjectivity raises possibly the largest obstacle for those seeking to automate the design process [28]: how can subjective creativity be accurately measured?

A crucial component of any Evolutionary Computation system is the fitness function, i.e. a way to reliably evaluate candidate solutions so that the population can be ranked by selection/replacement operators. In a creative design environment, how can one quantify subjective form in an automated fitness function? For example, how could an image generation system quantify whether one image is "better" than another?

Since aesthetic design can be highly subjective, the most basic solution to the dilemma of evaluation lies in interactive fitness functions. This allows the user to directly specify their preferences and assign fitness values to the population through methods such as ranking/sorting the population with respect to preference, or by simply selecting their preferred elite solutions. However, the use of human input in the evolutionary process presents a significant bottleneck in the overall system.

An alternative solution which bypasses this bottleneck lies in the more traditional use of mathematical analysis of evolved solutions in order to optimise some pre-set aspect of the solution (as in typical mathematical applications such as regression where the goal is to minimise some error metric). Such approaches can be used in cases where there are more than just aesthetic considerations, and aspects of the design beyond the original functionality can be objectively quantified. One such example would be in engineering design, where there are not only hard limits and constraints for the functional specification of the design, but well-defined objectives such as the minimisation of deflection or of self-weight.

1.3   Chapter Overview

The chapter continues as follows. Section 2 covers the representations identified in Sect. 1.1. Section 2.1 describes the use of Lindenmeyer systems in grammatical representations for evolutionary design, including GENR8, a popular architectural design tool using Grammatical Evolution. Shape grammars are detailed in Sect. 2.2. Alternative representations are described in Sect. 2.3, including Higher Order Functions and Graph Grammars.

Fitness evaluation in evolutionary design is covered in Sect. 3. The field of subjective interactive evolutionary design is outlined in Sect. 3.1, and Sect. 3.2 details objective numerical evaluation. A particular focus is made on engineering design applications of Grammatical Evolution in Sect. 3.2.2. Finally, the chapter concludes with Sect. 4.

2   Grammatical Representations for Evolutionary Design

In this section, we survey an number of historically popular representations of GE for evolutionary design: (1) Lindenmayer systems (2) Shape grammars (3) Other representations.

2.1   Lindenmayer Systems

Lindenmayer systems (L-systems) are a mathematical formalism which was proposed by Aristid Lindenmayer in 1968 as a foundation for an axiomatic theory of development [30]. An L-system consists of an alphabet of symbols that are used to write strings, and a collection of production rules for expanding each symbol into another string of symbols. An initial string, called an axiom, is used as the starting point for writing. L-system rules are recursive; this can lead to self-similarity, allowing for the expression of fractal-like forms.

Computer scientists study L-systems from the formal language theory perspective, e.g. as rewriting rules. L-systems have found widespread use in certain areas of computer graphics, including the generation of fractals and the realistic modelling

Fig. 2 A population of example images generated by L-systems using an interactive version of GE [19]

of plants [48]. L-systems tend to exhibit emergent behaviour, with results that can often surprise users [34]. A sample of simple images generated using L-Systems with an interactive version of PonyGE [19] is shown in Fig. 2.

A 2001 study on the advantages of generative grammatical encodings for physical design [26] investigated the automatic creation of designs. This study combined L-systems with evolutionary algorithms and applied them to the problem of generating table designs. Evolved designs contained an order of magnitude more parts than previous generative systems. Significantly, the generative version of the system produced designs with higher fitness and is faster than a non-generative system.

In [47], GE was used to design fractal curves with a given dimension. The ideas behind the evolution of grammars were used to automatically generate and evolve L-system grammars to represent fractal curves with a fractal dimension that approximates a pre-defined required value. When examined from the perspective of manual implementation for many dimensions, this is a non-trivial task. In addition, the task of taking a graphical object and attempting to derive an L-system to describe was shown to be a particularly hard problem [1].

Logo design can range from purely functional to highly expressive. Finished logos are intended to convey a clear meaning and to conform to a pre-defined style. L-systems were used for logo design in [42], with the resulting phenotypes expressed in the Postscript language. An interactive, "human-in-the-loop" fitness function was used for fitness evaluations, with all individuals being manually assigned a fitness value in sequence. Subsequent logo design work [33] allowed users to simply select desired elite solutions from a population of potential designs (as shown in Fig. 2). This interactive evaluation process was intended to demonstrate a range of attractive possibilities and to give the viewer an insight into the evolutionary design process. Evolved solutions were deemed of high enough quality to be entered into an evolutionary art competition.

As generated solutions exhibit emergent behaviour that can often produce unexpected results, L-systems are typically deployed for design exploration [26]. However, this emergent behaviour also has its downsides. Since a high degree of the generated phenotype is resultant from the generative aspects of L-systems themselves, the genetic encoding plays a comparatively diminished role in the definition of the overall solution [34]. Considering that standard implementations of Grammatical Evolution are noted to have locality issues [50], L-systems can yet further decrease locality, leading to a perceived increase in entropy in the system. While this may be desirable for design exploration (where the user is seeking new or surprising solutions), it means that small, fine-grained changes are difficult for such a system to make.

2.1.1 GENR8

GENR8 is an interactive evolutionary surface design tool created by Martin Hemberg and Una-May O'Reilly at MIT's Emergent Design Group [23, 46]. GENR8 uses a combination of Grammatical Evolution as an evolutionary engine and an extension of traditional L-systems, known as "Hemberg Extended Map L-Systems" (HEMLS) as an evolutionary representation [21]. HEMLS are based on Map L-systems, a specialised version of L-Systems used to re-write planar graphs with cycles. While traditional L-systems typically make use of recursion to "grow" an arboreal structure, map L-systems generate graphs that can be interpreted as surfaces [23]. HEMLS extend these Map L-Systems from two to three dimensions, allowing for three-dimensional surfaces to be generated [23].

The original concept for GENR8 arose from the Emergent Design Group in MIT, a collaboration between the School of Architecture and key computer scientists [23]. Architects sought a tool which could provide a range of candidate solutions, and which could adapt to changing desires and objectives during the design process. The main interface of GENR8 comprises an interactive three-dimensional design environment featuring variable attractors, repellors, boundaries, along with a fixed global gravitational force. Users can add, remove, or modify the various forces and limitations of the design environment in order to affect the growth of solutions within the environment. As such, only three things are needed for a surface to be created using GENR8: a starting point for the structure, known as a seed, a set of rules dictating how that seed will grow, and an environment in which the seed can grow [20].

GENR8 has been in use by both students and professional architects since 2003 [24, 25]. A survey of a number of noteworthy projects using GENR8 was completed in both [24] and [25]. Of note is the variety and distinction between projects; the authors reflect that since the GENR8 system (1) uses a generative, emergent representation (HEMLS), and (2) is extremely open-ended, there is a near impossibility to predict either *how* users will operate the system or *what* the system will produce. Therein, they argue, lies the crux of what makes a generative design aid like GENR8 such a useful prospect.

2.2 Shape Grammars

Shape grammars are a way to represent components of visual images as terminals in a formal grammar structure [51]. With shape grammars, terminals can be represented as elementary shapes or lines, in two or three dimensions. Boolean operations such as union, intersection, difference, and complement can be applied to these shapes, as well as Euclidean transformations such as translations, rotations, reflections, scalings, and compositions [51]. An example of a generative process using a shape grammar is shown in Fig. 3.

In an interdisciplinary collaboration between the schools of Computer Science, Architecture, and Engineering, O'Neill et al. [44] applied shape grammars to the

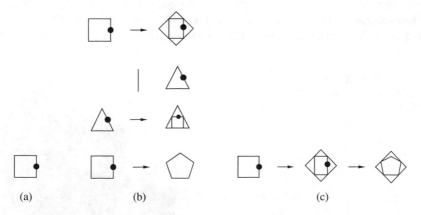

(a)   (b)   (c)

Fig. 3 An example of a shape grammar [45]. (**a**) shows an example start shape for a shape grammar. Example production rules are shown in (**b**), with non-terminals on the left of the arrow and production choices on the right separated by the "|" separator. Finally, (**c**) shows an example evolutionary progression of a shape grammar from the start shape defined in (**a**) using the production rules defined in (**b**)

area of architectural design. This work represented the first combination of shape grammars, already known to be a powerful way to encode human design knowledge [54], with a grammatical evolutionary algorithm.

In [44], shape grammars which generated a 250×250 pixel binary output image were represented in a similar fashion to GP-type symbolic expressions. A series of successively more complex binary target images were then generated, with the aim of evolving a matching target image. A basic fitness function was implemented to iterate over all pixels in a candidate solution image. Since pixels could only take binary values, the fitness of an individual was simply the number of correct pixels in the image. However, since this fitness measure only rewarded perfectly accurate re-creations of the target image, the system was less able to reward partial or near success. For example, if an individual was evolved to produce a perfect but slightly offset copy of the target image, it would not be recognized by this basic fitness function.

In a subsequent follow-up paper, the same authors replaced the basic fitness function with an interactive user-defined fitness function [45]. By implementing the entire GEVA system [43] as a plugin for the Blender 3D design suite [16], an interactive evolutionary design system was created. This system was used to design single-person shelters, under the supervision and direction of collaborators from the UCD School of Architecture. The shape grammars were extended into three dimensions, and the use of a 3D design suite enabled simple evolved solutions to be rendered in a visually attractive manner. An example evolved shelter is shown in Fig. 4.

One notable issue with the designs produced by the shape grammars described in [44] and [45] is that the combination of various shape elements through boolean operations does not necessarily mean the individual elements within a structure have "knowledge" of the other elements in the overall structure [35]. An example of this can be seen in the structure shown in Fig. 4, where the "roof" and "wall" components are connected through simple boolean intersection. In this instance, the

Fig. 4 A shelter designed using interactive Grammatical Evolution [45]

intersection of these two components is fortuitous; a direct connection now exists between them, allowing for this structure to be built. However, this intersection is either a product of random choice (i.e. through crossover or mutation) or is the intent of the designer (i.e. the user who evolved the structure using the interactive fitness function), rather than an inherent aspect of the shape grammars themselves. The use of shape grammars to define physical structures therefore means that "impossible" structures can be potentially created if the grammar is not carefully designed. Indeed, the structure shown in Fig. 4 implies the potential existence of an un-connected free-floating "roof" element in the population.

2.3   Other Representations

The use of arbitrary language context-free grammars to define the genotype-to-phenotype mapping process means that GE can be easily used to generate programs which interact with external programs, i.e. GE can be used in conjunction with other programs in order to control aspects of those programs. For example, a GE individual could be directly evaluated by an external fitness function [15], or a GE individual could describe a set of rules for modifying/controlling some external program [39].

In some cases, the representation can be so simple that a complex mapping process is not needed. In an engineering application of GE, Fenton et al. used a simple grammar that generated an arbitrary number of points within a 2-dimensional area [15]. These points were then deterministically connected using a Delaunay triangulation algorithm [11] in order to generate a fully triangulated truss.

On the other hand, if software already exists which can generate such complex representations, GE is perfectly placed to produce individuals in the form of pieces of code which can interact directly with that software. Such is the case with Nicolau and Costelloe's use of GE [39] to evolve images using Jenn3D, a 3-dimensional image generation program [40]. Their grammar produces settings for key parameters of the Jenn3D software, with the software acting as a "black box" from which aesthetically pleasing images are produced. Figure 5 shows an image generated by this system which was the winning entrant to the Evolutionary Art competition at the 2010 EvoStar conference in Turkey.

2.3.1   Higher Order Functions

Higher order functions (HOFs) are functions which can use other functions as either input arguments or output returns. This capacity allows for modularity and re-use of code, as a single function can perform many different actions depending on the input arguments [27]. The use of HOFs in grammatical encodings has four distinct advantages [34]:

Fig. 5 Winning image from
the Evolutionary Art
competition at the 2010
EvoStar conference [39]

1. they can make optimal solutions shorter, which usually increases the likelihood
   of being found,
2. their modularity and re-use aspects promote patterns in phenotypes,
3. they allow for non-entropic mutations, i.e. more consistent/constructive and less
   destructive mutations, and
4. they provide users and designers with a unique and natural way to express their
   artistic knowledge.

The use of HOFs in a formal grammar structure is particularly fitting, as they afford the user new pathways with which to instil bias towards desired outcomes [34]. Furthermore, the natural use of recursion and non-terminals in a grammar structure makes code re-use and HOFs intuitive in a grammatical setting. Example structures generated using HOFs are shown in Fig. 6.

2.3.2 Graph Grammars

In the context of design, shape grammars could be considered in some cases to be similar to pixel-based art. By contrast, graph grammars are closer to a vector-based representation [12, 31]. The principal feature of graph grammars is their use of nodes and edges in the phenotypic representation. Whereas individual elements of shape grammars do not necessarily connect to one another, the use of nodes and edges in a graph grammar dictates direct connections between individual elements in a design [31, 32] . This process is illustrated in Fig. 7.

Fig. 6 Bridge designs generated using a complex Higher Order Function grammar [13]

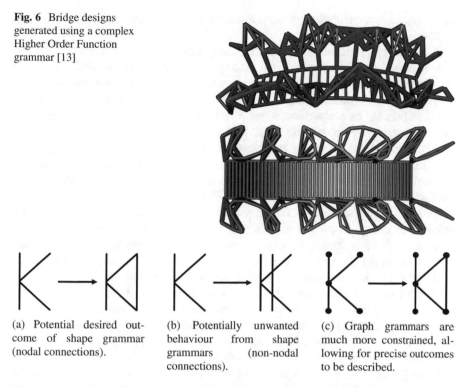

(a) Potential desired outcome of shape grammar (nodal connections).

(b) Potentially unwanted behaviour from shape grammars (non-nodal connections).

(c) Graph grammars are much more constrained, allowing for precise outcomes to be described.

Fig. 7 A major difference between shape and graph grammars is the use of nodes and edges to define individual elements [31, 32]. (**a**) Potential desired outcome of shape grammar (nodal connections). (**b**) Potentially unwanted behaviour from shape grammars (non-nodal connections). (**c**) Graph grammars are much more constrained, allowing for precise outcomes to be described

While shape grammars are successfully used for pure design applications such as art or product design [44, 45, 51, 52], the nature of graph grammars tends to better suit skeletal design applications such as structural engineering design.

3 Evaluation in Evolutionary Design

3.1 Interactive Evolutionary Design

The designer and end user judge a design not only by objective functionality, but also by subjective form. Despite the ability of evolutionary algorithms to produce creative and novel designs, they have primarily been used to aid the design process by optimising the *functionality* of a design, once it has been instantiated. Designers should be able to express their subjective and objective intentions with a design tool. To this end, several techniques that allow user input have been incorporated into evolutionary algorithms to allow the designer to express their aesthetic considerations [53].

The most common technique for expressing subjective preference is to allow the user to directly apply a fitness value to the generated designs. The designer directs the algorithm as an objective function would but this limits their role to that of an evaluator. This unfortunately causes a substantial fitness bottleneck due to the required number of evaluations; it can be appreciated that if the population size is large, this evaluation phase will take a long time [53].

The simplest way to reduce this fitness bottleneck is to use comparatively small population sizes. Nicolau and Costelloe [39] used an interactive fitness function for their image generation plugin to the Jenn3D image generation software [40]. As defined in Sect. 2.3, their system used GE to parametrically control the Jenn3D software to create an image. With a population size of only 10 individuals, each solution in the population was presented to the user sequentially, with the user assigning a discrete integer fitness value to each solution. Permissible values ranged from 1 (whereby the individual was instantly discarded from the population and replaced with a new randomly generated individual) to 5. Interestingly, the authors took advantage of the user-centric aspect of the overall system with a logical extension; no limit to the maximum number of generations was set, i.e. evolution was left open-ended. It was up to the user to end the evolutionary process.

Larger population sizes and sequential evaluation can significantly increase the time required to complete an evolutionary run. This time can be offset by either animating the changes or by presenting multiple images for the user to evaluate simultaneously. This can readily and easily be achieved through the use of novel interfaces and simplified evaluation approaches, as shown in Fig. 8. This will increase the number of possible evaluations in an efficient manner. However, it still acts as a bottleneck as users soon become tired of the evaluation process.

Novel interfaces and simpler rating systems can increase the number of evaluations carried out by the designer. One such approach described in [5] allowed the designer to directly manipulate a design they were interested in by allowing them to apply highly localised mutation operators. The results were presented as an animated array (similar to the array on the left hand side of Fig. 8) which allows the user to quickly evaluate the changes and also undo any mutations they did not like.

While novel interfaces can greatly improve the feedback and "feel" of the interactive evolutionary process, this in itself does not get to the crux of the problem. Design is a subjective process, and the designer needs to feel that they are actually designing rather than evaluating [6]. The fundamental subjectivity to the design process and the nebulous and ever changing goals of the designer mean that interactive evolutionary design still presents a challenge to evolutionary algorithms [53]. It is a mistake to treat the problem purely as an optimisation problem and instead it must be framed as an interface for allowing the designer to easily explore the search space of possible designs.

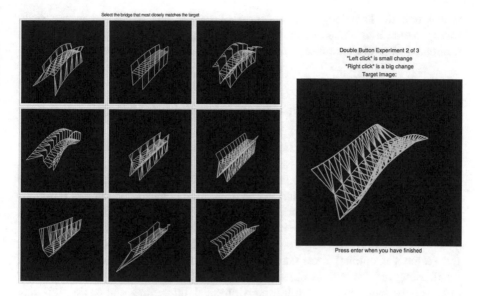

Fig. 8 Screenshot of interactive fitness function from [5]. Target image is shown on the right, with an array of 9 potential images on the left. Users are directed to select the image that most closely matches the target image

3.1.1 Representations Revisited

A certain quandary is inherent with interactive evaluation. While Evolutionary Computation systems are capable of having great detail in their representations, this may not necessarily be feasible when interactive fitness functions are in use. Indeed, a highly detailed representation may in fact hinder the evolutionary process in an interactive setting, as noted by Nicolau and Costelloe [39]:

> ... consider a toy evolutionary image generation task where the goal is to produce a simple black and white image on an N × N grid. The image could be encoded as a binary string of length N^2 – a representation that fits well with a Genetic Algorithm implementation.
>
> This simple representation is powerful in that it permits the construction of every possible 2-dimensional monochrome image for a given value of N. If this were a standard, non-interactive optimisation problem, this kind of representation would probably be suitable, since the space of all possible solutions is covered, meaning that with the right conditions, high-quality solutions are almost guaranteed as output from evolution.
>
> But in an interactive setting, this type of (fine-grained) representation makes the construction of even the most basic shapes on the canvas a slow and difficult process. Adding to the difficulty is the potentially destructive nature of the genetic operators of the GA.

Nicolau and Costelloe go on to note that for interactive applications (i.e. where user input is required, creating a computational bottleneck), the use of pre-defined elements in the building blocks of the representation is more likely to generate desirable high-quality solutions earlier on in the evolutionary process. The notion of such pre-defined elements ties in directly with grammar-based representations, where domain knowledge on the form of the desired solution can be easily incorporated. It is therefore clear to see how grammar-based systems such as Grammatical Evolution might prove appropriate in such applications.

3.2   Engineering Applications of Evolutionary Design

Design can be described as a marriage of exploration and purpose [17]. On the one hand, the search space must be explored to find a suitable concept or form, while on the other hand, the constraints of the original design specification dictate the function of the solution. Thus, there quite often exists a dichotomy, a famous conflict between form and function. While these two attributes of a design are not mutually exclusive, there can be a trade-off when realising a design [4, 38].

For pure subjective design applications (such as visual art or aural music), the search for optimal form can often satisfy the functional requirement in of itself. However, for certain objective design applications such as architecture or engineering, there are quite often hard physical limitations and constraints that must be imposed on the designs themselves. Whereas the optimisation of form can be said to be mostly subjective (and thus highly suited to "open-loop" interactive fitness functions, as described in Sect. 3.1), physical limitations and constraints can often be satisfied mathematically or in a boolean fashion through some inspection of elements of the design itself. This is particularly the case with engineering optimisation applications, where objective analyses on aspects such as weight or material and structural stresses and strains can deliver deep insights into the physical performance of the proposed design, providing the potential for non-interactive (i.e. "closed-loop") feedback to the system.

3.2.1   Engineering Constraints

An interesting point can be made in the case of constrained engineering problems. Readers familiar with Grammatical Evolution will be aware of the term "invalid" solutions. These are individuals whose chromosomes do not produce valid phenotypes, and thus cannot be evaluated. Since they cannot be evaluated, invalid solutions are typically given a bad "default" fitness value in GE [41].

In constrained engineering optimisation, there may exist multiple *soft* constraints. These constraints act as part of the fitness function, and may include such details as overall structural limits on deflection, or material limits such as stress or strain. Importantly, solutions which fail any or all of these constraints are still "valid" solutions. However, they are less desirable than solutions which pass all of the given constraints. Hence, a distinction must be made between *feasible* and *infeasible* solutions. Infeasible solutions are solutions that fail any or all soft constraints.

Evolutionary structural engineering optimisation will often require the designer to satisfy multiple parallel objectives. Since there may be overlaps between both design constraints and objectives, interaction between these constraints and the overall individual fitness may have a significant impact on the quality of the designs evolved. As such, a key challenge for designers when using evolutionary approaches is to find an accurate metric that will allow the designer to judge individual constraints, and to transform the performance of the individual relative to those constraints into a single coherent value for use by the fitness function. As such, it is important that infeasible solutions are penalised appropriately (i.e. with a gradient based on the severity of the constraint failures) in order to impose a gradient on the fitness landscape.

The use of soft engineering constraints can remove the need/use for multiple objective optimisation in some cases. Since design specifications in the form of maximum limits are usually given on critical aspects of the problem (such as structural deflection and material stress), any structure which does *not* violate these constraints is automatically deemed fit for purpose. Therefore, any further optimisation of *these particular aspects* of the solution beyond the pre-defined limits can be considered unnecessary, since the design is already fit for purpose. Evolution can then focus on the more critical aspects of the problem, such as minimising the self weight of the structure, or improving the aesthetic design. Essentially, once the necessary criteria for solving the problem are met, focussed optimisation can take place.

3.2.2   Engineering Applications of Grammatical Evolution

Formal grammars are well suited to engineering design since many design rules and specifications can be easily represented by a grammar, and moreover can often be readily parametrised to allow for more varied search [37, 49]. The use of Grammatical Evolution as an optimisation engine is particularly complementary to these assets, and its application to engineering design has proved to be quite successful [7, 9, 15].

A major factor in engineering design is the analysis of proposed designs. Engineering analyses can be (and have historically always been) performed by hand, but are more recently being performed by complex design and analysis software packages using methods such as finite element analysis [36]. The use of analysis packages allows for complete quantitative numerical information about all aspects of the proposed design. Viewed in the light of evolutionary optimisation, any number of these aspects can form the basis of an objective in a fitness metric. Analysis packages should thus be considered as an integral part of the overall fitness function for engineering optimisation.

There have been a number of pure engineering design applications of Grammatical Evolution over the years. Fenton et al. [14] proposed a grammatical framework for evolving planar (two dimensional) truss structures. This work is a particularly interesting use case of GE, as two genomes were evolved simultaneously. Each

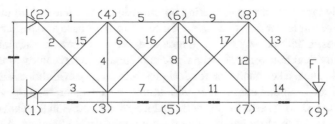

(a) Complete topological layout for cantilever truss.

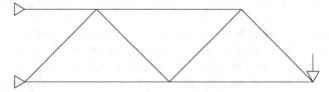

(b) Example of evolved solution to suit the design envelope specified in Fig. 9a.

Fig. 9 Example topological layout and subsequent optimised structure evolved using DO-GE
[14]. (**a**) Complete topological layout for cantilever truss. (**b**) Example of evolved solution to suit
the design envelope specified in (**a**)

genome controlled separate aspects of an individual, hence the title "DO-GE" (Dual
Optimisation in Grammatical Evolution). The first genome (Genome A) dealt with
the topological layout of the structure (i.e. the location and connectivity of nodes
and edges) via the usual mapping through a grammar. Once the topology of the
structure was defined by the first genome, the truss member sizes were set through
a direct GA-style one-to-one mapping from the second genome (Genome B).
Structural analysis was performed using the free open-source finite element analysis
program SLFFEA [29], with the single objective of minimising the self-weight of
the structure.[1] It was shown that the standard evolutionary process of Grammatical
Evolution is capable of handling multiple concurrent genetic components. An
example problem definition and derived solution is shown in Fig. 9.

A noted weak link of the work presented in [14] was the grammar itself.
This grammar was only capable of generating rectangular truss structures from
a small set of six pre-defined layouts, and ultimately could only generate 1890
unique phenotypes (note that this only describes the representation capabilities
of the grammar, and does not include all combinations of material sizes). This
representational limitation was addressed in a subsequent publication [15], with
the introduction of SEOIGE (Structural Engineering Optimisation In Grammatical
Evolution). Therein, a new technique for generating planar truss structures through

---

[1]Note that a single objective can be used when engineering constraints are implemented, as detailed
in Sect. 3.2.1.

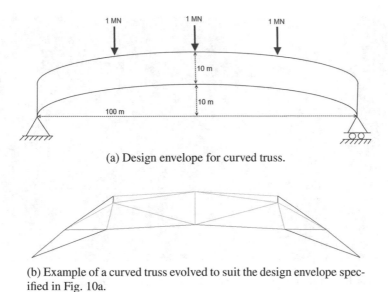

(a) Design envelope for curved truss.

(b) Example of a curved truss evolved to suit the design envelope specified in Fig. 10a.

Fig. 10 Example of a design envelope and subsequent optimised structure evolved using SEOIGE [15]. (**a**) Design envelope for curved truss. (**b**) Example of a curved truss evolved to suit the design envelope specified in (**a**)

the use of a node-based grammar was introduced. This new technique evolved the number and locations of nodes within a specified design envelope. Nodes were then connected using a deterministic Delaunay triangulation algorithm [11]. The use of a triangulation algorithm to connect evolved nodes means that all evolved structures are *guaranteed* to be kinematically stable, i.e. no kinetic mechanisms can be generated by such a system. This can be linked somewhat to the use of structural form and geometry as a proxy for in-depth structural analysis in GENR8 [22], although in the case of [15] a full analysis is also possible.

One additional feature of the node-based grammar from [15] is that the technique allows for evolution of a structure to fit any design envelope that can be represented as an equation. Since one dimension (y) is defined as a function of the other dimension (x), any shape that can be so defined can be represented by the grammar. A simple example is shown in Fig. 10, where a curved truss has been evolved to fit an arched design envelope.

The truss optimisation work by Fenton et al. [14, 15] is also notable as fully code-compliant hard and soft constraints were built into the fitness function, based on the contemporary building standards and design codes of practice [2, 3]. Furthermore, a discrete set of building materials was defined from real-world commercially available construction elements (the indexes of which were specified by Genome B in [14]). This is of particular note as the majority of the techniques polled from the literature allowed for continuous optimisation of member sizings, i.e. member sizes were optimised with no regard to construction viability. Despite the more limited

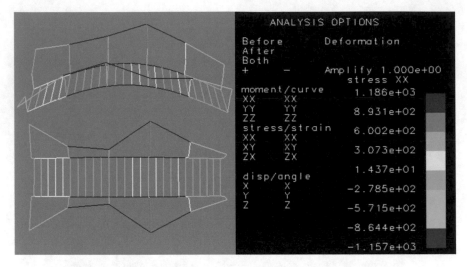

Fig. 11 Structural analysis of a simple timber bridge generated by GE [13]

representation space when compared with other techniques from the literature (in the case of material size optimisation) and the more difficult constraints (in the form of full standards compliance), both techniques were able to evolve comparable, and in most cases more efficient structures to those from the literature.

3.2.3 Multiple Objectives in Engineering Optimisation

Often engineering specifications require multiple conflicting objectives, such as the minimisation of cost, weight, or structural deflection. Furthermore, these quantitative numerical objectives may need to be combined with the subjective aspect of the form of the design. As such, that makes the use of multi-objective optimisation techniques key to many engineering design applications.

Byrne et al. [4] used NSGA-II [10] to evolve wooden bridge designs for the conflicting objectives of minimal stress and minimal material usage. As with [9, 14, 15], structural analysis was performed using the free open-source finite element analysis program SLFFEA [29]. The analysis visualisation for an example structure is shown in Fig. 11. Experiments showed that Grammatical Evolution was capable of driving towards Pareto-optimality, with combined results of a 34% reduction in material usage and a 41% reduction in average maximum stress.

Byrne et al. applied Grammatical Evolution to a real-world problem, evolving full-scale electricity transmission pylon towers for a design competition with the Royal Institute of British Architects [9]. Similar to the truss optimisation works detailed above [14, 15], this work combined real-world constraints and design codes of practice to evolve optimal pylon designs for a variety of loading conditions.

Fig. 12 Final evolved pylon design, as submitted to the Royal Institute of British Architects' 2011 pylon design competition [9]

Higher Order Functions (as described in Sect. 2.3.1) were used in the grammatical representation to ensure fully connected structures, while Sierpinski triangulation, a form of fractals similar to L-Systems, were used to enhance structural rigidity. Due to variety in the loading cases, multiple objective optimisation in the form of NSGA2 [10] was used to optimise pylons for minimal displacement and weight. The final evolved and (ultimately unsuccessful) submitted design is shown in Fig. 12.

An interesting application of multiple objective optimisation for design is the use of GE to evolve parametric aircraft models [7, 8]. Combining the use of a parametric vehicle design platform developed by NASA and Sterling Software [18] with fluid dynamics analysis, the authors used NSGA2 [10] to jointly optimise aircraft designs for the opposing objectives of maximal lift and minimal drag. In a number of case studies, the authors demonstrated that the wings of the popular Cessna 182 light aircraft were already highly optimal, with the original wing design lying very close to the optimised Pareto front of designs in terms of lift and drag optimisation. However, a case study of the Russian MIG-21 fighter aircraft showed that the original wing and tail sections were so highly adapted to supersonic flight that even random search was able to find optimally superior solutions for regular subsonic flight conditions.

3.3 Optimisation vs Design Exploration

As noted in Sect. 3.1, the use of interactivity in design optimisation can be a double-edged sword. While a fitness bottleneck may be created, the ability to directly impose preference or design intent on the evolutionary process affords the designer great power to exploit the system. However, both objective and subjective (i.e. interactive) fitness functions can be combined, allowing for a "best of both worlds" scenario where evolution can operate under either condition. Evolution under an *objective* fitness function is typically termed "optimisation", i.e. some defined aspect of the problem is being optimised; evolution under a *subjective* fitness function is typically termed "exploration", as subjective preference cannot be so easily defined.

A good example of this marriage can be seen in GENR8 [23], which uses a combination of interactive and automated fitness functions. In order to speed up the creative process, it is possible for GENR8 to be run autonomously. Fitness is calculated as a linear combination of five aspects of any given solution:

1. size,
2. smoothness,
3. soft boundaries,
4. subdivisions, and
5. symmetry.

The weighting of any and all parameters is a variable option open to change by the designer during the course of a run. This approach allows the designer to invest as little or as much input into the design process as they desire [46].

An interesting experiment from [4] combined an interactive aspect to the overall evolutionary process of bridge designs, marrying multi-objective quantitative fitness optimisation with a qualitative appraisal of subjective form. By presenting participants with a random selection of sample structures from both the first and last Pareto fronts produced by NSGA2 (i.e. a sampling of structures that were either highly or poorly fit in terms of engineering constraints), a survey of 28 participants found that engineering constraints were more often than not in direct opposition to aesthetic preferences. This suggested that aesthetic preferences had an inclination towards more "unconstrained" forms. As such, an interactive aspect to design could be used to trade off the seemingly opposed objectives of optimisation and design exploration by combining both objective and subjective fitness functions.

4 Conclusions

Grammatical Evolution has strong links to design for both objective optimisation and subjective exploration. The two main aspects are the design representation itself, and the evaluation of candidate designs. The use of a formal context-free grammar to define the representation of the system, combined with the separation between the genetic encoding and the phenotypic representation, provides a convenient and powerful platform which can allow designers complete freedom of expression. Furthermore, well known design representations such as Lindenmayer Systems can aid the explorative aspect of the design process by injecting a generative element into the evolutionary mix. Importantly, the use of grammars also supports the instillation of bias and structure, should the designers so desire.

The use of arbitrary fitness functions in Evolutionary Computation (EC) allows for a wide variety of fitness assessments to be coupled with the design process. Since design is quite often subjective, interactive fitness functions can be merged with many aspects of the EC process, including the specification of elite individuals, selection of individuals for variation, and ranking of populations. For objective design applications such as engineering optimisation, powerful analysis software can be used in more traditional objective fitness functions. Engineering design in particular can benefit from multiple objective optimisation, an area where EC techniques excel. Finally, subjective fitness appraisal can also be combined with traditional objective fitness functions in a "best of both worlds" scenario.

Acknowledgements This research is based upon works supported by Science Foundation Ireland under grant 13/IA/1850.

References

1. D. Beaumont, S. Stepney, Grammatical evolution of L-systems, in *IEEE Congress on Evolutionary Computation, 2009. CEC'09* (IEEE, New York, 2009), pp. 2446–2453
2. British Standards Institution, BS 449-2: 1969. The structural use of steel in building (1969)
3. British Standards Institution, BS 5950-1: 2000. Structural use of steelwork in building (2000)
4. J. Byrne, M. Fenton, E. Hemberg, J. McDermott, M. O'Neill, E. Shotton, C. Nally, Combining structural analysis and multi-objective criteria for evolutionary architectural design, in *European Conference on the Applications of Evolutionary Computation* (Springer, Berlin, 2011), pp. 204–213
5. J. Byrne, E. Hemberg, A. Brabazon, M. O'Neill, A local search interface for interactive evolutionary architectural design, in *International Conference on Evolutionary and Biologically Inspired Music and Art* (Springer, Berlin, 2012), pp. 23–34
6. J. Byrne, E. Hemberg, M. O'Neill, A. Brabazon, A methodology for user directed search in evolutionary design. Genet. Program Evolvable Mach. **14**(3), 287–314 (2013)
7. J. Byrne, P. Cardiff, A. Brabazon, M. O'Neill, Evolving parametric aircraft models for design exploration and optimisation. Neurocomputing **142**, 39–47 (2014)
8. J. Byrne, P. Cardiff, A. Brabazon, M. O'Neill, Evolving an aircraft using a parametric design system, in *International Conference on Evolutionary and Biologically Inspired Music and Art* (Springer, Berlin, 2014), pp. 119–130
9. J. Byrne, M. Fenton, E. Hemberg, J. McDermott, M. O'Neill, Optimising complex pylon structures with grammatical evolution. Inf. Sci. 316, 582–597 (2015)
10. K. Deb, A. Pratap, S. Agarwal, T. Meyarivan, A fast and elitist multiobjective genetic algorithm: NSGA-II. IEEE Trans. Evol. Comput. **6**(2), 182–197 (2002)
11. B. Delaunay, Sur la sphere vide. Izv. Akad. Nauk SSSR, Otdelenie Matematicheskii i Estestvennyka Nauk **7**(793–800), 1–2 (1934)

12. H. Ehrig, Introduction to the algebraic theory of graph grammars (a survey), in *International Workshop on Graph Grammars and Their Application to Computer Science* (Springer, Berlin, 1978), pp. 1–69
13. M. Fenton, Analysis of timber structures created using a GE-based architectural design tool. Master's thesis, University College Dublin, Ireland, 2010
14. M. Fenton, C. McNally, J. Byrne, E. Hemberg, J. McDermott, M. O'Neill, Automatic innovative truss design using grammatical evolution. Autom. Constr. **39**, 59–69 (2014)
15. M. Fenton, C. McNally, J. Byrne, E. Hemberg, J. McDermott, M. O'Neill, Discrete planar truss optimization by node position variation using grammatical evolution. IEEE Trans. Evol. Comput. **20**(4), 577–589 (2016)
16. S.B. Foundation, Blender 3D, 2009, http://www.blender.org/
17. J.S. Gero, Creativity, emergence and evolution in design. Knowl.-Based Syst. **9**(7), 435–448 (1996)
18. J.R. Gloudemans, P.C. Davis, P.A. Gelhausen, A rapid geometry modeller for conceptual aircraft, in *34th Aerospace Sciences Meeting and Exhibit, Reno, NV* (1996), pp. 15–18
19. E. Hemberg, J. McDermott, PonyGE, 2011, https://github.com/jmmcd/ponyge
20. M. Hemberg, U.-M. O'Reilly, GENR8 - using grammatical evolution in a surface design tool, in *GECCO* (2002), pp. 120–123
21. M. Hemberg, U.-M. O'Reilly, Extending grammatical evolution to evolve digital surfaces with GENR8, in *European Conference on Genetic Programming* (Springer, Berlin, 2004), pp. 299–308
22. M. Hemberg, U.-M. O'Reilly, Geometry as a substitute for structural analysis in generative design tools, 2005
23. M. Hemberg, U.-M. O'Reilly, P. Nordin, et al. GENR8 - a design tool for surface generation, in *GECCO Late Breaking Papers, pp160–167, San Francisco* (2001), pages 9–11
24. M. Hemberg, U.-M. O'Reilly, A. Menges, K. Jonas, M. Goncalves, S. Fuchs, Exploring generative growth and evolutionary computation for architectural design. *Art of Artificial Evolution* (Springer, Heidelberg 2006)
25. M. Hemberg, U.-M. O'Reilly, A. Menges, K. Jonas, M. da Costa Gonçalves, S.R. Fuchs, GENR8: architects' experience with an emergent design tool, in *The Art of Artificial Evolution* (Springer, Berlin, 2008), pp. 167–188
26. G.S. Hornby, J.B. Pollack, The advantages of generative grammatical encodings for physical design, in *Proceedings of the 2001 Congress on Evolutionary Computation, 2001*, vol. 1 (IEEE, New York, 2001), pp. 600–607
27. J. Hughes, Why functional programming matters. Comput. J. **32**(2), 98–107 (1989)
28. A. Jordanous, Evaluating evaluation: assessing progress in computational creativity research, in *Proceedings of the Second International Conference on Computational Creativity (ICCC-11). Mexico City, Mexico* (2011), pp. 102–107
29. S. Le, San Le's Free Finite Element Analysis (SLFFEA) (2008), http://slffea.sourceforge.net/
30. A. Lindenmayer, Mathematical models for cellular interactions in development I. filaments with one-sided inputs. J. Theor. Biol. **18**(3), 280–299 (1968)
31. J. McDermott, Graph grammars as a representation for interactive evolutionary 3d design, in *International Conference on Evolutionary and Biologically Inspired Music and Art* (Springer, Berlin, 2012), pp. 199–210
32. J. McDermott, Graph grammars for evolutionary 3d design. Genet. Program Evolvable Mach. **14**(3), 369–393 (2013)
33. J. McDermott, E. Hemberg, Logo design by grammatical evolution of L-Systems. GECCO art competition entry (2011)
34. J. McDermott, J. Byrne, J.M. Swafford, M. O'Neill, A. Brabazon, Higher-order functions in aesthetic EC encodings, in *2010 IEEE Congress on Evolutionary Computation (CEC)* (IEEE, New York, 2010), pp. 1–8
35. J. McDermott, J.M. Swafford, M. Hemberg, J. Byrne, E. Hemberg, M. Fenton, C. McNally, E. Shotton, M. O'Neill, String-rewriting grammars for evolutionary architectural design. Environ. Plann. B. Plann. Des. **39**(4), 713–731 (2012)

36. S. Moaveni, *Finite Element Analysis Theory and Application with ANSYS* (Pearson Education India, New Delhi, 2008)
37. S. Mullins, J. R. Rinderle, Grammatical approaches to engineering design, part I: an introduction and commentary. Res. Eng. Des. **2**(3), 121–135 (1991)
38. K. Murawski, T. Arciszewski, K. De Jong, Evolutionary computation in structural design. Eng. Comput. **16**(3), 275–286 (2000). ISSN 1435-5663. http://dx.doi.org/10.1007/PL00013716
39. M. Nicolau, D. Costelloe, Using grammatical evolution to parameterise interactive 3d image generation, in *European Conference on the Applications of Evolutionary Computation* (Springer, Berlin, 2011), pp. 374–383
40. F. Obermeyer, Jenn3D for visualizing coxeter polytopes, 2010, http://www.math.cmu.edu/~fho/jenn/
41. M. O'Neil, C. Ryan, *Grammatical Evolution* (Springer, Berlin, 2003)
42. M. O'Neill, A. Brabazon, Evolving a logo design using lindenmayer systems, postscript & grammatical evolution, in *IEEE Congress on Evolutionary Computation, 2008. CEC 2008. (IEEE World Congress on Computational Intelligence)* (IEEE, New York, 2008), pp. 3788–3794
43. M. O'Neill, E. Hemberg, C. Gilligan, E. Bartley, J. McDermott, A. Brabazon, GEVA: grammatical evolution in Java. ACM SIGEVOlution **3**(2), 17–22 (2008)
44. M. O'Neill, J.M. Swafford, J. McDermott, J. Byrne, A. Brabazon, E. Shotton, C. McNally, M. Hemberg, Shape grammars and grammatical evolution for evolutionary design, in *Proceedings of the 11th Annual Conference on Genetic and Evolutionary Computation* (ACM, New York, 2009), pp. 1035–1042
45. M. O'Neill, J. McDermott, J.M. Swafford, J. Byrne, E. Hemberg, A. Brabazon, E. Shotton, C. McNally, M. Hemberg, Evolutionary design using grammatical evolution and shape grammars: designing a shelter. Int. J. Des. Eng. **3**(1), 4–24 (2010)
46. U.-M. O'Reilly, M. Hemberg, Integrating generative growth and evolutionary computation for form exploration. Genet. Program Evolvable Mach. **8**(2), 163–186 (2007)
47. A. Ortega, A.A. Dalhoum, M. Alfonseca, Grammatical evolution to design fractal curves with a given dimension. IBM J. Res. Dev. **47**(4), 483–493 (2003)
48. P. Prusinkiewicz, J. Hanan, *Lindenmayer Systems, Fractals, and Plants*, vol. 79 (Springer Science & Business Media, Berlin, 2013)
49. J.R. Rinderle, Grammatical approaches to engineering design, part II: melding configuration and parametric design using attribute grammars. Res. Eng. Des. **2**(3), 137–146 (1991)
50. F. Rothlauf, M. Oetzel, On the locality of grammatical evolution, in *European Conference on Genetic Programming* (Springer, Berlin, 2006), pp. 320–330
51. G. Stiny, Introduction to shape and shape grammars. Environ. Plann. B. Plann. Des. **7**(3), 343–351 (1980)
52. G. Stiny, J. Gips, Shape grammars and the generative specification of painting and sculpture, in *IFIP Congress (2)*, vol. 2 (1971)
53. H. Takagi, Interactive evolutionary computation: fusion of the capabilities of EC optimization and human evaluation. Proc. IEEE **89**(9), 1275–1296 (2001). ISSN 0018-9219. https://doi.org/10.1109/5.949485
54. C.M. Vogel, J. Cagan, P. Boatwright, *The Design of Things to Come: How Ordinary People Create Extraordinary Products* (Wharton School Publishing, Upper Saddle River, 2005)

Grammatical Evolution and Creativity

Róisín Loughran

Abstract This paper considers the application of Grammatical Evolution (GE) to the concept of creativity both in theory and through the examination of two applied music generation systems. We discuss previous work on the application of evolutionary strategies to music generation and discuss current issues in the study of creativity and Computational Creativity (CC). In presenting and contrasting the development of two GE music generation systems, we can consider the multi-faceted aspects of creativity and how it may be approached from a computational perspective. The design of any such system is dependent on representation (what is music?) and fitness measure (what makes this music good?). In any aesthetic domain such questions are far from trivial. We conclude that it is vitally important to be clear on the purpose and aim in proposing any such system; systems may be either more generative or more autonomously creative if this is the a priori goal of the proposed experiment. Furthermore, we propose that evolutionary systems, and in particular GE, are highly suitable to the study of creativity as they can offer much scope in representation through grammars while allowing exploration and the possibility of self-adaptivity through the development of novel self-referential fitness measures.

1 Introduction

The ability to be creative is often thought to be a purely human quality; our creativity is that which makes us special, unique, more than one of the masses. Yet in recent years numerous computational methods have been applied to what would conventionally be considered creative tasks. Traditionally, creativity has been considered in terms of aesthetic talent; a person may be considered creative because they display exceptional ability in painting, music or writing. But creativity is merely an aspect of human intelligence. Creativity is not a specialised ability

R. Loughran (✉)
Natural Computing Research and Applications Group (NCRA), Michael Smurfit Graduate Business School, UCD, Dublin, Ireland
e-mail: roisin.loughran@ucd.ie

© Springer International Publishing AG, part of Springer Nature 2018   341
C. Ryan et al. (eds.), *Handbook of Grammatical Evolution*,
https://doi.org/10.1007/978-3-319-78717-6_14

afforded only to the lucky few, but a way of thinking available to us all. Most humans display creativity every time they solve a problem, hum a tune or make a witty remark. As the field of Artificial Intelligence (AI) progressed, researchers began to consider creativity not as an aspect of specifically human intelligence but one of general intelligence. The study of the exhibition of creativity from autonomous programs or machines has developed into the field of Computational Creativity (CC).

The field of CC is currently defined as the philosophy, science and engineering of computational systems which, by taking on specific responsibilities, exhibit behaviours that unbiased observers would deem to be creative [12]. This definition has been carefully refined over the past number of years and as such as few points should be noted: CC is the study of *systems*, not merely the artefacts produced; it considers *exhibited behaviour* without specifying that a physical artefact must be created; it refers to the perception of *unbiased observers* but not specifically human opinion; finally, the field studies *philosophical* along with engineering or technical principles. The definition has been refined in response to the development of the field of CC over the past decade. However, this definition is still circular in manner—CC is defined in terms of behaviour of a computational system deemed to be *creative*. Such circularity within a definition is understandable when we consider that creativity in itself is still such a difficult concept to define. The evaluation of a CC system is ideally based on the exhibition of novelty, value and intent by the system. While value and novelty can be attributed to any artefacts produced, the concept of intent can only be attributed to the system itself—did the system *mean* to undertake such behaviour and if so why? Such questions are the most difficult to address in any system, but intent has been proposed as one of the most important aspects in evaluating CC systems in recent years [21, 27].

In this chapter we consider the application of GE to the concept of creativity both in theory and through the examination of two applied systems. As noted throughout this book, GE is a powerful search algorithm based on the theory of evolution and natural selection. In considering representation and fitness we propose two music generation systems and contrast the functionality of both, examining how the GE approach to the two systems must consider this functionality from the outset. The following section reviews some previous work in music generation systems that use various evolutionary strategies before introducing CC and what must be considered in building a CC system. Section 3 describes the development of the first system from basic representation through the proposal of a self-adaptive music generation system. Section 4 proposes a different system that creates live-code for generating loops in ChucK [52]. Section 5 examines the ongoing issue of evaluation of CC systems and considers the important aspects of evaluating the systems proposed. Finally, some conclusions are drawn in Sect. 6.

2 Evolutionary Computation and Creativity

All evolutionary strategies, whether grammatical or not, solve a given problem by evolving a population of solutions; for any problem a number of solutions are created and the ideal solution is found through an iterative, stochastic combination of these solutions. This is well-suited to creative domains where one best or optimal solution may not exist. Could we ever define the best piece of art ever to be made? Such a question is frivolous, largely because it is subjective: people have differing opinions as to what is the 'best art'. Hence in artistic and aesthetic domains there are many local optima, and most likely no single global optimum. In this section we first consider EC as it has been applied to traditionally creative problems, before reviewing the various types of creativity and what should be considered before attempting to design any computational CC system.

2.1 Evolutionary Music

A variety of evolutionary strategies or methods have been applied to algorithmic music composition over the years. One of the most well-known systems, GenJam [1], employed a Genetic Algorithm (GA) to evolve jazz solos from pre-generated MIDI sequences. This has been developed into a real-time, interactive system that has been used in live performances in mainstream venues [2]. Genetic Programming (GP) has been used to recursively describe binary trees as genetic representation in evolving musical scores. The recursive mechanism of this representation allowed the generation of expressive performances and gestures along with the musical notation [14]. A wide range of evolutionary approaches to music generation and music composition are discussed throughout [39]. More recently, adapted GAs have been used with local search methods to investigate human virtuosity in composing with unfigured bass [40] and with non-dominated sorting in a multi-component generative music system that could generate chords, melodies and an accompaniment in a multi-objective system with two populations that are feasible (individuals which satisfy given constraints) and infeasible (those that violate given constraints) [45].

Grammars have been used in the description and generation of music for a number of years. A Generative Theory of Tonal Music (GTTM) [31] is a ground-breaking work that attempted to define the factors which underlie musical perception and lead to the realisation of musical order. GTTM was created as a musical analogy to Chomskian linguistics in that everything is based on a common fundamental grammar and that all tonal music can be explained as a hierarchical structure based on this grammar. While GTTM is useful as an analysis tool, it has not been applied to grammatical music generation. The use of grammars in systems for generating more general music (tonal or otherwise) was discussed in [38]. In recent years, grammars were used to augment live coding in creating music with Tidal [23].

The first system to specifically use GE was proposed in [16]. In this paper GE generated melodies for a specific processor, although the melodies produced were not discussed. GE has been implemented for composing short melodies in [43]. From four experimental setups of varying fitness functions and grammars they determined that users preferred melodies created with a structured grammar. GE was again employed for musical composition using the Wii remote for a generative, virtual system entitled Jive [48]. This system interactively modified a combination of piece-wise linear sequences to create melodic pieces of musical interest.

The above focus is on previous EC applications to music composition as it is evolutionary methods proposed in this chapter. However many other computing and machine learning methods such as Hidden Markov Models [42] and recurrent neural networks [11] have been applied to autonomous music generation. A comprehensive review of other computational methods applied to music composition can be found in [20].

2.2 Other Applications

The above review concentrates on musical applications, as two musical systems are described later in this chapter, but there have been many other creative applications of EC. Visual art in particular has been popular as a creative domain studied within the field of EC. Interactive fitness measures of visual art is much quicker and hence cheaper and easier to carry out than it is with music. Similarly visual results are easier to show in printed form. As such there have been many studies in visual art [32], but also in engineering such as in truss design [19], structural design [28] or fashion [37] which can use visual representations. EC has also been applied to numerous studies that use Natural Language Processing (NLP) in their representation such as in poetry creation in PoeTRYMe [41].

When considering a 'creative' application, one would be forgiven for immediately thinking of an aesthetic process such as music or art. Many early studies and discussions on creativity, however, use mathematical, scientific or logical examples to illustrate the concept. Margaret Boden's foundational book [4] discusses Kekule's discovery of the benzene ring at length as a creative discovery and proposes the idea of a 'necklace game' as a logical game for children that encourages creative reasoning. Creativity is not limited to aesthetic domains, but is relevant and observable in many actions requiring thought, reasoning or intelligence. Despite this importance of general creativity and creative thought over the aesthetic output, a distinct lack of work considering logical problems has been noted in recent work considered to be Computationally Creative [34].

2.3 Types of Creativity

Whether or not computers can genuinely exhibit creativity is still a hotly debated topic. Much research within the field of CC is centred on the philosophical question of how to define creativity and how it could be shown that a computer is capable of being creative. The problem with the definition of CC given in Sect. 1 is that it defines computational creativity in terms of being creative, while 'creative' itself is still such a difficult concept to define. It is accepted that there are two types of creativity: Historical (H) Creativity and Psychological (P) Creativity [5]. Ideas that are novel to the individual who generated it are considered P-Creative, whereas ideas that are novel to the world, that no-one has considered before are said to be H-Creative. By this reasoning H-Creativity is a special case of P-Creativity. Although it may be tempting to concentrate on systems that can generate H-creative artefacts, it is P-Creativity that is of most interest to researchers. Focussing on the general concept (P-Creative) rather than impressive results (H-Creative) is the best method towards understanding the underlying nature of general creativity.

Boden has proposed three different types of creativity: combinational, explorational and transformational. She suggests that computers may display creativity in one of three ways [4]:

- In combining novel ideas;
- In exploring the limits of conceptual space;
- In the transformation of established ideas that enable the emergence of new or unknown ideas.

These three processes can be considered analogous to the operation of grammar-based EC methods such as GE. The combination of ideas can be likened to the crossover operator, while the mutation operator is a more explorational method for searching within any given search space. The grammars used in GE, and other grammar-based EC systems, allow the mapping or transformation of information from one domain to another. The combination of all three processes indicates that GE would appear to be an appropriate approach to problem solving in any creative domain.

2.4 Designing a System

As the field of CC has developed, many systems that tackle creative problems with varying degree of autonomy have begun to emerge. Whether a system can be considered to show creativity rather than *mere generation* has become a hotly debated topic in CC research [50]. For a system to be considered truly autonomously creative, rather than generative, it must exhibit behaviour that displays novelty, value and intentionality. While novelty and value can generally be attributed to the artefact created by the system, intent lies within the behaviour of the system itself. The problem of intent is intrinsic to the autonomy of the system; if the system is to have created something itself, it must have intended to create it and hence must have had reason to create it. This idea of 'Addressing the Why' by looking at intent in CC systems has been considered in [21] whereby it was found that the case-studies considered could not satisfactorily answer the *why?* due to a lack of intrinsic goal-ownership. The goal of intent has been identified as one of the most important aspects of building a CC system [51]. In this study a systematic process is proposed for designing a CC system based on domain, representation, knowledge-base, aesthetic, generation and both genotypic and phenotypic evaluation. All steps may not be relevant to every type of system, but this does offer a systematic starting point for anyone approaching the field.

As noted throughout this book, GE is an evolutionary strategy whereby individuals are mapped to their meaningful domain using a grammar and evolved according to a fitness measure. Hence the grammar controls the representation and the fitness measure controls the selection of individuals. These are the key two elements in designing a GE system for music generation: how do we represent 'music' and how do we measure the 'goodness' of that music. The representation of music is a complicated issue; what do we mean by *music*?

It has been argued that there is in fact no such thing as music but only our perception of the concept [54]:

> *'Music, in its own right, doesn't exist'*

This argument states that when we talk about 'music' what we are actually referring to is a specific representation of music such as an audio recording, a live show or a musical score. We perceive these objects as music through our brains' interpretation of them. By this reasoning, music only truly exists in our minds. Although this may be a philosophical stance, it is an important one to consider from the outset when trying to establish how to represent music in a computational system. Music can be represented by computers digitally, for instance in .wav or .mp3 format, but such representations are very large and perceptually meaningless. Hence many systems represent music through MIDI values, score notation, chord progressions or some other specific language. It is philosophically debatable as to whether or not such systems actually produce music at all. A system that produces musical scores can only be read by someone who can read music and can only be heard if someone plays said music. Furthermore, regardless of the representation, there are many varieties in which systems can create music. Systems may be intended to create novel melody lines or responses to given melodies, accompaniments to solos, chord progressions, ornamentation, soundscapes or any other variation of what we deem music. This point is not to debunk the algorithmic composition of music but to ensure that the programmer understands their own representation and its limitations. In computational musical systems, it is more appropriate to consider all systems to be working in the musical domain, rather than assuming there is one type of representation of music that must be used.

GE offers an approach to this as the grammar is developed by the programmer to create a meaningful solution in the problem domain—in this case a pre-defined musical domain. To illustrate musical use of GE we describe the development of two distinct systems. Both systems are implemented in Python using PonyGE to generate music, but with differing grammars resulting in different musical representation. The first system uses a grammar to create short Musical Instrument Digital Interface (MIDI) messages whereas the second creates individual files that can be looped in the Live-coding language ChucK. As will be discussed later, the two representations lead to a different focus and different level of musical creativity in each system.

3 Case Study: The Composing Pony

The first system, developed over a number of experiments, we have come to refer to as *The Composing Pony*. Implemented in PonyGE, all versions of this system create short individual MIDI files that can be played through any digital sequencer, for example GarageBand. MIDI messages can be played as any specified MIDI instrument, or used to trigger audio samples. For these experiments we use a MIDI piano sound, designing a grammar that can specify pitch and duration for the individual notes.

3.1 Grammar

The Composing Pony uses a context free grammar in Backus-Naur Form (BNF) to create short melodies from the given genome by mapping to a series of notes by specifying a pitch, octave and duration. A level of musicality is introduced to the grammar by allowing not just individual notes but by also including chords, turns and arpeggios. The grammar is based on the following:

```
<piece>  ::= <event>|<piece><event>|<piece><event><event>
         |<piece><event><event><event>
<event>  ::= <style>,<oct>,<pitch>,<dur>,

<style>  ::= <note>|<note>|<note>|<note>|<note>|<note>|<note>
         |<chord>|<chord>|<chord>|<chord>|<turn>|<arp>
<chord>  ::= <int>,0,0|<int>,<int>,0 |12,0,0|<int>,0,0|<int>,0,0
         |<int>,0,0 |<int>,<int>,<int>
<turn>   ::= <dir>,<len>,<dir>,<len>,<stepD>
<arp>    ::= <dir>,<int>,<dir>,<int>,<ArpDur>

<int>    ::= 3|4|5|7|5|5|7|7
<len>    ::= <step>|<step>,<step>|<step>,<step>,<step>
         |<step>,<step>,<step>|<step>,<step>,<step>,<step>
<dir>    ::= up|down
<step>   ::= 1|1|1|1|1|2|2|2|2|2|2|2|2|3
<stepD>  ::= 1|2|2|2|2|2|2|4|4|4|4|4|4
<ArpDur> ::= 2|2|2|4|4|4|4|4|8|8
```

```
<oct>   ::=  3|4|4|4|4|4|5|5|5|5|6|6
<pitch> ::=  0|1|2|3|4|5|6|7|8|9|10|11
<dur>   ::=  1|1|1|2|2|2|4|4|4|8|8|16|16|32
```

This creates an individual (the `<piece>`) that consists of a number of musical events. Each of these events can be made up of either an individual note, a chord, a turn (series of notes with small intervals) or an arpeggio (series of notes with larger intervals). Each note is completely described by its given octave number, pitch and duration. A chord is described by these values plus the interval value from the root to each of the upper notes. Turns and arpeggios are described using the number of steps, the step-size and the direction of flow of the steps. Interval sizes and step-sizes can be altered to favour harmonic or dissonant relationships, thus changing the likely harmonicity of the resulting melodies. This grammar results in a population of individuals whose phenotypes can be played as MIDI messages through any sequencer. The evolutionary search through such a space is then determined by the fitness measure: how should we measure if one of these melodies is 'better' than another?

3.2   The Problem of Fitness

Deciphering the merit of a monophonic melody such as those created by this system is far from simple; we must obtain an objective measure from a subjective decision. Using a human to give a fitness measure, known as Interactive EC, would give a subjective measure but this is highly costly and time consuming and simultaneously retracts from the automation of the system. Some music generation EC studies have created populations whereby each individual is known to be highly musical, thus allowing a random fitness measure as in GenDash [53] or using the whole population in the one composition [2, 17]. Ideally, however, an EC system would encompass an objective measure of what results in a strong or weak melody. The various attributes used in the evaluation of melodies based on pitch and rhythm measurements have been considered in recent years [15]. It was concluded that previous approaches to formalise a fitness function for melodies have not comprehensively incorporated all measures.

As an initial approach to this problem we considered the level of tonality within the given melody. As found through GTTM, western tonal music contains a strong sense of tonal hierarchy. This is based on the major or minor tonal scale whereby certain tones are given preference and repeated throughout the piece. Variations on such hierarchies across other cultural music indicates that an expected tonality is more reliant on perception and cognition than on an innate acoustic relationship [30]. Tonal Induction [29], whereby a listener identifies the key of given music, has been shown to be perceivable by Westerners in both Western and Indian music [9]. This implies that there is no 'ideal' tonality, but that a preferred tonal hierarchy could be induced by a system with no a priori knowledge and hence no pitch expectations. Similarly the distributional view of key identification [49] implies that a perceived pitch key may be induced by enforcing a repetition of a given set of pitches. Such a relationship is used as the basis of the fitness measure within our system. As can be noted from the above grammar the `<pitch>` line allows any degree of the scale with equal likelihood. Such a line will enforce 12-tone music rather than music that fits to any typical Western tonal key. To create a tonal-based fitness measure, we consider the relationship between the pitches present in the given melody.

An initial fitness is defined to ensure the melody is of acceptable length:

$$\text{fitness}_{\text{initial}} = (\text{Len} - 200)^2 + 1 \tag{1}$$

where *Len* is the length, in integer values, of the current phenotype. Due to the variations in note values permitted through the grammar, this initial length value of 200 allows much variation in the duration of the resultant melody. This length was chosen experimentally to result in phenotypes long enough to produce music of acceptable duration while ensuring it did not continue indefinitely. The addition of the constant 1 is to prevent a fitness of zero as this initial fitness is now adjusted by multiplication according to the statistical relationship between the pitches.

For an emergent tonality, one pitch should be the most frequently played within the melody, with an unequal distribution of the remaining pitches. In the fitness the *primary* is defined as the pitch value with most instances and the *secondary* as that with the second highest number of instances. Thus for a good (low) fitness the number of primary pitches must be significantly higher than the number of secondary pitches. We define the number of instances of the seven most frequently played notes as Top7 and the number of instances of the top nine most frequently played notes as Top9.

The fitness is multiplied by 1.3 if any of the following inequalities hold:

$$\frac{\#\text{ instances of primary}}{\#\text{ instances of secondary}} < 1.3 \tag{2}$$

$$\frac{\text{Top7}}{\text{Total number of played notes}} < 0.75 \tag{3}$$

$$\frac{\text{Top9}}{\text{Total number of played notes}} < 0.95 \tag{4}$$

This forces the primary tone to have significantly more instances than the secondary and encourages most of the notes played to be within the top seven or top nine notes. In uniformed pitch-distributed music these Top7 and Top9 ratios would work out to be 0.58 and 0.75 respectively whereas in Western tonal music all notes, bar accidentals, would be contained in the top seven pitches. These limits of 0.75 and 0.95 result in more tonality than 12 tone serialism but will not create a melody with typical Western tonality. It must be noted that this fitness measure is reliant only on a statistical measure of the frequency of notes within the melody; the fitness is not related to the order in which notes are played or any temporal relationship

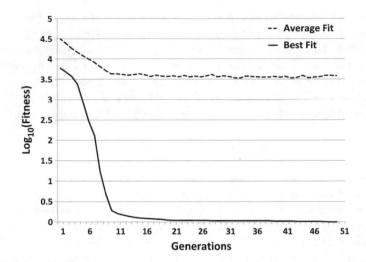

Fig. 1 Best and average fitness of melodies evolved over 50 generations, averaged over 30 runs

between one note and the next. The temporal arrangement of notes emerges from the grammar through the presence of note events.

A series of 30 experiments were run with a population of 100 for 50 generations. For these experiments all other parameters were left to the default settings in PonyGE: the mutation coefficient was set to 0.01, crossover was set to 0.7 and there was an elite size of 1. In comparison to many EC studies, these experimental runs were very short, taking less than 30 s to complete. A plot of the average and best fitnesses of the runs over 50 generations can be seen in Fig. 1. This clearly shows a rapid drop in fitness in early generations, as the initial fitness based on length is reached, followed by a slower tapering off of fitness as the statistical measures are satisfied.

As the grammar can produce melodies containing runs and turns of notes, a number of the resultant melodies can immediately (from generation 0) sound somewhat musical. Evolution searches towards the ideal statistical relationships given in the fitness function. As noted, however, these statistical measures do not affect the temporal (horizontal) arrangement of the notes. This fitness function cannot objectively measure pleasantness or 'goodness' of the music; it merely specifies a numerical goal according to which the space should be searched. A such, it is possible to have a musical sounding individual from the initial population which does not survive through subsequent generations. There is no direct link between this measure of fitness and the more abstract concept of 'musicality'; the concept of musical merit or fitness is much more complex than this.

A single individual phenotype is short, resulting in a short melody snippet. To create longer melodic compositions, the top four individuals were concatenated together. This makes use of the population aspect of evolution: instead of producing one single good result, a run has produced a population of results. As evolution converges towards a solution, the top few individuals will have similarly good fitness values. This results in a number of the top melodies being similar but not identical. Concatenating similar melodies together leads to the emergence of melodic themes that is audible in a number of the resultant compositions. This variation on a theme concept is highly suitable for musical works. A selection of melodies created using this system are available to listen at:

https://soundcloud.com/user-529879178/sets/composingponymelodies.

Melodies 1–3 are all final generation results from the above system. While it may be possible to have a musical individual at generation 0, as explained above, longer compositions that exhibit the emergence of a theme is only possible after many generations. MelodyAccompany 1 and 2 were created by an extended version of this system that generates accompaniments [36] and MelodyCritic 1 and 2 were created by the self-adaptive Critic system described in the following section.

3.3   Self-Adaptive System

The above system successfully uses GE to evolve musical phrases, but its search method is based on a pre-defined fitness metric. While this is justifiable from the tonality perspective as defined above, this does not actually constitute a *subjective* measure. Subjectivity implies that the choice of a given individual is due to the *preference* of the entity making the decision. As humans we justify our preferences by stating it's what we 'like' but how does that translate to the preference exhibited by an autonomous agent or algorithm?

Many computational compositional systems such as those reviewed in Sect. 2 use a pre-defined idea of what constitutes a successful composition, according to a given style or a series of rules. Systems learn these rules or abstract patterns from styles and create music that conforms to what it has learned. While such systems have been successful, they are ultimately confined to conform to music already created— by humans. With the current computational possibilities, an alternative and possibly more interesting question may lie in the pursuit of creations that do not conform to what has been seen before, but which can emerge from a self-adaptive system. The purpose of such a system would not be to create music to appease our current tastes, but to explore the emergence of a new preference, one that is wholly dependent on the workings of the system, rather than outside influence.

For an EC compositional system to be considered autonomously creative in this instance, the fitness function should be meaningful (i.e. not merely random) and not pre-defined to conform to previously decided musical rules, human preferences or style. Ideally, the fitness function should respond or adapt to the system in an explainable manner. It has been argued that in creative EC systems there must be a logical and explainable method for assigning fitness *even if* this fitness assignment is not what a human would choose [13]. Instead of assuming that the human ideal must be the computational ideal in a creative task, they developed a preference function by measuring qualities such as specificity, transivity and reflexivity to determine choice. These were taken as measures of the ordering of the individuals, rather than aspects of the individuals on their own. This function may not agree with what a human may choose but, more importantly, it showed a consistency in agreeing with itself. We developed a cyclical development of the Composing Pony to explore this possibility of creating a fitness measure that responded to the system itself.

This system creates a 'Critic' that can give a numerical output of one of the given melodies and thus be used as the fitness measure for a consequent EC run in creating a new melody. Evolving the Critic enables the creation of one that constitutes a justifiable preference measure, thus avoiding the problem of creating a subjective fitness measure for evolving subsequent music. This compositional system consists of three evolutionary phases:

- The evolution of an initial musical corpus;
- The evolution of a best *Critic* that conforms to the Critic population's preference of melodies;
- The use of this best Critic as the fitness function in evolving a new melody, which then replaces one melody in the original corpus.

The corpus consists of 40 melodies evolved using the Composing Pony as described above. These melodies can be played as each note has a given pitch and duration. For representation in the second phase, each melody is reduced to the number of times each degree of the scale and each note duration is played. Thus each melody is reduced to 18 distinct values—12 for each degree of the scale followed by 6 allowed note durations. These values can then be used with the Critic grammar shown below.

```
<expr> ::= <O><T1><O><T2><O><T3><O><T4>
    <O><T5><O><T6><O><T7><O><T8><O><T9>
    <O><T10><O><T11><O><T12><O><D1><O>
    <D2><O><D4><O><D8><O><D16><O><D32>
<O> ::= <op><scalar>
<op> ::= + | - | *
<scalar> ::= 1 | 2 | 3 | 4 | 5
```

This grammar takes a linear combination of the 18 distinct melodic values and returns a scalar result. Each individual in the (Critic) population thus gives a numerical output for each of the 40 melodies in the corpus. Individually, this output has no meaning for each melody—but it allows the melodies to be ordered numerically. In this system, we attribute the concept of preference to this output. The melodies are thus 'ranked' 1–40 according to this numerical result by each Critic. In this manner, each Critic within the population is afforded its own opinion (i.e. its ranking) as to which melodies it prefers. These rankings are then averaged across all Critics within the population resulting in the averaged ranking among the (Critic) population. This averaged overall ranking of all 40 melodies is taken to be the consensus of the ranking of the melodies among the Critic population. The fitness of each individual Critic is then calculated according to its Kendall-Rank Correlation with this consensus. Selection, mutation and crossover are then performed in a typical EC with this Rank fitness (or preference) measure to evolve

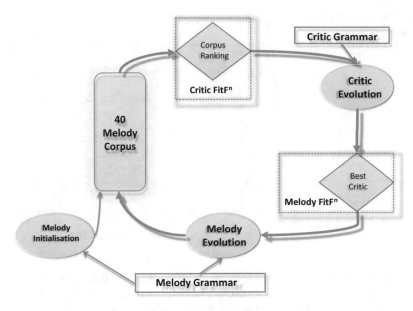

Fig. 2 Flow diagram of the cyclical Critic compositional system

one best Critic. Using this method, Critic individuals that rank melodies similar to the majority obtain better fitness, hence the idea of conforming to the population is encouraged throughout the evolution.

This best Critic outputs a numerical value for any of the melodies with the representation used with the Composing Pony. Thus, this can be incorporated as the fitness function in a new evolutionary run. In this manner, we have created a fitness measure that offers a meaningful and defendable measure of the music but is completely independent from the human designer. Furthermore, the melody created in the final phase can be used to replace one of the melodies in the corpus, thus creating a new Critic and the cycle repeats. In this manner, the system has become a self-adaptive complex system that can continue to run and create new melodies without user intervention. A graphical overview of the entire system is shown in Fig. 2.

Each of the evolutionary phases within the system was run with a population of size 100 over 50 generations using tournament selection of tournament size 2. Again all other parameters were set to those as in the Composing Pony described above. This complete cycle was repeated 40 times, with one melody from the original corpus being replaced by a newly generated melody in each cycle; after 40 cycles the system is running purely on melodies it has created itself. From listening to the melodies created by the system, it must be noted that there is no discernible 'improvement' in the melodies from the initial population to those created after many cycles. The melodies available through SoundCloud display the typical range of runs and chords audible in the earlier Composing Pony melodies. This is to be

Fig. 3 Diversity of melody corpus over 40 complete cycles of the system

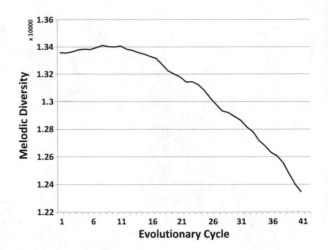

expected—at no point did we instruct the system to improve the melodies or inform it as to what constitutes a good melody. The purpose of this experiment was not to create better melodies but rather to examine a way of encouraging an autonomous system to determine its own preference for one melody over another through self-organisation. Over successive cycles this system becomes subjected to and develops responses on melodies created by itself, hence becoming more self-adaptive as the cycles repeat.

While we cannot expect to hear an expected different in the quality of the individual melodies, we can consider the change in the corpus of melodies as the corpus is replaced by those generated by the system. To do this, the diversity of the melody corpus was monitored as the corpus was re-filled by a newly evolved melody in each cycle. The diversity of the corpus was measured as the sum of the Levenshtein distances between the representation of each pair of melodies. The change in this diversity across 40 full evolutionary cycles is shown in Fig. 3. This shows that for approximately 10 evolutionary cycles, the diversity does not change dramatically from that of the initial corpus, but after 15 cycles, as the corpus is filled by newly evolved melodies there is a steady decrease in this measured diversity. The decrease is small, but nevertheless displays a definite trend. This shows that the process is having a directed effect on the melodies being produced, with newer melodies showing less diversity as they are created by the increasingly self-adaptive system.

This Composing Pony can create musical melodies but the resultant form is limited. Variations of the system has been considered that implement melodies with accompaniment [36], or arrange melody segments according to melodic distance [35] but regardless of the fitness measure used, the resultant melodies are heavily dependent on and limited by the grammar used. We discuss the implications of this in regards to evaluation of the system below in Sect. 5. The second proposed system again uses GE to create music but by developing a different grammar, with a different focus, creates music of a completely different form.

4   Case Study: Evolving Live Code

The second system we propose produces continuous or looped music using the live-coding language ChucK [52]. By the using the on-the-fly command programming capabilities of ChucK, shreds (each written as an individual file) can be added to a ChucK Virtual Machine (VM) by the user at the command line. The ChucK code is created through program synthesis using GE. A series of grammars that generate ChucK code for new shreds are presented. Each of these shreds can then be added or removed to the running VM by the programmer. In contrast to The Composing Pony presented above, this system focusses on representation and production of music, rather than in developing autonomous fitness. The generality of the system is dependent on the grammars used. We first describe creating highly specified files, each for a different instrument before considering generalising the grammars to enable a more powerful system.

4.1   Live Coding

Live coding is a practice where software that creates music (and sometimes visuals) is written and manipulated in real-time as part of a live performance [7]. Typically in a performance, the code is made visible on large screens, thus providing a more transparent experience to the audience. This leads to the possibility of glitches (or all-out crashes) within the software during the performance, the re-working or patching of which is part of the skill and nuance displayed by the composer [10]. While a number of specific coding environments have been developed specifically for live coding music (for e.g Supercollider, PureData, MaxMSP), live coding can be implemented in any computing language. The proposed system is developed using ChucK, a popular, strongly timed live coding programming language [52].

We propose introducing GE to generate live code in real time as a tool to help the performer. Instead of starting from scratch, the performer could run this GEChucK to create a number of initial ChucK files. They can then modify or remove these files as they see fit, saving the ones they like and re-running GE to create more in order to develop and enhance the live performance. It is important to note that this is not an Interactive GE system; the performer is not acting as the fitness function within the GE run but is instead evaluating the results at the end of each run, using the results they like and discarding those they do not wish to use. As such, we consider this to be a *co-creative* system: a system whereby the resultant creativity can be attributed to both performer and algorithm.

4.2 ChucK

ChucK is a strongly typed and strongly timed concurrent audio and multi-media programming language. It is strongly typed, although not statically typed, it is dynamic in that changes to the type system can take place (in a well-defined manner) at runtime. This dynamic aspect forms the basis for on-the-fly programming. It is compiled into virtual instructions which are immediately run on the ChucK VM. ChucK is strongly timed meaning that time is fundamentally embedded into the language—time and duration are native types. The keyword now is reserved to indicate the current logical point in time and time is progressed from now according to durations specified of type dur.

4.3 Instrument Grammars

The initial GEChucK system is based on an adaptation of the on-the-fly programming synchronisation examples provided by the creators of ChucK, Perry Cook and Ge Wang, available at http://chuck.cs.princeton.edu/doc/examples/. This system incorporates individual instrument grammars that can re-create a valid variation of each of the provided .ck files. GE was run independently multiple times, each time using a specific instrument grammar to create the corresponding instrument .ck file. Thus each GE run creates six individuals files. These can then be added or removed as ChucK shreds from the VM by the programmer at the command line.

Six distinct grammars were created, each of which is run with GE to create a distinct instrument that can be added as a ChucK shred. Each grammar begins with a code block to initialise the instrument, followed by a continuous loop.

```
<return> ::= <pre> L <code>
```

This states that the result will be comprised of some pre-code specified in <pre> followed by the body of code <code> and separated by the flag 'L'. For example in the first grammar, which creates the kick drum beat:

```
<pre> ::= .5::second => dur T;
       T - (now % T) => now;
       SndBuf buf => Gain g => dac;
       me.dir() + "data/kick.wav" => buf.read;
       .5 => g.gain;
```

This section of the grammar reads the sound file into the buffer, sets the gain and synchronises the resultant sounds to a period. In this version, this is currently hard-coded through the grammar as there are no non-terminals for GE to choose between. The remainder of the kick drum grammar consists of:

```
<code> ::= <line1> ; <line2> ; <line3> ;
<line1> ::= 0 => buf.pos
<line2> ::= <gain> => buf.gain
<gain> ::= 0.8 | 0.82 | 0.84 | 0.86 | 0.88 | 0.9
<line3> ::= <dur>::T => now
<dur> ::= 0.5 | 1 | 1
```

This grammar returns three lines of code. `<line1>` sets the play position to the beginning. `<line2>` offers a choice for the given gain and `<line3>` allows options for the duration, by advancing time. Note that the options for the `<gain>` are each equally likely, but there is a 2:1 bias towards advancing time by 1 rather than 0.5. Such biases can be introduced to the grammar as a design feature by the programmer. The grammars to create files controlling the snare, snare-hop, hi-hat and open hi-hat are based on variations of the grammar above.

The melodic content within these example files is created using Sin oscillators with a specified scale structure. For example, Grammar5 consists of:

```
<return> ::= <pre> L <code>
<pre> ::= .5::second => dur T;
     T - (now % T) => now;
     SinOsc s => dac;
     .25 => s.gain;
<scale>@=> int scale[];
<scale> ::= [0,2,4,7,9]|[1,3,8,9,11]|[0,1,2,3,4]|[4,5,7,10,11]

<code> ::= <line1> ; <line2> ; <line3> ;
<line1> ::= scale[Math.random2(0,4)] => float freq
<line2> ::= Std.mtof(21.0 + (Math.random2(0,3)*12 + freq))
     => s.freq
<line3> ::= <dur>::T => now
<dur> ::= 0.25 | 0.5
```

The `<scale>` options in such a grammar dictates the degrees of the scale that are playable by the evolved instrument. A Sin oscillator based on multiples of [0,2,4,7,9] for instance would be pleasantly harmonic, whereas [0,1,2,3,4] would lead to more dissident intervals created by the instrument.

These grammars are highly specified and quite limited. Each grammar creates a ChucK file of a specific instrument, but the choices offered within the grammar are few. While this may result in very little variation within the resultant phenotypes, it does ensure that the code generated is valid and error free. Subsequently, all individuals produce valid ChucK code. Ideally, we would like to evolve these according to which creates the 'best' music. But, as we discovered in developing The Composing Pony above, deciding which is the 'best' is a very complicated process. Furthermore, immediately generating a perfect loop is not the purpose of Live-coding. Live-coding is an interactive process, where the performer performs edits in a live environment. Hence we use the GEChucK system with a random fitness measure. Each final population will always result in valid code, but the performer will curate and modify the individuals they like. This initial system will create six .ck files every time the GE is run—four percussive and two melodic files. The performer can then play these files and keep or edit the ones they like in real time as is typical in a live-coding environment. The system can be re-run by the performer multiple times as they manage and edit their live performance. A video demonstration of the code being run can be found at https://youtu.be/GfFqIzYtDe8.

4.4   Generalised Grammar

To create a more powerful system, the grammars should be able to generalise to create more than one specific instrument. The level of generalisation would depend on the goals of the given run. The percussive grammar shown above could be easily amended to include a choice of the drum sound rather than hard-coding a specific sound. For instance:

```
me.dir() + <filename> => buf.read;
<filename> ::= "data/kick.wav"|"data/snare.wav"|"data/hhat.wav"
```

Similarly, there could be more options for the type of oscillators offered in the melodic grammars, instead of or along with the choices in the degree of scales. The following offers the possibility of either a sine, triangle or square wave oscillators:

```
<OscType> s => dac;
<OscType> ::= SinOsc | TriOsc | SqrOsc
```

The durations can also be manipulated in the grammars through the progression of time, if this is desired. Selecting a kick sound over a hi-hat, at least in a realistic setting, would most likely require a different duration between hits (the hi-hat being struck more rapidly that the kick drum). Such a relationship could be paired up within the grammar, but restrictions such as this limit the output of the system to what is predictable rather than taking advantage of the computational and explorative nature of the approach. The grammars will get more complex as more options for generators or sounds files are offered that can be played by the resultant code. As the grammars increase in complexity it is necessary to decide what level of constraint should be enforced on the possibilities of what is to be produced. Should the music be realistically playable or not constrained to such limits? Should the grammars be specific to certain instruments, enabling the user to intentionally choose what type of instrument they wish to hear, or should they be more general to result in a more ad-hoc, experimental performance? Such questions need to be addressed to design a meaningful, coherent system with which the end user would want to perform.

ChucK is a powerful language that can achieve much more variety than these instrument grammars can produce. As a programming language it offers all the typical operators, types and control structures you would expect from any high-level language. ChucK is object-oriented with a number of built in classes and the ability to create custom classes of specific types. Furthermore ChucK is able to run many processes or functions concurrently. A ChucKian process is called a *shred*. Creating and adding a new shred to the VM is called *sporking*. As ChucK is strongly-timed, functions or shreds can be called or sporked at any given time making parallel processes easy to manage. ChucK also has the capability to undertake many types of audio processing such as fourier analysis, filters and manipulating unit generators as well as dealing with MIDI or OSC events. Creating one BNF grammar that could utilise all of the functionality of ChucK would be a huge undertaking. Any one grammar could not automatically generate phenotypes that result in valid ChucK code. Using GE to generalise to explore the capabilities of ChucK would require a much more formalised method of measuring fitness.

4.5 Fitness Measure

This system is currently implemented with a random fitness measure. Random fitness is an alien concept to many EC researchers as it appears that there is no goal; a random fitness leads to no direction within the search. However, in creative applications such as GenDash [53] these have be used quite successfully. Such methods take advantage of the exploratory aspects of EC. Undirected search can explore the entire search space. However, this can only be employed when the space is highly constrained—so much so that any result is at least valid and arguably as useful as any other individual in the population. This can be used with the above system as the grammar only generates valid code, but it is undesirable as no directed search and hence no true evolution is taking place, rather it is akin to genetic drift. The only evaluation is taking place by the programmer after evolution has occurred. In effect, an interactive fitness measuring element (the human participant) of the experiment has been created but, rather than being used for search, instead performs evaluation between evolutionary runs. This is useful as an application to a live-coder; instead of starting from scratch the performer has a number of pre-made code snippets to start with and edit. But as an EC researcher, it feels as though we are not taking advantage of the power of the algorithm.

To enable more powerful evolution, the system should incorporate some meaningful measure of fitness. As this system creates code that creates music there are two fundamental aspects that may be measured: the code or the music. To develop an autonomous creative system, the system should ideally measure some aspect of the music created, but as has been discussed this is non-trivial. How could a function measure the fitness of a given loop? As the capabilities of ChucK are so broad, must we design grammars for specific instrument types and pair them with purpose created fitness measures, such as drum grammars with drum fitness functions and Sin generator grammars with Sin generator fitness function? Such a system may appear to make sense but inevitably this would lead to a deterministic system where the 'best' percussion and melodic content is pre-decided leaving no justifiable need for evolution. This raises the issue of exploration versus exploitation in computationally creative systems: in a complex system (such as GE combined with the full capabilities of ChucK) we must limit the space to have control and yet include enough freedom of exploration to allow the emergence of creativity. Combining individual grammars and fitness measures is unlikely to lead to such a balance.

Instead, in the next phase of this system, we propose to design a fitness measure that encourages well-written, meaningful code. EC has a long history of use for program synthesis and is becoming an increasingly popular approach in Software Engineering [22]. By developing fitness measures that are specifically designed to optimise ChucK code, GE would perform more meaningful evolution in optimising the code to offer the user. A variety of grammars would be developed so that the user could choose the function of the code they require—be it a unit generator, percussive element or audio effect—which would be functional from the start but which they could amend in a live environment to complement their performance. Such a system would be beneficial both to novices in ChucK who desire correctly compiled code and to more experienced users who wish to enhance the live-coding experience.

5 Evaluation

The difficulty in defining creativity naturally leads to a resultant difficulty in evaluating whether or not a computational system is creative. This has led to a number of authors doing self evaluation, minimal evaluation or no evaluation on their systems. The lack of evaluation in CC systems has been noted throughout the development of the field [3, 8, 25] and has led to much debate in the CC community as to how to evaluate the creativity of a system. The practice of evaluating creativity in terms of human opinion is nearly always assumed but rarely justified, which could arguably lead to limitations in the development of such systems [33]. Although some evaluation systems have been developed and their use is encouraged [26], there is still an argument that any system deemed to be creative should show intent and hence must have some level of self-awareness. Such systems are considered to be meta-creative and to possess creative autonomy [24]. Only through the verification of creative autonomy can it be stated that creativity is displayed by the system rather than via an extension of the programmers or users own personal creativity. Of course it is important to note that the concept of intent is the most philosophical aspect of creativity and there remains much argument that such a concept could never be properly achieved, or verified, in any real sense by a machine or computer program [46, 47].

An attempt to formalise a method of testing for creativity in a computer has been developed in the form of the Lovelace Test (LT) [6]. The test is named after Ada

Lovelace who in the 1840s showed remarkable foresight into the possibilities of the newly invented analytical machine. Lovelace posed that the machine could be used, not just for mere numerical calculations, but in time would be able to represent music and art. She further posed that it could be used in the study of creativity, but maintained that such machines would never be able to be truly creative as they were incapable of originating anything. Her arguments have been formalised into the Lovelace Questions [4]:

- Can computational ideas help us understand human creativity?
- Can computers ever do things that appear creative?
- Can computers ever recognise creativity?
- Can computers ever *really* be creative?

It is the fourth question above that remains the most interesting and controversial in relation to computers and creativity. The LT has been created as a method to test for an answer to this question. This test involves an artificial agent A, its output o and its human architect H. Simply put, the test is passed if H cannot explain how A produced o. While on the surface the test may seem easy to pass, it actually poses the problem of intent as we have discussed above. The test does not state that the programmer cannot merely *predict* the results—most computational systems would pass that—but that they cannot explain how the machine produced its results. Thus the machine must have developed its own reasoning for its actions without the programmer's knowledge.

In practice there can be logistical problems in creating creative systems that focus on intent. Later experiments conducted with the Composing Pony, such as the self-adaptive system described in Sect. 3 and those described in [35] are based on developing self-adaptive systems that have minimal influence from the programmer, in an effort to prioritise intent over quality of the produced output. Rather unsurprisingly, these systems do not produce traditionally impressive results from a human listener perspective. From listening to final generation melodies compared to those in the first generation, there is not necessarily an audible improvement—indeed why should there be? The system is not given any requirements to make 'good' music. Because of this however, the artefacts produced by such systems can be underwhelming, making it more difficult to convince the readers, the audience or even peers of their intrinsic merit. To combat this, evaluation of a creative system should always consider the purpose of the system and the workings within the system, rather than being solely based on the artefacts created.

5.1 Identifying the 'Why?'

The above argument amplifies why it is imperative for researchers to determine exactly what the purpose of any algorithmic compositional systems they are developing is from the outset. If a system generates music, the most natural way to investigate this system is in listening to the generated music. If, as the creator of this system, generating generically pleasing music is not your primary aim, it is important to state and address this. As CC evaluation is so problematic, the responsibility of explaining the functions and merits of the given system lies entirely with the programmer or creator of that system. The two systems presented in this chapter, although both GE music generation systems, result in completely different music, but also have very different purposes and goals in what they can achieve.

The Composing Pony The main purpose of The Composing Pony is to investigate self-adaptive fitness in a move towards complete creative autonomy. Listening to the resultant melodies is interesting, and we invite the reader to do so[1] but evaluating the system on the perceived merit of these melodies does not make sense. Arguably, the music could be improved by developing different grammars that would conform to a given style, either by genre or by composer, but such a change would be a result of the creativity of the programmer *not* the system. The strength of this system lies in the autonomy obtained from the self-adaptive fitness measure. This system itself is unable to create melodies that improve (in any human subjective way) from one generation to the next. It simply evolves towards a more stable version of its own autonomous 'opinion'.

GEChuck The purpose of GEChucK is to augment and complement the users experience in Live-coding with ChucK. While this should make the produced output music more interesting, meaningful and suitable for aural evaluation, we must remember that this is a co-creative system. Any recognised creativity from the output should be as much, if not more attributed to the performer as to the system. Ideally this system should be evaluated by users rather than by the audience. Even though the creativity is not as autonomous in such a system, developing a tool to augment a live-coding performance to assist the performer in such a way is clearly a worthwhile study into co-creativity. Typically, audience members at live-coding events are there as much to appreciate the code as the music, so the evolutionary generation of the initial code would hold great appeal to such a crowd. Music generation systems in particular have been recognised as falling somewhere on a scale between mere generation and creativity. Systems that achieve mere generation have been defended by the recognition that much music innovation has been achieved in Musical Metacreation (MuMe) from generative systems focussed on human-interactive co-creativity [18]. Any music generation system lies somewhere on a spectrum between pure generation (the artefact is most important) and pure computational creativity (the behaviour is most important). Meaningful and relevant evaluation of any system is dependent on where the system lies within such a spectrum.

Stating that the end result is not at all relevant in a music generation system is highly controversial, and has a tendency to unnerve people. Such a statement raises the question that if the music is not written for human enjoyment then who is the music *for*? We are not stating that systems such as the Composing Pony are

---

[1]https://soundcloud.com/user-529879178/sets/composingponymelodies.

composing music for themselves or any future autonomous agent to enjoy. The point we need to emphasise is that a focus on who the music is written for is again a pure judgement of the final artefact produced—rather than on the behaviour of the agent that created this music. We would suggest that the question is not to ask who the music is for but to completely disregard this notion of 'for' in an attempt to approach a more general evaluation of creativity.

6 Conclusion

We have presented a study on applying GE to creativity, both from a theoretical aspect and by considering two implemented systems. One of the most important findings from this chapter is that in planning any GE creative experiment, or indeed any computationally creative experiment, the level of creativity obtainable from a system is dependent on the manner in which the system operates and the specific purpose for which it was created. We presented two music compositional systems based on GE, the Composing Pony and GEChucK. The development of The Composing Pony was focussed on creating a system that could result in autonomous creativity. The autonomy was approached through the development of a self-referential fitness measure that resulted in a complex adaptive system with no influence from the programmer or user once the system had started. This first system had a focus on a high level of autonomous creativity. The second system, GEChucK, had a more user-based co-creative approach to music generation. In developing grammars to produce valid ChucK code, we described how this system could be used in a live-coding environment to augment the coding experience for both the user and audience.

We have discussed the application of GE to musical creativity, but creativity is not limited to the musical, or any specifically aesthetic, domain. Many of the original studies in creativity discuss mathematical and scientific examples of creative thinking. Of the three types of creativity described in Sect. 2—combinational, explorational and transformational—transformational creativity is said to result in the highest level of creativity [4, 44]. Boden has stated that the best examples of, or future possibilities for, achieving transformational creativity involve using evolutionary techniques [5]. We propose that the grammars employed in applying GE can enhance that possibility. The development and use of specific grammars in GE offer the potential to represent and examine problems in any given domain. Transformational creativity does, however, require more than a mere mapping that has been pre-defined by the programmer. Only if the system displays a true transformation from one concept to another can it be regarded as creative. Nevertheless, such grammars could be employed in exploring and representing numerous creative tasks and problems. The combination of appropriate grammars, the exploration of evolutionary search and the development of self-adaptive fitness measures are promising options in progressing towards an understanding and emergence of true computational creativity.

Acknowledgements This work is part of the App'Ed (Applications of Evolutionary Design) project funded by Science Foundation Ireland under grant 13/IA/1850.

References

1. J. Biles, GenJam: a genetic algorithm for generating jazz solos, in *Proceedings of the International Computer Music Conference* (International Computer Music Association, San Francisco, 1994), pp. 131–131
2. J.A. Biles, Straight-ahead jazz with GenJam: a quick demonstration, in *MUME 2013 Workshop* (2013)
3. M.A. Boden, Creativity and artificial intelligence. Artif. Intell. **103**(1), 347–356 (1998)
4. M.A. Boden, *The Creative Mind: Myths and Mechanisms* (Psychology Press, London, 2004)
5. M.A. Boden, Computer models of creativity. AI Mag. **30**(3), 23 (2009)
6. S. Bringsjord, P. Bello, D. Ferrucci, Creativity, the turing test, and the (better) lovelace test, in *The Turing Test* (Springer, Berlin, 2003), pp. 215–239
7. A.R. Brown, A. Sorensen, Interacting with generative music through live coding. Contemp. Music. Rev. **28**(1), 17–29 (2009)
8. A. Cardoso, T. Veale, G.A. Wiggins, Converging on the divergent: the history (and future) of the international joint workshops in computational creativity. AI Mag. **30**(3), 15 (2009)
9. M.A. Castellano, J.J. Bharucha, C.L. Krumhansl, Tonal hierarchies in the music of north india. J. Exp. Psychol. Gen. **113**(3), 394 (1984)
10. N. Collins, A. McLean, J. Rohrhuber, A. Ward, Live coding in laptop performance. Organised Sound **8**(3), 321 (2003)
11. F. Colombo, A. Seeholzer, W. Gerstner, Deep artificial composer: a creative neural network model for automated melody generation, in *International Conference on Evolutionary and Biologically Inspired Music and Art* (Springer, Berlin, 2017), pp. 81–96
12. S. Colton, G.A. Wiggins, et al., Computational creativity: the final frontier? in *Proceedings of the 20th European Conference on Artificial Intelligence ECAI'12*, vol. 12 (2012), pp. 21–26
13. M. Cook, S. Colton, Generating code for expressing simple preferences: moving on from hardcoding and randomness, in *Proceedings of the Sixth International Conference on Computational Creativity* (2015), p. 8
14. P. Dahlstedt, Autonomous evolution of complete piano pieces and performances, in *Proceedings of Music AL Workshop*. Citeseer (2007)
15. A.R. de Freitas, F.G. Guimaraes, R.V. Barbosa, Ideas in automatic evaluation methods for melodies in algorithmic composition, in *Sound and Music Computing Conference* (2012)
16. A.O. de la Puente, R.S. Alfonso, M.A. Moreno, Automatic composition of music by means of grammatical evolution, in *ACM SIGAPL APL Quote Quad*, vol. 32 (ACM, New York, 2002), pp. 148–155
17. A. Eigenfeldt, P. Pasquier, Populations of populations: composing with multiple evolutionary algorithms, in *Evolutionary and Biologically Inspired Music, Sound, Art and Design* (Springer, Berlin, 2012), pp. 72–83
18. A. Eigenfeldt, O. Bown, A.R. Brown, T. Gifford, Flexible generation of musical form: beyond mere generation, in *Proceedings of the Seventh International Conference on Computational Creativity* (2016)
19. M. Fenton, C. McNally, J. Byrne, E. Hemberg, J. McDermott, M. O'Neill, Automatic innovative truss design using grammatical evolution. Autom. Constr. **39**, 59–69 (2014)
20. J.D. Fernández, F. Vico, AI methods in algorithmic composition: a comprehensive survey. J. Artif. Intell. Res. **48**, 513–582 (2013)
21. C. Guckelsberger, C. Salge, S. Colton, Addressing the "why?" in computational creativity: a non-anthropocentric, minimal model of intentional creative agency, in *Proceedings of the 8th International Conference on Computational Creativity, Atlanta* (2017)

22. M. Harman, S.A. Mansouri, Y. Zhang, Search-based software engineering: trends, techniques and applications. ACM Comput. Surv. **45**(1), 11 (2012)
23. S. Hickinbotham, S. Stepney, Augmenting live coding with evolved patterns, in *International Conference on Evolutionary and Biologically Inspired Music and Art* (Springer, Berlin, 2016), pp. 31–46
24. K.E. Jennings, Developing creativity: artificial barriers in artificial intelligence. Mind. Mach. **20**(4), 489–501 (2010)
25. A. Jordanous, Evaluating evaluation: assessing progress in computational creativity research, in *Proceedings of the 2nd International Conference on Computational Creativity (ICCC-11), Mexico City, Mexico* (2011)
26. A. Jordanous, A standardised procedure for evaluating creative systems: computational creativity evaluation based on what it is to be creative. Cogn. Comput. **4**(3), 246–279 (2012)
27. A. Jordanous, B. Keller, Modelling creativity: identifying key components through a corpus-based approach. PloS one **11**(10), e0162959 (2016)
28. R. Kicinger, T. Arciszewski, K. De Jong, Evolutionary computation and structural design: a survey of the state-of-the-art. Comput. Struct. **83**(23), 1943–1978 (2005)
29. C.L. Krumhansl, Tonality induction: a statistical approach applied cross-culturally. Music. Percept. **17**(4), 461–479 (2000)
30. C.L. Krumhansl, L.L. Cuddy, A theory of tonal hierarchies in music, in *Music Perception* (Springer, Berlin, 2010), pp. 51–87
31. F. Lerdahl, R. Jackendoff, *A Generative Theory of Tonal Music* (MIT Press, Cambridge, 1985)
32. M. Lewis, Evolutionary visual art and design, in *The Art of Artificial Evolution* (Springer, Berlin, 2008), pp. 3–37
33. R. Loughran, M. O'Neill, Generative music evaluation: why do we limit to 'human'? in *Computer Simulation of Musical Creativity (CSMC). Huddersfield, UK* (2016)
34. R. Loughran, M. O'Neill, Application domains considered in computational creativity, in *Proceedings of the 8th International Conference on Computational Creativity, Atlanta* (2017)
35. R. Loughran, M. O'Neill, Clustering agents for the evolution of autonomous musical fitness, in *Evolutionary and Biologically Inspired Music, Sound, Art and Design* (Springer, Berlin, 2017)
36. R. Loughran, J. McDermott, M. O'Neill, Grammatical evolution with zipf's law based fitness for melodic composition, in *Sound and Music Computing Conference, Maynooth* (2015)
37. N. Lourenço, F. Assunção, C. Maçãs, P. Machado, Evofashion: customising fashion through evolution, in *International Conference on Evolutionary and Biologically Inspired Music and Art* (Springer, Berlin, 2017), pp. 176–189
38. J. McCormack, Grammar based music composition. Complex Syst. **96**, 321–336 (1996)
39. E.R. Miranda, J. Al Biles, *Evolutionary Computer Music* (Springer, Berlin, 2007)
40. E. Munoz, J. Cadenas, Y.S. Ong, G. Acampora, Memetic music composition. IEEE Trans. Evol. Comput. **20**(1), 1–15 (2016)
41. H.G. Oliveira, Poetryme: a versatile platform for poetry generation. Comput. Creat. Concept Invent. Gen. Intell. **6**(1), 21 (2012)
42. F. Pachet, The continuator: musical interaction with style. J. N. Music Res. **32**(3), 333–341 (2003)
43. J. Reddin, J. McDermott, M. O'Neill, Elevated pitch: automated grammatical evolution of short compositions, in *Applications of Evolutionary Computing* (Springer, Berlin, 2009), pp. 579–584
44. G. Ritchie, The transformational creativity hypothesis. N. Gener. Comput. **24**(3), 241–266 (2006)
45. M. Scirea, J. Togelius, P. Eklund, S. Risi, Metacompose: a compositional evolutionary music composer, in *International Conference on Evolutionary and Biologically Inspired Music and Art* (Springer, Berlin, 2016), pp. 202–217
46. J.R. Searle, Minds, brains, and programs. Behav. Brain Sci. **3**(3), 417–424 (1980)
47. J.R. Searle, Is the brain a digital computer? The American Philosophical Association Centennial Series (2013), pp. 691–710

48. J. Shao, J. McDermott, M. O'Neill, A. Brabazon, Jive: a generative, interactive, virtual, evolutionary music system, in *Applications of Evolutionary Computation* (Springer, Berlin, 2010), pp. 341–350
49. D. Temperley, E.W. Marvin, Pitch-class distribution and the identification of key. Music. Percept. **25**, 193–212 (2008)
50. D. Ventura, Mere generation: essential barometer or dated concept, in *Proceedings of the Seventh International Conference on Computational Creativity, ICCC* (2016)
51. D. Ventura, How to build a CC system, in *Proceedings of the 8th International Conference on Computational Creativity, Atlanta* (2017)
52. G. Wang, P.R. Cook, et al., Chuck: a concurrent, on-the-fly, audio programming language, in *Proceedings of the 2003 International Computer Music Conference ICMC* (2003)
53. R. Waschka II, Composing with genetic algorithms: GenDash, in *Evolutionary Computer Music* (Springer, Berlin, 2007), pp. 117–136
54. G.A. Wiggins, D. Müllensiefen, M.T. Pearce, On the non-existence of music: why music theory is a figment of the imagination. Music. Sci. **14**(1 suppl), 231–255 (2010)

Identification of Models for Glucose Blood Values in Diabetics by Grammatical Evolution

J. Ignacio Hidalgo, J. Manuel Colmenar, J. Manuel Velasco,
Gabriel Kronberger, Stephan M. Winkler, Oscar Garnica,
and Juan Lanchares

Abstract One the most relevant application areas of artificial intelligence and machine learning in general is medical research. We here focus on research dedicated to diabetes, a disease that affects a high percentage of the population worldwide and that is an increasing threat due to the advance of the sedentary life in the big cities. Most recent studies estimate that it affects about more than 410 million people in the world. In this chapter we discuss a set of techniques based on GE to obtain mathematical models of the evolution of blood glucose along the time. These models help diabetic patients to improve the control of blood sugar levels and thus, improve their quality of life. We summarize some recent works on data preprocessing and design of grammars that have proven to be valuable in the identification of prediction models for type 1 diabetics. Furthermore, we explain the data augmentation method which is used to sample new data sets.

1 Introduction

Diabetes is a group of metabolic diseases where blood glucose levels (also known as blood sugar) are higher than usual values. This is caused by either a defect in the secretion, or in the action of insulin, which is essential for the control of blood glucose levels.

J. I. Hidalgo (✉) · J. M. Velasco · O. Garnica · J. Lanchares
Adaptive and Bioinspired System Group, Universidad Complutense de Madrid, Madrid, Spain
e-mail: absys@ucm.es

J. M. Colmenar
Universidad Rey Juan Carlos, Móstoles, Spain
e-mail: josemanuel.colmenar@urjc.es

G. Kronberger · S. M. Winkler
University of Applied Sciences Upper Austria, Heuristic and Evolutionary Algorithms
Laboratory, Hagenberg, Austria
e-mail: Gabriel.Kronberger@fh-hagenberg.at; Stephan.Winkler@fh-hagenberg.at

© Springer International Publishing AG, part of Springer Nature 2018   367
C. Ryan et al. (eds.), *Handbook of Grammatical Evolution*,
https://doi.org/10.1007/978-3-319-78717-6_15

We distinguish the following three main types of diabetes[1]:

- **Type 1 diabetes** (T1DM[2]): It is an autoimmune disease and is caused by the immune system mistakenly attacking healthy insulin producers cells (β cells). The consequence of this attack is a chronic and permanent inability of the pancreas to generate insulin. Insulin is a hormone that facilitates the access of glucose into the cells of the human body. T1DM usually manifests in early childhood and the patient must inject synthetic insulin daily, usually in various doses and with meals.
- **Type 2 diabetes** (T2DM): with this type of diabetes, the body does not produce enough insulin or does not properly use the insulin it produces. People with type 2 diabetes often have to take pills or be treated with insulin. Type 2 diabetes is the most common form of diabetes (accounting for approximately 90% of diabetics) and usually occurs in higher ages. In early stages of the evolution of the illness it can be easily controlled by healthy eating and exercise practices.
- **Gestational diabetes** (GD): this type of diabetes occurs in some women during pregnancy. It increases the risk of developing another type of diabetes for life, especially type 2 diabetes. It also increases the risk of the child of becoming overweighted and developing diabetes. It is very common in overweight pregnant and in those who are late mothers. It can also be controlled with good dietary habits, but sometimes the injection of exogenous insulin is needed during pregnancy.

Diabetes is a serious illness that requires close monitoring. Except for rare occasions, having high sugar during fasting phases indicates that the patient is chronically ill. Anyone with diabetes should eat healthy foods, control their weight and do physical activity every day. In short, all diabetics must maintain blood glucose within a range that is usually between 70 and 180 mg/dl [1].

The good news is that it has been shown that a strict glycemic control reduces complications, improves performance and mitigates medical costs. Glucose level control is a demanding and difficult task both for patients and their families. To keep good levels of blood glucose, the patient must have some capacity of prognosis to know the level of glucose he/she would have after ingesting a certain amount of food or injecting with a quantity of a insulin of a certain kind. The main objective is to avoid not only long periods of hyperglycemia (glucose levels > 180 mg/dl), but also episodes of severe hypoglycemia (glucose levels < 40 mg/dl), that can lead to death [2].

One of the reasons why it is difficult to control blood glucose level is the lack of a general model of response to both insulin and other variables, due to the particularities of each patient. Models published in the literature apply classical

---

[1] There are other types of diabetes with lower incidence such as problems caused by genetic defects affecting insulin action, induced by drugs, or other syndromes.

[2] T1DM stands for Type 1 Diabetes Mellitus, from Latin *mel* ("honey").

modeling techniques, resulting in linear equations, defined profiles, or models with a limited set of inputs.

In this chapter we describe an ensemble of novel techniques that involves obtaining a set of patient models using grammatical evolution (GE), combined with data preprocessing and other techniques. The main objective of this research is to obtain models to predict future values of glucose for a given patient as a function of past values of glucose, insulin and ingestions and future values of insulin and food. One of the best known applications of genetic programming (GP) is symbolic regression, and the application of one of its variants, GE, allows us to obtain models that incorporate non-linear terms [3]. This is the first approach we describe in this chapter. We show the application of GE to find a custom regression model that describes and predicts the blood glucose level in a patient on the basis of previous glucose levels, ingested carbohydrates and injected insulin. Subsequently we explain how to increase the quality of the input data by means of data augmentation.

Section 2 explains glucose control strategies. In Sect. 3 we explain the acquisition and the preprocessing of the data we have used. In Sect. 4 we summarize the technique presented at [4] for getting more diversity in the data, in Sect. 5 we explain the motivation of using GE for this complex problem. We also explain the combination of the models in Sect. 4. Finally we present results in Sect. 6 and draw conclusions in Sect. 7.

2 Glucose models

Although there are numerous different glucose control strategies, we can differentiate among the following three main categories:

- Traditional therapies are based on *manual calculation and administration of the insulin protocol* [5]. The decisions regarding the administration of insulin is made entirely by the patient following their own experience and the indications of the medical staff. They need to measure glucose levels and take decisions on the administration of the multiple insulin manual injections. If the glucose levels are low, due to excessive exercise or because a wrong administration of insulin, patients need to eat some sugar. Sometimes it is necessary to inject additional doses of insulin to correct anomalous high values of glucose. All these steps should be done by measuring the glucose with a glucometer, which implies painful punctures, usually in the fingers. Continuous glucose monitoring systems (CGMS) are very valuable here because they measure the value of glucose reducing the number of punctures.
- *Insulin pump* therapies substitute manual injections by the use of continuous subcutaneous insulin infusion systems (CSIIS), also known as insulin pumps [6]. Sometimes the use of CSIIS is combined with a CGMS, which helps in automating some decisions such as stopping the pump in dangerous situations. The process of deciding the amount of insulin before the meals is done in

the same way as in the traditional therapies. As this is a supervised process, the patient still needs to be alert and to detect anomalous glucose situations, stopping the infusion of insulin or correcting values through the infusion of glucagon (the hormone that counteracts insulin by raising the glucose levels), insulin, or eating.

- The use of an *artificial pancreas* (AP) will be the ideal solution [7]. Unlike other artificial organs, an AP is a less invasive solution. Its main components are a CGMS, a set of glucose control algorithms to calculate the amount of insulin needed, and a CSIIS. An AP can also include bihormonal (insulin/glucagon) infusion pumps. There have been significant advances in the development of the AP, still the independence of the patients with AP is not completely safe at this stage of research because the predictions are not accurate enough for hours after intakes.

What is common to all the strategies is that blood glucose control in T1DM patients requires the prognosis, i.e. estimation of future glucose values on the basis (at least) of the amount of food intakes and/or the injection of insulin and/or glucagon. The actual level of glucose in the patient's blood depends on several factors, some of them intrinsic to its own organism functions. Unfortunately, data collection is not an easy task, and there is a high number of important variables that, although influencing the problem, can not be measured directly and non-invasively. For this reason we formulate the problem in a practical way and limit the variables that can appear in the expression of the model to those that can be directly and easily measured.

We will try to find a model of future values of blood glucose based on data we can collect such as previous glucose, carbohydrates, and insulin values and interpret this as a symbolic regression (SR) problem. SR tries to obtain a mathematical expression that explains one or a set of target variables as a white-box function of input variables. The data used in this chapter was collected from real patients using a continuous glucose monitoring system (CGMS) during 12 days at a hospital in Spain.[3] We use observations taken every 15 min, up to 1152 measurements for each patient; the records of the estimated carbohydrate units ingested and the injected insulin are also available.

Thus, for each measurement we have a set of four values (time, glucose, carbohydrates, insulin). It is important to note that values of carbohydrates (CH) are estimated by the patients, who were trained previously. The values of the insulin are recorded (and not estimated), and the measure of the glucose is made by an electronic system with a normal distributed error (5% absolute error on average). Table 1 shows a reduced version of our data set.

Our goal is to develop predictions for four time windows, namely for 30, 60, 90 and 120 min ahead. For example, for the 30 min horizon we need to obtain the following model:

---

[3]On June 6, 2012, the Clinical Research Ethics Committee of the Hospital of Alcalá de Henares (Spain) authorized the use of the data collected, provided that the privacy of the data is ensured and the informed consent of patients is made.

Table 1 Portion of a dataset for a patient

ID	Day	Hour	Type	G_{Sensor}	$\cdots$	CH	INS
$\cdots$	$\cdots$	$\cdots$	$\cdots$	$\cdots$	$\cdots$	$\cdots$	$\cdots$
36817	2016/03/31	15:43	0	61			
36818	2016/03/31	15:58	0	61			
36819	2016/03/31	16:13	0	71			
36820	2016/03/31	16:28	0	80			
36821	2016/03/31	16:43	0	83			
36822	2016/03/31	16:58	0	83			
36823	2016/03/31	17:23	4			1.0	
36823	2016/03/31	17:23	5				0.5
37035	2016/03/31	17:14	0	75			
37036	2016/03/31	17:29	0	64			
37902	2016/04/01	15:13	4			1.0	
37902	2016/04/01	15:13	5				1.0
38083	2016/04/01	15:09	0	122			
38084	2016/04/01	15:24	0	115			
38085	2016/04/01	15:39	0	110			
$\cdots$	$\cdots$	$\cdots$	$\cdots$	$\cdots$	$\cdots$	$\cdots$	$\cdots$

For each sample we have an identifier (ID), Day and Hour of the event and TYPE of the variable (0=Glucose,4=Carbohydrates, 5=Insulin). Glucose measured by the sensor (G_{Sensor}) is given as mg/dl, the carbohydrates as units (CH, $10\,\text{g} = 1$ unit), and insulin as units (INS). There is also information about errors and notes which are not relevant for the model and here represented by dots

$$\hat{G}_{t+30} = f_{t+30}(\{G_{t+i} : i \in (-240\ldots0)\}, \tag{1}$$

$$\{I_{t+j} : j \in (-240\ldots+30)\}, \{C_{t+k} : k \in (-240\ldots+30)\})$$

where time offsets are given in minutes, and

- G is the time series of measured blood glucose concentration values;
- $\hat{G}_{t+30}$ is blood glucose predicted for time t+30 min;
- $\{G_{t+i} : i \in (-240\ldots0)\}$ are glucose values registered from up to 4 h before the prediction is made;
- C is the amount of carbohydrate inputs as estimated by the patients;
- $\{C_{t+k} : k \in (-240\ldots0)\}$ are carbohydrates values estimated by the patient and registered up to 4 h before;
- $\{C_{t+k} : k \in (1\ldots+30)\}$ are carbohydrates values planned for the following 30 min;
- I is the time series of insulin inputs (pump and bolus);
- $\{I_{t+j} : j \in (-240\ldots0)\}$ are insulin values registered up to 4 h before;
- $\{I_{t+j} : j \in (1\ldots+30)\}$ are insulin values planned for the following 30 min.

Following the same notation we also forecast blood glucose $\hat{G}$ up to 120 min ahead:

$$\hat{G}_{t+60} = f_{t+60}(\{G_{t+i} : i \in (-240\ldots 0)\}, \tag{2}$$
$$\{I_{t+j} : j \in (-240\ldots +60)\}, \{C_{t+k} : k \in (-240\ldots +60)\})$$

$$\hat{G}_{t+90} = f_{t+90}(\{G_{t+i} : i \in (-240\ldots 0)\}, \tag{3}$$
$$\{I_{t+j} : j \in (-240\ldots +90)\}, \{C_{t+k} : k \in (-240\ldots +90)\})$$

$$\hat{G}_{t+120} = f_{t+120}(\{G_{t+i} : i \in (-240\ldots 0)\}, \tag{4}$$
$$\{I_{t+j} : j \in (-240\ldots +120)\}, \{C_{t+k} : k \in (-240\ldots +120)\})$$

where $\hat{G}_{t+60}$, $\hat{G}_{t+90}$ and $\hat{G}_{t+120}$ are blood glucose predicted for 60, 90 and 120 min. Again, at each time point t data from up to 4 h before are available for prediction. To generate the four prediction models f_{t+30}, f_{t+60}, f_{t+90}, f_{t+120} we used enhanced variants of GE for evolving models as explained in the following sections.

3 Modeling Glycemia by Grammatical Evolution with Data Preprocessing

Figure 1 shows a grammar we have applied for searching a representation of the relation between the glucose in 30 min (G_{t+30}) and the available input variables. Using this grammar, model expressions are formed as combinations of input variables, mathematical operators $\{+, -, *, /\}$ and functions exp, sin, cos and log. As in previous works [8–10], the first set of grammars is used to direct the search introducing some knowledge on it. Thus, the start symbol is always transformed into an expression in the form of:

```
<expr> ::= <gl> + <ch> - <ins>
```

which indicates that the final expression *(phenotype)* is a combination of glucose variables, `<gl>`, with carbohydrates variables, `<ch>`, that have a positive impact, and insulin variables, `<ins>`, that have a negative impact. The grammar supports the idea that meals (carbohydrates) always increase the glucose value, while insulin always reduce the glucose values.

We have implemented the GE process in Java using the ABSys JECO library [11] using compilable phenotypes to speed up the evaluation of individuals [12]. Variables `xi` correspond to the pre-processed input data, as explained in [3].

```
# Model expression
<func> ::= <expr>

<expr> ::= (<gl> + <ch> - <ins>)

# Glucose
<gl> ::= <preop> (<gl>) | <vargl> | <gl> <op> <gl> |
         (-1)*(<gl>)
<vargl> ::= x2|x3|x4|x5|x6|x7|x8

# CH
<ch> ::= <preop> (<ch>) | <varch> | <ch> <op> <ch>
<varch> ::= x9|x10|x11|x12|x13|x14|x15|x16|x17|x18|x19|x20|x21|x22|x23

# Insulin:
<varins> ::= x24|x25|x26|x27|x28|x29|x30|x31|x32|x33|x34|x35|x36|x37|x38
<op> ::= +|-|*|/
<preop> ::= Math.exp|Math.sin|Math.cos|Math.log
<cte> ::= <base>*Math.pow(10,<sign><exponent>)
<base> ::= <digit digit>
<digit> ::= 1|2|3|4|5|6|8|9
<sign> ::= +|-
```

Fig. 1 Grammar developed for solving the extraction of models of glycemia for G_{t+30}. It considers the pre-processed input data (xi variables) and includes some knowledge about the glucose prediction problem

3.1 Using a Traditional SR Grammar

The traditional approach in SR usually follows a more restrictive use of the number of variables, functions and operators. This approach has been investigated by other authors in both GE [13, 14], where authors developed and work with different grammars, and GP [15] where the authors reduced the number of features and still retrieved appealing results. Following this idea we also investigated a traditional SR grammar with reduction in the number of input variables [16].

The reduction of variables has been done after observing that the information of two consecutive values of preprocessed glucose values, for instance $G_{(t-[15...0[)}$ and $G_{(t-[30...15[)}$ are very similar and, therefore, the use of both them does not provide any relevant information. In the case of carbohydrates and insulin, instead of eliminating variables we add them by pairs. The reason is that we want to preserve all the inputs, i.e. we need all the information of insulin and carbohydrates. This approach also reduces the number of operators to the three basic arithmetic operations: $+$, $-$ and $*$. In most of the phenotypes, the division operation only incorporates complexity without being part of the best solutions. We have also reduced the complexity of the rules to generate constants for two reasons. First, since we have reduced the number of rules for the rest of the terminals, it is not convenient for the constants to consume a large number of genes on the chromosome, since it could lead to an increase in the number of wrappings, or the number of non-feasible solutions. Second, during the tuning of the algorithm in the preliminary experiments

```
<func> ::= <expr>

<expr> ::= (<expr> <op> <expr>) | (<cte> <op> <expr>)  |  <var>

<var> ::= <varch> | <varins> | <vargl>

<op> ::= + | - | *

<vargl> ::=  x2 | x4 | x7

<varch> ::= x9 | (x10 + x11) | (x12 + x13) | (x14 + x15) | (x16 + x17) |
       (x18 + x19) | (x20 + x21) | (x22 + x23)

<varins> ::= x24 | (x25 + x26) | (x27 + x28) | (x29 + x30) | (x31 + x32) |
       (x33 + x34) | (x35 + x36) | (x37 + x38)

<cte> ::=  <factor> * <digit>
<factor> ::= 0.1 | 0.01 | 0.001| 0.0001|  1
<digit> ::= 0 | 1 | 2 | 3 | 4 | 5 | 6 | 7 | 8 | 9 | 10
```

Fig. 2 Grammar developed for solving the extraction of models of glycemia for G_{t+120}. This grammar considers the pre-processed input data (xi variables) and shall lead to the reduction of the number of variables

we have observed that good solutions do not incorporate large constants. Hence, those complex constants can be simplified. Figure 2 shows the grammar used in this second approach for obtaining models for G_{t+120}. For the models of G_{t+30},G_{t+60} and G_{t+90}, we produced similar grammars using the available variables for each time horizon.

4 Enhancing Quality of Input Data with Data Augmentation

One the main obstacles that researches encounter when training models is the lack of significant amounts of data. Especially in medical data analysis, the collection of data is very complex, as data from real patients is not always easy to collect in sufficient quantity and quality. In this section we describe a methodology called *data augmentation* [4], which generates synthetic glucose time series from real data. These synthetic time series can be used to train a GE model or to produce several GE models that work together in a combined system.

The term data augmentation was coined by Tanner and Wong [17], and it relates to methods for constructing iterative sampling algorithms that introduce unobserved data or latent variables. More advanced approaches include simulation of data based on dynamic systems [18] or evolutionary systems [19]. The idea is to find a filter that, once applied to the real data, give us two time series: a smoothed version of the measured blood glucose and a remainder that follows a Gaussian distribution. We can then generate new time series by adding up new Gaussian time series to the smoothed version of the blood glucose. As a filter, we use a weighted moving average (WMA) whose parameters are optimized by an univariate marginal distribution algorithm (UMDA).

Thus, our technique is based on two steps:

- First, we estimate the WMA parameters using an UMDA algorithm, where the fitness function uses the p-value of the Shapiro-Wilk test so that the remainder of the glucose time series follows a Gaussian distribution.
- Second, we generate the synthetic time series sampling new values from the normal distribution and adding them up to the smoothed version.

4.1 Moving Averages

A moving average (MA) is a type of finite impulse response filter which calculates the convolution of the glucose values with a fixed weighting function using a rolling window. In this study we have used a weighted MA (WMA) in which each weight is different. The simplest way of calculating the WMA in a period of N observations is:

1. Add the values of the weighted glucose level of the last N observations.
2. Divide the result by the sum of the individual weights.

Equation (5) defines the WMA for the last N observations, given a glucose time series (G) consisting of at least M observations (N $\leq$ M). This calculation is done for the whole glucose time series.

$$\text{WMA}_M = \frac{\sum_{i=M-N}^{M} w_i \times G_i}{\sum_{i=M-N}^{M} w_i} \tag{5}$$

MAs have been used in numerous applications, e.g. to smooth out high-frequency variations and find the long-term trends. In Fig. 3 we can see the results of applying the WMA filter to blood glucose time series of Fig. 4.

4.2 Univariate Marginal Distribution Algorithm

The univariate marginal distribution algorithm (UMDA), proposed by Pelikan and Mühlenbein [20, 21], is a stochastic, evolutionary optimization method that belongs to the class of so-called estimation of distribution algorithms (EDAs). EDAs do not rely on the usual genetic operators for creating new individuals (crossover and mutation). Instead, they sample from a probabilistic distribution which is estimated from the best individuals of the previous generation. The UMDA algorithm is perhaps the simplest form of an EDA and uses the empirical univariate marginal probability (that is to say, the frequency of each component in the population).

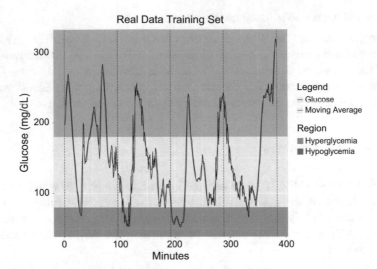

Fig. 3 Real glucose data with WMA

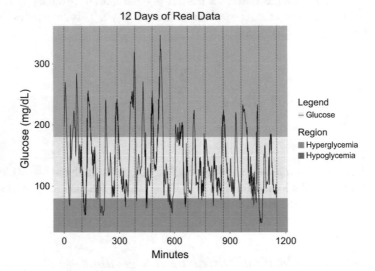

Fig. 4 Real glucose data—12 Days

As mentioned above, we use an UMDA for obtaining the N weights for the weighted moving average (WMA). We have experimented with different fitness functions. In this paper, we have used the p-value of the Shapiro-Wilk test [22].

$$P = \frac{(\sum_{i=1}^{N} A_i G_i)^2}{\sum_{i=1}^{N} (G_i - \text{MEAN}(G))^2} \tag{6}$$

Equation (6) shows the results of the Shapiro-Wilk test, where G_i are the blood glucose levels and A_i are factors obtained through a process that samples from a standard normal distribution and identically distributed random variables, and composes them with their covariance matrix.

4.3   Obtaining Models with Augmented Data

In Fig. 5 we show the complete workflow of the data augmentation approach. We start from 12 days of real data (top of the figure). Then we divide these 12 days into three portions of 4 days. The first 4 days of data are used to train a GE model using a grammar similar to the one presented in Fig. 1. Also, with these first 4 days, we generate a time series using a WMA where the weights were found using an UMDA. After that, we have explored two options to improve GE. We can either obtain a unique GE model with both real data and synthetic data, or look for several GE models where a final prediction is made using a weighted linear combination of each model (ensemble). The UMDA is trained using the second section of 4 days from the 12 days of real data. Models are validated using the last 4 days of the 12 day window.

5   Why Grammatical Evolution?

Recently there has been an interesting discussion about whether grammatical evolution works or it is simply a metaheuristic forced by the natural metaphor on which is inspired [23, 24]. As will be evident, our team is a strong supporter of the usefulness of evolutionary grammars as a powerful search and optimization tool. We consider that it has a theoretical basis that is firm and serious, although not fully developed (like other evolutionary computation theory). Let's see some reasons for our selection.

The search space in which we move to obtain models of blood glucose is immense and grammatical evolution allows us to work on it in an effective way and under different approaches. Although this chapter explains techniques which are essentially solutions to symbolic regression problems, our group has tested other interesting approaches that allow us to investigate other possibilities and incorporate knowledge through the grammars. For instance, in some of our works we have applied a grammar similar to the one in Fig. 6. This (portion of a) grammar incorporates important knowledge about the dynamics of the insulin and carbohydrates on the glucose. We can assume that the intake of carbohydrates and insulin are spread along a period of time, instead of being a discrete input associated to a time instant. Hence, we included in our grammars non-terminal symbols like <curvedCH>, that can be then mapped to the Bateman function represented by:

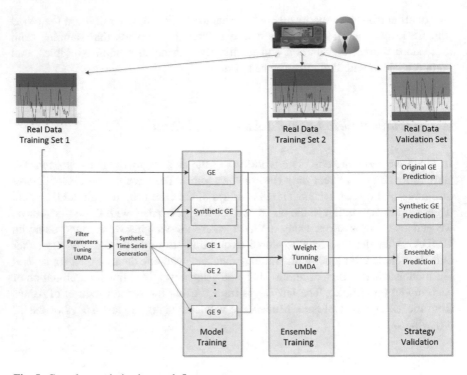

Fig. 5 Complete optimization work flow

```
beta(0.041*Math.min(24,getPrevDataDistance(1,k,1)),2,5)
```

where `beta` is the classical Beta distribution function and the function named `getPrevDataDistance` returns the number of recorded events since the last input of the variable (either carbohydrates or insulin).

This technique can be used also for obtaining an expression of the model for the dynamic behavior of insulin. Analogously, Fig. 7 replicated the process for the dynamic of the insulin. The important thing here is that the grammar allows us not only to incorporate knowledge, but also to obtain information about the best dynamic. If good solutions incorporate more frequently (or even better, always) one of the options, we can simplify the grammars and, at the same time, have an interpretation of the models according to a physiologic idea. That is was what we exactly did for our best results: incorporate the Bateman functions in the preprocessing of the data and simplify the grammars. With these data and grammars, the optimization process is similar to solving a SR problem.

Another reason to select GE as our optimization method, apart from our previous successful research, has to do with neutral mutation properties and solutions that have different genotypes but equal (or similar) phenotypes. In problems like the one treated in this chapter, the phenotype can have several interpretations. We can consider that the phenotype is the mathematical expression that represents

```
# Data 2h ago (24 elements of 5 min.) operated somehow.
<func> ::= predictedData(k-<idxCurr2h>) + <exprch> - <exprins>
# Real glucose can be, as sooner as two hours ago:
<idx4hto2hAgo> ::=
        24|25|26|27|28|29|30|31|32|33|34|35|36|37|38|39|40|41|42|43|44|45|46|47|48
# Predicted glucose could be the most recent one.
<idxCurr2h> ::= 1|2|3|4|5|6|7|8|9|10|11|12|13|14|15|16|17|18|19|20|21|22|23
# CH
<exprch> ::= (<exprch> <op> <exprch>)
        |<preop> (<exprch>)
        |(<cte> <op> <exprch>)
        |(getPrevData(1,k,1) * <cte> * <curvedCH>)
        | ......
        |<curvedCH>
        |<cte>
        |<exprch2>

<exprch2> ::= (getPrevData(1,k,1) <op> (getPrevDataDistance(1,k,1)))
        |(getPrevData(1,k,1) <op> getPrevDataDistance(1,k,1))
        |(getPrevData(2,k,1) <op> getPrevDataDistance(2,k,1))
        |(getPrevData(3,k,1) <op> getPrevDataDistance(3,k,1))
        |(getPrevData(4,k,1) <op> getPrevDataDistance(4,k,1))
        |(getPrevData(1,k,1) <op> getPrevDataDistance(1,k,1))
        |(getPrevDataDistance(1,k,1))
        |(getPrevDataDistance(2,k,1))
        |(getPrevDataDistance(3,k,1))
        |(getPrevDataDistance(4,k,1))
        |(getPrevData(1,k,1))
        |(getPrevData(2,k,1))
        |(getPrevData(3,k,1))
        |(getPrevData(4,k,1))

# CH in 2 (0.041,24), 3 (0.027,36) and 4 (0.02,48) hours with 3 shapes of beta:
<curvedCH> ::= beta(0.041*Math.min(24,getPrevDataDistance(1,k,1)),2,5)
        |beta(0.041*Math.min(24,getPrevDataDistance(1,k,1)),3,3)
        |beta(0.041*Math.min(24,getPrevDataDistance(1,k,1)),5,2)
        |beta(0.027*Math.min(36,getPrevDataDistance(1,k,1)),2,5)
        |beta(0.027*Math.min(36,getPrevDataDistance(1,k,1)),3,3)
        |beta(0.027*Math.min(36,getPrevDataDistance(1,k,1)),5,2)
        |beta(0.02*Math.min(48,getPrevDataDistance(1,k,1)),2,5)
        |beta(0.02*Math.min(48,getPrevDataDistance(1,k,1)),3,3)
        |beta(0.02*Math.min(48,getPrevDataDistance(1,k,1)),5,2)
```

Fig. 6 A grammar developed for the extraction of models of glycemia. (Part a)

the model. The phenotype can also be taken as the set of tuples (time, glucose, carbohydrates, insulin) expressing the blood glucose profile, both in the validation of the training model and in the prediction phases with new data. Two features may be highlighted in this approach:

- Different genotypes or chromosomes can lead to the same expression after the particular decoding and mapping processes of GE.
- Different mathematical expressions (hence, coming from different genotypes) can lead to equal tuples (or similar in the vast majority of points in space).

It has been demonstrated in previous work that this particularity is very useful in the search for solutions within evolutionary computing in general. There are works that tackle this theory outside GE, but that we clearly identify them with the search spaces that appear in this chapter [25, 26].

```
# Insulin:## Sum of insulins in past 2h minus the peak
## Curve for the peak in past 2h
<exprins> ::= (<exprins> <op> <exprins>)
         |<preop> (<exprins>)
         |(<cte> <op> <exprins>)
         |getVariable(2,k-<idx>)
         |((getSumOfValues(24,k,2) - getMaxValue(24,k,2)) <op>
         (getMaxValue(24,k,2) <op> <curvedINS>))

# INS in 2 (0.041,24), 3 (0.027,36) and 4 (0.02,48) hr. with 3 shapes of beta:
<curvedINS> ::= beta(0.041*Math.min(24,getMaxValueDistance(24,k,2)),2,5)
          |beta(0.041*Math.min(24,getMaxValueDistance(24,k,2)),3,3)
          |beta(0.041*Math.min(24,getMaxValueDistance(24,k,2)),5,2)
          |beta(0.027*Math.min(36,getMaxValueDistance(36,k,2)),2,5)
          |beta(0.027*Math.min(36,getMaxValueDistance(36,k,2)),3,3)
          |beta(0.027*Math.min(36,getMaxValueDistance(36,k,2)),5,2)
          |beta(0.02*Math.min(48,getMaxValueDistance(48,k,2)),2,5)
          |beta(0.02*Math.min(48,getMaxValueDistance(48,k,2)),3,3)
          |beta(0.02*Math.min(48,getMaxValueDistance(48,k,2)),5,2)

<op> ::= +|-|*|/
<preop> ::= Math.exp|Math.sin|Math.cos|Math.log
<cte> ::= <base>*Math.pow(10,<sign><exponent>)
.....
```

Fig. 7 A grammar developed for the extraction of models of glycemia. (Part b)

6 Experimental Results

After explaining the main techniques we employed in the previous sections, we here summarize some of the most important experimental results of our research.

The most frequently used metric for assessing the quality of regression solutions is the root squared mean error (RSME). However, this metric and also error functions that include average processes are not very useful in a problem such as our glucose model identification problem because a prediction with an error of 20 points can be very bad if the actual glucose is low, or maybe not so bad if the actual data belongs to the safe range of values. Thus, we here use the Clarke error grid (CEG) metric [27], a metric that better illustrates this behavior showing the differences between actual and predicted glucose values through regions on a Cartesian space. The idea is that a point (x, y) represents the situation where the actual glucose value is x and the predicted value is y. The golden prediction is $y = x$. The key point of this approach is that it defines five delimited zones (A to E) with different properties:

- Zones A and B: Values on Zone A represent the glucose values that deviate from the reference values by 20% or less and those that are in the hypoglycemic range (<70 mg/dl), not only the predicted value but also the reference value. Predicted values on zone B deviate from the reference values by more than 20% although the clinical treatment will be correct with a high probability. The samples in zones A and B are clinically exact or at least acceptable, and thus the clinical treatment will be correct. We will treat those classes as a combined category in the analysis of our experimental results.

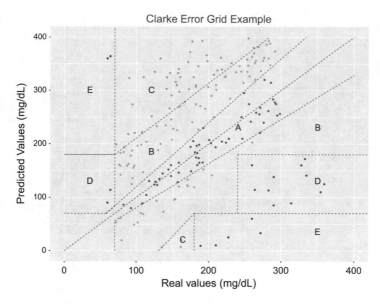

Fig. 8 An example of a Clarke Error Grid for a predictions. We can see points on different zones of the prediction space

- Zone C: The values in this zone could be dangerous in some situations. The goal is to minimize predictions in this category.
- Zones D-E: The values included in those areas are potentially dangerous, since the prediction is far from being acceptable and the indicated treatment will be different from the correct one. Again, the goal is to minimize predictions in this category.

There is no general consensus in the evaluation of prediction errors related to diabetic patients. In fact, the limits of the zones described by CEG were modified in [28] with little attention from the research community. Hence, we decided to use the definition formulated in the original paper. Figure 8 shows an example CEG diagram for predictions in $t + 60$.

6.1 Experimental Environment

We have implemented the GE algorithms in Java, and we have stored them in a public GitHub repository called JECO, which stands for Java Evolutionary Computation library [11]. In order to ease the utilization of this library by the community of researchers, we have decoupled the implementation of the algorithms, operators and utility methods from the problem specification. Hence, if a researcher wants to use JECO, it is only necessary to develop the code related to the particular

Fig. 9 Pancreas Model Tools application, training tab

problem that is tackling, which basically means the codification of a solution, the evaluation of a solution and the generation of the initial population.

In the case of the modeling of glucose in diabetic patients, we have developed an application that we have called Pancreas Model Tools (PMT). PMT includes a complete graphical user interface (GUI) that allows the user to configure the parameters of the experiments, and also to obtain information about the performance of the experiment, both graphically and in text formats.

In Fig. 9 we show the main window of PMT. We here see the "Training (GE)" tab, where the user can select the parameters for the training phase, where the GE algorithm is run. It can be seen that is easy to select the training file, the grammar file, the number of generations, the crossover probability, the population size, the mutation probability, the maximum number of wraps, the number of codons in the chromosome and the size of the tournament for selection. In addition, the method to initialize the population can be selected (random or sensible). Besides, the objective function can be chosen with a combo box. The default objective function is RSME, but the absolute error and the Clarke Error Grid (CEG) objectives can also be selected. Notice that a button labeled as "CEG penalty" is also available, clicking this leads to the display of a dialog where the researcher may define the penalty applied to the points in the regions B, C, D and E of the CEG fitness function.

On the right-hand side of the window the user can observe the progress of the optimization in the plot of the objective function values. In addition, a clock measuring the execution time is displayed, and a button to stop the execution is also available.

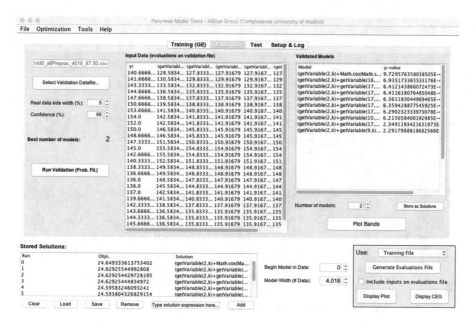

Fig. 10 Pancreas Model Tools application, validation tab

The bottom-right part of the window allows the user to both plot a graph where the solution is evaluated and display a CEG plot with these data. Besides, a CSV file can be generated to be used in a spreadsheet or in other tools, where the selected solution is evaluated according to the chosen file (training, validation or test files).

The bottom-left part of the window shows a component where the solutions of the experiments can be stored. This way, the researcher can run different experiments, store the solutions with the button "Store Solutions", and then validate the different models with our validation tool.

The "Validation" tab, displayed in Fig. 10, has a low number of parameters. On the one hand, a validation file is required and, on the other hand, a set of models from training executions is needed. In this phase, PMT performs a selection of the best models using Probabilistic Fitting. This technique makes use of the χ^2 test to select those models which, applied in combination, generate the best prediction with the confidence percentage determined by the user. All the given models are evaluated using the validation data and ranked according to their *p-value* with respect to the expected data. Then, the statistical test is run taking 2 models, then 3 models, then 4, etc., which leads to the *p-values* of these combinations. Hence, the validation ends with the selection of a number of models to be used. PMT also provides a button to plot the resulting models.

The "Test" tab, displayed in Fig. 11, allows to assess the performance of the validated models on a set of test data. In this case, the stored solutions (models) are evaluated on the test data. The resulting values are compared with the target glucose

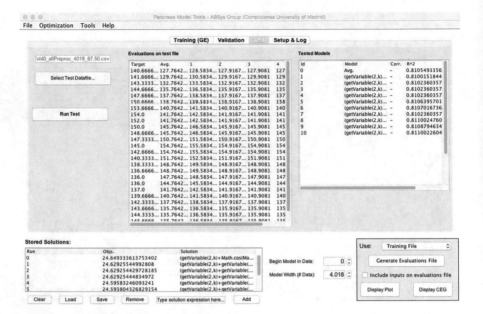

Fig. 11 Pancreas Model Tools application, testing tab

value, yr in the figure, and the R^2 value is shown. Therefore, the researcher can easily obtain a quality measure for the resulting models.

The last tab of the application is devoted to the setup and log tasks. As seen in Fig. 12, a text area displays the log of the execution of PMT. This log can be stored in a file for future applications, data such as the fitness of the best solution, deviation of the fitness on each generation and partial execution times are logged during the optimization. In the lower part of the tab the user can select the directory where the log file will be saved as well as the compilation directory. This last element is needed because PMT performs the compilation of phenotypes which, in this kind of models, accelerates the evaluation of the solutions [29].

PMT can also be run in console mode allowing long experiment runs on server machines. In this execution mode, a properties file is required, where each one of the parameters previously described (either in training, validation and test tabs) can be included. The properties file can be generated from the GUI through the corresponding menu option, and it can be also imported to the graphical mode.

Finally, we have embedded a simple grammar editor in PMT, shown in Fig. 13. Users can edit a grammar file directly in PMT and also verify the correctness of the grammar.

PMT is still under development, and some features need further improvements and corrections. However, we are confident that in a near future the tool will be finished and then made available to the researchers community.

Fig. 12 Pancreas Model Tools application, setup and log tab

Fig. 13 Grammar editor in Pancreas Model Tools

6.2 Results

We use two different datasets for the experiments:

- *Data Set 1*: 10 T1DM patients (n=10) have been selected for the observational study, based on conditions of good glucose control. Data from patients were acquired over multiple weeks using Medtronic (c) CGMs. Log entries were stored in 5-min intervals, and insulin was injected using a Medtronic Pump. In this dataset, we have at least 10 complete days of data for each patient. The patients were predominantly female (80%), their (average) age 42.3 ($\pm$11.07), the number of years of disease 27.2 ($\pm$10.32), the number years with pump therapy 10 ($\pm$4.98), their weight 64.78 ($\pm$13.31) kg, and their HbA1c 7.27% on average ($\pm$0.5%). The average number of days with data is 44.80 ($\pm$30.73).
- *Data Set 2*: 5 T1DM patients (n=5) were monitored in an observational study. Data from patients were acquired over 12 days with Abbot FreeStyle Libre (c) devices. We have observations every 15 min up to a total of 1152 measures. We also have recorded (estimated by the patient) carbohydrate units ingested and insulin injected by manual doses. The patients were also predominantly female (80%), their (average) age 36.4 ($\pm$10.60), the number of years of disease 21.18 ($\pm$10.13), the number of years with pump therapy is not available, their weight 68.63 ($\pm$15.58) kg, and their HbA1c 7.84% on average ($\pm$1.42%). The number of days with data is 12.

6.2.1 Results with GE with Data Preprocessing

First, we analyze results using GE with data preprocessing explained in Sect. 3. We obtained models for *Data Set 1* for prediction in 30, 60, 90 and 120 min time windows. We used the RSME as fitness function, and GE with 200 individuals, one point crossover with 0.65 probability, individual mutation probability of 0.05, 300 codons, 5 wrappings, and 250 generations. We used the identifier GE_spec to refer to the grammars like the one in Fig. 1 and GE_gen to the experiments with Fig. 2. We also compare results with a GP approach as the one explained in [3] (Table 2).

Additionally, we have used two baseline predictors. The first one considers the average glucose of the previous values in the past 2 h; we denote it here as Avg. The second baseline considers as the prediction the last known value of the glucose; it is here denoted as Last. For all the techniques the prediction accuracy is better for the short forecasting horizons and gradually become worse as the forecasting horizon is increased from 30 min to 2 h. GE variants performed best for 30 and 60 min and GP variants performed best for higher horizons although not with significant differences.

Table 2 Fractions of predictions (in percent) on independent test data

	t+30				t+60			
Alg	A + B	C	D	E	A + B	C	D	E
Avg	39.98 + 45.85	0.00	14.17	0.00	39.97 + 45.92	0.00	14.11	0.00
Last	71.82 + 25.23	0.22	2.68	0.01	53.85 + 39.84	1.19	4.79	0.35
GE_spec	77.90 + 19.93	0.26	1.87	0.01	57.21 + 37.17	1.19	4.21	0.23
GE_gen	80.67 + 17.51	0.38	1.43	0.01	58.65 + 35.80	1.28	4.07	0.21
GP	82.97 + 14.45	0.05	2.53	0.01	63.25 + 31.06	0.27	5.37	0.04
	t+90				t+120			
Alg	A + B	C	D	E	A + B	C	D	E
Avg	40.00 + 45.89	0.00	14.09	0.00	40.03 + 45.88	0.00	14.07	0.00
Last	44.41 + 45.56	2.84	6.16	1.05	39.13 + 47.96	4.14	6.88	1.88
GE_spec	46.91 + 43.85	1.98	6.74	0.52	42.18 + 44.47	2.28	10.92	0.15
GE_gen	47.58 + 43.38	2.27	6.14	0.62	41.74 + 47.01	2.16	8.18	0.89
GP	53.99 + 38.66	0.41	6.81	0.10	50.26 + 40.97	0.41	8.07	0.26

For each patients and prediction horizon, the best modeling results are highlighted

6.2.2 Results with GE with Data Augmentation

Second, we present results for testing the application of data augmentation. We augmented the training data of *Data Set 2* with new time series and got a new GE model trained with the original data plus ten more synthetic time series. The models were trained rolling a window of 4 h (16 observations) through the data to make a prediction with the different forecasting horizons (30, 60, 90 and 120 min). The fitness function for the GE models was again the RMSE. The results of this new model are presented in Fig. 14. It is important to point out that this model drastically decreases the predictions in the C zone, whereas the points in the B and A zones are more than 20% and more than 70%, respectively. There is a slight increase of points in the D zone and no predictions were in the most dangerous section, zone E.

In addition, the ten new time series were used to train ten new GE models. The full set of models (original model and the ten new ones) were combined into an ensemble model. This way, the prediction of the ensemble is the weighted sum of every individual prediction as explained above. The final prediction ($\hat{G}$) is a linear combination of every GE model's prediction $\hat{G}_i$. The prediction horizons are 30, 60, 90 and 120 min. To get the value of the weighs (W_i), the combining system was trained during the second section of the real data using and UMDA algorithm.

In Table 3 we summarize the results of all the experiments, which are labeled as follows:

- OrigGE, grammatical evolution model trained only with original data.
- SynthGE, GE model trained with original plus synthetic data.

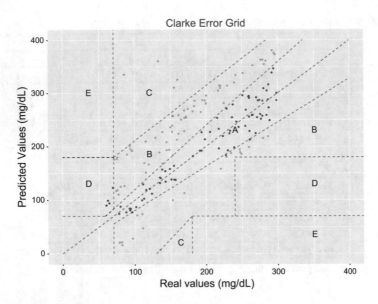

Fig. 14 Clarke Error Grid results for GE model trained with original and synthetic data

- EnsembleGE, system that combines the predictions of ten GE models.
- MAPE is the mean absolute percentage error for training (MAPE-T) and validation (MAPE-V) phases.

So, from Table 3 several conclusions arise:

- Prediction horizon 30 min:

  - All the strategies have similar performance with no points in the D and E zones.

- Prediction horizon 60 min:

  - This horizon seems to point out the frontier of safe predictions as all the strategies begin to have points in the D and E zones.
  - Although the GE model has fewer points in the D and E zones, a lot of predictions are in zone C. Please keep in mind that predictions in zone C can lead to unnecessary treatments.
  - The best model is EnsembleGE, almost 95% of the predictions are in the A and B zones (see also Fig. 15).

- Prediction horizon 90 and 120 min:

  - For greater horizons, all techniques get bigger MAPE-Vs and a lot of predictions in the most dangerous zones.
  - The percentage of points into the A and B zones remain around 80% for SynthGE and EnsembleGE, but the percentage in the A zone is reduced drastically in comparison to the previous horizons. Besides, the ratio of

Table 3 Clarke zones for predicted values

Strategy	Horizon = 30 min						
	Zones percentage						
	A	B	C	D	E	MAPE-T	MAPE-V
OrigGE	45.88	47.18	6.92	0.00	0.00	4.1	7.1
SynthGE	55.8	42.6	1.6	0.00	0.00	3.1	5.45
EnsembleGE	59.25	39.92	0.83	0.00	0.00	5.7	6.33
Strategy	Horizon = 60 min						
	Zones percentage						
	A	B	C	D	E	MAPE-T	MAPE-V
OrigGE	10.78	41.36	40.98	3.12	3.76	13.72	21.25
SynthGE	40.2	41.12	15.8	2.12	0.76	8.1	12.45
EnsembleGE	79.08	15.1	3.5	1.02	1.3	5.7	7.63
Strategy	Horizon = 90 min						
	Zones percentage						
	A	B	C	D	E	MAPE-T	MAPE-V
OrigGE	17.25	40.28	33.03	6.88	2.56	12.20	19.07
SynthGE	33.09	44.12	18.03	2.56	2.2	7.1	13.45
EnsembleGE	43.33	41.23	11.7	2.54	1.2	6.7	12.3
Strategy	Horizon = 120 min						
	Zones percentage						
	A	B	C	D	E	MAPE-T	MAPE-V
OrigGE	15.45	35.81	40.30	3.78	4.66	17.31	23.89
SynthGE	32.34	41.12	21.7	1.54	3.3	16.6	18.54
EnsembleGE	51.1	32.67	11.73	3.4	1.1	12.7	16.33

predictions in the D and E zones is within 4% and 5%. Both strategies improve the behavior of the OrigGE model, and the ensemble modeling strategy leads to slightly more robust results (fewer points in the C, D and E zones and lower MAPE-V values) (Fig. 15).

An example of one solution is shown on Fig. 16:

$$\hat{G}_{t+30} = -0.05 - 0.0008 * Variable(24, k) * (Variable(8, k) + \qquad (7)$$
$$+Variable(2, k) + 0.2 + Variable(24, k) + 0.01 \cdot Variable(6, k)$$

That translated to the variables of Glucose SR is:

$$\hat{G}_{t+30} = -0.05 - 0.0008 * I_{(t)} * G_{(t-[15...0[)} + \qquad (8)$$
$$+G_{(t)} + 0.2 + I_{(t)} + 0.01 \cdot G_{(t-[45...30[)}$$

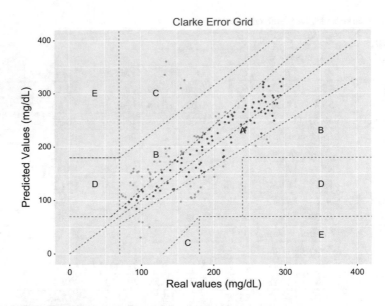

Fig. 15 Clarke Error Grid results for weighted ensemble

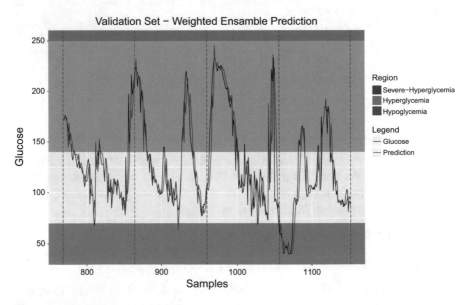

Fig. 16 Weighted ensemble prediction

7 Conclusions

In this chapter we presented several techniques to find prediction models for glucose prognosis. They are based on GE and data processing. We explain how to design effective grammars and share with the reader several data processing tools that improve robustness and quality of the predictions. We have implemented the GE algorithms in a public GitHub repository called JECO [11]. A complete GUI called Pancreas Model Tools is also available, that allows the user to configure the parameters of the experiments, and also to obtain information about performance, both graphically and in text formats.

We have developed a grammar which includes specific knowledge by considering that the prediction may depend on the previous values of glucose, carbohydrates ingestion, and insulin injection. This approach considers the preprocessing of the data. We also investigated a traditional symbolic regression grammar which considers a reduction in the number of input variables. This second approach also reduces the number of operators and the complexity of the rules to generate constants. We compared both with a traditional genetic programming approach for symbolic regression.

We also explained a technique, called Data Augmentation (DA), for enhancing grammatical evolution models in a context of data scarcity. With DA we are able to generate glucose time series from one sample, that can be used to train GE models. Experimental results show that the GE models trained with these synthetic time series get more robust predictions, decreasing significantly the number of dangerous predictions.

Acknowledgements This work was partially supported by the Spanish Government Minister of Science and Innovation under grants TIN2014-54806-R and TIN2015-65460-C2. J. I. Hidalgo also acknowledges the support of the Spanish Ministry of Education mobility grant PRX16/00216. S. M. Winkler and G. Kronberger acknowledge the support of the Austrian Research Promotion Agency (FFG) under grant #843532 (COMET Project Heuristic Optimization in Production and Logistics). The authors would like to thank the help of the medical staff: Marta Botella, Esther Maqueda, Aranzazu Aramendi-Zurimendi and Remedios Martínez-Rodríguez.

References

1. G. Sparacino, F. Zanderigo, S. Corazza, A. Maran, A. Facchinetti, C. Cobelli, Glucose concentration can be predicted ahead in time from continuous glucose monitoring sensor time-series. IEEE Trans. Biomed. Eng. **54**(5), 931–937 (2007)
2. J.I. Hidalgo, E. Maqueda, J.L. Risco-Martín, A. Cuesta-Infante, J.M. Colmenar, J. Nobel, gIUCmodel: a monitoring and modeling system for chronic diseases applied to diabetes. J. Biomed. Inform. **48**, 183–192 (2014)
3. J.I. Hidalgo, J.M. Colmenar, G. Kronberger, S.M. Winkler, O. Garnica, J. Lanchares, Data based prediction of blood glucose concentrations using evolutionary methods. J. Med. Syst. **41**(9), 142 (2017)
4. J.M. Velasco, O. Garnica, S. Contador, J.M. Colmenar, E. Maqueda, M. Botella, J. Lanchares, J.I. Hidalgo, Enhancing grammatical evolution through data augmentation: application to blood glucose forecasting, in *European Conference on the Applications of Evolutionary Computation* (Springer, Berlin, 2017), pp. 142–157
5. B. Hansen, I. Matytsina, Insulin administration: selecting the appropriate needle and individualizing the injection technique. Expert Opin. Drug Deliv. **8**(10), 1395–1406 (2011)
6. J. Weissberg-Benchell, J. Antisdel-Lomaglio, R. Seshadri, Insulin pump therapy. Diabetes Care **26**(4), 1079–1087 (2003)

7. P.A. Bakhtiani, L.M. Zhao, J. El Youssef, J.R. Castle, W.K. Ward, A review of artificial pancreas technologies with an emphasis on bi-hormonal therapy. Diabetes. Obes. Metab. **15**(12), 1065–1070 (2013)
8. J.I. Hidalgo, J.M. Colmenar, J.L. Risco-Martin, A. Cuesta-Infante, E. Maqueda, M. Botella, J.A. Rubio, Modeling glycemia in humans by means of grammatical evolution. Appl. Soft Comput. **20**, 40–53 (2014)
9. J.M. Velasco, S. Winkler, J.I. Hidalgo, O. Garnica, J. Lanchares, J.M. Colmenar, E. Maqueda, M. Botella, J.-A. Rubio, Data-based identification of prediction models for glucose, in *Proceedings of the Companion Publication of the 2015 Annual Conference on Genetic and Evolutionary Computation* (ACM, New York, 2015), pp. 1327–1334
10. J.M. Colmenar, S.M. Winkler, G. Kronberger, E. Maqueda, M. Botella, J.I. Hidalgo, Predicting glycemia in diabetic patients by evolutionary computation and continuous glucose monitoring, in *Proceedings of the 2016 on Genetic and Evolutionary Computation Conference Companion* (ACM, New York, 2016), pp. 1393–1400
11. Adaptive and Bioinspired Systems Group, ABSys JECO (Java Evolutionary COmputation) library (2016), https://github.com/ABSysGroup/jeco
12. J.M. Colmenar, J.I. Hidalgo, J. Lanchares, O. Garnica, J.-L. Risco, I. Contreras, A. Sánchez, J.M. Velasco, Compilable phenotypes: speeding-up the evaluation of glucose models in grammatical evolution, in *European Conference on the Applications of Evolutionary Computation* (Springer International Publishing, Berlin, 2016), pp. 118–133
13. M. O'Neill, C. Ryan, Grammatical evolution by grammatical evolution: the evolution of grammar and genetic code, in *European Conference on Genetic Programming* (Springer, Berlin, 2004), pp. 138–149
14. I. Dempsey, M. O'Neill, A. Brabazon, *Foundations in Grammatical Evolution for Dynamic Environments*, vol. 194 (Springer, Berlin, 2009)
15. D. Moreno-Salinas, E. Besada-Portas, J. López-Orozco, D. Chaos, J. de la Cruz, J. Aranda, Symbolic regression for marine vehicles identification. IFAC-PapersOnLine **48**(16), 210–216 (2015)
16. M. Kommenda, A. Beham, M. Affenzeller, G. Kronberger, Complexity measures for multi-objective symbolic regression, in *International Conference on Computer Aided Systems Theory* (Springer, Berlin, 2015), pp. 409–416
17. M.A. Tanner, W.H. Wong, From EM to data augmentation: the emergence of MCMC Bayesian computation in the 1980s. ArXiv e-prints, Apr. 2011
18. M. Yadav, P. Malhotra, L. Vig, K. Sriram, G. Shroff, ODE - augmented training improves anomaly detection in sensor data from machines. CoRR, abs/1605.01534 (2016)
19. A. Kumar, L. Cowen, Augmented training of hidden Markov models to recognize remote homologs via simulated evolution. Bioinformatics **25**(13), 1602–1608 (2009)
20. M. Pelikan, H. Mühlenbein, Marginal distributions in evolutionary algorithms, in *Proceedings of the International Conference on Genetic Algorithms Mendel*, vol. 98 (Citeseer, 1998) pp. 90–95
21. H. Mühlenbein, The equation for response to selection and its use for prediction. Evol. Comput. **5**, 303–346 (1997)
22. S.S. Shapiro, M.B. Wilk, An analysis of variance test for normality (complete samples). Biometrika **52**(3), 591–611 (1965)
23. C. Ryan, A rebuttal to Whigham, Dick, and Maclaurin by one of the inventors of grammatical evolution: commentary on "On the mapping of genotype to phenotype in evolutionary algorithms" by Peter A. Whigham, Grant Dick, and James Maclaurin. Genet. Program Evolvable Mach. **18**, 385–389 (2017)
24. P.A. Whigham, G. Dick, J. Maclaurin, On the mapping of genotype to phenotype in evolutionary algorithms. Genet. Program Evolvable Mach. **18**, 353–361 (2017)
25. S. Verel, G. Ochoa, M. Tomassini, Local optima networks of NK landscapes with neutrality. IEEE Trans. Evol. Comput. **15**(6), 783–797 (2011)
26. G. Ochoa, M. Tomassini, S. Vérel, C. Darabos, A study of NK landscapes' basins and local optima networks, in *Proceedings of the 10th Annual Conference on Genetic and Evolutionary Computation* (ACM, New York, 2008), pp. 555–562

27. W. Clarke, D. Cox, L. Gonder-Frederick, W. Carter, S. Pohl, Evaluating clinical accuracy of systems for self-monitoring of blood glucose. Diabetes Care **10**(5), 622–628 (1987)
28. J. Parkes, S. Slatin, S. Pardo, B. Ginsberg, A new consensus error grid to evaluate the clinical significance of inaccuracies in the measurement of blood glucose. Diabetes Care **23**(8), 1143–1148 (2000)
29. J.M. Colmenar, J.I. Hidalgo, J. Lanchares, O. Garnica, J.-L. Risco, I. Contreras, A. Sánchez, J.M. Velasco, Compilable phenotypes: speeding-up the evaluation of glucose models in grammatical evolution, in *European Conference on the Applications of Evolutionary Computation* (Springer, Berlin, 2016), pp. 118–133

Grammatical Evolution Strategies for Bioinformatics and Systems Genomics

Jason H. Moore and Moshe Sipper

Abstract Evolutionary computing methods are an attractive option for modeling complex biological and biomedical systems because they are inherently parallel, they conduct stochastic search through large solution spaces, they capitalize on the modularity of solutions, they have flexible solution representations, they can utilize expert knowledge, they can consider multiple fitness criteria, and they are inspired by how evolution optimizes fitness through natural selection. Grammatical evolution (GE) is a promising example of evolutionary computing because it generates solutions to a problem using a generative grammar. We review here several detailed examples of GE from the bioinformatics and systems genomics literature and end with some ideas about the challenges and opportunities for integrating GE into biological and biomedical discovery.

1 Introduction

Bioinformatics has its origins in the late 1970s with the convergence of DNA sequencing, internetworking, and microcomputers. Early demand for bioinformatics centered on the use of computers and the internet to store, manage, manipulate, and analyze DNA sequences derived from experimental studies in the biological and biomedical sciences. This demand exploded in the mid-1990s with the advent of high-throughput methods for measuring biomolecules such as messenger RNA levels in cells and tissues [17]. This explosion of data has continued and, when

J. H. Moore (✉)
Institute for Biomedical Informatics, Perelman School of Medicine, University of Pennsylvania, Philadelphia, PA, USA
e-mail: jhmoore@upenn.edu

M. Sipper
Institute for Biomedical Informatics, Perelman School of Medicine, University of Pennsylvania, Philadelphia, PA, USA

Computer Science Department, Ben-Gurion University, Beersheba, Israel
e-mail: sipper@upenn.edu

© Springer International Publishing AG, part of Springer Nature 2018   395
C. Ryan et al. (eds.), *Handbook of Grammatical Evolution*,
https://doi.org/10.1007/978-3-319-78717-6_16

combined with questions about the complexity of biological systems, creates computational challenges that often require machine learning and artificial intelligence (AI) approaches [6].

Evolutionary computation has emerged as a useful artificial intelligence approach for the study of complex biological systems because these methods are inherently parallel, conduct stochastic search through large solution spaces, capitalize on the modularity of solutions—which is an important characteristic of biological systems, have flexible solution representations, can utilize expert knowledge, can consider multiple fitness criteria, and are inspired by how evolution optimizes fitness through natural selection that is understood by biologists. Genetic programming (GP) is a population type of evolutionary computing [14, 26]. The goal of GP is to 'evolve' computer programs to solve complex problems. This is accomplished by first generating, or initializing, a population of random computer programs that are composed of the basic building blocks needed to solve or approximate a solution to the problem. The power of GP is its ability to recombine building blocks to create new solutions through an iterative process that involves selection of the best solutions. GP and its many variations have been applied successfully in a wide range of different problem domains including bioinformatics. The potential for evolutionary methods to impact complex problem solving was discussed in a recent editorial [27]. The goal of this chapter is to review bioinformatics and systems genomics applications of a type of GP called grammatical evolution (GE) that generates computer programs or solutions using a grammar. These grammar-based approaches provide tremendous flexibility.

Grammatical evolution (GE) was introduced by Ryan et al. [25] as a variation on genetic programming. Here, a Backus-Naur Form (BNF) grammar is specified that allows a computer program or model to be constructed by a simple genetic algorithm operating on an array of bits. BNF is a formal notation for describing the syntax of a context-free grammar as a set of production rules that consist of terminals and nonterminals [15]. Nonterminals form the left-hand side of production rules while both terminals and nonterminals can form the right-hand side. A terminal is essentially a model element while a nonterminal is the name of a production rule. The GE approach is appealing because only a text file specifying the grammar needs to be altered for different applications. There is no need to modify and recompile source code during development once the fitness function for evaluating solutions is specified.

We begin in the next section with a brief summary of GE applications and some thoughts about the future of this approach for solving complex biological and biomedical problems. We then review in some detail in the next two sections a bioinformatics application of GE for machine learning in human genetics and a systems genomics application of GE for simulating discrete dynamical systems.

2　A Survey of Grammatical Evolution Approaches to Bioinformatics and Systems Genomics

A search of the phrase "grammatical evolution" on PubMed revealed only 25 publications. In addition to the studies discussed below, several other applications of GE have been reported. For example, Smart et al. [28] used GE to do feature selection and feature engineering to analyze electroencephalogram (EEG) data from patients experiencing epileptic seizures. In this case, the GE performed as well as other methods and provided the added benefit of the grammar for rapid development and testing. As another example, Ferrante et al. [4] used GE to study the behavior of insects. They found that GE could model self-organized task specialization using low-level behavioral primitives as building blocks for more complex behaviors. As a third example, Hidalgo et al. [7] used GE to model and predict glucose concentrations in physiological systems. The results of this study have important implications for predicting insulin need in diabetic patients following carbohydrate intake. More recently, Fenton et al. [3] used grammatical genetic programming to evolve control heuristics for heterogeneous cellular networks. Finally, GE has been used in the context of artificial life experiments. For example, Alfonseca and Gil [1] used GE to study the ecology of mathematical expressions as a way to study biological evolution. We also searched for "grammatical evolution" and the keyword "bioinformatics" in the genetic programming bibliography to capture publications in computer science conferences and other venues not captured by PubMed. This search returned 13 publications nearly all of which will be discussed below.

3　A Grammatical Evolution Approach to Neural Network Analysis of Human Genetics Data

An important goal of human genetics and genetic epidemiology is to understand the mapping relationship between interindividual variation in DNA sequences, variation in environmental exposure, and variation in disease susceptibility. In other words, how do one or more changes in an individual's DNA sequence increase or decrease their risk of developing disease through complex networks of biomolecules that are hierarchically organized, highly interactive, and dependent on environmental exposures? Understanding the role of genomic variation and environmental context in disease susceptibility is likely to improve diagnosis, prevention, and treatment. Success in this important public-health endeavor will depend critically on the amount of nonlinearity in the mapping of genotype to phenotype and our ability to address it. Here, we define as nonlinear an outcome that cannot be easily predicted by the sum of the individual genetic markers. Nonlinearities can arise from phenomena such as locus heterogeneity (i.e. different DNA sequence variations leading to the same phenotype), phenocopy (i.e. environmentally determined phenotypes that don't have a genetic basis), and the dependence of genotypic effects on environmental exposure (i.e. gene-environment interactions or plastic reaction norms) and genotypes at other loci (i.e. gene-gene interactions or epistasis). The challenges associated with detecting each of these phenomena in big data has been reviewed and discussed by Moore et al. [20] who call for an analytical retooling to address these complexities.

The limitations of the linear model and other parametric statistical approaches for modeling nonlinear interactions have motivated the development of data mining and machine learning methods. The advantage of these computational approaches is that they make fewer assumptions about the functional form of the model and the effects being modeled [16]. In other words, data mining and machine learning methods are much more consistent with the idea of letting the data tell us what the model is rather than forcing the data to fit a preconceived notion of what a good model should be. Neural networks represent one machine learning approach that can complement parametric statistical approaches such as linear regression. Ritchie et al. [23, 24] introduced a GP approach to evolving neural networks (NN) for genetic analysis where both the architecture and the weights of the NN are optimized. This was later extended to include a grammar for generating NN models using GE [21]. The GENN approach was shown to be more powerful than GPNN for detecting and modeling gene-gene interactions in population-based studies of human disease susceptibility. More recent work has incorporated GENN into a pipeline [10] that includes multiple different data sources and that harnesses the power of feature selection [12, 13] (see also [9, 29]).

Holzinger et al. [10], who compared grammatical evolution neural networks (GENN) with grammatical evolution symbolic regression (GESR), noted that, "our results suggest that GENN is better at correctly and accurately detecting genetic models with no main effects ... In the simulated meta-dimensional data, Lasso had higher detection power for the full model than both GENN and GESR. However, when we used more powerful parameter settings, GENN was also able to identify the full model consistently ... Lasso is considerably faster than either GENN or GESR, so if computational resources are a major limitation, this may be the optimal method. However, Lasso is not robust to models with no main effects, so the overall benefit of a faster analysis would need to be weighted accordingly ... "

We now briefly review a simple example grammar for generating NN models with GE. The root of the grammar picks a node with a logistic activation function and transfer function with a mathematical function for combining multiple features (addition, subtraction, multiplication, division) along with some inputs that could be additional nodes and/or features with weights. The GE operates by generating an array of bits where each set of bits encodes and integer value that is used to execute the grammar. For example, an array of bits yielding integers [0,1,1,2] would generate a NN with a single node with a logistic activation function, a subtraction transfer function, and a single input of feature number three modified by a randomly generated weight. A slightly more complex NN example that could be generated from this grammar with the right integer set is shown in Fig. 1.

Fig. 1 A GE-evolved neural network with logistic activation nodes, arithmetic transfer functions, numeric weights, and feature inputs

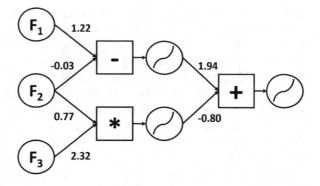

```
<root>       ::= <node> <input>
<node>       ::= <activation> <transfer>
<input>      ::= <input> <input>              0
               | <feature> <weight>           1
               | <node> <input>               2
<activation> ::= logistic                     0
               | linear                       1
<transfer>   ::= addition                     0
               | subtraction                  1
               | multiplication               2
               | division                     3
<feature>    ::= feature 1                     0
               | feature 2                     1
               | feature 3                     2
<weight>     ::= random number
```

Once a grammar is specified a genetic algorithm or any other optimization approach that operates on an array of bits can be applied. Neural networks constructed and optimized in this manner provide tremendous flexibility for modeling complex patterns in big data. A key question is whether these methods could be extended to deep learning or whether smaller networks optimized using GE could approximate the performance of much larger NN.

4 A Grammatical Evolution Approach to Systems Genomics Modeling and Simulation

Understanding how interindividual differences in DNA sequences map onto interindividual differences in phenotypes is a central focus of human genetics. Genotypes contribute to the expression of phenotypes through a hierarchical network of biochemical, metabolic, and physiological systems. The availability of biological information at all levels in the hierarchical mapping between genotype and phenotype has given rise to a new field called systems biology. One goal of systems biology is to develop a bioinformatics framework for integrating multiple levels of biological information through the development of theory and tools that can be used for mathematical modeling and simulation [11]. The promise of both human genetics and systems biology is improved human health through the improvement of disease diagnosis, prevention, and treatment. We illustrate here the use of GE to discover and optimize Petri net models of discrete dynamical systems.

Petri nets are a type of directed graph that can be used to model discrete dynamical systems [2]. Goss and Peccoud [5] demonstrated that Petri nets could be used to model molecular interactions in biochemical systems. The core Petri net consists of two different types of nodes: places and transitions. Using the biochemical systems analogy of [5], places represent molecular species. Each place has a certain number of tokens that represent the number of molecules for that particular molecular species. A transition is analogous to a molecular or chemical reaction and is said to fire when it acquires tokens from a source place and, after a possible delay, deposits tokens in a destination place. Tokens travel from a place to a transition or from a transition to a place via arcs with specific weights or bandwidths. While the number of tokens transferred from place to transition to place is determined by the arc weights (or bandwidths), the rate at which the tokens are transferred is determined by the delay associated with the transition. Transition behavior is also constrained by the weights of the source and destination arcs. A transition will only fire if two preconditions are met: (1) if the source place can completely supply the capacity of the source arc and, (2) if the destination place has the capacity available to store the number of tokens provided by the full weight of the destination arc. Transitions without an input arc act as if they are connected to a limitless supply of tokens. Similarly, transitions without an output arc can consume a limitless supply of tokens. The firing rate of the transition can be immediate, delayed deterministically, or delayed stochastically, depending on the complexity needed. The fundamental behavior of a Petri net can be controlled by varying the maximum number of tokens a place can hold, the weight of each arc, and the firing rates of the transitions.

Moore and Hahn [18, 19] developed a BNF grammar for Petri nets in BNF. For the Petri net models, the terminal set includes, for example, the basic building blocks of a Petri net: places, arcs, and transitions. The nonterminal set includes the names of production rules that construct the Petri net. For example, a nonterminal might name a production rule for determining whether an arc has weights that are fixed or genotype-dependent. We show below the production rule that was executed to begin the model building process for the study by [19].

```
<root> ::= <pick_a_gene> <pick_a_gene> <pick_a_gene>
<net_iterations> <expr> <transition> <transition> <place_noarc>
```

When the initial <root> production rule is executed, a single Petri net place with no entering or exiting arc (i.e. <place_noarc>) is selected and a transition leading into or out of that place is selected. The arc connecting the transition and place can be dependent on the genotypes of the genes selected by <pick_a_gene>. The nonterminal <expr> is a function that allows the Petri net to grow. The production rule for <expr> is shown below.

```
<expr> ::= <expr> <expr>    0
         | <arc>            1
         | <transition>     2
         | <place>          3
```

Here, the selection of one of the four nonterminals (0, 1, 2, or 3) on the right-hand side of the production rule is determined by a combination of bits in the genetic algorithm.

The base or minimum Petri net that is constructed using the <root> production rule consists of a single place, two transitions, and an arc that connects each transition to the place. Multiple calls to the production rule <expr> by the genetic algorithm chromosome can build any connected Petri net. In addition, the number of times the Petri net is to be iterated is selected with the nonterminal <net_iterations>. Many other production rules define the arc weights, the genotype-dependent arcs and transitions, the number of initial tokens in a place, the place capacity, etc. All decisions made in the building of the Petri net model are made by each subsequent bit or combination of bits in the genetic algorithm chromosome.

Figure 2 shows an example Petri net constructed by Moore and Hahn[19]. This model was evolved using GE to map genotypic variation across different genes to disease susceptibility determined by levels of protein product. Here, the GE evolved different arcs (A) connecting transitions (T) to molecular species (P) to be dependent on different genotypic values at a particular gene. Thus, the GE was able to evolve both the structure of the network and the parameter settings to reach some target behavior.

Fig. 2 A GE-evolved Petri net with different arcs (A) connecting transitions (T) to molecular species or places (P). Each arc, transition, and place has several different parameters evolved by the GE that govern its behavior

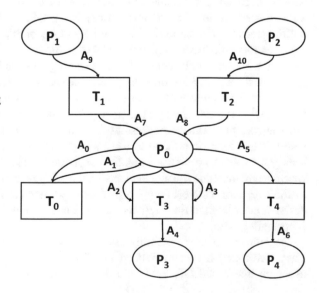

5 The Future of Grammatical Evolution Approaches to Bioinformatics and Systems Genomics

The potential impact of evolutionary computation in the biological and biomedical sciences is enormous [27]. Grammatical evolution has a place in this future given its flexible grammar-based method for representing solutions to complex problems. We list here several computational challenges that will need to be addressed for application of GE to biological problems. We then end with some of the hot new biological problems that GE might be useful for.

The most important challenge of using GE or other similar approaches is the inherent complexity of biological systems. Biological systems are driven by molecular, physiological, anatomical, environmental, and social interactions. Layer on top of this big data from technologies such as high-throughput DNA sequencing and the modeling challenges become manyfold more significant. No computational modeling approach is immune to these challenges. Here are a few research topics that will need to be explored in the coming years. First, what is the best way to adapt GE to handle diverse data types coming from different sources and technologies? Kim et al. [12, 13] have started to address this with the GENN system described above. Second, what is the best way to integrate expert knowledge into GE to help identify and exploit good building blocks? This is important to provide the GE with some direction in an effectively infinite search space. Fortunately, there are many sources of expert knowledge for biological systems including literature sources such as PubMed and biological knowledge bases such as the hetionet database that integrates 29 different sources of information about genes, diseases, drugs, pathways, anatomies, processes, etc. [8]. Third, what is the best way to parallelize GE for use in cluster or cloud computing technology? Fourth, what is the best way to store GE results and to create knowledge from those results that can in turn be used by the GE in future runs? Fifth, what is the best way to perform multiobjective optimization? This is important for biological problems where there are often multiple fitness objectives. For example, using GE to identify genetic risk factor for disease could benefit from rewarding models for the drugability of the genes it is finding in addition to measures such as classification accuracy. This helps the GE reward models with genes that are actionable in addition to being predictive. Finally, what is the best way to interpret GE models and results? This is perhaps the most important challenge because at the end of the day biologists want actionable results. They want to be able to learn something from a GE result that will make it easy for them to design a validation experiment. This is not easy and is an area where many machine learning and artificial intelligence efforts fall short. If we want to solve the world's most complex problems, we need to keep in mind the ability to derive impact from those solutions. This is something the deep learning community is struggling with.

Regarding the interpretability issue it is worth mentioning the work of [30]. They developed a system dubbed *G-PEA* (*G*P *P*ost-*E*volutionary *A*nalysis), for use with tree-based GP. First, one defines a functionality-based similarity score between expressions, which G-PEA uses to find subtrees that carry out similar semantic *tasks*. Then, the system clusters similar sub-expressions from a number of independently-evolved fit solutions, thus identifying important *semantic building blocks* ensconced within the hard-to-read GP trees. These blocks help identify the important parts of the evolved solutions and are a crucial step in understanding how they work. Though developed within the context of tree-based GP, ideas from G-PEA may well transfer to GE.

An emergent, important theme in artificial intelligence is that of usability and accessibility to a person not versed with machine learning. Towards this end [22] have developed PennAI, an accessible artificial intelligence whose ultimate goal is to deliver an open-source, user-friendly AI system that is specialized for machine learning analysis of complex data in the biomedical and healthcare domains. It would be interesting to examine the use of GE within the context of PennAI.

The biological and biomedical sciences are changing rapidly. We highlight here a few hot areas where GE could be focused in the coming years. First, cell biology and genomics continues to be transformed by high-throughput technologies such as DNA sequencing, mass spectrometry, and imaging. Each of these technologies generates massive amounts of data about different molecules and cellular processes. A central challenge in bioinformatics is the integration of these data to facilitate new scientific questions. Understanding how different molecular and cellular levels interact to influence a biological process or outcome is a place where grammatical evolution can have a significant impact given its inherent flexibility for program or solution representation. Second, mobile devices and remote sensors are starting to have a big impact on the biological and biomedical sciences. Remote sensors can track animals and plants in ecological settings while wearable devices can measure physiology and behavior of human subjects in their natural environment. These new technologies generate massive amounts of heterogeneous data that often have a time component adding an additional dimension of complexity. This is an area that could greatly benefit from GE. Finally, electronic health records (EHR) have exploded over the last several years for capturing, storing, integrating, and managing health data. There is an unprecedented opportunity to develop and apply methods such as GE for identifying patterns of health measures that are predictive of disease outcomes and drug response, for example. This is an emerging area that needs machine learning and artificial intelligence strategies for improving health and healthcare. An example application is the use of GE for real-time monitoring of patient data synced with clinical decision support systems that can provide instantaneous alerts to clinicians about patient characteristics that are urgent. Some of the technical challenges mentioned above will need to be solved for GE use in these domains to become a reality.

References

1. M. Alfonseca, F.J.S. Gil, Evolving an ecology of mathematical expressions with grammatical evolution. Biosystems **111**(2), 111–119 (2013)
2. J. Desel, G. Juhás, "What is a Petri net?" Informal answers for the informed reader, in *Unifying Petri Nets: Advances in Petri Nets* ed. by H. Ehrig, J. Padberg, G. Juhás, G. Rozenberg (Springer, Berlin/Heidelberg, 2001), pp. 1–25
3. M. Fenton, D. Lynch, S. Kucera, H. Claussen, M. O'Neill, Multilayer optimization of heterogeneous networks using grammatical genetic programming. IEEE Trans. Cybern. **47**(9), 2938–2950 (2017)
4. E. Ferrante, A.E. Turgut, E. Duéñez-Guzmán, M. Dorigo, T. Wenseleers, Evolution of self-organized task specialization in robot swarms. PLoS Comput. Biol. **11**(8), e1004,273 (2015)
5. P.J. Goss, J. Peccoud, Quantitative modeling of stochastic systems in molecular biology by using stochastic Petri nets. Proc. Nat. Acad. Sci. **95**(12), 6750–6755 (1998)
6. C.S. Greene, J. Tan, M. Ung, J.H. Moore, C. Cheng, Big data bioinformatics. J. Cell. Physiol. **229**(12), 1896–1900 (2014)
7. J.I. Hidalgo, J.M. Colmenar, G. Kronberger, S.M. Winkler, O. Garnica, J. Lanchares, Data based prediction of blood glucose concentrations using evolutionary methods. J. Med. Syst. **41**(9), 142 (2017)
8. D.S. Himmelstein, A. Lizee, C. Hessler, L. Brueggeman, S.L. Chen, D. Hadley, A. Green, P. Khankhanian, S.E. Baranzini, Systematic integration of biomedical knowledge prioritizes drugs for repurposing. eLife. **6**, 1–35 (2017)
9. E.R. Holzinger, C.C. Buchanan, S.M. Dudek, E.C. Torstenson, S.D. Turner, M.D. Ritchie, Initialization parameter sweep in ATHENA: optimizing neural networks for detecting gene-gene interactions in the presence of small main effects, in *Proceedings of the 12th Annual Conference on Genetic and Evolutionary Computation* (ACM, New York, 2010), pp. 203–210
10. E.R. Holzinger, S.M. Dudek, A.T. Frase, S.A. Pendergrass, M.D. Ritchie, ATHENA: the analysis tool for heritable and environmental network associations. Bioinformatics **30**(5), 698–705 (2013)
11. T. Ideker, T. Galitski, L. Hood, A new approach to decoding life: systems biology. Ann. Rev. Genomics Hum. Genet. **2**(1), 343–372 (2001)
12. D. Kim, R. Li, S.M. Dudek, M.D. Ritchie, ATHENA: Identifying interactions between different levels of genomic data associated with cancer clinical outcomes using grammatical evolution neural network. BioData Min. **6**(1), 23 (2013)
13. D. Kim, R. Li, S.M. Dudek, A.T. Frase, S.A. Pendergrass, M.D. Ritchie, Knowledge-driven genomic interactions: an application in ovarian cancer. BioData Min. **7**(1), 20 (2014)
14. J.R. Koza, *Genetic Programming: On the Programming of Computers by Means of Natural Selection*, vol. 1 (MIT Press, Cambridge, 1992)
15. M. Marcotty, H. Ledgard, *The World of Programming Languages* (Springer, Berlin, 1986)
16. B.A. McKinney, D.M. Reif, M.D. Ritchie, J.H. Moore, Machine learning for detecting gene-gene interactions. Appl. Bioinform. **5**(2), 77–88 (2006)
17. J.H. Moore, Bioinformatics. J. Cell. Physiol. **213**(2), 365–369 (2007). http://dx.doi.org/10.1002/jcp.21218
18. J.H. Moore, L.W. Hahn, Petri net modeling of high-order genetic systems using grammatical evolution. BioSystems **72**(1), 177–186 (2003)
19. J.H. Moore, L.W. Hahn, An improved grammatical evolution strategy for hierarchical Petri net modeling of complex genetic systems, in *EvoWorkshops* (Springer, Berlin, 2004), pp. 63–72
20. J.H. Moore, F.W. Asselbergs, S.M. Williams, Bioinformatics challenges for genome-wide association studies. Bioinformatics **26**(4), 445–455 (2010)
21. A.A. Motsinger-Reif, S.M. Dudek, L.W. Hahn, M.D. Ritchie, Comparison of approaches for machine-learning optimization of neural networks for detecting gene-gene interactions in genetic epidemiology. Genet. Epidemiol. **32**(4), 325–340 (2008)

22. R.S. Olson, M. Sipper, W. La Cava, S. Tartarone, S. Vitale, W. Fu, J.H. Holmes, J.H. Moore, A system for accessible artificial intelligence, in *Genetic Programming Theory and Practice XV* (Springer, New York, 2017). https://arxiv.org/abs/1705.00594 (to appear)
23. M.D. Ritchie, B.C. White, J.S. Parker, L.W. Hahn, J.H. Moore, Optimization of neural network architecture using genetic programming improves detection and modeling of gene-gene interactions in studies of human diseases. BMC Bioinforma. **4**(1), 28 (2003)
24. M.D. Ritchie, A.A. Motsinger, W.S. Bush, C.S. Coffey, J.H. Moore, Genetic programming neural networks: a powerful bioinformatics tool for human genetics. Appl. Soft Comput. **7**(1), 471–479 (2007)
25. C. Ryan, J.J. Collins, M. O'Neill, Grammatical evolution: evolving programs for an arbitrary language, in *Genetic Programming, First European Workshop, EuroGP'98*, Paris, France, 14–15 April 1998, Proceedings, pp. 83–96 (1998). https://doi.org/10.1007/BFb0055930
26. M. Sipper, *Machine Nature: The Coming Age of Bio-Inspired Computing* (McGraw-Hill, New York, 2002)
27. M. Sipper, R.S. Olson, J.H. Moore, Evolutionary computation: the next major transition of artificial intelligence? BioData Min. **10**(1), 26 (2017). https://doi.org/10.1186/s13040-017-0147-3
28. O. Smart, I.G. Tsoulos, D. Gavrilis, G. Georgoulas, Grammatical evolution for features of epileptic oscillations in clinical intracranial electroencephalograms. Expert Syst. Appl. **38**(8), 9991–9999 (2011)
29. S.D. Turner, S.M. Dudek, M.D. Ritchie, ATHENA: a knowledge-based hybrid backpropagation-grammatical evolution neural network algorithm for discovering epistasis among quantitative trait loci. BioData Min. **3**(1), 5 (2010)
30. K. Wolfson, S. Zakov, M. Sipper, M. Ziv-Ukelson, Have your spaghetti and eat it too: evolutionary algorithmics and post-evolutionary analysis. Genet. Program Evolvable Mach. **12**(2), 121–160 (2011)

Grammatical Evolution with Coevolutionary Algorithms in Cyber Security

Erik Hemberg, Anthony Erb Lugo, Dennis Garcia, and Una-May O'Reilly

Abstract We apply Grammatical Evolution (GE), and multi population competitive coevolutionary algorithms to the domain of cybersecurity. Our interest (and concern) is the evolution of network denial of service attacks. In these cases, when attackers are deterred by a specific defense, they evolve their strategies until variations find success. Defenders are then forced to counter the new variations and an arms race ensues. We use GE and grammars to conveniently express and explore the behavior of network defenses and denial of service attacks under different mission and network scenarios. We use coevolution to model competition between attacks and defenses and the larger scale arms race. This allows us to study the dynamics and the solutions of the competing adversaries.

1 Introduction

Cyber attacks have increased in frequency, sophistication, and severity, and have been the cause of numerous disruptions. Denial of service attacks target computer networks because critical data and transactions now flow through them. As a result, it is crucial to not only be aware of the capabilities of cyber attackers, but also to design more secure networks. The issue with the current state of cyber defenses, however, is that they are largely reactive in nature. It is sometimes only when an attack is experienced that a network defense is strengthened. When attackers consequently alter their strategies, the of reactive defensive behavior repeats. Our goal is to investigate this coevolutionary arms race in order to shed light on its dynamics and identify robust defenses in advance of deployment.

Grammatical Evolution, see Fig. 1, is initialized with a grammar expressed in Backus Naur Form (BNF) and search parameters. The grammar describes a language in the problem domain and its (rewrite) rules express how a sentence,

E. Hemberg (✉) · A. E. Lugo · D. Garcia · U.-M. O'Reilly
Computer Science and Artificial Intelligence Lab (CSAIL), MIT, Boston, MA, USA
e-mail: aelugo@alum.mit.edu; dagarcia@alum.mit.edu; unamay@csail.mit.edu

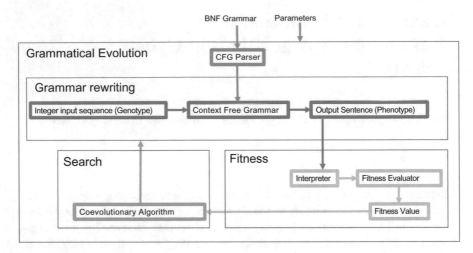

Fig. 1 Grammatical evolution takes a BNF grammar and search parameters as input. The grammar rewrites the integer input to a sentence. Fitness is calculated by interpreting the sentence and then evaluate it. The search component modifies the solutions using two central mechanisms: fitness based selection and random variation. We use coevolutionary algorithms

i.e. solution, can be composed by rewriting a start symbol, i.e. high level goal. In our system's GE component, the BNF description, upon input, is parsed to a context free grammar representation. GE genotypes are fixed length integer vectors. Sentences of the grammar are GE phenotypes. To decode a genotype, in sequence each of its integers is used to control the rewriting. This sentence is the phenotype. Fitness is calculated by interpreting the sentence and then evaluating it according to some objective(s). When we use our system to solve different problems, we only have to change the BNF grammar, the interpreter and the fitness function for each problem, rather than change the genotype representation. This modularity of GE and the reusability of the GE parser and rewriter are efficient software engineering and problem solving advantages. The grammar further helps us communicate our system's functionality to stakeholders because it enables conversations and validation at the domain level rather than at the algorithm level. This contributes to stakeholder confidence in solutions and our system.

Our system is named RIVALS [10]. Rather than manually tune and invent defenses for a network every time an attacker adapts and acts in a novel way, RIVALS assists during network design and hardening with the goal of anticipating attack evolution and identifying a robust defense that can circumvent the arms race and the reactive counter-measure postures. It uses coevolutionary algorithms [19] (and GE) to generate evolving network attacks and to evolve network defenses that effectively counter them, see Fig. 2. RIVALS's research is grounded by focusing on peer-to-peer networks, specifically the Chord protocol, and extreme distributed denial of service (DDOS) attacks. A peer-to-peer network is a robust and resilient means of securing mission reliability in the face of extreme DDOS attacks.

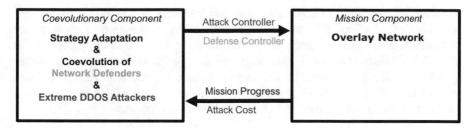

Fig. 2 RIVALS system overview. Defenders are marked in blue and attackers in red

RIVALS' premise is that its attention to the coevolutionary nature of attack and defense dynamics will to help identify robust network design and deployment configurations that support mission completion despite an ongoing attack.

RIVALS currently includes a peer-to-peer network simulator that runs the Chord [22] protocol. It models simple attacks and defenses on networks running on the simulator. It measures the performance of attackers and defenders through the concept of a mission. A mission is represented by a set of tasks to be completed. These tasks rely on the network's quality of service to succeed. An attacker's goal is to degrade the network so that the tasks, and in extension the mission, fail. Meanwhile, a defender's goal is to ensure the success of the mission. Mission completion and resource cost metrics serve as attacker and defender measures of success. DDOS attacks in RIVALS are modeled as multiple nodes being selected and, from a start time, being completely disabled for some duration.

To model the co-adaptive behavior of adversaries, RIVALS sets up separate populations of attackers and defenders and coevolves them under the direction of a coevolutionary algorithm. Over the course of many generations, a coevolutionary optimization process reveals dual collections of more effective defender and attacker strategies. At this point in time RIVALS has a suite of different coevolutionary algorithms with grammars for two simple problems. The algorithms explore archiving as a means of maintaining progressive exploration and support the evaluation of different solution concepts. All algorithms in our suite reuse the parser and rewriter component of GE.

The rest of this paper is organized as follows. In Sect. 2, we introduce similar work as well as necessary background information on peer-to-peer attacks and coevolutionary algorithms. Next, in Sect. 3, we present a brief overview of RIVALS. Section 4 presents the our experimentation and Sect. 5 shows the results. Finally, Sect. 6 concludes the paper and discusses potential future directions.

2 Related Work

Our project investigates proactive cyber security modeling by means of GE and coevolutionary search algorithms. This section of related work and background information considers cyber security, coevolutionary algorithms and GE in different combinations. In Sect. 2.1 we discuss projects at the intersection of evolutionary algorithms and cyber security, comparing them to RIVALS where relevant. In Sect. 2.2 we differentiate coevolutionary search algorithms from other EAs, independent of GE, and in Sect. 2.3 we discuss systems at the intersection of GE and coevolution. To date RIVALS is the only system that combines GE and coevolution in order to investigate a problem in the domain of cyber security.

2.1 Cyber Security and Evolutionary Algorithms

Moving Target Defense (MTD) projects, like RIVALS, use Evolutionary Algorithms (EAs) in a cyber security problem domain. The strategy of a MTD is to keep an attacker off guard by continually changing system configurations or information that the attacker needs to effectively attack. Strategies could involve changing the software underlying platforms, the location of sensitive data or the timing of system functions. For example, the system of [25] uses a GA to evolve adaptable adversarial strategies for defense against zero-day exploits. The system only adapts a defender population while RIVALS adapts both defender and attacker populations. In another contrast, it encodes strategies as binary chromosomes that represent finite state machines whereas RIVALS' uses a context free grammar. Arguably the important difference between RIVALS and this system is that evolution is used to address only two fixed scenarios while in RIVALS attackers compete with multiple defenders and defenders compete with multiple attackers.

Another work in this context and related to RIVALS is the coevolutionary agent-based network defense lightweight event system (CANDLES) [20]. It is designed to coevolve attacker and defender strategies in the context of a custom, abstract computer network defense simulation. CANDLES' attack and defense strategies are not expressed with grammars.

2.2 Coevolutionary Search

Coevolutionary algorithms are well suited to domains that have no intrinsic objective measure, also called *interactive* domains [19]. They can be distinguished as two types: (a) Compositional coevolutionary algorithms that are used to solve problems where a solution involves interaction among many components that together might be thought of as a team. This is often called cooperative coevolution. (b) Test-based coevolutionary algorithms that are used when the quality of a potential *solution* to the problem is determined by its performance when interacting with some set of *tests*. This is often called competitive coevolution.

Competitive coevolutionary algorithms are often applied in game search [19]. They are also related to game theory [19]. One advantage over game theory is that coevolutionary algorithms can be applied to larger search spaces [20].

There are a variety of examples of coevolutionary projects. One more theoretical project has investigated solution concepts for testcase coevolution with a no free lunch framework [23]. Others address application domains such as streaming data classification [13], complexification of solutions [21], simulations of behavior and bug fixes [16].

2.2.1 Solution Concepts for Coevolutionary Algorithms

Coevolutionary algorithms differ from other EAs in one respect because they have two interacting populations. These dual populations imply that the algorithm explores domains in which the quality of a *solution* is determined by its performance when interacting with a set of *tests*. In return, a *test*'s quality is determined by its performance when interacting with some set of *solutions*. For example, the *tests* of a network attack strategy are different network routing behaviors that could resist the attack, and inversely the *tests* of a network behavior are different attack strategies that could disrupt the network.

Because a *solution*'s performance is measured against multiple *tests*, coevolutionary algorithms use *solution concepts* to express fitness and clarify what constitutes a superior solution [19]. Solution concepts include:

Best Worst Case A *solution*'s fitness is its worst performance against the set of *tests* that it tries to solve or its performance against the fittest test case. The coevolutionary algorithm's goal is to optimize the best worse case solution.

Maximization of Expected Utility A *solution*'s fitness is its average performance against the test cases. It is usually assumed that *tests* have equal importance. The coevolutionary algorithm's goal is to optimize the average case solution.

Nash Equilibrium Solutions which lead to stable *solution* states in which no sole actor can their improve their state unilaterally are preferred. The coevolutionary algorithm's goal is to find solutions at a Nash equilibrium.

Pareto Optimality Each *test* is considered to be an independent objective and a *solution* is a multi-dimensional datum in this multi-objective space. From this space, a pareto optimal (non-dominated) set of *solutions* can be identified as superior *solutions*.

It should also be noted that the interactive aspect of *solution* fitness also implies the algorithm lacks an *exact* fitness measurement. That is, usually, Evolutionary Algorithms rely upon a fitness function, a function of the form $f : G \mapsto \mathbb{R}$ that assigns a real value to each possible genotype in G. Individual solutions are compared as $f(g_0)$ with $f(g_1)$ and their relative ranking based on fitness is always the same, i.e. exact. In contrast, in coevolutionary algorithms two individuals are compared based on their interactions with other individuals. and because these individuals are only samples from a population and may change as a population undergoes evolution, the ranking of an individual relative to another solution is essentially an estimate.

We now describe a set of coevolutionary algorithm challenges and how they are remedied.

2.2.2 Coevolutionary Algorithm Challenges and Remedies

Coevolutionary algorithms are challenging to work with because we have limited understanding of their detailed dynamics. Their two populations and dynamic solution concepts make them harder to interpret [8]. The search driver, i.e. the selection pressure, is difficult to control because fitness measurements are only estimates. Fitness estimation makes it hard to precisely determine whether the algorithm is making productive progress [19]. The problem of local optima still exists as it does with other EAs. The arms race we use coevolutionary algorithms for, in fact does not automatically appear since *tests* can be uninteresting, or not conform to some a priori goal [8]. This requires vigilant design and monitoring.

Coevolutionary search and optimization exhibits some unique pathologies that again arise from fitness being measured as a result of one or more interactions. One pathology is *intransitivity*, i.e. non transitive relations can exist between the competing solution spaces [8]. For example, consider the intransitive cycle in Rock-Paper-Scissors where Rock beats Scissors, Scissors beats Paper, and Paper beats Rock [4, 8, 14]. Some intransitive pathologies are:

Red Queen Effect Two populations continuously adapt to each other and their subjective fitness improves, but they fail to make any consistent progress along the objective metric. Conversely, they do make progress but the fitness estimate does not reflect this and falsely indicates a lack of progress [4].

Cycling The adversary (whether *solution* or *test*) drops some element of selection pressure so abilities can be "forgotten" only to reuse them.

Transitive dominance One *solution* can be superior to a *test* that at the same time is superior to the *solution* according to a different conflicting subjective metric [4].

A general remedy to intransitivity is to maintain diversity and make sure an informative search gradient is always available. Another remedy is to explicitly assure that useful *tests* persist. This can be accomplished by introducing memory. Memory is usually implemented by means of an archive (see Fig. 3), a repository of solutions that is maintained outside the algorithmic cycle of generational selection and variation, something like a *Hall of Fame*.

Another pathology is *disengagement* [4]. This occurs when one population is constantly superior to the other. At this point the subjective fitnesses of both populations become constant so there is no differential selection pressure and the search gradient is lost. Drift results. Memory also helps address disengagement. Another remedy is to search explicitly for lower difficulty *tests* by looking for those which create less disagreement among *solutions* [4].

Memory, of course, also addresses cycling by preventing a *test* that selects for a *solution* from evolving out of the population.

Fig. 3 A coevolutionary
algorithm with two archives

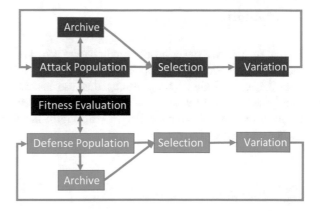

2.3   Coevolution and Grammatical Evolution

GE has previously been used in tandem with coevolutionary algorithms. In one use
case, [7], coevolution and GE are used together to cope with dynamic environments.
The GEGE method aims to find "modules" that can be reused when the environment
changes, it has a compact representation of a larger grammar with an increased
search space and strongly coupled grammars [3]. It uses cooperative coevolution
to simultaneously evolve the grammar and genetic code with a hierarchy of
grammars [7].

One study, [17, 18], used both GE and a Pareto-coevolutionary algorithm in
a supervised machine learning context to train classifiers with a multi-objective
fitness measure. It trained the classifiers via a two-population competition. Another
study used both GE and coevolution to develop an Artificial Life model for evolving a predator–prey ecosystem of mathematical expressions [2]. Coevolutionary
algorithms with GE have also been applied to financial trading using multiple
cooperative populations [1, 9].

In one competitive coevolution and GE example, spatial coevolution in age-
layered planes evolves robocode for robots [11]. In another, in the *STEALTH
(Simulating Tax Evasion And Law Through Heuristics)* [12] project, a coevolutionary and modeling methodology is used to explore how non-compliant tax strategies
evolve in response to abstracted auditing and regulatory attempts that evolve to
detect them. STEALTH shares the arms race element of this chapter's work because
in taxation, similar to cyber security, as soon as an evasion scheme is detected and
stopped, a new, slightly mutated, variant of the scheme appears.

3   Methods

In this section we describe the methods we use. We present them in the following order: peer-to-peer networks in Sect. 3.1, the RIVALS network simulator in Sect. 3.2, coevolutionary algorithms that use archives in Sect. 3.3 and grammar representations for cyber security in Sect. 3.4. Because grammars are expressions of problem solving behavior, Sect. 3.4 also introduces the two problems we use to demonstrate RIVALS.

3.1   Peer-to-Peer Network

DDOS attacks often target a specific server within a network. By overloading this server with work, the server effectively becomes useless and the network struggles to route traffic through it. In a centralized network an attacker could attack its key central server, e.g. the server that is responsible for directing traffic to all the other servers, and take down the entire network. Peer-to-peer networks are not so fragile. They distribute data and resources with redundancy and thus have no single point of failure making them inherently more robust to DDOS attacks. Peer-to-peer networks are also robust to topological changes. They can continue to function even as nodes drop out as what may happen during a DDOS attack. They also can integrate additional nodes should they come back online. As an example, the Chord protocol includes a stabilization service handles nodes that are joining and leaving the network.

3.1.1   Chord Overview

We now briefly describe important elements of the Chord protocol (for more details see [22]) and our implementation of it. A peer-to-peer network is an overlay of a physical network. In Chord the logical network topology is a ring. Location-wise, each peer has a successor node and a predecessor node in the ring. Requests for data from a node need to be looked up to identify which node has the data and the node needs to be efficiently accessed. For lookup Chord uses distributed key hashing. For routing Chord relies upon node-based finger tables. A finger table is a look-up table for neighboring peers. Each table holds information that helps to logarithmically decrease the cost of finding which node holds a queried key. The Chord protocol includes a stabilization service handles nodes that are joining and leaving the network.

3.2   RIVALS Network Simulator

In RIVALS we currently model Chord on a single workstation. Upon nodes leaving or joining the network, the original Chord protocol *eventually* stabilizes itself through periodic actions. In RIVALS' implementation every time a node leaves or joins the network, successor and predecessor pointers as well as the finger tables are immediately repaired. In RIVALS nodes in the Chord network become part of the circle by receiving an m-bit identifier obtained by hashing the nodes with SHA-1.[1]

The network simulator has two versions. One version, we call the "logical" version, and the other the "logical to physical" version. The differences between these two versions of the software are explained in the next two subsections.

3.2.1   Logical Network

The reason we name this version the "logical" version is because we assume the message gets sent via the hop series defined by the logical network. Figure 4 shows a simple physical network on the left, and the virtual (logical) Chord overlay network that gets constructed by the protocol on the right. In this example, if we are interested in finding a specific key in the network, we can ask any peer and that peer will use its finger table information to route the query to some peer that is closer to the target peer containing the desired key in the identifier circle. This series of queries

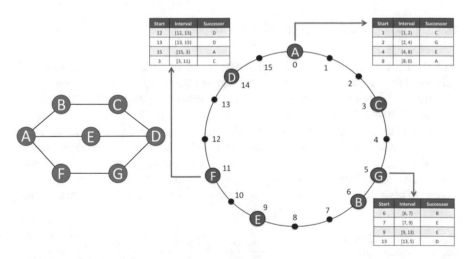

Fig. 4 Physical network on the left and its virtual(logical) Chord overlay representation on the right. The finger tables for nodes A, G, and F are shown

---

[1] In RIVALS' implementation, `Python`'s `random` library is used.

provides a hopping series of the nodes visited before reaching the target node with the key. For example, if we ask node F where the key with identifier 3 is, it would pass the query to node A, and then node A would find that the key is located at node C. This results in a hopping series of F, A, C. In the simulator implementation, rather than use the protocol as a means of finding a key in the network, we use it as a means to represent the sending of a message through the network. We achieve this by asking the peer we consider the starting node, or the node responsible for sending the message, to find the identifier associated with the target node. In this sense, the difference is that we now use the protocol to lookup target node identifiers instead of key identifiers.

3.2.2 Logical to Physical Network

The key difference between the "logical" version and the "logical to physical" version of the simulator is that this version increases the complexity and realism by simulating messages flowing through the physical layer of the network as opposed to just through the virtual Chord overlay ring. As a result, in this version, when sending a message, instead of modeling this as the message hopping through the ring and reaching its destination, each hop from one node to another overlays the message passing from the equivalent nodes but along the routes and routers of the actual physical network.

3.3 Coevolutionary Algorithms with Archives

In RIVALS we use multiple solution concepts and coevolutionary algorithms with GE, see Table 1. Our baseline algorithm, named Coev, is a simple coevolutionary algorithm without an archive [12] that uses a maximum expected utility solution concept. When it is configured to use a best worst solution concept instead, we call it MinMax. A third algorithm, MaxSolve uses the maximum expected utility solution concept and both a *solution* and a *test* archive [6]. It manages archive growth with a hard maximum size limit. Upon reaching maximum size, it winnows the archive according to how many attacks a defender resists or vice-verse, how many defense an attack is effective against. Our fourth algorithm is Incremental

Table 1 Coevolutionary algorithms used in RIVALS

Name	Archives	Solution concept
Coev	0	Maximum expected utility
MinMax	0	Best worst case
MaxSolve	2	Maximum expected utility
IPCA	1	Pareto optimality
rIPCA	2	Pareto optimality

Algorithm 1: `IPCA`, `rIPCA`

1: **procedure** IPCA(populations, generations)
2:    $t \leftarrow 0$
3:    $D^0 \leftarrow$ populations$_{\text{defenders}}$ ▷ Defender is *solution*
4:    $A^0 \leftarrow$ populations$_{\text{attackers}}$ ▷ Attacker is *test*
5:    $D^*, A^* \leftarrow \emptyset$ ▷ Best solutions
6:    **while** $t <$ generations **do**   ▷ Iterate for # generations
7:        $A^t \leftarrow$ NonDominated(D^t, A^t)   ▷ Extract attacker pareto-front
8:        **if** `rIPCA` **then**
9:            $D^t \leftarrow$ NonDominated(A^t, D^t)   ▷ Extract defender pareto-front
10:       $D \leftarrow$ GenerateDefenders(D^t)
11:       $A \leftarrow$ GenerateAttackers(A^t)
12:       $A' \leftarrow$ UsefulAttackers(A, A^t, D, D^t)   ▷ Get useful attackers
13:       $A^{t+1} \leftarrow A^{t+1} \cup A'$
14:       $D^{t+1} \leftarrow D^t$
15:       **for** $i = 1..|D|$ **do**
16:           **if** UsefulDefender(D_i, D^{t+1}, A^{t+1}) **then**   ▷ Get useful defenders
17:               $D^{t+1} \leftarrow D^{t+1} \cup D_i$
18:       **if** $D^{t+1} \neq D^t$ **then**
19:           $t \leftarrow t + 1$
20:       $D^*, A^* \leftarrow$ ExtractBest(D^{t+1}, A^{t+1})
21:   **return** D^*, A^* ▷ Returns best solutions found

Pareto-Coevolution Archive technique (`IPCA`), shown in Algorithm 1. `IPCA` uses a *solution* archive and the Pareto Optimal Set solution concept [5]. The archive is maintained by selecting *solutions* that are not dominated by other *solutions* in terms of which *tests* they solve, i.e. are useful. That is, if a *solution*, X, only solves tests A and B, and *solution*, Y, only solves test A, then *solution* X dominates Y and Y is removed from the archive. This provides monotonic evolutionary progress. Finally, our fifth algorithm is `rIPCA`, an extension of `IPCA` [10]. `rIPCA` applies the Pareto Optimal Set solution concept to both *solution* and *test* populations, as opposed to just the *solution* population as done in `IPCA` (see Algorithm 1 line 9). This unfortunately erases the monotonicity property of `IPCA` but it provides memory to both adversaries, rather than just one. For more details of `rIPCA` see [10]. In both `IPCA` and `rIPCA` we consider a *solution* to be a defense and a *test* to be an attack.

3.4 Problems and Grammars in RIVALS

RIVALS uses grammars to facilitate the expression and exploration of attack sequences and defender strategies. The grammars are very helpful in allowing domain knowledge to be naturally expressed. The ease of use of GE currently outweighs our concern regarding the low locality of GE operators [24]. We have two central grammars which each correspond to a problem we experiment with.

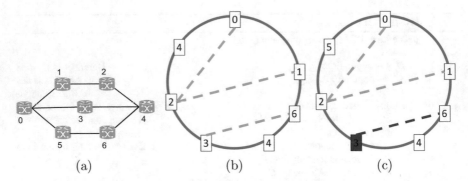

Fig. 5 Mobile asset placement problem example. (**a**) Physical network. (**b**) Virtual network with three tasks. (**c**) Virtual network with three tasks and the node 3 attacked. The task depending on node 3 fails. Dashed lines indicate the assets that are needed for the different tasks

3.4.1 Mobile Asset Placement

The mobile asset placement problem is to optimize the strategic placement of assets in a network. In a mission scenario we assume this optimization is determined before a mission and that the optimization only addresses assets which can feasibly be moved from one node to another or spun up at different nodes, i.e. that are "mobile".

While under the threat of node-level DDOS attack, the defense must enable a set of tasks. It does this by fielding feasible paths between the nodes that host the assets which support the tasks. A mobile asset is, for example, mobile personnel or a software application that can be served by any number of nodes. A task is, for example, the connection that allows a personnel member to use a software application. We show the concept of a task as a dashed line connecting nodes in Fig. 5. Attacks are models of DDOS attacks where a variable number of specific nodes are targeted and disabled. Any disabled node is considered unreachable. Thus an attack, to cause mission failure, must take down the nodes which host assets that support the tasks.

For example in Fig. 5 there are three tasks that need to be completed using six different assets. The physical network topology of the example is shown in Fig. 5a. The virtual (logical) overlay with the three tasks and assets are shown in Fig. 5b. An attack that results in a failed task on the network is shown in Fig. 5c.

To round out the definition of a problem it is necessary to state the fitness function of the attacker and of the defender. We state these in Sect. 4.2.

In the problem's defense grammar, each task is defined by its assets and where they are hosted. We currently assume a one-to-one mapping between assets and node identifiers, i.e. the node identifier is the same as the asset identifier.

The attack grammar for Fig. 5a, Topology 0, given start symbol `<Attacks>` is:

```
<Attacks> ::= DDOSAttack(<node>)
            | DDOSAttack(<node>), <Attacks>
<node> ::= 0 | 1 | 2 | 3 | 4 | 5 | 6
```

The corresponding grammar for the defending population with start symbol
<list> is:

```
<list> ::= [Task1(<assets1>, <assets1>), Task2(<assets1>, <assets1>),
            Task2(<assets1>, <assets1>), Task3(<assets1>, <assets1>),
            Task5(<assets1>, <assets1>), Task6(<assets1>, <assets1>)]
<assets1> ::= 0 | 1 | 2 | 3 | 4 | 5 | 6
```

Note that by defining different sets of assets the grammar can express constraints
as to where assets can be hosted. By defining different nodes in the attack grammar,
it is possible to express only the nodes reachable by the set of botnet compromised
nodes. Also note that while the grammars are low level abstractions of attacks or
defenses, this allows generality in the sense that they belie any number of mission
or attack goals, strategies, techniques and tactics at a higher level by the attacker
or defender. Finally, note that with a more complex simulator or an actual network
testbed, a simple grammar change could express task ordering and dependency.

3.4.2   Network Routing

The network routing problem is to complete a mission that is composed of tasks.
All tasks must complete for the mission to 100% succeed. Each task is completed if
source and destination nodes can be connected within a specified time interval, e.g.
a message can be sent between them.

The current RIVALS attack grammar for describing the behaviors in the network
routing problem is simple. An attack is one or more identifications of a node,
when it will start to be attacked and the duration of the attack. Given start symbol
<Attacks>, it is:

```
<Attacks> ::= DDOSAttack(<node>, <start_time>, <duration>)
            | DDOSAttack(<node>, <start_time>, <duration>), <Attacks>
<node> ::= 0 | 1 | 2 | 3 | 4 | 5 | 6
<start_time> ::= 0 | 1 | 2 | 3 | 4 | 5 | 6 | 7 | 8 | 9
<end_time> ::= 1 | 2 | 3 | 4 | 5 | 6 | 7 | 8 | 9
```

Note that the grammar is recursive and this allows an attack to target one or more
nodes.

An example of the attack grammar used in the logical to physical version of the
simulator upon receiving the start symbol <Attacks> is:

```
<Attacks> ::= {'physical_attacks': [<physical_attacks>],
              'logical_attacks': [<logical_attacks>]}
<physical_attacks> ::= DDOSAttack(<node>, <start_time>,
                <duration>), <physical_attacks>
                    | DDOSAttack(<node>, <start_time>,
                    <duration>)
```

```
<logical_attacks> ::= DDOSAttack(<node>, <start_time>,
                        <duration>),<logical_attacks>
                      | DDOSAttack(<node>, <start_time>, <duration>)
<node> ::= 0 | 1 | 2 | 3 | 4 | 5 | 6
<start_time> ::= 0 | 1 | 2 | 3 | 4 | 5 | 6 | 7 | 8 | 9
<end_time> ::= 1 | 2 | 3 | 4 | 5 | 6 | 7 | 8 | 9
```

In this grammar, because both the physical and virtual networks are utilized to represent the flow of a message, an attacker is allowed to target nodes at both the physical and virtual layers. The defense grammar in both versions of the simulator is simple because the problem assumes just three high level routing mechanisms (see Sect. 4.2.2). The grammar just chooses between them. This grammar, given the start symbol <Defense> is:

```
<Defense> ::= shortest_path_protocol
            | flooding_protocol
            | chord_protocol
```

4 Experiments

We conduct experiments using the RIVALS network simulator to demonstrate the combination of GE and coevolution for network related cyber security. The network simulator for our peer-to-peer network allows us to define three increasingly complex topologies and address two different problems for each of them. Each of these six combinations is what we call a *scenario*.

These experiments provide insights into how the algorithms perform as well as how they can scale over the different topologies. We present our experimental setup in Sect. 4.1 and scenarios in Sect. 4.2.

4.1 Experimental Setup

We experiment with a suite of 5 coevolutionary algorithms all with the same modular GE capability. They are presented in Table 1 and described in Sect. 3.3. Each experiment is one algorithm run 30 times (each time from different random initial conditions). Parameter settings for each run are presented in Table 2. Population and archive sizes reflect the search space size and time cost of running the network simulator. Other parameters are standard. We present results that are averaged over the 30 runs.

We perform our tests on an Intel(R) Xeon(R) CPU E5-2630 v4 @ 2.20GHz processor with 24 cores with 96GB of RAM. Tests are performed serially for greater accuracy and to eliminate any possible interference between tests. We report the execution time and the fitness of the best defender at the last generation as the final performance.

Table 2 Coevolutionary algorithm settings for the problems

Parameter setting	Value	Description
Population size	40(10 Topo 2)	Number of individuals in each population
Archive size	20	Max archive size (MaxSolve)
Generations	20	Number of times populations are evaluated
Max length	20	Max length of individual integer string
Parent archive probability	0.9	Probability of choosing parent from archive (MaxSolve)
Crossover probability	0.8	Probability of combining two individual integer strings
Mutation probability	0.1	Probability of integer change in individual

Coevolutionary algorithms specific settings are in brackets

4.2 Scenarios

Each network simulation or "run" explores one of six *scenarios*. A scenario is defined by a network topology and a problem. A problem is defined by objectives for the defender and attacker, their behaviors, which are expressed by grammars, and their fitness functions.

4.2.1 Network Topologies

The experimental topologies range in size and complexity. In order to keep the network simulation simple, we assume that every edge is unit-length.

Topology 0   We start with a simple topology, see Fig. 5a, that functions as a benchmark allowing us to explore simple mission scenarios exhaustively before scaling up to larger and more realistic topologies.

Topology 1   See Fig. 6. This topology has 25 nodes, arranged in four subnets with four nodes conceptually functioning as fully connected subnet routers. All 25 nodes are mapped to the logical peer-to-peer ring. Topologies 1 and 2 are assumed to be too large to conveniently enumerate all the combinations of attacks and defenses.

Topology 2   See Fig. 7. This topology has 36 nodes modeling subnet routers placed across a large geographic area. All 36 nodes are mapped to the logical peer-to-peer ring with an assumption that they serve sub nets that are not on the ring.

4.2.2 Problems

Each scenario solves one of two problems.

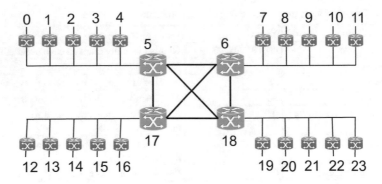

Fig. 6 Topology 1, larger network providing more nodes and a different topology

Fig. 7 Topology 2, possible network for a more realistic mission

1. **Mobile Asset Placement** This problem deals with the placement of network assets to serve tasks that support a mission. Optimal placement of the assets will minimize connectivity loss in an encounter with an attack. See Sect. 3.4.1 for the grammars and further details. The current version of the problem has six tasks. Each task uses two assets.

Attacker Fitness Function

$$f_a^{MAP} = \frac{n\_failed}{n\_tasks} - C\frac{n\_attacks}{n\_tasks}$$

n_tasks is the total number of tasks, n_failed is defined as how many tasks the attacker was able to disrupt, and $n\_attacks$ is the number of attacks the attacker used, $C = 1/1000$. This incentivizes attackers to disrupt tasks but with as few attacks as possible.

Defender Fitness Function

$$f_d^{MAP} = \frac{n\_successful}{n\_tasks} - n\_same\_nodes - n\_duplicate\_tasks$$

n_tasks is the same as before, $n\_successful$ is defined as the total successful tasks, n_same_nodes is the number of tasks such that the start and end node are the same (path to self), $n\_duplicate\_tasks$ is the number of duplicated tasks. This incentivizes defenders to succeed at as many tasks as possible while penalizing approaches that use trivial tasks (same start and end node) or duplicate tasks.

2. **Network Routing**   This problem defines a mission as the completion of tasks that successfully send a message between source and destination nodes within a specified time interval. Tasks represent different elements of a mission, e.g. coordination via chat between two users, using Internet Relay Chat (IRC), or transfer of a file using File Transfer Protocol (FTP) from one user to a server. A mission is successful if every task is completed one after the other in the time allowed per task. It is unsuccessful if any of the tasks of the mission fail. Currently, missions are limited to one task to allow us to reason about the results obtained. See Sect. 3.4.2 for the grammars.

Network Routing can be solved with either a "logical" or "logical and physical" network simulation. This does not change the fitness function of the defender but it does change that of the attacker. We first describe the defender's routing protocol choices and fitness function. Then we describe the attacker's fitness function assuming a "logical" network simulation where all hops occur just on the logical ring network. We then explain the difference between the two types of simulations and consequently provide the attacker's fitness function for the "logical and physical" simulations.

Defender Routing Protocols   The defender chooses among 3 different routing protocols that use shortest path, flooding or Chord's finger tables.

Shortest path protocol: At the beginning of a task, the network calculates the shortest path from a start node to an end node, and attempts to send the packet along this path. If at any point along the way the path becomes blocked due to node failure caused by an attacker, the network waits for the blocked node to become free before continuing. This protocol is more expensive in terms of time when a network is under attack. It is also more vulnerable to single nodes being attacked.

Flooding protocol: The flooding protocol works by sending multiple copies of the packet along all available paths and completes the task when the first packet reaches its destination through any of these paths. This is more expensive in hops but could be cheaper in time when under an attack.

Chord protocol: Chord chooses paths using its finger tables. Even under attack, its routing persists due to its stabilization when a node is lost or returns to service (see Sect. 3.1).

Defender Fitness Function We reward defenders that complete the mission quickly and with few hops and punish those that take longer and use more hops. For example, the flooding routing mechanism gives a better guarantee that the mission will be completed than the shortest path protocol, but floods the network and thus uses many hops around the network to do so. This behavior is taken into account into the fitness function and punished. The fitness function for the defender is

$$f_d^L = \frac{mission\_success}{overall\_time \cdot n\_hops}$$

where *overall_time* is the total time a specific routing protocol took to complete the mission and *n_hops* is total number of hops taken by the protocol to complete the mission.

Attacker Fitness Function on Logical Network We reward attackers for being able to disrupt a mission by attacking very few nodes for a short amount of time and punish attackers as the number of nodes and for how long they attack them increases. The fitness function for the attacker is

$$f_a^L = \frac{1 - mission\_success}{(n\_attacks \cdot total\_duration) + n\_attacks}$$

where *mission_success* describes whether the entire mission succeeded(1) or failed(0), *n_attacks* is the total number of nodes attacked in the network, and *total_duration* is the aggregated amount of time nodes were attacked. We include an additional *n_attacks* term in the denominator so as to prefer solutions with least amount of attacks.

Attacker Fitness Function on Logical to Physical Network This type of simulation is only relevant to routing with the Chord protocol. If a node finds cannot make a hop to another node in the ring, it scans its finger table to find the node produces the largest hop and is available. How we reward attackers changes because both logical nodes and physical nodes are available for attack. Given a definition that n_nodes = n_physical + n_logical, the new fitness function for attackers is:

$$f_a^{PL} = \frac{1 - mission\_success}{n\_nodes + (2 \cdot n\_physical \cdot p\_duration) + (n\_logical \cdot l\_duration)}$$

In this equation, *mission_success* still represents whether the mission succeeded (1) or failed (0), *n_physical* describes the number of attacks launched on nodes in the physical layer, *n_logical* represents the number of attacks launched on nodes in the virtual layer, *p_duration* represents the total aggregated time nodes in the physical layer were under attack, and *p_logical* represents the total aggregated time nodes in the logical layer were under attack. This fitness function penalizes attacks launched on the physical layer more heavily because taking out a node in the physical layer can require more effort than taking out the corresponding node in the virtual layer.

5   Results

Our first question compares the algorithms. In terms of the performance (best defender fitness) and execution time of the different ones, is the rIPCA algorithm an improvement upon them? Since it builds upon IPCA by using the same archive maintenance strategy for the *solutions* as IPCA uses for the *tests*, can it evolve better solutions? Or, because the monotonic progress guarantee of IPCA's archive is displaced by the second archive, will rIPCA evolve comparable or worse solutions? IPCA's archive keeps every solution (to guarantee monotonic fitness trajectory). Can the cost of monotonic progress be simultaneously lowered without significant loss of performance?

Our second question is specific to the network routing problem. In terms of the algorithms' performance, would each of them be able to consistently and correctly identify the Chord protocol implementation as the network defense mechanism that is best able to handle network attacks?

5.1   Mobile Asset Placement

We collected timing and performance results for the mobile asset placement problem. In Table 3 we show the averaged results over 30 runs for each topology and algorithm. We see that rIPCA has high execution time variance and that IPCA and rIPCA both yield high performance with rIPCA's being slightly lower. We observe that IPCA has a significantly longest execution time in all topologies, however as the network size grows performance becomes more similar.

Next, in Fig. 8, we show how each algorithm progresses over time on Topology 0. IPCA's trajectory shows its expected monotonic increasing performance and also has the highest average final performance. rIPCA, while not the best algorithm, is second in average final performance while consistently performing better in execution time (refer to Table 3).

Table 3 Mobile asset placement execution time and final defender fitness (averaged over 30 runs)

Algorithm	Exec time (s)	Final Perf.
Topology 0		
Coev	10.616 ± 0.444	0.132 ± 0.042
MinMax	8.603 ± 1.511	0.017 ± 0.050
MaxSolve	11.256 ± 0.507	0.282 ± 0.067
IPCA	24.661 ± 1.855	0.461 ± 0.069
rIPCA	8.079 ± 0.967	0.333 ± 0.166
Topology 1		
Coev	6.092 ± 1.249	0.380 ± 0.154
MinMax	4.213 ± 0.369	0.267 ± 0.200
MaxSolve	8.327 ± 0.429	0.267 ± 0.200
IPCA	12.990 ± 1.563	0.805 ± 0.063
rIPCA	5.932 ± 0.950	0.695 ± 0.259
Topology 2		
Coev	1.784 ± 0.328	0.182 ± 0.074
MinMax	1.482 ± 0.157	0.150 ± 0.094
MaxSolve	2.280 ± 0.127	0.184 ± 0.069
IPCA	4.188 ± 0.276	0.338 ± 0.074
rIPCA	2.245 ± 0.394	0.276 ± 0.132

5.2   Network Routing: Logical Simulation

Prior to running the experiments with the network routing problem, we exhaustively searched Topology 0 (Fig. 5a) for a solution. To do this, we set attacks to last the full duration of a task. We saw that *Chord* only fails if all the nodes are blocked. *Shortest path* fails if any node on the shortest path is blocked. *Flooding* fails if a start node is blocked, or an end node is blocked, or when at least one node in every path is blocked. This information provided us with a baseline of comparison outside the algorithms and it allowed us to verify algorithm correctness. It also points out that exhaustive search is possible in topologies with a small number of nodes and becomes increasingly difficult for a topology as large as the ones in Figs. 6 and 7.

We run the network routing mission simulation over 30 runs and then collect the average over the results. In Table 4 we show the average and standard deviation of both the wall-clock execution times as well as of the best fitness values per generation. We first consider Topology 0. The algorithms show different results, with IPCA and rIPCA showing superior average final performance. We conjecture this is due to the test archives for both IPCA and rIPCA as these archives help enforce monotonic performance increases. When looking at Topologies 1 and 2, we do not see much difference between the algorithms. This is due to the fact that the topologies are much larger in this case and the defenses are not as versatile. However, rIPCA is on par or better than IPCA in terms of execution time.

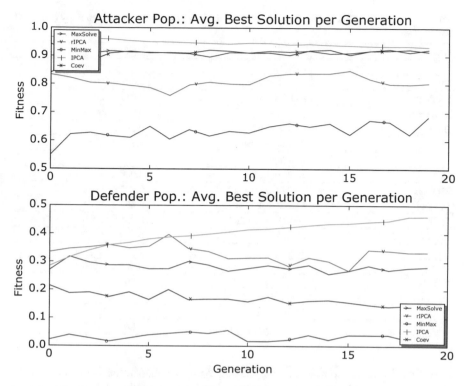

Fig. 8 Best fitness value average (over 30 runs) per generation for 20 generations on the mobile asset placement problem. Algorithms compared: IPCA, rIPCA, Coev, MinMax, MaxSolve

In Fig. 9, we examine the average fitness values for both attack and defense populations from one Coev run over Topology 0. In the attacker's average fitness plot, the average fitness for the attack population experiences a short increase in performance then quickly drops to 0. It then oscillates as the defense population converges on Chord. The variation in the algorithm allows non-optimal (i.e. non-chord) solutions to form part of the defense population. This, in turn, increases the average fitness of attacks as they face defenses which they can succeed against.

The network routing mission experiments show that IPCA and rIPCA perform better but are better suited at handling tasks where execution time isn't as important. We also show through our implementation of these coevolutionary algorithms that it is possible to model adversarial behavior on a network simulator. As expected, coevolution does not yield as strong defenders as for a fixed attack [10].

5.3 Network Routing: Physical and Logical Simulation

In these experiments, see Table 5, the trends in the defender fitness values across the topologies and algorithms closely resemble the trends we noted in Table 4. The

Table 4 Network routing execution time and final defender fitness on logical topology (averaged over 30 runs)

Algorithm	Exec time (s)	Final Perf.
Topology 0		
Coev	10.417 ± 1.650	0.091 ± 0.014
MinMax	9.802 ± 1.693	0.045 ± 0.028
MaxSolve	20.945 ± 1.336	0.088 ± 0.022
IPCA	66.576 ± 6.537	0.097 ± 0.021
rIPCA	47.754 ± 8.108	0.128 ± 0.055
Topology 1		
Coev	36.911 ± 13.290	0.008 ± 0.001
MinMax	34.745 ± 10.351	0.005 ± 0.002
MaxSolve	12.322 ± 19.236	0.007 ± 0.001
IPCA	266.382 ± 59.253	0.008 ± 0.000
rIPCA	267.784 ± 69.347	0.008 ± 0.000
Topology 2		
Coev	180.114 ± 80.664	0.005 ± 0.000
MinMax	158.955 ± 72.101	0.004 ± 0.001
MaxSolve	768.817 ± 342.642	0.005 ± 0.001
IPCA	1729.165 ± 623.941	0.005 ± 0.000
rIPCA	1566.194 ± 643.867	0.005 ± 0.000

difference, however, upon inspecting the outputs of the algorithms, is that rather than algorithms converging to the Chord protocol as the best solution for the defender, it varied in Topology 0 and Topology 1 between the Chord protocol and the flooding protocol. In the largest topology, the flooding protocol was always found by all of the algorithms as the best defender. Given these results, it is possible to recognize that increasing the complexity of the simulator to traverse the physical network between two nodes for every hop between the corresponding nodes in the virtual layer increased the number of hops the Chord protocol took to get the message to the destination. We also observed that the shortest path never evolved as a final solution. This indicated that the Chord protocol and the flooding protocol are more robust in terms of withstanding attackers.

6   Conclusions and Future Work

We have shown how to combine Grammatical Evolution and competitive coevolution so that it is possible to investigate adversarial problems and cyber arms races. In particular, we focused on network defenses and DDOS attacks. We grounded our work by considering peer to peer networks, specifically the Chord protocol, and node loss. Grammars were convenient for representing the search space of defender and attacker actions and we have embedded a GE module in each of our coevolutionary algorithms. When we use our system to solve different problems, we only

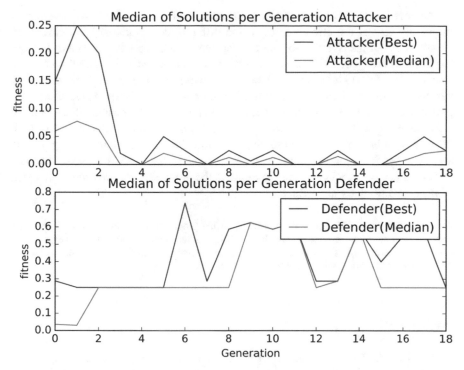

Fig. 9 Results from a `Coev` run for network routing on logical topology on network topology 0. Top: Median and best fitness results for attacker population over 20 generations. Bottom: Median and best fitness results for defender population over 20 generations

Table 5 Final defender fitness on each topology with physical and logical simulation (averaged over 30 runs)

Algorithm	Topology 0 Final Perf.	Topology 1 Final Perf.	Topology 2 Final Perf.
`Coev`	0.079 ± 0.010	0.007 ± 0.001	0.005 ± 0.000
`MinMax`	0.053 ± 0.023	0.004 ± 0.001	0.004 ± 0.001
`MaxSolve`	0.061 ± 0.018	0.006 ± 0.001	0.002 ± 0.001
`IPCA`	0.082 ± 0.009	0.007 ± 0.000	0.005 ± 0.001
`rIPCA`	0.095 ± 0.027	0.008 ± 0.001	0.005 ± 0.001

have to change the BNF grammar, the interpreter and the fitness function for each problem, rather than change the genotype representation. This modularity of GE and the reusability of the GE parser and rewriter are efficient software engineering and problem solving advantages. The grammar further helps us communicate with application domain stakeholders and increases their confidence in solutions and our system.

We have made progress in creating an end-to-end system where we have shown the ability to test the effectiveness of the different coevolutionary algorithms on simulated networks. We plan to continue this work and have ambitious goals laid out for future versions of RIVALS. In particular, we are interested in defending against low intensity DDOS attacks[15]. Attacks like these are hard to detect because they can be sent in small waves and thus are not easy to spot amongst regular traffic patterns. One element of future work is to extend the Chord protocol. Others include: experimenting with more scenarios, generating more complex missions, e.g. with different numbers of tasks and creating a *compendium* approach to pooling attacks and defenses from multiple runs to more explicitly choose an overall most robust defense. Finally, we will continue to improve the grammars, performance and speed of the coevolutionary algorithms.

Acknowledgements This material is based upon the work supported by DARPA. The views and conclusions contained herein are those of the authors and should not be interpreted as necessarily representing the official policies or endorsements. Either expressed or implied of Applied Communication Services, or the US Government.

References

1. K. Adamu, S. Phelps, Coevolutionary grammatical evolution for building trading algorithms, in *Electrical Engineering and Applied Computing* (Springer, Berlin, 2011), pp. 311–322
2. M. Alfonseca, S. Gil, Evolving a predator–prey ecosystem of mathematical expressions with grammatical evolution. Complexity **20**(3), 66–83 (2015)
3. R.M.A. Azad, C. Ryan, An examination of simultaneous evolution of grammars and solutions, in *Genetic Programming Theory and Practice III* (Springer, Berlin, 2006), pp. 141–158
4. J.C. Bongard, H. Lipson, Nonlinear system identification using coevolution of models and tests. IEEE Trans. Evol. Comput. **9**(4), 361–384 (2005)
5. E.D. de Jong, A monotonic archive for pareto-coevolution. Evol. Comput. **15**(1), 61–93 (2007)
6. E. De Jong, The maxsolve algorithm for coevolution, in *Proceedings of the 7th Annual Conference on Genetic and Evolutionary Computation* (ACM, New York, 2005), pp. 483–489
7. I. Dempsey, M. O'Neill, A. Brabazon, *Foundations in Grammatical Evolution for Dynamic Environments*, vol. 194 (Springer, Berlin, 2009)
8. S.G. Ficici, *Solution concepts in coevolutionary algorithms.* PhD thesis, Brandeis University, 2004
9. P. Gabrielsson, U. Johansson, R. Konig, Co-evolving online high-frequency trading strategies using grammatical evolution, in *2014 IEEE Conference on Computational Intelligence for Financial Engineering & Economics (CIFEr)* (IEEE, New York, 2014), pp. 473–480
10. D. Garcia, A.E. Lugo, E. Hemberg, U.-M. O'Reilly, Investigating coevolutionary archive based genetic algorithms on cyber defense networks, in *Proceedings of the Genetic and Evolutionary Computation Conference Companion* (ACM, New York, 2017), pp. 1455–1462
11. R. Harper, Evolving robocode tanks for Evo robocode. Genet. Program Evolvable Mach. **15**(4), 403–431 (2014)
12. E. Hemberg, J. Rosen, G. Warner, S. Wijesinghe, U.-M. O'Reilly, Detecting tax evasion: a co-evolutionary approach. Artif. Intell. Law **24**(2), 149–182 (2016)
13. M.I. Heywood, Evolutionary model building under streaming data for classification tasks: opportunities and challenges. Genet. Program Evolvable Mach. **16**(3), 283–326 (2015)

14. K. Krawiec, M. Heywood, Solving complex problems with coevolutionary algorithms, in *Proceedings of the 2016 on Genetic and Evolutionary Computation Conference Companion* (ACM, New York, 2016), pp. 687–713
15. A. Kuzmanovic, E.W. Knightly, Low-rate TCP-targeted denial of service attacks: the shrew vs. the mice and elephants, in *Proceedings of the 2003 Conference on Applications, Technologies, Architectures, and Protocols for Computer Communications* (ACM, New York, 2003), pp. 75–86
16. C. Le Goues, A. Nguyen-Tuong, H. Chen, J.W. Davidson, S. Forrest, J.D. Hiser, J.C. Knight, M. Van Gundy, Moving target defenses in the helix self-regenerative architecture, in *Moving Target Defense II* (Springer, Berlin, 2013), pp. 117–149
17. A.R. McIntyre, M.I. Heywood, Multi-objective competitive coevolution for efficient GP classifier problem decomposition, in *IEEE International Conference on Systems, Man and Cybernetics, 2007. ISIC* (IEEE, New York, 2007), pp. 1930–1937
18. A.R. McIntyre, M.I. Heywood, Cooperative problem decomposition in pareto competitive classifier models of coevolution, in *Genetic Programming* (Springer, Berlin, 2008), pp. 289–300
19. E. Popovici, A. Bucci, R.P. Wiegand, E.D. De Jong, Coevolutionary principles, in *Handbook of Natural Computing* (Springer, Berlin, 2012), pp. 987–1033
20. G. Rush, D.R. Tauritz, A.D. Kent, Coevolutionary agent-based network defense lightweight event system (candles), in *Proceedings of the Companion Publication of the 2015 on Genetic and Evolutionary Computation Conference* (ACM, New York, 2015), pp. 859–866
21. K.O. Stanley, R. Miikkulainen, Competitive coevolution through evolutionary complexification. J. Artif. Intell. Res. (JAIR) **21**, 63–100 (2004)
22. I. Stoica, R. Morris, D. Karger, M.F. Kaashoek, H. Balakrishnan, Chord: a scalable peer-to-peer lookup service for internet applications. ACM SIGCOMM Comput. Commun. Rev. **31**(4), 149–160 (2001)
23. D.R. Tauritz, A no-free-lunch framework for coevolution, in *Proceedings of the 10th Annual Conference on Genetic and Evolutionary Computation* (ACM, New York, 2008), pp. 371–378
24. P.A. Whigham, G. Dick, J. Maclaurin, C.A. Owen, Examining the best of both worlds of grammatical evolution, in *Proceedings of the 2015 on Genetic and Evolutionary Computation Conference* (ACM, New York, 2015), pp. 1111–1118
25. M.L. Winterrose, K.M. Carter, Strategic evolution of adversaries against temporal platform diversity active cyber defenses, in *Proceedings of the 2014 Symposium on Agent Directed Simulation* (Society for Computer Simulation International, 2014), p. 9

Evolving Behaviour Tree Structures Using Grammatical Evolution

Diego Perez-Liebana and Miguel Nicolau

Abstract Behaviour Trees are control structures with many applications in computer science, including robotics, control systems, and computer games. They allow the specification of controllers from very broad behaviour definitions (close to the root of the tree) down to very specific technical implementations (near the leaves); this allows them to be understood and extended by both behaviour designers and technical programmers. This chapter describes the process of applying Grammatical Evolution (GE) to evolve Behaviour Trees for a real-time video-game: the Mario AI Benchmark. The results obtained show that these structures are quite amenable to artificial evolution using GE, and can provide a good balance between long-term (pathfinding) and short-term (reactiveness to hazards and power-ups) planning within the same structure.

1 Evolving Behaviour Trees for Game Playing Control

The objective of this chapter is to demonstrate how Grammatical Evolution (GE) [1] can be used to evolve control structures for agents that interact in highly dynamic environments. An example of this application is the control of Non-Player Characters (NPCs) in computer games. These are highly dynamic environments, where NPCs must be able to react efficiently and effectively in previously unseen scenarios. In the concrete case of real-time games, these agents must be able to perform actions in a limited time budget, typically in just a few milliseconds. These actions must tackle both dynamic (enemies, power ups, moving structures) and static (level structure, path-finding) elements in the game. This requires the agent to be

D. Perez-Liebana (✉)
School of Electronic Engineering and Computer Science, Queen Mary University of London,
London, UK
e-mail: Diego.Perez@qmul.ac.uk

M. Nicolau
Natural Computing Research and Applications Group, University College Dublin, Dublin, Ireland
e-mail: Miguel.Nicolau@ucd.ie

© Springer International Publishing AG, part of Springer Nature 2018   433
C. Ryan et al. (eds.), *Handbook of Grammatical Evolution*,
https://doi.org/10.1007/978-3-319-78717-6_18

able to react to imminent hazards, as well as devising action plans to accomplish the goals that lead to winning the game.

An example of a platform game with these characteristics is the Mario AI Benchmark [2, 3]. In this environment, the goal is to reach the end of the level, avoiding (or killing) enemies or other hazards that may harm the player. The agent (Mario) must react to dynamic events that happen at close distance, and also plan ahead to make progress in the level. Section 3 describes this benchmark, the environmental information and the avatar effectors.

These two components, reactiveness and navigation, are closely related in this game environment: both make use of the same set of actuators (or actions) that Mario can employ. Section 4 describes two different approaches for tackling them, one using the same actuators for both needs, and another providing different sub-behaviours that deal with them separately.

Previous studies [4] have successfully applied GE to evolve Behaviour Trees (BTs) [5] for the Mario AI Benchmark. A BT is a tree structure composed of different types of nodes, including control nodes that permit control over the flow of execution, condition nodes that query the game state, and action nodes that execute actions in the game. Section 5 describes how BTs work and how they are implemented for the framework used in this study, and Sect. 6 details how to implement these structures using GE.

A set of approaches is compared in terms of evolvability, generalisation, and complexity of resulting controllers. Sections 7 and 8 describe the experimental study and results obtained, with conclusions and recommendations for their applicability, both to Mario AI and other dynamic environments, given in Sect. 9.

2   Related Work

This section reviews applications of GE to control environments including games, other approaches to create controllers for the Mario AI benchmark, and applications of BTs as game controllers.

From the onset, GE practitioners have used its grammar-based syntax specification to solve a multitude of problems, including controllers for a diverse range of environments. A typical example is the use of GE to solve the Santa Fe Ant Trail problem [6], which rapidly became a typical benchmark over many years. Other examples include its application to the Lawn-Mower problem [7], and its combination with a gene regulatory network, to solve the pole-balancing problem [8]. Regarding gaming environments, examples include the work of Galván-López et al. [9], who evolved controllers for Ms. PacMan, and Harper [10, 11], who used GE to co-evolve controllers for Robocode Tanks.

The application of GE to game environments is not limited to control agents, however. Other interesting applications include the design and optimisation of horse gate animations [12], and the design of levels [13] and personalised content [14] for the Mario AI environment.

Mario AI provides a suitable platform for research in the application of controllers to dynamic environments. Multiple approaches that aim at maximising the game score can be found in the literature. These include rule-based agents with higher-level, hand-designed conditions and actions [15], cuckoo search and its comparison with a standard genetic algorithm approach [16]), the evolution of finite-state machines created with genetic algorithms [17, 18], Q-Learning with full game information [19], Neural-Networks with Manifold Learning as a dimensionality-reducing technique [20] and, finally, the combination of Monte Carlo Tree Search with appropriate heuristics [21], creating agents that outperform the leading state of the art controllers in this game.

Most game environments are highly dynamic environments, often resulting in noisy fitness evaluation. This is also true for Mario AI, where a random seed can vary the events and levels generated with the same difficulty level, presence and absence of enemies, etc. There exists a large body of research in the area of noisy fitness environments. A recent example of such studies are the works of Liu et al. [22] and Kunanusont [23], who evolved game parameters for AI-assisted game design in a search space with noisy and expensive evaluations.

BTs, initially introduced as a means to encode formal system specifications [5], have gained popularity as a way to encode game controllers in a modular, scalable and reusable manner [24]. They have now been used in high-revenue commercial games, such as "Halo" [25], "Spore" [26], and other smaller indie games (such as "Façade" [27]) illustrating their importance in the game AI community.

The evolution of BT structures has been explored in the work of Lim et al. [28], where the authors used Genetic Programming [29] to evolve AI controllers for the *DEFCON* game. In this study, the resulting agent played against the standard *DEFCON* AI controller, achieving a success rate superior to 50%.

One of the main hurdles encountered in the work of Lim et al. was how to exchange typed BT structures between individuals. This issue is easily dealt with GE, which was also used to evolve BTs, as controllers for Mario AI [4]. The current chapter details those experiments, giving insight on the actual process of specifying the syntax of BTs through a grammar, and maximising the exchange of coherent genetic material between solutions, increasing the effectiveness of the search process.

3 Mario AI as a Dynamic Game Benchmark

Super Mario Bros is a popular two-dimensional platform game where the player controls Mario, who must reach the right end of the level by avoiding enemies, other hazards, and collecting bonus items and power-ups. Therefore, the Mario AI benchmark exemplifies a highly dynamic environment with a final goal that requires long term planning. This benchmark, an adaptation of an open source version of *Super Mario Bros* (by Markus Persson), is used for the experimental work developed for this chapter. The framework allows testing agents in multiple levels, customising them by difficulty, type (over or underground), length, time limit, creatures (presence or absence), dead ends, and random seed for the automatic generation of the level.

3.1   Game State Information

The playing agent is able to analyse the environment surrounding Mario by means of two matrices, one providing information about the geometry of the level, and the other indicating the presence of enemies.

The level of detail to be retrieved from both matrices can be set to three values: **Zoom 0** represents the world with a different integer for each entity in the game, whereas **Zoom 2** gives the simplest possible representation (1 meaning enemy or obstacle presence, and 0 the absence of it). As a mid point, **Zoom 1** provides the information categorised in useful groups, such as enemies that can be killed by stomping or shooting, different types of blocks, etc.

Mario itself can be in three different states during the game: *Small*, where an enemy or hazard hit causes the player to lose; *Big*, reachable by eating a mushroom from the *Small* state; and *Fire*, which permits the player to shoot fireballs. Being hit by an enemy changes Mario's state to the previous one. The benchmark also provides information about the state of the agent, plus its location in the level and extra information, such as if Mario is on the ground, if able to shoot, jump, or if carrying a turtle shell. Additional information is also available, including the game status (game running, won or lost), the time left to complete the level, the current score and a set of *kill statistics*, including the number of enemies killed and how they were eliminated (by stomp, by fire or by shell).

3.2   Game Actions

Mario can choose among several actions to be performed at each game step. These actions include three directions (*Left*, *Right* and *Down* - *Up* has no meaning in this implementation), *Jump*, and *Run/Fire*. If the agent is already moving right or left, applying the action *Run/Fire* makes Mario move faster. If *Jump* and *Run/Fire* are applied simultaneously, Mario jumps farther. Also, when in *Fire* mode, it makes the agent shoot a fireball. Therefore, the set of possible actions defines an action space of $2^5 = 32$ actions (although some of these are nonsensical, such as left and right pushed at the same time). As the agent is played in real-time, the action supplied at each frame must be provided every 40 ms, or the agent will be disqualified.

4 Mario Agents

The focus of this work is on the evolution of BT data structures that allow a hierarchical decomposition of tasks, by means of GE. The evolved structures need to be able to respond adequately to scenarios that propose dynamic hazards and an overall goal. In the case of Mario, GE evolves a BT that combines the two required aspects of the agent behaviour for this game, also identified in the introduction: reactiveness (dealing with close enemies and hazards) and navigation across the static elements in the level. Both were dealt with using basic game movements or combinations of these. Tables 4 and 5, at the end of the chapter, show the routines employed by GE, along with a brief explanation of each.

Two different approaches are analysed in this study, in order to assert the importance of the navigation component of the algorithm's behaviour. Each approach use a different set of routines. *ReactiveMario (NoAstar)* combines reactive and very basic navigation commands, while *PlanningMario (Astar)* uses A* for navigation in order to let the GE focus on the reactive part of the behaviour. Section 6 details the general structure of the evolved BTs and how reactiveness and navigation are integrated into a single approach.

4.1 A Reactive Mario

In this approach (NoAstar), the agent is exclusively focused on reacting to moving elements in the game, without employing any explicit path-finding. Therefore, the elements considered are the position of enemies and hazards, such as *goombas*, bullets, flying turtles, bonus mushrooms and fire flowers. GE is used here to evolve a BT that avoids these entities and navigates the agent through the levels. This controller, submitted to the Gameplay track of the 2010 Mario AI Competition, ranked 4th out of 8 entries [3] in this contest.

In this edition, one of the most difficult navigational hazards were dead ends. In those, the level presents more than one way to move ahead, but at least one of them is a *cul de sac*. An example of one of these is shown in Fig. 1, where it can be seen that the *cul de sac* is longer than the size of the environmental matrix. Two sub-trees (*UseRightGap* and *AvoidRightTrap*, see Table 5) have been specifically designed by hand to address this problem. The latter routine detects a dead end in front of Mario and moves him back until there is no obstacle over his head. The former sub-tree finds a platform which Mario can jump onto (or a gap to fall through), to overcome the trap by running through the open part.

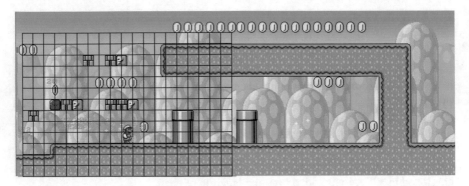

Fig. 1 Mario and environmental information. Both matrices are of size 21×21, centered in Mario

4.2 A Planning Mario

This second approach (Astar) employs A* to guide navigation through the level, while handing GE the task of dealing with reactiveness to the hazards of the game. However, in order to use A* for navigation, the game level must be represented as a navigable graph, a structure not supplied by the benchmark. Furthermore, due to the nature of the game, this graph needs to be modifiable. Changes in the blocks (which can be destroyed by Mario) or changes in the state of the avatar (i.e., from *Big* to *Small*) can make some old paths invalid. Therefore, this graph must be generated *dynamically*, at each step, by the agent. It is important to note that the map building process is independent from the use of GE to evolve the playing agents and it is not a functionality provided in the framework. The present section briefly summarises this process.

4.2.1 Mapping a Level

The first problem when dealing with path planning is the world representation. As the Mario AI Benchmark does not provide access to a complete map of the level, this has to be built as Mario moves through it, using the environment arrays described in Sect. 3.1. As this map is created for navigation, blocks that do not affect movement (items, enemies or coins) are not taken into account. However, it is possible to add meta-data information, such as the type of block (question or brick), enemies, and/or collectible items, which can be later used for queries in the BT (Fig. 2).

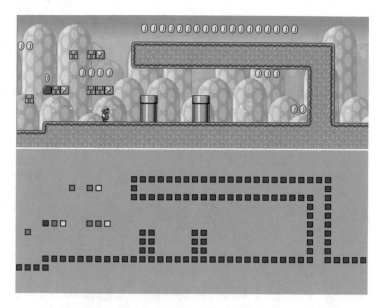

Fig. 2 Top: the original section of the level as seen in game. Bottom: the respective map generated from the environmental matrix received by the agent

4.2.2   Nodes for Path Planning

Once a representation of the geometry of the level is available, a graph for the A* algorithm can be built. Given the format of the data, the best solution is to build a tile-based graph approximation.

The first decision is where to place the nodes (or vertices) of the graph within the map; these nodes represent navigable spaces, i.e. positions where Mario can stand. Figure 3 (left) shows the level structure (as squares) and the graph nodes (as dots). It is worthwhile mentioning that this process identifies some nodes that are not accessible (such as the nodes inside the ceiling of the dead end), but the next step will filter these out of the graph in which Mario is located and can move.

4.2.3   Edges for Path Planning

Although most grid-based path finding networks consider the map as seen from a zenithal perspective (i.e. from the top), this game requires the graph built as seen from the player's perspective, sideways to the level. This incorporates an additional challenge, where horizontal and vertical edges cannot be used in the same way.

The edge creation process analyses the nodes to finish the graph construction, using different types of links. The following links are available for the graph, which are also shown in the example Fig. 3 (right).

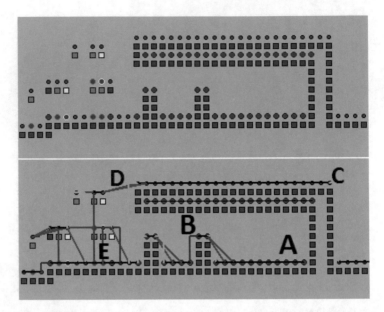

Fig. 3 Top: level structure (squares) and graph nodes (dots). Squares indicate different types of block—question mark, brick, or solid. Bottom: navigation graph representation. Different types of edges are Walk link (A), Jump link (B), Fall link (C), Faith jump link (D) and Break jump link (E)

- **Walk links**: These are the simplest ones, which can be used just by applying the right (or left) actions. These edges are bidirectional.
- **Jump links**: Unidirectional upward edges that join nodes vertically separated by no more than 3 cells and horizontally by 1 position. Therefore, they can be used to jump to a node that is over the starting node (with a maximum jump height) and one unit to the left or right.
- **Vertical jump links**: Some level formations can be jumped onto from below, keeping the same vertical. For these structures, unidirectional upward edges are created, which join nodes vertically separated by no more than 3 cells.
- **Fall links**: Unidirectional downward edges that join nodes vertically separated by any number of cells and horizontally by 1 position. Some of these links have as a counterpart a *jump* edge (some jump links can also be used to fall in the opposite direction). This distinction is important, because while the former have to be managed by jumping, the latter must be gone through moving in one direction and managing the fall in order to land in the proper place.
- **Faith jump links**: Bidirectional edges that link two nodes horizontally separated by no more than 4 cells. These edges are used to link nodes that are separated horizontally by more than one unit, and with a maximum vertical distance. These can be, in some cases, hard jumps to make, because of the long distance between starting and ending node.
- **Break jump links**: These are very similar to normal jump, but in this case there is a brick block in the trajectory of the jump, in the vertical of the node where

the edge starts. Because this block can (potentially) be destroyed, this link is included in the graph as it can become a regular *jump* link. It is also possible that the brick block does not break (becoming a solid block instead) and the link cannot be used. In that case, as the map and graph are repeatedly generated, this link will not be created again.

An important aspect of this game is that Mario can have different states (*Big* or *Small*), and some edges can only be traversed if Mario is *Small* (only one cell is required to pass through). This information is also included in the edges, and it is used not only to traverse the graph, but also to compute the cost of the edges for A*.

The *basic cost* of an edge is calculated as the Manhattan Distance[1] between its nodes. The *final cost* is computed as the basic cost multiplied by a factor determined by the link type. The reasoning is as follows: the factor of traveling an edge walking must be higher than jumping, because calculating the jump and managing landing takes longer and it has a higher associated risk (it is more likely to miss a jump than a simple walk movement). The *basic cost* of each link is therefore multiplied by a factor of 1.5 if the link involves a jump, with the exception of a *break jump* link, which factor is 3.0 due to the extra cost involved in trying to break the brick.

Once A* can be used to generate paths to different positions in the level, it is possible to design path finding routines for GE to use during the evolution of BTs. The next section gives a definition of BTs, and how are they used for this game.

5   Behaviour Trees for Decision Making

Behaviour Trees (BT) are data structures that allow to decompose a complex behaviour hierarchically in several sub-trees as tasks of reduced complexity. Their applicability is broad in the fields of AI and technology, such as management of control systems [30], robotics [31] and decision making behaviours in video-games [24–26], an area in which BTs have achieved great popularity.

In fact, along with Finite State Machines (FSM), BTs are one of the most prolific structures to implement complex Non Player Character (NPC) behaviours in games. In contrast to FSMs, BTs are more flexible, scalable and intuitive, easier to develop (even for non-technical developers and designers) and are able to incorporate multiple concerns such as path planning and path following [32].

For example, a soldier NPC can have different behaviours, such as patrolling, investigating and attacking. Each one of these tasks can be broken down in different sub-tasks (movement tactics, weapon management or aiming algorithms), which at the same time can be composed of lower level actions (playing sounds or animations). In the robotics domain, high level goals can be broken down in sub-goals, like recharging batteries or entering rooms, which in turn can be decomposed in opening, closing and forcing doors [31].

BTs establish a descending order of complexity from the root to the leaves, employing different node types. In the simplest implementation, all nodes can return

---

[1] The sum of absolute differences in Cartesian coordinates.

success or *failure* to their parent node (although other versions could return real values, enumerators, etc.). Nodes are divided into two major categories: the first type is control nodes, which manage the flow of execution through the tree:

- **Sequence** nodes execute its children from left to right until one returns *failure*. If all children return *success*, the sequence node itself also returns *success*. Otherwise, it will return *failure* to its parent. These nodes are represented with a right pointing arrow.
- **Selector** nodes execute its children from left to right until one returns *success*. If all children return *failure*, this node will return the same to its parent, and *success* otherwise. These nodes are represented with a question mark.
- **Parallel** nodes execute all its children in parallel. Termination conditions and return values can be diverse (i.e. breaking and returning the value from the first child to finish, returning a majority vote, etc.). These are typically represented with parallel right pointing arrows.
- **Decorator** or **Filter** nodes modify the normal execution flow in different ways (negating the value of its child node, loops, running a node until *failure*, etc.). These nodes typically have only one child. Decorators are normally represented with a diamond shape.

Leaf nodes are **Conditions** and **Actions**. The former query situations and features of the current environment, while the latter apply moves in the scenario the agent is in. Actions usually return *success* unless the action was not possible to be executed for some reason, while the returned value of a condition node depends on the query performed.

BTs can also incorporate handlers for data sharing and sub-behaviour re-use. For the former, *Blackboards* allow passing information between nodes and trees, and it is possible to introduce management mechanisms to coordinate access and usage of resources. For the latter, it is possible to use look-up tables to build a BT library that allows the designer to re-use sub-trees in multiple locations of the overall BT.

5.1 Behaviour Trees and Mario AI

Tables 4 and 5 (at the end of this chapter) include all conditions, actions, filters and sub-trees designed for the agent, and available to the evolutionary algorithm. Some sub-trees are only available for controllers without A*. These are used for navigational purposes, which are taken care of by A* routines in the other controllers. The leaf nodes described in these tables are also summarised here:

- **Conditions**: Used to provide information about the enemies (distance to the avatar and their type) and obstacles in the map (type and position of the blocks).

- **Actions**: The most useful action combinations are provided to the BT, based on those described previously (see Sect. 3.2). Examples are *Down*, *Fire*, *RunRight* (*Right* and *Run* both pressed), *NOP* (no buttons pressed) or *WalkLeft*. There are also actions to request paths to specific locations, when using A*.
- **Sub-trees**: These units are indivisible and require a concrete sequence of moves to be performed. Jumps are more effectively managed in sub-trees, as they require a frame in which the jump button is not pressed before the jump action is executed, and farther jumps can be made with consecutive repetitions of the key being pressed. Sub-trees are achieved by combining different filter and action nodes. Figure 4 shows the sub-tree to make long jumps to the right.

In this work, the BTs used are stored in XML files, with a hierarchical structure that defines the type of each node and the operation that it represents. Figure 4 includes the (simplified) XML code of the sample sub-tree from this chapter. Note that this implies that the GE grammar must be able to generate the behaviours in this format.

6 Building Behaviour Trees with Grammatical Evolution

Figure 4 shows the complexity of the syntax of the BT Controllers. GE's use of grammars can ensure that the evolved controllers maintain syntactic correctness, both keeping compatibility with the variety of BT control and leaf nodes, and also incorporating domain knowledge (as explained below). This is possible through the use of the grammar as an instrument to control of the syntax of solutions both in terms of data-structures and biases [33, 34].

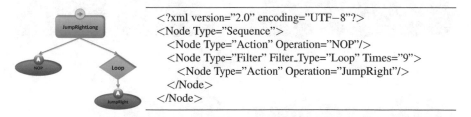

```
<?xml version="2.0" encoding="UTF-8"?>
<Node Type="Sequence">
  <Node Type="Action" Operation="NOP"/>
  <Node Type="Filter" Filter_Type="Loop" Times="9">
    <Node Type="Action" Operation="JumpRight"/>
  </Node>
</Node>
```

Fig. 4 Sub-tree for executing long jumps to the right. NOP ensures no button is pressed before the JumpRight command (Jump plus Right actions) is executed. The Loop filter makes sure JumpRight is executed during a given number of frames. On the left, graphical representation. On the right, BT XML Structure of this sub-tree

6.1 Structure of a Behaviour Tree

The grammar employed to evolve BTs specifies the (XML) syntax, containing all conditions, actions, sub-trees and filters designed. Earlier experimentation, where GE was free to combine these nodes without a rigid structure, showed that the evolved trees were badly structured (such as sequences of sequences, with NOP actions at their leaves), not human-readable, and computationally demanding.

In order to avoid these issues, a constrained structure for the syntax of BTs was imposed via the grammar. Although still variable in size, the BT structures are contrived to follow an *and-or* tree structure [35], the recommended way of building BTs for game AI [36]. Therefore, all evolved BTs have a selector node at the root with a variable number of *Behaviour Block* (BB) sub-trees, each one of them encoding a particular sub-behaviour. Each one of these BBs consists of a sequence one or more conditions, followed by a sequence of sub-trees or atomic actions.

The last child of the root node is an unconditioned BB, which is either a sequence of actions and sub-trees, or a default navigation behaviour (when using the Astar agent). Figure 5 exemplifies this structure.

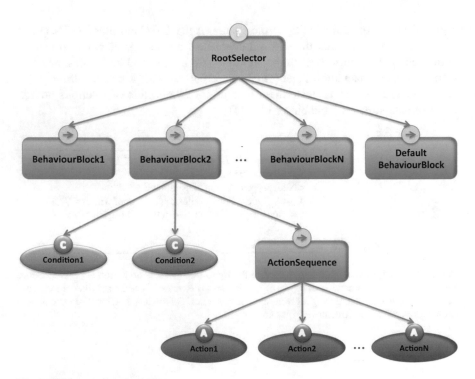

Fig. 5 Structure of evolved BTs

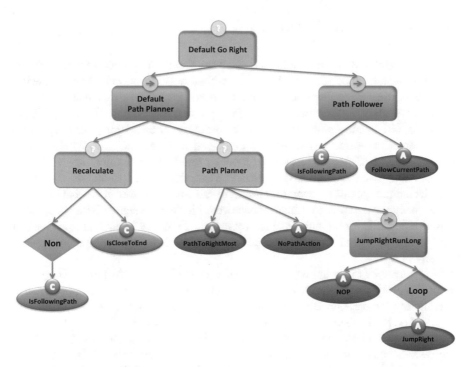

Fig. 6 Sub-tree for path finding. It calculates, if needed, the path to the rightmost position available

The root selector starts with the leftmost BB at the beginning of the BT execution. The BT will follow a left-to-right priority order in which each sub-tree will be executed if its stated condition(s) are fulfilled. Hence, the right-most block is the default behaviour, which will be executed in case all the previous conditioned BBs fail to trigger. The conditions provided are complex queries to the game state, which allows limiting the number of conditions associated to each BB to just one or two. The number of actions and sub-trees on each BB is left unlimited.

The default behaviour (right-most block) depends on the navigation used: without A*, it is simply composed of a sequence of actions, without associated conditions. However, if A* us used, a particular sub-tree is provided. Figure 6 shows this structure (sub-tree `Default Go Right`), which is composed of a selector node, with two sub-trees, `Default Path Planner` and `Path Follower`.

`Default Path Planner` is composed of two sub-trees. `Recalculate` decides if the default path has to be calculated; that can happen when no item is being targeted, or when a path was set but is almost finished. `Path Planner` (executed if the one before is successful) calculates the path to the rightmost position in the map (the direction to follow to the end of the level). In the rare event where a path is not found, Mario enters an emergency state: to keep moving, a default forward jump is executed.

6.2   Designing the Grammar

Given that each BB is a self-contained structure, due to the syntax described above, it is reasonable to permit individuals to exchange these between them. Specific crossover points were thus encoded into the grammar to allow this, using a special grammar symbol (`<GEXOMarker>`) to label crossover points [37, 38]. These constrain GE to only slice individuals according to these points, when applying crossover; a two-point crossover was employed to guarantee this. Without these markers, standard 1-point crossover would provide more exploration with less exploitation; given the high cost of the fitness function, this trade-off was necessary. This technique creates an operator similar to sub-tree crossover in GP, but allowing the exchange of a variable number of behaviour blocks between individuals. Finally, it is also possible for an individual to crossover with himself, which is equivalent to a sub-tree swap operator. In the presented grammar, this is very useful to modify the priority of a BB.

An extract of the grammar used (Astar variant) is shown in Fig. 7. The `<BT>` symbol merely defines the XML prelude, while the `<XMLPart>` symbol provides specific implementation BT tags. The following two symbols (`<RootNode>` and `<RootSelNode>`) define the and-or tree selector root node.

Its contents are defined in `<SeqsAndDefBB>`: a set of sequences, followed by the default behaviour. A first crossover marker is defined here, as the right-most place at which crossover can occur (just after all the defined filtered sequences, but before the default behaviour, which is equal for all individuals).

The set of filtered sequences (i.e. BBs) is defined by the symbol `<SeqNodes>`, which is just a recursively defined list of one or more BBs. Each of them, however, defined by `<SequenceNode>`, places a crossover marker at the start (i.e. left) of the definition of a BB, allowing for the exchange of BBs between individuals.

The definition of the remainder of the XML syntax proceeds in a similar fashion, and most of it is not shown for lack of space (the grammar is composed of 48 non-terminal symbols, and 541 lines). The definition of the `Default Go Right` sub-tree is worth mentioning (symbol `<DefaultGoRight>`): GE grammars can define a large sequence of text as a single terminal symbol.

7   Experimental Work

A series of experiments were ran to test several aspects of this approach. To ascertain if BTs are a good structure to evolve controllers for Mario AI, BTs were evolved using GE and their training and test performance were monitored over time, along with other statistical measurements. These experiments also measured if the separation of reactive and navigation routines led to improved results. Section 7.2 discusses in detail the different evolutionary approaches tested, aiming to deal with the noisy fitness evaluation that highly dynamic environments such as games can present.

```
<BT> ::= '<?xml version="2.0" encoding="utf-8"?>\n' <XMLPart>
<XMLPart> ::= '<Behavior>\n' <RootNode> '</Behavior>\n'

<RootNode> ::= '<Node Type="Root">\n'<RootSelNode>'</Node>\n'
<RootSelNode> ::= '<Node Type="Selector">\n' <SeqsAndDefBB> '</Node>\n'
<SeqsAndDefBB> ::= <SeqNodes> <GEXOMarker> <DefBB> '\n'

<SeqNodes> ::= <SequenceNode> | <SeqNodes> <SequenceNode>
<SequenceNode> ::= <GEXOMarker> '<Node Type="Sequence">\n'
                    <1to2Conditions> <FilterSeqActNLUTs> '</Node>\n'

<1to2Conditions> ::= <ConditionNode> | <ConditionNode> <ConditionNode>
                    | <ConditionedLUT>
<ConditionNode> ::= '<Node Type="Condition" />\n'

<FilterSeqActNLUTs> ::= <FilterHeader> <SeqActNLUTs> '</Node>\n'
                      | <SeqActNLUTs>
<FilterHeader> ::= <Loop> | <NON> | <UFL>
<Loop> ::= '<Node Filter_Type="Loop" Times="'<I>'" Type="Filter">\n'
<NON> ::= '<Node Filter_Type="NON" Type="Filter">\n'
<UFL> ::= '<Node Filter_Type="Until_Fail_Lim" Times="'<I>'" Type="Filter">\n'
<I> ::= 2 | 3 | 4 | 5 | 6 | 7 | 8 | 9

<SeqActNLUTs> ::= '<Node Type="Sequence">\n' <1PlusActOrLUTs> '</Node>\n'
<1PlusActOrLUTs> ::= <ActionOrLUT> | <1PlusActOrLUTs> <ActionOrLUT>
<ActionOrLUT> ::= <ActionNode> | <LUTNode>

<DefBB> ::= '<Node Type="Sequence">\n' <DefaultGoRight> '</Node>\n'
<DefaultGoRight> ::= '<Node Name = "DefGoRight" Type="Selector">
  <Node Name = "DefPathPlanner" Type="Sequence">
    <Node Name="Recalculate" Type="Selector">
      <Node Filter_Type="NON" Type="Filter">
        <Node Operation="IsFollowingPath" Type="Condition"/>
      </Node>
        <Node Operation="IsRightMostCloseToEnd" Type="Condition"/>
      </Node>
    <Node Name="PathPlanner" Type="Selector">
      <Node Operation="GetPathToRightMost" Type="Action"/>
      <Node Operation="NoPathAction" Type="Action"/>
      <Node Name="JumpRightRunLong" Type="Sequence">
        <Node Operation="NOP" Type="Action"/>
        <Node Filter_Type="Loop" Times="25" Type="Filter">
          <Node Operation="JumpRightRun" Type="Action"/>
        </Node>
      </Node>
    </Node>
  </Node>
  <Node Name="Path Follower" Type="Sequence">
    <Node Operation="IsFollowingPath" Type="Condition"/>
    <Node Operation="FollowCurrentPath" Type="Action"/>
  </Node>
</Node>'
```

Fig. 7 Extract of the grammar used, showing the incorporation of the XML syntax

7.1 Evaluating Behaviour Trees

A set of game levels is generated to test each evolved controller. Each *mapset* is composed of 10 levels (5 difficulty settings, with and without enemies), and is generated with a single random seed. The resulting fitness value (to be maximised)

is a weighted sum of distance traveled and the actual Mario AI Benchmark score (which includes enemy kills and collected items). Both game levels and BT controllers are deterministic: the same controller in a map always yields the same fitness.

7.2   Generality of Controllers

The Mario AI benchmark is able to randomly create multiple levels, ranging from very easy to physically impossible to terminate. Such a dynamic environment poses a generalisation problem, and the following approaches were tested aiming at tackling this issue (note that both non-A* and A* versions of these were used):

- **Single**: this approach always uses the same mapset for evaluation, with the same seed for all independent runs.
- **Five**: in this case, the same five mapsets are used to test each controller (kept for all runs). This increases the variety of situations each controller is evaluated on.
- **Change1**: this approach uses only one mapset for evaluation, but changing it at each generation. The same sequence of mapsets is used in all runs. This approach increases the variety of situations seen for each controller, while keeping the evaluation effort small. To ensure continuity between generations, the parent population is reevaluated with the new generation's mapset.
- **Change5**: this case uses five mapsets for each evaluation, but all five are replaced at each generation (same sequence for all runs). The parent population is reevaluated with the new mapsets at the start of each new generation.
- **Slide**: this approach also uses five mapsets for each evaluation, replacing one mapset with a new one at every generation, in a sliding window manner (12345, 23456, etc.). The same sequence is kept for all runs. The parent population is reevaluated with the new five mapsets at the start of each new generation.

Each of the 10 systems evaluated (five approaches described in Sect. 7.2, with and without A*) used the setup shown in Table 1.

As different approaches use a different number of mapsets for evaluation, and a single mapset took anywhere between 0.7 s and 6.0 s to evaluate (using a single core of a 2.8 GHz Intel Core i7 processor), different numbers of generations were used so that each approach used the same number of mapsets per run.

Table 1 Experimental setup

GE	Population size	500
	Evaluations	250,000
	Derivation-tree depth range (for initialisation)	20...30
	Derivation-tree max depth	*unset*
	Tail ratio (for initialisation)	50%
	Selection tournament size	1%
	Elitism (for generational replacement)	10%
	Marked 2-point crossover ratio	50%
	Marked swap crossover ratio	50%
	Average mutation events per individual	1
Mario	Level difficulties	0...4
	Level types	0 1
	Level length	320

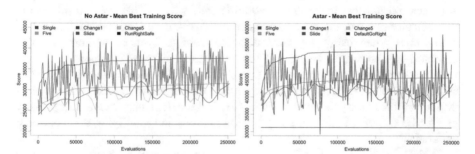

Fig. 8 Mean best training score across time, for all approaches not using (left) or using (right) A*. Note the difference in the scales on the Y axis

8 Results

8.1 Performance on Training

The mean best controller training score for all approaches is shown in Fig. 8. These plots also include the average performance of the respective reference behaviour (*RunRightSafe* without A*; *DefaultGoRight* for A*).[2]

The results confidently show that all approaches substantially outperform their respective reference behaviours. It seems evident that the BT approach can successfully add reactive elements to the controllers, enhancing its performance. A second observation that can be made is that there is a performance difference between the controllers that use A* navigation and those that do not. The *RunRightSafe*

---

[2]This and all results reported in this chapter are averaged over 30 independent runs. Videos of the best controllers of some runs are available online (http://tinyurl.com/gebtMarioAI).

controller has an average performance close to 22,000 points, while *DefaultGoRight* averages above 31,000. With the exception of the *Single* approach, this is at a par (or superior) to the average controller performance for the other approaches not using A*. This showcases the performance improvement of using a dedicated, deterministic algorithm for navigation.

The relative performance of each of the approaches is similar with or without A*. It is worthwhile highlighting that the *Single* approach has the best training performance. It is therefore quite successful at optimising the controller behaviour for the single mapset it is trained on, independently from the initial random seed. It shows the best evolvability, with a typical optimisation performance curve, achieving the best training score with or without A*. A similar result can be observed with the *Five* approach, providing a steady improvement in average performance across the five training mapsets. The final lower total score is due to a more diverse performance across the different mapsets.

Changing the mapset used for evaluation at each generation makes *Change1* approach the noisiest in terms of evolution across time. This noisy result shows the difficulty range of the levels generated in this framework with different random seeds, even when using the same difficulty setting. With or without A*, this approach has both the highest and lowest average score of all approaches, and with A*, sometimes performs worse than the default behaviour. *Change5* and *Slide* exhibit a similar performance. The evolution curves show the extreme range of difficulties due to the generated maps, but to a lesser extent than *Change1*, especially in the case of *Slide*, thanks to using several mapsets and modifying them between generations.

Table 2 shows the results of performing a linear regression to analyse the average learning rate of the different approaches. Although they are not linear, a simple linear model allows to make some observations: the intercept roughly represents the starting performance of each controller, the slope is an approximation of the learning rate of each approach, and the standard and residual errors are a measure of the noise present in the average learning performance.

As can be seen, the *Single* approach exhibits the best average learning rate across all runs. *Five* also shows a good learning rate, while *Slide* and *Change5* exhibit similar learning rates, but lower and with a higher noise. Finally, *Change1* has the lowest learning rate, which is actually negative when used in conjunction with A* navigation, and the highest residual error (an indication of the range of different maps explored and how hard it is to evolve controllers in such a dynamic environment).

8.2   Performance on Test

A generalisation test was carried out in order to measure the performance of the evolved controllers in unseen scenarios. This test consisted of 20 unseen maps (seeds 666 to 685), with the same parameters as the training mapsets. The individual that obtained the highest training fitness was tested every 5000 evaluations and the average results across all runs are shown in Fig. 9.

Table 2 Least-squares analysis of learning rates (bold face indicate approaches with the best training/test performance)

Approach	Train				Test			
	Intercept	Slope	Std. E.	Res. E.	Intercept	Slope	Std. E.	Res. E
No A*								
Single	3.49E+4	**1.40E−2**	4.84E−4	784.5	2.12E+4	2.26E−3	2.50E−4	127.7
Five	2.87E+4	1.36E−2	1.00E−3	739.3	2.24E+4	3.22E−3	6.29E−4	321
Change1	3.24E+4	8.64E−3	3.43E−3	3946	2.25E+4	**1.18E−2**	1.25E−3	639.1
Slide	2.75E+4	1.12E−2	2.03E−3	1383	2.29E+4	1.15E−2	1.34E−3	684.2
Change5	2.70E+4	1.25E−2	3.35E−3	1763	2.27E+4	1.17E−2	1.30E−3	667.1
RunRightSafe	2.18E+4	0.0	0.0	0.0	2.18E+4	0.0	0.0	0.0
A*								
Single	5.03E+4	**1.69E−2**	7.63E−4	1236	3.50E+4	−3.69E−3	4.53E−4	231.4
Five	4.28E+4	1.41E−2	9.29E−4	680.9	3.63E+4	4.45E−4	3.38E−4	172.6
Change1	4.55E+4	−5.81E−3	4.47E−3	5133	3.69E+4	1.04E−3	9.59E−4	489.6
Slide	4.16E+4	2.94E−3	2.16E−3	1467	4.06E+4	**1.61E−2**	1.76E−3	902.7
Change5	4.06E+4	4.34E−3	4.50E−3	2369	3.80E+4	8.16E−3	7.74E−4	395.2
DefaultGoRight	3.11E+4	0.0	0.0	0.0	3.11E+4	0.0	0.0	0.0

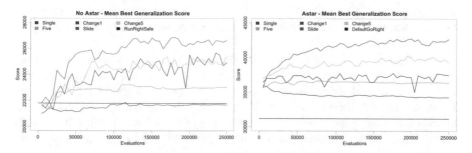

Fig. 9 Mean best test score of the best training individual every 5000 evaluations, for all approaches not using (left) or using (right) A*

The first result to notice in these tests is that the performance of all approaches decreases with respects to that of training. Given that these levels are unseen and not used for computing the fitness during training, this is to be expected. A* approaches fall from a 35,000–55,000 training performance range to 34,000–44,000 in test, while no A* behaviours drop from 25,000–40,000 to 21,000–27,000.

As can be observed, the *Single* approach clearly overfitted its single training mapset, and has the lowest generalisation score overall. It is interesting to see that, with no A*, it is even worse than the reference *RunRightSafe* behaviour, while with A* its average generalisation score worsens as evolution progresses. Despite of a few signs of training overfitting, the *Five* approach slightly improves its generalisation score over time without A*. With A* it quickly reaches its best performance without further improvement overtime. Its performance is again substantially better with A* (over 36,000 points) than without (around 23,000 points).

Table 3 Average test performance and std. deviation

Approach	Avg. score	Std. dev.	Approach	Avg. score	Std. dev.
No A*			*A**		
Single	21668.1	1531.9	Single	34224.1	1016.8
Five	23033.3	2210.9	Five	36350.1	468.6
Change1	24910.4	1860.2	Change1	37435.2	596.2
Slide	26629.3	1631.7	Slide	42616.7	731.7
Change5	25374.7	1609.9	Change5	39282.5	579.9
RunRightSafe	21790.2	0.0	DefaultGoRight	31173.8	0.0

Change1 and *Change5* steadily improve their generalisation performance, when used without A*. In spite of the very noisy average training performance, the large number of generations it is allowed to evolve can be a reason for this improvement. In the case if A*, both approaches show a better performance than their no A* counterparts, with *Change5* showing a better improvement than *Change1*. However, the approach that shows the best performance in the generalisation test is *Slide*, with a substantially better average score at all evaluation steps.

Table 3 shows the test performance of the best training controllers (again averaged across 30 runs). All A* approaches present significantly better test performance than their respective no A* behaviours, with mostly non-overlapping standard deviation intervals.

The right half of Table 2 presents the test score improvement rates of all approaches; these are very low for *Single* and *Five*. *Single* has a negative learning rate, when used with A* navigation. *Slide* and *Change5* show good test performance improvement over time, *Slide* with A* exhibiting the highest learning rate across all sets (in training and testing) and approaches (A* or not). Finally, it is worth highlighting that the learning rate of *Change1* (with A*), albeit very low, is positive, in contrast to its negative training learning rate.

8.3   Analysis

8.3.1   Fitness Analysis

Figure 10 provides an analysis of the specific fitness contributors (number of cells passed, number of kills and time left when Mario dies or finishes a level) of the best evolved controllers, averaged across the 20 test mapsets.

This analysis reinforces the idea that A* navigation makes an evident contribution to the survivability of Mario. The average number of cells passed with the *DefaultGoRight* controller is much higher, leading to a higher number of (random) kills. The time left with A* is also superior, due mainly to it not getting stuck in areas that are difficult to navigate.

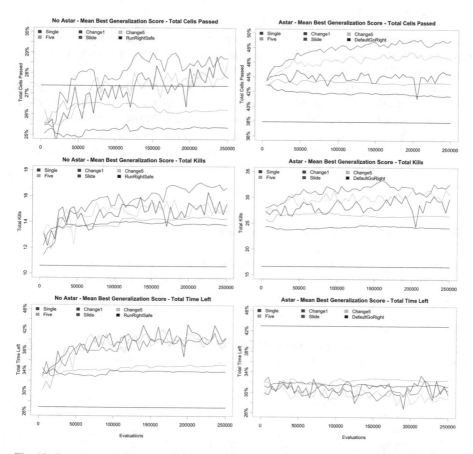

Fig. 10 Breakdown of average test performance of best evolved controllers, without A* (left) and with A* (right). The first row plots average percentage of passed cells; the second the average number of kills; and the last the percentage of time left

Controllers evolved with no A* show a worse test performance in terms of total cells passed than their reference behaviour (*RunRightSafe*). This is because BT structures need to be evolved to effectively combine navigation and reactiveness actions (such as killing enemies). *Single* and *Five*, despite of being poor at generalisation, are able to improve their average number of kills. They fail, however, at significantly evolving controllers that improve the number of cells passed or the total time left.

In the A* case, the BT structures are evolved mainly for reactiveness, with all approaches producing good reactiveness behaviour blocks. This allows them to improve the good navigation base given by the *DefaultGoRight* increasing the number of cells passed, as well as the number of kills (with a much higher improvement than controllers without A*).

This analysis provides another indication that the *Single* approach does not generalise well. It exhibits little or no improvement (apart from number of kills, when used without A*). *Five* performs slightly better, and all the other approaches evolve better generalisable behaviours across time.

It is also of interest the (non-)evolution of how much time was left after the game was completed when using A*. Even though better navigation means maps will be finished in less time, complex reactive behaviours and overall better survivability increase the amount of time spent in each map. Fitness-contributing behaviours, such as collection of items, were shown hard to evolve. Controllers with A* collected, on average, between 1 and 2 items, while no A* controllers achieved less than 1.

8.3.2   Structure and Size of the Solutions

Figure 11 (top) shows the average (genotypic) solution size, and it provides further evidence that the *Single* and *Five* approaches overfit their target maps. The size of the genotype steadily increases through evolution, which is more pronounced when A* is not used (hence solution size seems more stable with a pathfinding algorithm in the behaviour).

Although the genotype size (and hence number of nodes in the BT controllers) is comparable with or without A*, the actual structure of these trees is radically

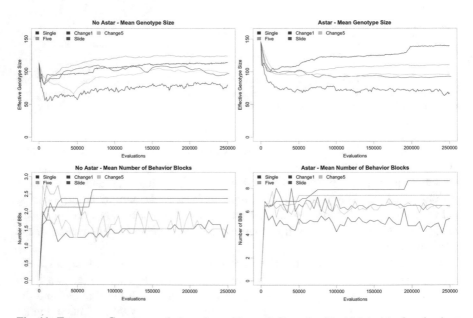

Fig. 11 Top row: Genotype solution size without (left) and with (right) A*, for the best individuals. Bottom row: Mean number of BBs for the best individuals, without (left) and with (right) A*

different with the two navigation approaches. Figure 11 (bottom) plots the number of Behaviour Blocks (BBs) in the best controllers as seen across time. As can be seen, this number is very stable, indicating that evolution is mainly focused on optimising the contents of each BB keeping a similar number in the BT.

Having a small number of BBs without A* corresponds with a very complex structure on each one of them. It is worth highlighting that this very small number limits the effectiveness of the crossover operator: each BB incorporates a complex mix of both navigation and reactiveness actions, which is difficulty to combine and inter-exchange properly. When using A* as a default behaviour for navigation, each BB is mostly a compact set of conditions and actions evolved for reactiveness, resulting in a larger number of BBs being evolved by each controller. These BBs are more easily exchanged through crossover as independent reactive sequences.

9   Conclusions and Future Work

This chapter analysed the application of GE to evolve Behaviour Trees, a structure that is able to incorporate reactive (short term) and planning (long term) concerns in highly dynamic environments. In particular, this chapter showed the application of this technique to evolve controllers for the Mario AI video-game.

The experiments showed that GE is suitable for this task, allowing the incorporation of domain knowledge and specific syntax restrictions into the generated solutions, through careful grammar design. Also, the specification of crossover points allowed for the definition and exchange of Behaviour Blocks, accelerating the evolutionary process. The resulting solutions are human readable, and easy to analyse and fine-tune. Not only this shows the applicability of this technique to produce usable and maintainable behaviours, but it also addresses one of the main concerns of the games industry regarding speed, applicability and understandability of solutions proposed by evolutionary approaches.

Possible extensions to this work include adopting a multi-objective approach, dividing the objective fitness score into some of its constituents (such as distance traveled or number of kills). Specifically related to the use of BTs, one could also record statistics such as the frequency of use, the number of kills and the complexity of each BB, and use this information to prune or inform the crossover operators. Some mechanisms would have to be in place to avoid early convergence to a very reduced set of BBs, but this could also be achieved through individual BB analysis.

Appendix: Actions, Conditions, Filters and Sub-trees for Mario

This section contains tables with the actions, conditions, filters and sub-trees used by the approaches described in this chapter to evolve Behaviour Trees. Note that some actions and conditions can be analogous in both the controllers with and without A* (i.e. *IsBreakableUp* vs. *UnderBrick*); they are, however, different: while the A* version checks the nodes in the graph, the no-A* implementation needs to analyse the contents of each cell. Also, note that actions use the terms *left* and *right*, which imply movement, while conditions use *ahead* (for right) and *back* (for left). Entries marked with a † denote sub-trees that have an analogous *left* (or *back*) variant (Tables 4 and 5).

Table 4 Filters available to the GE to evolve a BT

Filters			
Name	¬A*	A*	Description
Loop	✓	✓	Repeats the execution of its child sub-tree N times
Non	✓	✓	Negates the result given by its sub-tree
UntilFails	✓	✓	Repeats the execution of its sub-tree until it receives a *failure*
UntilFailsLimited	✓	✓	Repeats the execution of its sub-tree N times or until *failure*

Table 5 Conditions, actions and sub-trees available to the GE to evolve a BT

Name	¬A*	A*	Description
Conditions			
CanIFire	✓	✓	Checks if Mario is able to shoot fireballs
CanIJump	✓	✓	Indicates if Mario is able to jump (if he is on the ground)
IsFollowingPath	✓	✓	Indicates if Mario is following a path given by A*
IsStuck	✓	✓	Checks if Mario has been idle for many cycles
UnderBrick/ Question	✓	✓	Verifies if there is a brick/question block over Mario
EnemyAhead †	✓	✓	Checks if there is an enemy ahead of Mario
EnemyAhead Up/Down †	✓	✓	Queries for an enemy ahead and over/below Mario
JumpableEnemy Ahead †	✓	✓	Checks ahead for an enemy that can be stomped
NoJumpable EnemyAhead †	✓	✓	Checks ahead for an enemy that cannot be stomped
IsBulletToHead/ Feet	✓	✓	Checks for a bullet coming towards Mario's head/feet
AvailableJump Ahead †	✓		Verifies if there are no obstacles over and ahead of Mario
HoleAhead †	✓		Indicates if there is a hole ahead of Mario

(continued)

Table 5 (continued)

Name	¬A*	A*	Description
Conditions			
IsGapAhead †	✓		Indicates if there is a free gap in front of Mario
IsBreakableUp/ Ahead	✓		Checks for a breakable block above/ahead of Mario
IsClimbableUp/ Ahead	✓		Checks for a climbable platform over/ahead of Mario
IsJumpPlatform UpAhead †	✓		Verifies if there is a platform ahead and over Mario
IsPushable Up/Ahead	✓		Checks for a question mark block over/ahead of Mario
Obstacle Ahead †	✓		Verifies if there is an obstacle ahead of Mario
ObstacleHead †	✓		Indicates if there is an obstacle ahead, at Mario's head
Actions			
NOP, Down, Fire	✓	✓	No action and atomic actions for *Down* and *Fire*, resp.
WalkRight †	✓	✓	Atomic action *Right*
RunRight †	✓	✓	Combination of the atomic actions *Right* and *Fire*
GetPathTo ClosestBrick		✓	Uses A* to get a path to the closest brick block to Mario
GetPathTo ClosestQuestion		✓	Uses A* to get a path to the closest question mark block
GetPathTo ClosestItem		✓	Uses A* to get a path to the closest item to Mario
GetPathTo Ground		✓	Gets a path (with A*) to lowest position seen in the level
GetPathTo Top		✓	Gets a path to highest position seen in the level
GetPathTo Closest RightMost		✓	Gets a path to rightmost position seen in the level
GetPathTo ClosestLeft Most		✓	Gets a path to leftmost position seen in the level
Sub-trees			
UseRight Gap †	✓		Moves Mario to the right until no blocks are over him to then jump to a higher platform and continue from there
AvoidRight Trap †	✓		Attempts to overcome a dead end. Takes Mario back to the previous bifurcation point to then use *UseLeftGap*
GoUnder Right †	✓		Passes structures traversable only if Mario is small; or he runs, crouches and slides under it

(continued)

Table 5 (continued)

Name	¬A*	A*	Description
Conditions			
DefaultPath Planner		✓	Gets the path to the rightmost position on the screen
Path Follower		✓	Follows the last path calculated
JumpRight Long †	✓	✓	Shown in Fig. 4. Makes a long jump to the right. The filter executes the *JumpRight* action 9 frames
JumpRight RunLong †	✓	✓	As above, with JumpRightRun (*jump*, *right*, *run*)
JumpRight Short †	✓	✓	As *JumpRightLong*, with *JumpRight* executed 3 frames
JumpRight RunShort †	✓	✓	As the one above, with JumpRightRun
WalkRight Safe †	✓	✓	Moves Mario to the right, checking for hazards, trying to jump (or kill, if enemy can be stomped) over them
RunRight Safe †	✓	✓	As *WalkRightSafe*, but the input *run* is always on
Vertical JumpLong	✓	✓	As *JumpRightLong*, but the action is Jump (input *jump*)
Vertical JumpShort	✓	✓	As *JumpRightShort*, but the action is Jump

References

1. C. Ryan, J.J. Collins, M. O'Neill, Grammatical evolution: evolving programs for an arbitrary language, in *EuroGP 98* (1998), pp. 83–96. Available: https://doi.org/10.1007/BFb0055930
2. J. Togelius, S. Karakovskiy, J. Koutnik, J. Schmidhuber, Super Mario evolution, in *IEEE Symposium on Computational Intelligence and Games* (2009), pp. 156–161
3. S. Karakovskiy, J. Togelius, The Mario AI benchmark and competitions. IEEE Trans. Comput. Intell. AI Games **4**(1), 55–67 (2012)
4. M. Nicolau, D. Perez-Liebana, M. O'Neill, A. Brabazon, Evolutionary behavior tree approaches for navigating platform games. IEEE Trans. Comput. Intell. AI Games **9**(3), 227–238 (2017)
5. R. Colvin, I. Hayes, A semantics for behavior trees. ARC Centre for Complex Systems (ACCS), Technical report ACCS-TR-07-01 (2007)
6. M. O'Neill, C. Ryan, Evolving multi-line compilable c programs, in *Genetic Programming, 2nd European Workshop, EuroGP 99, Göteborg, May 26–27, 1999, Proceedings*, ed. by R. Poli, P. Nordin, W.B. Langdon, T.C. Fogarty. Lecture Notes in Computer Science, vol. 1598 (Springer, Berlin, 1999), pp. 83–92. Available: https://doi.org/10.1007/3-540-48885-5_7
7. J. M. Swafford, M. O'Neill, M. Nicolau, A. Brabazon, Exploring grammatical modification with modules in grammatical evolution, in *European Conference on Genetic Programming, EuroGP 2011, Torino, April 27–29, 2011, Proceedings*, ed. by S. Silva, J.E. Foster, M. Nicolau, P. Machado, M. Giacobini. Lecture Notes in Computer Science, vol. 6621 (Springer, Berlin, 2011), pp. 310–321

8. E. Murphy, M. Nicolau, E. Hemberg, M. O'Neill, A. Brabazon, Differential gene expression with tree-adjunct grammars, in *Parallel Problem Solving from Nature - PPSN XII, 12th International Conference, Taormina, September 1–5, 2012, Proceedings*, ed. by C.A.C. Coello, V. Cutello, K. Deb, S. Forrest, G. Nicosia, M. Pavone. Lecture Notes in Computer Science, vol. 7491 (Springer, Berlin, 2012), pp. 377–386

9. E. Galván-López, D. Fagan, E. Murphy, J.M. Swafford, A. Agapitos, M. O'Neill, A. Brabazon, Comparing the performance of the evolvable PiGrammatical evolution genotype-phenotype map to grammatical evolution in the dynamic Ms. Pac-Man environment, in *IEEE Congress on Evolutionary Computation* (2010), pp. 1587–1594

10. R. Harper, Co-evolving Robocode tanks, in *GECCO, Genetic and Evolutionary Computation Conference*, ed. by N. Krasnogor et al. (ACM, New York, 2011), pp. 1443–1450

11. R. Harper, Evolving Robocode tanks for Evo Robocode. Genet. Program Evolvable Mach. **15**(4), 403–431 (2014)

12. J.E. Murphy, M. O'Neill, H. Carr, Exploring grammatical evolution for horse gait optimisation, in *EuroGP 2009*, ed. by L. Vanneschi, S. Gustafson. Lecture Notes in Computer Science, vol. 5481 (Springer, Berlin, 2009), pp. 183–194

13. N. Shaker, M. Nicolau, G. Yannakakis, J. Togelius, M. O'Neill, Evolving levels for super mario bros using grammatical evolution, in *IEEE Conference on Computation Intelligence and Games, CIG 2012, Granada, September 11–14, 2012, Proceedings* (2012), pp. 304–311

14. N. Shaker, G.Y.J. Togelius, M. Nicolau, M. O'Neill, Evolving personalised content for super mario bros using grammatical evolution, in *AAAI Conference on Artificial Intelligence and Interactive Digital Entertainment, AIIDE-12, 8th Conference, Stanford, October 8–12, 2012, Proceedings* (AAAI, Palo Alto, 2012), pp. 75–80

15. S. Bojarski, C.B. Congdon, REALM: a rule-based evolutionary computation agent that learns to play Mario, in *IEEE Conference on Computational Intelligence and Games* (2010), pp. 83–90

16. E.R. Speed, Evolving a Mario agent using cuckoo search and softmax heuristics, in *International IEEE Consumer Electronics Society's Games Innovations Conference (ICE-GIC)* (2010), pp. 1–7

17. N.C. Hou, N.S. Hong, C.K. On, J. Teo, Infinite Mario Bross AI using genetic algorithm, in *IEEE Conference on Sustainable Utilization and Development in Engineering and Technology (STUDENT)* (2011), pp. 85–89

18. A.M. Mora, J.J. Merelo, P. García-Sánchez, P.A. Castillo, M.S. Rodríguez-Domingo, R.M. Hidalgo-Bermúdez, Creating autonomous agents for playing super Mario bros game by means of evolutionary finite state machines. Evol. Intell. **6**(4), 205–218 (2014)

19. J.-J. Tsay, C.-C. Chen, J.-J. Hsu, Evolving intelligent Mario controller by reinforcement learning, in *International Conference on Technologies and Applications of Artificial Intelligence (TAAI)* (2004), pp. 266–272

20. H. Handa, Dimensionality reduction of scene and enemy information in Mario, in *IEEE Congress on Evolutionary Computation* (2011), pp. 1515–1520

21. E.J. Jacobsen, R. Greve, J. Togelius, Monte Mario: platforming with MCTS, in *GECCO, Genetic and Evolutionary Computation Conference* (2014), pp. 293–300

22. J. Liu, J. Togelius, D. Perez-Liebana, S.M. Lucas, Evolving game skill-depth using general video game ai agents, in *IEEE Conference on Evolutionary Computation* (2017)

23. K. Kunanusont, R.D. Gaina, J. Liu, D. Perez-Liebana, S.M. Lucas, The N-tuple bandit evolutionary algorithm for automatic game improvement, in *IEEE Conference on Evolutionary Computation* (2017)

24. A. Champandard, M. Dawe, D.H. Cerpa, Behavior trees: three ways of cultivating strong AI, in *Game Developers Conference*. Audio Lecture (2010)

25. D. Isla, Managing complexity in the Halo 2 AI system, in *Game Developers Conference* (2005)

26. L. McHugh, Three approaches to behavior tree AI, in *Game Developers Conference* (2007)

27. M. Mateas, A. Stern, Managing intermixing behavior hierarchies, in *Game Developers Conference* (2004)

28. C.-U. Lim, R. Baumgarten, S. Colton, Evolving behaviour trees for the commercial game DEFCON, in *EvoApplications 2010*, vol. 6024 (Springer, Berlin, 2010), pp. 100–110

29. J.R. Koza, *Genetic Programming: On the Programming of Computers by Means of Natural Selection (Complex Adaptive Systems)*, 1st edn. (A Bradford Book, London, 1992)
30. A. Klöckner, Behavior trees for UAV mission management, in *INFORMATIK 2013: informatik angepasst an Mensch, Organisation und Umwelt* (2013), pp. 57–68
31. M. Colledanchise, P. Ögren, How behavior trees modularize hybrid control systems and generalize sequential behavior compositions, the subsumption architecture, and decision trees. IEEE Trans. Robot. **33**(2), 372–389 (2017)
32. I. Millington, J. Funge, *Artificial Intelligence for Games* (CRC Press, London, 2016)
33. M. Nicolau, Automatic grammar complexity reduction in grammatical evolution, in *GECCO, Genetic and Evolutionary Computation Conference Workshops* (2004)
34. R. Harper, GE, Explosive grammars and the lasting legacy of bad initialisation, in *IEEE Congress on Evolutionary Computation* (2010), pp. 2602–2609
35. N.J. Nilsson, *Artificial Intelligence, A New Synthesis* (Morgan Kaufmann Publishers, San Francisco, 1998)
36. A. Champandard, Behavior trees for Next-Gen game AI, in *Game Developers Conference*. Audio Lecture (2007)
37. M. Nicolau, I. Dempsey, Introducing grammar based extensions for grammatical evolution, in *IEEE Congress on Evolutionary Computation* (2006), pp. 2663–2670
38. M. Nicolau, D. Costelloe, Using grammatical evolution to parameterise interactive 3D image generation, in *EvoApplications 2011*. Lecture Notes in Computer Science, vol. 6625 (Springer, Berlin, 2011), pp. 374–383

Business Analytics and Grammatical Evolution for the Prediction of Patient Recruitment in Multicentre Clinical Trials

Gilyana Borlikova, Louis Smith, Michael Phillips, and Michael O'Neill

Abstract For a drug to be approved for human use, its safety and efficacy need to be evidenced through clinical trials. Optimisation of patient recruitment is an active area of business interest for pharma and contract research organisations (CRO) conducting clinical trials. The healthcare industry and CROs are gradually starting to adapt business analytics techniques to improve processes and help boost performance. Development of methods able to predict at the outset which prospective investigators/sites will succeed in patient recruitment can provide powerful tools for this business problem. In this chapter we describe the application of Grammatical Evolution to the prediction of patient recruitment in multicentre clinical trials.

1 Introduction

Clinical trials are an essential step in the approval process of any new drug and patient recruitment is the most time and resource consuming part of the majority of clinical trials [31]. Patient recruitment is critical to clinical trials as, if a required number of patients is not recruited, a trial cannot be completed [31]. Therefore, optimisation of patient recruitment is a critical point of interest for pharma and CROs. This business problem can be tackled from several different directions, including attempts to predict recruitment timelines and design relevant interventions [2, 3]; identification of eligible patients though trawling of Electronic Health Records (EHR) [18, 31] or better strategies of patient engagement [22, 24, 31]. However, neither approach by itself provides a universal fix to the challenging

G. Borlikova (✉) · M. O'Neill
Natural Computing Research & Applications Group, School of Business, University College Dublin, Dublin, Ireland
e-mail: gilyana.borlikova@ucd.ie; m.oneill@ucd.ie

L. Smith · M. Phillips
ICON plc, Dublin, Ireland
e-mail: louis.smith@iconplc.com; michael.phillips@iconplc.com

© Springer International Publishing AG, part of Springer Nature 2018
C. Ryan et al. (eds.), *Handbook of Grammatical Evolution*,
https://doi.org/10.1007/978-3-319-78717-6_19

461

problem of sourcing the required number of patients for a trial reliably. One way to facilitate successful patient recruitment is to ensure strategies for selection of investigators/clinical sites (sites) at the start of a trial that will achieve higher patient enrolment numbers. This study builds and extends upon previous work [7, 8] that used Grammatical Evolution (GE) [13, 26], a grammar-based Genetic Programming (GP) system [23] to evolve binary classification models, in order to predict the future patient enrolment performance of sites considered for a trial. To ensure business-applicability of any evolved classifiers, it is important to carefully consider performance of the classifiers on each of the two classes constituting the problem. The first part of the study presented here investigates the use of a range of classification performance metrics that take into account the contribution of each of the classes. The results show that classification metrics with a range of different degrees of each class contribution produce models that cover different parts of the problem space. However, it would be beneficial to be able to specifically develop models targeting particular sectors of the problem space. The second part of the study addresses this challenge by introducing a new fitness function that attempts to evolve classifiers that maximise performance on one class, while adhering to a particular threshold on the second class. Overall, the results demonstrate the ability of GE to evolve highly competitive customised patient recruitment classification models and show that a collection of such models can be used to address challenges of the real-world patient recruitment business scenarios.

2 Background

2.1 Patient Recruitment in Clinical Trials

Patient recruitment is critical for the successful completion of clinical trials [22, 24, 31]. Studies indicate that though majority of clinical trials eventually enroll the required number of patients, up to the nearly 50% of sites in a given trial fail to enroll planned number of patients and the timelines are usually pushed to nearly twice the original plan [34]. This results in the need to bring more sites into the study and to extend overall enrolment timelines, leading to financial waste, compromised timelines and an increase in the overall risk to the studies [24, 31].

Several components contribute to the success or failure of patient enrollment, such as the recruitment potential of the site, complexity and duration of the trial protocol, different strategies of patient engagement and other factors [22, 24, 31]. A lot of attention has been given recently to better ways of reaching target patient populations and maintaining patient engagement [31, 33]. There is also a growing effort to reduce trial protocol complexity [31]. However, notwithstanding recent progress, the process of improving patient recruitment remains an area of active business interest.

2.2 Different Approaches to Patient Enrolment Prediction

Most published research into patient recruitment is based on modelling enrolment rates and forecasting timelines to achieving certain number of enrolled patients [2, 3]. Another widely adapted approach is identifying patients and enrolment eligibility from analysis of the existing patient databases and electronic health records [1, 18, 31].

An alternative way to address this problem is to improve the quality of clinical sites selected to participate in a trial. This can be achieved by the development of predictive classification models based on the historical patient recruitment data. A recent study by Ni and colleagues [24] adapted a similar approach (classification based on historical data) to predict patients response to clinical trial invitations in the context of paediatric emergency department. They report that compared to the random response predictor that simulated current practice, the machine learning (ML) algorithms trained on historical data achieved significantly better performance.

2.3 Grammatical Evolution for Classification

GE [13, 26] was previously successfully applied to a range of classification problems in finance and evolved classifiers that were competitive with the results produced by other ML algorithms [9, 10, 35]. It was suggested that GE methodology has general utility for rule-induction applications. Especially attractive features of GE are the possibility of incorporating domain knowledge into the formulation of the problem at the grammar development stage [25], and an ease of incorporating different fitness functions to drive evolutionary process of model development. This study builds on our previous work [7, 8] that extended GE methodology into the domain of prediction of patient recruitment in multicenter clinical trials.

2.4 Scope of Research

In this application of GE to Business Analytics, we use the advantages of GE to evolve classification models for prediction of patient recruitment in multicentre clinical trials.

Performance of classification models can be fully characterized by a table called confusion matrix (CM) [29]. In the case of a two-class classification problem CM of a classifier has four cells (Table 1); cells on the main diagonal contain the number of correct predictions for each of the classes (True Positives, TP and True Negatives, TN); the cells on the contra-diagonal contain counts of errors made by the classifier (False Positives, FP and False Negatives, FN).

Table 1 Confusion matrix

		Actual condition	
		Condition positive	Condition negative
Predicted condition	Predicted positive	True positive (**TP**)	False positive (**FP**)
	Predicted negative	False negative (**FN**)	True negative (**TN**)

In our initial study we used GE to evolve classification models to predict the future patient enrolment performance of sites considered for a trial and have shown that prediction accuracy of the GE-evolved models is comparable or even better than the accuracy achieved by a range of ML algorithms widely used for classification [7]. However, the standard accuracy that was used as a fitness function in the study is a non-balanced score [30, 32] that does not account for an individual class's contribution to the metric. At the same time, model construction for this business problem necessitates careful consideration of the two classes as in most real-life patient recruitment situations, historic data is unbalanced (the proportion of poorly performing *vs.* successful sites is uneven) and misclassification costs differ between the classes. In the context of patient recruitment prediction we want to develop classifiers that distinguish between sites that will go on to show poor patient enrolment (class of interest or condition positive in terms of CM, Table 1) from sites that will perform (condition negative). In this situation one type of error, mistakenly predicting condition negative (FN in CM), will result in inclusion of a potentially weak site in the study, while another, mistakenly predicting condition positive (FP in CM), will lead to elimination of a potentially promising site from the study. The size of the penalty for each type of mistake will depend on the immediate business context/environment of a particular clinical trial.

In the first part of the study we address this aspect of the business problem by exploring the use of several balanced scores/metrics that account for the contribution of each class and provide an alternative to the standard accuracy in classification [30, 32]. We investigate the use of balanced accuracy, Yoden's J-statistic and F-score as the fitness functions to drive model development with GE and compare the results with that of the standard accuracy [17, 27, 32].

The second part of the study attempts to simultaneously address two aspects of the business challenge of site selection for patient recruitment, dependency of the misclassification costs on the business context at the model deployment stage (for example, the scarcity or abundance of sites available for inclusion into the study), and the fact that these costs are usually not known at the model development stage. For such situations Fawcett and Provost [29] advocate the use of Receiver Operating Characteristic (ROC) curve for model evaluation and selection, and the use of expected cost/benefit to frame evaluation of the probabilistic ML classifiers. If the costs were known in advance, the problem could be framed in a cost-sensitive learning framework [15]. In the GP field Zhang and colleagues developed different fitness functions [5] and diverse ensembles [6] to improve classification in the case of unbalanced data. Fawcett and Provost [28] introduced the idea of developing a robust hybrid classifier to address challenges of imprecise class distribution and misclassification costs. Recently several authors [4, 12, 21] extended this idea by developing multi-objective ROC Front (ROCF) methods. We set out to address this challenge by proposing a new fitness function that incorporates a misclassification threshold and utilising this function to develop a collection of models capable of addressing varying business scenarios. These models are compared with the standard ML algorithms and possible approaches to the selection of the best generalisable model are discussed.

3 Case Study: GE with Class-Balanced Fitness Functions

In this study, we address the problem of unbalanced classes and different misclassification costs by exploring a range of alternative fitness functions to drive GE. We formulate the business problem as a binary classification problem, construct a grammar adapted to the problem and then run GE with the standard accuracy as the fitness function to establish a baseline. We then investigate a range of well-established balanced-score classification metrics: balanced accuracy with equal weights, J-statistic and (F-measure) with three different values of beta [17, 27, 30, 32]. The GE models developed with these functions are compared with models developed using standard accuracy and performance of the benchmark ML algorithms.

3.1 Experimental Design

3.1.1 Model Data

The dataset used in the current study was constructed based on the de-identified historical operational data provided by ICON plc. on 21 Diabetes Mellitus Type II Phase III clinical trials and was described previously in [7]. The operational data provided by the company was supplemented by data from the outside sources. During data preparation, records with missing values were removed, as well as a few predictor variables with near-zero variance. The resultant dataset consisted of 1233 records containing 43 site related predictor variables. The dataset contained 35 numerical variables and 8 categorical variables describing different characteristic of prospective site and related clinical trial. The sites were allocated to two classes based on their patient enrolment performance. Prior to the beginning of experiments, the data was split into balanced training and testing subsets (70/30%) using *createDataPartition* function of the CARET package in R [19]. In all experiments model training and (where necessary) tuning was performed using the training subset and then performance of the best models was tested on the testing data subset to assess the evolved models generalisability to unseen data.

3.1.2   Evolutionary Model Representation and Run Parameters

In a similar way to our previous work [7, 8] we approached the business problem of patient enrolment prediction as a classification problem. GE was used to evolve decision-tree type discreet classifiers. Figure 1 shows the GE grammar used in the experiments. Construction of the grammar incorporated domain knowledge shared by business experts on clinical trials that informed grouping and different selection probabilities of particular features. The grammar used the function and terminal set detailed in Table 2. We confined the function set that operated on numerical variables to arithmetic operations in order to cover only linear transformations of the variables.

Table 3 details the evolutionary parameters setting. Sub-tree crossover was employed to ensure the validity of the resulting individuals. All experiments were run using a custom modification of the PonyGE2 system [16] with post-processing of the results using R and Python.

3.1.3   Fitness Functions, Performance Measurement and Benchmarking

The following functions were investigated [17, 27, 30, 32]:

$$Accuracy = \frac{(TP + TN)}{(TP + TN + FP + FN)} \tag{1}$$

$$Balanced\ Accuracy = \omega \times \frac{TP}{TP + FN} + (1 - \omega) \times \frac{TN}{TN + FP}, \ where\ \omega = 0.5 \tag{2}$$

$$J-statistic = \frac{TP}{TP + FN} + \frac{TN}{TN + FP} - 1 \tag{3}$$

$$F-measure = (1 + \beta^2) \times \frac{TP}{((1 + \beta^2) * TP + \beta^2 \times FN + FP)}, \ where\ \beta = 0.5, 1, 2 \tag{4}$$

To facilitate comparison of performance of models developed with different fitness functions, they were assessed in terms of True Positive Rate (TPR) and False Positive Rate (FPR) derived from confusion matrix data of a model, similarly to the ROC coordinates [11].

```
<s> ::= np.where(<pred>, <out>, <out>)

<out> ::= <s>|<class>
<class> ::= -1|1

<pred> ::=  np.logical_and(<pred>,<pred>)|
            np.logical_or(<pred>,<pred>)|
            np.logical_not(<pred>)|
            (<expr_num> <bool_num_comp> <expr_num>)|
            (<expr_num> <bool_num_comp> <expr_num>)|
            (<expr_num> <bool_num_comp> <expr_num>)|
            <expr_bool>|<expr_bool>|<expr_bool>

<bool_num_comp> ::= <|>|<=|>=

<expr_num> ::=  (<expr_num> <op_num> <expr_num>)|
                (<var_num> <op_num> <var_num>)|
                <var_num>

<op_num> ::= +|-|*

# thirty four numerical features arranged into three groups
<ft_num1> ::= x[0]|x[1]|x[2]|x[3]|x[4]|x[5]|x[6]|x[7]|x[8]|x[9]
<ft_num2> ::= x[10]|x[11]|x[12]|x[13]|x[14]|x[15]|x[16]|x[17]|x[18]|x[19]|x[20]
<ft_num3> ::= x[21]|x[22]|x[23]|x[24]|x[25]|x[26]|x[27]|x[28]|x[29]|x[30]|
              x[31]|x[32]|x[33]|x[34]

# numerical constants
<const_num> ::= -1|-0.9|-0.8|-0.7|-0.6|-0.5|-0.4|-0.3|-0.2|-0.1|0.0|
                0.1|0.2|0.3|0.4|0.5|0.6|0.7|0.8|0.9|1

<var_num> ::= <const_num>|<const_num>|
              <ft_num1>|<ft_num1>|<ft_num1>|
              <ft_num2>|
              <ft_num3>

# five boolean features
<ft_bool> ::= x[38]|x[39]|x[40]|x[41]|x[42]

<expr_bool> ::=  np.logical_and(<expr_bool>,<expr_bool>)|
                 np.logical_or(<expr_bool>,<expr_bool>)|
                 np.logical_not(<expr_bool>)|
                 <op_bool>|<op_bool>|
                 <ft_bool>|<ft_bool>|<ft_bool>|
                 <cat>|<cat>|<cat>

<op_bool> ::= np.logical_and(<ft_bool>,<ft_bool>)|
              np.logical_or(<ft_bool>,<ft_bool>)|
              np.logical_not(<ft_bool>)

# possible values of the three categorical features
<x35_1> ::= 1|2|3|4|5|6|7|8|9|10|11|12
<x35_2> ::= 13|14|15|16|17|18|19|20|21|22|23|24
<x35_3> ::= 25|26|27|28|29|30|31|32|33|34|35|36|37
<x36> ::= 1|2|3
<x37> ::= 1|2|3|4|5

<cat> ::= (x[35] <op_cat> <x35_1>)|
          (x[35] <op_cat> <x35_2>)|
          (x[35] <op_cat> <x35_3>)|
          (x[36] <op_cat> <x36>)|
          (x[37] <op_cat> <x37>)

<op_cat> ::= ==|!=
```

Fig. 1 Grammar used to construct GE classifier

Table 2 Function and terminal sets of GE classifier

Function set	Terminal set
+, −, *, /, and, or, not	35 numerical predictive variables: x0, …, x34
=, ≠	3 categorical predictive variables: x35, x36, x37
<, >, ≤, ≥	5 Boolean predictive variables: x38, …, x42
	20 random constants in −1.0, …, 1.0 with 0.1 step

Table 3 Evolutionary parameter settings

Parameter	Value
Initialisation	Ramped-half-and-half initialisation
Number of runs	30
Population size	1000
Number of generations	50
Selection	Tournament
Tournament Size	5 (0.5% of population size)
Replacement	Generational
Elite size	1
Crossover	Sub-tree
Crossover Probability	0.9
Mutation	Sub-tree
Mutation Probability	1 event per individual
Max derivation tree depth	9

$$TPR = \frac{TP}{TP + FN} \tag{5}$$

$$FPR = \frac{FP}{TN + FP} \tag{6}$$

Performance of the GE models was compared to the performance of three well-established ML algorithms, Classification and Regression Tree (CART), Random Forest (RF) and Support Vector Machine with Radial Basis Function Kernel (SVM) [20]. The two of the selected ML algorithms (CART and RF) are based on the decision trees and therefore provide a good comparison to the GE decision-tree models, while SVM is a powerful algorithm that uses a different principle to achieve classification. The R CARET package [19] was used to train, tune and test the ML models. Accuracy was used as a metric in tuning (tenfold cross-validation repeated 10 times) and training procedures and all ML models results are reported for the default class probability threshold of 0.5. Settings of the ML models are presented in Table 4.

Table 4 Benchmark machine learning (ML) model settings

Model	R CARET method	Parameter setting
Classification and Regression Tree (**CART**)	rpart	Complexity parmeter = 0.0249
Random Forest (**RF**)	rf	#randomly selected predictors = 7
Support Vector Machines, Radial Basis Function Kernel (**SVM**)	svmRadial	Sigma = 0.0149, cost = 0.5

3.2 Results and Analysis

Results of the evolutionary runs with different fitness functions are presented in Fig. 2. The possible range of fitness values in each case depends on a particular function. The best and average population fitness gradually increased over 50 GE generations in all experiments confirming the ability of all fitness functions to successfully drive evolutionary process (Fig. 2a, b). The median training performance of the 30 best-of-run classifiers evolved with each fitness function was 0.72 for accuracy, 0.69 for balanced accuracy, 0.39 for J-statistic, 0.60 for $F_{0.5}$-score, 0.63 for F_1-score and 0.77 for F_2-score (Fig. 2c). When these classifiers were applied to the previously unseen test subset, their performances degraded slightly comparing with the training performance. The median fitness levels achieved on the test were 0.66, 0.64, 0.30, 0.52, 0.60, 0.75 respectively (Fig. 2d).

To facilitate between-function comparison of models' performance, all models were then assessed in terms of TPR/FPR coordinates. Dot-plots of performance on test data of 30 individual best-of-run models developed with each function (Fig. 3) show that models evolved using different fitness functions group in different parts of the TPR/FPR space.

To investigate the relationship between a model's performance on training data with performance on testing data, we next created dot-plots of results of the best-of-run models evolved with each function in two coordinate systems—Fitness on train/TPR on test (Fig. 4) and TPR on train/TPR on test (Fig. 5). The visual examination of the dot-plots suggests that while there appears to be no defined relationship between a model's fitness on training and TPR on test (Fig. 4), there is a positive linear relationship trend between the TPR that a model showed on train and its TPR on test (Fig. 5).

Table 5 contains the highest TPR and corresponding FPR values achieved on the test subset by GE models evolved with different fitness functions and TPR/FPR values achieved by the three ML models with the 0.5 class threshold. The same data is visualised in Fig. 6. The figure and the table show a trade-off between increase in TPR and corresponding increase on FPR. In the extreme case the best classifier evolved using F_2-measure correctly predicts 99% of class of interest sites (TPR 0.99) at the price of misclassifying almost 80% of the opposite class (FPR 0.79).

Between the GE-evolved models, classifiers evolved using standard accuracy achieved the highest TPR of 0.57 with the corresponding FPR of 0.27, using $F_{0.5}$

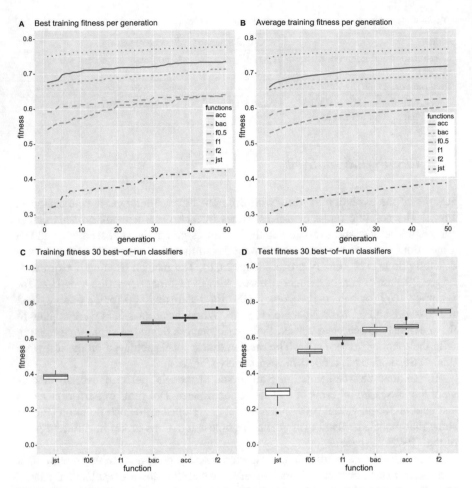

Fig. 2 GE with different fitness functions classification experiments. Best (**a**) and average (**b**) training fitness achieved by GE models driven by different fitness functions in 30 independent runs over 50 generations. (**c**) Fitness of the 30 best-of-run evolutionary classifiers on the training (**c**) and test (**d**) data. Note that the range of fitness values depends on the function

0.61/0.30, using J-statistic 0.73/0.38, using balanced accuracy 0.77/0.45, using F_1 0.84/0.52 and using F_2 0.99/0.79 (TPR/FPR respectively). For comparison, all three ML models with the default 0.5 class threshold showed lower TPR levels (Table 5). The results clearly demonstrate that GE evolves models that are comparable or even better than ML models, depending on the context.

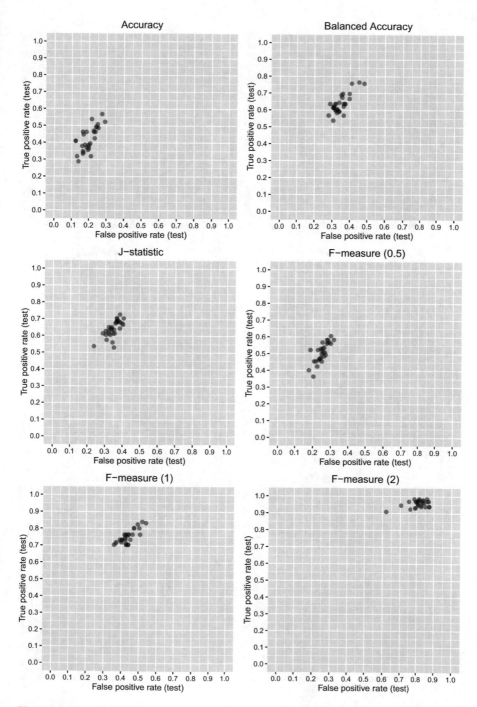

Fig. 3 Performance of the best-of-run GE models evolved with different fitness functions on test data (30 runs for each function)

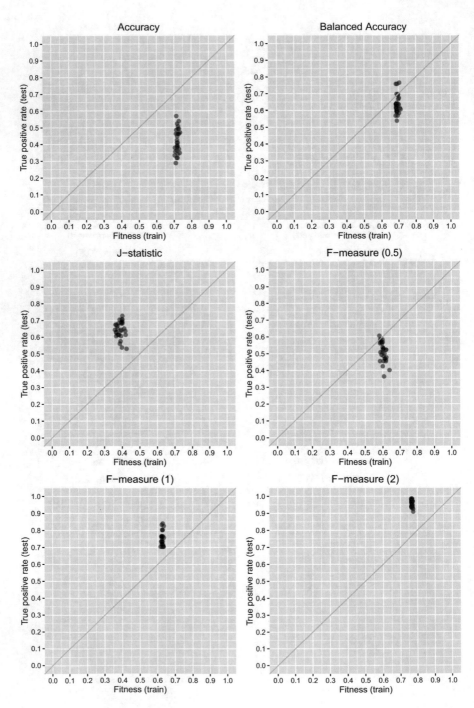

Fig. 4 Relationship between fitness on train and TPR on test of the best-of-run GE models evolved with different fitness functions

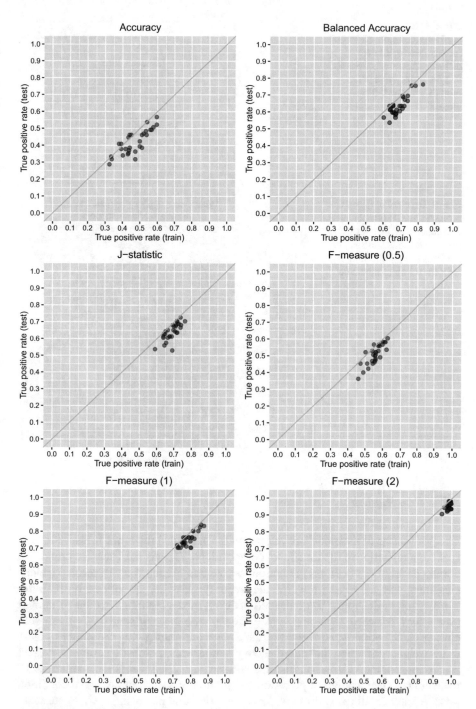

Fig. 5 Relationship between train and test TPR performance of the best-of-run GE models evolved with different fitness functions

Table 5 Best test performance achieved by GE models developed with different fitness functions and test performance of ML models with the 0.5 class threshold

Model	TPR	FPR
Accuracy	0.57	0.27
Balanced accuracy	0.77	0.45
J-statistic	0.73	0.38
F-metric (0.5)	0.61	0.30
F-metric (1)	0.84	0.52
F-metric (2)	0.99	0.79
CART	0.49	0.21
RF	0.56	0.25
SVM	0.39	0.17

Fig. 6 Best test performance achieved by GE models developed with different fitness functions and test performance of ML models with the 0.5 class threshold

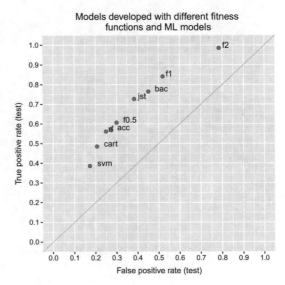

3.3 Conclusions

The positioning of the models developed with the studied functions in the TPR/FPR space is a reflection of the functions' compositions. The standard accuracy reflects a combined number of correct predictions across two classes and as a result develops classifiers that are biased towards the majority class i.e. are stricter on majority class misclassifications. The balanced accuracy takes separate account of correct predictions for each class and in the case of the ω coefficient $= 0.5$ gives both classes contribution equal weight in the final score, thus giving the minority class more weight in shaping the classifier. In a similar way, J-statistic combines correct predictions for each class, but this time without an explicit weighting coefficient. F-measure is a combination of precision (proportion of TP out of predicted condition positive) and recall (proportion of TP out of condition positive, TPR). F_1-measure (balanced F-score) gives equal weight to precision and recall, $F_{0.5}$-measure weighs precision more than recall (by attenuating the influence of FNs), while F_2-measure puts more weight on recall (by placing more emphasis on FNs) [27]. As the result, models developed with $F_{0.5}$-measure fitness function are closer to the ones evolved using standard accuracy, while models developed with F_2-measure are extremely liberal (heavily biased towards the class of interest).

Overall, the study demonstrates how the flexibility of GE allows for an easy utilisation of different fitness functions to drive model development. The fitness functions examined in this study help to develop models distributed along the strict/liberal model axis, thus enabling development of a collection of models that are better suited to different business scenarios.

4 Case Study: GE with a Threshold Fitness Function

Development of models for prediction of patient recruitment is further complicated by the fact that the target misclassification costs are usually not known at the model development stage and are business-context dependent. In this part of the study we address this challenge by proposing a new fitness function to develop a multi-model system of decision-tree type classifiers that optimise a range of possible trade-offs between the correct classification and errors. We apply this new fitness function to drive GE evolution and consider induced models in more detail.

4.1 Experimental Design

All experiments were conducted using the dataset described in Sect. 3.1. The data was split into train (70%) and test (30%) subsets while maintaining class balance and GE models were evolved on the train subset. The GE grammar, function and terminal sets and evolutionary parameters were the same as described earlier (Tables 1, 2 and 3, Sect. 3.1).

We introduced a new fitness function to facilitate evolving solutions that maximise performance in terms of TPR given FPR cut-off value:

$$Fitness = \begin{cases} TPR & \text{if } FPR \leq \text{cut-off} \\ -FPR & \text{if } FPR > \text{cut-off} \end{cases} \tag{7}$$

Using this function, the fitness of the solution is assigned value equal to its TPR if solution's FPR is below or equal to the set cut-off value, otherwise it is assigned the value equal to $-FPR$. The choice of the FPR cut-off values for the study was informed by the business needs. Depending on the business environment, the site selection might benefit from either more conservative/strict models or more liberal models that will be able to correctly identify more instances of the class of interest even at a price of more misclassification errors on the other class. We have projected

Table 6 Benchmark machine learning (ML) model settings

Model	R CARET method	Parameter setting
Classification and Regression Tree (**CART**)	rpart	Complexity parmeter = 0
Random Forest (**RF**)	rf	#randomly selected predictors = 13
Support Vector Machines, Radial Basis Function Kernel (**SVM**)	svmRadial	Sigma = 0.0000129, cost = 512

that from a business perspective the tolerable levels of FPR should not exceed 0.5 (50% of the majority class misclassification). Based on this assumption, four FPR cut-off values were investigated in this study: 0.2, 0.3, 0.4, 0.5.

An issue of model generalisation is critical for any applied model development. We investigate different approaches for selection of the best models, and compare visual selection of individual models based on plotting, selection based on a validation subset and selection based on performance as assessed by bootstrap resampling of the validation subset (50 repeated resamples with replacement).

To benchmark the best evolved GE classification models their performance was compared to performance of the three well-established machine learning (ML) algorithms widely used in classification problems CART, RF and SVM [20]. As previously, the R CARET package [19] was used to train and tune ML models and to test their performance on the data. Model parameters were tuned using tenfold cross-validation repeated 10 times with the Area Under the Curve (AUC) as the selection metric and the default 0.5 class threshold. Final models parameter settings are presented in Table 6.

4.2 Results and Analysis

The best and average population fitness gradually increased over 50 GE generations in experiments with all four FPR cut-offs confirming effectiveness of the proposed fitness function in driving evolutionary process (Fig. 7). As expected, the application of the fitness function with different FPR cut-offs resulted in different values of fitness achieved by the respective GE populations. Best training fitness per generation (Fig. 7a) provides an easily observed illustration of this point. In the experiment with the most stringent FPR cut-off of 0.2 the best training fitness achieved within the population gradually reaches 0.59 over 50 generations, while in the experiment with the most liberal FPR cut-off of 0.5 the best fitness within the population gradually reaches almost 0.85. The median training performance of the 30 best classifiers evolved in each independent evolutionary run was 0.52 (0.2 cut-off), 0.64 (0.3 cut-off), 0.73 (0.4 cut-off) and 0.83 (0.5 cut-off) (Fig. 7c). The average training fitness per generation and the fitness of the 30 best of run classifiers figures (Fig. 7b, c) also provide an illustration of the fact that independent

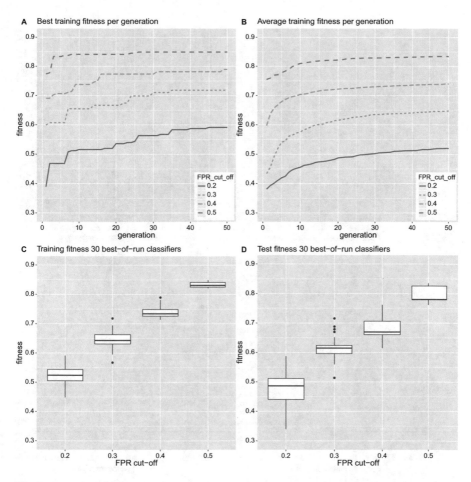

Fig. 7 GE with a threshold fitness function classification experiments. Best (**a**) and average (**b**) training fitness achieved by GE models driven by fitness function with different FPR cut-off values in 30 independent runs over 50 generations. (**c**) Fitness of the 30 best-of-run evolutionary classifiers on the training (**c**) and test (**d**) data

GE runs evolve models with "tightness" of the fitness distribution increasing along with the liberalisation of the imposed FPR cut-off. With the strict 0.2 FPR cut-off 30 independent runs result in models fairly dispersed in terms of the final fitness, while the most liberal cut-off of 0.5 FPR allows for the development of models that return nearly identical fitness.

Next, the performance of the 30 best-of-run GE-evolved classifiers was evaluated on the test data. As expected, in comparison with the median performance on the train subset, the median fitness levels achieved by these models on the test subset were lower (0.49, 0.62, 0.67 and 0.78 respectively), reflecting the challenge of generalisation (Fig. 7d). Dot-plots of the same data (Fig. 8) shows detailed

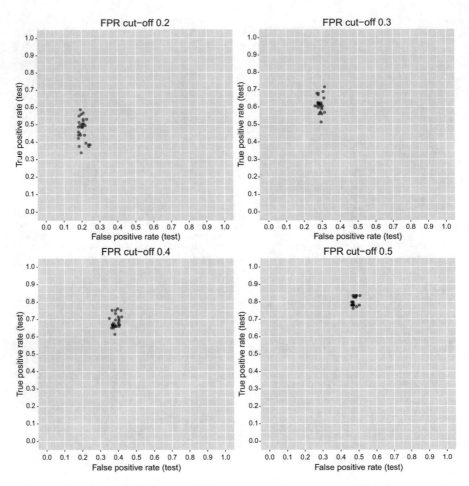

Fig. 8 Performance of the best-of-run GE models evolved with different fitness functions on test data (30 runs for each function)

distribution of the fitness values of the 30 models and confirms that the models retain positioning in terms of the FPR axis well overall (within 0.05 of FPR cut-off in most cases).

Examination of the performance of all 30 generated models on test data helps to assess the method in general (in the current case, performance of the new proposed fitness function utisiling different FPR cut-offs), but does not enable selection of the best model. At the same time, the business problem would benefit from selecting a particular, preferably the best, model from the 30 evolved so that it can be deployed to classify prospective clinical trial sites in the future.

To examine the relationship between performance in training and generalisation to the test subset we generated dot-plots for all models in coordinates TPR on train/TPR on test (Fig. 9). Visual examination of the plots suggested that in this case

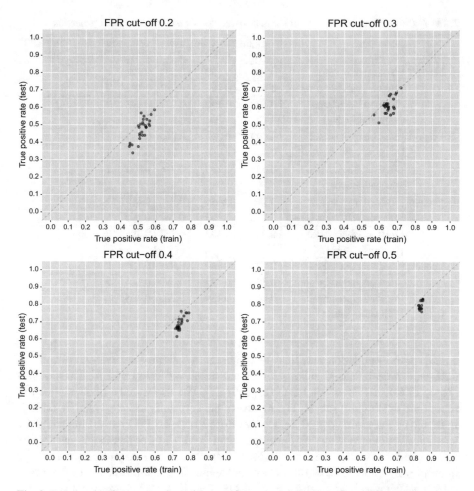

Fig. 9 Relationship between train and test performance of the best-of-run GE models evolved with different FPR cut-offs (30 runs per cut-off)

selection of the top performing model on train as a candidate for future deployment is a reasonable approach, as the top performing models generally align along the train/test coordinate diagonal. This is further confirmed by examination of the models' ranks. For FPR cut-offs of 0.2 and 0.3 the top model on the train set was also the top model on the test set, for 0.4 cut-off the top model on the train set was second on the test set. In the case of the most liberal FPR cut-off (0.5) the top model on the train set ranked seventh on the test set, while the second top model of the train set generalised top on the test. In fact, all 30 models developed with the 0.5 cut-off performed very close to each other on both train and test sets.

We decided to conduct an additional sub-investigation to further explore avenues to finding a reliable "best generalisable model". While using the pool of models developed on the train data subset, we divided the original test data subset into

Table 7 Comparison of the different methods of the "best generalisable model" selection

Cut-off threshold	Selection method	Test_fin TPR	Test_fin FPR	Test TPR	Test FPR	Test_fin TPR rank	Test TPR rank
0.2 cut-off	Best on train subset	0.589	0.190	0.587	0.192	2	1
	Best on validation subset	0.589	0.190	0.587	0.192	2	1
	Best on Bootstraped validation subset	0.589	0.190	0.587	0.192	2	1
0.3 cut-off	Best on train subset	0.699	0.299	0.716	0.315	1	1
	Best on validation subset	0.699	0.299	0.716	0.315	1	1
	Best on Bootstraped validation subset	0.699	0.299	0.716	0.315	1	1
0.4 cut-off	Best on train subset	0.740	0.356	0.752	0.415	2	2
	Best on validation subset	0.740	0.397	0.762	0.396	3	1
	Best on Bootstraped validation subset	0.740	0.397	0.762	0.396	3	1
0.5 cut-off	Best on train subset	0.822	0.489	0.826	0.485	9	7
	Best on validation subset	0.836	0.483	0.780	0.504	8	21
	Best on Bootstraped validation subset	0.822	0.489	0.780	0.465	30	27

equally sized validation and final test subsets, generating an overall split of the data into three balanced subsets - original train, validation and final test subset (70%, 15% and 15% of total data respectively). We also tested a bootstrapped (50 repetitions) validation subset. The results of the sub-study are presented in Table 7. It should be noted that the 30 models developed with 0.5 FPR cut-off threshold are less spread out than the models developed with the other three thresholds and display a very similar performance. The results indicate that there is no particular advantage in employing validation data subset or bootstrapped validation subset for the model selection. We observed a similar trend for positive linear relationship between TPR on train and TPR on test in the earlier part of the study (see Fig. 5). In the light of these findings, the model selection based on performance on the train subset is an acceptable approach and was adapted for the final analysis.

Table 8 presents AUCs of the tuned ML models on training and test data. However, for business application, we want to be able to select class threshold settings at model-development stage that will take into account business-informed FPR cut-offs while maximising possible TPR levels. One approach can be to select class thresholds to satisfy FPR cut-offs based on the training data and then apply them for classification of the test data. The class thresholds established by this method in the current study can be seen in the last columns of Table 8.

Table 9 contains TPR and FPR values resulting from evaluation on the test dataset of the GE models evolved with different FPR cut-offs, selected based on the best train performance and the ML models with class thresholds corresponding to the four training FPR cut-offs. The same data is visualised in Fig. 10.

Table 8 Performance of ML models and class thresholds corresponding to FPR cut-offs

Model	Train AUC	Test AUC	0.2 cut-off	0.3 cut-off	0.4 cut-off	0.5 cut-off
CART	0.846	0.750	0.28	0.19	0.17	0.15
RF	0.966	0.742	0.22	0.13	0.08	0.05
SVM	0.859	0.710	0.263	0.263	0.262	0.245

Table 9 Performance of the best GE models developed with different FPR cut-offs and ML models with the corresponding class thresholds on test

Model	Metric	0.2 cut-off	0.3 cut-off	0.4 cut-off	0.5 cut-off
GE	TPR	0.59	**0.72***	**0.75***	**0.83***
	FPR	**0.19**	**0.32**	**0.42**	**0.48**
CART	TPR	**0.66***	0.71	0.73	0.79
	FPR	**0.24**	**0.30**	**0.36**	0.44
RF	TPR	0.76	0.80	0.85	0.89
	FPR	0.32	0.43	0.54	0.64
SVM	TPR	0.66	0.71	0.72	0.82
	FPR	0.33	0.38	0.39	0.55

*Highest TPR levels achieved within 0.05 of FPR cut-off

Fig. 10 Comparison of test performance of GE models developed with different FPR cut-offs and ML models

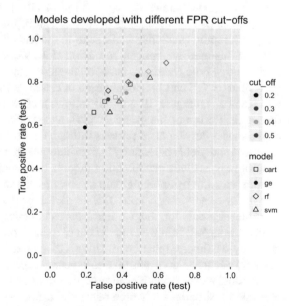

The results show that in all four experiments GE-evolved models maintain their positioning around FPR cut-off values on test data more consistently than ML models with class thresholds based on these cut-offs (in bold—actual FPR levels within ±0.05 of the desired FPR levels). Though in 6 cases ML models achieved higher levels of TPR they fail to maintain required FPR levels. Apart from the experiment with the strictest FPR cut-off (0.2), GE models achieve the highest TPR between models with "on test" FPR levels within ±0.05 of the desired FPR levels (in bold *).

4.3 Conclusions

Compared with the fitness functions that were used in the first study, the new fitness function allows to directly pre-set FPR levels during model development. The results show that the new function was able to successfully drive GE and evolve classification models that maximise correct identification of the class of interest while maintaining different levels of the other class misclassification. The observation that performance of a model on the training data can serve as an indicator of the model's performance on the test data greatly facilitates model selection stage. The models selected based on this approach showed generalisation to the previously unseen data that was superior to the generalisation of the benchmark ML models in maintaining pre-set FPR levels. This aspect of the GE-evolved models will be particularly important for real-world business application scenarios.

5 Conclusions and Future Developments

This study demonstrates the application of GE to Business Analytics to address the problem of improving patient recruitment in multicenter clinical trials. It does it by developing predictive classification models of future performance of clinical sites. In this area we built upon our previous work [7, 8] and used GE to evolve decision-tree type classifiers based on the historical records of the sites' recruitment performance. GE was previously used in classification problems [9, 10, 35] and has a range of advantages. GE grammar allows for incorporation of domain knowledge during the design of the grammar [25], and provides an option for an easy tuning of the model development process through the custom selected/constructed fitness functions and yields potentially human-interpretable models [9, 10, 25]. In addition, GE not only evolves classification models but simultaneously performs a form of feature selection by zooming onto a subset of predictor variables [9, 10, 25].

We have previously used GE to develop classification models for patient recruitment prediction that were at least as effective as the ML benchmarks. In the original work, we followed the default classification conventions and used standard accuracy as fitness function to drive GE and shape model selection. However, standard accuracy does not take into account the contribution of different classes to the score and is often biased towards the majority class, thus it is a sub-optimal measure for situations in which misclassification costs differ for two classes [30].

In the first part of this study, classifiers were evolved using a range of GE fitness functions that in various forms, combine the contribution of the two classes in one resultant score, balanced accuracy, Yoden's J-statistic and F-score with three different values of beta [17, 27, 32]. Results of these classifiers were compared with the results of the classifier evolved using standard accuracy and benchmarked against 3 ML algorithms widely used in classification. The results demonstrate that the use of these fitness functions produces classifiers with different TPR/FPR qualities. Taken together, the classifiers developed in this work cover different areas of the TPR/FPR space. To address the challenge of developing classifiers for imprecise environments, Fawcett and Provost [28] proposed an idea of the rodust hybrid classifier comprised of a group of classifiers that can maximise the coverage of different segments of the TPR/FPR space. It can be speculated that the classifiers developed in this work form a front akin to this robust hybrid classifier. The utilisation of a range of fitness functions representing different degrees of contribution of two classes to the final score can be used to address challenges of uneven misclassification costs in unbalanced data situation and guide evolution of customised patient recruitment classification models by GE. However, this approach has some limitations, as even though the developed models cover different areas along the FPR axis, it would be difficult to specifically direct model development to particular misclassification levels.

In the second part of this study we set out to use GE to evolve a system of classifiers that maximise correct classification of the class of interest while maintaining pre-set levels of the other class misclassification. To achieve this we proposed a new fitness function that incorporates cut-off values for the acceptable level of FPR. Based on the business context of clinical site selection we identified a range of potentially acceptable misclassification levels and used GE to evolve a system of models to accommodate these costs. We demonstrate that the resultant models show generalisation levels comparable with or even better than the well-established ML models, while maintaining the required levels of misclassification. However, care should be taken when projecting these generalisation results to future model deployment. Though the current study assessed models' generalisation on the previously unseen data, both data subsets (train and test) were produced by splitting one historical dataset. The generalisability of the models in future deployment might be negatively affected if new data differs substantially from this dataset. Our sub-study on approaches to the selection of models with good generalisability has shown that, at least in this particular case, the simple selection of models based on their training performance provides satisfactory results. In the future, an additional verification of this finding on different datasets will be needed. Notwithstanding these limitations, the demonstrated ability of the GE-evolved models to uphold misclassification error levels on the majority class while maximising correct classification of the class of interest is a very valuable feature from the perspective of clinical site selection.

We adopted an approach of solving this problem as single objective optimisation of a number of separate points, opting to maximise TPR for each FPR cut-off point separately. The same problem can be re-cast as a multi-objective optimisation problem of simultaneously optimising TPR and minimising FPR (or maximising specificity). Several recent studies successfully used Evolutionary Multiobjective Optimisation (EMO) to solve similar problems and simultaneously evolve a Pareto front of acceptable solutions [4, 6, 12, 14, 21]. We plan to investigate the utility of an EMO approach to development of classification models for patient recruitment business problem in future work. However, the GE model system developed here has the advantage of giving the business user explicit control over the selection of business-acceptable FPR thresholds at the model development stage.

The classification models developed in this study can be used at the site selection stage to screen out clinical sites that have propensity to underperform and jeopardise the trial. Incorporating this Business Analytics tool (screening) at the site selection stage can facilitate patient recruitment by improving quality of the study sites pool. It can substantially reduce costs associated with the need to initiate and maintain low-performing sites and to bring in emergency "rescue" sites later in the study. Furthermore, in-depth investigation of variables used by GE-evolved classification models might give some additional information about the factors influencing clinical site's success in patient recruitment.

Overall, the results of this study clearly demonstrate that GE has a range of advantages making it suitable for the use in this business domain. GE was shown to evolve highly tailored classification models adapted to the needs of prediction of patient recruitment in multicenter clinical trials. On a more general level, this study showcases successful application of GE in Business Analytics.

Acknowledgements This research is based upon work supported by ICON Plc.

References

1. P. Aegerter , N. Bendersky , T.C. Tran , J. Ropers , N. Taright , G. Chatellier, The use of DRG for identifying clinical trials centers with high recruitment potential: a feasibility study. Stud. Health Technol. Inform. **205**, 783–787 (2014)
2. V.V. Anisimov, Statistical modeling of clinical trials (recruitment and randomization). Comput. Stand. Theory Methods **40**(19–20), 3684–3699 (2011)
3. V.V. Anisimov, V.V. Fedorov, Modelling, prediction and adaptive adjustment of recruitment in multicentre trials. Stat. Med. **26**(27), 4958–4975 (2007)
4. S. Bernard, C. Chatelain, S. Adam, R. Sabourin, The multiclass roc front method for cost-sensitive classification. Pattern Recogn. **52**(C), 46–60 (2016)
5. U. Bhowan, M. Johnston, M. Zhang, Developing new fitness functions in genetic programming for classification with unbalanced data. IEEE Trans. Syst. Man Cybern. B Cybern. **42**(2), 406–421 (2012)
6. U. Bhowan, M. Johnston, M. Zhang, X. Yao, Evolving diverse ensembles using genetic programming for classification with unbalanced data. Trans. Evol. Comput. **17**(3), 368–386 (2013)
7. G. Borlikova, M. Phillips, L. Smith, M. O'Neill, Evolving classification models for prediction of patient recruitment in multicentre clinical trials using grammatical evolution, in *Applications of Evolutionary Computation. EvoApplications 2016*, ed. by G. Squillero, P. Burelli. Lecture Notes in Computer Science, vol. 9597 (Springer International Publishing, Berlin, 2016), pp. 46–57
8. G. Borlikova, M. Phillips, L. Smith, M. Nicolau, M. O'Neill, Alternative fitness functions in the development of models for prediction of patient recruitment in multicentre clinical trials, in *Operations Research Proceedings 2016*, ed. by A. Fink, A. Fügenschuh, M.J. Geiger, vol. 9597 (Springer International Publishing, Berlin, 2018), pp. 375–381
9. A. Brabazon, M. O'Neill, Diagnosing corporate stability using grammatical evolution. Int. J. Appl. Math. Comput. Sci. **14**(3), 363–374 (2004)
10. A. Brabazon, M. O'Neill, Credit classification using grammatical evolution. Informatica **30**(3), 325–335 (2006)

11. A.P. Bradley, The use of the area under the ROC curve in the evaluation of machine learning algorithms. Pattern Recogn. **30**(7), 1145–1159 (1997)
12. C. Chatelain, S. Adam, Y. Lecourtier, L. Heutte, T. Paquet, A multi-model selection framework for unknown and/or evolutive misclassification cost problems. Pattern Recogn. **43**(3), 815–823 (2010)
13. I. Dempsey, M. O'Neill, A. Brabazon, *Foundations in Grammatical Evolution for Dynamic Environments*. Studies in Computational Intelligence, vol. 194 (Springer, Berlin, 2009)
14. R. Dilão, D. Muraro, M. Nicolau, M. Schoenauer, Validation of a morphogenesis model of drosophila early development by a multi-objective evolutionary optimization algorithm, in *Evolutionary Computation, Machine Learning and Data Mining in Bioinformatics. EvoBIO 2009*, ed. by C. Pizzuti, M.D. Ritchie, M. Giacobini. Lecture Notes in Computer Science, vol. 5483 (Springer, Berlin, 2009), pp. 176–190
15. C. Elkan, The foundations of cost-sensitive learning, in *Proceedings of the Seventeenth International Joint Conference of Artificial Intelligence*, Seattle, Washington (2001), pp. 973–978
16. M. Fenton, J. McDermott, D. Fagan, S. Forstenlechner, E. Hemberg, M. O'Neill, Ponyge2: grammatical evolution in python, in *Proceedings of the Genetic and Evolutionary Computation Conference Companion. GECCO '17* (ACM, New York, 2017), pp. 1194–1201
17. C. Ferri, J. Hernandez-Orallo, R. Modroiu, An experimental comparison of performance measures for classification. Pattern Recogn. Lett. **30**(1), 27–38 (2009)
18. F. Kopcke, D. Lubgan, R. Fietkau, A. Scholler, C. Nau, M. Sturzl, R. Croner, H.U. Prokosch, D. Toddenroth, Evaluating predictive modeling algorithms to assess patient eligibility for clinical trials from routine data. BMC Med. Inform. Decis. Mak. **13**, 134 (2013)
19. M. Kuhn, Building predictive models in R using the caret package. J. Stat. Softw. **28**(5), 1–26 (2008)
20. M. Kuhn, K. Johnson, *Applied Predictive Modeling* (Springer, New York, 2013)
21. J.C. Levesque, A. Durand, C. Gagne, R. Sabourin, Multi-objective evolutionary optimization for generating ensembles of classifiers in the roc space, in *Proceedings of the 14th Annual Conference on Genetic and Evolutionary Computation. GECCO '12* (ACM, New York, 2012), pp. 879–886
22. L. Marks, E. Power, Using technology to address recruitment issues in the clinical trial process. Trends Biotechnol. **20**(3), 105–109 (2002)
23. R.I. McKay, N.X. Hoai, P.A. Whigham, Y. Shan, M. O'Neill, Grammar-based genetic programming: a survey. Genet. Program Evolvable Mach. **11**(3/4), 365–396 (2010)
24. Y. Ni, A.F. Beck, R. Taylor, J. Dyas, I. Solti, J. Grupp-Phelan, J.W. Dexheimer, Will they participate? predicting patients' response to clinical trial invitations in a pediatric emergency department. J. Am. Med. Inform. Assoc. **23**(4), 671–680 (2016)
25. M. Nicolau, M. Saunders, M. O'Neill, B. Osborne, A. Brabazon, Evolving interpolating models of net ecosystem co2 exchange using grammatical evolution, in *Genetic Programming*. Lecture Notes in Computer Science, vol. 7244 (Springer Berlin, 2012), pp. 134–145
26. M. O'Neill, C. Ryan, *Grammatical Evolution: Evolutionary Automatic Programming in a Arbitrary Language, Genetic Programming*, vol. 4 (Kluwer Academic Publishers, Boston 2003)
27. D.M. Powers, Evaluation: from precision, recall and F-measure to ROC, informedness, markedness and correlation. J. Mach. Learn. Technol. **2**, 37–63 (2011)
28. F. Provost, T. Fawcett, Robust classification for imprecise environments. Mach. Learn. **42**(3), 203–231 (2001)
29. F. Provost, T. Fawcett, *Data Science for Business: What You Need to Know About Data Mining and Data-Analytic Thinking* (O'Reilly Media, Inc., Sebastopol, 2013)
30. G. Santafe, I.n. Inza, J.A. Lozano, Dealing with the evaluation of supervised classification algorithms. Artif. Intell. Rev. **44**(4), 467–508 (2015)
31. P. Schuler, B. Buckley, *Re-engineering Clinical Trials: Best Practices for Streamlining the Development Process* (Academic, Amsterdam, 2014)

32. M. Sokolova, N. Japkowicz, S. Szpakowicz, Beyond accuracy, F-score and ROC: a family of discriminant measures for performance evaluation, in *Australasian Joint Conference on Artificial Intelligence* (Springer, Berlin, 2006), pp. 1015–1021
33. S. Treweek, E. Mitchell, M. Pitkethly, J. Cook, M. Kjeldstrøm, M. Johansen, T.K. Taskila, F. Sullivan, S. Wilson, C. Jackson, R. Jones, P. Lockhart, Strategies to improve recruitment to randomised controlled trials. Cochrane Database Syst. Rev. **14**(4), MR000013 (2010)
34. Tufts: Csdd impact report - 89% of trials meet enrolment, but timelines slip, half of sites under-enrol, vol. 15(1) (2013). http://csdd.tufts.edu/files/uploads/jan-feb_2013_ir_summary.pdf
35. C. Tuite, A. Agapitos, M. O'Neill, A. Brabazon, A preliminary investigation of overfitting in evolutionary driven model induction: implications for financial modelling, in *Applications of Evolutionary Computation*, ed. by C. Di Chio, A. Brabazon, G. Di Caro, R. Drechsler, M. Farooq, J. Grahl, G. Greenfield, C. Prins, J. Romero, G. Squillero, E. Tarantino, A.B. Tettamanzi, N. Urquhart, A.Ş.a. Uyar. Lecture Notes in Computer Science, vol. 6625 (Springer, Berlin, 2011), pp. 120–130

Index

Printed in the United States
By Bookmasters